POLITICS
in States and
Communities

POLITICS
in States and Communities

FIFTEENTH EDITION

Thomas R. Dye
Florida State University, Emeritus

Susan A. MacManus
University of South Florida

With the assistance of
Sandra L. Waldron
Ashleigh E. Powers
Research Associates

Boston Columbus Indianapolis New York San Francisco Upper Saddle River
Amsterdam Cape Town Dubai London Madrid Milan Munich Paris Montréal Toronto
Delhi Mexico City São Paulo Sydney Hong Kong Seoul Singapore Taipei Tokyo

Executive Editor: Charlyce Jones-Owen
Program Manager: LeeAnn Doherty
Editorial Assistant: Maureen Diana
Executive Marketing Manager: Wendy Gordon
Marketing Coordinator: Theresa Rotundo
Project Manager: Carol O'Rourke

Full Service Vendor: PreMediaGlobal
Art Director: Maria Lange
Cover Art: Erich Schlegel/Getty Images
Procurement Specialist: Mary Ann Gloriande
Printer/Binder: Courier, Kendallville
Cover Printer: Lehigh-Phoenix Color Corp.

Credits and acknowledgments borrowed from other sources and reproduced, with permission, in this textbook appear on the appropriate page within text and on page 545.

Library of Congress Cataloging-in-Publication Data

Dye, Thomas R.

Politics in states and communities / Thomas R. Dye, Florida State University, Emeritus, Susan A. MacManus, University of South Florida; With the assistance of Sandra L. Waldron, Ashleigh E. Powers, Research Associate. — Fifteenth edition.
    pages cm

Includes bibliographical references and index.
ISBN-13: 978-0-205-99472-4
ISBN-10: 0-205-99472-5
1. State governments--United States. 2. Local government—United States. I. MacManus,
    Susan A. II. Title.
JK2408.D82 2013
320.80973--dc23

2013045703

10 9 8 7 6 5 4 3 2—V011— 15 14

www.pearsonhighered.com

ISBN-10:   0-205-99472-5
ISBN-13: 978-0-205-99472-4

CONTENTS

9. COURTS, CRIME, AND CORRECTIONAL POLICY 249

10. GOVERNING AMERICA'S COMMUNITIES 289

PREFACE

Politics in States and Communities is distinguished by:

Its focus on politics.

Its comparative approach.

Its concern with explanation.

Its interest in policy.

Its focus is on conflicts in states and communities and the structures and processes designed to manage conflict.

This "conflict management" theme emphasizes the sources and nature of conflict in society, how conflict is carried on, how key decision makers in states and communities act in conflict situations, and how "politicos" emerge and determine "who gets what." The political conflict management theme guides the discussion of formal governmental structures: federalism, state constitutions, parties and primaries, apportionment, legislative organizations, gubernatorial powers, court procedures, nonpartisanship, mayor and manager government, metropolitan government, community power, school boards and superintendents, tax systems, budget making, and so on.

An equally important theme is that states and communities in America play an important role in the political life of the nation. State and local governments do more than merely provide certain services such as education, road building, and fire protection. They also perform a vital political function by helping to resolve conflicts of interest in American society.

NEW TO THE FIFTEENTH EDITION

- Learning objectives at the beginning of each chapter and inserted into the text where each topic is discussed.
- Chapter Highlights—concise chapter summaries updated.
- New Visuals to Enhance State Comparisons—50 state maps on marijuana legalization, abortion law restrictiveness, voter ID requirements, professionalism in state legislatures, workers' right-to-work laws, the death penalty, the 2012 presidential election results, and unauthorized immigrants.

The fifteenth edition presents more in-depth and up-to-date coverage of the following:

- Demographics is destiny—one of the dominant themes of the 2012 post-presidential election coverage; the political impact of changing demographics and political cultures across and within states; changes in participation rates and party affiliations of Hispanics and Asians; changing racial/ethnic composition of younger voters and their growing share of the electorate.
- Generational politics—the growing political clout of the Millennial generation, especially in swing states; higher turnout, election of more young mayors and state legislators, bigger role as key staffers for state legislators; clashes between young and old on moral and economic issues, the future solvency of Social Security and other age-based programs; upswing in age discrimination cases; baby boomers versus the Millennials; role reversal—older Americans now voting more Republican, Millennials voting more Democratic but more independent leaning than strongly attached to parties.
- Immigration—how one becomes a citizen; conflicts over immigration reform; state laws dealing with undocumented immigrants' access to drivers licenses and college tuition; state DREAM Acts.
- Shifting opinions on moral issues—same-sex marriage, recreational use of marijuana, online gambling, contraceptives, abortion, physician-assisted suicide, and gun control; growing ideological and public policy divide between red and blue states.

- Privacy and individual rights debates—state and local government use of drones, security cameras, red light cameras; release of gun ownership and registration data; protection of privacy rights in government records (cybersecurity).

- Campaigns and elections—lower turnout rates in swing states; possible impact of negative ad saturation; the impact of early voting on campaigns; "big data" and micro-targeting in get-out-the-vote efforts; polling flaws; campaign spending reform battles; continued debate over the presidential primary "first" position of the Iowa Caucus and New Hampshire primary led by diverse states.

- The "nationalization" of judicial, mayoral, and school board races; infusion of outside interest group money into local races due to ideologically divisive issues national in scope.

- Continuing election system controversies—voter IDs, voter eligibility (felons, noncitizens), online and same-day registration, early voting, polling place location, time in line, mail ballots, absentee voting; partisan priorities: Democrats focused on preventing voter suppression, Republicans on preventing voter fraud.

- Changing media habits—of voters, elected officials; reduced presence of state public affairs networks and the capitol press corps.

- Increased violence against judicial system officials and at public schools and universities (shootings, bullying); renewed demands for more funding and support for better mental health programs.

- The Occupy Wall Street and Tea Party movements—the disappearance of street-level protests, the incorporation of key ideas into major parties' platforms (Tea Party—national debt; Occupy Wall Street—income inequality).

- Declining party competition in state legislatures; more safe seats; fewer states with divided party control (governor vs. legislature).

- State exasperation with federal inaction on critical issues; the emergence of the new "bottoms-up" phase of federalism; state-initiated lawsuits challenging federal policies.

- Reforms of institutions and policies aimed at improving the effectiveness of state and local government service delivery; reforms aimed at improving education (charter schools; No Child Left Behind, Race to the Top, Virtual Schools, Common Core Standards, college tuition hikes, differential funding for majors with more job potential); welfare (means-tested federal-state assistance programs; incentive programs; Medicaid expansion; the wealth gap); transportation (high speed rail, bus rapid transit, MAP-21; mega-commuters); the environment (Keystone pipeline, CAFÉ standards, smart growth, recycling, hazardous waste removal and storage); health care (ObamaCare; Medicaid expansion; Medicare).

- Battles over public employee unions, right-to-work laws, and privatization of prisons.

- Lingering effects of the Great Recession—municipal bankruptcies; state takeovers of failing cities and school districts; employee cutbacks; public employee pension restructuring and benefit reduction; service mergers; taxes; debt; the financial resiliency goal.

- The punishment versus rehabilitation debate; pendulum swings toward rehabilitation; community alternatives to jail; probation; parole; declining crime rates.

- Affirmative action policies; battles over university admission policies; government contracting policies.

- Direct democracy—citizen-led efforts to expand the initiative and recall processes in some states; efforts to limit them in others.

- Money in politics—the *Citizens United* v. *Federal Elections Commission* ruling; the rise of self-financed candidates; escalating campaign costs; new efforts at campaign finance reform: more-detailed and timely disclosure laws, Clean Election laws, public financing; court rulings on contributions to judicial candidates.

- Redistricting—controversies over methods (legislative vs. independent commission); impacts of post-2010 redistricting; racial and partisan gerrymandering.

- Civil rights policy—the expansion of civil rights battlefields beyond just race to gender, disability, age, and sexual preference issues; new court rulings on race and gay rights (LGBT).

- Fraud and corruption—concerns about absentee balloting and online voting; scandals involving big state governors; ethics laws and regulations; ethics training for elected officials and public employees.

- Lieutenant governors—more visibility; how selected; relationship to governor; roles and responsibilities; clearer gubernatorial succession laws (who steps in when a vacancy occurs).
- Expanded responsibilities of attorneys general, secretaries of state, auditors, comptrollers, and treasurers.
- The rise of independents and third parties—more registering as independents; the rise of independent candidates for major state offices; party-switching candidates and what the public thinks of them; difficulties faced by newly emerging third parties.
- Metropolitics—changes in the social distance between cities versus suburbs; rebirth of downtowns as magnets for young residents; shrinking employment–resident gap in suburbs.
- Growing emphasis on citizens' quality of life—Gallup's new "well-being" ratings; commute lengths; the urban sustainability movement; disaster-proofing disaster-prone areas.

FOCUS OF BOXED INSERTS

We begin each chapter with real-life situations designed to make the materials that follow more relevant. Individuals featured in our **"People in Politics"** are up-and-coming state and local officials rising to national prominence, from a wide variety of backgrounds, states, and positions. The new **"Did You Know?"** features inform students about new developments and long-standing controversies, like states losing their challenge to the Affordable Care Act (ObamaCare), attacks on judges and law enforcement officers, the status of the Tea Party and Occupy Wall Street movements, legislators who later became president, metro area mega-commuters, and term limits. **"Up Close"** features include Arizona v. United States on Immigration; The Sandy Hook Shootings and the Right to Bear Arms; Nation versus States: Legalizing Pot; How to Read Political Polls Like a Pro; A Conflicting View: Eliminating Campaign Spending; Privatizing Prisons: The Pros and Cons; A Radioactive Waste Dump Proposal Divides a Small Town; The Decline of the Golden State; The Federalist Society: Proponents of Judicial Restraint; and Mental Health and Mass Murders.

The following are the **popular features that have been revised and retained**: Federalizing Crime; Getting into Politics; Broadcast Television Coverage of Local Campaigns Is Limited; Historic Landmarks in the Development of American Federalism; Americans Serve Their Communities by Volunteering; Which States Rank Highest on the Gallup-Healthways "Well-Being" Index?; California's "Top Two" Primary System: Bipartisanship Promise Appeals to Other States; Three Scandal-Ridden Governors Embarrass Their States; A Showdown over Public Employee Union Power; How to Win at the Budget Game; Exposing Political Corruption; "Diversity" in Universities: Continued Legal Challenges to Affirmative Action in Admissions; and Welfare Reform Success Tied to Work.

RACIAL AND ETHNIC POLITICS

As in previous editions, **special attention has been given to racial and ethnic conflict, cooperation, and clout,** including new material on Hispanic, Asian, and Native American population growth and political power. The racial/ethnic-related subjects covered in each chapter are as follows.

Chapter 1: "Race and Ethnicity," "The Politics of Immigration," "The DREAM Act," "Arizona v. the United States," "State Political Cultures," "Civil Rights," and "The Commonwealth of Puerto Rico" (moving toward statehood).

Chapter 2: "The Politics of State Initiatives" (including affirmative action and racial preferences and illegal immigration); and individual state votes on Civil Rights initiatives.

Chapter 3: Federalism and slavery and segregation, civil rights policies and court rulings, and grants-in-aid to minority businesses.

Chapter 4: "Explaining Voter Turnout" (socioeconomic explanations of voting habits), "Continuing Election Controversies," "Race, Ethnicity, and Political Participation (changing participation rates and party affiliations)," "Securing the Right to Vote" (ending discriminatory voting practices), and "Minorities in State Politics" (affirmative racial gerrymandering; racial polarization; Hispanic power); and civil disobedience and civil rights battles.

Chapter 5: Racial discrimination argument against runoff elections; racial/ethnic makeup of political party supporters.

Chapter 6: "Minorities and Women in State Legislatures (expanded coverage of Native American state legislators)," Rankings of the States: Asians and Native Americans, and "Legislative Apportionment and Districting."

Chapter 7: "The Making of a Governor—Race and Ethnicity," "Minority and Women Governors," including growing numbers of Hispanics and Asian Americans in the gubernatorial ranks and minority women in pathbreaking roles.

Chapter 8: "Bureaucracy, Democracy, Representativeness, and Responsiveness" (minority employee presence, affirmative action, and state equal opportunity requirements).

Chapter 9: The race/ethnicity of judges, racial issues in jury selection, hate crimes, issues related to police crackdowns and the "Broken Windows" policy, race, and the death penalty.

Chapter 10: Minority responses to satisfaction with their community, affect of local elections systems on minorities (the Civil Rights Act, court rulings, and minority representation on city councils and school boards).

Chapter 11: Minority turnout patterns in local elections, party identification trends of minorities and voting coalitions, minority mayors, city managers, and council members, policy implications of minority representation; multiracial voting coalitions, and multilingual communicators in city hall; San Antonio Mayor Julian Castro—rising star on national stage.

Chapter 12: "Ethnic and Racial Diversity in Metropolitan Areas," the racial composition of cities and suburbs, changing immigration patterns (different countries of origin), majority-minority MSAs, the concentration of social problems in the inner city (racial tensions and rioting), and racial politics in metropolitan reform efforts including city-county consolidation efforts—racial imbalance, inequities, and school segregation.

Chapter 13: Minority attitudes toward growth and environmental policy, the relocation of poor minorities, the racial composition of neighborhoods, and environmental injustice.

Chapter 14: Impact of employee layoffs and budget cutbacks on minorities; appointment of African American emergency financial manager to rescue bankrupt City of Detroit.

Chapter 15: "Politics and Civil Rights," "Struggle against Segregation," "Continuing Racial Separation and 'White Flight', " "Policy Consequences of Minority Representation," discussions of racial balance in schools, affirmative action and racial preference battles, employment equity, fairness in housing, and federal court rulings; and representational and governance issues affecting Hispanics and Native Americans (including tribal governments).

Chapter 16: "Education," addresses a variety of topics including racially biased educational testing—SAT tests and achievement tests used to measure teacher and school performance under No Child Left Behind, racial differences in dropout rates, and black representation on school boards.

Chapter 17: Discusses the disproportionate number of minorities who are chronically poor, on welfare, and without adequate health care.

GENDER AND POLITICS

We have also **greatly expanded our coverage of gender in politics.**

Chapter 1: Civil rights issues facing women.

Chapter 2: Abortion-related referenda; voter referenda and court rulings on domestic partners and same-sex marriage.

Chapter 3: Violence Against Women Act; the Equal Rights Amendment; and women's political groups and lobbyists.

Chapter 4: "Securing the Right to Vote" (the Nineteenth Amendment); female registration and turnout rates and voting patterns; "Women in State Politics (women in state and local offices, candidacy challenges, the gender gap).

Chapter 5: Gender makeup of political party supporters, profile of a female state political party chair (Democrat Allison Tant of Florida), and gains in number of Republican women governors.

Chapter 6: Women in state legislatures—racial and ethnic representation; candidacies, electoral successes, and challenges; in leadership posts; policy preferences; decision-making styles and impacts.

Chapter 7: "The Making of a Governor" (varieties of background and gender); "Minority and Women Governors" (historical timeline); minority women governors (Nikki Haley and Susan Martinez) as trailblazers and rising stars; and the impact of women as running mates (lieutenant governors) for governors.

Chapter 8: "Bureaucracy, Democracy, Representativeness and Responsiveness"—discusses the presence of women, employment discrimination, and state equal opportunity requirements.

Chapter 9: Women judges—representation on different types of courts, racial/ethnic makeup, and underrepresentation overall; the pipeline grows—more women in law school; hate crimes (on the basis of gender identity); upswing in crimes committed by women; sentencing injustices; and women on death row.

Chapter 10: Women in elected local offices; hiring difficulties faced by women school administrators when competing for school superintendent positions; and representation on school boards.

Chapter 11: "Recruiting City Council Candidates" (gender differences);"Women in Local Politics" (backgrounds and electoral successes as candidates, mayors, city council members, county commissioners, and school board members); women as city managers; female governance styles and policy impacts.

Chapter 12: Traditional and nontraditional households in cities and suburbs.

Chapter 13: Women's attitudes toward growth policies.

Chapter 14: Impact of employee layoffs and budget cuts on women.

Chapter 15: "Gender Equality" covers a variety of topics including historical differential treatment of rights and responsibilities of men and women, and discussions of sexual harassment, affirmative action, gender equality, education, age-based laws, the earnings gap, comparable worth, abortion rights, and sexual orientation rights.

Chapter 16: Female educational attainment rates—K–12, higher education, and representation on school boards.

Chapter 17: The feminization of poverty; female-headed households and chronic poverty; public assistance programs for women and their children; pregnancies; and dependency on welfare.

Finally, the fifteenth edition **continues the popular feature** *"Rankings of the States"* **with new rankings in some chapters.** The topics covered are population growth, income and education, Hispanic and African American populations, religion and ideology (liberalism) in the states, state gun laws and firearms death rates, reliance on federal aid, registered lobbyists, voter turnout, women and minorities in state legislatures, governors' formal powers, government spending and employment, crime and incarceration rates, general-purpose and special-purpose local governments, citizen voluntarism rates, Metropolitan Statistical Areas in the states, road mileage and gasoline taxes, tax revenues and burdens, state spending and borrowing, educational performance (SAT scores and high school graduation rates), financing public schools, poverty rates, and enrollment in Temporary Assistance for Needy Families and Medicaid programs.

INSTRUCTIONAL FEATURES

This book includes multiple instructional features designed to provide timeliness and relevance, to capture students' attention and interest, to involve students interactively with political questions, and to aid in the study of state and local politics. While the instructional features should aid in teaching state and local politics, the text material is not "dumbed down." It still includes the most important research by scholars in the field.

"Learning Objectives" Each chapter opens with a list of Learning Objectives for students to think about as they read through the material. Each objective is then placed in the chapter where discussion of the subject begins.

"People in Politics" These features are designed to personalize politics for students, to illustrate to them that the participants in the struggle for power are real people. They discuss where prominent people in politics went to school, how they got started in politics, how their careers developed, and how much power they came to possess. Featured are two young mayors (Tashua Allman, Glenville, West Virginia, and Svante Myrick, Ithaca, New York), Martin Luther King, Jr., minority female governors Susana Martinez and Nikki Haley, Wisconsin governor Scott Walker, San Antonio mayor Julian Castro, Chicago mayor Rahm Emanuel, and National Teacher of the Year Jeff Charbonneau.

"Up Close" These features illustrate the struggle over who gets what. They range over a wide variety of current political conflicts, such as the Arizona immigration law, state constitutions and the right to bear arms, the Sandy Hook Elementary School shootings, scandalous governors, the decline of the Golden State, the removal of radioactive waste, and the diversity factor in university admissions.

"Rankings of the States" Comparative analysis is used throughout the text both to describe and to explain differences among states and communities in governmental structure, political processes, and public policy. Through the Rankings of the States boxes, students can observe their own state in relation to all other states.

"Did You Know?" These features, designed to be both instructive and entertaining, inform students about various aspects of American states and communities—everything from how many governors later became president to the fate of the Tea Party and Occupy Wall Street protests and the economic realities of mega-commuting.

Chapter Pedagogy Each chapter contains learning objectives, a running glossary in the margin, and chapter highlights designed to help students better master the information as they read and review the chapters.

SUPPLEMENTARY PACKAGE

Pearson is pleased to offer a robust package of resources for both instructors and students using *Politics in States and Communities,* 15e. Our goal is to make teaching and learning from this book even more effective and enjoyable. Several of the supplements for this book are available at the Instructor Resource Center (IRC), an online hub that allows instructors to quickly download book-specific supplements. Please visit the IRC welcome page at http://www.pearsonhighered.com/irc/ to register for access.

MySearchLab

MySearchLab for Politics in States and Communities moves students from studying and applying concepts to participating in politics. MySearchLab contains an eTextbook and a collection of tools and resources that can help students in any course. The Pearson eText, included in the MyLab, is accessible on Apple and Android tablets through the Pearson eText app. The eText app provides full-text search capabilities, highlights, notes, bookmarks, and support for multimedia content. Also included as part of the MySearchLab are:

- **Pre-Tests and Post-Tests** help students move from diagnostic assessment to mastery with personalized study plans and follow-up reading, video, and multimedia.
- **Chapter Exams** test mastery of each chapter.
- The **Pearson eText** allows students to take notes, print key passages, and more.
- **Flashcards** reinforce terms and concepts in a fun, interactive platform.
- With **Grade Tracker**, instructors can easily monitor students' work on the site and progress with each activity.

Use ISBN 0133745767 to order MySearchLab with this book. To learn more, please visit http://mysearchlab.com or contact your Pearson representative.

Instructor's Manual/Test Bank (0133745694)

This resource includes learning obejectives, chapter summaries, class discussion questions, activities/projects, true/false questions, multiple choice questions, short answer questions, and essay questions for each chapter.

Pearson MyTest (0205982166)

This powerful assessment generation program includes all of the items in the test bank. Questions and tests can be easily created, customized, saved online, and then printed, allowing flexibility to manage assessments anytime and anywhere. To learn more, please visit http://www.pearsonmytest.com or contact your Pearson representative.

PowerPoint Presentation (0133745686)

Organized around a lecture outline, these multimedia presentations also include photos, figures, and tables from each chapter. Available exclusively on the IRC.

ACKNOWLEDGMENTS

The authors are deeply indebted to the research scholars whose labors produced the insight and understanding that we try to convey to our readers. This text contains more than 500 research citations relevant to state and local politics in America. Hundreds of scholars have contributed to this impressive body of literature. We have tried our best to accurately describe and interpret their work; we apologize for any errors in our descriptions or interpretations.

Thomas R. Dye

Susan A. MacManus

CHAPTER ONE

POLITICS IN STATES AND COMMUNITIES

LEARNING OBJECTIVES

1.1 Explain how the problems that governments address are inherently political in nature.

1.2 Compare the public policies of various states and communities in areas such as population growth, income, and education.

1.3 Describe both the current racial and ethnic composition of the United States and how it has changed over time.

1.4 Identify those who immigrate to the United States, current and proposed immigration policies, and the politics underlying legal and illegal immigration.

1.5 Compare the ideological profiles of liberal and conservative states.

1.6 Explain how differences in states' political cultures affect their ideological profiles.

1.7 Describe how the religious profiles of states affect the politics and attitudes about wedge issues such as abortion.

1.8 Assess how political leaders influence politics in states and communities through policy entrepreneurship.

1.9 Describe the major policy responsibilities held by states and communities, including education, health and welfare, transportation, public safety, civil rights, the physical environment of our communities, and taxes.

1.10 Trace the admission of states into the union, and explain the political status of the District of Columbia, Puerto Rico, and the U.S. territories.

Explain how the problems that governments address are inherently political in nature.

A POLITICAL APPROACH TO STATES AND COMMUNITIES

Politics is the management of conflict. Disagreements are often fierce at the state and local levels over everything from the death penalty, stem cell research, and student testing, to which neighborhood will get a new park, what taxes to impose, and how to deal with race and religious controversies. An understanding of "politics" in American states and communities requires an understanding of both the major conflicts confronting society and the political processes and governmental organizations designed to manage conflict. State and local governments do more than provide public services such as education, highways, police and fire protection, sewage disposal, and garbage collection. These are important functions of government to be sure; but it is even more important that government deal with racial tensions, school disputes, growth problems, economic stagnation, minority concerns, poverty, drugs, crime, and violence. These problems are primarily *political* in nature; that is, people have different ideas about *what* should be done, or *whether* government should do anything at all.

Moreover, many of the service functions of government also engender political conflict. Even if "there is only one way to pave a street," political questions remain. Whose street will get paved? Who will get the paving contract? Who will pay for it? Shouldn't we build a new school instead of paving the street?

 1.2

Compare the public policies of various states and communities in areas such as population growth, income, and education.

THE COMPARATIVE STUDY OF STATES AND COMMUNITIES

The task of political science is not only to *describe* politics and public policy in American states and communities, but also to *explain* differences through comparative analysis. We want to know *what* is happening in American politics, and we want to know *why*. Which states allow their citizens to vote directly on controversial issues and which states don't? Which states place limits on abortion? Which states tax their citizens heavily and which states have no income tax? What are the most influential lobbying groups in the states? Which states generally vote Democratic and which states can usually be counted on by Republicans? In which states are women most successful in winning office? Which states spend the most on schools? Which states have the death penalty and actually use it? Which cities are leading the "green" revolution and which metropolitan areas have the most traffic congestion? Why do some states *lead* while others *lag* in tackling tough issues? What we really want to understand are the "whos, whats, whens, wheres, hows, and whys" of state and local politics. Most of us will move to vastly different locations several times in our lifetimes and will likely encounter situations that upset us to the point where we want to get involved and hold *somebody* accountable. It is hard to fix blame if we do not have a clue about how politics works in different states and communities.

In the past, the phrase "comparative government" applied to the study of foreign

Each state's politics reflects its own unique history and culture. Hawaii's elected officials wear with pride clothing and flowered leis that have come to symbolize the state, just as many Texas officials love to don cowboy hats.

governments, but American states and communities provide an excellent opportunity for genuine **comparative study**, which compares political institutions and behaviors from state to state and community to community in order to identify and explain similarities or differences.

Comparison is a vital part of explanation. Only by comparing politics and public policy in different states and communities can we arrive at any comprehensive explanations of political life. Comparative analysis helps us answer the question *why*.

American states and communities provide excellent "laboratories" for applying comparative analysis. States and communities are not alike in social and economic conditions, in politics and government, or in their public policies. These differences are important assets in comparative study because they enable us to search for relationships between different socioeconomic conditions, political system characteristics, and policy outcomes. For example, if differences among states and communities in educational policies are closely associated with differences in economic resources or in party politics, then we may assume that economic resources or party politics help "explain" educational policies.

State politics are often affected by unique historical circumstances. (See Figure 1–1 and Table 1–1.) Louisiana is distinctive because of its French–Spanish colonial background and the continuing influence of this background on its politics today. For nine years Texas was an independent republic (1836–1845) before it was annexed as a state by Congress. Eleven southern states were involved in a bloody war against the federal government from 1861 to 1865. Hawaii has a unique history and culture, combining the influence of Polynesian, Chinese, Japanese, and European civilizations. Alaska's rugged climate and geography and physical isolation set it apart. Wisconsin and Minnesota reflect the Scandinavian influences of their early settlers. Utah was initially settled by members of the Church of Jesus Christ of Latter-day Saints, popularly known as the Mormons, and it retains much of its distinctly Mormon culture today.

These unique historical and cultural settings help to shape state political systems and public policies. However, the mere identification of unique traits or histories does not really "explain" why politics or public policy differs from state to state. Ad hoc explanations do not help much in developing general theories of politics. For example, only Texas has the Alamo and only New York has the Statue of Liberty, but the stories about these landmarks do not explain why New York has a state income tax and Texas does not. Students of state politics must search for social and economic conditions that appear most influential in shaping state politics over time in all the states. Despite the uniqueness of history and culture in many of our states, we must *search for explanations* of why state governments do what they do.

Since it is impossible to consider all the conditions that might influence state politics, we must focus our attention on a limited number of variables. We can begin with economic development—one of the most influential variables affecting state politics and public policy. **Economic development** is defined broadly to include three closely related components: population growth, income, and education.

Population Growth

America has always been a rapidly changing society. As its people change—in numbers, race, ethnicity, income, education, culture—new conflicts arise, some old conflicts burn out, and other conflicts reignite.

The total population of the United States grew by almost 10 percent between 2000 and 2010. But states grew unevenly. The fastest growing states between 2000 and 2010 were the "Sunbelt" states of the West and South. Texas, the nation's second largest state, gained the most numbers of new residents—4.3 million; California gained—3.4 million, followed by Florida—2.8 million, Georgia—1.5 million, North Carolina—1.5 million, and Arizona—1.3 million. These six states accounted for 54 percent of the overall population growth for the United States during the decade.

COMPARATIVE STUDY

In politics, comparing political institutions and behaviors from state to state and community to community in order to identify and explain similarities or differences.

ECONOMIC DEVELOPMENT

Broadly defined as population growth and the income and educational levels of a state's population.

FIGURE 1–1 State Histories

By the Treaty of Paris, 1783, England gave up claim to the 13 original Colonies, and to all land within an area extending along the present Canadian border to the Lake of the Woods, down the Mississippi River to the 31st parallel, east to the Chattahoochee, down that river to the mouth of the Flint, east to the source of the St. Mary's, down that river to the ocean. Territory west of the Alleghenies was claimed by various states but was eventually all ceded to the nation.

In 1803 President Thomas Jefferson engineered the Louisiana Purchase from France; it was the largest acquisition of territory in U.S. history, more than doubling the size of the nation.

American invasions of Canada were failures in both the Revolutionary War and the War of 1812. In the Rush–Bagot Treaty of 1817, the border between the United States and Canada was demilitarized and fixed at the 49th parallel. Later, in 1846, the British relinquished their claims to the Oregon territory south of the 49th parallel.

In 1819 Spain ceded Florida to the United States in the Adams–Onis Treaty, after General Andrew Jackson and his Tennessee volunteers invaded the territory in a war with the Seminole Indians.

Following battles at the Alamo in San Antonio and at the San Jacinto River, Texas declared its independence from Mexico in 1836, but the Mexican government refused to recognize the new republic. In 1845 Congress annexed Texas at the republic's request, ending nine years of independence. In 1846 Congress declared war on Mexico, and following the American army's capture of Veracruz and Mexico City, the United States forced its southern neighbor to cede the territories that became California, Nevada, Utah, Arizona, and New Mexico. Later, in 1853, the Gadsden Purchase from Mexico extended the U.S. border farther south.

Beginning with South Carolina on December 20, 1860, 11 southern states seceded from the United States of America, forming their own Confederate States of America. After their defeat, they were readmitted to the Union after they agreed to ratify the Thirteenth Amendment that abolished slavery (1865), and later the Fourteenth Amendment that guaranteed equal protection of the laws (1868), and the Fifteenth Amendment that prevented denial or abridgment of the right to vote on account of "race, color, or previous condition of servitude."

Twice the size of Texas, Alaska was purchased from Russia for $7.2 million in 1867. (At the time Secretary of State William Henry Seward was criticized for his extravagance, and Alaska was dubbed "Seward's folly" and "Seward's icebox.") Hawaii was annexed as a territory to the United States by congressional resolution in 1898 without consulting its residents.

Following victories in the Spanish–American War in 1898, Spain ceded Puerto Rico, Samoa and Guam, and the Philippines, which remained a U.S. territory until granted independence in 1946. The Virgin Islands were purchased from Denmark in 1917.

TABLE I–I   The States of the Union

State	Capital	Date Admitted to Union	Chronological Order of Admission to Union
Alabama	Montgomery	Dec. 14, 1819	22
Alaska	Juneau	Jan. 3, 1959	49
Arizona	Phoenix	Feb. 14, 1912	48
Arkansas	Little Rock	June 15, 1836	25
California	Sacramento	Sept. 9, 1850	31
Colorado	Denver	Aug. 1, 1876	38
Connecticut	Hartford	Jan. 9, 1788[a]	5
Delaware	Dover	Dec. 7, 1787[a]	1
Florida	Tallahassee	March 3, 1845	27
Georgia	Atlanta	Jan. 2, 1788[a]	4
Hawaii	Honolulu	Aug. 21, 1959	50
Idaho	Boise	July 3, 1890	43
Illinois	Springfield	Dec. 3, 1818	21
Indiana	Indianapolis	Dec. 11, 1816	19
Iowa	Des Moines	Dec. 28, 1846	29
Kansas	Topeka	Jan. 29, 1861	34
Kentucky	Frankfort	June 1, 1792	15
Louisiana	Baton Rouge	April 30, 1812	18
Maine	Augusta	March 15, 1820	23
Maryland	Annapolis	April 28, 1788[a]	7
Massachusetts	Boston	Feb. 6, 1788[a]	6
Michigan	Lansing	Jan. 26, 1837	26
Minnesota	St. Paul	May 11, 1858	32
Mississippi	Jackson	Dec. 10, 1817	20
Missouri	Jefferson City	Aug. 10, 1821	24
Montana	Helena	Nov. 8, 1889	41
Nebraska	Lincoln	March 1, 1867	37
Nevada	Carson City	Oct. 31, 1864	36
New Hampshire	Concord	June 21, 1788[a]	9
New Jersey	Trenton	Dec. 18, 1787[a]	3
New Mexico	Santa Fe	Jan. 6, 1912	47
New York	Albany	July 26, 1788[a]	11
North Carolina	Raleigh	Nov. 21, 1789[a]	12
North Dakota	Bismarck	Nov. 2, 1889	39
Ohio	Columbus	March 1, 1803	17
Oklahoma	Oklahoma City	Nov. 16, 1907	46
Oregon	Salem	Feb. 14, 1859	33
Pennsylvania	Harrisburg	Dec. 12, 1787[a]	2
Rhode Island	Providence	May 29, 1790[a]	13
South Carolina	Columbia	May 23, 1788[a]	8
South Dakota	Pierre	Nov. 2, 1889	40
Tennessee	Nashville	June 1, 1796	16
Texas	Austin	Dec. 29, 1845	28
Utah	Salt Lake City	Jan. 4, 1896	45
Vermont	Montpelier	March 4, 1791	14
Virginia	Richmond	June 25, 1788[a]	10
Washington	Olympia	Nov. 11, 1889	42

(continued)

TABLE 1-1   The States of the Union (Continued)

State	Capital	Date Admitted to Union	Chronological Order of Admission to Union
West Virginia	Charleston	June 20, 1863	35
Wisconsin	Madison	May 29, 1848	30
Wyoming	Cheyenne	July 10, 1890	44

[a]Date of ratification of U.S. Constitution.

Source: Derived from *Book of the States*, 2012, Volume 44, Table 10.2, pp. 554–555. Printed with permission from the Council of State Governments.

Population growth *rates*—the percentage of population increase over the decade—may be better indicators of the changing requirements of state governments to provide public services, as well as the changing politics in the states. Nevada, the fastest growing state for five decades, grew by 35 percent, followed by Arizona (25 percent), Utah (24 percent), Idaho (21 percent), and Texas (21 percent). The slowest growing were Rhode Island, Louisiana, and Ohio—all of which grew by less than 2 percent. Michigan actually lost 0.6 percent of its population over the decade. The top five fastest growing states between 2000 and 2030 are projected to be Nevada (114 percent), Arizona (109 percent), Florida (80 percent), Texas (60 percent), and Utah (56 percent). (See "*Rankings of the States:* Population Size and Projected Growth Rate, 2010–2030.")[1] The Census Bureau predicts that soon Florida will edge past New York into third place in total population.

Income

Rising personal **income** indicates increased worker productivity and the creation of wealth. Per capita personal income in the United States grew from about $4,000 in 1970 to about $39,791 in 2010. Income is not evenly distributed throughout the states (see "*Rankings of the States:* Income and Education"). Per capita personal income in Connecticut is more than $56,000, but it is less than $32,000 in Mississippi.

Education

Many economists have asserted that economic growth involves an upgrading in the workforce, the development of professional managerial skills, and an increase in the volume of research. These developments involve a general increase in the *educational levels* of the adult population. In 1970 about 11 percent of the U.S. adult population had completed four years or more of college; by 2011 that figure had risen to 30 percent. But high levels of educational attainment do not prevail uniformly throughout the states (see "*Rankings of the States:* Income and Education").

The extent to which economic development—population growth, income, and education—affects the politics of the states is an important question, which we return to again in the chapters that follow.

1.3 RACE AND ETHNICITY

Describe both the current racial and ethnic composition of the United States and how it has changed over time.

Differences in the racial and ethnic composition of state populations account for much of the variation in the politics of states and cities throughout the nation. Later we examine racial and ethnic cleavages in voting behavior and political participation (Chapter 4), state legislative politics (Chapter 6), community politics (Chapter 11), and civil rights policy (Chapter 15).

African Americans

Today the nation's 41 million blacks comprise 13 percent of the total population of the United States. (The distribution of blacks among the 50 states is shown in "*Rankings of the States:* Hispanic and African American Populations.") In 1900, most African Americans

Population Size and Projected Growth Rate, 2010–2030

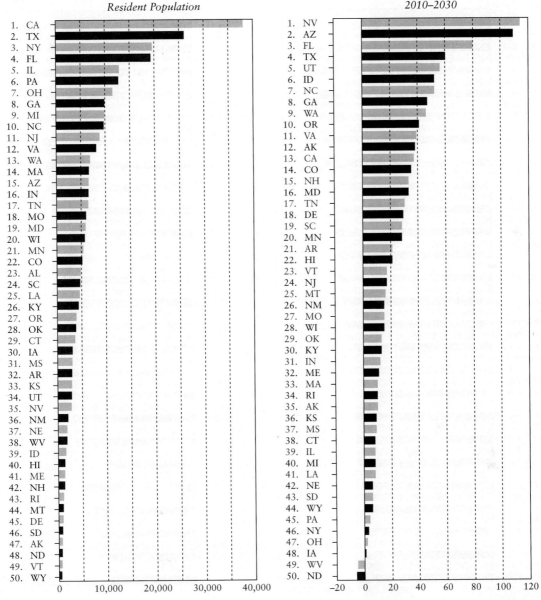

Resident Population

1.	CA
2.	TX
3.	NY
4.	FL
5.	IL
6.	PA
7.	OH
8.	GA
9.	MI
10.	NC
11.	NJ
12.	VA
13.	WA
14.	MA
15.	AZ
16.	IN
17.	TN
18.	MO
19.	MD
20.	WI
21.	MN
22.	CO
23.	AL
24.	SC
25.	LA
26.	KY
27.	OR
28.	OK
29.	CT
30.	IA
31.	MS
32.	AR
33.	KS
34.	UT
35.	NV
36.	NM
37.	NE
38.	WV
39.	ID
40.	HI
41.	ME
42.	NH
43.	RI
44.	MT
45.	DE
46.	SD
47.	AK
48.	ND
49.	VT
50.	WY

Projected Growth Rate (Percentage Change): 2010–2030

1.	NV
2.	AZ
3.	FL
4.	TX
5.	UT
6.	ID
7.	NC
8.	GA
9.	WA
10.	OR
11.	VA
12.	AK
13.	CA
14.	CO
15.	NH
16.	MD
17.	TN
18.	DE
19.	SC
20.	MN
21.	AR
22.	HI
23.	VT
24.	NJ
25.	MT
26.	NM
27.	MO
28.	WI
29.	OK
30.	KY
31.	IN
32.	ME
33.	MA
34.	RI
35.	AK
36.	KS
37.	MS
38.	CT
39.	IL
40.	MI
41.	LA
42.	NE
43.	SD
44.	WY
45.	PA
46.	NY
47.	OH
48.	IA
49.	WV
50.	ND

Note: Data are for 2012. In thousands.
Source: U.S. Census Bureau, "Annual Estimates of the Population for the United States, Regions, States, and Puerto Rico," Table 1. Available at http://www.census.gov/popest/data/state/totals/2012/tables/NST-EST2012-01.xls.

Source: U.S. Census Bureau, *Statistical Abstract of the United States,* 2010, Table 14. Available at http://www.census.gov/prod/2009pubs/10statab/pop.pdf.

Income and Education

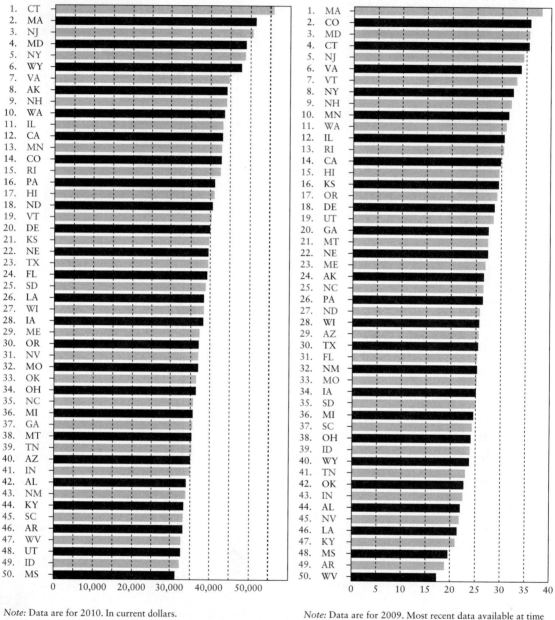

Personal Income Per Capita ($)

1. CT
2. MA
3. NJ
4. MD
5. NY
6. WY
7. VA
8. AK
9. NH
10. WA
11. IL
12. CA
13. MN
14. CO
15. RI
16. PA
17. HI
18. ND
19. VT
20. DE
21. KS
22. NE
23. TX
24. FL
25. SD
26. LA
27. WI
28. IA
29. ME
30. OR
31. NV
32. MO
33. OK
34. OH
35. NC
36. MI
37. GA
38. MT
39. TN
40. AZ
41. IN
42. AL
43. NM
44. KY
45. SC
46. AR
47. WV
48. UT
49. ID
50. MS

0   10,000   20,000   30,000   40,000   50,000

Percentage with Bachelors Degree

1. MA
2. CO
3. MD
4. CT
5. NJ
6. VA
7. VT
8. NY
9. NH
10. MN
11. WA
12. IL
13. RI
14. CA
15. HI
16. KS
17. OR
18. DE
19. UT
20. GA
21. MT
22. NE
23. ME
24. AK
25. NC
26. PA
27. ND
28. WI
29. AZ
30. TX
31. FL
32. NM
33. MO
34. IA
35. SD
36. MI
37. SC
38. OH
39. ID
40. WY
41. TN
42. OK
43. IN
44. AL
45. NV
46. LA
47. KY
48. MS
49. AR
50. WV

0   5   10   15   20   25   30   35   40

Note: Data are for 2010. In current dollars.
Source: U.S. Census Bureau, *Statistical Abstract of the United States,* 2012, Table 681. Available at http://www.census.gov/compendia/statab/2012/tables/12s0681.pdf.

Note: Data are for 2009. Most recent data available at time of publication.
Source: U.S. Census Bureau, "Educational Attainment in the United States: 2009," Table 2, February 2012. Available at http://www.census.gov/prod/2012pubs/p20-566.pdf.

(89.7 percent) were concentrated in the South. But World Wars I and II provided job opportunities in large cities of the Northeast and Midwest. Blacks could not cast ballots in most southern counties, but they could "vote with their feet." The migration of blacks from the rural South to the urban North was one of the largest internal migrations in our history. But blacks have steadily been moving back to the South. Today, 55 percent of the nation's black population lives in the South.[2]

African American candidates have been increasingly successful in winning city and county offices and state legislative seats. (See Chapter 4 for a discussion of voting rights laws and their impact on the election of minorities.) The largest numbers of black elected officials are found in the southern states. In 1989 the nation's first elected black governor, Douglas Wilder, moved into Virginia's statehouse, once the office of Jefferson Davis, president of the Confederacy. Black candidates have also been increasingly successful in winning elections in large cities throughout the nation and community organizer, Barack Obama, became the first black president of the United States. Later in this book we describe black representation in city councils (Chapter 11) and in state legislatures (Chapter 6), as well as civil rights policy (Chapter 15).

Hispanics

Perhaps the most significant change in the nation's ethnic composition over the last decade is the growth in the numbers and percentage of Hispanic Americans. In 2000, Hispanics became the nation's largest minority. More than one in six people in the United States are of Hispanic origin. (The term *Hispanic* refers to persons of Spanish-speaking ancestry and culture, regardless of race, and includes Mexican Americans, Cuban Americans, Central and South Americans, and Puerto Ricans.) Today Hispanics outnumber African Americans in the U.S. population (see "*Rankings of the States:* Hispanic and African American Populations"). The largest subgroup is Mexican Americans, some of whom are descendants of citizens living in Mexican territory that was annexed to the United States in 1848 (see Figure 1–1), but most of them have come to the United States in accelerating numbers in recent years. The largest Mexican American populations are in New Mexico, California, Texas, and Arizona. The second largest subgroup is Hispanics from Central and South America, who are concentrated in the Northeast, South, and West. Third largest is Puerto Ricans, many of whom retain ties to the island and move back and forth to the mainland, especially to New York City and now central Florida. Fourth largest are Cubans, most of whom have fled from Castro's regime and live in the Miami metropolitan area. While these groups share a common language and faith (Catholic), they often differ in their political leanings and participation rates due to varied cultural backgrounds and length of residency in the United States[3] (see Chapter 15).

Asians and Pacific Islanders

The Asian population, nearly 16 million (5 percent of the nation's total), is actually growing more rapidly than any other minority. One-half of Asians and Pacific Islanders live in the West. California has the largest Asian population (4.7 million), but Asians are a majority of the population of Hawaii, the only state with a "majority minority" population. Asians, like Hispanics, are not a monolithic group either

Ethnic-based holidays are often adopted by the community-at-large. In Texas, Cinco de Mayo (5th of May) celebrations, commemorating the victory of the Mexicans over the French at the Battle of Puebla in 1862, are quite popular. Cinco de Mayo festivities feature music, dance, food, and beverages unique to Mexico and reflect the influence that Mexican American immigrants have had on the culture and politics of the state.

Hispanic and African American Populations

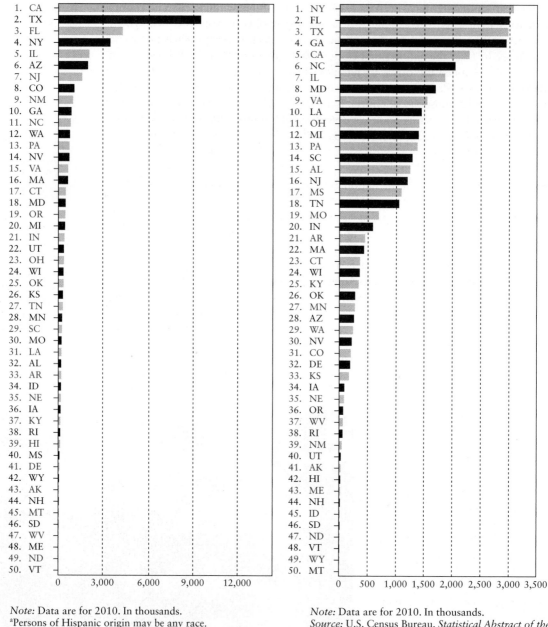

Hispanic[a] Population

Rank	State
1.	CA
2.	TX
3.	FL
4.	NY
5.	IL
6.	AZ
7.	NJ
8.	CO
9.	NM
10.	GA
11.	NC
12.	WA
13.	PA
14.	NV
15.	VA
16.	MA
17.	CT
18.	MD
19.	OR
20.	MI
21.	IN
22.	UT
23.	OH
24.	WI
25.	OK
26.	KS
27.	TN
28.	MN
29.	SC
30.	MO
31.	LA
32.	AL
33.	AR
34.	ID
35.	NE
36.	IA
37.	KY
38.	RI
39.	HI
40.	MS
41.	DE
42.	WY
43.	AK
44.	NH
45.	MT
46.	SD
47.	WV
48.	ME
49.	ND
50.	VT

Horizontal axis: 0, 3,000, 6,000, 9,000, 12,000

African American Population

Rank	State
1.	NY
2.	FL
3.	TX
4.	GA
5.	CA
6.	NC
7.	IL
8.	MD
9.	VA
10.	LA
11.	OH
12.	MI
13.	PA
14.	SC
15.	AL
16.	NJ
17.	MS
18.	TN
19.	MO
20.	IN
21.	AR
22.	MA
23.	CT
24.	WI
25.	KY
26.	OK
27.	MN
28.	AZ
29.	WA
30.	NV
31.	CO
32.	DE
33.	KS
34.	IA
35.	NE
36.	OR
37.	WV
38.	RI
39.	NM
40.	UT
41.	AK
42.	HI
43.	ME
44.	NH
45.	ID
46.	SD
47.	ND
48.	VT
49.	WY
50.	MT

Horizontal axis: 0, 500, 1,000, 1,500, 2,000, 2,500, 3,000, 3,500

Note: Data are for 2010. In thousands.
[a]Persons of Hispanic origin may be any race.
Source: U.S. Census Bureau, *Statistical Abstract of the United States*, 2012, Table 18. Available at http://www.census.gov/prod/2011pubs/12statab/pop.pdf.

Note: Data are for 2010. In thousands.
Source: U.S. Census Bureau, *Statistical Abstract of the United States*, 2012, Table 19. Available at http://www.census.gov/prod/2011pubs/12statab/pop.pdf.

ethnically or politically.[4] There are significant language and cultural differences among Chinese, Japanese, Koreans, Cambodians, Malaysians, Pakistanis, Filipinos, Thais, Hmong, Laotians, and Vietnamese Americans. Pacific Islanders, those with origins in Hawaii, Guam, Samoa, or other Pacific Islands, also have unique heritages.

Native Americans

It is estimated that 10 million Native Americans (American Indians and Alaska Natives) once inhabited the North American continent. By 1900 the Native American population had been reduced to barely a half million by war, disease, and forced privations inflicted upon them. Today, Native Americans number nearly 4 million, or 1 percent of the U.S. population. There are more than 562 Indian tribes and Alaska Native groups that speak more than 250 languages. Each tribe has its own culture, history, and identity.[5] The 10 largest American Indian tribal groups are the Cherokee, Navajo, Latin American Indian, Choctaw, Sioux, Chippewa, Apache, Blackfeet, Iroquois, and Pueblo. The four largest Alaska Native tribal groups are Eskimo, Tlingit-Haida, Alaska Athabascan, and Aleut. The 11 states with the largest Native American populations are, in descending order, California, Oklahoma, Arizona, Texas, New Mexico, New York, Washington, North Carolina, Michigan, Alaska, and Florida (see Chapter 15). Approximately half of all Native Americans live on semiautonomous reservations in various states.

THE POLITICS OF IMMIGRATION

America is a nation of immigrants, from the first "boat people," the Pilgrims, to the latest Haitian and Cuban refugees. Continuing immigration, together with differences in birth and death rates, is expected to change the ethnic composition of the nation considerably over the next half century (see Figure 1–2). The Census Bureau predicts that the United States will become a majority-minority nation for the first time in 2043. By 2060, minorities are projected to comprise 57 percent of the population.

Most immigrants come to the United States for economic opportunity. Others come to escape oppression and discrimination. Most personify the traits we typically think of as American—enterprise, ambition, perseverance, initiative, and a willingness to work hard.

1.4

Identify those who immigrate to the United States, current and proposed immigration policies, and the politics underlying legal and illegal immigration.

FIGURE 1–2 Projected Racial and Ethnic Characteristics of U.S. Population

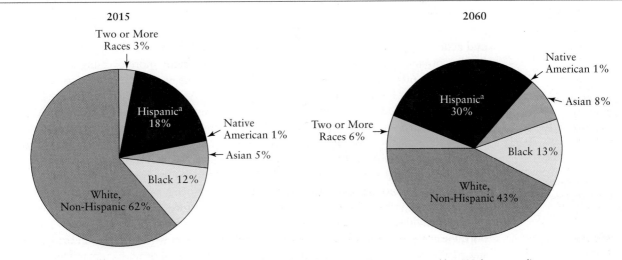

2015

- Two or More Races 3%
- Hispanic[a] 18%
- Native American 1%
- Asian 5%
- Black 12%
- White, Non-Hispanic 62%

2060

- Native American 1%
- Asian 8%
- Hispanic[a] 30%
- Two or More Races 6%
- Black 13%
- White, Non-Hispanic 43%

Note: Current and future population figures are from a 2011 estimate based on 2010 Census. Figures may not add to 100 due to rounding.
[a]Persons of Hispanic origin may be any race.
Source: U.S. Census Bureau, "Percent of the Projected Population by Race and Hispanic Origin for the United States: 2015 to 2060," Table 6, December 2012. Available at http://www.census.gov/population/projections/data/national/2012/summarytables.html.

As immigrants have always done, they frequently take dirty, low-paying, thankless jobs that other Americans shun. When they open their own businesses, they often do so in blighted, crime-ridden neighborhoods long since abandoned by other entrepreneurs.

National Immigration Policy

Immigration policy is a responsibility of the national government. Today, roughly a million people per year are admitted to the United States as "lawful permanent residents" (persons who have needed job skills or who have relatives who are U.S. citizens) or as **political refugees** (persons with "a well-founded fear of persecution" in their country of origin). Another 36 million people are awarded temporary visas to enter the United States for study, business, or pleasure.

The easiest way to become a U.S. citizen is to be born here, regardless of whether your parents are here legally or not. If you were born outside of the United States, the golden ticket is the "green card"—the U.S. government–issued document granting you permanent residency status allowing you to live and work in the country. Green cards are issued for family reasons and for special employment. A person may apply for a green card if a spouse, child, or sibling is a U.S. citizen. Persons may also apply if an employer is willing to hire them and to assert that their job skills are crucial. Preferences are given to medical professionals, advanced degree holders, and executives of multinational corporations.

Persons who have resided in the United States for at least five years, who are over age 18, who can read and speak English, who possess "good moral characters" (no felony convictions), and who can pass a modest citizenship test are eligible for naturalization as citizens.

Citizens of the United States are entitled to a passport, issued by the U.S. State Department upon presentation of a photo plus evidence of citizenship (a birth certificate or naturalization papers). A passport entitles holders to reenter the United States after travel abroad. A visa is a document or stamp on a passport, issued by a foreign country, that allows a citizen to enter that country.

Illegal Immigration

In theory, a sovereign nation should be able to maintain secure borders, but in practice the United States has been unwilling and unable to do so. Estimates of **illegal immigration** vary wildly, between official statistics provided by the U.S. Department of Homeland Security and unofficial estimates provided by other organizations like the Pew Hispanic Center and the Center for Immigration Studies. The Department of Homeland Security estimates that over 11 million unauthorized immigrants currently reside in the United States. Other, unofficial estimates range from 12 to 15 million or more. The number varies depending on the economy and actions by state and local governments. Many undocumented immigrants slip across U.S. borders or enter ports with false documentation, while many more overstay tourist or student visas. Nearly 60 percent of these unauthorized immigrants were born in Mexico; the remainder come from other Latin and South American countries, Asia, and elsewhere.[6] Eighty-five percent of all unauthorized immigrants in the United States come from 10 countries (Mexico, El Salvador, Guatemala, Honduras, China, the Philippines, India, Korea, Ecuador, and Vietnam).

Immigration "reform" was the announced goal of Congress in the Immigration Reform and Control Act of 1986, also known as the Simpson–Mazzoli Act. It sought to control immigration by placing principal responsibility on employers; it set fines for knowingly hiring **undocumented, or unauthorized, immigrants.** However, it allowed employers to accept many different forms of documentation (which, as it turned out, could be easily forged) and at the same time subjected them to penalties for discrimination against legal foreign-born residents. To win political support, the act granted **amnesty** to undocumented immigrants who had lived in the United States since 1982. But the act failed to reduce the flow of either legal or undocumented immigrants.

Border control is an expensive and difficult task. The federal agency responsible for border security is **U.S. Immigration and Customs Enforcement (ICE)**, a branch of the Department of Homeland Security. Localized experiments in border enforcement have indicated

POLITICAL REFUGEES
Those residing in the United States because they have "a well-founded fear of persecution" in their country of origin.

ILLEGAL IMMIGRATION
The unlawful entry of people from other nations into the United States.

UNDOCUMENTED, OR UNAUTHORIZED, IMMIGRANTS
Persons residing illegally in a nation.

AMNESTY
Government forgiveness of a crime, usually granted to a group of people.

U.S. IMMIGRATION AND CUSTOMS ENFORCEMENT (ICE)
Federal agency responsible for the enforcement of immigration and customs laws.

that illegal immigration can be reduced by half or more, with significant increases in ICE personnel and technology. However, political opposition to increased border enforcement and reduced immigration comes from a variety of sources. Hispanic groups have been especially concerned about immigration enforcement efforts that may lead to discrimination against all Hispanic Americans. Powerful groups benefit from the availability of undocumented immigrants, such as the agriculture, restaurant, clothing, and hospital industries; they regularly lobby in Washington to weaken enforcement efforts. Some employers prefer hiring undocumented immigrants ("los indocumentados") because they are willing to work at hard jobs for low pay and few, if any, benefits. Even high-tech firms have found it profitable to bring in English-speaking immigrants as computer programmers.

DREAM Act

Congress considered but failed to pass a DREAM (Development, Relief, and Education for Alien Minors) Act in 2010. The DREAM Act would offer permanent residency to undocumented aliens, who came into the United States as minors, who are under the age of 30, who have lived in the country continuously for five years, and who enrolled in a college or university for two or more years or served honorably in the U.S. military. The bill failed to overcome a filibuster in the U.S. Senate, falling short of the 60 votes necessary. But in 2012, President Barack Obama announced that his administration would not deport young undocumented aliens who matched the DREAM Act's requirements. The U.S. Citizenship and Immigration Service (CIS) now accepts application under this Deferred Action for Childhood Arrivals program.

Immigration and Federalism

Although the federal government has exclusive power over immigration policy, its decisions have significant effects on states and communities—on their governmental budgets, on the use of their public services, on the security of their residents, and even on their social character. Immigration is by no means uniform across the states. Border states in the southwest and southeast (Florida) have the highest concentrations of unauthorized immigrants. (See Figure 1–3.) Immigration-related politics and policies often differ across the states on issues ranging from allowing undocumented immigrants to secure a driver's license to giving in-state tuition to children of undocumented immigrants.

Increasingly, states and cities have attempted to enact their own versions of immigration reform. In 1994 California voters approved a referendum, Proposition 187, which would have barred welfare and other benefits to persons living in the state illegally. A federal court later declared major portions of Proposition 187 unconstitutional. And the U.S. Supreme Court has held that a state may not bar the children of undocumented immigrants from attending public schools. Some cities with politically liberal electorates, for example San Francisco, have declared themselves to be "sanctuary" cities, ordering their police officers not to enforce federal immigration laws or even to ask suspects about their immigration status. Some cities with more conservative voters have adopted ordinances making it illegal for landlords to rent to undocumented immigrants or employers to hire them. Federal courts have invalidated most of these laws as an unconstitutional interference in the exercise of federal power.[7] The U.S. Supreme Court's propensity to restrict state laws that appear to infringe on federal power was evident in its 2012 ruling (*Arizona* v. *U.S.*) that certain portions of Arizona's tough immigration enforcement law cracking down on undocumented immigrants undermined federal authority. (See "*Up Close:* Arizona v. the United States on Immigration.")

Additional state issues involving immigration continue to arise. Can states deny driver's licenses to persons who cannot prove that they are in the country legally? Should states offer in-state tuition to students who graduated from high school but who are not in the country legally? (State versions of the DREAM Act have been passed in 12 states as of 2013, including Texas, California, and New York. Maryland voters approved a state DREAM Act in 2012 by a 59 percent vote.) And can states act to deny voter registration

FIGURE 1–3 Proportion of Undocumented Immigrants by State

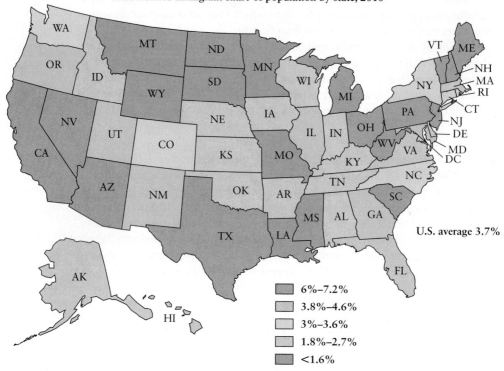

Unauthorized immigrant share of population by state, 2010

U.S. average 3.7%

- 6%–7.2%
- 3.8%–4.6%
- 3%–3.6%
- 1.8%–2.7%
- <1.6%

Note: Data are for 2010.
Source: Pew Hispanic Center, "Unauthorized Immigrant Population: National and State Trends, 2010," February 1, 2011. Available at http://www.pewhispanic.org/2011/02/01/appendix-c-maps.

to persons who cannot prove their citizenship? In 2004, Arizona voters approved a state constitutional amendment that required proof of citizenship in order to register to vote. In 2013, the U.S. Supreme Court, in *Arizona* v. *Inter-Tribal Council of Arizona,* ruled it unconstitutional. The Court, in a 7–2 ruling, said that Arizona's requirement went beyond registration procedures spelled out in the National Voter Registration Act of 1993 (the "motor voter" law) and that federal law trumps state law.

Conflict over Immigration Reform

To date, the intense conflict over immigration policy in Washington has prevented any effective action to halt illegal immigration, determine the status of millions of undocumented immigrants, or decide how many aliens should be admitted each year and what the criteria for their admission should be. Beginning during the George W. Bush administration and continuing to Obama's presidency, Congress has struggled over how to resolve this intensifying problem. Debates have centered on how to compromise diverse interests—employers seeking to keep immigration as open as possible, immigrants seeking a legal path to citizenship, and citizens seeking border security and opposed to any form of amnesty for undocumented aliens. Intense debates have also taken place over strengthening border enforcement, including funding 700 miles of fencing along the 2,000-mile Mexican border; providing a path to citizenship that includes criminal background checks, paying fines and fees, and acquiring English proficiency; establishing a temporary (two-year) guest worker program; and shifting the criteria for legal immigration from family-based preferences to a greater emphasis on skills and education. So far it has been extremely difficult to build consensus on these divisive issues.

Citizens opposed to giving amnesty to undocumented immigrants currently in the United States complain that undocumented immigrants receive services like health care for free while they do not.

The failure of the federal government to enforce existing federal immigration laws inspired Arizona to pass its own illegal immigration act in 2010. It made it a *state* crime to be in the country illegally.

The law allowed state and local police in "any lawful contact . . . where reasonable suspicion exists that a person is an alien who is unlawfully present in the United States, when practicable to determine the immigration status of the person . . ." Once identified as illegal immigrants, persons could be taken into custody, prosecuted for violating Arizona law, were turned over to the federal Immigration and Customs Enforcement (ICE) for deportation. "Reasonable suspicion" may involve a combination of circumstances, but the law specifically prohibits officers from using race or ethnicity as determining factors.

The U.S. Department of Justice filed suit against the Arizona law arguing that it violated the Supremacy Clause of the Constitution. "A state may not establish its own immigration policy or enforce state laws in a manner that interferes with federal immigration laws. The Constitution and federal immigration laws do not permit the development of a patchwork of state and local immigration policy throughout the country." (*United States* v. *Arizona*, Federal District Court Brief, July 28, 2010).

The Supreme Court agreed that federal immigration laws preempt any state laws on the topic, as provided by the Supremacy Clause of the Constitution. The Constitution grants to Congress the power to "establish an uniform Rule of Naturalization" (Art.I, Sec 8, Cl 4). And according to the Court, federal law intends a "single integrated all-embracing system." Even complementary state regulation of immigration is impermissible. Federal immigration law is "complex and comprehensive" and Congress has not specified any role for the states in this area. The states cannot make illegal immigration a state crime, state officials cannot arrest an alien not lawfully present in the United States, states cannot require registration of aliens, and states cannot impose criminal penalties on employers who hire illegal aliens. The Court did not order Arizona police to stop inquiring about alien status, or reporting to ICE when they encountered an illegal alien.

Arizona v. *United States*, June 25, 2012.

LIBERALISM AND CONSERVATISM IN THE STATES

State politics differ in their prevailing ideological predispositions—that is, whether they are predominantly "liberal" or "conservative." There are various ways of defining and measuring ideological predispositions.[8] One way is to look at policy enactments. For example, "policy **liberalism**" might be defined as the adoption of relaxed eligibility standards for receipt of welfare and medical benefits, decriminalization of marijuana possession, elimination of the death penalty, extensive regulation of business, state ratification of the Equal Rights Amendment, and the adoption of progressive state income taxes. "Policy **conservatism**" would be defined as the opposite of these enactments. Scholars frequently construct new policy liberalism rankings for states based on key ideological issues of the day such as gun control, abortion laws, welfare eligibility and work requirements, tax progressivity, and unionization.[9]

Compare the ideological profiles of liberal and conservative states.

LIBERALISM
Referring to a state's tendency to expand welfare benefits, regulate business, adopt progressive state income taxes, and generally use the resources of government to achieve social change.

Another way to identify the ideological profiles of the 50 states is to use voters' self-identification. A common question on opinion polls is "How would you describe your views on most political matters? Generally do you think of yourself as liberal, moderate, or conservative?" Using this definition, Gallup surveys have identified the most liberal states as Massachusetts, Oregon, Vermont, Delaware, and Connecticut. Among the most conservative are Alabama, North Dakota, Wyoming, Mississippi, and Utah.[10] (See "*Rankings of the State:* Importance of Religion and Liberalism.") Ideology and party affiliation tend to go hand-in-hand. Of the 10 most liberal states, all are reliably Democratic voting states in national elections, and of the 10 most conservative states, all regularly vote Republican in national elections.

Nationally, among voters, 23 percent describe their ideological disposition as liberal, 36 percent as moderate, and 38 percent as conservative.[11] Historically researchers have found that voters' ideological identification correlates closely with measures of policy liberalism and conservatism.[12]

1.6 STATE POLITICAL CULTURES

Explain how differences in states' political cultures affect their ideological profiles.

Do the states exhibit separate and identifiable political cultures? That is, are there political differences among the states that cannot be accounted for by demographic characteristics, for example, race, ethnicity, income, or education? It does appear that some states have developed historical traditions of Democratic and Republican party affiliation, as well as cultural patterns of liberal and conservative politics, that are independent of any demographic features of their populations. For example, Minnesota has developed a liberal and Democratic tradition, Indiana a conservative and Republican tradition, and neither can be fully explained by the socioeconomic composition of their populations. The liberal politics of Massachusetts, Rhode Island, and Oregon as well as the conservative politics of Tennessee, North Dakota, and Utah are not fully explained by characteristics of these states' populations or by specific historical events. So we attribute to **"political culture"** the differences across states that take into account the values and ways of life of early settler and immigrant groups.

Early attempts at developing different classifications of state political cultures began with examinations of the content and language of each state's original constitution. These documents were seen as reflecting the cultural values of the early settlers, which were passed down from one generation to the next and became part of the state's political fabric. More recent attempts have used a combination of race and ethnic origins, religious affiliations, and social structures to classify states and, in turn, to examine how closely cultural differences reflect political and public policy differences across the states.

The newest research[13] uses U.S. Census and religious survey data to classify all U.S. counties into 11 regional subcultures that represent distinctive differences in race, ethnicity, religion, social class, historical settlement patterns, language, regionalism, sectionalism, and new streams of immigration and migration. (See Figure 1–4.) With the exception of the Rurban subculture, the study's subcultures represent historical and cultural extensions of earlier settler and immigrant waves. To measure state culture, the study computed the respective proportions of the total statewide population that are under the influence of each subculture.

The state-by-state distribution of regional subcultures shows why each state is unique. Pennsylvania, for example, is dominated by a Germanic subculture, while neighboring West Virginia is dominated by a Heartland subculture. The Rurban subculture is dominant in Oregon, while the Global subculture is dominant in neighboring California. Arkansas has a border-dominated politics, while Mississippi's remains under the sway of a Blackbelt subculture. Politics in New Mexico continues to be dominated by a Latino subculture, while neighboring Texas now lacks a dominant subculture and is truly multicultural. The regional political subculture measure, a *composite* of social, economic, ethnic heritage, immigration, and migration factors, is a more powerful predictor of state party affiliation, voting patterns, and public policy outcomes than any single factor.

FIGURE 1-4 Regional Subcultures of the United States

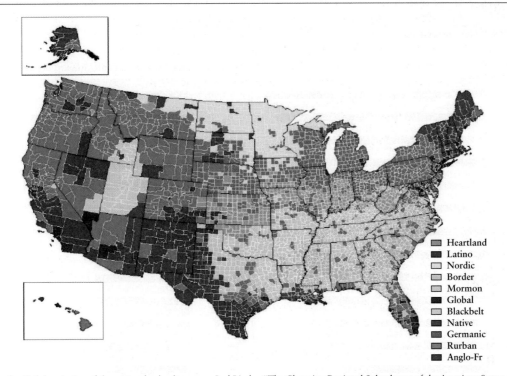

Heartland
Latino
Nordic
Border
Mormon
Global
Blackbelt
Native
Germanic
Rurban
Anglo-Fr

Note: For a more detailed description of the regional subcultures, see Joel Lieske, "The Changing Regional Subcultures of the American States and the Utility of a New Cultural Measure." *Political Research Quarterly* 63 (2010), 538–552.
Source: Courtesy of Joel Lieske, "The Changing regional Subcultures of the American States and the Utility of a New Cultural Measure." Political Research Quarterly 63 (2010), 538–552..

Some scholars have examined the link between cultural-religious values and citizen attitudes toward immigration reform. For example, "agreement with three values—continuing our heritage as a nation of immigrants, following the Golden Rule, and protecting the dignity of every person—predicts higher support for a path to citizenship for illegal immigrants."[14]

RELIGION IN THE STATES

The religious profiles of the states vary significantly and are becoming more important in explaining why states act differently politically, particularly on highly divisive, politically explosive moral issues.[15] A voter's position on these media-grabbing issues may be grounded in religious beliefs and may be a stronger voting cue than one's political party affiliation, although the two are often related.[16] Consequently, moral issues (like same-sex marriage, contraceptive coverage, abortion, gambling, marijuana legalization) are increasingly being used by political parties and candidates as **wedges**, designed to cause voters to cross party lines on those hot-button issues alone. Putting such issues on the ballot in the form of an amendment is seen as a way to boost turnout among religious conservatives, regardless of whether they are Republicans or Democrats. Liberals, in turn, use such amendments as tools to turn out their own voters, many of whom are more concerned about the blurring of church and state than the issue itself.

There are several ways to define a person's religiosity. The four most common measures are the importance of religion in a person's life, frequency of attendance at worship services, frequency of prayer, and belief in God.[17] States differ significantly in the degree to which their citizens say religion is important in their lives. Southern states rank highest; New England states rank lowest. (See "*Rankings of the State:* Religion and Ideology (Liberalism)

1.7

Describe how the religious profiles of states affect the politics and attitudes about wedge issues such as abortion.

WEDGES
Moral issues designed to cause someone to cross party lines.

RANKINGS OF THE STATES

Religion and Ideology (Liberalism)

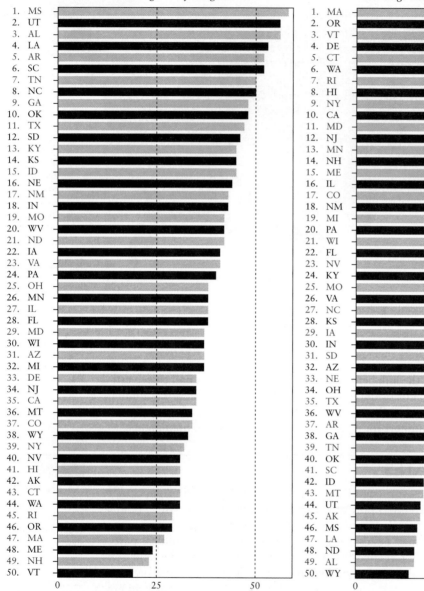

Percentage "Very Religious"

1. MS
2. UT
3. AL
4. LA
5. AR
6. SC
7. TN
8. NC
9. GA
10. OK
11. TX
12. SD
13. KY
14. KS
15. ID
16. NE
17. NM
18. IN
19. MO
20. WV
21. ND
22. IA
23. VA
24. PA
25. OH
26. MN
27. IL
28. FL
29. MD
30. WI
31. AZ
32. MI
33. DE
34. NJ
35. CA
36. MT
37. CO
38. WY
39. NY
40. NV
41. HI
42. AK
43. CT
44. WA
45. RI
46. OR
47. MA
48. ME
49. NH
50. VT

Percentage Residents Identifying as Liberal

1. MA
2. OR
3. VT
4. DE
5. CT
6. WA
7. RI
8. HI
9. NY
10. CA
11. MD
12. NJ
13. MN
14. NH
15. ME
16. IL
17. CO
18. NM
19. MI
20. PA
21. WI
22. FL
23. NV
24. KY
25. MO
26. VA
27. NC
28. KS
29. IA
30. IN
31. SD
32. AZ
33. NE
34. OH
35. TX
36. WV
37. AR
38. GA
39. TN
40. OK
41. SC
42. ID
43. MT
44. UT
45. AK
46. MS
47. LA
48. ND
49. AL
50. WY

Note: Data are for January–December 2012.
Source: Frank Newport, "Mississippi Maintains Hold as Most Religious U.S. State," Gallup Inc., February 13, 2013. Available at http://www.gallup.com/poll/160415/mississippi-maintains-hold-religious-state.aspx. Copyright © 2013 All rights reserved. The content is used with permission; however, Gallup retains all rights of republication.

Note: Data are for January–December 2012.
Source: Frank Newport, "Alabama, North Dakota, Wyoming Most Conservative States," Gallup, Inc., February 1, 2013. Available at http://www.gallup.com/poll/160196/alabama-north-dakota-wyoming-conservative-states.aspx#2. Copyright © 2013 All rights reserved. The content is used with permission; however, Gallup retains all rights of republication.

Actually, it is the frequency of a person's religious service attendance more than an individual's specific faith that is often the best determinant of their stance on moral issues and their likelihood of voting.

STATE POLITICAL LEADERSHIP

Political leadership in a state also helps shape its politics and public policy. While we can systematically examine the influence of population size and growth, income, education, race, and ethnicity on state politics, we must also remind ourselves that from time to time individual leaders have brought about political change in their states—change that might not have occurred without their efforts. Electoral politics in states and communities as well as the nation encourage **political entrepreneurship**—that is, electoral politics provides incentives for candidates to propose policy innovations in order to publicize themselves and win votes.

1.8

Assess how political leaders influence politics in states and communities through policy entrepreneurship.

POLICY RESPONSIBILITIES OF STATES AND COMMUNITIES

Despite the glamour of national politics, states and communities carry on the greatest volume of public business, settle the greatest number of political conflicts, make the majority of policy decisions, and direct the bulk of public programs. They have the major responsibility for maintaining domestic law and order, for educating children, for providing highways that allow Americans to move from place to place, and for caring for the poor and the ill. They regulate the provision of water, gas, electric, and other public utilities; share in the regulation of insurance and banking enterprise; regulate the use of land; and supervise the sale of ownership of property. Their courts settle by far the greatest number of civil and criminal cases. In short, states and communities are by no means unimportant political systems. Each state determines for itself via the state constitution or state laws whether a function will primarily be funded and performed by the state government or by various local governments—cities, counties, school districts, or other local entities. In many instances, both state and local government dollars help support a specific service.

1.9

Describe the major policy responsibilities held by states and communities, including education, health and welfare, transportation, public safety, civil rights, the physical environment of our communities, and taxes.

POLITICAL ENTREPRENEURSHIP
The tendency of candidates in electoral campaigns to propose policy innovations in order to publicize themselves and win votes.

Education

Education is the biggest expenditure for state and local governments *combined*. (See Figure 1–5.) However, local governments spend a larger portion of their budgets on education than state governments, but each helps fund this critical activity. States and communities are responsible for decisions about what should be taught in public schools, how much should be spent on the education of each child, how many children should be in each classroom, how often they shall be tested, how much teachers should be paid, how responsibilities in education should be divided between state and local governments, what qualifications teachers must have, what types of rates and taxes shall be levied for education, and many other decisions that affect the life of every child in America. Support for higher education, including funds for state and community colleges and universities, is now a major expenditure of state governments. The federal government has never contributed more than 10 percent of the nation's total expenditures for education.

Health and Welfare (Social Services and Income Maintenance)

States and communities continue to carry a heavy burden in the fields of health and welfare—despite an extensive system of federal grants-in-aid for this purpose. (See Figure 1–5.) States and communities must make decisions about participation in federal programs and allocate responsibilities among themselves for health and welfare programs. While the federal government administers Social Security and Medicare, state governments administer the

Education is one of the most costly functions performed by state and local governments. Some of the most intense fights in state legislatures are over how much money to spend on K–12 education versus higher education (community colleges and universities).

largest public assistance programs—Temporary Assistance for Needy Families (cash aid, formerly Aid to Families with Dependent Children), Medicaid (health care for the poor), and food stamps, as well as unemployment compensation. Within the broad outlines of federal policy, states and communities decide the amount of money appropriated for health and welfare purposes, the benefits to be paid to recipients, the rules of eligibility, and the means by which the programs will be administered. States and communities may choose to grant assistance beyond the limits supported by the national government.

Transportation

The United States has over 4 million miles of surfaced roads and over 240 million registered motor vehicles. States and communities must make decisions about the allocation of money for streets and highways, sources of funds for highway revenue, the extent of gasoline and motor vehicle taxation, the regulation of traffic on the highways, the location of highways, the determination of construction policies, the division of responsibility between state and local governments for highway financing administration, and the division of highway funds between rural and urban areas. While the federal government is deeply involved in highway construction, state and local governments fund well over half of the costs of all highway improvements. For years, mass transit has gotten shortchanged next to highways because a majority of Americans prefer to travel in their own cars over riding buses or taking the subway. Historically, high-speed rail has fared even worse than other forms of mass transit, although there are some signs it is becoming a higher priority. The federal American Recovery and Reinvestment Act of 2009 (the Economic Stimulus Package) budgeted $8 billion for building high-speed rail systems connecting major urban areas. Only a handful of states, California being the largest, applied for the funds. For others, the price of such a major infrastructure project was just too high, especially in the middle of a recession. Today, construction of a high-speed rail system is still largely on the drawing boards in many states, although the planning is further along.

FIGURE 1–5 How State and Local Governments Spend Their Money

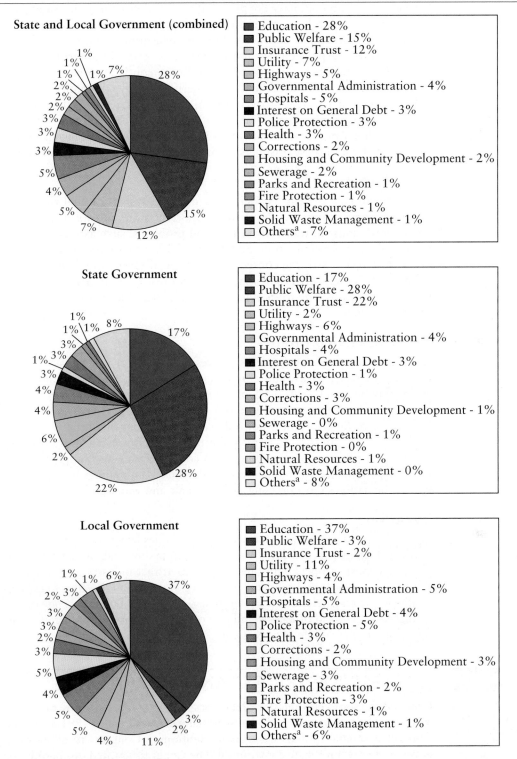

State and Local Government (combined)

- Education - 28%
- Public Welfare - 15%
- Insurance Trust - 12%
- Utility - 7%
- Highways - 5%
- Governmental Administration - 4%
- Hospitals - 5%
- Interest on General Debt - 3%
- Police Protection - 3%
- Health - 3%
- Corrections - 2%
- Housing and Community Development - 2%
- Sewerage - 2%
- Parks and Recreation - 1%
- Fire Protection - 1%
- Natural Resources - 1%
- Solid Waste Management - 1%
- Others[a] - 7%

State Government

- Education - 17%
- Public Welfare - 28%
- Insurance Trust - 22%
- Utility - 2%
- Highways - 6%
- Governmental Administration - 4%
- Hospitals - 4%
- Interest on General Debt - 3%
- Police Protection - 1%
- Health - 3%
- Corrections - 3%
- Housing and Community Development - 1%
- Sewerage - 0%
- Parks and Recreation - 1%
- Fire Protection - 0%
- Natural Resources - 1%
- Solid Waste Management - 0%
- Others[a] - 8%

Local Government

- Education - 37%
- Public Welfare - 3%
- Insurance Trust - 2%
- Utility - 11%
- Highways - 4%
- Governmental Administration - 5%
- Hospitals - 5%
- Interest on General Debt - 4%
- Police Protection - 5%
- Health - 3%
- Corrections - 2%
- Housing and Community Development - 3%
- Sewerage - 3%
- Parks and Recreation - 2%
- Fire Protection - 3%
- Natural Resources - 1%
- Solid Waste Management - 1%
- Others[a] - 6%

Note: Figures may not add to 100 due to rounding. Data are for 2010.
[a]Other expenditures include employment security administration, veterans' services, general expenditures, liquor stores, protective inspection and regulation, air transportation, parking, libraries, and sea and inland port facilities.
Source: U.S. Census Bureau, "State and Local Government Finances by Level of Government and by State: 2010," Table A-1. Available at http://www2.census.gov/govs/estimate/summary_report.pdf.

Public Safety

States and communities have the principal responsibility for public safety in America. Over 2.4 million state and local government jobs are in the protective services (police, firefighters, and correctional officers), second only to education. Some state police have important highway safety responsibilities and cooperate with local authorities in the apprehension of criminals. However, community police forces continue to be the principal instrument of law enforcement and public safety. Sheriffs and their deputies are still the principal enforcement and arresting officers in rural counties. States and communities also have the principal responsibility for maintaining prisons and correctional institutions. Each year several million Americans are prisoners in jails, police stations, juvenile homes, or penitentiaries. The bulk of these prisoners are in state and local, rather than federal, institutions.

Civil Rights

The national government has defined a national system of civil rights, but these rights cannot become realities without the support of state and local authorities. States and communities must deal directly with racial problems, such as racial isolation in the public schools, job discrimination, and segregated housing patterns in the cities. They must also deal directly with the consequences of racial tension, including violence. But in the twenty-first century, civil rights battles are not just racial in nature. Claims of discrimination are on the upswing from older workers, gays and lesbians, women, disabled persons, and immigrants.

Physical Environment

Local governments have the principal responsibility for our physical environment. They must plan streets, parks, and commercial, residential, and industrial areas and provide essential public utilities for the community. The waste materials of human beings—rubbish, garbage, and sewage—exceed one ton every day per person. The task of disposal is an immense one; the problem is not only collecting it, but finding ways to dispose of it. If it is incinerated, it contributes to air pollution; and if it is carried off into streams, rivers, or lakes, it contributes to water pollution. A community's water supply may also be contaminated if pollutants and toxins are buried. Thus, communities are largely responsible for two of the nation's most pressing problems: air and water pollution.

Taxation

To pay for public programs, states and communities levy taxes. They must decide what tax burdens their citizens can carry and whether to tax income, sales, or property. At the same time, they must compete with one another to attract industry and commerce. If taxes are too high, businesses and residents may leave along with jobs. But if taxes are too low, the quality of life may deteriorate. Finding the right level of taxation is one of the toughest jobs facing state and local officials—and one of the most perilous politically. And proposing to raise taxes in the middle of a recession can be particularly risky.

1.10

Trace the admission of states into the union, and explain the political status of the District of Columbia, Puerto Rico, and the U.S. territories.

"STATES," "DISTRICTS," AND "TERRITORIES"

How did the states become states? The original 13 states did so by ratifying the U.S. Constitution. The first new states to be admitted were Vermont in 1791 and Kentucky in 1792. States that sought admission began by petitioning Congress to allow them to elect delegates and draw up a state constitution. The Congress granted this permission in a series of enabling acts. Later, when the territorial voters approved the new constitution, the territory formally applied for admission and presented its constitution to Congress for approval. Congress accepted the application by a joint resolution of both houses, and a new star was added to the flag. The last admissions were Alaska and Hawaii in 1959.

Of course, from a political perspective, admission was not always an easy process. Long before the Civil War (or "The War Between the States" as it is still called in parts of the Old South), states were admitted roughly in pairs of free and slave states, so as not to upset the delicate balance in the U.S. Senate. Iowa and Wisconsin were admitted as free states in 1846 and 1848, while Florida and Texas were admitted in 1845 as slave states. When California was admitted as a free state in the famous Compromise of 1850, the balance was tilted toward the free states. The balance was further tipped when Minnesota was admitted in 1858 and Oregon in 1859. The Civil War followed in 1861.

Eleven states seceded from the Union in 1860—Alabama, Arkansas, Florida, Georgia, Louisiana, Mississippi, North Carolina, South Carolina, Tennessee, Texas, and Virginia. Although the Supreme Court later voided the acts of secession as unconstitutional, Congress required all of these states to reapply for admission to the Union. After the war, these states were under military occupation by U. S. troops. The military governments drew up new state constitutions, registered black voters, and sent black representatives to Congress. Congress required these governments to ratify the Thirteenth, Fourteenth, and Fifteenth Amendments in order to be readmitted to the Union. The "reconstructed" southern state governments did so, and all were readmitted by 1870.

Hawaii and Alaska were the last states admitted to the Union (1959). Hawaii is the only state with an Asian majority population (64 percent). For many years after it became a territory in 1898, Hawaii depended primarily on sugar and pineapple exports to support its economy. But today its economy depends heavily on tourism, not only from "the mainland" but also from Japan. Living costs in both Hawaii and Alaska are high.

The District of Columbia

The U.S. Constitution, Article I, Section 8, specified in 1787 that "the seat of the government of the United States" shall be in a "district not exceeding ten square miles" ceded to the federal government by the states (Maryland and Virginia). The District of Columbia was to be governed by Congress. In defense of a separate district, Alexander Hamilton wrote:

> [Congressional control] of the seat of government . . . is an indispensable necessity. Without it not only the public authority may be insulted and its proceedings interrupted with impunity, but a dependence of the members of the general government of the state comprehending the seat of government . . . might bring the national councils an imputation of awe or influence . . . dishonorable to the government.[18]

Hamilton's language is stiff and formal, but his meaning is clear: Making Washington a state would generate undue local pressure on Congress.

The Twenty-third Amendment, ratified in 1961, gives Washington full participation in presidential elections. Because Congress has also granted it, by law, full home rule, the city has its own elected mayor and city council. In 1978, Congress passed another constitutional amendment that would grant the District full congressional representation and the right to vote on ratification of future constitutional amendments. However, the necessary three-quarters of the states failed to ratify this amendment. So while DC residents can vote in presidential elections, they are not represented by voting members in the U.S. Senate or House of Representatives. However, DC is represented by an elected nonvoting delegate to the

District of Columbia residents frequently take to the streets to call attention to the fact that they are taxed but have no elected representatives in the U.S. Congress. They want Congress to admit the District to the Union as a state.

Puerto Rico is a territory of the United States. Puerto Ricans who permanently move to the United States are entitled to register to vote immediately because all territorial residents are full U.S. citizens. Consequently, candidates running in states with sizable Hispanic populations are more likely to target newly arrived Puerto Ricans than Hispanics from Colombia, Venezuela, Mexico, or other Latin American countries who must first become naturalized citizens before they are eligible to register to vote.

U.S. House of Representatives who can vote and serve on a committee but cannot vote on any passage of legislation.

Having failed to gain congressional representation by constitutional amendment, District residents and their supporters in Congress turned to a new strategy—calling on Congress to admit the District to the Union as a state. (While the Constitution specifies that Congress shall govern over "such District not exceeding ten miles square . . . as the seat of the government," presumably Congress could satisfy this constitutional mandate by reducing "the seat of the government" to a few blocks surrounding the Capitol, while admitting the bulk of the District as a state.) This strategy not only reduces the barrier in Congress from a two-thirds vote to a simple majority vote of both houses, but, more important, eliminates the need to secure ratification by three-quarters of the states. Nonetheless, so far Congress has refused to vote for District statehood (presumably the state would be named "Columbia"). Troubles with District self-government have convinced many Congress members that Washington is not ready for statehood. But the District's residents and its nonvoting representative in Congress never quit trying. Politically, Washington is heavily Democratic, liberal, and black. Its 632,000 residents are likely to support larger social welfare programs, an expanded bureaucracy, and increased federal spending. Opponents of these policies are not likely to be enthusiastic about the District's representation in Congress.

The Commonwealth of Puerto Rico

Nearly 4 million people live on the Caribbean island of Puerto Rico, a population greater than that of 23 states. They are American citizens, who can move anywhere in the United States; and have been subject to the draft in wartime. (Congress granted Puerto Ricans citizenship in 1917.)

The government of Puerto Rico resembles a state government, with a constitution and an elected governor and legislature. However, Puerto Rico has no voting members of Congress and no electoral votes in presidential elections. But Puerto Ricans are represented in the U.S. House of Representatives by a nonvoting representative, just like the District of Columbia.

The United States seized Puerto Rico in 1898 in the Spanish–American War. In 1950, its voters chose to become a "**commonwealth**," and self-governing commonwealth status was officially recognized in 1952. In a 1967 plebiscite, 60 percent of Puerto Ricans voted to remain a commonwealth, 39 percent voted for statehood, and less than 1 percent voted for independence. In nonbinding referenda in 1991, 1993, and 1998, Puerto Ricans continued to support commonwealth status. That changed in 2012. In a two-part referendum, 52 percent first voted against keeping their current U.S. commonwealth status. Then, when asked if they wanted to become a U.S. state, an independent country, or a freely associated state (a type of independence in close alliance with the United States), 61 percent of those who answered the second question opted for statehood. But because over 470,000 voters had intentionally left the second question blank, opponents of statehood were quick to point out that only 45 percent of all those casting ballots—less than a majority—supported statehood. Puerto Ricans remain divided between statehood and commonwealth status and Congress seems to be in no hurry to push for statehood. Many Congress members worry that statehood would cause their own states to lose federal funding and representatives in Congress. Article IV, Section 3 of the U.S. Constitution gives the U.S. Congress the power to grant statehood.

Under commonwealth status Puerto Ricans pay no U.S. income tax, although local taxes are substantial. Yet, they receive all of the benefits to which U.S. citizens are entitled—Social Security, public assistance, food stamps, Medicaid, and Medicare. If Puerto Rico were to become a state, its voters could participate in presidential and congressional elections; but its taxpayers would not enjoy the same favorable cost–benefit ratio they enjoy under commonwealth status. Some Puerto Ricans also fear that statehood would dilute the island's cultural identity and perhaps force English upon them as the national language.

U.S. Territories

In addition to the Commonwealth of Puerto Rico, the United States has 12 "territories," also known as possessions. The major territories are the U.S. Virgin Islands, American Samoa, Guam, and the Northern Mariana Islands. The residents of all U.S. territories are full U.S. citizens (with the exception of those on American Samoa who are U.S. nationals, but not citizens). These residents possess all the rights and obligations of U.S. citizens, including Social Security payments and benefits and service in the armed forces, *except for* the right to vote in presidential elections or to vote for representatives in U.S. Congress. Like the District of Columbia, each territory elects a nonvoting delegate at-large to the U.S. House of Representatives who can participate in committees but cannot vote on legislation. However, both the Democratic and Republican parties seat voting delegations from the District of Columbia, Puerto Rico, and the territories at their presidential nominating conventions.[19]

COMMONWEALTH
Although four states call themselves "commonwealths" (Pennsylvania, Virginia, Massachusetts, and Kentucky), the term refers to any self-governing community and currently describes the government of Puerto Rico, a territory of the United States.

CHAPTER HIGHLIGHTS

■ Politics is the management of conflict. Aside from understanding the major conflicts confronting society, one must also understand the political processes and governmental organizations designed to manage conflict.

■ The task of political science is not only to *describe* politics and public policy but also to *explain* differences, through comparative analysis, among states and among communities. Comparative analysis helps us answer the question *why*.

■ Economic development, defined broadly to include population growth, income, and education, is key to a state's politics and public policies. Changing growth rates (fastest in the West and South) and the need to increase educational opportunity can create conflict in and among states.

■ Perhaps the most significant change in the nation's ethnic composition over the last decade is the growth in the numbers and percentage of Hispanic Americans, with Mexican Americans as the largest subgroup.

■ Most immigrants come to the United States for economic opportunity, including work and education, while others come to escape oppression and discrimination. Approximately 1 million immigrants come legally and roughly three times that many come illegally.

■ Although immigration policy is the responsibility of the federal government, conflict over the issue has prevented any effective action to halt illegal immigration, determine the status of undocumented immigrants, or decide on the number of aliens to admit every year and what the admission criteria should be.

■ The newest immigration policy debates have focused on the rights of undocumented children (minors) brought to the United States by undocumented adult immigrants.

■ The path to becoming a citizen is fairly straightforward; it is the length of time it takes that is often the biggest barrier.

■ Ideological predispositions—liberal, moderate, or conservative—of states and communities can be defined chiefly by the kinds of policies enacted and voters' self-identification. Ideological leanings can also depend on a state's historical patterns of party affiliation, voters' religious fervor (frequency of attendance at worship), political cultures and subcultures, and, on occasion, the political leadership of an individual.

■ Compared to the national government, state and local governments settle the greatest number of political conflicts, make the majority of policy decisions, and direct the bulk of public programs.

■ Of all state and local programs, education is the most costly. But states and local governments also carry heavy responsibilities for health and welfare, highways, public safety, and the environment. One of the toughest responsibilities is finding a level of taxation that won't drive out jobs and residents.

■ Achieving statehood is a difficult process requiring congressional approval. The District of Columbia and Puerto Rico have come the closest to becoming new states.

CHAPTER TWO

DEMOCRACY AND CONSTITUTIONALISM IN THE STATE

LEARNING OBJECTIVES

2.1 Trace the constitutional tradition in the states, and list the ways in which constitutions limit governments and influence politics at the state level.

2.2 Describe the key features that state constitutions share and the limits that they place on state governments.

2.3 Examine the various methods used to change state constitutions: legislative proposals, popular initiatives, constitutional conventions, and constitutional commissions.

2.4 Trace the development of direct democracy in the states, assess the effectiveness of its variants, and compare it to representative democracy.

2.5 Evaluate whether direct or representative democracy is a better approach for governing the states.

2.6 Discuss how state initiatives have been used to move public policies in both liberal and conservative directions, and assess the current ideological trend of state initiates.

2.7 Evaluate whether the proliferation of initiatives and initiative campaigns in some states is problematic, and trace efforts to institute congressional term limits through the initiative process.

CONSTITUTIONAL GOVERNMENT IN THE STATES

State constitutions are frequently the center of intense, hard-fought, multimillion-dollar political battles over everything from school vouchers, medical malpractice, and gambling to cigarette taxes and sexual assault. Constitutions contain principles worth fighting for—or against. And they are much easier to amend than the U.S. Constitution. Constitutions govern governments. They set forth the structure and organization of government; they distribute powers among branches of government; and they prescribe the rules by which decisions will be made. Most important, constitutions limit the powers of government and protect the rights of citizens. All 50 states have written constitutions.

Limited Government

LIMITED GOVERNMENT

The principle that government power over the individual is limited, that there are some personal liberties that even a majority cannot regulate, and that government itself is restrained by law.

CONSTITUTIONALISM

A government of laws, not people, operating on the principle that governmental power must be limited, that government officials should be restrained in their exercise of power over individuals.

The true meaning of **constitutionalism** is limited government. Today most of the world's governments, including even the most authoritarian regimes, have written constitutions that describe the government's formal structure. But the constitutions of authoritarian regimes rarely place any restrictions on the government's powers. In the English and American political heritage, constitutionalism means that the power of government over the individual is clearly limited, that there are some aspects of life that even majorities cannot regulate, and that government itself is restrained by a higher law. Constitutional government places individual liberty beyond the reach of governments, even democratic governments. Thus, if a majority of voters wanted to prohibit communists, or atheists, or racists, from writing or speaking or organizing, voters could not do so under a constitutional government that protected free speech, press, and assembly.

All 50 state constitutions limit the powers of state government and protect individual liberty. While we have come to rely principally on the U.S. Constitution for the protection of individual liberty, every state constitution also contains a bill of rights that protects individuals from deprivations of personal liberty by their state government. Most of these state constitutional guarantees merely reiterate rights guaranteed to all Americans in the U.S. Constitution, but some state documents extend rights *beyond* the federal guarantees.

Legal Status

State constitutions are the supreme law of the state. They take precedence over any state *law* in conflict with them. Since constitutions govern the activities of governments themselves, they are considered more fundamental than the ordinary laws passed by governments.

The U.S. Constitution is the *supreme law* of the nation. State constitutions take precedence over state law, but they are subordinate to the U.S. Constitution and the laws of the United States. The U.S. Constitution mentions state constitutions once, and only to assert the supremacy of the U.S. Constitution and the laws and treaties of the United States. Article VI states:

> This constitution, and the laws of the United States which shall be made in pursuance thereof; and all treaties made, or which shall be made, under the authority of the United States, shall be the supreme law of the land; and the judges in every state shall be bound thereby, *anything in the constitution or laws of any state to the contrary notwithstanding.* (emphasis added)

Origins of Written Constitutions

Probably no other people in the world are more devoted to the idea of written constitutions than are Americans. This devotion has deep roots in national traditions. In 1215 a group of English lords forced King John to sign a document, later known as the Magna Carta, which guaranteed them certain feudal rights and set a precedent for constitutional government. Although the British political tradition eventually rejected formal written constitutions, the idea of a written constitution was strongly reinforced by the experience in the Thirteen Colonies. The Colonies were created by charters given to companies establishing settlements in America. These charters became more elaborate as the colonial ventures succeeded, and dependence on a written code for government organization and operation became strongly entrenched.

Colonial History

Colonial charters, or **"constitutions,"** were granted through royal action, by recognizing proprietary rights, as in Maryland, Delaware, and Pennsylvania, or by granting royal commissions to companies, as in Virginia, Massachusetts, New Hampshire, New York, New Jersey, Georgia, and North and South Carolina. In two colonies, Connecticut and Rhode Island, royal charters were granted directly to the colonists, who participated in drawing up the charter for submission to the Crown. The important point is that these charters, whatever their origin, were present in all the Colonies, and many political traditions and expectations grew up around them.

All the Colonies were subject to royal control. Yet colonists looked to their charters for protection against British interference in colonial affairs. This was particularly true in Connecticut and Rhode Island, which had elected governors and legislatures whose acts were not subjected to a royal governor's veto, nor sent to England for approval. The political importance of these early charters is illustrated by the conflict over the Fundamental Orders of Connecticut. In 1685 King James issued an order for the repeal of Connecticut's charter. In 1687 Sir Edmund Andros went to Hartford and in the name of the Crown declared the government dissolved. The charter was not surrendered, however, but hidden by Captain John Wadsworth in an oak tree, which is now displayed for sightseers. Immediately after the English revolution of 1688, the document was taken out of the "Charter Oak" and used again as the fundamental law of the colony. Succeeding British monarchs silently permitted this colonial defiance. After the Declaration of Independence, new constitutions were written in 11 states; Connecticut retained its charter as the fundamental law until 1818, and Rhode Island kept its charter until 1842. The colonial experience, together with the earlier English heritage, firmly implanted the tradition of written constitutions.

State Constitutional Politics

Theoretically, constitutional decision making is deciding *how to decide*. It is deciding on the rules for policymaking; it is not policymaking itself. Policies are to be decided later, according to the rules set forth in a constitution.

But in reality, all state constitutions not only specify organizations and processes of decision making, but also undertake to determine many substantive policy questions. Unlike the U.S. Constitution, state constitutions contain many policy mandates on topics as diverse as tax rates, utility regulation, labor–management relations, insurance regulation, debt limits, educational funding, gambling, and a host of other policy matters. In nearly every election, voters are asked to decide on proposed amendments to their state constitutions. Most of these amendments deal with policy questions about which the voters have little knowledge or information. The result, of course, is that most state constitutions have become ponderous tomes that look more like law books than constitutions. While the U.S. Constitution contains only about 8,700 words, the average state constitution contains 26,000, and some run to over 100,000 (see Table 2–1). Length itself is not the problem but, rather, that these constitutions are laden with detailed policy decisions.

Why have so many policy mandates crept into state constitutions? Inasmuch as constitutions govern the actions of governors, legislators, executive agencies, and courts, many groups have sought to place their own policy preferences in constitutions. This places these preferences beyond the immediate reach of government officials, who are bound by constitutional mandates. If a policy preference is enacted into state law, it can be changed by ordinary actions of the legislature and governor. But if a policy preference is written into the state constitution, it can be changed only by extraordinary procedures—for most states a two-thirds vote in both houses of the legislature and majority approval of the voters in a statewide referendum.

COLONIAL CHARTERS
Documents granted to American colonies by English kings establishing governments; fostered American tradition of written constitutions.

CONSTITUTION
The legal structure establishing governmental bodies, granting their powers, determining how their members are selected, and prescribing the rules by which they make their decisions. Considered basic or fundamental, a constitution cannot be changed by ordinary acts of governmental bodies.

TABLE 2–1 General Information on State Constitutions

State	Number of Constitutions*	Year(s) of Adoption	Effective Year of Present Constitution	Estimated Length (Words)	Number of Amendments		
					Submitted to Voters	Adopted	Passage Rate (%)
Alabama[a]	6	1819, 1861, 1865, 1868, 1875, 1901	1901	376,006[a]	1180	855	72
Alaska	1	1956	1959	13,479	42	29	69
Arizona	1	1911	1912	47,306	266	147	55
Arkansas	5	1836, 1861, 1864, 1868, 1874	1874	59,120	196	98	50
California	2	1849, 1879	1879	67,048	891	525	59
Colorado	1	1876	1876	66,140	336	155	46
Connecticut[b]	4	1818, 1965	1965	16,401	31	30	97
Delaware[c]	4	1776, 1792, 1831, 1897	1897	25,445	N/A[c]	142	N/A
Florida	6	1839, 1861, 1865, 1868, 1886, 1968	1969	56,705	154	118	77
Georgia	10	1777, 1789, 1798, 1861, 1865, 1868, 1877, 1945, 1976, 1982	1983	41,684	94	71	76
Hawaii	1	1950	1959	21,498	131	110	84
Idaho	1	1889	1890	24,626	210	123	59
Illinois	4	1818, 1848, 1870, 1970	1971	16,401	18	12	67
Indiana	2	1816, 1851	1851	11,476	79	47	59
Iowa	2	1846, 1857	1857	11,089	59	54	92
Kansas	1	1859	1861	14,097	125	95	76
Kentucky	4	1792, 1799, 1850, 1891	1891	27,234	75	41	55
Louisiana	11	1812, 1845, 1852, 1861, 1864, 1868, 1879, 1898, 1913, 1921, 1974	1975	69,876	239	168	70
Maine	1	1819	1820	16,313	205	172	84
Maryland	4	1776, 1851, 1864, 1867	1867	43,198	261	225	86
Massachusetts	1	1780	1780	45,283	148	120	81
Michigan	4	1835, 1850, 1908, 1963	1964	31,164	68	30	44
Minnesota	1	1857	1858	11,734	215	120	56
Mississippi	4	1817, 1832, 1869, 1890	1890	26,229	161	125	78
Missouri	4	1820, 1865, 1875, 1945	1945	69,394	175	114	65
Montana	2	1889, 1972	1973	12,790	56	31	55
Nebraska	2	1866, 1875	1875	34,934	350	228	65
Nevada	1	1864	1864	37,418	232	136	59

Table 2–1 General Information on State Constitutions (Continued)

State	Number of Constitutions*	Year(s) of Adoption	Effective Year of Present Constitution	Estimated Length (Words)	Number of Amendments		
					Submitted to Voters	Adopted	Passage Rate (%)
New Hampshire	2	1776, 1784	1784	13,060	287	145	51
New Jersey	3	1776, 1844, 1947	1948	26,360	80	45	56
New Mexico	1	1911	1912	33,198	293	160	55
New York	4	1777, 1822, 1846, 1894	1895	44,397	295	220	75
North Carolina	3	1776, 1868, 1970	1971	17,177	37	30	81
North Dakota	1	1889	1889	18,746	265	150	57
Ohio	2	1802, 1851	1851	53,239	286	172	60
Oklahoma	1	1907	1907	81,666	354	187	53
Oregon	1	1857	1859	49,016	490	249	51
Pennsylvania	5	1776, 1790, 1838, 1873, 1968	1968	26,078	36	30	83
Rhode Island[b]	3	1842, 1986	1843	11,407	12	10	83
South Carolina	7	1776, 1778, 1790, 1861, 1865, 1868, 1895	1896	27,421	686	497	72
South Dakota	1	1889	1889	27,774	227	214	94
Tennessee	3	1796, 1835, 1870	1870	13,960	61	38	63
Texas	5	1845, 1861, 1866, 1869, 1876	1876	86,936	631	456	73
Utah	1	1895	1896	17,849	163	111	69
Vermont	3	1777, 1786, 1793	1793	8,565	211	53	25
Virginia	6	1776, 1830, 1851, 1869, 1902, 1970	1971	21,899	51	43	85
Washington	1	1889	1889	32,578	174	101	59
West Virginia	2	1863, 1872	1872	33,324	121	71	59
Wisconsin	1	1848	1848	15,102	194	145	75
Wyoming	1	1889	1890	26,349	125	98	78

*The constitutions referred to in this table include those Civil War documents customarily listed by the individual states.

aThe Alabama constitution includes numerous local amendments that apply to only one county.

bColonial charters with some alterations served as the first constitutions in Connecticut (1638, 1662) and in Rhode Island (1663).

cProposed amendments are not submitted to the voters in Delaware.

Source: For more detailed information, see *Book of the States,* 2012, Volume 44, Table 1.1, p. 11. Data as of January 1, 2012. Printed with permission from the Council of State Governments.

Interest Groups and Citizens' Movements

Interest groups frequently strive to "constitutionalize" their policy preferences. In Texas, for example, higher education proponents successfully persuaded the voters to approve a constitutional amendment expanding the number of schools benefitting from the proceeds of the public endowment that supports state universities. Similarly, grassroots citizens' movements in the United States, often displaying a distrust of elected officials, have sought to bind officials by constitutional mandates. Indeed, referenda on proposed state constitutional amendments confront voters in many states in almost every election.

Growth of State Constitutional Law

Along with interest groups and citizens' movements, lawyers and judges have contributed to the growth of state constitutional law. In a significant number of cases, state court judges have interpreted their own constitutions independently of the U.S. Constitution regarding civil rights and other controversies (see "Judicial Federalism" in Chapter 9). An emerging body of state constitutional law is a reminder of the legal importance of state constitutions.

Reformers' Influence

Over the years, specific constitutional amendments have resulted in lengthy documents. The more detailed and specific a state's constitution, the more likely it is to require more amendments to meet changing circumstances over time, thus leading to an even longer document. Constitutional reformers and "good government" groups have sought for many years to take policy matters out of the state constitution. They argue that governors and legislators should not be bound by constitutional details, that they need flexibility in confronting new challenges, and that state government should be strengthened, not weakened, in the modern era. These reform efforts have met with some success; newer state constitutions tend to be shorter than older ones. But it has become more difficult for reformers to convince politicians or the public that a state's constitution needs a complete overhaul.

<table>
<tr><td>2.2</td><td></td></tr>
</table>

Describe the key features that state constitutions share and the limits that they place on state governments.

STATE CONSTITUTIONS: AN OVERVIEW

Bill of Rights

BILL OF RIGHTS
In state constitutions, written protections for basic freedoms; most resemble the Bill of Rights in the U.S. Constitution but some extend these rights.

All state constitutions have a **bill of rights**, which asserts the basic freedoms of speech, press, religion, and assembly. (See "*Up Close:* The Sandy Hook Shootings and the Right to Bear Arms" and "*Rankings of the States:* State Gun Law Restrictiveness and Firearms Death Rate.") There are frequent references to basic procedural rights, such as the writ of habeas corpus, trial by jury, protection against double jeopardy and self-incrimination, prohibitions against ex post facto laws, imprisonment for debt, unreasonable searches and seizures, and excessive bail. Most of these protections merely duplicate the guarantees of the U.S. Constitution. However, frequently one finds in the state constitutions interesting "rights" that are not found in the national Constitution. For example, the Florida Constitution guarantees "every natural person the right to be let alone and free from government intrusion into his private life"; Mississippi guarantees the right of crime victims to speak in court and receive restitution; Indiana prohibits "unnecessary rigor" in punishment for crime. Some state constitutions have "little ERAs"—equal rights amendments—guaranteeing gender equality under law. Moreover, a *state* supreme court may place a different interpretation on a state constitutional right than the *federal* courts place on the same guarantee in the U.S. Constitution. (See "Judicial Federalism" in Chapter 9.)

Separation of Powers

SEPARATION OF POWERS
The constitutional allocation of powers among the three branches of government: legislative, executive, and judicial.

All state constitutions reflect the American political tradition of **separation of powers**, with separate legislative, executive, and judicial articles establishing these separate branches of government, and ensuring a system of checks and balances. Generally, however, state

UP CLOSE

The Sandy Hook Shootings and the Right to Bear Arms

On December 14, 2012, a gunman entered the Sandy Hook Elementary School in Newtown, Connecticut, and fatally shot 20 children and 6 teachers. The killer used a Bushmaster XM-15 assault rifle to blast his way through a locked glass door into the school building. In a first grade classroom he murdered the teacher and 15 of 16 pupils. A six-year-old girl was the sole survivor; she played dead until the killer left, then ran from the school covered with blood. The principal and school psychologist rushed to the room and were immediately shot and killed. The gunman reloaded his thirty-round magazine frequently. He proceeded to kill five other children in another classroom as well as three more teachers, some of whom died trying to protect the pupils. After firing 50 to 100 rounds, the gunman committed suicide by shooting himself in the head. Later it was found that he had killed his mother at home and taken his weapons from her lawful collection.

The Right to Bear Arms

The Second Amendment to the U.S. Constitution declares: "A well regulated Militia, being necessary to the security of a free State, the right of the people to keep and bear Arms, shall not be infringed." Many state constitutions include a provision guaranteeing the right to bear arms. Most of the state guarantees do not refer to a militia, but rather to the specific right of people to bear arms in self-defense. For example, Florida's Constitution states: "The right of people to keep and bear arms in defense of themselves and of the lawful authority of the state shall not be infringed."

The Right of Individuals to Bear Arms in Self-Defense

Over the years it was argued that the Second Amendment protects only the *collective* right of the states to form militias—that is, their right to maintain National Guard units. The argument focused on the qualifying phrase "a well regulated Militia, being necessary to the security of a free State." Yet another view was that the Second Amendment confers on Americans an *individual* constitutional right, like the First Amendment freedom of speech or press; that is, the right to own and bear arms. The history surrounding the adoption of the Second Amendment reveals the concern of colonists with attempts by despotic governments to confiscate the arms of citizens and render them helpless to resist tyranny. James Madison wrote in the *Federalist Papers* No. 46 that "the advantage of being armed which the Americans possess over the people of almost every other nation, forms a barrier against the enterprise of [tyrannical] ambition."

Enter the Supreme Court

The U.S. Supreme Court finally resolved the meaning of the Second Amendment in two important cases in 2008 and 2010. In *District of Columbia* v. *Heller* (2008) the Court held in a 5–4 decision that "The Second Amendment protects an individual right to possess a firearm unconnected with service in a militia and to use that arm for traditionally lawful purposes, such as self-defense within the home." The Court held that the District of Columbia's ban on handguns in the home violated the individual's right under the Second Amendment "to keep and bear arms." Yet because this case dealt with a *federal* jurisdiction, proponents of gun control hoped that it did not prohibit states and localities from banning guns. But in *McDonald* v. *Chicago* (2010), a case challenging Chicago's complete ban on handguns, the Supreme Court ruled (again by 5–4) that the Second Amendment incorporated a fundamental right that states and localities cannot abridge. The majority opinion stated: "it is clear that the Framers and ratifiers of the Fourteenth Amendment counted the right to keep and bear arms among those fundamental rights necessary to our system of ordered liberty." However, the opinion also stated that the Second Amendment right is not unlimited. Various government restrictions on guns may be constitutional. The Supreme Court left open the issue of exactly which gun controls are constitutional and which are not.

New York Acts Quickly

The Sandy Hook shootings inspired the New York State Legislature to enact the nation's toughest state gun regulations. Governor Andrew Cuomo signed the law in January, 2013, less than an hour after its final passage in the legislature. The law bans assault weapons (automatic and semi-automatic rifles and machine pistols), as well as high-capacity magazines (those that carry more than seven bullets). It requires background checks for both gun and ammunition buyers. It also creates a comprehensive databank on people barred from owning guns. Supporters hailed the legislation as a model for the national government.

A Presidential Proposal

President Barack Obama responded to the shooting and other mass gun violence with a multi-pronged proposal which included: reinstatement of a 1994 federal ban on assault weapons that had expired in 2004; a ten-round limit on ammunition magazines; criminal background checks on all gun sales, including those at "gun shows" and other private sales; elimination of armor piercing bullets; provision of mental health services in schools; federal funds to hire more police as school resource officers. He also issued a series of executive orders designed among other things to improve federal background checks.

constitutions emphasize legislative power over executive power. The historical explanation is that governors were appointed by the king in most colonies and the early constitutions reflected the colonists' distaste for executive authority. Yet the fact that constitutions are usually written by legislatures, legislative commissions, or constitutional conventions that resemble legislatures may also explain why legislative power is emphasized. Finally, the curtailment of executive power may reflect the desires of important interest groups in the states, who would prefer to deal with independent boards and commissions in the executive branch rather than with a strong governor. (See Chapter 7 for further discussion.)

Weak Governors

Whether the reasons are historical or political, the executive branches of most state governments are weakened and divided by state constitutions. Executive powers are divided between the governor and many separately elected executive officers—attorney general, secretary of state, treasurer, auditor, lieutenant governor, state school superintendent, and others. State constitutions also curtail executive authority by establishing a multitude of boards or commissions to head executive departments. Membership on these boards and commissions is generally for long overlapping terms, which are not coextensive with the term of the governor.

Legislative Powers

BICAMERAL
A legislative body that consists of two separate chambers or houses.

Only the Nebraska Constitution provides for a unicameral legislature. All other state legislatures are **bicameral**—divided into an upper and a lower chamber—making a total of 99 state legislative bodies. In many states the basis for apportioning these bodies is set forth in the state constitution. However, since the guarantee of the U.S. Constitution that no state shall deny to any person the "equal protection of the laws" takes precedence over state constitutions, federal courts require state legislative apportionment in both houses to meet the constitutional standard of one person, one vote. (See Chapter 6.)

Local Governments

All state constitutions have provisions regarding the organization and powers of local governments. Local governments are really subdivisions of state governments; they are not independent governmental bodies. State constitutions generally describe the organization of counties, cities, towns, townships, boroughs, school districts, and special districts. They may delegate responsibilities to them for public safety, police, fire, sanitation, sewage and refuse disposal, hospitals, streets, and public health. State constitutions may establish tax and debt limits for local governments, describe the kinds of taxes they may levy, and prescribe the way in which their funds may be spent. In the absence of constitutional provisions governing local governments, these subordinate units must rely upon state legislatures for their organization and powers. In recent years there has been a movement toward greater home rule for communities. More than half the states have provided for some semblance of home rule, which removes some of the internal affairs of communities from the intervention of state legislatures. Of course, when a "home rule" charter is granted to a community by an act of the legislature, it can be readily withdrawn or revised by the legislature. Constitutional home rule is a more secure grant of power to communities than legislative home rule. (See Chapter 10 for further discussion.)

Interest Group Regulation

Since state constitutions take precedence over state laws and are more difficult to amend, interest groups prefer to see special protections written into the state's fundamental document. This prevents legislatures from meddling in important business affairs each legislative session. Even reformers sometimes support the inclusion of regulatory language in the state's constitution, out of fear that later lobbying efforts by business could easily change

State Gun Law Restrictiveness and Firearms Death Rate

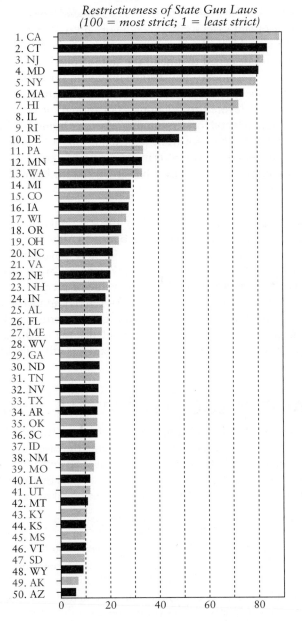

Restrictiveness of State Gun Laws
(100 = most strict; 1 = least strict)

1. CA
2. CT
3. NJ
4. MD
5. NY
6. MA
7. HI
8. IL
9. RI
10. DE
11. PA
12. MN
13. WA
14. MI
15. CO
16. IA
17. WI
18. OR
19. OH
20. NC
21. VA
22. NE
23. NH
24. IN
25. AL
26. FL
27. ME
28. WV
29. GA
30. ND
31. TN
32. NV
33. TX
34. AR
35. OK
36. SC
37. ID
38. NM
39. MO
40. LA
41. UT
42. MT
43. KY
44. KS
45. MS
46. VT
47. SD
48. WY
49. AK
50. AZ

0   20   40   60   80

Firearms Death Rate per 100,000

1. WY
2. LA
3. AL
4. MS
5. AR
6. MT
7. NV
8. TN
9. AK
10. NM
11. OK
12. SC
13. MO
14. WV
15. AZ
16. ID
17. GA
18. KY
19. FL
20. NC
21. CO
22. IN
23. TX
24. MI
25. KS
26. VA
27. PA
28. OR
29. UT
30. MD
31. SD
32. ND
33. WA
34. VT
35. DE
36. ME
37. OH
38. CA
39. IL
40. WI
41. NE
42. IA
43. NH
44. MN
45. RI
46. CT
47. NY
48. NJ
49. HI
50. MA

0   3   6   9   12   15   18   21

Note: Data are for 2011. The strength of gun laws in a state is based on a ranking system developed by the Brady Campaign, which assigns points based on the presence of specific laws related to curbing firearm trafficking, strengthening background checks, enhancing child safety, banning military style assault weapons, and restricting guns in public places.
Source: Brady Campaign to Prevent Gun Violence, 2011 Brady Campaign State Scorecard. Available at http://www.bradycampaign.me/sites/default/files/2011_Brady_Campaign_State_Scorecard_Rankings.pdf.

Note: Data are for 2009. Most recent data available at time of publication.
Source: "Number of Deaths Due to Injury by Firearms per 100,000 Population" The Kaiser Family Foundation State Health Facts. Data Source: Centers for Disease Control and Prevention, National Center for Health Statistics. Underlying Cause of Death 1999–2010. http://www.kff.org/other/state-indicator/firearms-death-rate-per-100000/

state laws. So most state constitutions include long sections on regulation of insurance, utilities, corporations, alcoholic beverages, railroads, mining, medicine, real estate, the state bar association, and education.

Taxation and Finance

All state constitutions have articles on taxation and finance. Frequently these place severe restrictions on the taxing power of state and local governments. Taxpayer groups distrust state legislatures and wherever possible seek to restrict taxing powers by constitutional mandate. Many referenda votes are designed to amend the state's constitution to limit tax burdens. (See Chapter 14.) Local governments may also be limited in state constitutions to specific tax sources and upper limits or "caps" on local taxation. Certain classes of property may be protected, such as that devoted to religious, educational, or charitable uses; government property; some agricultural or forestry land; and even "**homesteads,**" that is, owner-occupied homes. Some constitutions may grant tax exemptions to new industries in order to attract industrial development. Constitutions may "earmark" certain tax revenues for specific purposes; for example, gasoline taxes may be earmarked for highway use only.

Debt Limitation

Most state constitutions limit debt that can be incurred by the state only or by local governments. Many states *must* have a balanced operating budget. (Although such a constitutional command does not always succeed, on the whole, state governments are less burdened by debt than is the federal government.) Local governments are frequently limited to a debt that cannot exceed a fixed percentage of the value of property in the community. Moreover, state constitutions generally require a local referendum to approve any increase in local debt. Occasionally, however, state and local governments devise ways to get around constitutional debt limits; for example, they may pledge the revenues of a new project ("revenue bonds") to pay off the debt, rather than taxes ("full faith and credit bonds"). (See Chapter 14.)

2.3   CONSTITUTIONAL CHANGE IN THE STATES

Examine the various methods used to change state constitutions: legislative proposals, popular initiatives, constitutional conventions, and constitutional commissions.

The U.S. Constitution has been amended only 77 times in 200 years (and the first 10 amendments, the Bill of Rights, were really part of the process of ratifying the original document). But state constitutions are so detailed and restrictive that they must be amended frequently. Nearly every year state voters must consider constitutional amendments on the ballot.

Throughout the 50 states, there are four methods of constitutional change:

■ *Legislative proposal:* Amendments are passed by the state legislature and then submitted to the voters for approval in a referendum. This method is available in all states. (However, in Delaware amendments passed by the legislature need not be submitted to the voters.)

■ *Popular initiative:* A specific number of voters petition to get a constitutional amendment on the ballot for approval by the voters in a referendum. This method is available in 17 states.

■ *Constitutional convention:* Legislatures submit to the voters a proposal for calling a constitutional convention, and if voters approve, a convention convenes, draws up constitutional revisions, and submits them again for approval by the voters in a referendum. This method is available in at least 41 states.

■ *Constitutional commission:* Constitutional commissions may be created by legislatures to study the constitution and recommend changes to the state legislature, or in the case of Florida (only), to submit its recommendations directly to the voters in a referendum.

Over the years, the record of voters' response to state constitutional amendment (Table 2–2) shows that voters are more accepting of individual amendments submitted to them by *state legislatures* than any other method of constitutional change. A somewhat higher percentage of citizen initiatives are defeated at the polls, as are most amendments proposed by

TABLE 2-2 The Success of State Constitutional Amendments by Method of Initiation

Method of Initiation	Total Proposals									Percentage Adopted								
	1996–97	1998–99	2000–01	2002–03	2004–05	2006–07	2008–09	2010–11	2011–12	1996–97	1998–99	2000–01	2002–03	2004–05	2006–07	2008–09	2010–11	2011–12
All Methods	233	296	212	232	166	200	132	191	186	76	77	72	71	68	78	64	70	63
Legislative Proposal	193	266	180	208	127	167	98	170	125	82	79	91	75	75	87	69	72	74
Popular (Citizen) Initiative	40	21	32	24	39	33	30	21	61	48	52	41	36	44	33	43	57	43
Constitutional Convention																		
Constitutional Commission		9					4				89					75		

Source: Book of the States, 2012, Volume 44, Table A, p. 4; 2012 data from University of Southern California Initiative & Referendum Institute, *Ballotwatch*, November 2012. Available at http://www.iandrinstitute.org/BW%202012-3%20Election%20results%20v1.pdf. Printed with permission from the Council of State Governments.

constitutional conventions. These figures suggest the key role that state legislatures play in constitutional change. While it is true that many legislative proposals are merely "editorial," voters seem to prefer limited, step-by-step constitutional change, rather than sweeping reform initiated by citizens.

Legislative Proposal

The most common method of amending state constitutions is by **legislative proposal**. Many states require that a constitutional amendment receive a two-thirds vote in both chambers of the legislature before submission to the voters; a few states require a three-fifths majority in both houses, while others require only simple legislative majorities. Some states require that a constitutional amendment be passed by two successive legislative sessions before being submitted to the voters. Every state except Delaware requires constitutional amendments proposed by the legislature to be submitted to the voters for approval in a referendum. (See Table 2–3.)

Popular Initiative

Popular initiative of constitutional revision was introduced during the Progressive Era at the beginning of the twentieth century; this method usually requires that an initiative petition be signed by 5, 10, or 15 percent of the number of voters in the last governor's election. The petition method allows citizens to get an amendment on the ballot *without the approval of the state legislature*. It is not surprising that measures designed to reduce the powers of legislators—for example, *tax limitation* measures and *term limits* for legislators—have come about as a result of citizen initiatives.

Constitutional Convention

While there has been only one national Constitutional Convention, in 1787, there have been over 230 state constitutional conventions. State constitutional conventions are generally proposed by state legislatures, and the question of whether or not to have a convention is generally submitted to the state's voters. (Some state constitutions require periodic submission to the voters of the question of calling a constitutional convention.) The legislature usually decides how convention delegates are to be elected and the convention organized. More important, the legislature usually decides whether the convention's work is to be *limited* to specific proposals or topics, or *unlimited* and free to write an entire new constitution.

In recent years, however, neither legislators nor voters have shown much enthusiasm for state constitutional conventions. No state conventions were held in the 1990s. (The Louisiana legislature convened itself as the "Louisiana Convention of 1992," but the meeting was really only a special session of the legislature; moreover, its proposed constitutional revision failed by a wide margin at the polls. Hawaii voters came close to calling a convention in 1996; they cast more "Yes" than "No" votes but not the necessary majority of *all* votes after blank votes were counted.) Indeed, voters have regularly *rejected* convention calls in the states that require periodic votes on whether or not to hold a convention. For example, in 2012, voters in Alaska, New Hampshire, and Ohio all rejected calling a constitutional convention—with nearly two-thirds voting against it in each state.

Political leaders and citizens alike appear wary of calling a constitutional convention. They are suspicious of "reform" and fearful about "runaway" conventions making unwanted changes in the political system. This is true of voters despite the fact that they always have the opportunity of later voting on the constitutional changes proposed by a convention. The current fear of conventions may also be a product of low levels of trust and confidence in government, as well as a lack of political consensus on many "hot-button" issues such as abortion, affirmative action, gambling, gun control, and tax limitations. Advocates on both sides of these kinds of issues may be unsure of the outcome of a

TABLE 2–3 State Constitutional Amendment by Legislatures

	Legislative Vote Required for Proposal	Consideration by Two Sessions Required	Referendum Vote Required for Ratification
Alabama	3/5	No	Majority vote on amendment
Alaska	2/3	No	Majority vote on amendment
Arizona	Majority	No	Majority vote on amendment
Arkansas	Majority	No	Majority vote on amendment
California	2/3	No	Majority vote on amendment
Colorado	2/3	No	Majority vote on amendment
Connecticut	(a)	(a)	Majority vote on amendment
Delaware	2/3	Yes	Not required
Florida	3/5	No	3/5 vote on amendment
Georgia	2/3	No	Majority vote on amendment
Hawaii	(b)	(b)	Majority vote on amendment
Idaho	2/3	No	Majority vote on amendment
Illinois	3/5	No	(c)
Indiana	Majority	Yes	Majority vote on amendment
Iowa	Majority	Yes	Majority vote on amendment
Kansas	2/3	No	Majority vote on amendment
Kentucky	3/5	No	Majority vote on amendment
Louisiana	2/3	No	Majority vote on amendment
Maine	2/3	No	Majority vote on amendment
Maryland	3/5	No	Majority vote on amendment
Massachusetts	Majority	Yes	Majority vote on amendment
Michigan	2/3	No	Majority vote on amendment
Minnesota	Majority	No	Majority vote in election
Mississippi	2/3	No	Majority vote on amendment
Missouri	Majority	No	Majority vote on amendment
Montana	2/3	No	Majority vote on amendment
Nebraska	3/5	No	Majority vote on amendment
Nevada	Majority	Yes	Majority vote on amendment
New Hampshire	3/5	No	2/3 vote on amendment
New Jersey	(d)	(d)	Majority vote on amendment
New Mexico	Majority	No	Majority vote on amendment
New York	Majority	Yes	Majority vote on amendment
North Carolina	3/5	No	Majority vote on amendment
North Dakota	Majority	No	Majority vote on amendment
Ohio	3/5	No	Majority vote on amendment
Oklahoma	Majority	No	Majority vote on amendment
Oregon	Majority	No	Majority vote on amendment
Pennsylvania	Majority	Yes	Majority vote on amendment
Rhode Island	Majority	No	Majority vote on amendment
South Carolina	2/3	Yes	Majority vote on amendment
South Dakota	Majority	No	Majority vote on amendment
Tennessee	2/3	Yes	Majority vote in election
Texas	2/3	No	Majority vote on amendment
Utah	2/3	No	Majority vote on amendment
Vermont	Majority	Yes	Majority vote on amendment
Virginia	Majority	Yes	Majority vote on amendment

(continued)

TABLE 2–3   **State Constitutional Amendment by Legislatures (Continued)**

	Legislative Vote Required for Proposal	Consideration by Two Sessions Required	Referendum Vote Required for Ratification
Washington	2/3	No	Majority vote on amendment
West Virginia	2/3	No	Majority vote on amendment
Wisconsin	Majority	Yes	Majority vote on amendment
Wyoming	2/3	No	Majority vote in election

[a]3/4 vote at one session, or majority vote in two sessions between which an election has intervened.

[b]2/3 vote at one session or majority vote in two sessions.

[c]Majority voting in election or 3/5 voting on amendment.

[d]3/5 vote in session or majority vote in two sessions.

Source: Book of the States, 2012, Volume 44, Table 1.2, pp. 13–14. Printed with permission from the Council of State Governments.

convention and therefore unite to oppose calling for one. Rhode Islanders reflected these concerns when they defeated such a call by a 52 to 48 percent margin in 2004. Comments by one citizen blogger analyzed the dilemma well: "I guess it's a matter of cynicism. If you think an honest group of engaged citizens can get together and debate good reforms for our government, vote yes. If you're worried that a slate of unaccountable insiders will stack the delegate deck or simple majorities will want to roll back things like gay rights or reproductive rights, vote no."[1]

Constitutional Revision Commissions

These commissions are created by legislatures to "study and recommend" constitutional changes. Legislatures generally prefer a constitutional commission to a convention, because a commission can only study and report to the legislature. In addition, a commission can relieve the state legislature of a great deal of work. The typical commission is appointed by an act of the legislature, and its membership usually includes legislators, executive officials, and prominent citizens. Its recommendations are usually handled in the legislature like regular constitutional amendments, although they may be more sweeping than ordinary amendments.

Constitutional revision commissions have also been declining in number in recent years. (However, three of the nation's largest states—California, New York, and Florida—together with Arkansas and Utah created constitutional revision commissions in the 1990s.) The value of these commissions is in their supposed ability to review fundamental governmental processes, to inspire citizen participation in this review, and perhaps to provide an opportunity for legislatures to shift some especially controversial issues away from themselves and onto the shoulders of independent bodies.[2] And, of course, legislatures still retain control of the revision process, since commissions must usually make their recommendations to their legislatures, which then decide whether to place them on the ballot for voter approval. More often than not, legislators have ignored commission recommendations or watered them down before submitting them to the voters.

DEMOCRACY

Popular participation in government. (The Greek root of the word means "rule by the many.")

REPRESENTATIVE DEMOCRACY

Popular participation in government through the selection of public officials by a vote of the people in periodic, competitive elections in which candidates and voters can freely express themselves.

2.4 DEMOCRACY IN THE STATES

Trace the development of direct democracy in the states, assess the effectiveness of its variants, and compare it to representative democracy.

Democracy means popular participation in government. (The Greek root of the word means "rule by the many.") But popular participation can have different meanings. To our nation's Founders, who were ambivalent about the wisdom of democracy, it meant that the voice of the people would be *represented* in government. **Representative democracy** means the selection of government officials by a vote of the people in periodic elections open to competition in which candidates and voters can freely express themselves. (Note that "elections" in which only one party is permitted to run candidates, or where candidates are not free to express their views, do not qualify as democratic.) The Founders believed that government rests ultimately on the consent of the governed. But their notion of "republicanism" envisioned decision making by representatives of the people, rather than direct decision making by the people. The U.S. Constitution has no provision for direct voting by the people on national policy questions.

Direct democracy means that the people themselves can initiate and decide policy questions by popular vote. The Founders were profoundly skeptical of this form of democracy. They had read about direct democracy in the ancient Greek city-state of Athens, and they believed that "the follies" of direct democracy far outweighed any virtues it might possess. It was not until over 100 years after the U.S. Constitution was written that widespread support developed in the American states for direct voter participation in policymaking. Direct democracy developed in states and communities, and it is found today *only* in state and local government.

History of Direct Democracy in the States

At the beginning of the twentieth century, a strong populist movement in the midwestern and western states attacked railroads, banks, corporations, and the political institutions that were said to be in their hands.[3] The populists were later joined by progressive reformers who attacked "bosses," "machines," and parties as corrupt. The populists believed that their elected representatives were ignoring the needs of farmers, debtors, and laborers. They wished to bypass governors and legislatures and directly enact popular laws for railroad rate regulation, relief of farm debt, and monetary expansion. They believed that both the Democratic and Republican parties of their era were controlled by the trusts and monopolies. The progressives and reformers viewed politics as distasteful. They did not believe that government should be involved in resolving conflicts among competing interests or striving for compromises in public policy. Instead, government should serve "the public interest"; it should seek out the "right" answer to public questions; it should replace politicians with managers and administrators. The progressive reform movement was supported by many upper middle-class, white, Anglo-Saxon, Protestant groups, who felt that political "machines" were catering to the votes of recent immigrants such as Irish, Italians, eastern and southern Europeans, working-class people, Catholics, and Jews.[4] The progressive reform movement brought about many changes in the structure of municipal government. (See "Reformers and Do-Gooders" in Chapter 11.) The movement also brought about some interesting innovations in state government.

In order to reduce the influence of "politics," "parties," and "politicians," the populists and progressives advocated a wide range of devices designed to bypass political institutions and encourage direct participation by voters in public affairs. They were largely responsible for replacing party conventions with the primary elections we use today. They were also successful in bringing about the Seventeenth Amendment to the U.S. Constitution requiring that U.S. senators be directly elected by the voters, rather than chosen by state legislatures. They also supported women's suffrage, civil service, and restrictive immigration laws.

The populists and progressives were also responsible for the widespread adoption of three forms of direct democracy: **initiative, referendum**, and **recall**. These reforms began in the farm states of the Midwest and the mining states of the West. The populists provided much of the early support for these devices, and the progressives and reformers carried them to fruition. President Woodrow Wilson endorsed initiative, referendum, and recall, and most adoptions occurred prior to World War I.

Initiative

This device allows a specific number or percent of voters, through the use of a petition, to have a proposed state constitutional amendment or a state law placed on the ballot. This process bypasses the legislature and allows citizens to both propose and adopt laws and

DIRECT DEMOCRACY
Popular participation in government through direct voter initiation of policy (usually by petition) and voter approval or rejection of policy decisions by popular vote.

INITIATIVE
A device by which a specific number or percentage of the voters may petition to have a constitutional amendment or law placed on the ballot for adoption or rejection by the electorate; found in some state constitutions but not in the U.S. Constitution.

REFERENDA
Proposed laws or constitutional amendments submitted to the voters for their direct approval or rejection; found in some state constitutions but not in the U.S. Constitution.

RECALL
An election to allow voters to decide whether to remove an elected official before his or her term expires; found in some state constitutions but not in the U.S. Constitution.

constitutional amendments. Table 2–4 lists the states that allow popular initiatives for constitutional amendments, and those that allow popular initiatives for state law. Note that Alaska, Idaho, Maine, Utah, Washington, and Wyoming permit citizen initiatives for state *laws,* but not for constitutional *amendments.* Historically, use of the initiative process has been highest in Oregon, California, Colorado, North Dakota, and Arizona, according to the Initiative and Referendum Institute.

Referendum

This device requires the electorate to approve decisions of the legislature before these become law or become part of the state constitution. As we noted earlier, most states require a favorable referendum vote for a state constitutional amendment. Referenda on state laws may be submitted by the legislature (when legislators want to shift decision-making responsibility to the people), or referenda may be demanded by popular petition (when the people wish to change laws passed by the legislature).

TABLE 2–4   Initiative and Recall in the States

Initiative for Constitutional Amendments (Signatures Required to Get on Ballot)[a]	Statutory Initiative (for State Laws)	Recall (Signatures Required to Force a Recall Election)[b]
Arizona (15%)	Alaska	Alaska (25%)
Arkansas (10%)	Arizona	Arizona (25%)
California (8%)	Arkansas	California (12%)
Colorado (5% of votes cast for sec. state in last election)	California	Colorado (25%)
Florida (8% of statewide votes cast in last presidential election)	Colorado	Georgia (15%)
Illinois (8%)	Idaho	Idaho (20%)
Massachusetts (3%)	Maine	Illinois (15%)
Michigan (10%)	Massachusetts	Kansas (40%)
Mississippi (12%)	Michigan	Louisiana (33%)
Missouri (8%)	Missouri	Michigan (25%)
Montana (10% of qualified electors in state at large)	Montana	Minnesota (25%)
Nebraska (10% of registered voters)	Nebraska	Montana (10%)
Nevada (10% of total votes in last general election)	Nevada	Nevada (25%)
North Dakota (4% of state population)	North Dakota	New Jersey (25%)
Ohio (10%)	Ohio	North Dakota (25%)
Oklahoma (15% of votes cast for office receiving the highest number of votes in the last state election)	Oklahoma	Oregon (15%)
Oregon (8%)	Oregon	Rhode Island (15%)
South Dakota (10%)	South Dakota	Washington (25%)
	Utah	Wisconsin (25%)
	Washington	
	Wyoming	

[a]Figures expressed as percentage of vote in last governor's election unless otherwise specified; some states also require distribution of votes across counties and districts.

[b]Figures are percentages of voters in last general elections of the official sought to be recalled.

Source: Statutory and Constitutional Initiative Powers from National Conference of State Legislatures, "Signature Requirements for Initiative Proposals: 2012 Elections," September 20, 2012. Available at http://www.ncsl.org/Portals/1/Documents/legismgt/elect/2012_SigReqs.pdf. © 2012 National Conference of State Legislatures. Recall powers from National Conference of State Legislatures, "Recall of State Officials," July 2011. Available at http://www.ncsl.org/legislatures-elections/elections/recall-of-state-officials.aspx. © 2011 National Conference of State Legislatures

Recall

Recall elections allow voters to remove an elected official before his or her term expires. Usually a recall election is initiated by a petition. The number of signatures required is generally expressed as a percentage of votes cast in the last election for the official being recalled (frequently 25%). Currently 19 states provide for recall election for some or all of their elected officials (see Table 2–4). The impeachment and removal of Illinois governor Rod Blagojevich (D) led that state's voters in 2010 to approve a constitutional amendment enabling recall elections of governors in their state. Recall efforts increase during economic downturns when voters are angry at elected officials' for budget cuts or proposed tax and fee increases. Although officials are often publicly threatened with recall, rarely is anyone ever removed from office through this device. But it does happen. Regardless of the outcome, the recall process is often very expensive and divisive because it first involves an expensive petition drive, then a costly election campaign against the incumbent. Recent examples were gubernatorial recall elections in California and Wisconsin. In 2003, Californians removed California governor Gray Davis (D) from office in an election that cost nearly $70 million. In 2012, Wisconsin governor survived a recall effort that cost an estimated $81 million.

DIRECT VERSUS REPRESENTATIVE DEMOCRACY

2.5

Evaluate whether direct or representative democracy is a better approach for governing the states.

The U.S. Constitution has no provision for national referenda. Americans as a nation cannot vote on federal laws or amendments to the national constitution. But voters in the *states* can express their frustrations directly in popular initiatives and referenda voting.

Arguments for Direct Democracy

Proponents of direct democracy make several strong arguments on behalf of the initiative and referendum devices.[5]

- Direct democracy enhances government responsiveness and accountability. The threat of a successful initiative and referendum drive—indeed sometimes the mere circulation of a petition—encourages officials to take popular actions.
- Direct democracy allows citizen groups to bring their concerns directly to the public. Taxpayer groups, for example, who are not especially well represented in state capitals, have been able through initiative and referendum devices to place their concerns on the public agenda.
- Direct democracy stimulates debate about policy issues. In elections with important referendum issues on the ballot, campaigns tend to be more issue oriented. Candidates, newspapers, interest groups, and television news are all forced to directly confront policy issues.
- Direct democracy stimulates voter interest and improves election-day turnout. Controversial issues on the ballot—the death penalty, abortion, gun control, taxes, gay rights, English only, and so on—bring out additional voters. There is some limited evidence that elections with initiatives on the ballot increase voter turnout by three to five percentage points over elections with no initiatives on the ballot.[6]
- Direct democracy increases trust in government and diminishes alienation. While it is difficult to substantiate such a claim, the opportunity to directly affect issues should give voters an increased sense of power.

Arguments for Representative Democracy

Opponents of direct democracy, from our nation's Founders to the present, argue that representative democracy offers far better protection for individual liberty and the rights of minorities than direct democracy. The Founders constructed a system of **checks and balances** not so much to protect against the oppression of a ruler, but to protect against

CHECKS AND BALANCES Constitutional provisions giving each branch of the national government certain checks over the actions of other branches.

the tyranny of the majority. Opponents of direct democracy echo many of the Founders' arguments:

- Direct democracy encourages majorities to sacrifice the rights of individuals and minorities. This argument supposes that voters are generally less tolerant than elected officials, and there is some evidence to support this supposition. However, there is little evidence that public policy in states with the initiative and referendum is any more oppressive than public policy in states without these devices. Nonetheless, the potential of majoritarian sacrifice of the liberty of unpopular people is always a concern.

- Direct democracy facilitates the adoption of unwise and unsound policies. Although voters have rejected many bad ideas, frequently initiatives are less well drafted than legislation.

- Voters are not sufficiently informed to cast intelligent ballots on many issues. Many voters cast their vote in a referendum without ever having considered the issue before going into the polling booth.

- A referendum does not allow consideration of alternative policies or modifications or amendments to the proposition set forth on the ballot. In contrast, legislators devote a great deal of attention to writing, rewriting, and amending bills, and seeking out compromises among interests.

- Direct democracy enables special interests to mount expensive initiative and referendum campaigns. Although proponents of direct democracy argue that these devices allow citizens to bypass special-interest-group-dominated legislatures, in fact only a fairly well-financed group can mount a statewide campaign on behalf of a referendum issue. And the outcome of the vote may be heavily influenced by paid television advertising. So money is important in both "representative" and "direct" democracy.

- Ballot initiatives also create an environment that encourages citizens to distrust their elected officials. By putting citizens in an "adversarial relationship with their governments," they begin to criticize the regular political process and view public officials as "untrustworthy."[7]

The chief justice of California's Supreme Court in a speech on "The Perils of Direct Democracy" argued that there needs to be "some fundamental reform of the voter initiative process [otherwise] we shall continue on a course of dysfunctional state government, characterized by a lack of accountability on the part of our officeholders as well as the voting public."[8]

The Decline of Representative Government

Direct, popular participation in government in the American states has been growing in strength at the expense of representative democracy. State legislatures, and indeed state governments generally, are perceived by the American public as largely unresponsive, frequently unethical, and dominated by special interests. Whether or not this popular image is accurate, it drives the political movement toward increasing numbers of popular initiatives and referenda votes. National surveys report overwhelming support for "laws which allow citizens to place initiatives directly on the ballot by collecting petition signatures."[9] In American state and local government, "Participatory democracy is here to stay; there is no turning back."[10] Citizens have, in effect, become "Election Day lawmakers."[11]

| 2.6 | THE POLITICS OF STATE INITIATIVES |

Discuss how state initiatives have been used to move public policies in both liberal and conservative directions, and assess the current ideological trend of state initiates.

In theory the initiative device is ideologically neutral; both liberal and conservative groups can use this device to bypass state legislatures. During the Progressive Era at the beginning of the twentieth century, many *liberal* reforms were advanced by popular initiative. In recent years, as the general public has moved in a *conservative* direction, many citizen initiative efforts have reflected conservative themes. It is true, however, that the ideological makeup of a state affects the type of initiatives that end up on the ballot. This explains why citizens in the more liberal states, such as Oregon, Colorado, and California, sign petitions to put medicinal marijuana issues on the ballot, while those in the more conservative Deep South states offer amendments defining marriage as solely between a man and a woman (see Table 2–5).

TABLE 2–5 State Votes on Selected Propositions in the 2000s

Taxes

		Outcome
Oklahoma (2004)	Create property tax exemption for disabled veterans and surviving spouses	Pass
Alaska (2006)	Tax commercial passenger ships visiting the state	Pass
Colorado (2006)	Prohibit tax deduction of wages paid to undocumented immigrants	Pass
Florida (2008)	Property tax exemption for conservation property	Pass
Massachusetts (2008)	Repeal state income tax	Fail
Georgia (2010)	New fee on car tags for new trauma trust fund	Fail
California (2012)	Increase income taxes on wealthy and increase sales tax	Pass

Civil Rights

Nevada (2000)	Prohibit same-sex marriages	Pass
Arizona (2004)	Require proof of citizenship to register to vote; require state agencies to check the immigration status of program beneficiaries	Pass
Michigan (2006)	Prohibit racial preferences/affirmative action	Pass
Rhode Island (2006)	Allow felons to vote after leaving prison	Pass
California (2008)	Define marriage as solely between one man and one woman	Pass
Arizona (2010)	Bar preferential treatment in public employment, education, and contracting	Pass
Maine (2012)	Legalizes same-sex marriage	Pass
Oklahoma (2012)	Prohibits discrimination or preferential treatment based on race, sex, ethnicity, and national origin	Pass

Drugs

Colorado (2000)	Allow marijuana for medicinal purposes	Pass
Alaska (2004)	Legalize persons age 21 or older to grow, sell, use, or give away marijuana	Fail
Arizona (2006)	Limit probation for methamphetamine convicts	Pass
Massachusetts (2008)	Decriminalize the possession of marijuana	Pass
Michigan (2008)	Allow medical use of marijuana	Pass
California (2010)	Legalize and tax possession of marijuana	Fail
Colorado (2012)	Legalizes and taxes marijuana	Pass

Education

California (2000)	Establish school voucher system	Fail
Michigan (2000)	Establish school voucher system	Fail
South Dakota (2004)	Allow state to provide food and transportation funding for children who attend religious schools	Fail
Ohio (2006)	Allow slot machines; dedicate revenue for college scholarships	Pass
Arkansas (2008)	Authorize state lottery with money dedicated to education	Pass
Oregon (2008)	Require teacher compensation to be based on classroom performance	Fail
Idaho (2012)	Approve or repeal a law tying teacher pay to student performance on standardized tests	Fail (Repealed)

Abortion

Colorado (2000)	Require waiting period for abortions	Fail
Florida (2004)	Authorize legislature to pass a law requiring parental notification when teens seek an abortion	Pass
Oregon (2006)	Waiting period and parental notification for abortion by minor	Fail
South Dakota (2008)	Prohibit abortion except in case of rape, health of mother	Fail
Colorado (2008)	Defines a "person" to be any human being from moment of fertilization	Fail
Mississippi (2011)	Defines "personhood" as beginning at the moment of fertilization, cloning or the functional equivalent	Fail
Montana (2012)	Requires parental notification before a minor's abortion	Pass

(continued)

Other		Outcome
Alaska (2004)	Prevent intentional baiting and feeding of bears	Fail
Georgia (2006)	Preserve the "tradition of fishing and hunting"	Pass
Missouri (2006)	Allow stem cell research	Pass
Missouri (2008)	Establish English as the language of all governmental meetings	Pass
Washington (2008)	Allow physician-assisted suicide	Pass
California (2010)	Suspend greenhouse gas reduction mandate until unemployment rate drops below 5.5%	Fail
Massachusetts (2012)	Permits physician-assisted suicide	Fail

Source: Book of the States, annual publications. 2012 data from University of Southern California Initiative & Referendum Institute, *Ballotwatch,* November 2012. Available at http://www.iandrinstitute.org/BW%202012-3%20Election%20results%20v1.pdf. Printed with permission from the Council of State Governments2.

Tax Limitation Initiatives

PROPOSITION 13

A constitutional amendment to reduce property taxes passed by California voters; has come to symbolize tax revolts.

The nation's "tax revolt" got its start with citizen initiatives in the states, beginning with California's **Proposition 13** in 1978, a constitutional amendment initiative to reduce property taxes. "Prop 13" was funded by real estate developers, business, and agricultural interests. Opposition was led by public officials who believed the amendment would cripple public services. The political establishment was joined by public employee unions, teachers, and environmental groups, in making dire predictions about the impact of the amendment. But California voters went to the polls in record numbers to approve Proposition 13 by better than a two-to-one margin. By 1980 Democrats and Republicans across the nation were campaigning as "tax cutters." Later, President Ronald Reagan would interpret it as part of a general mandate for lower taxes and less government, and as a forerunner to his own federal income tax cuts. But not all states joined in the "tax revolt."

In the years since Proposition 13, however, almost as many states *defeated* tax limitation referenda as passed them. And California voters surprised anti-tax forces in 1998 by approving a citizens' initiative to raise cigarette taxes by 50 cents a pack, then again in 2012 when they approved higher taxes for the wealthy. (Chapter 14 will devote more discussion to the politics of taxation.) Scholars have tried to distinguish between states in which the tax revolt was successful and those where it was not. It turns out that the states with constitutional provisions for citizen initiatives are more likely to join the "tax revolt"—that is, to pass tax limitation constitutional amendments—than states without provisions for citizen initiatives.[12] Cigarette tax increases are the exception— they seem to pass nearly everywhere, especially if the tax is earmarked for health programs for the poor.

Steep property tax increases, often due to higher land valuations, frequently generate citizen protests and often result in tax limitation ballot initiatives. Tax revolts have long characterized politics in America, beginning with the Boston Tea Party.

Crime and Drugs

"Getting tough on crime" has generally been popular with referendum voters. For years, the death penalty was approved everywhere it has appeared on the ballot, including Massachusetts. More recently, support for the death penalty has softened a bit. Voters in some states have been successful in prompting their legislators to reject the death penalty (New Jersey, 2007; Maryland, 2013).

Recent referendum votes have also shown that citizens are far less enthusiastic about the "War on Drugs" than most politicians proclaim to be. Governors and legislators apparently feel uncomfortable taking the lead in reducing penalties for drug possession or allowing marijuana use for medicinal or recreational purposes.

Voters in California approved an initiative statute, placed on the ballot by citizen petition, that substitutes treatment for prison as a consequence for unlawful drug possession and use. This initiative requires judges to impose probation and drug treatment, not incarceration, for possession, use, or transportation of controlled substances. Only the manufacture and sale of drugs remains a prison offense. Moreover, the initiative authorized the dismissal of charges after completion of drug treatment.

Constitutional amendments allowing medical use of marijuana have been approved by voters in several states. However, federal law prohibits it and the U.S. Supreme Court has held that federal law prevails over state law in drug regulation.

Early on voters in Arizona, California, Alaska, Colorado, Nevada, Oregon, Montana, and Washington approved referenda allowing the medical use of marijuana. By 2013, 18 states had approved medical marijuana use. (While the U.S. Supreme Court has held that federal law prohibiting such use prevails over state law, the federal government has not been aggressive in enforcing the law.) In 2012, the marijuana battle took a different turn. Voters in Washington and Colorado approved the recreational use of marijuana. It appears voters were swayed by proponents' arguments that making it legal could raise much needed revenue (it would be taxed) and relieve overcrowded jails. Again, the U.S. attorney general expressed little interest in prosecuting these states. (The reticence of the federal government to get involved in the marijuana issue will be discussed in more detail in Chapter 3 on Federalism.)

Abortion and Physician-Assisted Suicide

Both abortion and physician-assisted suicide remain controversial issues among both citizens and legislators. In some states, referendum votes have prohibited the use of state funds for abortion, while in other states such a prohibition has failed. (The U.S. Congress, in its controversial "Hyde Amendment," prohibits the use of federal funds for abortions, except to protect the life of a woman or in cases of rape or incest. See "Battles over Abortion" in Chapter 15.) Limits on abortion have been hotly contested in various state referendum votes; abortion opponents have lost more of these referendum votes than they have won. And no consensus appears to have developed in the states regarding physician-assisted suicide. In 1998, voters in Michigan defeated an initiative allowing it as did Massachusetts voters in 2012. But voters approved it in Oregon in 2000 and Washington in 2008.

Prohibiting Same-Sex Marriages

Following a decision by the Supreme Court of Vermont that recognized the validity of same-sex marriages in that state, several states moved quickly to amend their constitutions to prohibit such marriages and to deny recognition to them. When a Massachusetts Supreme Judicial Court ruled in February 2004 that the state's prohibition against gay marriage violated the state constitution, a number of other states rushed to put amendments outlawing same-sex marriages on their ballots. Referendum voters have approved such prohibitions when they have appeared on the ballot. The longest lasting amendment-related battle over same-sex marriage has been in California. In 2008, the California Supreme Court held that banning same-sex marriages was an unconstitutional denial of the Equal Protection Clause of the Fourteenth Amendment. But that same year California voters passed a state constitutional amendment, Proposition 8, declaring that "only marriage between a man and a woman is valid or recognized in California." California officials, including the governor, refused to defend Proposition 8 in federal courts. Lower federal courts held that Proposition 8 was unconstitutional. But when the case was presented to the Supreme Court, it held on a technicality that the parties to the case had no "standing" before the Court. But the effect of the Courts decision was to let the lower federal courts' rulings stand, thus approving same-sex marriages in California. *Hollingsworth* v. *Perry,* June 26, 2013.

School Vouchers

Proposals to grant school vouchers to parents to spend at any school they choose, including private schools, have met with voter disapproval in several key referendum votes including California (in 1993 and again in 2000) and Michigan. These losses set back the advocates of "school choice." However, the movement regained momentum as the number of failing schools increased, some minority leaders pushed for choice casting it as a civil rights issue, and state and local budgets needed to be balanced. But it remains a contentious issue.

Affirmative Action and Racial Preferences

No referendum issue has generated more controversy than the California Civil Rights Initiative, approved in 1996. Proposition 209 bans "granting preferential treatment to any individual or group" on the basis of "race, sex, color, ethnicity or national origin" in state employment, education, or contracting. Arizona's Proposition 200 amendment, passed in 2004 (56% Yes vote), was nearly as explosive. It requires people registering to vote to prove their citizenship and those voting in person on Election Day to show identification. It also requires proof of citizenship or of legal residency when applying for nonfederally funded public assistance and establishes fines for state and local government employees who fail to check. Proponents (Protect Arizona Now) saw it as a way to discourage undocumented immigrants from influencing Arizona elections. Opponents (Hispanic groups such as the League of United Latin American Citizens [LULAC], the Mexican American League Defense and Educational Fund [MALDEF], and the National Council of La Raza) viewed the proposition as harassment against immigrants—both legal and undocumented. Even the Mexican government weighed in against it, predicting it "will lead to discrimination based on racial profiling while limiting access to basic health and educational services."[13] The antiracial-preference issue extended to Michigan where voters in 2006 also approved such an amendment. Proposal 2 prohibits giving preferential treatment on the basis of race in public education, public contracts, and public employment. The constitutionality of the Proposal was challenged in court, specifically the use of racial preferences in the admission practices of state public universities (the University of Michigan). The case was appealed all the

Impassioned critics of school vouchers, like this Texas woman, often protest against using public tax dollars to fund private schools.

way to the U.S. Supreme Court. Before that case was resolved, the U.S. Supreme Court ruled on another affirmative action case involving the University of Texas, Austin. The case was brought by a white female, Abigail Fisher, who sued the university after being denied admission in 2008. In *Fisher* v. *University of Texas (2013)*, the Supreme Court reaffirmed its "strict scrutiny" doctrine in holding that the University of Texas, Austin, program that used race as part of an "index" for evaluating admissions applications was unconstitutional. The burden of proof that racial classifications meet strict scrutiny requirements rests with universities; lower federal courts cannot simply assume that universities are in compliance. Not all states approve anti–affirmative action proposals.

Immigration

Services to undocumented immigrants have put more fiscal pressure on state and local governments than on the federal government since states and localities deliver most of the services. Arizona voters approved denying bail to undocumented immigrants charged with committing a serious felony and prohibited them from collecting punitive damages from civil suits. Colorado's voters ratified an amendment directing the state attorney general to sue the federal government to get it to enforce existing federal immigration laws. More recently, Montana and Maryland voters approved amendments limiting services to undocumented immigrants.

Redistricting

Every 10 years, after completion of the Census, states have to redraw congressional and state legislative districts to reflect population shifts. Districts are redrawn to make sure each district has the same number of constituents (the principle of one person, one vote). Redistricting is often referred to as the fiercest of political battles because it sets the political landscape for the next decade. In recent years, voters in several states have been asked to approve changes to the process, often moving it out of the hands of legislators into those of an independent commission. In 2008, for example, California voters approved an amendment giving a nonpartisan independent commission the responsibility for redistricting but in 2012, Ohio voters rejected such a proposal.

Eminent Domain

Local governments have the power to "take" private property to use for public purposes (e.g., roads, schools), although the property owner must be paid for the land taken by the government. But when the U.S. Supreme Court ruled in *Kelo* v. *City of New London* (2005) that private property could be condemned via eminent domain proceedings and used for economic development purposes (which might mean taking private property for private sector gain if a developer were involved), citizens in many states were outraged. On the heels of the ruling, voters in many states approved constitutional amendments restricting such practices. (For example, California voters passed Proposition 99 prohibiting state and local governments from using eminent domain to take a person's privately owned residence.) The issue of taking private property for economic

A U.S. Supreme Court ruling (*Kelo* v. *City of New London,* 2005) that local governments could use their eminent domain powers to condemn private property, then, in turn, allow the property to be used for *private* gain under the guise of "economic development" have prompted many state legislatures to place anti-taking amendments on the ballot. Property rights groups keep a close eye on these proposals; most have passed easily.

development remains controversial, especially after the major corporation (Pfizer) that was enticed to locate in New London moved out five years later and the planned urban village development never came to fruition.[14]

2.7 | INITIATIVE CAMPAIGNS

SPECIAL INTERESTS
Specific groups bound together by their common preferences on key policy issues.

Over time, initiative campaigns have become more sophisticated and costly. Supporters must first circulate their petitions, often using paid as well as volunteer workers to obtain the necessary signatures.[15] Television, radio, and newspaper advertising usually accompanies the drive. Once on the ballot, an initiative campaign can become expensive, with television "infomercials," celebrity endorsements, and get-out-the-vote work on Election Day. There are political consulting firms that specialize in developing campaign strategies for the passage or defeat of ballot initiatives rather than candidates.

Some initiative campaigns are sponsored by "**special interests**"—specific businesses or industries; labor unions, including government employees; religious organizations; environmental groups; and public interest groups.[16] The gambling industry, for example, often backs "citizens' initiatives" to legalize gambling. Many of the designated sponsoring groups for petitions—for example, "Citizens for Tax Justice" (tax limits) and "Eight is Enough" (term limits)—are organized and funded by established lobbying groups that have failed to accomplish their goals through the legislative process.

Opposition campaigns to initiatives may also be well funded by organized interests. Lobbying groups that are well entrenched in state capitals—public employee unions, teachers' unions, and utility, insurance, and liquor industries (see Chapter 6)—are usually leery of citizens' initiatives. Political officeholders are also generally skeptical of citizen initiatives, even though they may occasionally endorse particularly popular ones. After all, the initiative process is designed to *bypass* the state capital and its power holders. A proposal in New Jersey in 1992 to adopt the initiative process was successfully defeated by a strong coalition of well-established interest groups that mounted "an unprecedented joint lobbying effort."[17] Occasionally opposition groups have resorted to the "counterinitiative"— deliberately adding an initiative to the ballot that is designed to undermine support for a popular citizen initiative. There is a tendency for voters to vote against initiatives when the issues are complex and confusing. Occasionally state supreme courts have denied an initiative a place on the ballot, not only for procedural reasons, but also because in the court's opinion it violated the U.S. Constitution.

Initiatives Impact a Candidate's Campaign

Candidates for office are certainly attentive to issues that will be listed on the same ballot as they are for two reasons. First, they will undoubtedly have to take a public stand on them. One well-known political consultant warns: "Political candidates fool themselves into thinking campaigns are about the candidates and not the issues."[18] A candidate's stance on a high-profile ballot issue is often an important determinant of whether that candidate will get a voter's support.[19] Second, ballot initiatives can "skew voter turnout and create competition for money, interests, and votes."[20] Turnout in nonpresidential election years is higher, particularly among regular *party-line* voters, when a high-profile citizen initiative is on the ballot.[21]

The Threat of Initiatives

Legislatures may be goaded at times into enacting legislation by the threat of a popular initiative. Recognizing that a popular initiative may gain a position on the ballot and win voter approval, legislatures may prefer to preempt an initiative movement by writing their own version of the policy. Indeed there is some evidence that legislatures in initiative states are more sensitive to majority preferences among voters than legislatures in states without the initiative device.[22] Another threat is to rights of petition signers. In 2010, the

U.S. Supreme Court ruled 8 to 1 in *Doe* v. *Reed* that ballot-measure petitions are public records and that making them so would help guard against election fraud in the petition-gathering process. The ruling stemmed from a Washington state group (Project Marriage Washington) that sued the state to keep petition signatures private so as to protect signees from harassment and harm by referendum opponents. Their petition had proposed repealing a 2009 state law giving gay and lesbian couples registered as domestic partners marriage-like benefits. The Court did, however, leave the door open to groups petitioning to keep names confidential should they be able to offer "a reasonable probability" that disclosing names would lead to threats, harassment, and reprisals.

Reform Proposals

Reformers have argued that initiative voting is becoming too common, that multiple initiatives on the ballot overload and confuse voters, that initiatives are often poorly drafted, and that voters are often poorly informed about the real purposes and intent of an initiative. They often urge that neutral voter guides be printed by the state, summarizing arguments for and against initiative questions; that the names and affiliations of major contributors to initiative campaigns be published; and that courts scrutinize titles on initiatives to ensure that they accurately reflect their purposes and intent.

Americans overwhelmingly support the initiative process. Indeed, 64 percent of Americans say that it is a good idea to let citizens place issues directly on the ballot by collecting petition signatures.

Many states have laws that allow citizens to place initiatives directly on the ballot by collecting petition signatures. If the initiative is approved by voters on Election Day, it becomes law. Is this a good idea?[23]

Yes	64%
No	17%
Not sure	19%

Yet only 18 states currently have a statewide constitutional initiative process (see Table 2–4). Despite the popularity of the initiative and referendum process, legislators in a majority of states are unlikely to grant initiative rights to their citizens in the near future.

Citizens' Initiatives and Term Limits

Citizen initiatives to limit the terms of public officials—Congress members, state legislators, and other state and local officials—have enjoyed great success whenever they have appeared on the ballot. The U.S. Supreme Court has held that a state *cannot* impose term limits on *members of Congress*. However, states, and citizens in states with the popular initiative and referenda, can limit the terms of their own *state legislators*. And indeed, term limits have usually won by landslide margins whenever they have appeared on referenda ballots (see Table 2–6).

Opponents of term limits, including state legislators themselves, have pursued

Groups in favor of term limits want "citizen legislators" rather than career politicians. They feel that long-time officeholders care more about how issues play out in the media or in polls than how they affect the daily lives of their constituents back home. Those who oppose term limits cite the right of every voter to elect his or her candidate of choice, regardless of how long that person may have served in elective office.

TABLE 2–6 Term-Limited State Legislators

State	Year Enacted	House		Senate		% Voted Yes
		Limit	Year of Impact	Limit	Year of Impact	
Maine	1993	8	1996	8	1996	67.6
California	1990	12*	1996	12*	1998	52.2
Colorado	1990	8	1998	8	1998	71.0
Arkansas	1992	6	1998	8	2000	59.9
Michigan	1992	6	1998	8	2002	58.8
Florida	1992	8	2000	8	2000	76.8
Ohio	1992	8	2000	8	2000	68.4
South Dakota	1992	8	2000	8	2000	63.5
Montana	1992	8	2000	8	2000	67.0
Arizona	1992	8	2000	8	2000	74.2
Missouri	1992	8	2002	8	2002	75.0
Oklahoma	1990	12*	2004	12*	2004	67.3
Nebraska	2000	n/a	n/a	8	2006	56.0
Louisiana	1995	12	2007	12	2007	76.0
Nevada	1996	12	2010	12	2010	70.4

*In California and Oklahoma, a legislator may serve a total of 12 years in the legislature during his or her lifetime. The total time may be split between the two chambers, or spent in its entirety in a single chamber. Before 2012, California's limits were identical to those in Arkansas: six years in the assembly and eight years in the senate.

Source: National Conference on State Legislatures, "The Term Limited States," January 2013. Available at: http://www.ncsl.org/legislatures-elections/legisdata/chart-of-term-limits-states.aspx. © 2013 National Conference of State Legislatures.

TERM LIMITS

Constitutional limits on the number of terms or the number of years that a public official may serve in the same office.

the two-pronged strategy against the measure: persuade the voters to reject it and, if that fails, persuade a court to declare it unconstitutional. Supporters of term limits clearly have public opinion on their side. (See "*Did You Know?* Term Limits Are Still Controversial.") And voters are not at all supportive of legislators' efforts to relax term limits once they have been voted in. In 2004, citizens of Arkansas and Montana overwhelmingly rejected proposals to allow legislators to serve longer before being "term-limited" out of office. And in 2012, West Virginia voters rejected a legislative proposal to eliminate term limits for sheriffs.

Constitutional arguments against term limits have led to prolonged litigation in the courts. Opponents argued that term limits placed an unconstitutional barrier on the right to be a candidate for public office, and that they violated the right of voters to cast their ballots for candidates of their choice. These arguments were rejected first by the California Supreme Court, and later by the U.S. Court of Appeals (together with the argument that voters did not understand what they were voting for on term limits referenda).[24] The U.S. Supreme Court has declined to hear appeals of cases upholding the constitutionality of term limits.[25]

U.S. Supreme Court Rejection of Congressional Term Limits by States

When the voters of Arkansas adopted a state constitutional amendment in 1992 setting term limits for their U.S. senators and representatives, the U.S. Supreme Court ruled in 1995 that this action violated the U.S. Constitution by setting forth qualifications for Congress members beyond those found in Article I. Only three qualifications are specified in the U.S. Constitution: age, citizenship, and residence. (The Arkansas term limit amendment actually set qualifications for eligibility for name placement on the ballot; Arkansas argued

Did YOU KNOW?

Term Limits Are Still Controversial

Distrust of politicians and declining confidence in the ability of government to confront national problems fueled grassroots movements in many states to limit the terms of public officials—both Congress members and state legislators. However, the enthusiasm of the general public for term limits was seldom matched by legislators—either in Washington or in state capitals—who were reluctant to limit their own legislative careers. Hence, citizens in states with the popular initiative and referenda turned to these instruments of direct democracy.

Arguments for Term Limits

Proponents of term limits argue that "citizen legislators" have largely been replaced by career "professional politicians." People who have held legislative office for many years become isolated from the lives and concerns of average citizens. Career politicians respond to the media, to polls, and to interest groups, but they have no direct feeling for how their constituents live. Term limits, proponents argue, would force politicians to return home and live under the laws that they make.

Proponents also argue that term limits would increase competition in the electoral system. By creating "open seat" races on a regular basis, more people would be encouraged to seek public office. Incumbents do not win so often because they are the most qualified people in their districts, but, rather, because of the many electoral advantages granted by incumbency—name recognition, campaign contributions from special interests, pork barrel and casework, and office staff (see "The Great Incumbency Machine" in Chapter 6). These incumbent advantages discourage good people from challenging officeholders.

Arguments against Term Limits

Opponents of term limits argue that they infringe on the voters' freedom of choice. If voters are upset with the performance of their state legislators, they can always "throw the rascals out." If they want to limit a legislator's term, they can do so simply by not re-electing him or her. But if voters wish to keep popular, able, experienced, and hard-working legislators in office, they should be permitted to do so. Experience is a valuable asset in state capitals; voters may legitimately desire to be represented by senior legislators with knowledge and experience in public affairs.

Opponents also argue that inexperienced legislators would be forced to rely more on the policy information supplied to them by bureaucrats, lobbyists, and staff people. Term limits, they argue, would weaken the legislature, leaving it less capable of checking the power of the special interests. But proponents counter this argument by observing that the closest relationships in state capitals develop between lobbyists and senior legislators who have interacted professionally and socially over the years, and that the most powerful lobbying groups strongly oppose term limits.

---

that this was a permissible exercise of power to regulate "times, places and manner of holding elections" granted to the states in Article I. But the Court dismissed this argument as an "indirect attempt to accomplish what the Constitution prohibits.") The Court held that a state cannot limit the terms of members of Congress:

> Allowing individual states to adopt their own qualifications for Congressional service would be inconsistent with the framers' vision of a uniform national legislature representing the people of the United States. If the qualifications set forth in the text of the Constitution are to be changed, that text must be amended.[26]

Justice John Paul Stevens, writing for the majority in the controversial 5–4 decision, set forth two key arguments in opposition: first, that the power to set term limits is *not* among the powers reserved to the states by the Tenth Amendment, and second, that the Founders intended age, citizenship, and residency to be the *only* qualifications for members of Congress.

The ruling was rather disappointing to many Americans. Polls show that 75 percent would vote for a law limiting the number of terms of U.S. Senators and Representatives. Support for term limits differs little across party lines (82% of Republicans, 79% of independents, and 65% of Democrats).[27]

Term Limits Kick In

Term limits are taking their toll on state legislatures in the 15 states across the country that have them.[28] Significant numbers of state legislators have been "term-limited" out of office, resulting in an increase in the number of "freshman" legislators in most of them (Arizona, California, Florida, Maine, Michigan, Missouri, Ohio, Oregon, and South Dakota).

State legislators themselves are strongly opposed to term limits. The National Conference of State Legislatures reports that 83 percent of state legislators polled oppose term limits. Even many of those who originally favored limits now say they were mistaken: "Originally, I believed that fresh blood would be good; however, experience, understanding of the process and historical knowledge are lost. The same debates occur year after year."[29] Another complaint is that eight-year terms encourage early and continuing political jousting for leadership positions (e.g., speaker of the House, presiding officer of the Senate, key committee chairs). A majority of legislators say that term limits have added to the influence of legislative staff and lobbyists. However, interestingly, both staffers and lobbyists oppose term limits; staffers fear losing their jobs when new legislators bring in their own new staffers, and lobbyists must work to establish new relationships with new legislators rather than rely on old acquaintances in the legislature. Some legislatures report taking proactive steps to mitigate the inexperience of new legislators by initiating pre-session training into the legislative process.

CHAPTER HIGHLIGHTS

- Constitutions limit the powers of state government and protect individual liberty.
- All 50 states have a written constitution as well as a bill of rights. State constitutions are the supreme law of the states and take precedence over state law, but they are subordinate to the U.S. Constitution and the laws of the United States.
- The idea of written constitutions originated with the Magna Carta in England in 1215 and evolved through the experience of the Thirteen Colonies.
- Theoretically, a constitution sets out the rules for policymaking but does not make policy. In reality, all state constitutions contain policy mandates influenced by interest groups and citizen movements.
- State constitutions endow greater power in the legislature than the governor. They also determine the organization and powers of local governments, such as counties, towns, and school districts.
- No constitutional right is absolute. The Second Amendment right to "keep and bear arms," for example, allows states to form militias (National Guards) and, depending on one's interpretation, an individual's right to own guns, but does not prohibit reasonable restrictions such as registration and waiting periods. The Sandy Hook shootings reignited tensions between the federal and state governments over gun laws.
- Because state constitutions are long and detailed, they must be amended frequently. Amendments can be made through legislative proposal (usually the most successful method), popular initiative (petition), constitutional convention, and constitutional revision commission.
- The nation's Founders envisioned a *representative democracy* in which the people elect government officials to make policy decisions, as opposed to *direct democracy* in which the people initiate and decide policy by popular vote.
- The use of direct democracy devices—initiative, referendum, and recall—is a growing trend. Citizens in a number of states have used these devices for a variety of policies, including imposing tax limits or allowing tax increases, allowing recreational use of marijuana, prohibiting or permitting same-sex marriages, disallowing affirmative action in college admission and job hiring, restricting eminent domain, and imposing term limits on officeholders. These direct democracy devices have become very costly and divisive, especially the recall when it involves statewide elected officials (governors).

CHAPTER THREE

STATES, COMMUNITIES, AND AMERICAN FEDERALISM

LEARNING OBJECTIVES

3.1 Analyze the relationships between different levels of government in federal, confederal, and unitary systems.

3.2 Describe the advantages of federalism for the United States.

3.3 Describe the disadvantages of federalism for the United States.

3.4 Compare the powers of the national and state governments in the U.S. federal system.

3.5 Describe the role of the states in the constitutional amendment process using the proposed Equal Rights Amendment, the proposed District of Columbia amendment, and the Twenty-Seventh Amendment as examples.

3.6 Outline how Congress has used its powers both to tax and to spend as a way to enhance the power of the national government.

3.7 Analyze the merits, at both the state and national levels, of the various types of government from dual federalism through "bottom-up" federalism, including the effect each had on the relationship between the nation and the states.

3.8 Illustrate the concept of devolution using the 1996 welfare reform legislation as an example.

3.9 Evaluate how recent Supreme Court decisions have affected the balance of power between the states and the national government.

3.10 Explain the constitutional requirements pertaining to the full faith and credit clause, extradition, and interstate compacts.

WHAT IS FEDERALISM?

Analyze the relationships between different levels of government in federal, confederal, and unitary systems.

FEDERALISM

A constitutional arrangement whereby power is divided between national and subnational governments, each of which enforces its own laws directly on its citizens and neither of which can alter the arrangement without the consent of the other.

UNITARY SYSTEM

Constitutional arrangement whereby authority rests with the national government; subnational governments have only those powers given to them by the national government.

CONFEDERATION

Constitutional arrangement whereby the national government is created by and relies on subnational governments for its authority.

Virtually all nations of the world have units of local government—states, republics, provinces, regions, cities, counties, or villages. Decentralization of the administrative burdens of government is required almost everywhere. But not all nations have federal systems of government.

Federalism is a system in which power is divided between national and subnational governments with both exercising separate and autonomous authority, electing their own officials, and taxing their own citizens for the provision of public services. Moreover, federalism requires that the powers of the national and subnational governments be guaranteed by a constitution that cannot be changed without the consent of both national and subnational populations.[1]

The United States, Canada, Australia, India, the Federal Republic of Germany, and Switzerland are generally regarded as federal systems. But Great Britain, France, Italy, and Sweden are not. While these nations have local governments, they are dependent on the national government for their powers. They are considered **unitary systems** rather than federal systems, because their local governments can be altered or even abolished by the national governments acting alone. In contrast, a system is said to be a **confederation** if the power of the national government is dependent upon local units of government. While these terms—unitary and confederation—can be defined theoretically, in the real world of politics it is not so easy to distinguish between governments that are truly federal and those that are not. Indeed, it is not clear whether the U.S. government today retains its federal character.

What is clear is that this unique arrangement often creates interesting politics between the two levels of government. Some draw parallels between national–state government relationships and family interactions. Sometimes the two levels get along famously (a "love-in"), most notably when Washington sends millions of dollars to state capitals to fund everything from highways to health care to disaster relief. Other times, they are at one another's throats (a "family feud"), such as when the U.S. Department of Defense proposes to close more military bases in one state than another. Or when the national government orders states to revamp their driver's licenses or purchase new voting machines but doesn't give them sufficient funds to do so. When certain types of issues arise, the two would rather go their separate ways ("live and let live"). Individual states may like to set their own policies on taxing out-of-state Internet sales or defining "marriage," "life," and "privacy rights" without being overruled by Congress or the federal courts that might see these issues as more national in scope. As with families, interactions among the various levels of government are constantly changing as the players change. And the most intense conflicts, by far, are over money, power, and control.

WHY FEDERALISM?

Describe the advantages of federalism for the United States.

Why have state and local governments anyway? Why not have a centralized political system with a single government accountable to national majorities in national elections—a government capable of implementing uniform policies throughout the country?

"Auxiliary Precautions" against Tyranny

The nation's Founders understood that "republican principles," while they should be nurtured and cherished, would not be sufficient in themselves to protect individual liberty. Periodic elections, party competition, voter enfranchisement, and political equality may function to make governing elites more responsive to popular concerns. According to the Founders, "A dependence on the people is, no doubt, the primary control of government, but experience has taught mankind the necessity of auxiliary precautions."

Among the most important "auxiliary precautions" devised by the Founders to control government are federalism—dividing powers between the national and state governments—and **separation of powers**—the dispersal of power among the separate executive, legislative, and judicial branches of government.

> In the compound republic of America, the power surrendered by the people is first divided between two distinct governments, and then the portion allotted to each subdivided among distinct and separate departments. Hence a double security arises to the rights of the people. The different governments will control each other, at the same time that each will be controlled by itself.[2]

Dispersing Power

Decentralization distributes power more widely among different sets of leaders. Multiple leadership groups are generally believed to be more democratic than a single set of all-powerful leaders. Moreover, state and local governments provide a political base of offices for the opposition party when it has lost national elections. In this way, state and local governments contribute to party competition in America by helping to tide over the losing party after electoral defeat so that it may remain strong enough to challenge incumbents at the next election. And finally, state and local governments provide a channel of recruitment for national political leaders. National leaders can be drawn from a pool of leaders experienced in state and local politics.

Increasing Participation

Decentralization allows more people to participate in the political system. There are more than 89,000 governments in America—states, counties, townships, municipalities, towns, special districts, and school districts. Nearly a million people hold some kind of public office. Most are elected at the state and local levels. (Only 542 are federal officials—1 President, 1 Vice President, 100 U.S. Senators (two from each state), 435 U.S. Representatives, 4 Delegates to the House of Representatives from U.S. territories and the District of Columbia, and 1 Resident Commissioner from the Commonwealth of Puerto Rico.) State and local governments are widely regarded as being "closer to the people." Thus, by providing more opportunities for direct citizen involvement in government, state and local governments contribute to the popular sense of political effectiveness.

Improving Efficiency

Decentralization makes government more manageable and efficient, especially in a diverse nation where a "one size fits all" approach to delivering services does not always work well. Imagine the bureaucracy, red tape, and confusion if every government activity in every local community—police, schools, roads, firefighting, garbage collection, sewage disposal—were controlled by a centralized administration in Washington. If local governments did not exist, they would have to be invented. Government becomes arbitrary when a bureaucracy far from the scene directs a local administrator to proceed with the impossible—local conditions notwithstanding. Decentralization softens the rigidity of law.

Ensuring Policy Responsiveness

Decentralized government encourages policy responsiveness. Multiple competing governments are more sensitive to citizen views than monopoly government. The existence of multiple governments offering different packages of benefits and costs allows a better match between citizen preferences and public policy. People and businesses often can "vote with their feet" by relocating to those states and communities that most closely conform to their own policy preferences. Americans are mobile. In a given year, some 11 percent of Americans move. Of those, the vast majority (63%) move within the same county, 19 percent to a different county within the same state, 14 percent to a different state, and

3 percent from abroad. Business and industry are also increasingly mobile. Mobility not only facilitates a better match between citizen preferences and public policy, it also encourages competition between states and communities to offer improved services at lower costs.

Encouraging Policy Innovation

Federalism encourages policy experimentation and innovation. Federalism may be perceived today as a "conservative" idea, but it was once viewed as the instrument of "progressivism." A strong argument can be made that the groundwork for Franklin D. Roosevelt's New Deal in the 1930s was built in state policy experimentation during the Progressive Era earlier in the century. Federal programs as diverse as the income tax, unemployment compensation, countercyclical public works, Social Security, wage and hour legislation, bank deposit insurance, and food stamps all had antecedents at the state level. Indeed, the compelling phrase "laboratories of democracy" is generally attributed to the great progressive jurist, Supreme Court Justice Louis D. Brandeis, who used it in defense of state experimentation with new solutions to social and economic problems.[3] Competition among governments provides additional incentives for inventiveness and innovation in public policy.[4]

Managing Conflict

Political decentralization frequently reduces the severity of conflict in a society. Decentralization is a classic method by which different peoples can be brought together in a nation without engendering irresolvable conflict. Conflicts between geographically defined groups in America are resolved by allowing each to pursue its own policies within the separate states and communities; this avoids battling over a single national policy to be applied uniformly throughout the land.

<hr>

3.3

Describe the disadvantages of federalism for the United States.

FEDERALISM'S FAULTS

Federalism is not without its faults. It may create confusion about which level of government is responsible for action and anger when needed action is delayed. Federalism can also obstruct action on national issues, or contradict national policy. (See "*Up Close: Nation versus States: Legalizing Pot.*") Although decentralization may reduce conflict at the national level, it may do so at the price of "sweeping under the rug" some serious, national injustices.

Protecting Slavery and Segregation

Federalism in America remains tainted by its historical association with slavery, segregation, and discrimination. An early doctrine of "nullification" was set forth by Thomas Jefferson in the Virginia and Kentucky Resolution of 1798, asserting states' right to nullify unconstitutional laws of Congress. Although the original use of this doctrine was to counter congressional attacks on a free press in the Alien and Sedition Acts, the doctrine was later revived to defend slavery. John C. Calhoun of South Carolina argued forcefully in the years before the Civil War that slavery was an issue for states to decide and that under the Constitution of 1787, Congress had no power to interfere with slavery in the southern states or in the new western territories.

In the years immediately following the Civil War, the issues of slavery, racial inequality, and black voting rights were nationalized. The Thirteenth, Fourteenth, and Fifteenth Amendments to the Constitution were enforced with federal troops in the southern states during Reconstruction. But following the Compromise of 1876 federal troops were withdrawn from the southern states, and legal and social segregation of blacks became a "way of life" in the region. Segregation was denationalized; this reduced national conflict over race, but the price was paid by black Americans. Not until the 1950s and 1960s were

Nation versus States: Legalizing Pot

The Supremacy Clause of the U.S. Constitution asserts the superiority of federal laws over the constitutions and laws of the states. The federal government prohibits the sale, possession, or growth of marijuana for any purpose. The Food and Drug Administration lists marijuana as a Schedule 1 substance under the Controlled Substances Act "classified as having a high potential for abuse and no currently accepted medical use."

Yet, a number of states have undertaken to legalize marijuana for medical use (see below). Many of these states have done so through ballot propositions. Majorities of Americans approve the use of marijuana for medical purposes. There is a clear conflict between federal and state laws over medical marijuana.

In partial recognition of this conflict, Attorney General Eric Holder announced the 2009 "clarifying guidelines.... For the use of federal investigative and prosecutorial resources." The Drug Enforcement Administration (DEA) will not arrest or prosecute individual marijuana users who are in compliance with state laws authorizing marijuana for medical purposes. "These guidelines do not legalize marijuana. But it is not the practice of the DEA to target individuals with serious medical conditions who comply with state laws authorizing their use for medical purposes." In other words, the federal government will not enforce federal law it states which have passed laws approving the use of marijuana for medical purposes.

Colorado and Washington are the first states to legalize the recreational use of marijuana. In 2012, voters in both states passed referenda repealing their laws prohibiting the recreational use of marijuana and replacing them with state regulations. (Both states continue to ban the open public use of marijuana.) These state laws are in direct conflict with federal law.

The issue creates a political problem for the Obama administration. The president's political support in the

Legalization of Marijuana by State

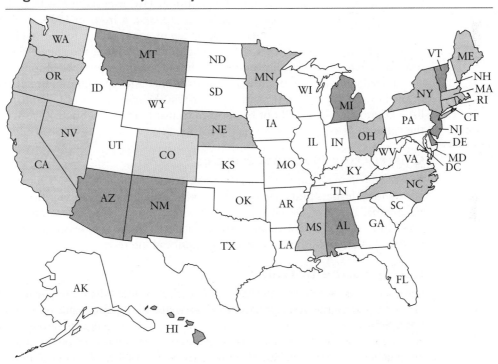

■ States with legalized medical marijuana

■ State that have removed jail time for possessing small amounts of marijuana

■ State that both have a medical marijuana law and have removed jail time for possessing small amounts of marijuana

■ States that have legalized medical marijuana and adult use of marijuana.

Note: Data are for 2013. Maryland has a limited medical marijuana defense for possession only. In Alaska, the courts have found that the state constitution's right to privacy includes the right to possess modest amounts of marijuana in one's home.
Source: Marijuana Policy Project, "State Policy," 2013. Available at http://www.mpp.org/states/.

electorate is strong among young people and young people tend to approve of the legalization of marijuana. But the president is charged with enforcing federal law. The U.S. Justice Department issued a strong admonishment to pot users: "The Department's responsibility to enforce the Controlled Substances Act remains unchanged." But it is not clear whether the Obama Administration will take any action against Colorado or Washington or pot users in these states. Initially, no action was taken. Administration officials announced it was a low priority compared to economic recovery.

MARIJUANA LAWS IN THE STATES

States Legalizing Recreational Use

    Colorado

    Washington

States Legalizing Medical Use

    Alaska

    Arizona

California
Colorado
Connecticut
Delaware
Hawaii
Main
Massachusetts
Nevada
New Jersey
New Mexico
Oregon
Rhode Island
Vermont
Washington

Source: National Organization for the Reform of Marijuana Laws. www.norml.org.

questions of segregation and equality again made into national issues. The civil rights movement asserted the supremacy of national law, especially the U.S. Supreme Court's decision in *Brown* v. *Board of Education of Topeka, Kansas* in 1954, that segregation violated the Fourteenth Amendment's guarantee of equal protection of the law, and later the national Civil Rights Act of 1964. Segregationists asserted the states' rights argument so often in defense of racial discrimination that it became a code word for racism.

Indeed, only now that national constitutional and legal guarantees of equal protection of the law are in place is it possible to reassess the true values of federalism. Having established that federalism will not be allowed to justify racial inequality, we are free to explore the values of decentralized government.

Obstructing National Policies

Federalism allows state and local officials to obstruct action on national problems. It allows local leaders and citizens to frustrate national policy, to sacrifice the national interest to local interests. Decentralized government provides an opportunity for local "NIMBYs" (not in my backyard) to obstruct airports, highways, waste disposal plants, public housing, and many other projects in the national interest.

Racing to the Bottom?

Competition among the states, a major feature of federalism, may lead to a "race to the bottom" among the states with regard to welfare assistance and other programs for the poor. States may be encouraged to continuously reduce benefit levels in order to avoid becoming "welfare magnets," that is, to avoid the migration of the poor to states with more generous welfare programs. But research shows little direct evidence of poor families moving to states for higher benefit levels, or other states lowering benefits to avoid the migration of poor people.[5]

Allowing Inequalities

Finally, under federalism the benefits and costs of government are spread unevenly across the nation. For example, some states spend twice as much to educate a child in the public schools as other states (see Chapter 16). Welfare benefits in some states are twice as high as in other states (see Chapter 17). Taxes in some states are twice as high per capita as in other states (see Chapter 14).

THE STRUCTURE OF AMERICAN FEDERALISM

In deciding in 1869 that a state had no constitutional right to secede from the Union, Chief Justice Salmon P. Chase described the legal character of American federalism:

> The preservation of the states and the maintenance of their governments, are as much within the design and care of the constitution as the preservation of the union and the maintenance of the national government. The constitution, in all of its provisions, looks to an indestructible union, composed of indestructible states.[6]

What is meant by "an indestructible union, composed of indestructible states"? American federalism is an indissoluble partnership between the states and the national government. The U.S. Constitution allocated power between two separate authorities, the nation and the states, each of which was to be independent of the other. Both the nation and the states were allowed to enforce their laws directly on individuals through their own officials and courts. The Constitution was the only legal source of authority for the division of powers between the states and the nation. The American federal system was designed as a strong national government, coupled with a strong state government, in which authority and power are shared, constitutionally and practically.

The framework of American federalism is determined by (1) the powers delegated by the Constitution of the national government, and its declared supremacy; (2) the constitutional guarantees reserved for the states; (3) the powers denied by the Constitution to both the national government and the states; (4) the constitutional provisions giving the states a role in the composition of the national government; and (5) the subsequent constitutional and historical development of federalism.

Delegated Powers and National Supremacy

Article I, Section 8, of the U.S. Constitution lists 18 grants of power to Congress. These **"delegated," or "enumerated," powers** include authority over matters of war and foreign affairs, the power to declare war, raise armies, equip navies, and establish rules for the military. Another series of delegated powers is related to control of the economy, including the power to coin money, to control its value, and to regulate foreign and interstate commerce. The national government has been given independent powers of taxation "to pay the debts and provide for the common defense and general welfare of the United States." It has the power to establish its own court system, to decide cases arising under the Constitution and the laws and treaties of the United States and cases involving certain kinds of parties. The national government was given the authority to grant copyright and patents, establish post offices, enact bankruptcy laws, punish counterfeiting, punish crimes committed on the high seas, and govern the District of Columbia. (See Figure 3–1.) Finally, after 17 grants of express power came the power "to make all laws which shall be necessary and proper for carrying into execution the foregoing powers, and all other powers vested by this constitution in the government of the United States or in any department or officer thereof." This is generally referred to as the **Necessary and Proper Clause** or the **Implied Powers Clause**.

These delegated powers, when coupled with the **National Supremacy Clause** of Article VI, ensured a powerful national government. The Supremacy Clause was specific regarding the relationship between the national government and the states. In questions involving conflict between the state laws and the Constitution, laws, or treaties of the United States:

> This constitution, and the laws of the United States which shall be made in pursuance thereof; and all treaties made or which shall be made under the authority of the United States shall be the supreme law of the land; and the judges in every state shall be bound thereby, anything in the constitution or laws of any state to the contrary notwithstanding.

DELEGATED, OR ENUMERATED, POWERS

Powers specifically mentioned in the Constitution as belonging to the national government.

NECESSARY AND PROPER CLAUSE

Clause in Article I, Section 8, of the U.S. Constitution granting Congress the power to enact all laws that are "necessary and proper" for carrying out those responsibilities specifically delegated to it. Also referred to as the Implied Powers Clause.

IMPLIED POWERS CLAUSE

Powers not mentioned specifically in the Constitution as belonging to Congress but inferred as necessary and proper for carrying out the enumerated powers.

NATIONAL SUPREMACY CLAUSE

Clause in Article VI of the U.S. Constitution declaring the constitution and laws of the national government "the supreme law of the land" superior to the constitutions and laws of the states.

FIGURE 3–1 Constitutional Distribution of Powers

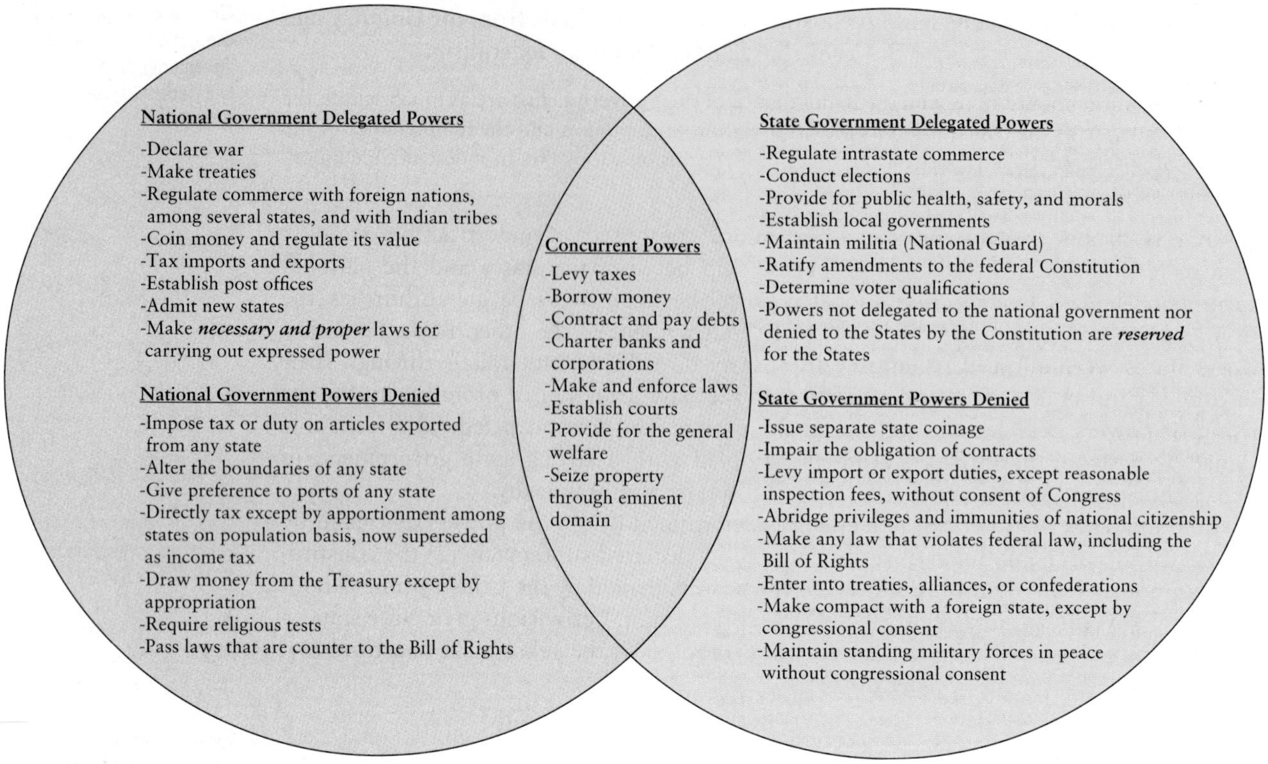

National Government Delegated Powers

-Declare war
-Make treaties
-Regulate commerce with foreign nations, among several states, and with Indian tribes
-Coin money and regulate its value
-Tax imports and exports
-Establish post offices
-Admit new states
-Make *necessary and proper* laws for carrying out expressed power

National Government Powers Denied

-Impose tax or duty on articles exported from any state
-Alter the boundaries of any state
-Give preference to ports of any state
-Directly tax except by apportionment among states on population basis, now superseded as income tax
-Draw money from the Treasury except by appropriation
-Require religious tests
-Pass laws that are counter to the Bill of Rights

Concurrent Powers

-Levy taxes
-Borrow money
-Contract and pay debts
-Charter banks and corporations
-Make and enforce laws
-Establish courts
-Provide for the general welfare
-Seize property through eminent domain

State Government Delegated Powers

-Regulate intrastate commerce
-Conduct elections
-Provide for public health, safety, and morals
-Establish local governments
-Maintain militia (National Guard)
-Ratify amendments to the federal Constitution
-Determine voter qualifications
-Powers not delegated to the national government nor denied to the States by the Constitution are *reserved* for the States

State Government Powers Denied

-Issue separate state coinage
-Impair the obligation of contracts
-Levy import or export duties, except reasonable inspection fees, without consent of Congress
-Abridge privileges and immunities of national citizenship
-Make any law that violates federal law, including the Bill of Rights
-Enter into treaties, alliances, or confederations
-Make compact with a foreign state, except by congressional consent
-Maintain standing military forces in peace without congressional consent

Under the Constitution of 1787, certain powers were delegated to the national government, other powers were shared by the national and state governments, and still other powers were reserved for state governments alone. Similarly, certain powers were denied by the Constitution to the national government, other powers were denied to both the national and state governments, and still other powers were denied only to state governments. Later amendments especially protected individual liberties.
Source: United States Constitution.

RESERVED POWERS

Powers not granted to the national government or specifically denied to the states in the Constitution that are recognized by the Tenth Amendment as belonging to the state governments. This guarantee, known as the Reserved Powers Clause, embodies the principle of American federalism.

Reserved Powers

Despite these broad grants of power to the national government, the states retained a great deal of authority over the lives of their citizens. The Tenth Amendment reaffirmed the idea that the national government had only certain delegated powers and that all powers not delegated to it were retained by the states:

> The powers not delegated to the United States by the constitution, nor prohibited by it to the states, are reserved to the states respectively, or to the people.

The states retained control over the ownership and use of property; the regulation of offenses against persons and property (see "*Up Close:* Federalizing Crime"); the regulation of marriage and divorce; the control of business, labor, farming, trades, and professions; the provision of education, welfare, health, hospitals, and other social welfare activities; and provision of highways, roads, canals, and other public works. The states retained full authority over the organization and control of local government units. Finally, the states, like the federal government, possessed the power to tax and spend for the general welfare.

Powers Denied to the Nation and States

The Constitution denies some powers to both national and state governments; these denials generally safeguard individual rights. Both nation and states are forbidden to pass ex post facto laws or bills of attainder. The first eight amendments to the

Political office holders in Washington are continually pressured to make a "federal crime" out of virtually every offense in society. Neither Democrats nor Republicans, liberals nor conservatives, are willing to risk their political futures by telling their constituents that crime fighting is a state and local responsibility. So Washington lawmakers continue to add common offenses to the ever lengthening list of federal crimes.

Traditionally, federal crimes were limited to a relatively narrow range of offenses, including counterfeiting and currency violations; tax evasion, including alcohol, tobacco, and firearm taxes; fraud and embezzlement; robbery of federally insured banks; murder or assault of a federal official; and violations of customs and immigration laws. While some federal criminal laws overlapped state laws, most criminal activity—murder, rape, robbery, assault, burglary, theft, auto theft, gambling, and sex offenses—fell under state jurisdiction. Indeed, the *police power* was believed to be one of the "reserved" powers states referred to in the Tenth Amendment.

But over time Congress has made more offenses *federal* crimes. Today federal crimes range from drive-by shootings to obstructing sidewalks in front of abortion clinics. Any violent offense motivated by racial, religious, or ethnic animosity is a "hate crime" subject to federal investigation and prosecution. **"Racketeering" and "conspiracy"** (organizing and communicating with others about the intent to commit a crime) is a federal crime. The greatest impact of federal involvement in law enforcement is found in drug-related crime. Drug offenders may be tried in either federal or state courts or both. Federal drug laws, including those prohibiting possession, carry heavier penalties than those of most states.

The effect of federalizing crime is to subject citizens to the possibility of being tried twice for the same crime—in federal court and in state court for an offense that violates both federal and state criminal codes. The U.S. Supreme Court has held that such multiple prosecutions do *not* violate the Double Jeopardy Clause of the Fifth Amendment, "nor shall any person be subject for the same offense to be twice put in jeopardy of life or limb."[a] In the well-publicized Rodney King case, a California state jury acquitted police officers of beating King, but a federal court jury later convicted them of violating King's civil rights.

Only recently has the U.S. Supreme Court recognized that federalizing crime may impinge upon the reserved powers of states. In 1994 Congress passed a popular Violence Against Women Act that allowed victims of "gender-motivated violence,"

[a]*Health* v. *Alabama*, 474 U.S. 82 (1985).
[b]*U.S.* v. *Morrison*, May 15, 2000.

including rape, to sue their attackers for monetary damages in federal court. Congress defended its constitutional authority to involve itself in crimes against women by citing the Commerce Clause, arguing that crimes against women interfered with interstate commerce, the power over which is given to the national government in Article I of the Constitution. But in 2000 the Supreme Court rejected this argument, "If accepted, this reasoning would allow Congress to regulate any crime whose nationwide, aggregate impact has substantial effects on employment, production, transit, or consumption. Moreover, such reasoning will not limit Congress to regulating violence, but may be applied equally as well to family law and other areas of state regulation since the aggregate effect of marriage, divorce, and childbearing on the national economy is undoubtedly significant. The Constitution requires a distinction between what is truly national and what is truly local, and there's no better example of the police power, which the Founders undeniably left reposed in the states and denied the central government, than the suppression of violent crime in vindication of its victims."[b] In Justice Scalia's opinion, allowing Congress to claim that violence against women interfered with interstate commerce would open the door to federalizing all crime: "would allow general federal criminal laws, because all crime affects interstate commerce."

RACKETEERING AND CONSPIRACY

Organizing and communicating with others about the intent to commit a crime.

Federal, state, and local laws prohibit drugs and guns in a school zone.

Constitution, "the Bill of Rights," originally applied to the federal government, but the Fourteenth Amendment, passed by Congress in 1866, provided that the states must also adhere to fundamental guarantees of individual liberty. "No state shall make or enforce any law which shall abridge the privileges or immunities of the citizens of the United States; nor shall any state deprive any person of life, liberty or property without due process of law; nor deny to any person within its jurisdiction equal protection of the laws."

Some powers were denied only to the states, generally as a safeguard to national unity, including the powers to coin money, enter into treaties with foreign powers, interfere with the obligations of contracts, levy duties on imports or exports without congressional consent, maintain military forces in peacetime, engage in war, or enter into compacts with foreign nations or other states.

The National Government's Obligations to the States

The Constitution imposes several obligations on the national government in its relations with the states. First of all, the states are guaranteed *territorial integrity*: No new state can be created by Congress out of the territory of an existing state without its consent. (Nonetheless, Congress admitted West Virginia to the Union in 1863 when the western counties of Virginia separated from that state during the Civil War. Later a "reconstructed" Virginia legislature gave its approval.) The national government must also guarantee to every state "*a republican form of government.*" A republican government is a government by democratically elected representatives. Presumably this clause in the Constitution means that the national government will ensure that no authoritarian or dictatorial regime will be permitted to rule in any state. Apparently this clause does *not* prohibit popular initiatives, referenda, town meetings, or other forms of direct democracy. The Supreme Court has never given any specific meaning to this guarantee. Each state is also guaranteed *equal representation in the U.S. Senate*. Indeed, the Constitution, Article V, prohibits any amendments that would deprive the states of equal representation in the Senate. Finally, the national government is required to *protect each state against foreign invasion and domestic violence*. The protection against foreign invasion is unequivocal, but the clause dealing with domestic violence includes the phrase "upon application of the legislature or the Executive (when the legislature cannot be convened)." Governors have called upon the national government to intervene in riots to maintain public order. But the national government has also intervened *without* "application" by state officials in cases where federal laws are being violated. Perhaps the most important direct intervention was President Dwight Eisenhower's decision to send federal troops to Little Rock High School in Arkansas in 1956 to enforce the Supreme Court's desegregation decision in *Brown* v. *Board of Education of Topeka, Kansas* (see Chapter 15).

State Role in National Government

The states also play an important role in the composition of the national government. U.S. representatives must be apportioned among the states according to their population every 10 years. Governors have the authority to fill vacancies in Congress, and every state must have at least one representative regardless of population. The Senate of the United States is composed of two senators from each state regardless of the state's population. The times, places, and manner of holding elections for Congress are determined by the states. The president is chosen by electors, allotted to each state on the basis of its senators and representatives. (See Figure 3–2.)

Finally, amendments to the U.S. Constitution must be ratified by three-fourths of the states. (See Figure 3–3.)

FIGURE 3–2 Electoral College Votes in the 2012 Election: A Political Map (States Drawn in Proportion to Electoral Votes)

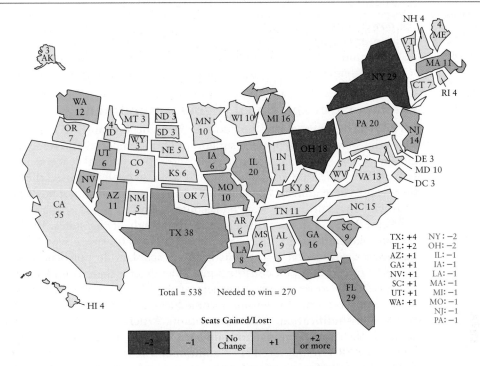

TX: +4	NY: −2
FL: +2	OH: −2
AZ: +1	IL: −1
GA: +1	IA: −1
NV: +1	LA: −1
SC: +1	MA: −1
UT: +1	MI: −1
WA: +1	MO: −1
	NJ: −1
	PA: −1

Total = 538   Needed to win = 270

Seats Gained/Lost:

−2	−1	No Change	+1	+2 or more

Source: Courtesy of Professor Josh Putnam, Davidson College. Map is available at http://frontloading.blogspot.com.

FIGURE 3–3 The States' Role in Constitutional Amendment

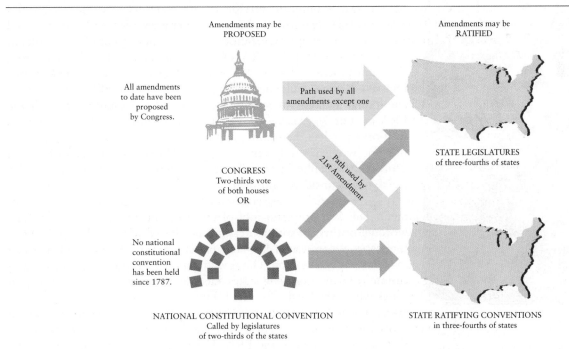

Amendments may be PROPOSED

All amendments to date have been proposed by Congress.

Path used by all amendments except one

Amendments may be RATIFIED

STATE LEGISLATURES of three-fourths of states

CONGRESS
Two-thirds vote of both houses
OR

Path used by 21st Amendment

No national constitutional convention has been held since 1787.

NATIONAL CONSTITUTIONAL CONVENTION
Called by legislatures of two-thirds of the states

STATE RATIFYING CONVENTIONS
in three-fourths of states

Source: United States Constitution, Washington, DC.

BATTLES IN THE STATES OVER CONSTITUTIONAL AMENDMENTS

3.5

Describe the role of the states in the constitutional amendment process using the proposed Equal Rights Amendment, the proposed District of Columbia amendment, and the Twenty-Seventh Amendment as examples.

The power of the states in the American federal system has been demonstrated in several battles over constitutional amendments passed by Congress. According to Article V of the U.S. Constitution, the Constitution cannot be amended without the approval of three-fourths of the states, either by their state legislatures or by state constitutional ratifying conventions.

The Defeat of the Equal Rights Amendment

EQUAL RIGHTS AMENDMENT (ERA)

A constitutional amendment proposed by Congress but never ratified by the necessary three-fourths of the states. It would have guaranteed "equality of rights under law" for women and men.

In 1972 when Congress sent the **Equal Rights Amendment (ERA)** to the states for ratification, it did so with overwhelming support of both Democrats and Republicans in the House and the Senate. National opinion polls and most national leaders, including Presidents Richard Nixon, Gerald Ford, and Jimmy Carter, strongly endorsed the simple language of the proposed amendment: "Equality of rights under law shall not be denied or abridged by the United States or by any State on account of sex."

The ERA won quick ratification in about half of the states. By 1978, 35 state legislatures had ratified the ERA. (See Figure 3–4.) (However, five states voted to rescind their earlier ratification. Most constitutional scholars do not believe a state can rescind its earlier ratification of a constitutional amendment; there is no language in the Constitution referring to rescissions.) Leaders of the ERA movement called upon Congress to grant an unprecedented extension of time beyond the traditional seven years to continue the battle for ratification. (The Constitution, Article V, does not specify how long states can consider a constitutional amendment.) In 1978, Congress (by simple majority vote) granted the ERA an unprecedented additional 3 years for state ratification; the new limit was 1982, a full 10 years after Congress proposed the original ERA.

Arkansas women marched through the streets of Washington DC with women from every state in the union in pushing for ratification of the Equal Rights Amendment.

The "Stop ERA" movement gained strength in the states over time. Under the leadership of conservative spokeswoman Phyllis Schlafly, an active group of women successfully lobbied *against* the ERA in state legislatures. In spite of overwhelming support for the ERA from Democratic and Republican presidents and congresses, leading celebrities from television and film, and even a majority of Americans surveyed by national polling organizations, these "ladies in pink" were influential in the defeat of the ERA. (The phrase "ladies in pink" refers to a common practice of anti-ERA women lobbyists wearing pink, dressing well, baking apple pies for legislators, and otherwise adopting the traditional symbols of femininity.) Most of the lobbying against the ERA in state legislatures was done by women's groups. While not as well organized as the leading feminist groups (the National Organization for Women, the League of Women Voters, the Women's Political Caucus), the "ladies in pink" were very much in evidence when state legislatures considered ratification.[7]

Three-quarters of the states *must* concur in a constitutional amendment. This is a powerful tool of the states in our federal system. The wording of the Constitution cannot be altered without the approval of the states, regardless of how much support such a change in wording may have in Washington. The amendment fell *three states short* of ratification by the necessary 38 states. Last-ditch attempts to pass the ERA in states where the battle was close (Florida, Illinois, and North Carolina) failed in 1982. But there is a renewed effort in a number of states to ratify the amendment. "All we need is three," is the rallying cry of current-day supporters of the ERA. The biggest problem they face is the belief by many citizens that there already *is* an equal rights amendment

FIGURE 3–4 ERA in the States

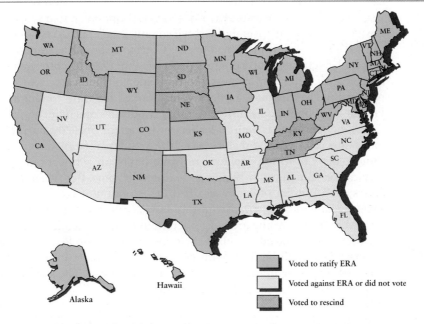

Voted to ratify ERA

Voted against ERA or did not vote

Voted to rescind

Source: United States Library of Congress, Washington, DC.

in the U.S. Constitution. It is less likely that state legislators will put a high priority on its passage without pressure from grassroots organizations.

The Defeat of the District of Columbia Amendment

The Constitution grants Congress the power to govern the District of Columbia, but over time Congress has delegated considerable home rule to the District. Washington elects its own mayor and council, levies city taxes, and provides municipal services to its residents. The Twenty-third Amendment, ratified by the states in 1961, gives Washingtonians three *presidential* electors, but residents of the city have never had voting members of Congress. (The District's only congressional representation is its *nonvoting* delegates to the House and Senate, who may serve on committees and participate in debates on the floor.) In 1978 Congress passed and sent to the states a constitutional amendment to grant the District of Columbia two U.S. senators and as many representatives as their population would warrant if it were a state (currently one). Congress placed a seven-year time limit on ratification by the states in the amendment itself, thus preventing a time extension by simple majority vote of the House and Senate.

The DC amendment passed both houses of Congress with well over the necessary two-thirds majority and the support of both Democrats and Republicans. But opposition in the states arose quickly. Much of the opposition was political: The District was seen as predominantly black, liberal, and Democratic. Less than 8 percent of the District's voters are registered as Republicans. The District itself has a less-than-reassuring record of self-government. By the 1985 deadline only 16 states, well short of the necessary 38, had ratified the amendment.

The Surprise Passage of the Twenty-Seventh Amendment

As part of the Bill of Rights, Congress in 1789 sent to the states an amendment that would prohibit a pay raise for members of Congress until after the intervention of an election for House members. The amendment had no time limit for ratification attached to it. But only 6 of the original 13 states ratified James Madison's pay raise amendment, and it was largely forgotten. However, as congressional scandals mounted in the 1980s and public confidence in Congress plummeted, the old amendment was rediscovered. (By one account, a University of Texas student ran across the amendment in 1982 and realized it had no time limit. Using his own money he undertook a national campaign that resulted in 26 states ratifying the amendment. Surprisingly, he received only a "C" on his research paper.)[8] As more states ratified the 200-year-old amendment, Congress should have realized that their behavior was under scrutiny. But Congress proceeded in 1989 to vote itself a 50 percent pay raise, touching off a storm of protest. (Nationwide polls indicated that 82 percent of Americans opposed the pay increase.) Angry voters looked for ways to rein in an arrogant Congress. Fifteen additional states rushed to ratify Madison's amendment.

Some scholars, as well as leaders in Congress, argued that ratification of the amendment after 203 years did not meet "the standard of timeliness." They argued that even though the Constitution placed no time limits on ratification, Article V "implied" that ratification should occur within a "reasonable" time. But when the archivist of the United States, Don Wilson, officially certified the adoption of the Twenty-seventh Amendment in 1992 as he was authorized to do by law, congressional leaders were stymied. Although they were irate over the archivist's action, they were unable to reverse it. Individual members of Congress raced to join in the popular sentiment, fearing that any effort to undo the amendment would be dealt with severely by the voters in the next election. Both houses voted nearly unanimously to endorse the amendment. The states had succeeded in administering an unexpected reprimand to Congress.

3.6 HOW MONEY SHIFTED POWER TO WASHINGTON

Outline how Congress has used its powers both to tax and to spend as a way to enhance the power of the national government.

Over the years the national government has acquired much greater power in the federal system than the Founders originally envisioned. (See *Up Close:* Historic Landmarks in the Development of American Federalism.") The "delegated" powers of the national government are now so broadly defined—particularly the power to tax and spend for the general welfare—that the government in Washington is involved in every aspect of American life. (The argument that constitutionally Congress can tax and spend only in support of its *enumerated* powers was rejected by the Supreme Court.)[9] Today, there are really no segments of public activity fully "reserved" to the states or the people.

Earliest Federal Aid

It is possible to argue that even in the earliest days of the Republic, the national government was involved in public activities that were not specifically delegated to it in the Constitution.[10] The first Congress of the United States in the famous Northwest Ordinance, providing for the government of the territories to the west of the Appalachian Mountains, authorized grants of federal land for the establishment of public schools, and by so doing, showed a concern for education, an area "reserved" to the states by the Constitution. Again in 1863, in the Morrill Land Grant Act, Congress provided grants of land to the states to promote higher education.

Money, Power, and the Income Tax

The date 1913, when the Sixteenth Amendment gave the federal government the power to tax income directly, marked the beginning of a new era in American federalism. Congress had been given the power to tax and spend for the general welfare in Article I of the Constitution. However, the Sixteenth Amendment helped to shift the balance of financial power from the states to Washington, when it gave Congress the power to tax the incomes of corporations and individuals on a progressive basis. The income tax gave the federal government the power to raise large sums of money, which it proceeded to spend for the general welfare as well as for defense. It is no coincidence that the first major grant-in-aid programs (agricultural extension in 1914, highways in 1916, vocational education in 1917, and public health in 1918) all came shortly after the inauguration of the federal income tax.

The American federal system is a product of more than its formal constitutional provisions. It has also been shaped by court interpretations of constitutional principles as well as the history of disputes that have occurred over state and national authority.

Marbury v. Madison (1803): Expanding Federal Court Authority

Chief Justice John Marshall, who presided over the Supreme Court from 1801 to 1835, became a major architect of American federalism. Under Marshall, *the Supreme Court assumed the role of arbiter in disputes between state and national authority.* It was under Marshall that the Supreme Court in *Marbury* v. *Madison* assumed the power to interpret the U.S. Constitution authoritatively. The fact that the referee of disputes between state and national authority has been the *national* Supreme Court has had a profound influence on the development of American federalism. Since the Supreme Court is a *national* institution, one might say that in disputes between nation and states, one member of the two opposing teams is also serving as umpire. Constitutionally speaking, then, there is really *no* limitation on national as against state authority *if* all three branches of the national government—the Congress, the president, and the Court—act together to override state authority.

McCulloch v. Maryland (1819): Expanding Implied Powers of the National Government

In *McCulloch* v. *Maryland*, Chief Justice Marshall provided a broad interpretation of the Necessary and Proper Clause:

> Let the end be legitimate, let it be within the scope of the Constitution, and all means which are appropriate, which are plainly adopted to the end, which are not prohibited but consistent with the letter and the spirit of the Constitution, are constitutional.[a]

The *McCulloch* case firmly established the principle that the Necessary and Proper Clause gives Congress the right to choose its means for carrying out the enumerated powers of the national government. Today, Congress can devise programs, create agencies, and establish national laws on the basis of long chains of reasoning from the most meager phrases of the constitutional text because of the broad interpretation of the Necessary and Proper Clause.

Secession and the Civil War (1861–1865): Maintaining the "Indestructible Union"

The Civil War was, of course, the greatest crisis of the American federal system. Did a state have the right to oppose national law to the point of secession? In the years preceding the Civil War, John C. Calhoun argued that the Constitution was a compact made by the *states* in a sovereign capacity rather than by the *people* in their national capacity. Calhoun contended that the federal government was an agent of the states, that the states retained their sovereignty in this compact, and that the federal government must not violate the compact, under the penalty of state nullification or even secession from the Union.

The issue was decided in the nation's bloodiest war. What was decided on the battlefield between 1861 and 1865 was confirmed by the Supreme Court in 1869: "Ours is an indestructible union, composed of indestructible states."[b] Yet the states' rights doctrines, and political disputes over the character of American federalism, did not disappear with Lee's surrender at Appomattox. The Thirteenth, Fourteenth, and Fifteenth Amendments, passed by the Reconstruction Congress, were clearly aimed at limiting state power in the interests of individual freedom. The Thirteenth Amendment eliminated slavery in the states; the Fourteenth Amendment granted citizenship to blacks (and to anyone born or naturalized in the United States) and prohibited states from denying a person's civil rights; and the Fifteenth Amendment prevented states from discriminating against blacks in the right to vote. These amendments delegated to Congress the power to secure their enforcement. Yet for several generations these amendments were narrowly construed and added little, if anything, to national power.

National Labor Relations Board v. Jones and Laughlin Steel Corp. (1937): Expanding Interstate Commerce

The Industrial Revolution in America created a *national* economy with a nationwide network of transportation and communication and the potential for national economic depressions. Yet for a time, the Supreme Court placed obstacles in the way of national authority over the economy, and by so doing the Court created a "crisis" in American federalism. For many years, the Court narrowly construed interstate commerce to mean only the movement of goods and services across state lines, insisting that agriculture, mining, manufacturing, and labor relations were outside the reach of the delegated powers of the national government. However, when confronted with the Great Depression of the 1930s and President Franklin D. Roosevelt's threat to "pack" the Court with additional members to secure approval of his New Deal measures, the Court yielded. In *National Labor Relations Board* v. *Jones and Laughlin Steel Corporation* in 1937, the Court recognized the principle that production and distribution of goods and services for a national market could be regulated by Congress under the Interstate Commerce Clause. The effect was to give the national government effective control over the national economy.

Brown v. Board of Education (1954): Guaranteeing Civil Rights

After World War I, the Supreme Court began to build a national system of civil rights that was based on the Fourteenth Amendment. In early cases, the Court held that the Fourteenth Amendment prevented states from interfering with free speech, free press, or religious practices. Not until 1954, in the Supreme Court's landmark desegregation decision in *Brown* v. *Board of Education of Topeka, Kansas,* did the Court begin to call for the full assertion of national authority on behalf of civil rights.[c] The Supreme Court's use of the Fourteenth Amendment to ensure a national system of civil rights supported by the power of the federal government was an important step in the evolution of the American federal system.

Voting Rights Act (1965) and *Bush v. Gore* (2000): *Federal Oversight of Elections*

The Voting Rights Act of 1965 plunged the federal government into direct oversight of state and local as well as federal elections in an effort to end discriminatory practices. The Act and subsequent amendments to it require the Justice Department to approve any election law changes in states and communities covered by the Act. It provides that intent to discriminate need not be proven if the results demonstrate a discriminatory impact on minorities.

In the contested presidential election of 2000, the U.S. Supreme Court confirmed national oversight of Electoral College voting and vote counting in *Bush v. Gore*. In this landmark case the Court reversed a Florida Supreme Court interpretation of that state's election laws and ruled that voting and vote counting are entitled to Equal Protection and Due Process under the Fourteenth Amendment.

Federation of Independent Business *v. Sebelius* (2012): *Expanding the Taxing Power*

The Patient Protection and Affordable Care Act of 2010 ("ObamaCare") imposes a tax on Americans who *do* not obtain government approved health insurance. Twenty-six states, several

individuals, and the Federation of Independent Business filed suit in federal court challenging the constitutionality of the Act. They argued that it exceeded Congress's power under the Interstate Commerce Clause to force their citizens to buy a product. Chief Justice John Roberts, in writing for the majority of the Court, agreed that the Commerce Clause could not justify the "mandate" on citizens to buy insurance. But in a surprise 5-4 decision Roberts held that Congress could impose a tax on people who do not by health insurance in the exercise of their power to "lay and collect taxes" (Article I, Section 8). The Court's opinion appears to open a whole new source of federal power.

The U.S. Supreme Court's controversial decision in *Bush v. Gore,* issued in December 2000, effectively determined the outcome of the 2000 presidential election. It also affirmed that voting and vote counting processes in states must adhere to equal protection and due process under the Fourteenth Amendment to the U.S. Constitution.

[a]*McCulloch v. Maryland,* 17 U.S. 316 (1819).
[b]*Texas v. White,* 7 Wallace 700 (1869).
[c]*Brown v. Board of Education of Topeka, Kansas,* 347 U.S. 483 (1954).

Federal Grants-in-Aid

The federal "grant-in-aid" has been the principal instrument in the expansion of national power.[11] Today, the federal government spends over $500 billion annually on grants-in-aid to state and local governments, making it the third largest item in the federal budget after Social Security and national defense.[12] More than one-third of all state and local government expenditures are currently from monies derived from federal grants. This money is paid out through a staggering number and variety of programs. Federal grants may be obtained to assist in everything from the preservation of historic buildings, the development of minority-owned businesses, the education of the disabled, the construction of airports, to the funding of disaster relief and tree preservation.

The largest portion of federal grant-in-aid money (47%) is devoted to health, including Medicaid (health care for the poor), the state children's health insurance program, and funds for substance abuse and mental health services. Only about 10 percent is used for highways and transit, and only about 16 percent for education, training, employment, and social services. (See Figure 3–5.) Typically, Congress appropriates funds to a federal agency that is charged with administering the grant program, such as health grant funds to the

FIGURE 3–5 Federal Grants-in-Aid by Major Function

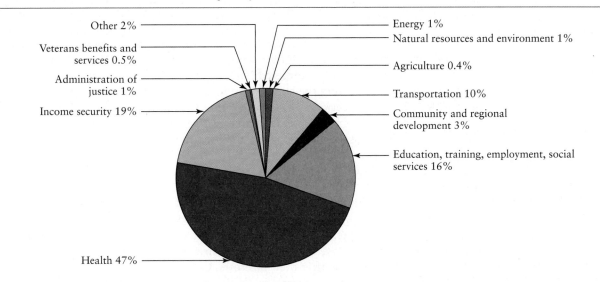

Other 2%

Veterans benefits and services 0.5%

Administration of justice 1%

Income security 19%

Health 47%

Energy 1%

Natural resources and environment 1%

Agriculture 0.4%

Transportation 10%

Community and regional development 3%

Education, training, employment, social services 16%

Note: Data are for 2011.
Source: U.S. Census Bureau, *Statistical Abstract of the United States,* 2012, Table 432. Available at http://www.census.gov/prod/2011pubs/12statab/stlocgov.pdf.

Department of Health and Human Services. The agency, in turn, distributes the grant funds to the states. States may award subcontracts or subgrants at the local level, depending on how the grant is structured.

Money with Strings Attached

Today, grant-in-aid programs are the single most important source of federal influence over state and local activity. A **grant-in-aid** is defined as payment of funds by one level of government (national or state) to be expended by another level (state or local) for a specified purpose, usually on a matching-funds basis (the federal government puts up only part of the funding, the state or locality the rest) and "in accordance with prescribed standards of requirements." No state or local government is *required* to accept grants-in-aid. Participation is voluntary. So in theory, if conditions attached to the grant money are too oppressive, state and local governments can simply decline to participate. Yet it is often asserted that states are "bribed" by the temptation of much-needed federal money and "blackmailed" by the thought that other states will get the money, which was raised in part by federal taxes on the state's own citizens.

Currently, federal grants-in-aid can be described as either "**categorical grants**" or "**block grants**," depending on the extent of federal oversight of how the money is spent.

> *Categorical Grants:* Most federal aid money is distributed as categorical grants for specific, narrow projects. Grants are offered by federal administrative agencies to state or local governments that compete for project funds in their applications. Federal agencies have a great deal of discretion in selecting specific projects for support, and they can exercise direct control over the projects. Most categorical grants are distributed to state or local governments according to a fixed formula set by Congress. Federal administrative agencies may require reports and adherence to rules and guidelines, but they do not choose which specific projects to fund.

> *Block Grants:* These grants are for a general governmental function, such as health, social services, law enforcement, education, or community development. State and local governments have fairly wide discretion in deciding how to spend federal block grant money within a functional area. For example, cities receiving "community development" block grants can decide for themselves about specific neighborhood development projects, housing projects, and community facilities. All block grants are distributed on a formula basis set by Congress.

GRANTS-IN-AID

Payments of funds from the national government to state or local governments or from a state government to local governments for specific purposes.

CATEGORICAL GRANTS

Federal grants-in-aid to state or local governments for specific purposes or projects.

BLOCK GRANTS

Federal grants-in-aid for general governmental functions, allowing state and local governments to exercise some flexibility in use.

Grantsmanship

Federal money flows unevenly among the states and some states rely on it more than others (see "*Rankings of the States:* Reliance on Federal Aid"). The federal grant system is not neutral in its impact on the states, nor is it intended to be. Many grant programs are based on formulas that incorporate various indications of need and financial ability. Federal aid is supposed to be "targeted" on national problems.[13] The effect of differential grant allocations among the states, combined with differences among state populations in federal tax collections, is to *redistribute* federal money throughout the nation. The big winners in the federal grant game are generally the poorer rural states like West Virginia and Mississippi; the losers are the urban states. But not always—a prime exception being funding for homeland security. Funding battles are always a principal source of conflict between governments—"the time-honored bone of intergovernmental contention."[14]

The rush to Washington to ensure that states and cities receive their "fair share" of federal grant money, together with concerns over federal interference in the conduct of state and local government, has produced a great deal of intergovernmental lobbying at the nation's capital. Most individual states now maintain offices in Washington with staff committed to looking after their interests. Cities have also hired Washington-based lobbyists to look after their interests in the federal grants game, particularly since during the Bush administration, more federal aid was directed at local governments than in the past.[15]

From the earliest days of the Republic, American statesmen have argued over federalism. In recent years, political conflict over federalism—over the decision between national versus state and local responsibilities and finances—has tended to follow traditional "liberal" and "conservative" political cleavages. Generally, liberals seek to enhance the power of the *national* government because they believe that people's lives can be changed—and bettered—by the exercise of national governmental power. The government in Washington has more power and resources than do state and local governments, which many liberals regard as too slow, cumbersome, weak, and unresponsive. Thus liberalism and centralization are closely related in American politics.

The liberal argument for national authority can be summarized as follows:

- State and local governments are not sufficiently aware of social problems. The federal government must take the lead in civil rights, equal employment opportunities, care for the poor and aged, the provision of adequate medical care for all Americans, and the elimination of urban poverty and blight. Grants-in-aid permit the government to set national goals and priorities in all levels of government.

- Grants-in-aid provide the necessary impetus for social change. It is difficult to achieve change when reform-minded citizens must deal with 50 state governments and over 89,000 local governments. Change is more likely to be accomplished by a strong central government.

- Grants-in-aid provide an opportunity for the national government to ensure a uniform level of public service throughout the nation—for example, federal grants-in-aid help ensure a minimum level of existence for the poverty-stricken regardless of where they live. This aspect of federal policy assumes that in some parts of the nation, state and local governments are unable, or perhaps unwilling, to devote their resources to raising public service levels to minimum national standards.

Conservatives, in contrast, are skeptical about the "good" that government can do and believe that adding to the power of the national government is not an effective way of resolving society's problems. On the contrary, they often argue that "government is the problem, not the solution." Excessive federal government regulation, burdensome taxation, and big spending combine to restrict individual freedom, penalize work and savings, and destroy incentives for economic growth. Government should be kept small, controllable, and close to the people.

Reliance on Federal Aid

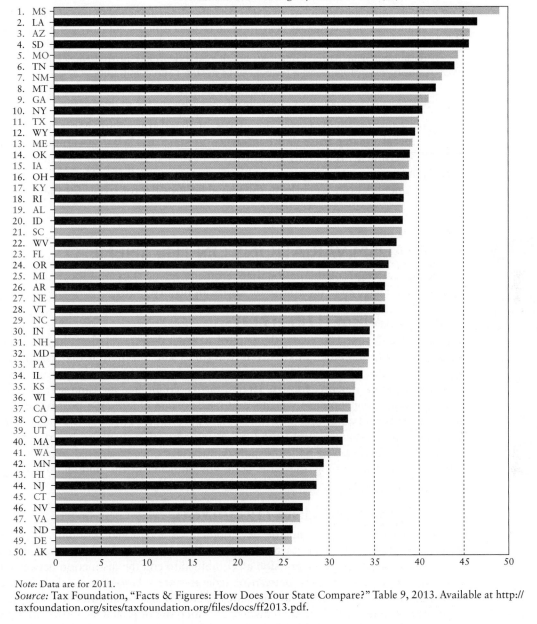

Federal Aid as Percentage of Total Revenue (%)

1. MS
2. LA
3. AZ
4. SD
5. MO
6. TN
7. NM
8. MT
9. GA
10. NY
11. TX
12. WY
13. ME
14. OK
15. IA
16. OH
17. KY
18. RI
19. AL
20. ID
21. SC
22. WV
23. FL
24. OR
25. MI
26. AR
27. NE
28. VT
29. NC
30. IN
31. NH
32. MD
33. PA
34. IL
35. KS
36. WI
37. CA
38. CO
39. UT
40. MA
41. WA
42. MN
43. HI
44. NJ
45. CT
46. NV
47. VA
48. ND
49. DE
50. AK

0   5   10   15   20   25   30   35   40   45   50

Note: Data are for 2011.
Source: Tax Foundation, "Facts & Figures: How Does Your State Compare?" Table 9, 2013. Available at http://taxfoundation.org/sites/taxfoundation.org/files/docs/ff2013.pdf.

Conservative objections to federal grant-in-aid programs can be summarized as follows:

■ Grassroots government promotes a sense of self-responsibility and self-reliance. State and local government can better adapt public programs to local needs and conditions. Federal grants-in-aid are invariably accompanied by federal standards or "guidelines," which must be adhered to if states and communities are to receive their federal money. While no state is required to accept a federal grant and its restrictions, it is difficult for states and communities to resist the pressure to accept federal money.

- Federal grants cause state and local officials to overspend what looks to them like "free" money. Overspending on programs or services that local residents would not be willing to pay for out of their *own* tax revenues creates waste and inefficiency and contributes to the overall growth of government. Federal money is not "free": It comes from the *nation's* taxpayers. Local governments are sometimes pressured to apply for funds for projects they do not really need, simply because federal funds are available.

- The grant-in-aid system assumes that federal officials are better judges of goals and priorities at all levels of government than are state or local officials. In many grant programs federal officials must approve each funded project—a housing project in Des Moines, a sewage disposal system in Baton Rouge, an urban renewal project in Alabama. Block grants, which allocate federal funds on a formula basis to states and communities for general purposes like "community development" or "mental health," provide more flexibility than project grants. But Congress cannot resist attaching directions for the use of these grants.

Americans are divided over the merits of these arguments. Most national opinion surveys reveal greater trust and confidence in state and local government than in the federal government. But many Americans believe that the federal government can do a better job handling specific issues such as protecting civil rights. There is no way to settle these arguments about federalism; they have been heard for over 200 years in American politics.

3.7

FEDERALISM: VARIATIONS ON THE THEME

Analyze the merits, at both the state and national levels, of the various types of government from dual federalism through "bottom-up" federalism, including the effect each had on the relationship between the nation and the states.

The relative strength of the national government versus state and local governments has constantly changed over the course of American history.

Dual Federalism (1787–1913)

DUAL FEDERALISM

Early concept of federalism in which national and state powers were clearly distinguished and functionally separate.

For the nation's first 100 years, the pattern of federal–state relations has been described as **dual federalism**. Under this pattern, the states and the nation divided most governmental functions. The national government concentrated its attention on the "delegated" powers—national defense, foreign affairs, tariffs, commerce crossing state lines, coining money, establishing standard weights and measures, maintaining a post office and building post roads, and admitting new states. State governments decided the important domestic policy issues—slavery (until the Civil War), education, welfare, health, and criminal justice. This separation of policy responsibilities was once compared to a "layer cake,"[16] with local governments at the base, state governments in the middle, and the national government at the top.

Cooperative Federalism (1913–1964)

COOPERATIVE FEDERALISM

Model of federalism in which national, state, and local governments work together exercising common policy responsibilities.

The Industrial Revolution and the development of a national economy, an income tax that shifted financial resources to the national government, and the challenges of two world wars and the Great Depression all combined to end the distinction between national and state concerns. The new pattern of federal–state relations was labeled **cooperative federalism**. Both the nation and the states exercised responsibilities for welfare, health, highways, education, and criminal justice. This merging of policy responsibilities was compared to a "marble cake." "As the colors are mixed in a marble cake, so functions are mixed in the American federal system."[17]

The Great Depression of the 1930s forced states to ask for federal financial assistance in dealing with poverty, unemployment, and old age. Governors welcomed massive federal public works projects. In addition, the federal government intervened directly in economic affairs, labor relations, business practices, and agriculture. Through the grant-in-aid device, the national government cooperated with the states in public assistance, employment services, child welfare, public housing, urban renewal, highway building, and vocational education.

Yet even in this period of shared national–state responsibility, the national government emphasized cooperation in achieving common national and state goals. Congress generally acknowledged that it had no direct constitutional authority to regulate public health, safety, or welfare.

Centralized Federalism (1964–1980)

Over the years it became increasingly difficult to maintain the fiction that the national government was merely assisting the states in performing their domestic responsibility. By the time President Lyndon B. Johnson launched the "Great Society" in 1964, the federal government clearly set forth its own "national" goals. Virtually all problems confronting American society—from solid waste disposal and water and air pollution to consumer safety, home insulation, noise abatement, and even metric conversion—were declared to be national problems. Congress legislated directly on any matter it chose, without regard to its "enumerated powers" and without pretense to financial assistance. The Supreme Court no longer concerned itself with the "reserved" powers of the states; the Tenth Amendment lost most of its meaning. The pattern of national–state relations became centralized. As for the cake analogies, one commentator observed: "The frosting had moved up to the top, something like a pineapple upside-down cake."[18]

CENTRALIZED FEDERALISM

Model of federalism in which the national government assumes primary responsibility for determining national goals in all major policy areas and directs state and local government activity through conditions attached to money grants.

New Federalism (1980–1985)

From time to time efforts have been made to reverse the flow of power to Washington and return responsibilities to state and local government. The phrase "**New Federalism**" originated in the administration of President Richard M. Nixon, who used it to describe general revenue sharing—federal sharing of tax revenues with state and local governments with few strings attached. Later, "New Federalism" was used by President Ronald Reagan to describe a series of proposals designed to reduce federal involvement in domestic programs and encourage states and cities to undertake greater policy responsibilities.

General Revenue Sharing began in 1972 as a conservative alternative to categorical grants by federal agencies for specific projects. It was argued that unrestricted federal money grants to state and local government were preferable to centralized bureaucratic decision making in Washington. Revenue sharing promised to reverse the flow of power, end excessive red tape, and revitalize state and local governments. Revenue sharing was strongly supported by state and local government officials, who were happy to have the federal government collect tax money and then turn it over to them to spend. But the Reagan administration, confronting high federal deficits and wanting to reduce Washington's role in domestic policy, undertook a long and eventually successful effort in 1986 to end General Revenue Sharing.

Another Reagan approach was greater reliance on the block grant. Congress endorsed many block grants in the early 1980s, but the struggle between categorical grant advocates (liberals and Democrats) and the consolidationists (Reagan and the Republicans) was really a draw. Many categorical grant programs were merged (notably in health services; alcohol, drug abuse, and mental health; social services; maternal and child health; community services; community development; and education), but many others remained independent.

The New Federalism also temporarily lessened the dependence of state and local governments on federal money. In the years prior to 1980, state and local governments had become increasingly dependent on federal grants as sources of revenue. Federal grants rose to over one-quarter of all state–local expenditures in 1980 (see Table 3–1). Total federal aid dollars continued to rise during the Reagan years, but not at the same rate as in previous years. The result was a decline in state–local dependence on federal money to less than 20 percent.

By the 1990s, under Republican President George H. W. Bush as well as Democratic President Bill Clinton, however, the flow of federal aid dollars to the states rose.

NEW FEDERALISM

A reference to efforts first in the Nixon administration to return some federal tax funds to the states (general revenue sharing) and later efforts in the Reagan administration to consolidate federal grant-in-aid programs into block grants.

GENERAL REVENUE SHARING

Federal sharing of tax revenues with state and local governments with few strings attached; program ended in 1986.

TABLE 3–1 Trends in Federal Grants-in-Aid

Year	Total Federal Grants (Billion Dollars)	Federal Grants as a Percentage of	
		Total Federal Spending	State and Local Expenditures
1980	91	15.5	39.9
1985	106	11.2	29.6
1990	135	10.8	25.2
1995	225	14.8	31.5
2000	286	16.0	27.4
2003	389	18.0	31.0
2006	434	16.3	29.7
2007	444	16.3	28.3
2008	461	15.5	26.9
2009	538	15.3	33.1
2010	608	17.6	37.5
2011, est.	625	16.4	(NA)

Note: NA = Not Available

Source: U.S. Census Bureau, *Statistical Abstract of the United States,* 2012, Table 431. Available at http://www.census.gov/prod/2011pubs/12statab/stlocgov.pdf.

Representational Federalism (1985–1996)

Despite centralizing tendencies, it was still widely assumed prior to 1985 that the Congress could not directly legislate how state and local governments should go about performing their traditional functions. However, in its 1985 *Garcia* v. *San Antonio Metropolitan Transit Authority* decision,[19] the U.S. Supreme Court appeared to remove all barriers to direct congressional legislation in matters traditionally reserved to the states. The case arose after Congress directly ordered state and local governments to pay minimum wages to their employees. The Court dismissed arguments that the nature of American federalism and the Reserved Powers Clause of the Tenth Amendment prevented Congress from directly legislating in state affairs. The Court declared that there were *no* "a priori definitions of state sovereignty," *no* "discrete limitations on the objects of federal authority," and *no* protection of state powers in the U.S. Constitution. According to the Court: "State sovereign interests . . . are more properly protected by procedural safeguards inherent in the structure of the federal system than by judicially created limitations on federal power." It said that the only protection for state powers was to be found in the states' role in electing U.S. senators, members of the U.S. House of Representatives, and the president.

The Supreme Court's *Garcia* case ruling became known as "**representational federalism.**" The United States is said to retain a federal system because national officials are selected from subunits of government—the president through the allocation of Electoral College votes to the states, and the Congress through the allocation of 2 Senate seats per state and the apportionment of representatives to states based on population. Whatever protection exists for state power and independence must be found in the national political process—in the influence of state and district voters on their senators and congress members. Representational federalism does not recognize any constitutionally protected powers of the states.

However, the Supreme Court may be unwilling to jettison altogether the notion of federalism as the division of power between nation and states. Justice Sandra Day O'Connor, a former Arizona legislator and appellate court judge, staunchly defended federalism on the Supreme Court. Quoting from the *Federalist* and citing the Tenth Amendment, Justice O'Connor wrote the majority opinion in a case considering whether Congress's

REPRESENTATIONAL FEDERALISM

The notion that federalism is defined by the role of the states in electing members of Congress and the president rather than any constitutional division of powers.

Age Discrimination Employment Act invalidated a provision of the Missouri Constitution requiring judges to retire at age 70.[20] She cited the "constitutional balance of federal and state powers" as a reason for upholding the Missouri Constitution. Only a "clear statement" by Congress of its intent to override a traditional state power would justify doing so. This "clear statement" rule presumably governs federal laws that may be in conflict with state laws or constitutions. The rule does not prevent Congress from directly regulating state government activity, but it requires Congress to say unambiguously that this is its intent.

Coercive Federalism: Preemptions and Mandates (1997–2010)

Can Congress *directly* regulate the traditional functions of state and local governments? We know that Congress can influence the actions of state and local governments by offering them grants of money and then threatening to withdraw it if they do not meet federal rules, regulations, or "guidelines." But can Congress, in the exercise of its broad constitutional powers, legislate directly about traditional functions of state and local governments—schools, streets, police and fire protection, water and sewers, refuse disposal? Can the national government by law treat the states as administrative units required to carry out the mandates of Congress?

Certainly the historical answer to this question was "No." A typical nineteenth-century description of federalism by the U.S. Supreme Court asserted that the federal government could not intrude or interfere with the independent powers of state governments and vice versa:

> There are within the territorial limits of each state two governments [state and national], restricted in their spheres of action, but independent of each other, and supreme within their respective spheres. Each has its separate departments, each has its distinct laws, and each has its own tribunes for their enforcement. Neither government can intrude within the jurisdiction of the other or authorize any interference therein by its judicial officers with the action of the other.[21]

Perhaps this separation and independence never really characterized relations between the national government and the state governments. But at least state governments were viewed as independent authorities that could not be directly coerced by the national government in their traditional functions. Today, many state officials believe their independence is slowly being whittled away by actions of Congress and the federal courts. Federalism scholars agree with this assessment. The federal government has continued centralizing and nationalizing policy in major areas formerly controlled by states and localities (education testing, sales tax collection, emergency management, infrastructure, and election administration) through use of **mandates** and **preemptions**. Some have labeled this "opportunistic federalism" on the part of the federal government.[22]

- *Congressional regulation of state taxes.* More than a century ago, the U.S. Supreme Court held that Congress could not levy taxes on the states or on their bonds or notes.[23] Intergovernmental tax immunity was believed to be an integral part of the Tenth Amendment's guarantee of the reserved powers of the states. The states could not tax federal bonds and the nation could not tax state bonds. But in 1987, the U.S. Supreme Court shocked state and local officials and the municipal bond market by holding that Congress could if it wished levy taxes on the interest received from state and local bonds. In a dissent, Justice Sandra Day O'Connor observed that "the Court has failed to enforce the constitutional safeguards of state autonomy and self-sufficiency that may be found in the Tenth Amendment and the Guarantee Clause, as well as in the principles of federalism implicit in the Constitution."[24]

- *Federal preemptions.* The supremacy of federal laws over those of the states, spelled out in the Supremacy Clause of the Constitution, permits Congress to decide whether or not state laws in a particular field are preempted by federal law. To date, Congress has passed over 500 preemption statutes and the number is on the rise.[25] Total preemption refers to the federal

MANDATES
In federal–state relations, the federal government's orders to state (or local) governments to provide particular services or perform specific services.

PREEMPTIONS
In federal–state relations, the federal government's assumption of regulatory powers in a particular field to the partial or full exclusion of state powers.

government's assumption of all regulatory powers in a particular field—for example, copyrights, bankruptcy, railroads, and airlines. No state regulations in a totally preempted field are permitted. Partial preemption stipulates that a state law on the same subject is valid as long as it does not conflict with the federal law in the same area. For example, the Occupational Safety and Health Act of 1970 specifically permits state regulation of any occupational safety or health issue on which the federal Occupational Safety and Health Administration (OSHA) has *not* developed a standard; but once OSHA enacts a standard, all state standards are nullified.

■ *Federal mandates.* Federal mandates are orders to state and local governments to comply with federal laws. Federal mandates occur in a wide variety of areas—from civil rights and voter rights laws to conditions of jails and juvenile detention centers, minimum wage and worker safety regulations, air and water pollution controls, and requirements for access for disabled people. (See Table 3–2.)

■ *"Unfunded" mandates.* When no federal monies are provided to cover these costs, the mandates are said to be "**unfunded mandates.**" Governors, mayors, and other state and local officials (including Bill Clinton, when he served as governor of Arkansas) have often urged Congress to stop imposing unfunded mandates on states and communities. Private industries have long voiced the same complaint. Regulations and mandates allow Congress to address

---

TABLE 3–2 Selected Federal Mandates

Examples of Federal Mandates to State and Local Governments

- *Age Discrimination Act 1986* Outlaws mandatory retirement ages for public as well as private employees, including police, firefighters, and state college and university faculty.
- *Asbestos Hazard Emergency Act 1986* Orders school districts to inspect for asbestos hazards and remove asbestos from school buildings when necessary.
- *Safe Drinking Water Act 1986* Establishes national requirements for municipal water supplies; regulates municipal waste treatment plants.
- *Clean Air Act 1990* Bans municipal incinerators and requires auto emission inspections in certain urban areas.
- *Americans with Disabilities Act 1990* Requires all state and local government buildings to promote handicapped access.
- *National Voter Registration Act 1993* Requires states to register voters at driver's licensing, welfare, and unemployment offices.
- *No Child Left Behind Act 2001* Requires states and their school districts to test public school pupils and provide vouchers to pupils from consistently below average scoring schools.
- *Help America Vote Act 2002* Requires states to modernize registration and voting procedures and voting technology.
- *Homeland Security Act 2002* Requires states and communities as "first responders" to train, equip, and prepare for terrorist attacks.
- *Real ID Act 2005* Designed to prevent terrorism, reduce fraud, and improve the reliability and accuracy of identification documents that state governments issue. The Act requires that a REAL ID driver's license be used for "official purposes," as defined by the Department of Homeland Security.
- *Patient Protection and Affordable Care Act of 2010* (Health Care Reform) Requires states to expand eligibility to the Medicaid program to persons falling below 133% of the federal poverty limit. Initially, 100% of the direct costs of covering these new enrollees will be borne by the federal government. But within a few years, the federal match will fall to 90%, leaving states to come up with 10% of the funding. This will amount to millions of dollars in states experiencing sharp increases in the number of Medicaid enrollees.

Note: Some of these mandates are partially funded by the federal government, but state and local officials still see them as "unfunded" because they are not totally funded.

---

problems while pushing the costs onto others. In 1995, Congress finally responded to these complaints by requiring that any bill imposing unfunded costs of $58 million on state and local governments (as determined by the Congressional Budget Office) would be subject to an additional procedural vote; a majority must vote to waive a prohibition against unfunded mandates before such a bill can come to the House or Senate floor.

Federal officials often define "unfunded mandates" differently than state officials. A Congressional Budget Office report in the early 2000s concluded that only two unfunded mandates exceeding the Unfunded Mandates Reform Act of 1995 have been passed by Congress (an increase in the federal wage in 1996, a reduction in federal reimbursement of state Food Stamp administrative costs in 1998). But the National Governors Association disagrees. It regards as "unfunded" any *under*funded grant-in-aid program that state and local governments cannot realistically reject or opt out of once they are passed by Congress.[26] The Homeland Security, No Child Left Behind, the Help America Vote, and Real ID Acts (requiring states to provide uniform, tamperproof driver's licenses) are seen by many state officials as examples of underfunded, de facto mandates.

"Bottom-Up" Federalism (2011–Present)

The newest phase of federalism, labeled by some as "**bottom-up federalism**," is "characterized by states having to address pressing fiscal and social issues without federal assistance as well as state and local pushback against federal policy."[27] In the midst of the Great Recession some states refused to participate in federal programs ranging from health insurance exchanges to high-speed rail initiatives, fearing federal funds would be insufficient to cover the high costs over time.[28] Others filed lawsuits challenging federal policy mandates on a wide range of issues such as ObamaCare, immigration, guns, education, and the environment), fearing the economic consequences they would impose on states which, unlike the federal government, have to balance their budgets. Economics also drove some states to pass laws conflicting with federal laws on social issues like marijuana legalization and same-sex marriage, often justifying their "defiance" on economic grounds (more tax dollars to fund state and local programs and projects). Like states, local governments have stepped up their challenges of, and resistance to, politics imposed on them from the federal government.[29]

This new phase of federalism reflects a strong reaction by states and localities to a long period of top-down preemption and coercion on the part of the federal government. (The backlash against the perceived expansion of federal power even resulted in a citizen-generated petition to the White House asking for the right to secede from the United States.[30]) State reactions to coercive federalism have not always been in the same direction, reflecting sharp demographic, socioeconomic, and political differences across the 50 states. For example, the more liberal states have led the way on same-sex marriage and marijuana legalization, while the more conservative states successfully challenged the federal government's authority to impose coercive penalties on states that refused to enact ObamaCare's Medicaid expansions.

Differences across the states on key issues have forced the U.S. Congress and the U.S. Supreme Court to react to actions taken by state and local governments rather than the other way around. In the process, "states have been reaffirmed as laboratories of democracy and laboratories for social change." Some have predicted that this "bottom-up" phase of federalism will be riddled with intergovernmental conflict: "The states are going to be in different places, and in different places than the national government. There are going to be huge wedges driving differences between states and the federal government. And states themselves."[31] Others see the period ahead as one of greater cooperation and collaboration between states, localities, and the private sector—by necessity in light of a dysfunctional federal government unable to respond to profound economic changes facing the nation.[32]

BOTTOM-UP FEDERALISM
States taking the lead in policymaking in critical economic and social areas, often in reaction to inaction or coercion by the federal government.

CONGRESS AND DEVOLUTION

Controversy over federalism—which level of government should do what and who should pay for it—is as old as the nation itself. Beginning in 1995, debates over federalism were renewed. The new phrase was **devolution**—the passing-down of responsibilities from the national government to the states.[33]

DEVOLUTION

Passing-down of responsibilities from the national government to the states.

Devolution and Welfare Reform

Welfare reform turned out to be the key to devolution. President Bill Clinton once promised "to end welfare as we know it," but it was a Republican Congress in 1996 that did so. After President Clinton had twice vetoed welfare reform bills, he and Congress finally agreed to merge welfare reform with devolution by:

- Ending a 60-year-old federal entitlement program for cash welfare aid (Aid to Families with Dependent Children), and substituting block grants with lump-sum allocations to the states for welfare payments (now known as Temporary Assistance to Needy Families).
- Granting the states broad flexibility in determining eligibility and benefit levels for persons receiving such aid.
- Allowing states to increase welfare spending if they choose but penalizing states that reduce their spending for cash aid below 75 percent of their 1996 levels.
- Allowing states to deny additional cash payments for children born to women already receiving welfare assistance and allowing states to deny cash payments to parents under age 18 who do not live with an adult and attend school.

Devolution resulted in a dramatic reduction of welfare caseloads—an average of more than 50 percent throughout the states, although part of this reduction may have been due to the healthy national economy because caseloads rose sharply during the Great Recession. (For more information on welfare policy, see Chapter 17.)

Political Obstacles to Federalism

It is not likely that presidents or members of Congress will ever be motivated to restrain their own power. Even when they recognize that they may be overstepping the enumerated powers of the national government, political pressures to "DO SOMETHING!" about virtually every problem that confronts individuals, families, or communities inspire them to propose federal interventions. Politicians gain very little by telling their constituents that a particular problem—violence in the schools, domestic abuse, physician-assisted suicide—is not a federal responsibility and should be dealt with at the state or local level of government.

THE SUPREME COURT AND THE REVIVAL OF FEDERALISM

The U.S. Supreme Court reconsidered the nature of American federalism in several recent cases. For the first time in many years, the Court declared laws of Congress unconstitutional because they exceeded the enumerated powers of Congress in Article I and tread upon the powers reserved to the states in Article X of the Constitution.

Federalism Revived

When a student, Alfonso Lopez, was apprehended at his high school carrying a .38 handgun, federal agents charged him with violating the federal Gun-Free School Zones Act of 1990. He was convicted and sentenced to six months in prison. His attorney appealed on the ground that it was beyond the constitutionally delegated powers of Congress to police local school zones. In *U.S.* v. *Lopez* (1995) the U.S. Supreme Court issued its first opinion in more than 60 years that recognized a limit to Congress's power over interstate commerce and reaffirmed the Founders' notion that the federal government has only the powers enumerated in the U.S. Constitution. Attorneys for the federal government argued that the Gun-Free School Zones Act was a constitutional exercise of its interstate commerce power because "possession of a firearm in a school zone may result in violent crime and that violent crime can be expected to affect the functioning of the national economy." But the Court rejected this argument, holding that such reasoning would remove virtually all limits to federal power: "To uphold the Government's contentions here, we would have to pile inference upon inference in a manner that would bid fair to convert congressional activity under the Commerce Clause to a general police power of the sort retained by the states."[34]

The U.S. Supreme Court again invalidated a provision of a law of Congress—the Brady Handgun Violence Prevention Act—by deciding that its command to local law enforcement officers to conduct background checks on gun purchasers violated "the very principle of separate state sovereignty." The Court affirmed that the "federal government may neither issue directives requiring the states to address particular problems, nor command the state's officers, or those of their political subdivisions, to administer or enforce a federal regulatory program."[35]

States Shielded from Lawsuits

The Supreme Court ruled in 1996 in *Seminole Tribe* v. *Florida* that the Eleventh Amendment shields states from lawsuits by private parties that seek to force states to comply with federal laws enacted under the commerce power.[36] And by the same division of votes (Majority: Rehnquist, O'Connor, Scalia, Kennedy, Thomas; Minority: Stevens, Souter, Ginsburg, Breyer), the Court held in 1999 in *Aldin* v. *Maine* that states were also shielded in their own courts from lawsuits in which private parties seek to enforce federal mandates. In an opinion that surveyed over 200 years of American federalism, Justice Kennedy wrote, "Congress has vast power but not all power. . . . When Congress legislates in matters affecting the states, it may not treat these sovereign entities as mere prefectures or corporations."[37] But in 2003, the Court took a slightly different direction. In a 6–3 ruling, it held that state employees could sue their state in federal court to enforce rights granted by the federal Family and Medical Leave Act of 1993 (*Nevada Department of Human Resources* v. *Hibbs*).[38]

Limits on the Commerce Power

In 2000, to the surprise of many observers, the Supreme Court held that Congress's Violence Against Women Act was an unconstitutional extension of federal power into the reserved police powers of states. Citing its earlier *Lopez* decision, the Court held that noneconomic crimes are beyond the power of the national government under the Interstate Commerce Clause. "Gender-motivated crimes of violence are not, in any sense, economic activity." The Court rejected Congress's argument that the aggregate impact of crime nationwide has a substantial effect on interstate commerce. "The Constitution requires a distinction between what is truly national and what is truly local, and there is no better example of the police power, which the Founders undeniably left reposed in the States and denied the central government, than the suppression of violent crime and vindication of its victims."[39] A similar argument was made by the states challenging a provision in the Affordable Health Care Reform Act of 2010 that requires everyone to buy health insurance. However, the U.S. Supreme Court rejected it. (See *Did You Know?*: "The States Lose Their Fight against "ObamaCare".")

Federalism's Future

It may be too early to judge the impact of these decisions on federalism—whether they represent the return to the traditional notions of enumerated powers of Congress and reserved powers of the states. The decisions invalidated some popular laws of Congress—laws with broad political support across the country—but validated some unpopular ones. And these decisions were made by a 5–4 vote of the Justices, suggesting that the replacement of a single Justice might greatly alter the federal system.

The States Lose Their Fight against "ObamaCare"

The Patient Protection and Affordable Care Act of 2010 ("ObamaCare") includes a mandate that every individual in the country obtain government approved health insurance. Twenty-six state Attorneys General joined together in a lawsuit challenging the Act as an unconstitutional expansion of federal power over the citizens of their states. Never before had the federal government mandated that individuals buy a product. The states argued that the Tenth Amendment's "reserved powers" insures that the national government is one of limited and enumerated powers.

Arguments over the Act were highly partisan. It was passed in Congress without a single Republican vote. Democrats claimed that the mandate was justified under the Commerce Clause because healthcare and health insurance is a form of interstate commerce. They also claimed that the mandate is constitutional under the Sixteenth Amendment because it is structured as a tax on income.

Chief Justice John Roberts wrote the majority, 5–4, opinion in this important case. He first determined that the individual mandate *cannot* be upheld under Congress's power to regulate interstate commerce. Allowing Congress to command people to buy a product—health-insurance—would open a vast new domain of federal power. The Founders gave Congress the power to *regulate* commerce not to *compel* it. Ignoring this distinction, Roberts wrote, would undermine the principle that the federal government is a government of limited and enumerated powers.

However, in a surprise turnabout, Roberts concluded that the individual mandate is a constitutional exercise of Congress's power to "lay and collect taxes" (Article I, Section 8). The Act itself refers to a "penalty" for noncompliance. But Roberts held that "every reasonable construction must be resorted to, in order to save the statute from unconstitutionality." He reasoned that the individual mandate can be interpreted as a tax on those who chose to go without insurance. He observed that the tax is administered and collected by the Internal Revenue Service.

Thus, while Roberts acknowledged restrictions on Congress's interstate commerce power, he appeared to open a whole new source of federal power over the states and their citizens under the taxing power.

Source: Federation of Independent Businesses v. *Sebelius,* June 28, 2012.

Explain the constitutional requirements pertaining to the full faith and credit clause, extradition, and interstate compacts.

HORIZONTAL FEDERALISM

Relationships between the states.

FULL FAITH AND CREDIT

The clause in the U.S. Constitution requiring states to legally recognize the official acts of other states.

INTERSTATE RELATIONS AND HORIZONTAL FEDERALISM

Full Faith and Credit

The U.S. Constitution provides that "**full faith and credit** shall be given in each state to the public acts, records, and judicial proceedings of every other state." As more Americans move from state to state, it becomes increasingly important that the states recognize each other's legal instruments. This constitutional clause is intended to protect the rights of individuals who move from one state to another, and it is also intended to prevent individuals from evading their legal responsibilities by crossing state lines. Courts in Illinois must recognize decisions made by courts in Michigan. Contracts entered into in New York may be enforced in Florida. Corporations chartered in Delaware should be permitted to do business in North Dakota.

One of the more serious problems in interstate relations today is the failure of the states to meet their obligations under the Full Faith and Credit Clause in the area of domestic relations, including same-sex marriage, divorce, alimony, child support, and

Out-of-state students often complain about having to pay higher tuition than in-state students at public universities and colleges.

custody of children. The result is now a complex and confused situation in domestic relations law. Full faith and credit–based battles in courtrooms across the United States are destined to intensify, as states pass sharply different laws defining marriage, life, privacy, and guardianship rights. Legal scholars are already arguing about whether same-sex marriages in some states will be recognized in other states where marriage is defined as solely between a man and a woman. Even though the two same-sex marriage cases decided by the U.S. Supreme Court in 2013 (*United States* v. *Windsor and Hollingsworth* v. *Perry)* were viewed as major victories for gay rights proponents, the rulings did not make same-sex marriage legal across all 50 states. But the rulings have prompted many jurisdictions across the United States to move in that direction, believing that the "full faith and credit" provision will ultimately prevail in future court rulings.

Privileges and Immunities

The Constitution also states: "The citizens of each state shall be entitled to all **privileges and immunities** of citizens in the several states." Apparently the Founding Fathers thought that no state should discriminate against citizens from another state in favor of its own citizens. To do so would seriously jeopardize national unity. This clause also implies that citizens of any state may move freely about the country and settle where they like, with the assurance that as newcomers they will not be subjected to unreasonable discrimination. The newcomer should not be subject to discriminatory taxation; nor barred from lawful occupations under the same conditions as other citizens of the state; nor prevented from acquiring and using property; nor denied equal protection of the laws; nor refused access to the courts. However, states have managed to compromise this constitutional guarantee in several important ways. States establish residence requirements for voting and holding office, which prevent newcomers from exercising the same rights as older residents. States often require periods of residence as a prerequisite for holding a state job or for admission into professional practice such as law or medicine. States discriminate against out-of-state students in the tuition charged in public schools and colleges. Finally, some states are now seeking ways to keep "outsiders" from moving in and presumably altering the "natural" environment.

Extradition

The Constitution also provides that "A person in any state with treason, felony, or other crime who shall flee from justice and be found in another state, shall on the demand of the executive authority from the state from which he/she fled, be delivered up, to be removed

PRIVILEGES AND IMMUNITIES
The clause in the U.S. Constitution preventing states from discriminating against citizens of other states.

EXTRADITION
The surrender by one state of a person accused or convicted of a crime in another state.

Did YOU KNOW?

Which States Rank Highest on the Gallup-Healthways "Well-Being" Index?

Spirited debates are often engendered by rankings of states (or cities) by their "livability" or "well-being." The Gallup-Healthways Well-Being Index is one such ranking that gets a lot of attention. It is calculated on a scale of 0 to 100, where a score of 100 represents ideal well-being. The score is an average of six subindexes:

1. **Life evaluations**—individual ratings of the quality of their present and future lives.
2. **Emotional health**—incidence of daily smiling or laughter, learning or doing something interesting, being treated with respect, enjoyment, happiness, worry, sadness, anger, stress, and diagnosis of depression.
3. **Work environment**—job satisfaction, ability to use one's strengths at work; supervisor's treatment (more like a boss or a partner), and the formation of a trusting work environment.
4. **Physical health**—sick days in the past month, disease burden, health problems that get in the way of normal activities, obesity, feeling well rested, daily energy, daily colds, daily flu, and daily headaches.
5. **Healthy behaviors**—not smoking, eating healthy, weekly consumption of fruits and vegetables, and weekly exercise frequency.
6. **Access to basic necessities**—to clean water, medicine, a safe place to exercise, and affordable fruits and vegetables; having enough money for food, shelter, health care, health insurance, doctor and dentist visits; being satisfied with the community, the community getting better as a place to live, and feeling safe walking alone at night.

Rank	State	Well-Being Rating	Rank	State	Well-Being Rating
1	Hawaii	71.1	26	Delaware	66.6
2	Colorado	69.7	27	Texas	66.6
3	Minnesota	68.9	28	Illinois	66.6
4	Utah	68.8	29	Pennsylvania	66.5
5	Vermont	68.6	30	New York	66.2
6	Montana	68.5	31	Alaska	66.1
7	Nebraska	68.5	32	New Jersey	66.1
8	New Hampshire	68.4	33	Georgia	66.1
9	Iowa	68.1	34	Florida	65.8
10	Massachusetts	68.1	35	North Carolina	65.7
11	Maryland	68.0	36	Michigan	65.6
12	South Dakota	68.0	37	Rhode Island	65.5
13	Wyoming	67.9	38	Missouri	65.5
14	Virginia	67.7	39	Nevada	65.2
15	Washington	67.7	40	South Carolina	65.2
16	Connecticut	67.6	41	Oklahoma	65.2
17	Kansas	67.6	42	Indiana	65.1
18	California	67.4	43	Louisiana	64.7
19	North Dakota	67.4	44	Ohio	64.6
20	Wisconsin	67.3	45	Alabama	64.2
21	Maine	67.3	46	Arkansas	64.1
22	Idaho	67.1	47	Tennessee	64
23	Arizona	67.1	48	Mississippi	63.6
24	Oregon	67.1	49	Kentucky	62.7
25	New Mexico	66.7	50	West Virginia	61.3

Note: Data collected January 2, 2012–December 30, 2012.
Source: Gallup-Healthways Well-Being Index, "2012 State of Well-Being: Community, State and Congressional District Well-Being Reports," 2013. Available at http://www.well-beingindex.com/stateCongresDistrictRank.asp. Copyright © (2013) Gallup, Inc. All rights reserved. The content is used with permission; however, Gallup retains all rights of republication.

to the state having jurisdiction of the crime." In other words, the Constitution requires governors to extradite fugitives from another state's justice system.

Governors have not always honored requests for extradition, but since no state wants to harbor criminals of another state, extradition is seldom refused. Historically, some of the reasons advanced for the occasional refusals have been (1) the individual has become a law-abiding citizen in his or her new state; (2) a northern governor did not approve of the conditions in Georgia chain gangs; (3) a black returned to a southern state would not receive a fair trial; (4) the governor did not believe that there was sufficient evidence against the fugitive to warrant her or his conviction in the first place; and (5) the governor opposes the death penalty which is the punishment in the state to which the accused is to be returned.

Interstate Compacts

The Constitution provides that "No state shall without the consent of Congress . . . enter into any agreement or compact with another state." The National Center for Interstate Compacts defines an interstate compact as "a contract between two or more states creating an agreement on a particular policy issue, adopting a certain standard or cooperating on regional or national matters." They help build consensus among the states. Over 215 interstate compacts now serve a wide variety of interests, such as interstate water resources; conservation of natural resources, including oil, wildlife, and fisheries; the control of floods; the development of interstate toll highways; the coordination of civil defense measures; the reciprocal supervision of parolees; the coordination of welfare and institutional care programs; the administration of interstate metropolitan areas; and the resolution of interstate tax conflicts. The average number of compacts a state is involved in is 25.[40] Two compacts involve all 50 states: the Interstate Compact on the Placement of Children and the Uniform Interstate Compact on Juveniles. In practice, Congress has little to do with these compacts; the Supreme Court has held that congressional consent is required only if the compact encroaches upon some federal power. Otherwise, the negotiation and ratification of interstate compacts lies with the legislatures of the states involved. Their decisions are often guided by whether they believe a proposed compact will help or hinder their state's "well-being" (see *Did You Know? Which States Rank Highest on the Gallup-Healthways "Well-Being" Index?"*).

Conflicts between States

States are not supposed to make war on each other, although they did so from 1861 to 1865. They are supposed to take their conflicts to the U.S. Supreme Court. The U.S. Constitution gives the Supreme Court the power to settle all cases involving two or more states. In recent years the Supreme Court has heard disputes between states over boundaries, the diversion of water, fishing rights, and the disposal of sewage and garbage.

■ Federalism is a system of government in which power is divided between national and subnational governments. Federalism, as well as the separation of powers among branches of government, was intended as double security for individual rights against the tyranny of a governing elite.

■ Arguments for federalism include the dispersal of power among leaders, increased participation of citizens, improved government efficiency, increased policy responsiveness, policy innovation, and reduced conflict among opposing groups. Arguments against federalism include confusion about responsibility, obstructed action on national issues, and uneven distribution of government costs and benefits across the nation.

■ The U.S. Constitution *enumerates* certain powers of the national government and, as affirmed by the Tenth Amendment, *reserves* other powers to the states.

■ The states' role in national government is to contribute members to Congress and ratify constitutional amendments. Amendments guaranteeing equal rights for women and granting statehood to the District of Columbia failed to get the necessary number of state ratifications, but an amendment restricting pay raises to Congress won approval.

■ Federal power has been expanded by the courts, especially in *Marbury* v. *Madison, McCullough* v. *Maryland, NLRB* v. *Jones & Laughlin Steel Corp., Brown* v. *Board of Education, Bush* v. *Gore,* and *Federation of Independent Business* v. *Sibelius.*

■ Using revenue generated by income tax (a power granted in the Sixteenth Amendment), the federal government distributes money to the states to carry out various programs. Liberals favor this enhanced power as necessary to effect social change. Conservatives believe federal grants reduce state and local control and lead to overspending and inefficiency.

■ State and local governments—and often the private sector—typically complain that grants-in-aid are "unfunded mandates," that is, federal laws with little or no funding to states and localities to carry them out.

■ Historically, the balance of power between the federal government and the states has tilted in one direction, then another (different phases of federalism). During the late 1990s, the federal government had the upper hand, with its imposition of preemptions and mandates on states. Beginning in the 2010s, the pendulum began swinging a bit toward the states. "Bottom-up" federalism saw states tackling the big issues facing them that were being ignored at the federal level.

■ The U.S. Constitution requires states to recognize each other's contracts and other legal instruments, allow citizens to move about the country without discrimination, and extradite fugitives. States may also enter into legal agreements with each other (interstate compacts) when cooperation on an issue is deemed advantageous.

CHAPTER FOUR

PARTICIPATION IN STATE POLITICS

LEARNING OBJECTIVES

4.1 Enumerate the different types of political participation, and understand the frequency with which Americans participate in politics.

4.2 Evaluate whether it is rational to vote, and identify the various factors that influence voter turnout.

4.3 Explain how differences in election laws between the states may influence both voter turnout and which candidates will be victorious.

4.4 Compare patterns in voter turnout among whites, African Americans, Hispanics, and Asians.

4.5 Explain the methods the federal government has employed to gradually expand the right to vote, tracing this expansion from creation of the Constitution through the adoption of the Twenty-Sixth Amendment.

4.6 Describe how states have drawn political districts to increase the number of racial and ethnic minorities elected to public office and what the Supreme Court has said about these efforts.

4.7 Compare the participation of men and women in state politics, and assess the significance of the recent influx of women in state and local political office.

4.8 Describe how political views and clout differ at different levels of government.

4.9 Describe the various interest groups that attempt to influence state politics and the role that lobbyists play in the process.

4.10 Describe the tactics used by lobbyists to promote group interests, and compare these tactics to those employed at the national level.

4.11 Explain why interest groups are more powerful in some states than in others.

4.12 Describe the differences between protests, political disobedience, and violence; and outline how state and local governments respond to these types of political participation.

THE NATURE OF POLITICAL PARTICIPATION

Enumerate the different types of political participation, and understand the frequency with which Americans participate in politics.

Recent elections have seen a modest upswing in voter participation in most states. More Americans than ever registered and voted, logged on to political Web sites, attended politically oriented events (concerts, movies, rallies, meet-ups, protests), wore their political preferences (shirts, hats, buttons, wristbands, flip-flops), and gave money to candidates and politically oriented advocacy groups. Civic engagement is seen by many as on the upswing—at least in presidential election years. But political participation rates lag in non-presidential election years, when many states and localities elect their officials.

Historically, campaigns have turned to the young for energy and innovation. It is certainly the case in the twenty-first century as young voters are being heavily targeted by both Democratic and Republican candidates. Because college students are more likely to get engaged in political discussions and activities than their non-college-attending friends,[1] candidates at all levels (federal, state, local) are visiting college campuses more than at any time since the 1960s. The candidates are not always just combing for votes. They seek young volunteers to help them design their Web sites; survey potential voters going door-to-door, recording their responses using "high-tech" hand-held PDAs; work phone banks; stuff envelopes; organize campus forums; make signs; pass out leaflets; chalk sidewalks; drive candidates to/from airports; staff large political rallies; and do anything else that comes to mind.

Popular participation in politics is the very definition of democracy. Individuals can participate in politics in many ways. They may run for, and win, public office; participate in marches, demonstrations, and sit-ins; make financial contributions to political candidates or causes; attend political meetings, speeches, and rallies; write letters or send e-mails to public officials or to newspapers; wear a political button or place a bumper sticker on a car; belong to organizations that support or oppose particular candidates or take stands on public issues; attempt to influence friends while discussing candidates or issues; vote in elections; or merely follow an issue or a campaign in the media.

This listing constitutes a ranking of the forms of political participation in order of frequency. (See Figure 4–1.) Less than 1 percent of the population *ever* runs for public office (see "*Up Close:* Getting into Politics"). Typically, only around half of the voting age population votes in presidential elections. Far fewer vote in state and local elections. Over one-third of the population is politically apathetic: They do not vote at all, and they are largely unaware of the political life of the nation. Ironically, many who do not consider themselves "political" participate in the life of their community as volunteers for various groups and organizations. They are unaware that volunteering at a local soup kitchen or tutoring disadvantaged elementary school kids are both examples of civic participation that make one's community a better place in which to live.

FIGURE 4–1 Political Participation

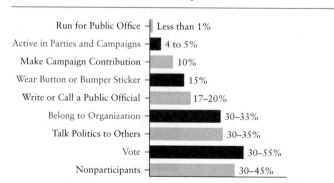

Source: Data from the American National Election Studies www.electionstudies.org.

Sustained political participation—voting consistently in election after election for state and local offices as well as Congress and the president—is rare. One study of voter participation over ten elections (including presidential, congressional, gubernatorial, and state and local legislative elections) showed that only 4 percent of the voting age population voted in 9 or all ten of the elections; only 26 percent voted in half of the ten elections; and 38 percent did not vote in any election.[2] Age is the best predictor of sustained political activity; older citizens are more likely than young people to be regular voters. Knowing this, candidates often target their campaigns to older voters, which, in turn, further alienates younger voters,[3] especially in state and local elections when younger voter turnout is considerably lower than that of persons age 50 and older. On the other hand, younger citizens are more likely than many older voters to participate in community volunteer efforts.[4]

SUSTAINED POLITICAL PARTICIPATION

Consistently voting in presidential and nonpresidential elections.

EXPLAINING VOTER TURNOUT

A sign of the times: A bumper sticker reads, "DON'T VOTE. IT JUST ENCOURAGES THEM." Around half of America's eligible voters stay away from the polls, even in a presidential election. **Voter turnout** is even lower in congressional midterm elections, where turnout falls to about 35 percent of the voting age population in the off years (when presidential candidates are not on the ballot). Turnout rates in gubernatorial elections are roughly similar to turnout rates for congressional races, rising and falling depending on whether the election is held simultaneously with a presidential election (see Figure 4–2).

4.2

Evaluate whether it is rational to vote, and identify the various factors that influence voter turnout.

VOTER TURNOUT

The percentage of the voting age population that cast ballots in an election.

FIGURE 4–2 The Trend in Voter Turnout

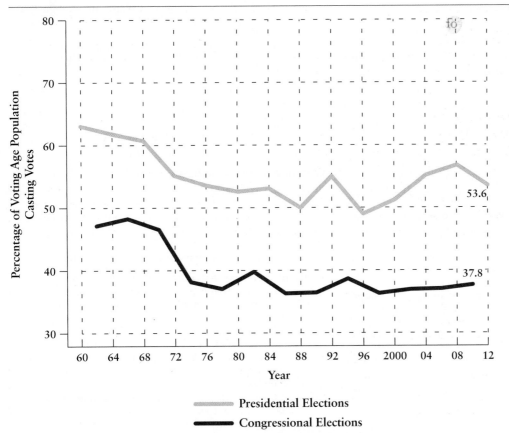

Source: Federal Election Commission. Data drawn from Congressional Record Service reports, Election Data Services Inc., and State Election Offices. 2010 and 2012 data from the United States Elections Project. Available at http://elections.gmu.edu/Turnout_2010G.html and http://elections.gmu.edu/Turnout_2012G.html.

Politics attracts both "amateurs" and "professionals." Amateurs may be defined as people who continue in a full-time job or occupation while engaging in politics part time, mainly for friendship and association or out of a sense of civic duty. Professionals are people who devote all their time and energy to politics, running for and occupying public office themselves, or working for candidates with the expectation of appointment to office upon the victory of their chosen candidate.

Get Involved

The most common way to get into politics is to get involved in the community. Look into various organizations in your community, including:

- Neighborhood associations
- Chambers of commerce, business associations
- Churches and synagogues (become an usher, if possible, for visibility)
- Political groups (Democratic or Republican clubs, League of Women Voters)
- Service clubs (Rotary, Kiwanis, Civitan, Toastmasters)
- Recreation organizations (Little League, flag football, soccer leagues, running and walking clubs, for example, as participant, coach, or umpire).

You can find out when and where such groups meet by looking in the neighborhood section of your local newspaper, or watching the community calendar on TV. Become an active member and gain some visibility in your community.

Learn about Public Affairs

It is essential that you learn about the public issues confronting your community and state as well as the duties and responsibilities of various government offices. You should:

- Attend meetings of your council or commission or attend state legislative sessions and committee hearings.
- Become familiar with current issues and officeholders, and obtain a copy of and read the budget.
- Learn the demographics of your district (racial, ethnic, and age composition; occupational mix; average incomes; neighborhood differences).

Run for Public Office

Many rewards come with elected office—the opportunity to help shape public policy; public attention and name recognition; and many business, professional, and social contacts. But there are many drawbacks as well—the absence of privacy; constant calls, meetings, interviews, and handshaking; and perhaps most onerous of all, the continual need to solicit donations. Before deciding to run, potential candidates should seriously consider the tremendous amount of work required. If you decide to run, begin by contacting your county elections department and obtain the following:

- Qualifying forms and information
- Campaign financing forms and regulations
- District and street maps for your district
- Recent election results in your district
- Election-law book or pamphlet
- Voter registration lists

Also contact your party's county chairperson and ask for advice and assistance. Convince the party's leaders that you can win. Ask for a copy of their list of regular campaign contributors.

Raise Money

Perhaps the most difficult task in politics is that of raising campaign funds. The easiest way to finance a campaign is to be rich enough to provide your own funds. Failing that, you must:

- Establish a campaign fund, according to the laws of your state.
- Find a treasurer/campaign-finance chairperson who knows large numbers of wealthy, politically involved people.
- Identify, call, and meet personally with potential contributors and solicit pledges, or better yet, checks.
- Invite wealthy, politically involved people to small coffees, cocktail parties, dinners; give a brief campaign speech and then have your finance chairperson solicit contributions.
- Don't be shy in approaching potential contributors; use the direct approach (e.g., "I know you want to help, Jim. How much can I put you down for?").
- Follow up fund-raising events and meetings with personal phone calls.
- Be prepared to continue fund-raising activities throughout your campaign; file accurate financial disclosure statements as required by law in your state.

Organize Your Campaign

Professional campaign managers and management firms almost always outperform volunteers. (Many firms advertise in the monthly magazine *Campaigns and Elections*, which can be accessed online at www.campaignline.com.) If you cannot afford professional management, you must rely on yourself or trusted friends to perform the following:

- Prepare and memorize a brief (preferably less than seven seconds) answer to the question, "Why are you running?"
- Ask a diverse group of friends to meet and serve as a campaign committee.
- Decide on a campaign theme; research issues important to your community; develop brief, well-articulated positions on these issues. A good theme will grab people's attention, capture your personality, and give depth to your campaign.
- Create a Facebook page and a Twitter account. Update them *frequently* with campaign events, news, your issue positions, and plenty of photos. Make sure you have frequent and meaningful "personal" interactions with those who visit your page. Also, provide a link to your official Web site.

- Create a Web site that is easy to navigate, clearly tells your story and your goals, and features ways for visitors to contribute time and money. Make sure to include a timely and busy event calendar.
- Open a campaign headquarters with desks and telephones. Use call forwarding; stay in contact. Use your garage if you can't afford an office.
- Arrange to meet with newspaper editors, editorial boards, TV station executives, and political reporters. Be prepared for tough questions.
- Hire a media consultant or advertising agency, or appoint a volunteer media director who knows Internet, television, YouTube, and newspaper advertising.
- Arrange a press conference to announce your candidacy. Notify all media well in advance. Arrange for an overflow crowd of supporters to cheer and applaud.
- Produce eye-catching, inspirational 15- or 30-second television and YouTube ads that present a favorable image of you and stress your campaign theme.
- Prepare and print attractive campaign brochures, signs, and bumper stickers.
- Prepare a schedule of community events, meetings, and other public happenings, and plan to make an appearance.
- If funds permit, hire a local survey-research firm or pollster to conduct continuous telephone surveys of voters in your district, to stay up to date with the issues that are important to voters.

Campaign Hard

Fund-raising, organizing, developing issues, writing speeches, and polling continue up to Election Day. Campaigns may be primarily *media centered* or primarily *door-to-door* ("retail") or some combination of both.

- Attend every community gathering possible, just to be seen, even if you do not give a speech. Keep all speeches *short*. Focus on one or two issues that your polls show are important to voters.
- Recruit paid or unpaid volunteers to canvass neighborhoods door-to-door to hand out literature and whenever possible to engage potential voters in friendly, favorable conversations about you. Record names and addresses of voters who say they support you.

- Do door-to-door canvassing yourself with a brief (seven-second) self-introduction and statement of the reason you are running. Use registration lists to identify members of your own party, and address them by name.
- Organize a phone bank, either professional or volunteer. Prepare *brief* introduction and phone statements. Your phone bank should become increasingly active as the election nears. Record names of people who say they support you.
- Know your opponent: Research his or her past affiliations, indiscretions, if any, previous voting record, and public positions on issues.
- Be prepared to "define" your opponent in negative terms. Negative advertising works. But be fair: Base your comments about your opponent on supportable facts.

On Election Day

Turning out *your* voters is the key to success. Election Day is the busiest day of the campaign for you and especially your staff. It is important to realize that, in many states, voting occurs in two phases: early voting (in person and absentee) and on Election Day. This means that you must campaign like tomorrow is Election Day beginning long before Election Day arrives. To be effective, you should divide supporters into two groups, those likely to participate in early voting and those likely to vote on Election Day. Develop voter turnout strategies for each.

- Use your phone bank to place as many calls as possible to your party members in your district (especially those who have indicated that they support you). Remind them to vote; make sure your phone workers can tell each voter where to go to cast their vote. Ask if they need a ride to the polls.
- Prepare volunteer drivers to take anyone to the polls that needs a ride. Send cars, clearly marked with your name but willing to assist anyone, to condominiums, nursing homes, and neighborhoods.
- Assign workers to as many polling places as possible. Most state laws require that they stay a specified distance from the voting booths. But they should be in evidence with your signs and literature to buttonhole voters before they go into the booth.
- Be ready with a victory and concession statement.

City and county elections, when they are held separately from national elections, usually produce turnouts of 25 to 35 percent. However, turnout can shoot up sharply if a local contest features interesting and unique candidates or centers on highly contentious moral or pocketbook issues. Such situations tend to spark more media coverage and prompt more "get out the vote" efforts by candidates and advocacy groups.

Is Voting Rational?

Why is voter turnout so low? Actually, we could reverse the question and ask why people vote at all. A **"rational" voter** (one who seeks to maximize personal benefits and minimize costs) should vote only if the costs of voting (the time and energy spent first in registering, then in informing oneself about the candidates, and finally going to the polls on Election Day) are exceeded by the expected value of having the preferred candidate win (the

RATIONAL VOTER
One who votes after deciding the personal benefits outweigh the costs.

personal benefits to be received from the winner) multiplied by the probability that one's own vote will be the deciding vote.[5] But under this "rational" notion, not many people would vote: Few Americans receive direct personal and tangible benefits from the election of one candidate versus another. And most Americans know that the likelihood of one vote determining the outcome of the election is remote. Yet millions of Americans vote anyway.

In order to rescue the "rational" model, political theorists have added "the intrinsic rewards of voting" to the equation.[6] These rewards include the ethic of voting, patriotism, a sense of duty, and allegiance to democracy. In other words, people get psychic rewards from voting itself rather than tangible benefits, and these psychic rewards do not depend on who wins or whether a single vote determines the outcome. So more people vote out of a sense of civic duty and commitment to democracy than on a purely rational basis.

Who Fails to Vote

For years, studies have found that the young, the poor, the unemployed, and the least educated are the least likely to vote and the most likely to feel alienated or turned off by politics.[7] (See Table 4–1.)

Nonvoters are also more prevalent among:

- First-generation immigrants, especially non-English speaking[8]
- Those who seldom participate in organized religious activities
- Newcomers to a community[9]
- People with little or no interest in politics, little trust in government, no belief that voting is a civic duty, and no belief they can make a difference by voting
- Persons with physical disabilities[10]
- Blue-collar and service-sector workers
- Asians and Latinos
- Single parents living in poor neighborhoods
- Independents
- Persons who have not been contacted by a candidate or party
- Renters (vs. homeowners)
- Residents of solidly one-party dominated states (nonswing states)

Socioeconomic Explanations

Much of the variation in voter turnout among the states can be explained by the socioeconomic characteristics of their residents—their overall educational level, income, racial and ethnic mix, and age profile. For example, income and educational levels are higher, and the white population is larger, in Minnesota and Wisconsin. Turnout is much higher in these states than in many Deep South states, whose populations are poorer, less educated, younger, and more racially diverse. (Rising turnout rates among these southern states have been attributed somewhat to socioeconomic shifts—more newcomers from the North—and to federal civil rights laws and black and Hispanic voter mobilization efforts.)

Partisan Competition-Related Explanations

Turnout tends to go up when a voter feels his or her vote can truly make a difference in the election outcome. Turnout is considerably higher, especially in presidential elections, in battleground or swing states. (These states are sometimes referred to as "purple" states—as opposed to "red" states—solidly Republican or "blue" states—solidly Democratic.) Voters in these states are much more likely to have visits from the candidates or their surrogates and be subjected to a lot more direct appeals for their votes via television ads. In the 2012 presidential election, 96 percent of the spending on television ads between April and Election Day by presidential campaigns and allied groups was in the 10 battleground states.

Voter Turnout Rate: 2012 Presidential Election

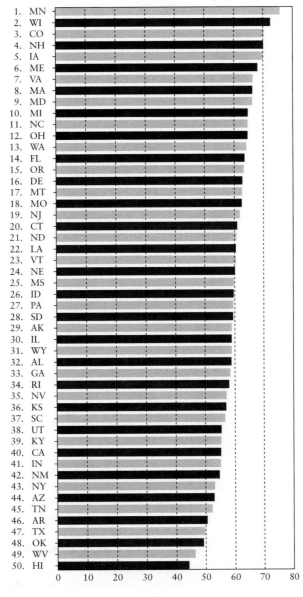

Voter Turnout 2012 (%)

1.	MN
2.	WI
3.	CO
4.	NH
5.	IA
6.	ME
7.	VA
8.	MA
9.	MD
10.	MI
11.	NC
12.	OH
13.	WA
14.	FL
15.	OR
16.	DE
17.	MT
18.	MO
19.	NJ
20.	CT
21.	ND
22.	LA
23.	VT
24.	NE
25.	MS
26.	ID
27.	PA
28.	SD
29.	AK
30.	IL
31.	WY
32.	AL
33.	GA
34.	RI
35.	NV
36.	KS
37.	SC
38.	UT
39.	KY
40.	CA
41.	IN
42.	NM
43.	NY
44.	AZ
45.	TN
46.	AR
47.	TX
48.	OK
49.	WV
50.	HI

Note: Turnout is the percentage of citizens of voting age who voted.
Source: Michael P. McDonald, *United States Election Project*, "2012 General Election Turnout Rates,"
Dec. 31, 2012. Available at http://elections.gmu.edu/Turnout_2012G.html.

TABLE 4–1 Characteristics of Voters in 2000, 2004, 2008, and 2012 Presidential Elections

Characteristics	2000 Percentage Reporting They Voted	2004 Percentage Reporting They Voted	2008 Percentage Reporting They Voted	2012 Percentage Reporting They Voted
Sex				
Male	53.1	56.3	55.7	59.7
Female	56.2	60.1	60.4	63.7
Race				
White	56.4	60.3	59.6	64.1
Black	53.5	56.3	60.8	66.2
Hispanic[a]	27.5	28	31.6	48.0
Asian	25.4	29.8	32.1	47.3
Age				
18–20	28.4	41	41	37.4
21–24	24.2	42.5	46.6	44
25–34	43.7	46.9	48.5	53.5
35–44	55	56.9	55.2	61.2
45–64	64.1	66.6	65	67.9
65 and over	67.6	68.9	68.1	72
Employment				
Employed	55.5	60	60.1	63.4
Unemployed	35.1	46.4	48.8	51.9
Education				
8 Years or less	26.8	23.6	23.4	37.1
High School Graduate	49.4	52.4	50.9	52.6
College Graduate	72	74.2	73.3	75

[a]Persons of Hispanic origin may be any race.

Source: U.S. Census Bureau, *Statistical Abstract of the United States 2012*, Table 399. Available at http://www.census.gov/compendia/statab/cats/elections/voting-age_population_and_voter_participation.html. 2012 data from U.S. Census Bureau, 2013, "Voting and Registration in the Election of November 2012," Tables 1, 2, 5, 6, 13. Available at http://www.census.gov/hhes/www/socdemo/voting/publications/p20/2012/tables.html.

Likewise, 99 percent of the campaign stops by the presidential or vice presidential candidates were in the battleground states.[11] Voter turnout rates were considerably higher in the highly competitive swing states.

In state and local elections, especially legislative contests, turnout tends to be considerably higher when districts are more evenly balanced between Democrats and Republicans and lower in safe, or one-party dominated, districts. Redistricting efforts completed after every Census are either done by legislators or independent redistricting commissions.

Media Predicting Winners Early Explanation

Election 2000 also reopened other debates about the impact of media coverage on voter turnout in different time zones.[12] The network practice of using exit polls to "call" elections before the polls have closed everywhere has long been under attack, especially by political parties and candidates on the West Coast. The National Commission on Federal Election Reform recommended this practice be stopped, at least in the 48 contiguous states. Although the national television networks have become more cautious and no longer "officially" call a state until all its polls are closed (important in states with multiple time zones), they still refuse to wait until all polls in every state are closed to report projections based on pre-election polls. Newsgathering is a highly competitive business—being first is a high priority. Yet a network "calling" a presidential race over before the polls have closed is seen by candidates for state and local offices that day as unfairly tamping down turnout in *their* races.

Legal and Procedural Explanations

There are two steps involved in the election process: registration and voting. States differ considerably in how they structure each step in the process. It is not surprising, then, that some turnout rate differentials are attributed to statutory (legal) differences across the states.

Differences in Registration Procedures. Voter registration procedures differ significantly across the 50 states. Several states allow Election Day registration (Maine, Minnesota, Wisconsin, Wyoming, New Hampshire, Idaho, Colorado, Montana, Iowa, and Connecticut). Election Day registration will be legal in California in 2015 after the state creates the integrated statewide voter registration database required by the federal Help America Vote Act. Several other states permit same-day registration at early voting sites, while one state has no registration requirement at all (North Dakota).[13] A larger number of states require a person to register 15–30 days in advance of the election in order to give election officials time to prepare voter lists for each voting precinct's poll workers. Such requirements are designed to reduce voter fraud and maintain the integrity of the voting process. But some voter advocacy groups claim they depress turnout, especially among those who have recently moved. The debate over whether Election Day registration (EDR), or same day registration (SDR), significantly increases voter turnout has been ongoing. One post-2012 election study found that states with Election Day registration had an average turnout rate of 71 percent, compared to 59 percent among states without EDR. Minnesota, the state with the highest turnout, estimates that Election Day registrations account for 5 to 10 percent of voter turnout.[14] Since the 2012 election, a number of other states are considering switching to Election Day registration.

Newer registration-related issues that were raised during the 2012 election cycle centered on how one could register (online vs. in-person), documentation needed (proof of citizenship, type of voter ID accepted), who could register voters (groups or just election officials), and how quickly registration forms collected by groups had to be turned in to election officials and fines for failure to do so (Florida). Debates over these issues reflected the larger vote suppression versus vote fraud schism, with Democrats typically more focused on halting registration practices they see as voter suppression and Republicans favoring those they perceived as preventing fraudulent registration and voting.[15]

Federally Mandated "Motor Voter" Registration Law. Although Congress had previously passed voting rights laws designed to protect minorities, it had never directly intervened in the general process of state election administration prior to 1993. But with strong Democratic support, Congress passed the National Voter Registration Act of 1993, popularly known as the "motor voter" act. It mandates that the states offer people the opportunity to register when they apply for a driver's license or apply for welfare services. States must also offer registration by mail, and they must accept a simplified registration form prepared by the Federal Election Commission. Finally, the act bars states from removing the names of people from registration lists for failure to vote.

What is the impact of the motor voter law on voter turnout in the states? Early studies showed that states that had enacted their own motor voter registration laws before the federal mandate appear to have increased their turnout rates.[16] However, although the law has increased voter *registration,* the evidence is mixed on whether it adds significantly to *turnout.*[17] Why? "Making registration easier does not provide citizens with a reason to vote."[18] What seems to be more effective are **post-registration laws** that require each registrant to be mailed a sample ballot and information about polling place location, providing a longer voting day, and requiring firms to give their employees time off to vote. One study has found that most of these increase young voter turnout.[19] So, too, does allowing early registration of pre-18-year-olds who will become eligible to vote by Election Day.

POST-REGISTRATION LAWS
Methods to enhance voter turnout after a person registers. Most effective with young voters.

Differences in the Actual Voting Experience: Time, Place, Equipment, Ballots, and Poll Workers. There is tremendous variation across the states in how easy each makes it for a voter to cast a ballot. Many, but not all, believe that turnout can be increased by:

- Making it easier to vote *before* Election Day by mail using an absentee ballot (with no excuse for absence required) or in person at a polling location. Twenty-seven states offer "no excuse" absentee voting, two states provide mail ballots, and 32 states have some form of early voting in-person.[20]
- Conducting an entire election by mail (such as Oregon does).[21]
- Making it easier to vote *on* Election Day with provisional ballots for those who believe they are registered and have erroneously been kept off of the precinct list of registered voters; or voting by Internet.
- Making polling places more accessible to persons with physical disabilities (curbside voting, selection of more accessible polling places and voting booths).
- Purchasing more and better voting equipment (more reliable, easier to use, less prone to tampering).
- Designing better ballot layouts (no more "butterfly ballots"; Braille ballots and large print for visually impaired voters).
- Better training of America's millions of poll workers in how to assist voters, especially first-time voters.
- Easier procedures for restoring the voting rights of felons.
- Better voter education programs targeted at all age groups, but especially among younger citizens (e.g., Kids Vote, State Mock Elections).
- More uniform procedures in place to count votes, define what is a legally cast ballot, and spell out when, who, and how recounts are to be conducted.
- Better procedures in place to distribute, collect, then count absentee ballots cast by military personnel and citizens living overseas in a timely fashion.

Many of these suggestions emerged in the aftermath of the presidential election in 2000, the closest race in modern American history, when the need to revamp many state election codes became obvious. Several state associations, along with a number of prominent commissions, such as the National Commission on Federal Election Reform cochaired by former presidents Jimmy Carter and Gerald Ford, and the U.S. Congress all conducted analyses that came to the same conclusion—America's state election systems needed to be overhauled. In response, Congress ended up passing the Help America Vote Act in 2002, which mandated states to reform their election systems.[22]

4.3 CONTINUING ELECTION CONTROVERSIES

Explain how differences in election laws between the states may influence both voter turnout and which candidates will be victorious.

More than a decade later, scholars are divided on whether some of the reforms implemented by some states after the 2000 election have actually worked as they were intended. Up for debate is whether early voting has actually increased turnout or simply shifted the time at which people vote.[23] There is also still considerable debate over what type of voting equipment, if any, is tamperproof.[24] And easing the absentee process has raised the issue of whether it also increases the likelihood of fraud.[25] The newest round of election-related controversies have centered on reforms related to voter eligibility and verification, voting locations, ease of voting, and use of the Internet for online registration, absentee ballot requests, and voting.

Election reform efforts have become considerably more partisan since the 2008 election, and are particularly intense in states with high levels of party competition. Partisan views of what is the biggest threat to the integrity of the election system are strikingly different; for Democrats, it is voter suppression; for Republicans, it is fraud. The closeness of major statewide elections (presidential, gubernatorial) prompts both major parties to pay more attention to election system reforms. Strong one-party control of both the state legislature and the governor's office enhances the likelihood of the "out" party's use of litigation to challenge the majority party's legislatively enacted election reforms.[26]

Voter Eligibility and Verification (IDs)

Controversies over voter eligibility and what is required to prove it have escalated in recent years. Most states accept the federal government's proof of citizenship (a requisite for registering to vote), which requires registrants to sign a statement swearing that they are a citizen under penalty of perjury. Some states, most notably Arizona, have argued they have the right to require physical evidence such as a birth certificate, naturalization papers, or a U.S. passport to prove citizenship. Arizona's more rigorous approach was challenged and reached the U.S. Supreme Court in 2013. The Court ruled it unconstitutional (*Arizona* v. *Inter-Tribal Council of Arizona*), and said that Arizona's requirement that a registrant provide actual proof of U.S. citizenship is preempted by the National Voter Registration Act's mandate that states "accept and use" the federal form. States also differ in requirements for reinstating the voting rights of convicted felons. In 15 states, it is automatic immediately upon release from prison; in others, it may require a formal request, a waiting period, restitution of damages, or approval by a state board. It may even depend on the nature of the crime.[27]

Another area of controversy is voter list maintenance—the updating of voter registration lists by local election officials. State procedures for removing (purging) deceased voters, convicted criminals (felons), or inactive voters from voter registration rolls differ. Use of national databases to remove noncitizens from the rolls has been particularly controversial in some border states, as has the motive for and timing of voter purges.

Over half the states have some form of voter ID requirement. Of those that do, there is a lot of variation. (See Figure 4–3.) According to the National Conference of State Legislatures, the two key distinctions are whether a law is *strict* or not, and whether or not the ID must include a photo.[28]

> **Strict versus Nonstrict:** In the "strict" states, a voter cannot cast a valid ballot without first presenting ID. Voters who are unable to show ID at the polls are given a provisional ballot. Those provisional ballots are kept separate from the regular ballots. If the voter returns to election officials within a short period of time after the election (generally a few days) and presents acceptable ID, the provisional ballot is counted. If the voter does not come back to show ID, that provisional ballot is never counted.
>
> **Photo versus Nonphoto:** Some states require that the ID presented at the polls must show a photo of the voter. Some of these are "strict" voter ID laws, in that voters who fail to show photo ID are given a provisional ballot and must eventually show photo ID in order to get that provisional ballot counted. Others are "nonstrict," and voters without ID have other options for casting a regular ballot. They may be permitted to sign an affidavit of identity, or poll workers may be able to vouch for them if they know them personally. In these "nonstrict" states, voters who fail to bring ID on Election Day aren't required to return to election officials and show ID in order to have their ballot counted. In the other voter ID states, there is a wide array of IDs that are acceptable for voting purposes, some of which do not include a photo of the voter. Again, some of these states are "strict" in the sense that a voter who fails to bring ID on Election Day will be required to vote a provisional ballot, and that provisional ballot will be counted only if the voter returns to election officials within a few days to show acceptable ID.

Voter IDs have become a lightning rod for partisan battles. The charge against them has been led by voter protection groups, mostly liberal and Democratic-leaning, who firmly believe that such laws reduce registration and turnout rates among young and minority voters.[29] However, legislators in states adopting tougher ID laws defend them on the grounds that they prevent fraud and thereby protect the integrity of the vote. They often cite public opinion polls that have consistently shown that a majority of Americans favor voter ID laws.

FIGURE 4-3 Voter ID Requirements

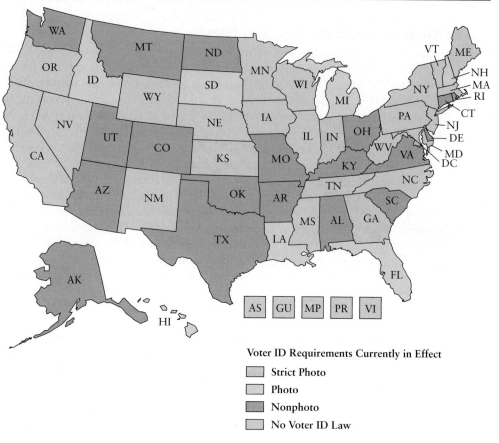

Voter ID Requirements Currently in Effect

- Strict Photo
- Photo
- Nonphoto
- No Voter ID Law

Please Note:

- Enforcement of Pennsylvania's voter ID law was enjoined for the November 2012 election by a state Judge. A legal challenge to the law is presently scheduled for July 2013. The voter ID law will *not* be applied in the May 21, 2013, primary elections.
- Alabama will become a photo ID state in 2014 if its new law receives pre-clearance under Section 5 of the Voting Rights Act.
- Mississippi and Texas have new strict photo ID laws, which may take effect in future elections if they receive pre-clearance under Section 5 of the Voting Rights Act.
- Wisconsin's new strict photo ID law was held unconstitutional on March 12, 2012.
- Virginia has passed legislation that puts their law in the "strict photo ID" category, but it does not take effect until July 1, 2014.
- Arkansas has passed legislation that puts their law in the "strict photo ID" category, but it will take effect either January 1, 2014, or when funds for the issuance of free IDs for voting purposes have been appropriated and are available.

Note: Data are for 2013.
Source: National Conference of State Legislatures, "Voter ID: State Requirements," Updated April 2, 2013.
Available at http://www.ncsl.org/legislatures-elections/elections/voter-id.aspx. © 2013 National Conference of State Legislatures.

Voting Locations and Ease of Voting

The nation's aging electorate—and the growing number of voters with sight, hearing, and/or mobility limitations—has also prompted states to reexamine the location of their polling places, along with the accessibility of their voting booths, ballot design, and voting technology, and to place more emphasis on training poll workers. So, too, has the federal Voting Accessibility for the Elderly and Handicapped Act (VAEHA), enacted in 1984. Under the Act, states are responsible for ensuring that polling places for federal elections are accessible to elderly voters and voters with disabilities.

At the same time, it is becoming more difficult to secure polling locations using traditional venues like churches, schools, nonprofit headquarters, and small businesses due to their structural inadequacies and liability concerns. For example, many schools have become "off-limits" as polling stations due to concerns about child security. Fewer polling locations can cause longer lines on Election Day. Long lines in key battleground states like Florida were such a high-profile problem in 2012 that President Obama created the Presidential Commission on Election Administration, even though nationally the average Election Day wait time in 2012 (13 minutes) was shorter than in 2008 (14 minutes) and wait times were actually longer during early voting (20 minutes) than on Election Day (13 minutes).[30] The new commission was charged with making recommendations on how to more efficiently run elections "in order to ensure that all eligible voters have the opportunity to cast their ballots without undue delay, and to improve the experiences of voters facing other obstacles in casting their ballots, such as members of the military, overseas voters, voters with disabilities, and voters with limited English proficiency."

One solution to the long-line problem may be to rely more on larger public facilities (community centers, libraries) than on smaller neighborhood-level locations. However, this more central vote center approach can prompt a political backlash from citizens used to having a close-by polling location. Closing of polling places in minority or poor neighborhoods can also yield claims of discrimination. Long lines might also be alleviated by more voting machines (but they cost $3,000 to $6,000 per machine), more and better trained poll workers, shorter and better designed ballots reducing the time voters spend in the booth, and, of course, early voting, *if* there are enough locations.[31]

Another factor affecting the ease of voting (and confidence in the results) is the *type of voting equipment available*. The vast majority of Americans cast their ballots on two primary types of voting equipment: paper ballots with optical scan (56%) and electronic voting machines called DREs—direct recording electronic machines (39%).[32] DRE systems have been under attack almost from their inception for their unreliability, vulnerability to tampering, and lack of a paper trail in the event of a needed recount. Consequently, many states have abandoned them in favor of optical scan paper-based systems similar to standardized test scantrons. But DREs are viewed more favorably by some disabled voters who worry a paper trail will jeopardize their right to a secret ballot. The Director of the Disability Vote Project of the American Association of People with Disabilities has testified that electronic touch-screen machines are the only "certified, tested, and proven equipment" that provide full access to disabled voters and provide a secret ballot.[33]

Online (Internet) Registration, Ballot Requests, and Voting

The growing number of Americans connected to the Internet raises the question of whether voting online would promote democracy or permit fraud. Some analysts believe it would substantially increase voter turnout because of its convenience. They argue it would give voters more time to think about how to vote on complex ballot initiatives and confusing bond referenda. Others are more skeptical. They worry about how to verify a voter's eligibility and identification and how to prevent hackers from "stealing" an election. Another concern is the "digital divide" that still exists between rich and poor in America and between men and women,[34] although the gap continues to narrow.

Online-based voting-related procedures are becoming more widespread reflecting the technological revolution that has many Americans "wired in" to the Web. A number of states now allow persons to register online, change addresses, and to request absentee ballots. Online registration has been particularly effective in increasing registration among younger voters and online requests for absentee ballots have increased among military and overseas personnel, rising from 22 percent in 2010 to 52 percent in 2012.[35] But the fear remains that any Web-based activity or resulting database can easily be hacked. Florida was the first state to experience cyberattacks against a U.S. elections system when, in 2012, hackers illegally requested more than 2,500 absentee ballots from registered voters in Miami-Dade County who had not asked for them.[36] The hackers were never identified.

Interest in actually voting via the Internet has increased largely in the context of making it possible for military service and overseas personnel to cast a ballot in a timely fashion to ensure it will be counted. The process has yet to be refined. A big concern is that those choosing to vote online will be giving up the secrecy of their ballot. Some caution that "the secrecy of the ballot is no small thing to give up—it is how we protect voters from coercion and prevent voters from selling their votes."[37] Safeguards against this have yet to be developed.

RACE, ETHNICITY, AND POLITICAL PARTICIPATION

Compare patterns in voter turnout among whites, African Americans, Hispanics, and Asians.

Racial and ethnic minorities are growing in numbers and percentages of the U.S. population (see "Race and Ethnicity" in Chapter 1) and in political power.

African Americans

For years, black voter turnout rates lagged behind white turnout, primarily due to discrimination. (More is said about this later in the chapter.) But this gap has closed in recent years. Now, black voter turnout often exceeds white turnout, especially in areas where blacks make up a sizable portion of the voting age population, when a minority person is a candidate in a high-profile election or the first minority to run for the office, and in places where black churches are proactive in voter mobilization and education.[38]

In the 2012 presidential election, black voter turnout surpassed white voter turnout for the first time in U.S. history. According to the U.S. Census Bureau, 66.2 percent of eligible black voters cast ballots in 2012, up from 64.7 percent in 2008. In contrast, non-Hispanic white turnout in 2012 was 64.1 percent, which fell from 66.1 percent four years earlier. As recently as 1996, blacks had turnout rates 8 percentage points lower than non-Hispanic whites.

CO-ETHNIC VOTING

A practice where minority voters vote for candidates of their own ethnicity.

Hispanics

Voter participation rates among Hispanics still trail black and white turnout. However, when allowances are made for education, income, age, and mobility, this turnout gap almost disappears.[39] Nonetheless, Hispanic voter participation overall is on the upswing and gap between Hispanics and African Americans is gradually narrowing. In the 2012 presidential election, Hispanics cast 10 percent of the total vote (up 1% from 2008), compared to African Americans who cast 13 percent—the same as in 2012. Hispanics, like blacks, are more likely to vote for Latinos—a practice known as "co-ethnic voting."[40]

Various explanations have been advanced for the lower voter participation of Hispanics. For starters, language can be a steep hurdle to jump, especially for newly arrived immigrants. The good news is that the emergence of Spanish-speaking television, radio, and newspapers is

Hispanics, the nation's fastest growing ethnic group, are becoming more active politically. Democrats and Republicans alike have stepped up their voter education and get-out-the-vote programs targeted at this large bloc of potential supporters. In 2012, Democrat Barack Obama got a larger share of the Hispanic vote than Republican Mitt Romney, prompting Republicans to re-vamp their outreach strategies, especially among young Hispanics.

helping candidates reach out to this population more easily than in the past.[41] So, too, is the availability of ballots in Spanish. Hispanic voter turnout is also affected by one's country of origin. There is less interest among immigrants from certain Central and South American countries where politics is largely reserved for elites and for men (patriarchal societies). It is no surprise that naturalized Hispanic citizens, with the exception of Cuban Americans, still vote at lower rates than their American-born peers. But this is changing rapidly as the Hispanic population continues to explode in the United States.[42]

As Hispanics emerge as the nation's largest minority, both Democratic and Republican parties vie for their votes. To remain competitive, Republicans must win a substantial portion of Hispanic voters, inasmuch as African American voters are solidly Democratic. In the 2012 presidential election, 93 percent of the African American vote was cast for Democratic candidate Barack Obama. (See Table 4–2.) The Latino vote in 2012 split 71 percent for Democrat Obama to 27 percent for Republican Mitt Romney (a loss of 4% for the Republicans over 2008). Eight years earlier, the Republican Bush brothers (President George W. Bush and Florida Governor Jeb Bush) made special efforts to recruit Hispanic voters to their party. Both speak Spanish (Jeb better than George W.). Both brothers had attempted to deal with Hispanic concerns as governors of their states, Texas and Florida, and both succeeded in winning over substantial portions of the Hispanic voters in those states. But by the 2008 election, Democrats had successfully recaptured some of the Hispanic vote and continued their dominance into 2012. Many Republicans, including a number of Republican state governors, are fearful it will be difficult to win back the Hispanic support they once had in light of their party's tough stances on immigration.

Asians

Asian Americans are the highest-income, best-educated and fastest-growing racial group in the United States, even though they make up only a small proportion of the total U.S. population (nearly 6%). Historically, Asian voter turnout rates have lagged behind those of whites, blacks, and Hispanics.[43] Some attribute their higher levels of nonvoting to

TABLE 4–2 Minority Voting in the 2004, 2008, and 2012 Presidential Elections

2004	White	African American	Latino	Asian
Share % of Total 2004 Vote	77	11	8	2
Republican Bush	58	11	44	44
Democrat Kerry	41	88	53	56
Independent Nader	0	0	2	☆
2008	**White**	**African American**	**Latino**	**Asian**
Share % of Total 2008 Vote	74	13	9	2
Republican McCain	55	4	31	35
Democrat Obama	43	95	67	62
Other	2	1	2	3
2012	**White**	**African American**	**Latino**	**Asian**
Share % of Total 2012 Vote	72	13	10	3
Republican Romney	59	6	27	26
Democrat Obama	39	93	71	73
Other	2	1	2	1

Note: ☆ represents an insufficient number of respondents.
Source: Data from Voter News Service exit poll, November 2008; National Election Poll (or NEP) Exit Poll, conducted by Edison/Mitofsky, November 2008 (available at http://www.cnn.com/ELECTION/2008/results/polls/#val=USP00p1); 2012 data from 2012 CNN Exit Poll, November 2012. Available at http://www.cnn.com/election/2012/results/race/president.

more pervasive language and cultural barriers. Others point to the higher-than-average tendency of newly registered Asians to register as independents, rather than Democrats or Republicans.[44] (As noted previously, partisans are higher turnout voters than independents.) While Asian Americans are still more prone to be independents compared with other racial and ethnic groups, they have become more Democratic in their political party preferences and presidential voting patterns over the past decade. In the 2012 presidential election, the vast majority of Asian Americans (73%) voted for President Obama—higher even than among Hispanics. (See Table 4–2.) There are, however, some partisan differences among the Asian subgroups. The highest support for Democrats is among Indian Americans and Japanese Americans. For Republicans, it is among U.S. Vietnamese and Filipinos.[45]

4.5

Explain the methods the federal government has employed to gradually expand the right to vote, tracing this expansion from creation of the Constitution through the adoption of the Twenty-Sixth Amendment.

SECURING THE RIGHT TO VOTE

The only mention of voting requirements in the U.S. Constitution as it was originally adopted is in Article I: "The electors in each state shall have the qualifications requisite for electors for the most numerous branch of the state legislature." Of course, "electors" (voters) for the most numerous branch of the state legislature are determined by *state* laws and constitutions. The effect of this constitutional provision was to leave to the states the power to determine who is eligible to vote in both state and federal elections. Over the years, however, a combination of constitutional amendments, congressional actions, and U.S. Supreme Court decisions has largely removed control over voting from the states and made it a responsibility of the national government.

Elimination of Property Qualifications

Early in American history, voting was limited to males over 21 years of age, who resided in the voting district for a certain period and owned a considerable amount of land or received a large income from other investments. So great was the fear that the "common man" would use his vote to attack the rights of property that only 120,000 people out of 2 million were permitted to vote in the 1780s. Men of property felt that only other men of property had a sufficient "stake in society" to exercise their vote in a "responsible" fashion. Gradually, however, Jeffersonian and Jacksonian principles of democracy, including confidence in the reason and integrity of the common man, spread rapidly in the new republic. Most property qualifications were eliminated by the states in the early nineteenth century.

Fifteenth Amendment

The first constitutional limitation on state powers over voting came with the ratification of the Fifteenth Amendment: "The right of the citizens of the United States to vote shall not be denied or abridged by the United States or any state on account of race, color, or previous condition of servitude." The object of this amendment, passed by the Reconstruction Congress and adopted in 1870, was to extend the vote to former black slaves and prohibit voter discrimination on the basis of race. The Fifteenth Amendment also gives Congress the power to enforce black voting rights "by appropriate legislation." Thus, the states retained their right to determine voter qualifications *as long as they do not practice racial discrimination,* and Congress was given the power to pass legislation ensuring black voting rights.

Nineteenth Amendment

Following the Civil War many of the women who had been active abolitionists, seeking to end slavery, turned their attention to the condition of women in America. They had learned to organize, conduct petition campaigns, and parade and demonstrate, as abolitionists, and later they sought to improve the legal and political rights of women. In 1869 the Wyoming territory adopted woman's suffrage; later several other western states followed suit. But it was not until the Nineteenth Amendment to the U.S. Constitution in 1920 that women's voting rights were constitutionally guaranteed.

The "White Primary"

For almost 100 years after the adoption of the Fifteenth Amendment, white politicians in the southern states were able to defeat its purposes. Social and economic pressures and threats of violence were used to intimidate many thousands of would-be African American voters. There were also many "legal" methods of disenfranchisement.

For many years the most effective means of banning black voting was a technique known as the "**white primary.**" So strong was the Democratic Party throughout the South that the Democratic nomination for public office was tantamount to election. This meant that *primary* elections to choose the Democratic nominee were the only elections in which real choices were made. If blacks were prevented from voting in Democratic primaries, they could be effectively disenfranchised. Thus southern state legislatures resorted to the simple device of declaring the Democratic Party in southern states a private club and ruling that only white people could participate in its elections, that is, in *primary* elections. Blacks would be free to vote in "official," general elections, but all whites tacitly agreed to support the Democratic, or "white man's," party, in general elections, regardless of their differences in the primary. Not until 1944, in *Smith* v. *Allwright,* did the U.S. Supreme Court declare this practice unconstitutional.[46]

Discrimination

Black voting in the South increased substantially after World War II. (From an estimated 5% of voting age blacks registered in southern states in the 1940s, black registration rose to an estimated 20% in 1952, 25% in 1956, 28% in 1960, and 39% in 1964.) But as late as 1965 the black voter turnout rate was little more than half of the white rate. In hundreds of rural counties throughout the South, blacks were prevented from registering and voting. Despite the Fifteenth Amendment, many local registrars in the South succeeded in barring black registration by means of an endless variety of obstacles, delays, and frustrations. Application forms for registration were lengthy and complicated; even a minor error would lead to rejection, such as underlining rather than circling in the "Mr.–Mrs.–Miss" set of choices. Literacy tests were the most common form of disenfranchisement. Many a black college graduate failed to interpret "properly" the complex legal documents that were part of the test. White applicants for voter registration were seldom asked to go through these lengthy procedures.

Civil Rights Act of 1964

The Civil Rights Act of 1964 made it unlawful for registrars to apply unequal standards in registration procedures or to reject applications because of immaterial errors. It required that literacy tests be in writing and made a sixth-grade education a presumption of literacy.

Twenty-Fourth Amendment

The Twenty-fourth Amendment to the Constitution was ratified in 1964, making poll taxes unconstitutional as a requirement for voting in national elections. In 1965 the U.S. Supreme Court declared poll taxes unconstitutional in state and local elections as well.[47]

Voting Rights Act of 1965

In Selma, Alabama, in early 1965, civil rights organizations effectively demonstrated that local registrars were still keeping large numbers of blacks off the voting rolls. Registrars closed their offices for all but a few hours every month, placed limits on the number of applications processed, went out to lunch when black applicants appeared, delayed months before processing applications from blacks, and used a variety of other methods to keep blacks disenfranchised. In response to the Selma-to-Montgomery March, Congress enacted a strong Voting Rights Act in 1965. The U.S. attorney general, upon evidence of voter discrimination, was empowered to replace local registrars with federal registrars, abolish literacy tests, and register voters under simplified federal procedures.[48] However, it turned out that federal registrars were sent to only a small number of southern counties. Many southern counties that had previously discriminated in voter registration hurried to sign up black voters just to avoid the imposition of federal registrars. The Voting Rights Act of 1965 has been extended and amended several times: 1970, 1975, 1982, and 2006. (The "Fannie Lou Hamer, Rosa Parks, and Coretta Scott King Voting Rights Act Reauthorization and Amendments Act of 2006" extends the Act for 25 more years, until 2031.) Hispanics and other language minorities were added to the Act's coverage in the 1975 revisions. The impact of the Act has been to largely eliminate discrimination in registration and voting. It has also increased the opportunity of black and Latino voters to elect representatives of their choice by providing a vehicle for challenging discriminatory election methods that may dilute minority-voting strength. The Act has been called "the single most effective piece of civil rights legislation ever passed by Congress."[49]

One component of the Voting Rights Act of 1965 had been rather controversial for a number of years—the preclearance requirement. The Act imposed a preclearance requirement on certain states and counties, mostly in the South, that met a coverage formula standard. The preclearance required state and local governments that were attempting to change registration or voting requirements in any way to submit these changes to the U.S. Department of Justice for its prior approval. The coverage formula was based on decades old voting turnout figures (voter turnout less than 50% in the 1964 presidential election) and voting procedures that had long been discarded by the states. In one of the U.S. Supreme Court's most controversial rulings (*Shelby County* v. *Holder,* 2013), the Court struck down the "coverage formula" in the preclearance requirement of the Voting Rights Act of 1965. The Court observed that the coverage formula was out of date: "Nearly 50 years later, things have changed dramatically." The Court upheld all other sections of the Voting Rights Act, and invited the Congress to draft another formula based on current conditions.

Eighteen-Year-Old Voting

Before 1970 only 3 of the 50 states permitted residents 18 to 21 years of age to vote— Georgia, Kentucky, and Alaska. All other states, in the exercise of their constitutional responsibility to determine the qualifications of "electors," had set the voting age at 21.

Congress passed and President Bush signed into law the Fannie Lou Hamer, Rosa Parks, and Coretta Scott King Voting Rights Act Reauthorization and Amendments Act of 2006, extending the federal Voting Rights Act until 2031. Each of the women played a vital role in the battle for civil rights for African Americans.

The movement for 18-year-old voting received its original impetus in Georgia in 1944 under the leadership of Governor Ellis Arnall, who argued successfully that 18-year-olds were then being called upon to fight and die for their country in World War II and, therefore, deserved to have a voice in the conduct of government. However, this argument failed to convince adult voters in other states; qualifications for military service were not regarded as the same as qualifications for rational decision-making in elections. In state after state, voters rejected state constitutional amendments designed to extend the vote to 18-year-olds.

Congress intervened on behalf of 18-year-old voting with the passage of the Twenty-sixth Amendment to the Constitution in 1971.[50] The states quickly ratified this amendment, during a period

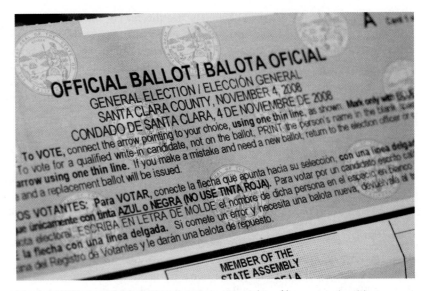

The federal Voting Rights Act protects the voting rights of language minorities. Election officials are responsible for translating ballot language into Spanish in Santa Clara County, California, which has a large Hispanic population.

of national turbulence over the Vietnam War. Many supporters of the amendment believed that protests on the campuses and streets could be reduced if youthful protesters were given the vote. Moreover, Democrats believed that their party would gain from the youth vote, and liberal candidates believed that idealistic young voters would spark their campaigns.

It turned out, however, that young people cast their votes for parties and candidates in the same proportions as older voters. The image of the idealistic, activist student was not an accurate image of the young voter in America at that time. However, all that has changed in the twenty-first century. Today's youngest generation, the Millennials, is by far more liberal than older generations. Some scholars have even labeled them the most solidly Democratic-voting age bloc. What *is* still true is that college students are more likely to be activists and to vote than their non-college-educated counterparts. In 2012, the voter turnout rate of young people was 63 percent compared to just 36 percent among young non-college-educated persons.[51] It is not surprising, then, that candidates focus more of their attention on college students and college campuses at election time.

MINORITIES IN STATE POLITICS

Racial and ethnic conflict remains a central factor in the politics of nearly every state. In recent years, conflict over voting and representation has centered on the effects of various institutional arrangements on minority influence in government.

Describe how states have drawn political districts to increase the number of racial and ethnic minorities elected to public office and what the Supreme Court has said about these efforts.

Diluting Minority Votes

Congress strengthened the Voting Rights Act in 1982 by outlawing any electoral arrangements that had the *effect* of weakening minority voting power. This "effects" test replaced the earlier "intent" test, which required black plaintiffs to prove that a particular arrangement was adopted with the specific intent of reducing black voting power.[52] (An **"intent" test** invalidates laws or practices only if they are designed to discriminate; an **"effects" test** invalidates laws or practices that adversely affect racial minorities regardless of the original intent.) For example, at-large elections or multimember districts for city councils, county commissions, or state legislative seats may have the effect of weakening minority voting power if a white majority in such districts consistently prevents blacks or Hispanics from winning office. Congress stopped short of directly outlawing such districts but

INTENT TEST
For an electoral law or practice to be proven discriminatory, minority plaintiffs had to prove it was designed to discriminate against them; now outlawed.

established a **"totality of circumstances"** test to be used to determine if such districts had a discriminatory effect. The "circumstances" to be considered by the courts include whether or not there has been a history of racial polarization in voting and whether minority candidates have ever won election to office in the district.[53]

Affirmative Racial Gerrymandering

The U.S. Supreme Court requires states and cities to provide minorities with a "realistic opportunity to elect officials of their choice." In the key case of *Thornburg* v. *Gingles*,[54] the Court interpreted the Voting Rights Act Amendments of 1982 to require state legislatures to draw election district boundary lines in a way that guarantees that minorities can elect minority representatives to governing bodies. The burden of proof was shifted *from* minorities to show that district lines diluted their voting strength to state lawmakers to show that they have done everything possible to maximize minority representation. The effect of the Court's decision was to inspire **affirmative racial gerrymandering**—the creation of predominantly black and minority districts wherever possible. (**Gerrymandering** is drawing a district to give an advantage to a political party, candidate, or racial/ethnic or language minority group.)

Racial gerrymandering dominated the redistricting process in all of the large states following the 1990 Census. In many states Republican legislators allied themselves with black and Hispanic groups in efforts to create minority districts; Republicans understood that "packing" minority (usually Democratic) voters into selected districts would reduce Democratic votes in many other districts.[55] The U.S. Justice Department also pressed state legislatures to maximize the number of **"majority-minority" congressional and state legislative districts.** With the assistance of sophisticated computer models, state legislatures and federal courts drew many odd-shaped minority congressional and state legislative districts.

Continuing Constitutional Doubts

Yet the U.S. Supreme Court has expressed constitutional doubts about bizarre-shaped districts based solely on racial composition. In a controversial 5–4 decision, Justice Sandra Day O'Connor wrote: "Race gerrymandering, even for remedial purposes, may balkanize us into competing racial factions... A reapportionment plan that includes in one district individuals who have little in common with one another but the color of their skin bears an uncomfortable resemblance to political apartheid."[56] (See Figure 4–4.) Later the Court held that the use of race as the "predominant factor" in dividing district lines is unconstitutional: "When the state assigns voters on the basis of race, it engages in the offensive and demeaning assumption that voters of a particular race, because of their race, think alike, share the same political interests and will prefer the same candidates at the polls."[57] But the Court stopped short of saying that all race-conscious districting is unconstitutional. Several states redrew the boundaries of majority-minority districts trying to conform to the Court's opinions.

More recently the battles have been over how to define a "majority" minority district. Should it simply be a district in which a minority group makes up a numerical majority of the voting age population? Or should it be a district in which more than one minority group works together to form a majority (a *coalition district*)? Or in instances where a numerical majority-minority district cannot be drawn, should states create *influence districts* in which the minority can influence the outcome of an election even if its preferred candidate cannot be elected? Or should *crossover* districts be drawn in which a minority can persuade enough nonminority voters to cross over to and vote for the minority's preferred candidate? In *Bartlett* v. *Strickland* (2009), the U.S. Supreme Court was asked to rule on whether the state of North Carolina could be required to draw a *crossover* district under Section 2 of the federal Voting Rights Act. In a 5–4 decision, it ruled that to comply with Section 2, the legislature would have to draw a numerical majority district, not an influence, crossover, or coalition district. It did not prohibit the state from doing so,

FIGURE 4–4 Affirmative Racial Gerrymandering

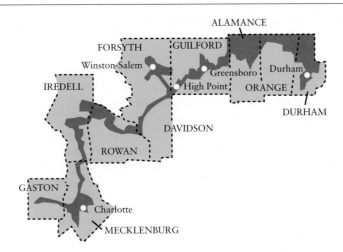

Note: North Carolina's 12th congressional district was drawn up to be a "majority-minority" district by combining African American communities over a wide region of the state. The U.S. Supreme Court in *Shaw* v. *Reno* (1993) ordered a court review of this district to determine whether it incorporated any common interest other than race. The North Carolina legislature redrew the district in 1997, lowering its black population percentage from 57 to 46, yet keeping its lengthy connection of black voters from Charlotte to Greensboro.
Source: North Carolina 12th Congressional District.

but merely ruled it was not required to do so under the Act. The constitutional status of affirmative racial gerrymandering remains unclear.

Increased Black Representation

Black representation in state and local governments, as well as in the U.S. Congress, rose dramatically in the 1990s. The total number of blacks elected to state and local office rose rapidly after 1980. New minority districts in many states boosted black representation in state legislatures. Today, roughly 9 percent of all 7,382 state legislators in the nation are African Americans. There are almost 1,000 black elected officials at the county level, over 4,000 at the municipal level, and nearly 20,000 black school board members across the country. The South has the largest number of black elected officials, while the small far western states have the fewest. We return to the question of minority representation in state legislatures in Chapter 6 and on city councils in Chapter 11.

Racial Polarization

Increases in the number of African American officeholders in state and local government are primarily the result of the creation of more black majority districts in cities and states. Few blacks win office in majority white city council, county commission, school board, or state legislative districts, although the number is increasing over time. In legislative districts where the black population is 65 percent or more, black candidates win 98 percent of the legislative seats. Majority white districts elect black candidates to about 2 percent of their legislative seats. While a few notable black political leaders have won electoral support across racial lines, racial polarization in voting remains a fact of life in many communities.[58]

Hispanic Power

The progress of Hispanics in state and local politics in recent years is reflected in the election of several governors and increasing numbers of state legislators, city and county commission members, and school board members. However, Hispanic political influence in the states is still limited. Latinos make up 3 percent of all state legislators. Latinos have been more successful at capturing school board seats—almost 1,900—and municipal offices—over 1,600. More than 500 have also been elected to county posts. Hispanic voter turnout is much lower than that for other ethnic groups in America. Many Hispanics are resident aliens and therefore are not eligible to vote. Language barriers may also present an obstacle to full participation. Finally, Hispanic voters divide their political loyalties. Cuban Americans tend to vote Republican. They are economically successful, they are concentrated in the Miami area, and they are a major force in city and state politics in Florida. The largest Hispanic group, Mexican Americans, tends to vote Democratic; their power is concentrated in California, Texas, Arizona, and New Mexico.[59] Puerto Ricans, the second largest Hispanic subgroup, is largely concentrated in New York, Florida, New Jersey, and Pennsylvania. They also tend to vote Democratic, although some research has found that Puerto Ricans coming straight from the island tend to have weaker attachments to either political party because of their lack of familiarity with the U.S. party system. Campaigns designed to reach them focus more on events that permit personal interactions with the candidate or surrogates who speak Spanish well.

4.7 WOMEN IN STATE POLITICS

Compare the participation of men and women in state politics, and assess the significance of the recent influx of women in state and local political office.

Traditionally women did not participate in politics as much as men. Women were less likely than men to contribute money, lobby elected officials, and run for or win public office.

Why was this so? Several explanations have been offered: (1) Women were socialized into more "passive" roles from childhood; (2) women with children and family responsibilities could not fully participate in politics; and (3) women did not have educations, occupations, and incomes equivalent to those of men. Perhaps all of these factors were at work in reducing female political participation, but today they are less important than they once were.

Women in State Offices

Women have made impressive political gains in state politics in recent years. Almost one-fourth of the nation's 7,383 state legislators are women. Women hold 21 percent of the 1,972 state senate seats and 25 percent of the 5,411 state house or assembly seats. Thirty-five women have served as governors of 26 states.[60] Seventy-five of the 320 statewide executive offices across the country (about 23%) are held by women—38 are Democrats and 37 are Republicans. In the 113th Congress—2013–2014—women make up 18 percent of all Congress members (see Table 4–3); 77 women serve in the U.S. House and 20 in the U.S. Senate. While these figures are modest, they represent significant advances over the recent past. In 1969 only 4 percent of the nation's state legislators were women.

Until the election of Ella Grasso (D–Connecticut) and Dixy Lee Ray (D–Washington) in the late 1970s, no woman had won election to the governor's office on her own; earlier women governors had succeeded their husbands to that office. Women are making even more rapid gains in city and county offices. The total number of women officeholders in local government has more than tripled over the past decade. As of January 2012, of the 1,248 mayors of U.S. cities with populations over 30,000, 217, or 17 percent, were women.[61] This influx of

More women running for office are stressing their business expertise.

TABLE 4–3 Women in National and State Elective Offices (Percentage of Total)

Level of Office	1981	1983	1985	1987	1989	1991	1993	1995	1997	1999	2001	2003	2005	2007	2010	2013
U.S. Congress	4	4	5	5	5	6	10	10	11	12	14	14	15	16	17	18
Statewide Elective	11	11	14	14	14	18	22	26	26	28	28	26	26	24	23	23
State Legislatures	12	13	15	16	17	18	21	21	22	22	22	22	23	24	24	24

Source: Center for American Women and Politics, Eagleton Institute of Politics, Rutgers University, "Women in Elective Office 2013," April 2013. Available at http://www.cawp.rutgers.edu/fast_facts/levels_of_office/documents/elective.pdf.

women at the grassroots level is now contributing to the success of women in running for and winning higher state and national offices, although some women from the corporate world are choosing to bypass local politics and make statewide or congressional races their first run for office.

Election Challenges

Women continue to confront special challenges when running for office.[62] In some places, political party leaders still tend to assist male more than female candidates.[63] In general, female candidates enjoy a slight advantage over male candidates in public perceptions of honesty, sincerity, and caring. However, women candidates are often perceived as "not tough enough" to deal with hard issues such as drugs and crime. When women candidates seek to prove that they are "tough," they risk being branded with adjectives like "strident" or "abrasive."

The Political Gender Gap

The **gender gap** in politics refers to differences between women and men in political views, party affiliation, and voting choices. This gap has narrowed slightly in recent years, with women currently more likely to identify with the Democratic Party and men as Republicans. Indeed, at the presidential level, national polls indicate that the majority of men voted for Republicans George H.W. Bush in 1992, Bob Dole in 1996, and George W. Bush in 2000 and 2004, and that a majority of women favored Bill Clinton in 1992 and 1996, Al Gore in 2000, John Kerry in 2004, and Barack Obama in 2008 and 2012. This gender gap extends into state politics as well, with women frequently giving Democratic gubernatorial candidates 5 to 10 more percentage points than men, although the gap varies across states.

GENDER GAP

In politics, a reference to differences between men and women in political views, party affiliations, and voting choices.

Women and Policymaking

Do greater numbers of women in state and local elected offices make any significant difference in public policy? Political scientists have attempted to answer this question but have had only mixed results. Male legislators support feminist positions on ERA, abortion, employment, education, and health just as often as female legislators. However, there is some evidence that women legislators give higher *priority* to these issues. Women are more likely than men to have as their "top legislative priority" bills focusing on women's and children's issues. However, state legislatures with larger percentages of women do *not* pass feminist legislation any more often than state legislatures with fewer women legislators.[64] (Women's priority issues are discussed in Chapter 15.)

There may also be gender-based attitudinal differences that affect a wide range of policy issues. For example, women state legislators may be more likely to view social problems such as crime in a larger societal context, leading them to focus on preventive and interventionist policies. Male legislators may view crime as an individual act that can be curtailed by certain swift and severe punishment. Over time as women increase their numbers in state legislatures and city councils, we might expect subtle changes in both the style and substance of policymaking.[65]

YOUNG AND OLD IN STATE POLITICS

Describe how political views and clout differ at different levels of government.

GENERATION GAP
In politics, a reference to differences between young and old in political views and policy preferences.

Generational conflict is intensifying in the nation and the states. The **generation gap** in politics—differences between young and old in political views and policy preferences—is not yet as great as differences among races and ethnic groups or among educational and income classes. But the generation gap has been widening in presidential elections since 2004. (See Figure 4–5.) Studies have found sharp ideological differences between the

FIGURE 4–5 Generation Gap and the Partisan Divide

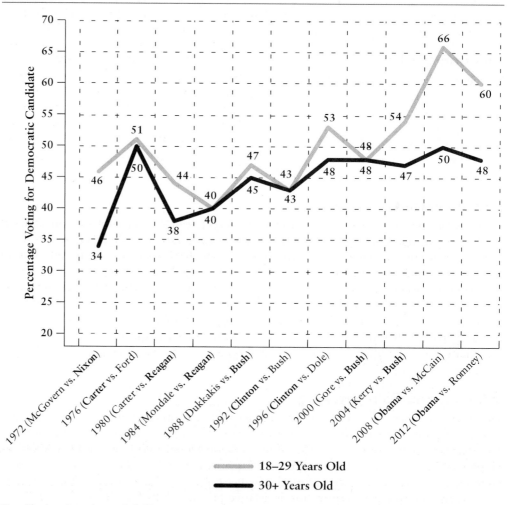

Note: Election winners' names in bold.
Source: Pew Research Center for the People & the Press, "Young Voters Supported Obama Less, But May Have Mattered More," November 26, 2012. Available at http://www.people-press.org/2012/11/26/young-voters-supported-obama-less-but-may-have-mattered-more/.

youngest and oldest generations on a wide range of policy issues, ranging from same-sex marriage to racial intermarriage and immigration. Younger voters aged 18 to 29 (the Millennials) are more liberal than their elders on most social and governmental issues.[66]

Millennials are a much more racially and ethnically diverse generation than older generations. Nonwhite voters make up 42 percent of the voting eligible population among 18- to 29-year-olds, but only 24 percent among voters aged 30 and over.[67] The breakdown of nonwhite voters among the Millennials is 18 percent Hispanic, 17 percent African American, and 7 percent mixed-race or some other race. Among voters 30 and older 12 percent are African American and 10 percent Hispanic.[68] Young voters are well acquainted with the changing face of America and overwhelmingly think diversity is good for the country.

Generational Clout Differs in Presidential and Nonpresidential Elections

In 2012, young voters made up a larger proportion of the electorate than seniors 65 and older (19% of voters were 18 to 29 years of age while just 16% were age 65 and older). They were also more cohesive in their voting patterns and in some key battleground states (Ohio, Florida, Virginia, and Pennsylvania), they were the key to President Obama winning the state and the election. But senior citizens often hold the upper hand in determining the outcome of state and local elections held in nonpresidential election years because their turnout rates are considerably higher than that of the Millennials.[69] In some states, the voting power of senior citizens in these elections may even be twice that of younger voters in state and local elections held in nonpresidential election years when young voter turnout plummets. It is important to note that the senior vote is gradually becoming less Democratic.[70] The passing of the once most solidly Democratic voting generation (the FDR-era seniors) and its replacement by the somewhat more conservative Baby Boomer generation has made the senior vote less cohesive and more Republican leaning. Today, it is the youngest generation that is the most solidly Democratic in its voting patterns, even though a sizable proportion describes themselves as independents.

Generational Policy Agendas

There is actually a great deal of misunderstanding about the priorities of the different generations and a lot of mislabeling, such as "greedy geezers," "selfish GenXers," or "Me-Millennials." (GenXers were born 1965–1981; Millennials were born 1982–2000.) In reality, on many state and local issues, the young and the old often agree on what are the big problems. Where they differ is on which problem should be tackled first. Surveys have shown that the priorities of different age cohorts often vary:

On economics:

- Young: economy and jobs
- Old: taxes and government spending

On noneconomic domestic issues:

- Young: education, environment, crime, moral issues (liberal)
- Old: health, social services, crime, moral issues (conservative)

These same surveys have shown that the generations also differ on the causes and cures of problems:

- Young: identify economic causes; favor solutions with a preventive emphasis; look more to government for solutions.
- Old: point to lapses in individual responsibility as major cause; favor reactive approaches; are more likely to believe the private sector, nongovernmental entities, and individuals produce better solutions to societal problems than government.

INTEREST GROUPS IN STATE POLITICS

Describe the various interest groups that attempt to influence state politics and the role that lobbyists play in the process.

INTEREST GROUPS

People who come together to exercise influence over government policy.

POLITICAL PARTY

An organization of people with similar political views whose primary purpose is to elect its members to public office.

Both interest groups and political parties organize individuals to make claims upon government, but these two forms of political organizations differ in several respects. An **interest group** seeks to influence specific policies of government—not to achieve control over government as a whole. A **political party** concentrates on winning public office in elections and is somewhat less concerned with policy questions. An interest group does not ordinarily run candidates for public office under its own banner, although it may give influential support to party candidates. Finally, the basic function of a political party in a two-party system is to organize a *majority* of persons for the purpose of governing. In contrast, an interest group gives political expression to the interests of *minority* groups.

Interest groups arise when individuals with a common interest decide that by banding together and by consolidating their strength they can exercise more influence over public policy than they could as individuals acting alone. The impulse toward organization and collective action is particularly strong in a society of great size and complexity. Over time, individual action in politics gives way to collective action by giant organizations of businesspeople, professionals, and union members, as well as racial, religious, and ideological groups.

Organized Interests

Groups may be highly organized into formal organizations with offices and professional staffs within the capitals of every state: The U.S. Chamber of Commerce, the National Association of Manufacturers, the AFL-CIO, and the National Education Association are examples of highly organized interest groups that operate in every state. Other groups have little formal organization and appear at state capitals only when an issue of particular concern arises, for example, when motorcyclists assemble to protest mandatory helmets, or when commercial fishermen come to complain about banning of nets.

Interest groups may be organized around *occupational or economic interests* (e.g., the Association of Real Estate Boards, the Association of Broadcasters, the Bankers Association, the Automobile Dealers Association, the Cattleman's Association, the Home Builders Association, the Insurance Council, the Association of Trial

Global warming—not a real problem.

Global warming—a real problem.

Lawyers), or on *racial or religious bases* (e.g., the National Association for the Advancement of Colored People, the Christian Coalition, the National Council of Churches, the Anti-Defamation League of B'nai B'rith), or around *shared experiences* (e.g., the American Legion, the Veterans of Foreign Wars, the League of Women Voters, the Automobile Association of America), or around *ideological positions* (e.g., Americans for Democratic Action, Common Cause, Americans for Constitutional Action). *Labor unions,* especially those representing employees of governments and school districts (e.g., the National Education Association, the American Federation of Teachers, the American Federation of State, County, and Municipal Employees), as well as industrial unions and the state AFL-CIO federation, are well organized and well represented in virtually all state capitals.[71] *Government officials* and governments themselves organize and help exert pressure on higher levels of government (e.g., the National Governors' Conference, the Council of State Governments, the National League of Cities, U.S. Conference of Mayors, the National Association of Chiefs of Police, the National Association of Counties). Even the *recipients of government services* have organized themselves (e.g., the Michigan Welfare Rights Organization).

Overall, economic interests are more frequently encountered in state politics than noneconomic interests. But certainly the proliferation of active noneconomic groups in America, from the environmentalists' Sierra Club to the senior citizens' AARP and the liberal-oriented Common Cause, testifies to the importance of organization in all phases of political life. Particularly active at the state level are the businesses subject to extensive regulation by state governments. Banks, truckers, doctors and lawyers, insurance companies, the gaming industry, utilities, hospitals, and liquor interests are consistently found to be among the most highly organized groups in state capitals. Chapters of the National Education Association are also highly active in state capitals, presenting the demands of educational administrators and teachers. And local governments and local government officials are well organized to present their demands.

A national survey of interest group activity in all 50 state capitals identified groups that were rated "most effective" in the states (see Table 4–4).

Professional Lobbyists

Often groups and corporations choose to be "represented" in state capitals by professional lobbyists. Many successful professional lobbyists are former legislators (see Chapter 6), former executive officials, or former top gubernatorial or legislative aides who have turned their state government experience into a career. They "know their way around" the capital. They offer their services—access to legislative and executive officials, knowledge of the lawmaking process, ability to present information and testimony to key policymakers at the right time, political skills and knowledge, personal friendships, and "connections"— to their clients at rates that usually depend on their reputation for influence. Occasionally their compensation is tied to their success in getting a bill passed; a six-figure fee may rest on the outcome of a single vote. Some professional lobbyists are attached to law firms or public relations firms and occasionally do other work; others are full-time lobbyists with multiple clients.

Most professional lobbyists publicly attribute their success to hard work, persistence, information, and ability to get along with others. They cite such qualities as "Being prepared, personal credibility"; "Legislators know I'm going to present the facts whether they're favorable to my client or not"; "I'm a forceful advocate—determined"; "Doing my homework on the issues"; "Knowledge of the issues I'm dealing with and knowledge of the system"; "I try to understand the political pressures on elected officials." Yet in more candid moments professional lobbyists will acknowledge that their success is largely attributable to personal friendships, political experience, and financial contributions: "Close friends I made in the legislature while I served as Speaker of the House"; "I raise a lot of money for people"; "My client has the largest political action committee in the state."[72]

LOBBYISTS
Individuals, groups, or organizations that actively seek to influence government policy.

TABLE 4–4 Heavy Hitters: The 25 Most Influential Interests in the States

Rank	Interest	Number of States in Which Interest Seen as Most Effective
1	General business (state chambers of commerce, etc.)	39
2	School teachers' organizations (NEA and AFT)	31
3	Utility companies and associations (electric, gas, water, telephone, telecommunications)	28
4	Manufacturers (companies and associations)	25
5	Hospital/nursing home associations	24
6	Insurance: general and medical (companies and associations)	22
7	Physicians, state medical associations	21
8	Contractors, builders, developers	21
9	General local government organizations (municipal leagues, county organizations, elected officials)	18
10	Lawyers (predominantly trial lawyers, state bar associations)	20
11	Realtors' associations	20
12	General farm organizations (state farm bureaus)	14
13	Bankers' associations	15
14	Universities and colleges (institutions and employees)	14
15	Traditional labor associations (predominantly the AFL-CIO)	15
16	Individual labor unions (Teamsters, UAW)	13
17	Gaming interests (race tracks, casinos, lotteries)	13
18	Individual banks and financial institutions	11
19	State agencies	10
20	Environmentalists	8
21	K–12 education interests (other than teachers)	12
22	Agricultural commodity organizations (stock growers, grain growers)	8
23	Tourism, hospitality interests	11
24	Retailers (companies and trade associations)	10
25	State and local government employees (other than teachers)	9

Source: Anthony J. Nownes, Clive S. Thomas, and Ronald J. Hrebenar, "Interest Groups in the States," in Virginia Gray and Russell L. Hanson, *Politics in the American States: A Comparative Analysis,* 9th ed. (Washington, DC: CQ Press, 2008), p. 117, most recent data at time of publication.

Lobby Registration

It is difficult to get a comprehensive picture of interest group activity in state capitals. Many organizations, businesses, legal firms, and individuals engage in interest group activity of one kind or another, and it is hard to keep track of their varied activities. Most states require the registration of "lobbyists" and the submission of reports about their membership and finances. (See *Rankings of the States:* Registered Lobbyists.) These laws do not restrain lobbying (that would probably violate the First Amendment freedom to "petition" the government for "redress of grievances"). Rather, they are meant to spotlight the activities of lobbyists. However, many hundreds of lobbyists never register under the pretext that they are *not really lobbyists,* but, instead, businesses, public relations firms, lawyers, researchers, or educational people. Usually, only the larger, formal, organized interest groups and professional lobbyists are *officially* registered as lobbyists in their states. While some states are more rigorously monitoring the registration and reporting of lobbyists, often it is the news media that are the most intense "lobbyist watchdogs." On the other hand, statehouse reporters are the first to admit they rank lobbyists as great sources of information about what is going on in the legislature.[73]

Registered Lobbyists

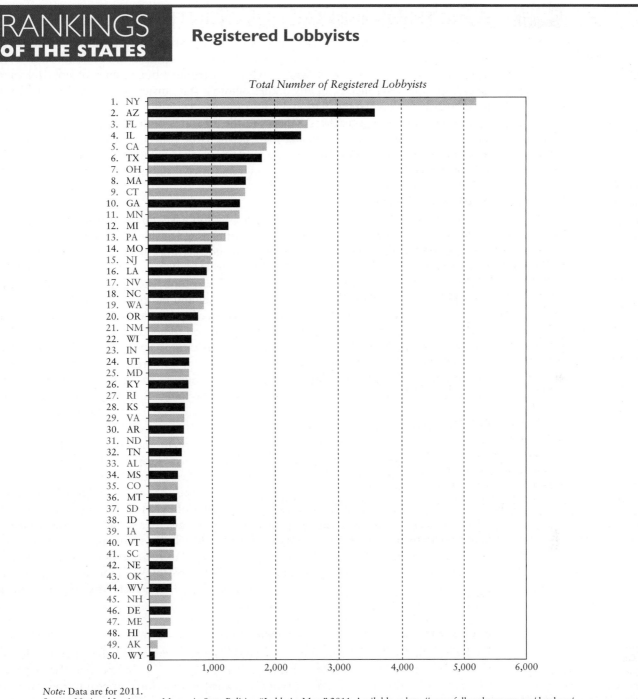

Total Number of Registered Lobbyists

1. NY	
2. AZ	
3. FL	
4. IL	
5. CA	
6. TX	
7. OH	
8. MA	
9. CT	
10. GA	
11. MN	
12. MI	
13. PA	
14. MO	
15. NJ	
16. LA	
17. NV	
18. NC	
19. WA	
20. OR	
21. NM	
22. WI	
23. IN	
24. UT	
25. MD	
26. KY	
27. RI	
28. KS	
29. VA	
30. AR	
31. ND	
32. TN	
33. AL	
34. MS	
35. CO	
36. MT	
37. SD	
38. ID	
39. IA	
40. VT	
41. SC	
42. NE	
43. OK	
44. WV	
45. NH	
46. DE	
47. ME	
48. HI	
49. AK	
50. WY	

Note: Data are for 2011.
Source: National Institute on Money in State Politics, "Lobbyist Map," 2011. Available at http://www.followthemoney.org/database/graphs/lobbyistlink/lobbymap.phtml?p=0&y=2011&l=1.

FUNCTIONS AND TACTICS OF INTEREST GROUPS

Describe the tactics used by lobbyists to promote group interests, and compare these tactics to those employed at the national level.

Interest group techniques are as varied as the imaginations of their leaders. Groups are attempting to advance their interests when a liquor firm sends a case of bourbon to a state legislator; when the League of Women Voters distributes biographies of political candidates; when an insurance company argues before a state insurance commission that rates must be increased; when the National Education Association provides state legislators with information comparing teachers' salaries in the 50 states or state teachers unions protest against proposals aimed at reducing their pensions or collective bargaining rights; when railroads ask state highway departments to place weight limitations on trucks; or when the American Civil Liberties Union supplies lawyers for civil rights demonstrators.

Typical Tactics

Typical lists of lobbying activities as supplied by lobbyists themselves usually begin with testifying at legislative committee hearings, contacting legislators directly, and helping to draft legislation. These lists usually go on to include getting constituents to contact legislators, inspiring letter-writing campaigns, and entering coalitions with other groups to lobby about particular pieces of legislation. Somewhat fewer lobbyists admit to making monetary contributions to legislators and performing personal and political favors for them, but we know from campaign contribution records and anecdotal evidence that these practices are common. Some lobbying organizations focus more on filing lawsuits or otherwise engaging in court litigation; indeed, some larger organizations have semiautonomous "legal defense" branches to carry on such activity. Relatively few interest groups resort to protests and demonstrations. None admit to direct bribery, but, as we shall see, reports of direct payments to legislators or their campaign funds in exchange for votes are not uncommon.

Bill Monitoring

More time is spent by lobbyists on monitoring the content and progress of bills affecting their clients and members than on any other activity. Just "keeping tabs" on what is going on each day in government is a time-consuming task. Lobbyists must be aware of any provisions of any bills affecting their clients, even provisions that are buried in a bill that does not mention them in its title or summary. Typically lobbyists may identify 100 or more bills that might affect their clients or members each legislative session, although they are likely to closely monitor the progress of only 20 or 30 bills that have a chance of becoming enacted.[74] (Less than 25% of bills introduced in a legislature are ever enacted in any form into law; see Chapter 6.) Lobbyists must be watchful: Nothing is more embarrassing to a lobbyist than to find that the legislature has passed a bill adversely affecting their client's interests without their ever knowing about it.

Lobbying

LOBBYING

Communications directed at government decision makers with the purpose of influencing policy.

Lobbying is defined as any communication, by someone acting on behalf of a group, directed at a government decision maker with the hope of influencing that person. Direct persuasion is usually more than just a matter of argument or emotional appeal to the lawmaker. Often it involves the communication of useful technical and political information. Many public officials are required to vote on, or decide about, hundreds of questions each year. It is impossible for them to be fully informed about the wide variety of bills and issues they face. Consequently, many decision makers depend on skilled lobbyists to provide technical information about matters requiring action, and to inform them of the policy preferences of important segments of the population. (See "Lobbying in State Legislatures" in Chapter 6.)

The behavior of lobbyists depends on the interests they represent and the characteristics of the state political system in which they function. Some interests hire full-time lobbyists; others rely on attorneys or firms who lobby on behalf of more than one group. This tends to be true in larger, more diverse states with more interest groups needing lobbyists' help. (See *Ranking of the States:* Total Number of Lobbyist Clients.) Still other interests rely on volunteers. Some maintain active contact with legislators or make campaign contributions. Some formulate a legislative agenda each session and trace the progress of bills in which they are interested. Indeed, one study of lobbying on behalf of the aging in four separate states revealed much variation in lobbying activity even on the same issues.[75]

Bribery and Corruption

Lobbying in state capitals may be somewhat cruder—if not more corrupt—than lobbying in Washington. In interviewing lobbyists and legislators in Washington, Lester Milbrath found that they considered state lobbying much more corrupt than national lobbying. "'Lobbying is very different before state legislators; it is much more individualistic. Maybe this is the reason they have more bribery in state legislatures than in Congress.' 'In the state legislatures, lobbying is definitely on a lower plane. The lobbyists are loose and hand out money and favors quite freely.' 'Lobbying at the state level is cruder, more basic, and more obvious.'"[76] Needless to say, it is difficult to document such statements. However, it seems reasonable to believe that state legislators might be more subject to the appeals of organized interest groups than members of Congress.

State legislators, unlike most members of Congress, are only part-time lawmakers. They must manage their own business, professional, and investment interests in addition to their legislative duties. They may have personal business or professional or real estate or legal ties with the same interests that are seeking to influence their legislative behavior. Such "**conflicts of interest**"—legislators voting in committee or on the floor on issues in which they have a personal financial interest—are not uncommon. Indeed, some interests occasionally seek to establish business or professional ties with legislators just to win their support.

Bribery is the offering of anything of value to government officials to influence them in the performance of their duties. Vote buying is illegal but not unheard of in state capitals. Instead of bribery, organized interests may contribute to a legislator's campaign chest without mentioning any specific quid pro quo.

Grassroots Lobbying, Media Campaigns, and Public Relations

Most people think of interest group tactics as direct attempts to influence decision makers, but many groups spend more of their time, energy, and resources in general public relations activities than anything else. The purpose of a continuing public relations campaign is to create an environment favorable to the interest group and its program. It is hoped that a reservoir of public goodwill can be established, which can be relied on later when a critical issue arises.

Lobbyists know that legislators pay attention to their constituents. **Grassroots lobbying** involves interest group efforts to get constituents to call or write their legislator on behalf of the group's position on pending legislation. Grassroots campaigns are now highly professional. They "rely totally on mass marketing, high technology, and public relations ploys reminiscent of political campaigns."[77] Form letters supplied by interest groups to constituents to sign and send to their legislator may not be effective. But direct calls, personal letters, e-mails, and faxes, especially from constituents who have previously contributed to a legislator's campaign, are seldom ignored.

Media campaigns are effective, but also expensive. These involve paid advertisements on radio or television designed to influence public opinion on pending legislation. Heavy media campaigns are more likely to be undertaken by lobbyists in Washington, DC, than in state capitals. Only about 20 to 30 percent of lobbyists in the states report having directly advertised in the media.[78]

Political Action Committee Money in the States

Because political campaigns are expensive, it is always difficult for a candidate to find enough money to finance a campaign. This is true for officeholders seeking reelection as well as new contenders. It is perfectly legal for an interest group to make a contribution to

CONFLICTS OF INTEREST
Legislators voting on an issue in which they have a personal financial interest.

BRIBERY
Offering anything of value to government officials with the purpose of influencing them in the performance of their duties.

GRASSROOTS LOBBYING
Influencing legislators by contacting their constituents and asking them to contact their legislators.

a candidate's campaign fund. Ordinarily, a respectable lobbyist would not be so crude as to exact any specific pledges from a candidate in exchange for a campaign contribution. He or she simply makes a contribution and lets the candidate figure out what to do when in office to ensure further contributions to the candidate's next campaign. (For further discussion, see "Money in State Politics" in Chapter 5.) There is, however, some evidence that contributions do influence a legislator's vote *if* the "vote means the difference between a contributing group's success or defeat on a bill."[79] The organizational strength of a group can also affect public policy. One study of the impact of labor unions on state public policy found that the greater the organizational strength of labor, the more states spend on welfare and education.[80]

PACS

Political action committees; organizations formed to raise and distribute campaign funds to candidates for public office.

Interest groups, operating through political action committees, or **PACs,** are becoming a major source of campaign funding for state office. As campaign costs increase, reliance on PAC money increases. In large urban states such as California and New York, where campaigns for state legislature may cost $250,000 or more, PAC contributions are the largest source of campaign funding.

PACs are politically sophisticated contributors. They do not like to back losers. Since incumbent members of state legislatures running for reelection seldom lose (see "The Great Incumbency Machine" in Chapter 6), PAC contributions are heavily weighted in favor of incumbents over challengers and candidates from the political party that controls each house of the legislature.

In states where there are campaign contribution limits, interest groups find other ways to support their preferred candidate. They may spend money on an advocacy ad, give an endorsement, or contribute to the state political party of which the candidate is a member.[81]

4.11 COMPARING INTEREST GROUP POWER IN THE STATES

Explain why interest groups are more powerful in some states than in others.

INTEREST GROUP INFLUENCE

The extent to which interest groups as a whole influence public policy as compared with other components of the political system.

How do interest group systems in the states differ? Why do some states have strong, influential interest groups shaping public policy, while in other states the influence of interest groups is moderated by group competition, party rivalry, and electoral politics?

We might define overall **interest group influence** in a state as "the extent to which interest groups as a whole influence public policy when compared to other components of the political system, such as political parties, the legislature, the governor, etc."[82] Using this definition researchers have attempted to categorize the states as having a "dominant," "complementary," or "subordinate" interest group system, in terms of its policy impact relative to the parties and the branches of government.

Over time interest group influence appears to be increasing in all of the states. A major factor is their increasing role in campaign finance. The more money coming from interest groups to political candidates, the greater is the influence of the interest group system.

Yet interest group influence in some states is greater than in other states, and our task is to search for explanations. One thing to remember is that some types of interest groups are powerful in one state, but not another. In such instances, these powerhouses often reflect key components of a state's economy (e.g., automobile lobbying groups in Michigan, tobacco interest groups in North Carolina, mining industry groups in Montana and West Virginia).

The Economic Diversity Explanation

Wealthy urban industrial states (Connecticut, Massachusetts, Michigan, New Jersey, New York, Rhode Island) have weaker interest group systems because of the diversity and complexity of their economies. No single industry can dominate political life. Instead, multiple competing interest groups tend to balance each other, and this cancels the influence of interest groups generally. In contrast, in rural states with less economic diversity, a few dominant industries (oil and gas in Louisiana, coal in West Virginia) appear to have more influence. The reputation for influence for particular industries in these states causes them to be viewed as strong pressure group states.

The Party Explanation

According to political scientist Sarah McCally Morehouse, "Where parties are strong, pressure groups are weak or moderate; where parties are weak, pressure groups are strong enough to dominate the policy-making process."[83] Where competitive political parties are strong—where the parties actively recruit candidates, provide campaign support, and hold their members accountable after the election—interest groups are less powerful. Policymakers in these states look to the party for policy guidance rather than to interest groups. Interest group influence is channeled through the parties; the parties are coalitions of interest groups; no single interest group can dominate or circumvent the party. Strong party states (Connecticut, New York, Minnesota, North Dakota, Rhode Island, Wisconsin, Massachusetts, Colorado) have weak interest group systems. Weak party states (primarily the one-party southern states) have strong interest group systems.

Strong governors and strong legislative leadership, exercising their influence as party leaders, can provide a check on the lobbying efforts of interest groups. When the special interests lose, it is usually on issues on which the governor and the party leadership have taken a clear stand[84] or when the governor is of one party and the legislature is controlled by the other (divided control) and the governor vetoes a piece of legislation.

The Professionalism Explanation

State legislatures are becoming more professional over time. In Chapter 6 we define a professional legislature as a well-paid, full-time, well-staffed body, as opposed to an amateur legislature, which meets only a few weeks each year, pays its members very little, and has few research or information services available to it. Professional legislatures have less turnover in members and more experience in lawmaking. Clearly, these characteristics of legislatures affect the power of interest groups. Interest groups are more influential when legislatures are *less* professional. When members are less experienced, paid less, and have little time or resources to research issues themselves, they must depend more on interest groups, and interest groups gain influence. Interest groups also frequently have more clout in states with legislative term limits, which have the effect of creating less-experienced lawmakers who turn more to interest groups to help them draft bills and raise campaign funds.[85]

PROFESSIONALISM
In legislatures, the extent to which members have the services of full-time, well-paid staff, as well as their access to research and sources of information.

The Governmental Fragmentation Explanation

It is also likely that states with weak governors, multiple independently elected state officials, and numerous independent boards and commissions have strong interest group systems. In states with fragmented executive power (Florida, South Carolina), interest groups have additional points of access and control, and executive officials do not have counterbalancing power. Strong governors (as in New York, Massachusetts, New Jersey, Connecticut, Delaware, and Minnesota) are better able to confront the influence of interest groups when they choose to do so. (We discuss governors' powers in Chapter 7.)

Fortunately, we do not have to choose one explanation to the exclusion of others. Economic diversity, party strength, professionalism, and governmental fragmentation all contribute to the explanation of interest group strength in the states.

PROTEST AS POLITICAL PARTICIPATION

4.12

Organized protests—marches, demonstrations, disruptions, civil disobedience—are important forms of political activity. Protest marches and demonstrations are now nearly as frequent at state capitols and city halls as in Washington. It is a lot easier to travel to the state capital than all the way to DC. But sometimes like-minded citizens choose to stand along busy streets or hold an announced rally at a public park to express their opinions on various issues of concern to them. Such gatherings often generate local news coverage

Describe the differences between protests, political disobedience, and violence; and outline how state and local governments respond to these types of political participation.

Civil disobedience acts, which often result in arrest, are designed to call attention to the existence of injustice. People for the Ethical Treatment of Animals (PETA) have used this tactic quite frequently in its effort to stop local stores from selling furs.

PROTEST

In politics, public activities designed to call attention to issues and influence decision makers.

CIVIL DISOBEDIENCE

A form of protest that involves peaceful nonviolent breaking of laws considered to be unjust.

and effectively recruit others to join "the cause." Both the Tea Party and the Occupy Wall Street movements expanded in just that way. (See "*Did You Know?*: Tea Party and Occupy Wall Street Protests Falter but Ideas Stick.") Even more common these days are protests via the Web—the "netroots" revolution.

It is important to distinguish between *protest, civil disobedience,* and *violence,* even though all may be forms of political activity. Most *protests* do *not* involve unlawful conduct and are protected by the constitutional guarantee of the First Amendment to "peaceably assemble and petition for redress of grievances." A march on city hall or the state capitol, followed by a mass assembly of people with speakers, sign waving, songs, and perhaps the formal presentation of grievances to whichever brave official agrees to meet with the protesters, is well within the constitutional guarantees of Americans.

Protest

"**Protest**" refers to direct, collective activity by persons who wish to obtain concessions from established power holders. Often the protest is a means of acquiring bargaining power by those who would otherwise be powerless. The protest may challenge established groups by threatening their reputations (in cases in which they might be harmed by unfavorable publicity), their economic position (in cases in which noise and disruption upset their daily activity), or their sense of security (when the threat exists that the protest may turn unruly or violent). The strategy of protest may appeal especially to powerless minorities who have little else to bargain with except the promise to stop protesting.

Protests may also aim at motivating uncommitted "third parties" to enter the political arena on behalf of the protesters. The object of the protest is to call attention to the existence of some issue and urge others to apply pressure on public officials. This strategy requires the support and assistance of the news media. If ignored by television and newspapers, protests can hardly be expected to activate support. However, the news media seldom ignore protests with audience interest; protest leaders and journalists share an interest in dramatizing "news" for the public.

Protests do not necessarily have to take place "in the streets." The Internet has made it possible for interest groups to protest electronically via highly organized e-mail campaigns to public officials. Some have labeled this new form of protest as "electronic activism." "You can hear the netroots screaming," wrote one columnist for the *New York Times* who was describing an Internet poll being taken by a protest group.[86]

Civil Disobedience

Civil disobedience is a form of protest that involves breaking "unjust" laws. Civil disobedience is not new: It has played an important role in American history, from the Boston Tea Party to the abolitionists who illegally hid runaway slaves, to the suffragettes who demonstrated for women's voting rights, to the labor organizers who picketed to form the nation's major industrial unions, to the civil rights workers of the early 1960s who deliberately violated segregation laws. The purpose of civil disobedience is to call attention, or to "bear witness," to the existence of injustice. In the words of Martin Luther King, Jr., civil disobedience "seeks to dramatize the issue so that it can no longer be ignored."[87] True civil disobedience has no violence, and only "unjust" laws are broken. Moreover, the law is broken "openly, lovingly" with a willingness to accept the penalty. Punishment is actively sought rather than avoided, since punishment will help to emphasize the injustice of the law. The object is to stir the conscience of an apathetic majority and win support for measures that will eliminate injustices. By willingly accepting punishment for the violation

Tea Party and Occupy Wall Street Protests Falter but Ideas Stick

Historically, protest movements in the United States have emerged in times of economic hardship. Protest arises slowly, gains ground, then dies away, but not without impact. Two cases in point: the Tea Party and Occupy Wall Street.

A global recession in 2008, combined with the federal government's intervention in the mortgage housing crisis and corporate bankruptcies, aroused fears of economic insecurity and anger over the use of taxpayer money. Recalling the tax revolt that led to the Boston Tea Party in 1773, irate citizens railed against a growing list of "big government" issues, spreading their ideas through rallies and social media, with backing from conservative advocacy groups and national TV and radio show hosts. By 2010, a number of Republican Party candidates had affiliated with the Tea Party and won election, including Libertarian Rand Paul in Kentucky who won a U.S. Senate seat that year. Emboldened Tea Partiers spoke out against health care reform, immigration, abortion, contraception, and gay marriage. They abandoned moderate incumbents in the primaries and ran candidates who toed the Tea Party's hard line. But by 2012 enthusiasm for the Tea Party appeared to wane. Many Republicans, including Senator Marco Rubio of Florida (a Tea Party favorite), distanced themselves from the Tea Party and sought to appeal to a broader section of Americans.

As the opposite end of the spectrum, Occupy Wall Street emerged out of anger toward "big business," particularly Wall Street's powerful influence on Congress. The movement's first public manifestation occurred on September 17, 2011, when a thousand protesters marched on Wall Street and then encamped in a nearby park. The activists argued that Wall Street financiers were destroying the economy by causing innumerable foreclosures, creating high unemployment, and widening the gap between rich and poor. Hand-made signs, "We are the 99%," broadcast on television and the Internet won the sympathy of ordinary Americans resentful of the 1 percent super-rich. On subsequent days in other U.S. cities, like-minded protesters called for higher taxes on the wealthy, reform of the banking system and campaign finance, stronger regulation of business, and government spending to create jobs. Similar protests erupted in Europe, Asia, and Australia. Lacking leadership and locked into consensus-only decision-making, occupiers began losing support as bums and derelicts sought haven among them and police clashed with militants. On November 15, New York police, following Mayor Michael Bloomberg's order, evicted occupiers from the park. Within weeks, other occupier camps were closed down. Calls for future action in the spring fell on deaf ears.

Despite the fizzling of both movements, many of their ideas took hold in Election 2012 campaigns and in policy debates thereafter. Tea Party support for reducing the national debt, blocking tax increases, and limiting government became key components of Republican campaigns while Occupy Wall Street cries for addressing wealth inequity, reining in the shortcomings of a free-market economy, and reviving the dream of upward mobility for everyone were front and center in Democratic candidates' campaigns.

of an unjust law, people who practice civil disobedience demonstrate their sincerity. They hope to shame public officials and make them ask themselves how far they are willing to go to protect the status quo.

As in all protest activity, the participation of the news media, particularly television, is essential to the success of civil disobedience. The dramatization of injustice makes news; the public's sympathy is won when injustices are spotlighted; and the willingness of demonstrators to accept punishment is visible evidence of their sincerity. Cruelty or violence directed *against* demonstrators by police or others plays into the hands of the protesters by further emphasizing injustices.[88]

Violence

Violence can also be a form of political participation. To be sure, it is criminal, and it is generally irrational and self-defeating. However, political assassination; bombing and terrorism; and rioting, burning, and looting have occurred with uncomfortable frequency in American politics. Violence is a tool used by groups on both the left and the right ends of the political spectrum. For example, violent protests at the 1999 World Trade Organization meeting in Seattle mostly came from the left, whereas violence against abortion clinics in the 1990s came from the right. The plane crashes into the Twin Towers of the World

Trade Center in New York and the Pentagon on September 11, 2001, were an even more recent reminder that violence is often the primary way extremist groups call attention to their political agendas.

It is important to distinguish violence from protest. Peaceful protest is constitutionally guaranteed. Most protests are free of violence. Occasionally there is an implicit *threat* of violence in a protest—a threat that can be manipulated by protesters to help gain their ends. However, most protests harness frustrations and hostilities and direct them into constitutionally acceptable activities. Civil disobedience should also be distinguished from violence. The civil disobedient breaks only "unjust" laws, openly and without violence, and willingly accepts punishment without attempting escape. Rioting, burning, and looting—as well as bombing and assassination—are clearly distinguishable from peaceful protest and even civil disobedience.

News Media

The real key to success in protest activity is found in the support or opposition of the news media to protest group demands. Virtually all of the studies of protest activity have asserted that it is the response of "third parties," primarily the news media, and not the immediate response of public officials, that is essential to success.[89] This is a plausible finding because, after all, if protesters could persuade public officials directly, there would be no need to protest. Indeed, one might even distinguish between "interest groups," which have a high degree of continuous interaction with public officials, and "protest groups," which do not regularly interact with public officials and must engage in protest to be heard. Furthermore, to be heard, reports of their protests must be carried in newspapers and on television, which increasingly are reporting protests taking place in the **blogosphere**.

The Effectiveness of Protests

Several conditions must be present if protest is to be effective.[90] First of all, there must be a clear goal or objective of the protest. Protesters must aim at specific concessions or legislation they desire; generally, complex problems or complaints that cannot readily be solved by specific governmental action are not good targets for protest activity. Second, the protest must be directed at public officials capable of granting the desired goal. It is difficult to secure concessions if no one is in a position to grant them. Third, the protest leaders must not only organize their masses for protest activity, but they must also simultaneously bargain with public officials for the desired concessions. This implies a division of labor between "organizers" and "negotiators."

Official Responses to Protests

When faced with protest activity, public officials may greet the protesters with smiles and reassurances that they agree with their objectives. They may dispense *symbolic* satisfaction without actually granting any tangible payoffs. Once the "crisis" is abated, the bargaining leverage of the protest leaders diminishes considerably. Public officials may dispense *token* satisfactions by responding, with much publicity, to one or more specific cases of injustice, while doing little of a broad-based nature to alleviate conditions. Or public officials may *appear to be constrained* in their ability to grant protest goals by claiming that they lack the financial resources or legal authority to do anything—the "I-would-help-you-if-I-could-but-I-can't" pose. Another tactic is to *postpone action* by calling for further study while offering assurances of sympathy and interest. Finally, public officials may try to *discredit* protesters by stating or implying that they are violence-prone or unrepresentative of the real aspirations of the people they seek to lead. This tactic is especially effective if the protest involves violence or disruption or if protest leaders have "leftist" or criminal backgrounds.

BLOGOSPHERE
An "area" on the Internet dominated by Web-logs. "Bloggers" often protest various societal ills via their space on the Internet.

State and Local Governments Bear Costs of Protests

Protests—peaceful and violent—occur in a particular state and locality. The targeted audience may extend beyond where the protest is taking place (to national or international television audiences). But it is the responsibility of the state or local government serving the area where the protest is occurring to protect the public and to respond when tragedies strike. Sometimes these situations can break the budget. Early estimates of the costs of the attacks on the World Trade Center in New York were in the billions. And even though Congress approved a substantial amount of federal fiscal assistance, the costs to both the State of New York and the City of New York created tremendous fiscal pressures on their budgets.

CHAPTER HIGHLIGHTS

▪ Around half of America's eligible voters don't vote, even in a presidential election. Reasons include confusing registration requirements, unawareness of alternatives to in-person voting, absence of high-profile candidates or hot issues, and lack of civic education.

▪ More people vote out of a sense of civic duty and commitment to democracy.

▪ Those least likely to vote are the young, the poor, the unemployed, and the least educated.

▪ Voting and political power of blacks has improved markedly in recent years, while that of Hispanics and Asians continues to be weak when compared to their proportion of the population.

▪ Voter turnout can be affected by the strength and competitiveness of a state's political parties, registration procedures (motor voter; same day) and follow-up, voting logistics (time, place, equipment, access for persons with disabilities), training of poll workers, and the media's predictions of winners based on early returns.

▪ Continuing election controversies involve voter eligibility and identification (IDs), voting locations, and online registration and voting.

▪ States have lost their control of voting to the federal government through constitutional amendments, court decisions, and federal laws broadening the right to vote.

▪ The Voting Rights Act of 1965 and its subsequent extensions and amendments have removed many legal barriers to minority voting.

▪ The Twenty-sixth Amendment lowered the voting age in national and state elections from 21 to 18. It was passed during the Vietnam War on the rationale that if 18-year-old men could be drafted into military service, they should have the right to vote.

▪ Recent efforts to strengthen minority voting power include the outlawing of any electoral arrangements that dilute that power and the drawing of election districts in a way that guarantees the election of minorities to governing bodies, prompting controversies about "racial gerrymandering."

▪ Women have made impressive gains in political power in recent years but still face challenges in public perceptions. When in office, they tend to put a higher priority on women's and children's issues.

▪ Senior citizens are the most politically powerful age group in the population, and have twice the voting power of the young in midterm, but not presidential, elections. Older voters are becoming slightly more Republican, while young Millennials have become more solidly Democratic in their voting patterns. Both old and young, however, agree on what are the big societal problems but differ on what are the causes and solutions.

▪ Most interest groups at the state level focus on economic issues, often hiring lobbyists to monitor bills and provide information to legislators and the media. Vote buying is illegal but not unheard of in state government.

▪ Interest group influence tends to be weaker in states dominated by specific industries or a single political party and in states with "professional" legislatures and strong governors.

▪ As state political campaign costs have increased, political action committees (PACs) have become a major source of campaign funding.

▪ Organized protests (marches and demonstrations) and civil disobedience (breaking laws viewed as unjust and accepting the punishment) rely heavily on media coverage for effectiveness. Peaceful protest is constitutionally guaranteed, but violence (riots, looting, bombing) is criminal. Street-level protests are hard to sustain but protesters' concerns often get incorporated into the platforms of major political parties.

CHAPTER FIVE

PARTIES AND CAMPAIGNS IN THE STATES

LEARNING OBJECTIVES

5.1 Assess the effectiveness of political parties in the contemporary political arena.

5.2 Compare the different ways in which political parties are involved in the process of selecting candidates for public office.

5.3 Describe the activities of state and local party organizations, and compare how these activities differ during and between elections.

5.4 Analyze how the fortunes of the Democratic Party and the Republican Party in the states have changed over time.

5.5 Compare divided and unified party government in the states, and determine whether divided government is a major contributor to legislative gridlock.

5.6 Analyze how party competition influences the operation of political parties within the states.

5.7 Describe the professionals who are involved with state and local political campaigns, and outline how they use the tools of their trade.

5.8 Examine the differences in campaign financing from state to state, and assess why these differences are often substantial.

5.9 Evaluate the effectiveness of state and national laws that limit campaign financing in order to increase the perceived efficacy of the electoral process.

Assess the effectiveness
of political parties in the
contemporary political arena.

PARTY

An organization that seeks to
achieve power by winning public
office in elections.

AMERICAN POLITICAL PARTIES: IN DISARRAY OR EXPERIENCING A REBIRTH?

For every news story that proclaims political parties to be dying—irrelevant and out of touch with most voters—there is another that points to the heightened role that state and local political **party** organizations play in registering voters and in GOTV—get-out-the-vote—operations. News operations (and political scientists, too) routinely "color" states and counties red (Republican) or blue (Democrat) to visually describe which party has the most registrants or to report which party's candidate won the most votes in an election contest. They tend to use green to "describe" independents—voters who do not identify with either of the major parties.

Throughout the often-heated campaign season, pollsters repeatedly take snapshots of potential voters "sliced and diced" by age, race/ethnicity, gender, education, income, religious affiliation, and ideology. They often use catchy terms ("Wal-Mart Moms," "NASCAR Dads") to describe groups on which they are focusing. Their main purpose is to see who is identifying themselves with the two major parties (Democrat, Republican), with minor parties (such as Libertarian, Green, Reform, Tea), or as independents (no party affiliation) and how they plan to vote on Election Day (strictly along party lines, for the other party's candidates, or by splitting their vote between the parties).

After a major election, *academics and scholars* at various think tanks analyze the links between voter attributes, party identification, and voting patterns. Their primary goal is to determine if there have been any seismic shifts in the composition of political parties in the nation at large and in specific states and localities. New typologies (categories) of the electorate generally emerge as the quality and quantity of data improves, along with the software used to probe the data.

Post-election analyses by *party activists and professional campaign consultants* in each state tend to focus more on trying to understand why one party's candidates won and another's lost. Here the bulk of the attention is on analyzing and comparing the effectiveness of state and local party organizations. How well did each do in recruiting volunteers, energizing the electorate (registering voters, promoting absentee balloting, getting people to the polls), identifying solid core supporters and the undecideds, organizing local political forums and rallies, and raising money?

Political parties are still central features on the American political landscape, although more Americans are describing themselves as "independents." In some families, party loyalties are a way of life, passed on like religion. In others, there is little discussion about politics at home, which leaves the establishment of party loyalty, if any, more in the hands of schools, social networks, or the mass media.

Staunch supporters of political parties today often cite scholars who have concluded that were it not for parties, there would be no democracy: "Political parties created modern democracy and modern democracy is unthinkable save in terms of parties."[1] While many agree with this broad assessment, there is less consensus about whether today's political parties have successfully played all the roles that early party supporters proclaimed that they could. There is an ongoing debate between the "purists" and the "realists" about the degree to which political parties do all that was initially expected of them or whether it really matters.[2] Others debate whether the American system of government is more party-centered or more candidate-centered. Do voters pay more attention to the party affiliation of a candidate or to the candidate's personal attributes—age, looks, gender, race, campaign style, political ads, and debate skills?

The Responsible Party Model

RESPONSIBLE PARTIES

A party system in which
each party offers clear policy
alternatives and holds their
elected officials responsible
for enacting these policies in office.

Initially, political parties were viewed as the principal instrument of majority control of public policy. "**Responsible parties**," as perceived by the "purists," are supposed to (1) develop and clarify alternative policy positions for the voters; (2) educate the people about the issues and simplify choices for them; (3) recruit candidates for public office who agree with the parties' policy positions; (4) organize and direct their candidates' campaigns to win office; (5) hold their elected officials responsible for enacting the parties' policy positions after they are elected; and (6) organize legislatures to ensure party control of policymaking. In carrying out these functions, responsible parties are supposed to modify the demands of special interests, build a consensus that could win majority support, and provide simple and identifiable, yet meaningful, choices for the voters on Election Day. In this way, disciplined, issue-oriented, competitive parties are seen as the principal means by which the people would direct public policy and hold elected officials accountable. Critics say such a party system would make bipartisanship more difficult.

Problems with the Model

Over the years, the "realists" have outlined many shortcomings of the "responsible party" model. Among the most commonly cited are:

- *The parties do not offer the voters clear policy alternatives.* Instead, each tries to capture the broad center of most policy dimensions, where it believes most Americans can be found. There is no incentive for parties to stand on the far right or far left when most Americans are found in the center. So the parties echo each other, and critics refer to them as "Tweedledee and Tweedledum."

- *Voter decisions are not motivated primarily by policy considerations.* Most voters cast their votes on the basis of candidate "image," the "goodness" or "badness" of the times, and traditional voting habits. This means there is little incentive for either parties or candidates to concentrate on issues. Party platforms are seldom read by anyone. Modern campaign techniques focus on the image of the candidate—compassion, warmth, good humor, experience, physical appearance, ease in front of a camera, and so forth—rather than positions on the issues.

- *American political parties have no way to bind their elected officials to party positions or even their campaign pledges.* Parties cannot really discipline members of Congress or state legislatures for voting against the party position; only voters can do this at the ballot box. Party cohesion, where it exists, is more a product of like-mindedness among Democratic or Republican legislators than it is of party control.

The Rise of Candidate-Centered Elections

In addition to these underlying problems, over time candidate-centered politics has been on the upswing due to:

- *The rise of primary elections.* Party organizations cannot control who the party's nominee shall be. Nominations are won in primary elections. Progressive reformers introduced primary elections at the beginning of the twentieth century to undercut the power of party machines in determining who runs for office. Nominees now establish personal organizations in primary elections and campaign for popular votes; they do not have to negotiate with party leaders, especially if they are self-financed candidates. Of course, the party organization may endorse a candidate in a primary election, but this is no guarantee of success with the party's voters.

- *The decline of party identification.* Democratic and Republican party loyalties have been declining over the years. Most people remain registered as Democrats or Republicans in order to vote in party primary elections, but increasing numbers of people identify themselves as "independent" and cast their vote in general elections without reference to party. Split-ticket voting (where a single voter casts his or her vote for a Democrat in one race and a Republican in another) has also increased in some states.

- *More focus on the candidate, less on his or her party affiliation.* Primary elections, the decline in party identification, and the importance of direct media communication with the voters have all combined to create **candidate-centered politics**. Candidates raise their own campaign funds, create their own personal organizations, and hire professional consultants to produce their own ads (many no longer even include their party affiliation in the advertising[3] or, if they do, the party label is minimized so as not to call attention to it).

PARTY IDENTIFICATION
Self-described identification with a political party, usually in response to the question: "Generally speaking, how would you identify yourself: as a Republican, Democrat, independent, or something else?"

CANDIDATE-CENTERED POLITICS
Individual candidates rather than parties raise funds, create personal organizations, and rely on professional consultants to direct their campaigns.

A growing number of Americans do not identify with either the Republican or Democratic Party. Consequently, in many states, there has been a surge in the number of voters who either register as independents or with third parties (Libertarian, Reform, Green, Socialist, and others).

■ *The influence of the mass media, particularly television and the Web.* Candidates can come directly into the voter's living room via television (broadcast, cable) and into a citizen's computer and wireless devices via the Internet. Cyberspace-related campaigning has become more essential, particularly in large, fast-growing states where it is more difficult to reach a large proportion of the voters by going door-to-door (**shoe leather campaigning**). Utilizing social networking sites is a must for today's campaigns.

■ *The decline of patronage.* Civil service reforms, at the national, state, and even city levels, have reduced the tangible rewards of electoral victory. **Party "professionals"**—who work in political campaigns to secure jobs and favors for themselves and their friends—are now being replaced by **political "amateurs"**—who work in political campaigns for the emotional satisfaction of supporting a "cause." Amateurs work intensely during campaigns, while professionals work year-round, in off-years and election years, building party support with small personal favors for the voters. These party "regulars" are disappearing.

■ *The rise of single-issue interest groups, PACs, and "527s."* Parties have always coexisted with broad-based interest groups, many of whom contribute money to both Democratic and Republican candidates in order to ensure access regardless of who wins. But many of the more militant single-issue groups require a "litmus test" of individual candidates on single issues—abortion, gun control, immigration. Their support and money hinge on the candidate's position on a single issue. Most PAC (political action committee) money goes directly to candidates, although some does go to state party organizations. The fastest growing type of group, a **"527" organization** (named after the portion of the IRS tax code that covers it), can spend unlimited amounts of money on campaign ads or activities but is expressly prohibited from coordinating its efforts with either a party or a candidate.

Parties Are Survivors

Despite the debate over whether we *should* have a pure responsible party system, the bottom line is that we do not have one for all the reasons laid out above. Nonetheless, American political parties "have demonstrated amazing adaptability and durability."[4] The political reality is that both the major parties (Democratic and Republican) and various minor or third parties continue to perform important political functions:

■ *Parties organize elections and narrow the choices of political office seekers confronting the voters.* In most state elections, the field of candidates in the November general election is narrowed to the Democratic and Republican Party nominees. Few independents are ever elected to high political office in the states. Only five governors in recent decades—Angus King and James Longley of Maine, Walter Hickel of Alaska, Lowell Weicker of Connecticut, and Lincoln Chafee of Rhode Island—have been elected as independents. Jesse Ventura, the Reform Party candidate, won election as Governor of Minnesota over his Democratic and Republican opponents. There are fewer than a dozen independent state legislators in the nation. Nebraska has the nation's only nonpartisan state legislature. Party nominees—for governor, attorney general, and other statewide executive offices, as well as state legislative seats—are selected in party primary elections in most states or by party conventions or caucuses in others.

SHOE LEATHER CAMPAIGNING
Door-to-door campaigning by candidates or party workers.

PARTY PROFESSIONALS
Those who participate in campaigns and party politics year-round, often to get jobs for themselves or their friends and to strengthen their party.

POLITICAL AMATEURS
Part-timers who participate in campaigns and party politics primarily during elections usually to support a specific candidate or cause.

"527" ORGANIZATION
An independent advocacy group that can spend an unlimited amount of money for or against a candidate.

■ *Parties continue to play an important role in voter choice.* It is true that political parties have lost much of their attractiveness to voters—a development described as **dealignment**. That is, fewer people identify themselves as "strong" Democrats or as "strong" Republicans; more people call themselves "independents," and more people split their votes between candidates of different parties, although this is less the case in highly competitive, evenly divided states. Party labels remain an important influence on voter choice. People who identify themselves as Democrats tend to vote for Democratic candidates, just as people who identify themselves as Republicans vote for Republican candidates. Nationwide the Democratic and Republican parties have inspired popular images of themselves (see Table 5–1). Both parties maintain fairly stable coalitions of supporters—called core voters or the party's "base." These national images and coalitions extend into the politics of most, but certainly not all, states. Party identifiers in some states are more conservative or more liberal than their counterparts in others. A Mississippi Democrat is typically more conservative than a Massachusetts Democrat!

DEALIGNMENT

A decline in party loyalty among voters and a rise in independent and split-ticket voting.

TABLE 5–I   Democratic and Republican Party Supporters Nationwide

	Supporters[a]	
	Republican (%)	**Democratic (%)**
Gender		
Male	29	29
Female	27	40
Race/Ethnicity		
White	34	28
Black	5	76
Hispanic	16	42
Ideology		
Conservative	51	18
Moderate	18	36
Liberal	5	64
Age Group		
18–29	23	36
30–49	27	32
50–64	29	36
65+	34	36
Education		
Less than high school	28	36
Some college	30	33
College graduate	29	32
Post graduate	25	39
Income		
Under $20,000	20	42
$20,000–$29,999	23	40
$30,000–$49,999	29	35
$50,000–$74,999	31	33
$75,000–$99,999	30	32
$100,000–$149,999	30	32
$150,000 and above	36	30

Note: Data are for 2012.
[a]Row percentages do not add up to 100% because independents are excluded from the table.
Source: Pew Research Center for the People and the Press, "Detailed Party Identification Tables," Table 1, 2012. Available at http://www.people-press.org/files/legacy-detailed_tables/Detailed%20tables%20for%20Party%20ID.pdf.

■ Party organizations and activists in the states play an important role in guiding their party and in shaping its image with the voters. **Party activists** are the people who serve on city, county, or state party committees, or who serve on the staffs of these committees. They regularly work in campaigns and serve on their state's delegation to the national party conventions. Many elected officials owe their start in politics to being involved in local party activities. Democratic and Republican state party organizations are found in every state. (Each national party's Web site typically has links to the individual state party organizations, and the state party Web site to local party organizations.) In some states these organizations are more powerful than in other states, but in all 50 states, party organizations are becoming increasingly efficient and more professional in their operations.

■ *The Democratic and Republican parties perform the central task of organizing state legislatures.* Only Nebraska has an official nonpartisan legislature. But in every other state, legislative leadership—for example, the house speaker and senate president—as well as committee chairs, are selected on a party basis. The majority party regularly votes for its own candidates for these posts. (See Chapter 6.)

5.2

PARTIES AND PRIMARIES

Compare the different ways in which political parties are involved in the process of selecting candidates for public office.

Party **primary elections** nominate most candidates for public office in America. For the nation's first century, candidates were nominated by party conventions, not primary elections, and as a result party organizations were far more influential than they are today. Primary elections were a key reform in the Progressive movement of the early twentieth century. Primaries "democratized" the nomination process and reduced the power of party bosses.

Filing

Primary elections are governed by state law; anyone can *file* a petition with a minimum number of voter signatures, or pay a small fee, to have his or her name placed on the primary ballot of either party for practically any public office. A candidate does *not* have to have experience in the party, or even the support of party officials, in order to file for elective office.

Endorsements

Primaries, then, reduce the influence of party organizations in the political process. It is possible, of course, for party organizations at the city, county, or state levels to *endorse,* officially or unofficially, candidates in primary elections. But party endorsements at the primary election stage may create intra-party friction so it is more common for party organizations to endorse at the general election stage. The importance of endorsements varies with the strength and unity of party organizations. Where party organizations are strong at the city or county level, the word can be passed down to precinct committee members to turn out the party's faithful for the endorsed candidate. Party endorsement in a statewide race appears to have less value.

Presidential primary elections play an integral part in the nomination process, which helps explain why so many states want to be "first."

Closed and Open Primaries

Primary elections in most states are **closed primaries**—that is, only voters who have *previously* registered as members of a party may vote in that party's primary. (See Table 5–2.) Only registered Democrats vote in the Democratic primary, and only registered Republicans vote in the Republican primary. **Semi-closed primaries** allow voters to change party registration on Election Day. Primaries in other states are **open primaries**. One type of open primary allows voters to choose when they enter the polling place which party's primary they wish to vote in. Another type of open primary, the top two primary, allows all voters, regardless of party, to vote in the same primary election. Every voter gets the same ballot and the two top vote-getters for each office, regardless of their party affiliation, face off against each other in the general election (Louisiana, Washington, and California). However, in Louisiana, if a candidate receives a majority of the primary vote, he or she wins the office outright. Not so in the other two states. At one time, Alaska, California, and Washington had **blanket primaries** in which voters could vote in *both* party primaries simultaneously—voting for one party's candidate for one office, and for another party's candidate for another office. But the U.S. Supreme Court ruled blanket primaries unconstitutional in 2000,[5] which thrilled leaders in both parties who did not like them because they allowed "outsiders" to influence the nomination of their party's candidate.

In 2010 California voters approved the **voter-nominated "top two" primary** whereby the top two vote-getters in primary races for congressional, state legislative, and statewide offices (but not the presidency) run against each other in the general election. Californians, fed up with the state's squabbling politicians and a growing budget deficit, approved Proposition 14 by a 54 to 46 percent vote. (For a more detailed look at the arguments for and against this new top two primary system, see "*Did You Know?* California's "Top Two" Primary System: Bipartisanship Promise Appeals to Other States.")

Party leaders generally prefer the closed primary because they fear **crossover voting** and raiding. Crossovers are voters who choose to vote in the primary of the party that they usually do not support in the general election. **Raiding** is an organized attempt to cross over and vote in order to defeat an attractive candidate running for the opposition party's nomination. However, there is no evidence that large numbers of voters connive in such a fashion.

Runoff Primaries

(The following discussion is not relevant to the three states where voters, not the parties, nominate candidates to run in the general election.) In most states, the **plurality winner** of the party's primary election—the candidate receiving the most votes, whether a majority or not—becomes the party's nominee. But in some states, a candidate must win a **majority** of votes in a primary election to become the party's nominee. If no candidate succeeds in winning a majority in the first primary, a **runoff primary** is held between the top two vote-getters.

Runoff primaries are linked to the traditional one-party politics of the southern states. Runoff primaries prevent a candidate with a minority of party voters from capturing the nomination in a race with three or more contenders. Presumably the runoff primary encourages candidates to seek majority support and prevents extremist candidates from winning nominations. No one can win a nomination by relying on splits among multiple opponents.

First primary front-runners have a better-than-even chance of winning the runoff. Overall, front-runners win about two-thirds of runoff primaries for state legislative seats, although they win only slightly more than half of the runoffs for governor and U.S. senator.[6]

Runoff primaries have been attacked as racially discriminatory. In districts where there is a large but less than majority black population and a history of racial bloc voting, black candidates who win a plurality of votes in the first primary may be defeated in the runoff if white voters unite behind the white runner-up. (It is possible, of course, for the reverse to occur in a majority black district.) One study of local runoff primaries in Georgia found

CLOSED PRIMARIES
Primary elections in which voters must declare (or have previously declared) their party affiliation and can cast a ballot only in their own party's primary election.

SEMI-CLOSED PRIMARIES
Primary elections in which voters must declare (or have previously declared) their party affiliation and can cast a ballot only in their own party's primary election; voters can change party registration on primary Election Day.

OPEN PRIMARIES
Primary elections in which a voter may cast a ballot in either party's primary election.

BLANKET PRIMARY
An open primary in which candidates from both parties appear on the same ballot.

VOTER-NOMINATED "TOP TWO" PRIMARY
The top two vote-getters in primary races for congressional, state legislative, and statewide offices (but not the presidency), regardless of their party affiliation run against each other in the general election.

CROSSOVER VOTING
Voters affiliated with one party casting votes in the other party's primary election.

RAIDING
An organized attempt to cross over and vote in another party's primary in order to defeat an attractive candidate who might beat your own party's candidate in the general election.

PLURALITY WINNER
The candidate receiving the most votes, whether a majority or not.

MAJORITY WINNER
The candidate receiving 50 percent plus one of the vote.

RUNOFF PRIMARY
An additional primary held between the top two vote-getters in a primary where no candidate has received a majority of the vote.

TABLE 5–2 Primary Elections in the States

Type of Primary					Second Primary
First Primary					
Closed: Proper party registration required	**Semi-closed: Voters may register or change party on Election Day**	**Open: Voter decides in which primary to vote in voting booth**	**Open: All voters; ballot lists all candidates; top two vote-getters advance to general election**	**Blanket**	**Runoff Primary**
Colorado	Alaska (Rep)	Alabama	California	Formerly used in Alaska, California, and Washington	Alabama
Connecticut	Arizona	Alaska (Dem)	Louisiana[a]	Declared unconstitutional by courts	Arkansas
Delaware	Idaho (Dem)	Arkansas	Washington		Georgia
Florida	Illinois	Georgia			Mississippi
Hawaii (Rep)	Massachusetts	Hawaii (Dem)			North Carolina
Idaho (Rep)	Nebraska	Indiana			Oklahoma
Iowa	New Hampshire	Kansas (Dem)			South Carolina
Kansas (Rep)	North Carolina[b]	Michigan			South Dakota
Kentucky	Ohio	Minnesota			Texas
Maine	Rhode Island	Mississippi			
Maryland	Washington (Dem)	Missouri			
Nevada	West Virginia	Montana			
New Jersey		North Dakota (Dem)			
New York		South Carolina			
North Dakota (Rep)		South Dakota (Dem)			
Oklahoma		Tennessee			
Oregon		Texas			
Pennsylvania		Utah (Dem)			
South Dakota (Rep)		Vermont			
Utah (Rep)		Virginia			
Washington (Rep)		Wisconsin			
Wyoming					

Note: Data from April 2012; Some states have different types of primaries for different political parties.

[a]Louisiana has semi-closed primaries for congressional elections, but state/local elections are voter-nominated "top two" vote-getters primaries. The presidential election is a closed primary. If a candidate receives more than 50% of the vote in a voter-nominated "top two" primary in Louisiana, that candidate is elected to office.

[b]Unaffiliated voters, by state statute and permission of a party, may vote in a party primary. Currently, both the Democratic and Republican parties allow this.

Source: *Book of the States,* 2012, Volume 44, Table 6.4, pp. 336–339. Printed with permission from the Council of State Governments.

that black plurality winners in the first primary were somewhat less likely to win a runoff against a white runner-up (50% black runoff victories) than white plurality winners against a black runner-up (84% white runoff victories).[7] However, more extensive and recent studies have concluded that runoff elections do not have the racially discriminatory impact that they were once perceived to have.[8] Race aside, because turnout in runoff primaries is often quite low while the costs remain high, some states, such as Florida, have eliminated them.

Did YOU KNOW?

California's "Top Two" Primary System: Bipartisanship Promise Appeals to Other States

In a change that is likely to have a far-reaching effect upon the state's political parties, California voters approved a state constitutional amendment in 2010, known as Proposition 14, the Top Two Primaries Act. From now on, California primary elections will be open to all candidates and all voters, regardless of party affiliation. All candidates for major state and federal offices, including the U.S. Senate and House of Representatives, governor, and state legislature, will appear on the same primary ballot. Candidates may or may not choose to have a party affiliation next to their name on the ballot. The two candidates receiving the most votes in the primary will appear on the November general election ballot, regardless of their party affiliation, if any.

This "top two" primary system strips the parties of their central function: selecting candidates for the general election. Supporters believe that it is a cure for "partisanship," and that it reduces the power of the most loyal, interested, and active party members in the selection of candidates. No longer will Democratic candidates be obliged to espouse "liberal" positions to attract the votes of ideologically motivated activists in the Democratic primary, and then shift their positions to the center for the general

election. Similarly, Republican candidates will no longer have to take "conservative" positions in the party's primary, only to shift to the center in the general election. All candidates will be encouraged to become "centrists" to appeal to all voters in both the primary and general elections.

The Top Two Primaries Act was placed on the ballot by a Democratic-controlled state legislature, it was supported by Republican governor Arnold Schwarzenegger; and it was approved by a vote of 54 to 46 percent. The proposition does not apply to presidential elections. Third parties, such as the Green Party and the Libertarian Party, will not be able to access the general election ballot, unless their candidate wins one of the top two spots in the open primary.

The top two proposition was born out of frustration over partisan gridlock in the state capital, especially party deadlocks over the state budget. A two-thirds majority in both the state House and Senate are required to raise taxes or to pass a budget. (See Chapter 14, "Up Close: The Decline of the Golden State.")

Opponents argued, unsuccessfully, that Proposition 14 only "masquerades as reform," that it reinforces incumbent advantage, and that it squeezes out third parties. It limits voter choice by minimizing policy differences between candidates so that personality trumps substance. Louisiana and Washington have experimented with similar primary systems, but few believe that these two states were successful in electing more moderates to office. (Washington adopted it in 2004; Louisiana discontinued it in 2008 but reinstated it in 2012.) The top two system may increase overall costs of running for office by requiring candidates to spend money to appeal to the full electorate in two separate elections.

The question of whether other states will follow California's decision came up in 2012. Voters in Arizona soundly rejected a proposal to move to a top two open primary in 2012. Proposition 121 was defeated by a 67 to 33 percent vote. But Arizona is a more conservative one-party-dominated state than California.

Who do you think is right? Will other states follow California's lead?

Conventions

State conventions continue in a handful of states. In New York and Connecticut, statewide **party conventions** nominate candidates; however, candidates can "challenge" the convention nominee to a primary election if the challenger receives a specified share of the convention vote (25% in New York, 20% in Connecticut).

Statewide party organizations seldom have much influence over primary outcomes. State party chairs and state party committee members generally don't like to publicly "take sides," often seeing it as equivalent to having to pick which of your offspring you love the most. Plus by avoiding endorsements during the primary stage of an election, it makes it easier to mount a united front behind the party's nominee in the general election.

Presidential Primaries and Caucuses

Every four years, state parties play a major role in nominating the party's candidate for president. In most states, each party holds a **presidential primary election**, usually, but not always, on the same day. But in some states, like Iowa, parties may use caucuses to select the presidential candidate they would like to see officially nominated at the national party convention. A **party caucus** is a meeting of voters at some officially designated location for the purpose of choosing who they prefer to be their party's standard-bearer in the race for president.

Beginning with the 2008 presidential election cycle and continuing to 2012, a number of states began moving up the date of their primaries (front-loading)—even defying national party calendar rules—to have more influence over the selection of the nominee. Florida and Michigan, two large diverse highly urbanized states, defied party-adopted calendars in both years and held their primaries ahead of the schedule agreed upon by both the Republican National Committee and the Democratic National Committee. These maverick states argued that beginning the presidential nomination process in two small, rural states (Iowa, New Hampshire) would yield a party nominee that would have trouble winning the more diverse battleground states with lots of Electoral College votes.

Every four years, the "calendar debate" between national party leaders and state party officials is revived. Each state's party leaders want their voters to have a major influence on who their party will nominate for president, which is precisely what prompts front-loading. The battle over the 2016 presidential primary calendar began in March 2013, when Nevada and Arizona launched moves designed to challenge Iowa and New Hampshire's status as the nation's first caucus and primary of the presidential cycle.

5.3 STATE PARTY ORGANIZATIONS AND ACTIVISTS

State **party organizations** are "highly variable, elusive to find, difficult to define, and frustrating to study."[9] Indeed, both Democratic and Republican party organizations at the state and local levels are ill defined, fluid, and often "unoccupied," particularly right after an election. It is more difficult to get people to engage in party activities between elections than in the heat of a "campaign season." Then it is fairly easy to fill party posts, especially in a highly competitive, two-party state.

Nonetheless, a small core of Democratic and Republican Party activists willing to be involved year-round can be found in every state. They occupy positions on city, county, and state Democratic and Republican committees, and in the county and state conventions of their party. They represent their party on the national party committees and in the national party presidential nominating conventions. At the lowest level, they continue to keep in contact with neighbors, urging residents to register and vote, handing out party literature, maintaining party Web sites, inviting newcomers to get involved, and perhaps even trying to do small favors for their loyal voters.

Activists as Ideologues

While parties may be pushed toward the ideological center in order to win elections, the activists in the parties tend to be strong **ideologues**—people who take consistently "liberal" or "conservative" positions on the issues. Republican Party activists tend to be more conservative than the general public, and Democratic Party activists tend to be more liberal than the general public. This is true even though activists in both parties tend to be more conservative in a conservative state and more liberal in a liberal state.[10]

In the southern and border states, as the Republican Party has grown in strength, Democratic and Republican Party activists have clearly separated themselves along ideological lines. Today, there are fewer conservatives among Democratic Party activists in the South than in previous eras. As conservatives drift toward the Republican Party, the liberal strength within the Democratic Party increases. Blacks have assumed increasingly active and influential roles in southern Democratic Party organizations, while fundamentalist white Protestants have become an increasingly active force in Republican circles.[11] The result is greater ideological cleavage between the parties.

IDEOLOGUE

A person who consistently takes a liberal or conservative stance on issues.

Activists as Potential Candidates

Party activists—people who serve in party posts as committee members or chairpersons at the city, county, or state level, or as delegates to party conventions—constitute a recruitment pool for candidates for public office. Often these people initially volunteered for party work with the expectation of eventually running for public office. Their party activity provides technical knowledge as well as personal contacts that become useful in their own future campaigns. Party workers generally have voter registration lists available to them as well as information regarding ballot access, filing dates, campaign expenditure reporting, and other useful information. And, of course, party workers come into personal contact with key campaign contributors.

State Party Organizations

American political parties are decentralized in their organization. Power flows from the bottom up, not the top down. (See Figure 5–1.) It is not really surprising in the American system of federalism—when only the president and vice-president have *national* constituencies, and senators, representatives, governors, state legislators, and county and city officials all have *state and local* constituencies—that the American parties are decentralized.

At the national level, the Democratic and Republican parties consist of a national committee; a House and Senate party conference; and various national clubs, such as Young Democrats and Young Republicans. There are also *50 state parties,* which are composed of state committees and county and city organizations. This structure is tied together loosely. **State committees** are generally involved in important statewide elections—governors, U.S. senators, and representatives in the smaller states. City and **county committees** are generally responsible for county and municipal offices, state legislative seats, and congressional seats in the larger states. The Democratic and Republican National Committees exist primarily for the purpose of holding national conventions every four years to select the party's presidential candidate. Since each level of party organization has "its own fish to fry," each operates quite independently of the other levels.

STATE COMMITTEES

Governing bodies of state party organizations.

COUNTY COMMITTEES

Governing bodies of county party organizations.

State Laws Govern Parties

Party affairs are governed largely by the laws of the states. Each state sets forth the conditions that an organization must meet to qualify as a political party and to get its candidates' names printed on the official election ballots. Each state sets the qualifications for membership in a party and the right to vote in the party's primary election. State laws determine the number, method of selection, and duties of various party officials, committees, and conventions. The states, rather than the parties, decide how the parties shall

FIGURE 5–1 Political Parties Are Built from the Bottom Up

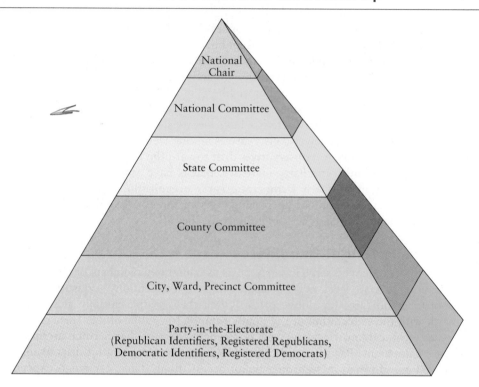

National Chair

National Committee

State Committee

County Committee

City, Ward, Precinct Committee

Party-in-the-Electorate
(Republican Identifiers, Registered Republicans,
Democratic Identifiers, Registered Democrats)

nominate candidates for public office. Most states require that party nominations be made by direct primaries, but several states still nominate by party caucuses or conventions. Most states also attempt to regulate party finances, although with little success.

State Committees

State party organizations officially consist of a "state committee," a "state chairman," or "chairwoman," and perhaps a state executive director and an office staff working at the state capital. Democratic and Republican state committees vary from state to state in composition, organization, and function. Membership on the state committee may range from about a dozen up to several hundred. The members may be chosen through party primaries or by state party conventions. Generally, representation on state committees is allocated to counties, but occasionally other units of government are recognized in state party organization. A state party chairman or chairwoman generally serves at the head of the state committee; these people are generally selected by the state committee, but their selection is often dictated by the party's candidate for governor.

In recent years state party organizations have strengthened themselves, despite the rise of candidate-centered politics. They have become "service agencies"[12] providing an array of technical services to their candidates—telephone polling facilities, Web site designs, lists of potential contributors, direct mail and telemarketing systems, links to media outlets throughout the state (with reporters' names and phone numbers listed), access to campaign and media consultants, Spanish-language training, advice on election law compliance and campaign finance reporting, research (including "oppo research" on the weaknesses of opponents), and even seminars on campaign techniques. Virtually all state parties now have permanent headquarters in the state capital. Most state parties today have full-time professional staff in addition to part-time help and volunteers. They are geared up to hold press conferences and issue press releases on a moment's notice, often in response to some activity or pronouncement by the opposition party.

Yet, state party organizations are only a part of the broader network that includes candidate organizations, interest groups regularly aligned with the party (unions and teacher organizations are especially important to Democrats), professional political campaign consultants, and professional fund-raisers.

It is difficult to assess whether or to what extent the strength of state party organizations contributes to electoral success in a state. So many other factors affect electoral success that it is difficult to estimate the *independent* effect, if any, of party organizational strength. But it is widely believed among party activists that sophisticated organizations improve prospects of victory for the party's candidates.

State Party Chairpersons

State party chairpersons are by no means political hacks. Most state chairpersons have been successful business people, lawyers, or public officials who may even serve their posts without salaries to satisfy their interest in politics and public affairs. Some come up through the ranks of local party organizations and have never held elective office; others started in elective politics. While in that position, they routinely interact with local party leaders who then become their supporters when they seek the state party chair position. (See *People in Politics:* State Party Chairs—Two Paths to Leadership.)

State party chairpersons can play different roles from state to state. Some see themselves as mere "political agents" of their governor; others are independently powerful. In general, chairpersons of the party out of power have more independence and power than those of the party in power. The latter are overshadowed by their governor. Party chairpersons do not hold on to their jobs very long—the average is less than three years.[13]

County Committees

Party organizations at the county level can be found almost everywhere. The organizations include:

- An active chairperson and executive committee, plus a few associated activists, who in effect make most of the decisions in the name of the party, who raise funds, who occasionally seek out candidates to fill out the party's slate in the general election (or approve the candidates who select themselves), and who speak locally for the party.
- A ward and precinct organization in which only a few local committee members are active and in which there is little door-to-door canvassing or other direct voter contact.
- The active participation in organizational matters of some of the party's elected public officials, who may share effective control of the organization with the official leadership of the party organization.
- Financial contributors to the party and its candidates, together with leaders of local interest groups that generally ally themselves with the party.

Republican and Democratic county chairpersons probably constitute the most important building blocks of party organization in America. City and county party officers and committees are chosen locally and cannot be removed by any higher party authority. In short, authority is not concentrated in any single statewide organization but is divided among many city and county party organizations.

Party volunteers operate phone banks, which often survey party members about what issues they regard as the most important for candidates to address. These grass-roots volunteers are also critical to Get-Out-The-Vote (GOTV) efforts—reminding voters to go to the polls or to vote absentee and even offering rides to the polls.

H ow does one become the head of a state's political party? One way is holding public office, and another is rising through the ranks.

Holding Public Office. **Jim Brulte** worked as a state legislator for 14 years before becoming state chair of the California Republican Party in March 2013. He started in politics in his college days, working for U.S. Senator S.I. Hayakawa. Early jobs with the Republican National Committee, in the Defense Department, and as White House advance man for Vice President George Bush furthered his political and government experience. He was elected to the California State Assembly, serving from 1990 to 1996. Term limits prevented his running again, so he ran for the California State Senate. He served from 1996 to 2004 and again came up against the term limits barrier. But he had made his mark, focusing on education, regulatory reform, reduction of crime, and measures to improve the state's business climate. During his last four years in office, he was Senate Republican leader and at one time was considered

the most powerful elected Republican in the state. To keep his hand in policymaking, he joined California Strategies, a public affairs consulting firm. In 2012, fellow Republicans, discouraged by the outcome of state elections, urged him to run for state party chair, which he won easily.

Rising through the Ranks. **Allison Tant** became state chair of the Florida Democratic Party in January 2013, defeating another long-time party activist for the top job. Key factors in her selection were her impressive organizing and fund-raising abilities. In 2012, she led statewide efforts for Barack Obama's reelection, chairing a local finance council that raised $330,000 for his Florida campaign. Four years earlier, in Obama's initial run for the presidency, she organized Tallahassee Women for Obama, building grassroots support in Northwest Florida. Her fund-raising activities extended to Democratic candidates running for Congress, the Legislature, and local office. She also took part in party strategy and management, chairing the Leon County Democratic Executive Committee, serving on the National Democratic Rules Committee, and assisting with efforts to improve research and messaging guidance to candidates. Her organizational skills reflected years of advocacy on behalf of children with disabilities. Among other accomplishments, she helped change the state's assessment of disabilities, worked to enhance therapy services, and established a scholarship program for educational opportunities beyond high school.

Local Party Organizations

Few local organizations have a full-time staff, or a permanent headquarters, or even a telephone listing,[14] but they usually have a Web site. (Many local parties get young party activists to design these.) Most rely on volunteers—precinct and county committee members—who seldom meet in nonelection years. Few local organizations have any budget. Most engage in election year efforts at distributing campaign literature, organizing campaign events, putting up posters and lawn signs, conducting registration drives, and even some door-to-door canvassing. The role of local party organizations is mostly supplementary to that of the candidates' own organizations.

However, when it comes to statewide races (gubernatorial, U.S. Senate, presidential contests), local party organizations are often seen as a vital part of state party-driven GOTV efforts. Thousands of volunteers are needed to chair precinct committees, call potential supporters urging them to vote, and wave signs and give last-minute pitches for their party's candidates at every polling place.

REPUBLICAN AND DEMOCRATIC PARTY FORTUNES IN THE STATES

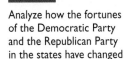

Analyze how the fortunes of the Democratic Party and the Republican Party in the states have changed over time.

Throughout history, Democratic and Republican Party fortunes have swung back and forth. National public opinion polls show that for many years, a far greater percentage of Americans identified themselves as Democrats than Republicans. Republicans began closing the gap in the 1990s, especially in the southern states, which at one time were solidly Democratic. The trend toward a more competitive party system across the states has continued. From 2008 to 2012 alone, the number of solidly Democratic states (as measured by voter self-identification) declined from 30 to 14, while the number of solidly Republican states increased from 4 to 9. (Solid states are defined as those in which one party has at least a 10-percentage point advantage over the other in party affiliation.)[15]

Changing Party Fortunes in Gubernatorial Races

The Republican Party enjoyed its greatest resurgence in nearly half a century in congressional and state politics in 1994. In that year Republicans captured control of the U.S. House of Representatives for the first time since 1954. At the state level, the GOP gained a majority of governorships for the first time in over three decades (see Figure 5–2). Following the 2004

FIGURE 5–2 Party Control of Governorships

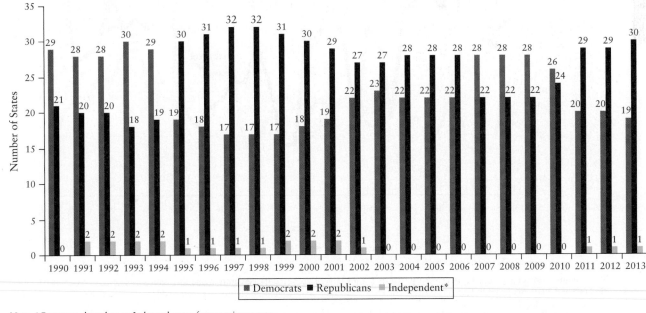

Note: *Governor elected as an Independent or from a minor party.
Source: Based on United States Census Bureau Elections: Gubernatorial and State Legislatures Accessed at http://www.census.gov/compendia/statab/cats/elections/gubernatorial_and_state_legislatures.html

elections, Republicans occupied governor's chairs in 28 states, including four of the nation's five largest states—California, New York, Texas, and Florida. But by 2006, the pendulum had swung back to the Democrats. Expectations were that it would swing back to the Republicans in 2010 and it did. An anti-incumbent, anti-Washington wave that year swept many Republican governors into office, including a number of Republican women governors.

Changing Party Fortunes in State Legislatures

The Democratic Party long enjoyed dominance over state legislatures. In the mid-1970s, the Democratic Party controlled over 30 state legislatures, while the Republican Party controlled only 4. The others were split between the two parties. But the Republican Party's fortunes in state legislatures improved significantly in the 1990s (see Figure 5–3). Following the 2004 state legislature elections, Republicans controlled 21 legislatures, Democrats 17, with 11 split between the parties. But, as with governors, control shifted back to Democrats in 2006, with expectations that it might swing back toward the GOP in the early 2010s, which it did. Some Democratic Party leaders attribute this shift to Republican-controlled redistricting processes following the 2010 Census and a rise in the number of safe seats making it harder for Democrats to close the gap. (The

FIGURE 5–3 Democratic and Republican Control of State Legislatures

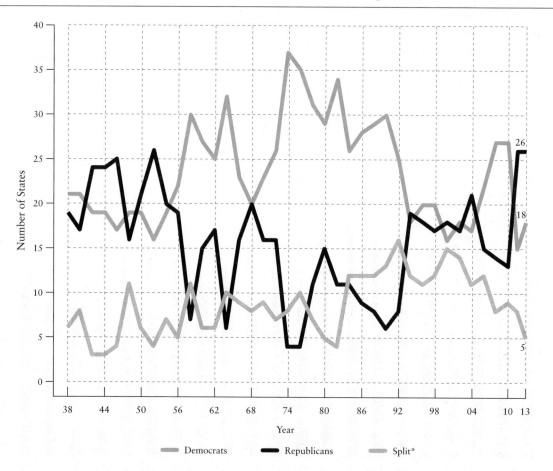

Note: Numbers do not add to 50 because Nebraska has a unicameral legislature and its legislators are nonpartisan.

*In 2008 and 2010, Alaska and Montana had ties between a Democratic- and Republican-controlled Senate and House, respectively. They are considered to have split legislatures.

Source: National Conference of State Legislatures, "Statevote 2012 Election Night Results Map," 2012, available at http://www.ncsl.org/legislatures-elections/elections/statevote-2012-election-night-results-map.aspx. © 2012 National Conference of State Legislatures.

redistricting process will be discussed in more detail in Chapter 6.) Regardless of the reason, Republican state party leaders know the pendulum can easily swing the other way. Politics is volatile, especially in states with large blocs of independents who tend to be swing voters.

Party Switchers: Genuine Conversion or Political Opportunism?

Occasionally, elected officials change their political party affiliation. They are usually welcomed with open arms by leaders of their new party at highly publicized press conferences. But when such events happen, the public tends to be skeptical, wondering whether the "switcher" truly had a change of heart or had simply read polls showing growing disfavor with the abandoned party. In 2010, Pennsylvania's Democratic primary voters defeated Senator Arlen Specter who publicly admitted to abandoning the Republican Party "so I can win." Alabama's Representative Parker Griffith, who switched from Democrat to Republican, met the same fate in the GOP primary. Occasionally, high-profile leaders abandon political parties altogether and run as independents, as did Senator Joseph Lieberman from Connecticut who left the Democratic Party and Rhode Island governor Lincoln Chafee who left the Republican Party, Voters seem a bit more amenable to that type of decision.

DIVIDED PARTY GOVERNMENT IN THE STATES

Overall, the frequency of **divided party government** (where the executive branch is controlled by one party, and one or both houses of the legislative branch are controlled by the other party) rose in the American states in the 1980s. Since 1984 more than half of the states have had divided government; the high was 31 states after both the 1988 and 1996 elections. But that trend has tapered off in recent years to the point where one party controls both the legislature and the governorship in all but a dozen states.[16]

Unified Party Government

A **unified party government**—where the same party controls both houses of the legislature as well as the governorship—is often *presumed* to be better able to enact its program into law. More important, perhaps, voters are better able to attribute praise or blame for the direction of state government. Under a unified party government, the dominant party cannot escape responsibility for poor performance by blaming it on the opponent party's control of one house or branch of state government.[17] When that does occur, it is usually because of *intraparty* squabbles. The greater the control one party has, the more likely it is that factions will emerge within that party's elected officials, usually along ideological or geographical lines or both.

Does Divided Government Mean "Gridlock"?

Legislative gridlock—the failure to enact significant pieces of legislation—is often attributed to divided party government. Studies of state legislatures have shown that the overall output of a legislature (the number of bills passed) is *not* affected by divided party government. However, it has been shown that divided party government makes the passage of *controversial* legislation more difficult. When a governor faces a legislature with one or more houses controlled by the opposite party, it becomes more difficult to pass legislation in areas where there are high levels of conflict, often welfare, crime, education, moral issues, and the environment. (See "Divided Government: Governor versus the Legislature" in Chapter 7.) Legislative gridlock under divided government is worse in states with strong interest group systems. Yet in less controversial areas of legislation, such as agriculture, economic development, and transportation, divided party government does not appear to impede the passage of legislation.[18]

DIVIDED PARTY GOVERNMENT

In state politics, where the governorship is controlled by one party and one or both houses of the legislature is controlled by the other party.

UNIFIED PARTY GOVERNMENT

In state politics, where the governorship and both houses of the state legislature are controlled by the same party.

LEGISLATIVE GRIDLOCK

The failure to win gubernatorial and legislative support to enact significant legislation.

5.6

Analyze how party competition influences the operation of political parties within the states.

PARTY COMPETITION AND POLICY DIFFERENCES WITHIN THE STATES

Party competition within the 50 states is uneven and dynamic. A state's competitiveness may change as the composition of its population shifts. But just exactly how competitive are the political parties in each of the 50 states? The answer to the question differs according to how one is measuring competition. One way of measuring party competitiveness is to track how often there is a change in the party affiliation of the winning candidate (*party turnover*) for top-of-the-ticket offices—president, governor, U.S. senator, or other statewide executive officials—or how wide is the winning candidate's *margin of victory*. Another is to count how often the governor is from one political party at the same time both houses of the state legislatures are controlled by the other party (*divided control*). Comparing the *percentage of voters who register with (or identify with) each party* is also a means of determining competitiveness—the more equal the percentages, the more competitive the party system is assumed to be.

Party leaders, campaign strategists, and political analysts use each of these measures to gauge the odds they will face in any campaign. Relying on just one could be deceiving and shortsighted. For example, Florida is not competitive if one merely uses the divided control measure but it is competitive if one uses margin of victory, party registration/identification parity measures, or electoral histories (Figure 5–4 groups states by margin of victory over the past three presidential elections). The perceived level of competition affects a party's ability to recruit candidates (particularly for down ballot races), raise money (both inside and outside the state), and engage volunteers. It also

FIGURE 5–4 "Color-Coded" State Party Competitiveness in National Elections

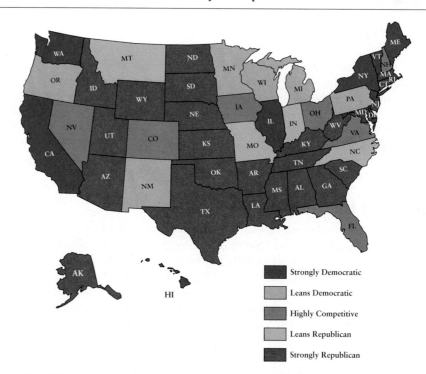

Strongly Democratic
Leans Democratic
Highly Competitive
Leans Republican
Strongly Republican

Note: Color code applies to presidential elections.
Source: Alan I., Abramowitz, Larry J. Sabato's crystal ball senior columnist. "The Electoral College: Democrats' Friend?" August 25, 2011. Available at http://www.centerforpolitics.org/crystalball/articles/aia2011082502.

affects how often a presidential candidate may visit a state in a highly competitive presidential election year.

Republican Party strength is greatest in states in the South and Mountain West, while Democratic Party strength is strongest in states in the Northeast, Rust Belt, and Pacific Coast. (See Figure 5–5.) However, states change as their demographic makeup shifts. For example, some states in the Mountain West have become more Democratic following an influx of Californians. Generally, however, party competition in many states is stronger today than at any time in recent history due to changes in their population mix. At the same time, the public's overall trust in the two major parties is lower, driven in large part by their exasperation with partisan gridlock at the national level, specifically by Congress' inability to resolve the nation's economic problems. As previously noted, fewer voters now identify with either party and choose instead to call themselves independents. That means that those who still strongly identify with the Republican or Democratic parties are more ideologically driven and more staunchly partisan.

Parties' Policy Differences

Party competition is most likely to produce policy differences if there is a bimodal distribution of voters' preferences in a state; and if the parties have strong organization and ideologically motivated activists, then the parties in that state will offer clear policy alternatives. This notion can be diagrammed as follows: where there is a **bimodal distribution of opinion** (voters divide into liberals and conservatives), the parties are more likely to take different policy positions. (Think of it as a camel with two humps and know that the farther apart they are, the more difficult it is to come together to work out a compromise

BIMODAL DISTRIBUTION OF OPINION

This occurs when most voters are clearly divided in their ideologies and policy preferences, thereby causing the parties to take divergent policy positions.

FIGURE 5–5 2012 Presidential Election Results Show Regional Party Strength Patterns

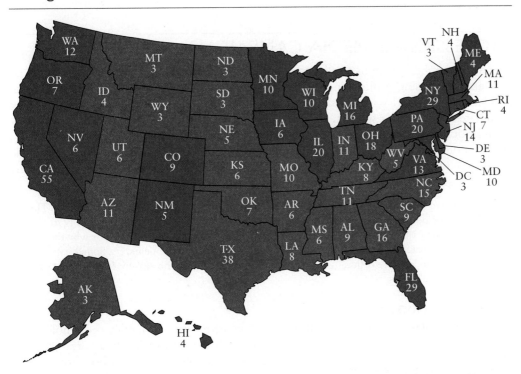

Source: RealClearPolitics, 2012. Available at http://www.realclearpolitics.com/epolls/2012/president/obama_vs_romney_final_results_map.html.

FIGURE 5–6 Bimodal Distribution of Opinion

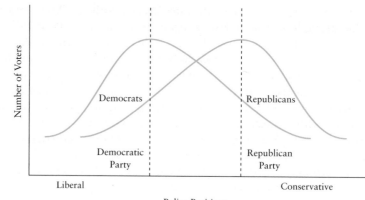

In states where voters are more divided along ideological lines (a bimodal distribution of opinion), the two major political parties are more likely to take different policy positions, making it more difficult to work out compromises on critical issues.

on tough issues.[19]) (See Figure 5–6.) In contrast, where there is a **unimodal distribution of opinion** (voters are less divided ideologically), the parties differ less in their policy positions.

Party conflict over policy questions is most frequent in those states in which the Democratic Party represents central-city, low-income, ethnic, and racial constituencies, and the Republican Party represents middle-class, suburban, small-town, and rural constituencies. In these states, the Democratic and Republican parties will tend to disagree over taxation and appropriations, welfare, education, moral values, and regulation of business and labor—that is, the major social and economic controversies that divide the national parties.[20] These schisms make it easier for professional campaign consultants to target a party's key, core constituents.

5.7

Describe the professionals who are involved with state and local political campaigns, and outline how they use the tools of their trade.

PROFESSIONAL MEDIA CAMPAIGNS

Professional public relations specialists, pollsters and focus group gurus, creative webmasters, and advertising geniuses now play a bigger role in the design and management of political campaigns than they used to before the professionalization of campaigns.[21] Few candidates for governor, senator, or any other statewide office rely exclusively on the party organization to handle their campaigns. Most create their own campaign organizations, and then turn to the whole new "image industry" to manage their mass media campaigns, which often seem to be nonstop. Political campaign communication experts describe the pervasiveness of campaigns in today's media-dominated world:

> Whether we like it or not . . . we can scarcely avoid taking part in the campaign process. Those who choose not to participate directly become involved at some level even if it is only to explain to friends why they are refusing to respond to a candidate's telephone survey, or why they are turning off the television to avoid political programs and advertisements. . . . Somebody is always seeking elective office. . . . The modern campaign knows no season. It seems that as one ends, another begins.[22]

Public Relations Firms

Some public relations firms are all-purpose organizations that plan the whole campaign; select a theme; monitor the electorate with continuous polling; produce television and online commercials, newspaper advertisements, and radio spots; select clothing and hairstyles for their candidates; write speeches and schedule appearances (or avoid them if the candidates cannot speak well); and even plan the victory party.

Other organizations limit themselves to particular functions, such as polling or television production. Some firms specialize by party, handling only Democratic or Republican candidates; a few firms specialize by ideology, handling liberal or conservative clients. Still other firms are strictly professional, providing services to any candidate who can afford them.

Polling

Frequently, **polling** is at the center of strategic campaign decision-making. At the beginning of the campaign, polls test the "recognition factor" of the candidate and assess which political issues are uppermost in the minds of voters. Special polling techniques can determine what a "winning candidate profile" looks like in a district. The results of these polls will be used to determine a general strategy—developing a favorable "image" for the candidate and focusing on a popular campaign "theme." Early polls can also detect weaknesses in the candidate, which can then be overcome in advertising (too rich—then show her in blue jeans reading to young children in a poor neighborhood; too intellectual—then show him in a hog-calling contest). Polls can tell whether the party is stronger than the candidate (then identify the candidate as loyal to the party) or whether the candidate is stronger than the party (then stress the candidate's independent thinking).

During the campaign polls can chart the progress of the candidate and even assess the effectiveness of specific themes and "media events." A "**media event**" is an activity generated to attract news coverage, for example, walking the entire length of the state to show "closeness to the people," or carrying around a broom to symbolize "house cleaning," or spending occasional days doing manual work in a factory or on a farm. Finally, polls can identify the undecided vote toward the end of the campaign and help direct the time and resources of the candidate.

Polling can be highly political and quite unrepresentative of the voting public. Some campaigns intentionally release polls that do not meet professional standards established by groups like the American Association of Public Opinion Research. Why do they do this? First, because they know that polls will almost always get media attention. Second, they know that few voters really understand how to read or interpret polls and, consequently, will not question the results. To counter the spread of badly biased polling, there are now guides on how to read and interpret polls available to both journalists and citizens. (See *Did You Know?* How to Read Political Polls Like a Pro.)

Name Recognition

The first objective is to increase the candidate's **name recognition** among the voters. Years ago, name recognition could be achieved only through years of service in minor public or party offices (or having a well-known family name). Today, expert media advisors (and lots of money) can create instant celebrity. "Exposure" is the name of the game, and exposure requires attracting the attention of the news media. (As one commentator observed: "To a politician there is no such thing as indecent exposure. Obscurity is a dirty word and almost all exposure is decidedly decent.") A millionaire land developer (former governor and later U.S. senator Bob Graham of Florida) attracted attention by simply working a few days as a ditch digger, busboy, and bulldozer operator to identify with the "common people" and received a great deal of news coverage.

Campaign Themes

The emphasis of the professional public relations campaign is on simplicity: a few themes, brief speeches, uncluttered ads, quick and catchy spot commercials. Finding the right theme or slogan is essential; this effort is not greatly different from that of launching an advertising campaign for a new detergent. A campaign theme should not be controversial. It might be as simple as "A leader you can trust"; the candidate would then be "packaged"

POLLING
Questioning a representative sample of the population (or of likely voters) to determine public opinion about candidates and issues.

MEDIA EVENT
An activity designed to attract news coverage of a candidate (free media).

NAME RECOGNITION
The likelihood that people recognize a candidate's name when questioned in opinion polls.

How to Read Political Polls Like a Pro

What to Do	Reason
■ Be careful of polls taken more than six weeks before an election	Most voters make up their minds about who they will vote for shortly before Election Day—Polls taken too early detect off-the-cuff responses that are often not accurate. [In many states, there are multiple "Election Days" due to early voting.]
■ Expand margin of error by half or more	Polls are purported to be a snapshot in time. But polls are based on many assumptions that make the analogy of a snapshot faulty. Polls are estimates.
■ Look at the source	Do the people paying for the poll have an interest in a certain result? A candidate's internal poll can be particularly dangerous. Use reputable polls for reputable data.
■ Be careful of polls that don't use a random sample	Internet polls are a common unscientific poll. Unless a poll is scientific and each person has an equal chance of being selected, it does not necessarily give a true glimpse of public opinion.
■ Look at question wording	Even subtle differences in the wording of a question can change the outcome of the poll. Make sure that there is no the use of loaded words.
■ Be careful of comparison among subgroups	A poll's margin of error is for the entire sample. Any subgroup comparison is less accurate. The smaller the size of the sample, the less accurate the information will be.
■ Look for the missing facts	There are 12 pieces of information you should be able to find:

- Whether the poll was scientific (respondents chosen randomly).
- Margins of sampling error for each group [even small groups] whose opinion is estimated.
- The number polled; if less than 600, it probably isn't worth reading and will be unreliable because of a large margin of error.
- Who was polled (e.g., adults, registered voters, likely voters).
- How those people were identified (from voter registration lists, taking their word).
- The actual wording of key questions.
- The dates of the poll.
- Who conducted the poll.
- Who paid for the poll.
- How the poll was conducted (telephone, Internet, in-person, mail).
- The response rate; if it dips much below 50 percent, it isn't a scientific poll and margins of error are meaningless.
- The language used in the interview (if in any area with a lot of non-English speakers).

Source: John McManus, "How to Read Political Polls Like a Pro." http://gradethenews.org, accessed May 25, 2006.

as competent and trustworthy. Equally important is to make sure a candidate "stays on message." Why? Message discipline makes those phrases more potent, and consistency increases the likelihood that voters will believe what you are saying.[23]

Grassroots Campaigning

Door-to-door campaigning (personal contacting) by candidates or party workers is effective when used, but it is labor and time intensive, and limited in the proportion of voters who can be reached. This is why statewide candidates have to rely more on mass media–based campaign techniques. However, local party organizations may play the role of surrogates for the candidate, walking through neighborhoods handing out brochures, leaving door hangers for those not home, and contacting potential supporters by phone or e-mail.[24] But **grassroots campaigning** by statewide candidates themselves is less common than "shoe leather campaigning" by candidates for the state legislature or other local offices. One positive outcome of door-to-door campaigning? Candidates campaigning that way usually lose weight!

Media Campaigning

Media campaigning concentrates on obtaining the maximum "free" exposure on the evening news, as well as saturating television, newspapers, and the Web with paid advertising. To win favorable news coverage, candidates and their managers must devise attractive media events with visuals and sound bites too good for the television news to ignore. News coverage of a candidate is more credible than paid commercials. So candidates must do or say something interesting and "newsworthy" as often as possible during the campaign.

Television "spot" advertisements incur costs in both production and broadcast time. Indeed, television may consume up to three-quarters of all campaign costs; about one-third of TV costs go for production of ads and two-thirds to buying time from television stations. The Federal Communications Commission requires broadcasters to make available broadcast time to political candidates for federal office at the same rates charged to product advertisers, but this does not apply to candidates for state and local offices. Ads are big business for professional campaign consultants and for local television stations. The estimated cumulative spending on TV political ads by presidential, state, and local candidates, political parties, and independent political groups in a single election cycle is in the billions. No surprise here. The average cost of a *single* 30-second spot aired on prime-time network television can cost in the hundreds of thousands of dollars. (To put

Republican party mascots capture the attention of young and old alike. They also often end up in local television and newspaper stories highlighting a campaign event.

Cell phones, tablets, and digital cameras make it easy to grab footage of exciting campaign events and candidate blunders which can, in turn, be used in candidate ads and posted online at candidate and political party Web sites, as well as on YouTube.

things in perspective, the average rate for a 30-second spot during the Super Bowl is over $4 *million* and rising every year.)

Deciding where to "run" an ad is becoming more difficult as the media habits of Americans change, especially across different generations. No single source of news today is as dominant as network news was in the early 1990s.[25] Increasingly, candidates are turning to cable television and radio because they are cheaper and more easily targeted to specific groups of voters (they reach more segmented audiences). Web-based advertising is also on the upswing as more Americans are going online for campaign information. Increasingly Web-based ads are being placed in nonpolitical Web sites; a political ad placed on a fishing-oriented site would certainly catch the eye of the viewer who did not expect to see that type of ad at that location. It is a good example of **microtargeting**.

Many Americans are choosing the news they wish to watch on the basis of the perceived ideological bent of specific broadcast and cable news outlets and their anchors, news magazine show hosts, and reporters. The same holds true for which radio stations they select, which Internet Web sites they visit, and whose Facebook or Twitter pages they would "like" or "follow."

MICROTARGETING

Aiming an ad at a specific subgroup of potential voters.

Negative Ads

Professional media campaigns have increasingly turned to the airing of television commercials and Internet video ads depicting the opponent in negative terms. The original negative TV ad is generally identified as the 1964 "Daisy Girl" commercial, aired by the Lyndon B. Johnson presidential campaign, which portrayed Republican opponent Barry Goldwater as a nuclear warmonger. Over time the techniques of negative ads have been refined; weaknesses in opponents are identified and dramatized in emotionally forceful 30- and 20-second spots. There is little agreement over whether an ad is negative or unfair: What one person labels a "negative" ad, another person may say is "true" depending on their own partisan or ideological bent.

While reformers bemoan "mudslinging," negative advertising can be effective. Such advertising seeks to "define" or "brand" an opponent in negative terms. Many voters cast their ballots *against* candidates they have come to dislike. Research into the opponent's public and personal background, often via "Googling" or "Binging," provides the

A highly competitive party primary, with multiple televised debates, can result in an intensely negative campaign which may, in turn, depress voter turnout. Such was the case in the Republican presidential primary contest in 2012 in several swing states.

data for **negative campaigning.** Previous speeches or writings can be mined for embarrassing statements, and previous voting records can be scrutinized for unpopular policy positions. Personal scandals can be exposed as evidence of "character." Victims of negative ads can be expected to counterattack with charges of "mudslinging" and "dirty" politics. If candidates fear that their personal attacks on opponents might backfire, they may "leak" negative information to reporters and hope that the media will do their dirty work for them.

NEGATIVE CAMPAIGNING
Soliciting voter support by attacking one's opponent.

Analyses of the impact of negative ads show it varies by who is delivering the message, who is receiving the message, and by whether the criticism is a personal attack or an attack on a candidate's issue position. Negative ads focusing on issues have a greater impact than attacks on a candidate's personal qualities, incumbents are criticized more for running them than challengers, and negative information about a candidate from the press is more harmful to a candidate than negative television ads aimed at that candidate. Studies also find that political novices are more influenced by negative ads than "old hands."[26]

The record-breaking number of negative ads aired in the 2012 presidential election[27] has raised a new question: Does too much negativity depress voter turnout among some key constituency bases? Nationally, and in some key battleground states (Florida, Ohio), turnout in the 2012 election dropped. Some scholars attribute at least some portion of the blame for turnout decline to a combination of ad over-saturation (with constant airing of conflicting back-to-back ads) and ad negativity. The possible link has sent party officials and campaign consultants scurrying to do further research.

Free Air Time

Candidates also seek free airtime on public service programs and televised debates. Underfunded candidates are more dependent upon these opportunities than their more affluent opponents. Thus, well-funded and poorly funded candidates may argue over the number and times of public debates and who is eligible to participate. (Many local television stations limit debate participation to candidates who receive a certain level of support from voters surveyed by a major polling firm.)

Campaigning on the Web

A well-designed Web site is now a must for candidates. Webmasters have become vital members of campaign staffs charged with designing and updating the Internet-based portion of a candidate's campaign. The more interactive the site, the better. Web sites play a big part in soliciting volunteers, raising money, informing voters about upcoming campaign events, and keeping enthusiastic supporters on the bandwagon. Major news media (television, radio, newspapers) routinely promote links to candidate Web sites in their regular news coverage. A particularly clever Web site feature might well be the centerpiece of a prime-time story—free media for the candidate. One thing is certain: the Web site had better be good. The average surfer looks at a site for no more than 20 seconds before deciding whether to "click onward."

M-Campaigning: Mobile Technologies as Campaign Vehicles

Mobile technologies are vital to improving GOTV efforts. The explosion of smartphones, tablets and other handheld devices has made them an integral part of campaigns and campaign coverage. "Candidates, voters, activists, and reporters are using these vehicles for a wide range of activities—public outreach, fund-raising, field organization, political persuasion, media coverage, and government accountability."[28] Mobile apps, mobile advertising, and text messaging have become essential components of campaigns at the national, state, and local levels. This move to greater reliance on mobile technologies reflects the fact that well over 80 percent of all smartphone and tablet users are registered to vote.[29]

| 5.8 | MONEY IN STATE POLITICS |

Examine the differences in campaign financing from state to state, and assess why these differences are often substantial.

Running for statewide offices in large states may cost millions, but even running for city council and school board seats can cost thousands. Candidates who do not have enough personal wealth to finance their own campaigns must find contributors. Fund-raising is one of the least pleasant aspects of politics. The mere thought of having to ask family, friends, and strangers for money keeps many citizens from running for office. However, there are firms that specialize in fund-raising—if a candidate can afford them—or friends who are experienced in raising money for local charities and organizations and have good "money networks" who can help. The prevailing rule of thumb is this: "Raising money is about asking. It is a numbers game. The more people you ask for money, the more money you will raise. . . . You must ask the right people the right way. That takes preparation, coordination, and organization."[30]

What Money Can Do

Can money buy elections? Not always, but money can make a significant difference in the outcome. Let us summarize what research has shown:

- Campaign spending is generally more important in contested primary elections than general elections. In primary elections there are no party labels and the electorate is more easily influenced by the kinds of campaigning that money can buy.
- "Early money"—a sizable campaign treasury available at the beginning of the campaign—is usually more valuable than money coming in later and closer to Election Day, especially in states with Early Voting. A candidate who can raise a lot of money early is perceived as a more credible, viable candidate than one who cannot. In the early stages of a campaign, the press routinely compares the fund-raising totals of the various candidates.
- Campaign spending in primary elections is closely related to electoral outcome where the party organizations are weak; money is less important where parties are strong and they endorse a primary candidate.[31] Primary voters are more likely than general election voters to be more ardently partisan.
- Campaign spending is more important in larger jurisdictions, where face-to-face campaigning is not possible and mass media appeals are essential. Television ads cost more in big markets and so does direct mail because it must be sent to many more voters.

- After a certain level of campaign spending is reached, additional expenditures do not produce the same effect. A law of diminishing returns seems to operate to reduce the impact of heavy campaign spending.[32]
- Incumbent officeholders have a strong advantage over challengers in soliciting and receiving campaign contributions.[33]
- However, the advantage of incumbency itself is greater than the advantage of heavy campaign spending. While it is true that incumbents have an easier time obtaining campaign contributions than challengers, only part of the advantage of being an incumbent derives from easier access to money. Most of the incumbent's advantage is in name recognition and greater news media coverage.[34]
- Candidates who outspend their opponents win in two out of three elections. Of course, the higher-spending candidates are usually incumbents, and incumbents tend to win even when they are outspent. But in elections in which there is no incumbent seeking reelection, the candidate who spends the most money can be expected to win three out of every four of these open-seat contests.[35]
- Most contributors want to be personally asked for money by the candidate. A major time commitment by the candidate is needed to raise money (some call it "dialing for dollars").

Fund-raising

The need to raise millions of dollars for political campaigns, especially for costly television advertising, has stimulated the development of many new fund-raising techniques. Campaign financing has moved beyond the small, face-to-face circle of contributing friends, supporters, and partisans. An important source of campaign money now is political action committees, or PACs, which mobilize group financial support for candidates. PACs have been organized by corporations, unions, trade and professional associations, environmental groups, and liberal and conservative ideological groups. The wealthiest PACs are based in Washington, but PAC contributions are becoming increasingly important in state gubernatorial and legislative campaigns as well.[36] They are far less likely to be involved in local campaigns, which cost much less to run.

Individual contributions are now sought through a variety of solicitation techniques, including the Internet, direct mail to persons designated by computer programs to be likely contributors, direct telephone solicitation by a candidate or via a recorded message, and live appeals by workers at telephone banks. About 10 percent of the population now claims to have ever contributed to candidates running for public office. But less than one-half of 1 percent contribute in any particular election cycle. Contributors disproportionately represent high-income, well-educated, older political partisans, although Internet appeals have prompted the less well heeled to give. There are, indeed, networks of contributors.[37] Some candidates have been able to tap into these networks through specialized mailing lists, telephone directories, and e-mail network listservs.

These specialized techniques supplement the more traditional fund-raising dinners, barbecues, fish fries, and cocktail parties. A successful fund-raising dinner usually includes an appearance by a national political figure, perhaps even the president, or an appearance by a show business celebrity. Tickets are sold in blocks to PACs and to wealthy, individual contributors who will give even more to have a "photo op" with the famous guest. Successful techniques may vary with the political culture of the state—for example, celebrity rock concerts in California versus barbecues in Texas.

Big Money in the States

States vary in their principal sources of campaign money because they differ in their economic bases and population makeup. In virtually every state, lawyers, lobbyists, and realtors are among the top 10 categories of contributors, although the rank order is different. States differ in the degree to which other types of contributors play a major role in state elections, reflecting differences in their economies: mining in Montana, unions in California and New York, and telecom services and equipment in Vermont.

Campaign Contributions to Presidential and State-Level Candidates

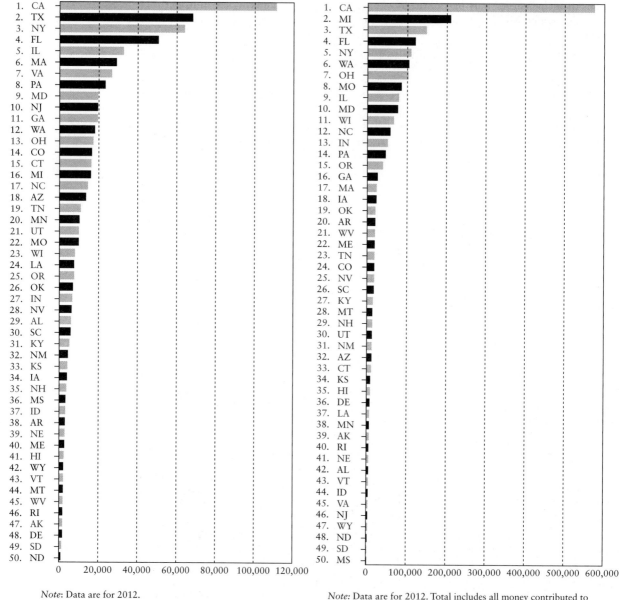

Presidential Candidates, 2012
Total Raised (in thousands of dollars)

1.	CA
2.	TX
3.	NY
4.	FL
5.	IL
6.	MA
7.	VA
8.	PA
9.	MD
10.	NJ
11.	GA
12.	WA
13.	OH
14.	CO
15.	CT
16.	MI
17.	NC
18.	AZ
19.	TN
20.	MN
21.	UT
22.	MO
23.	WI
24.	LA
25.	OR
26.	OK
27.	IN
28.	NV
29.	AL
30.	SC
31.	KY
32.	NM
33.	KS
34.	IA
35.	NH
36.	MS
37.	ID
38.	AR
39.	NE
40.	ME
41.	HI
42.	WY
43.	VT
44.	MT
45.	WV
46.	RI
47.	AK
48.	DE
49.	SD
50.	ND

x-axis: 0, 20,000, 40,000, 60,000, 80,000, 100,000, 120,000

State-Level Candidates, 2012
Total Raised (in thousands of dollars)

1.	CA
2.	MI
3.	TX
4.	FL
5.	NY
6.	WA
7.	OH
8.	MO
9.	IL
10.	MD
11.	WI
12.	NC
13.	IN
14.	PA
15.	OR
16.	GA
17.	MA
18.	IA
19.	OK
20.	AR
21.	WV
22.	ME
23.	TN
24.	CO
25.	NV
26.	SC
27.	KY
28.	MT
29.	NH
30.	UT
31.	NM
32.	AZ
33.	CT
34.	KS
35.	HI
36.	DE
37.	LA
38.	MN
39.	AK
40.	RI
41.	NE
42.	AL
43.	VT
44.	ID
45.	VA
46.	NJ
47.	WY
48.	ND
49.	SD
50.	MS

x-axis: 0, 100,000, 200,000, 300,000, 400,000, 500,000, 600,000

Note: Data are for 2012.
Source: Open Secrets.org Center for Responsive Politics, "Top States Funding Candidates," March 25, 2013. Available at http://www.opensecrets.org/pres12/pres_stateAll.php?list=all.

Note: Data are for 2012. Total includes all money contributed to all state-level candidates and committees during 2012.
Source: National Institute on Money in State Politics, "National Overview Map," 2012. Available at http://www.followthemoney.org/database/nationalview.phtml?l=0&f=0&y=2012&abbr=1.

Individual self-financed candidates and state political parties are also consistently big money sources in state elections. Interestingly, self-financed candidates (those who raise more than half of all campaign contributions from themselves or an immediate family member) make up only around 8 percent of all state-level candidates. They really don't fare all that well. Over the past nine years, only 11 percent of them have won their races.[38]

Campaign Spending in the States

Campaign spending in the state elections varies enormously from state to state. A gubernatorial campaign in a small state may cost only $1–6 million, but campaigns in California, New York, Texas, and Florida can easily top $20 million.[39] Special elections can cost even more because the candidates have to reach a lot of voters in a hurry and that spells television advertising.

State legislative campaigns may range in cost from less than $1,000 to nearly $850,000 for seat winners, depending on their competitiveness and the size of the district.[40] For example, in Maine, on average about $34,270 per candidate was spent on campaigns for a two-year state senate in 2012. However, $454,414 was spent in a race between two candidates competing to represent the Bangor area, for a job that pays $13,852 per year. Why such a difference even within the same state? Because the top-dollar, highly competitive district was seen as a swing seat—one that could determine the balance of power in the state's Senate. Each party desperately wanted to win it.[41] In general, campaign costs are usually much lower in less populous, more rural states where one political party tends to dominate. For example, candidates for the Idaho Senate on average spent $17,917 while those running for the state house spent $8,940 each.[42]

Critics of current campaign finance laws argue that the growing amounts of money pouring into campaigns is having a corrupting influence on politics, or at the least, adding to the public's perception of corruption and their cynicism toward politics in general. That is certainly the opinion of most minor party candidates.

Third-Party Candidates Face Long Odds

Third parties range from the Libertarian, Progressive, Green, and Reform parties to more single issue–focused ones like the Right-to-Life, Family Values, Real Food, TEA (Taxed Enough Already), Surfers, and Veterans parties.[43] (Each state makes its own laws spelling out how a group can formally become a political party.) In one study of third parties across the states, some 100 third parties fielded over 6,000 candidates—fewer than 20 percent of all candidates running for state offices across the United States. Just 2 percent won. Why? Third-party candidates struggle mightily to get high enough name recognition to compete with major party candidates. They need money to do that, and raising money is difficult. Consequently, third-party candidates are more likely to self-finance their campaigns than are Republican or Democratic candidates. According to the same study of third party candidates, third party candidates fared best in Vermont, worst in California. The most successful candidates have run from the Independent and Progressive parties. The least successful have been Libertarians and Green Party candidates. Historically, third-party candidates have done best during tough economic times when voters get really angry with incumbents (regardless of whether they are Democrats or Republicans). But often their greatest success is in forcing the two major parties to incorporate some of their popular ideals.[44]

STATE CAMPAIGN FINANCE REFORM

Public opinion surveys consistently show that the public thinks too much money is spent on political campaigns. They also believe that lobbyists and big donors "buy" elections and that after the election, these "money bags" gain greater access to elected officials than is available to the average citizen. These attitudes have prompted many states to pass

Evaluate the effectiveness of state and national laws that limit campaign financing in order to increase the perceived efficacy of the electoral process.

legislation addressing the money side of political campaigns and to make it easier for citizens to access information about a candidate's contributors and expenditures.[45] Over half the states have also established independent "watchdog" commissions to monitor candidate adherence to campaign finance laws.

State Campaign Finance Laws

Most states have enacted laws designed to bring greater "ethics" into political campaigning and reduce the importance of large campaign contributions. Generally these laws attempt to do one or more of the following:

- Limit the size of campaign contributions to a specific race by certain groups (usually political action committees, corporations and unions) and individuals (excluding the candidate); 37 states limit the amount of contributions to candidates by individuals, political parties, and political action committees; 46 states regulate corporate contributions to candidates (25 states set limits on the amount that can be contributed; 21 states prohibit any corporate contribution).[46]

- Limit the overall spending of candidates and parties; usually applies when candidates take public funds for their campaign; several have voluntary limits, such as Hawaii and Colorado, but fewer than half the states impose spending limits.

- Require financial disclosure of a candidate's personal finances as well as campaign contributions and expenditures—"Who gave it? Who got it?" All states require some disclosure from candidates, committees, and political parties, but some require more detail than others and for reports to be filed in a more timely fashion, often electronically via the Internet.

- Require more detailed financial disclosure of corporate and union spending (in response to the U.S. Supreme Court ruling that lets corporations and unions spend unlimited amounts of money on independent campaign-related advertising).

- Establish public funding of campaign expenses. Fourteen states currently have some type of public financing programs for candidates and/or political parties. Laws differ on how funding is provided (on a matching basis or not) and to which candidates.[47] But in every case, participation in such programs is optional. Funds are generated in many different ways, depending on the state: tax check-offs, voluntary surcharges, tax credits, or direct state appropriations. Seven states—Arizona, Connecticut, Maine, New Mexico, North Carolina, Vermont, and West Virginia—have adopted "Clean Elections" programs. This variation on public campaign financing allows eligible candidates to finance their campaigns almost entirely with public funds. Once a candidate qualifies by collecting a specified number of small contributions (perhaps as low as $10 or $25), he or she agrees not to collect any more contributions from private sources, but instead to receive a grant from the state to finance his or her campaign. Proponents argue Clean Election reforms free candidates from relying on special interest campaign cash and, once elected, allows them to "consider legislation on the merits without worrying about whether they are pleasing well-heeled donors and lobbyists."[48] Opponents of public funding of campaigns cite studies showing it has not been effective.[49]

- Establish regulatory agencies, or "commissions," to oversee campaign practices.

Federal Campaign Finance Laws

The initial model for the various campaign finance–related state laws was the Federal Election Campaign Act of 1974, which placed limits on the size of individual campaign contributions, required disclosure of campaign finances, provided for public funding of presidential elections through a tax check-off on federal income tax returns, and established a Federal Elections Commission to supervise presidential elections and distribute public funds to candidates.

In 2002, Congress passed the **Bipartisan Campaign Reform Act** (BCRA), also known as the McCain-Feingold bill. The specifics of this Act, some of which have already been

BIPARTISAN CAMPAIGN REFORM ACT 2002

Spells out rules for campaign contributions and spending in *federal* elections (presidential; congressional).

overturned by the U.S. Supreme Court, apply to *federal* elections (presidential and congressional):

- Prohibition on **soft money** contributions to the *national* parties. However, state and local parties can solicit soft money contributions of up to $10,000 for get-out-the-vote activities in federal elections. "Soft money" refers to contributions made to parties rather than directly to the campaign chests of candidates. Soft money is supposed to be spent for "party-building" activities, get-out-the-vote drives, or general party advertising (e.g., "Vote Republican" or "Vote Democratic"). But state and local parties cannot use soft money for activities directly affecting federal elections.

- Contributions from individuals to federal candidates are limited to $2,500 in 2012 (raised from $2,300 in 2008).

- Campaign ads by corporations, unions, and interest groups, in support of federal candidates, cannot be run 60 days before a general election, 30 days before a primary election (now unconstitutional).

- Expenditures by independent groups made on the candidates' behalf must be reported to the Federal Elections Commission. Individuals, corporations, and organizations may not pay for any "electioneering communication," which is defined as any broadcast that refers to a candidate for federal office that is aired within 30 days of a federal primary election or 60 days of a federal general election.

The U.S. Supreme Court and Campaign Finance

The U.S. Supreme Court has recognized that limitations on campaign *contributions* help further a compelling government interest—"preventing corruption and the appearance of corruption" in election campaigns. But the Court has been reluctant to allow governments to limit campaign *expenditures* because paying to express political views is necessary in the exercise of free speech. In an important early case, *Buckley* v. *Valeo* (1976), the Court held that limiting a candidate's campaign expenditures that are made from one's own personal funds violated the First Amendment's guarantee of free speech.[50]

Later, when called upon to consider the constitutionality of the BCRA, the Court upheld limitations on contributions directly to candidates and to national parties.[51] It also upheld limits on "soft money" contributions to state and local parties, recognizing that these provisions were designed to prevent circumventions of valid prohibitions on campaign contributions. And the Court also upheld a prohibition on spending for "electioneering communications" by individuals and interest groups that are controlled or coordinated with parties or candidates. The Court struck down an attempt by Congress to prohibit children from making campaign contributions.

But still later, the U.S. Supreme Court reconsidered the BCRA's provisions limiting individual and organization electioneering communications. The Court distinguished between "**express advocacy**" on behalf of a candidate or party and "**issue ads**" that are not the functional equivalent of express advocacy.[52] (In other words, ads that do not urge viewers or listeners to vote for or against a particular candidate or party.) "When it comes to defining what speech qualifies as the functional equivalent of express advocacy, the Court should give the benefit of the doubt to speech, not censorship." The effect of the decision is to permit political contributors to support organizations unaffiliated with a candidate or party, including nonprofit "527" organizations, that air television ads not expressly endorsing a candidate right up to Election Day.

In 2010, the U.S. Supreme Court went even further in equating money and speech in *Citizens United* v. *Federal Elections Commission*. The Court ruled that corporations and unions have the same political speech rights as individuals and can therefore use their profits to support or oppose individual candidates for federal offices.[53] "Because speech is an essential mechanism of democracy—it is the means to hold officials accountable to the people—political speech must prevail against laws that would suppress it by design or inadvertence." It also struck down the part of the 2002 McCain-Feingold campaign

SOFT MONEY

Campaign contributions given to party organizations for activities such as party building and voter registration, but not to be used directly for their candidates' campaigns. Soft money contributions to *national* parties were banned in 2002, but can still be made to state and local party organizations.

EXPRESS ADVOCACY

An ad for a federal candidate paid for by an individual or interest group that asks a voter to support (or reject) a particular candidate or party

ISSUE ADS

Ads paid for by an individual or interest group that have an opinion on key policies but do not urge voters to vote for a specific candidate or party.

Political speech is the heart of the First Amendment. Expenditures for political speech must be constitutionally protected. Spending money to broadcast one's political views, regarding candidates, issues, and public affairs generally, is an integral part of political speech. Speech must be heard by others to be effective, and in today's society this means spending money to gain access to the mass media. Limitations on political spending in effect limit political speech and therefore violate the First Amendment's guarantee of freedom of speech. Any "undue influence" of money in politics is outweighed by the loss for democracy resulting from restrictions on free speech.

The U.S. Supreme Court was correct in its 2010 holding that corporations and unions could not be prohibited from engaging in political speech. The Court said "Because speech is an essential mechanism for democracy—it is the means to hold officials out of both to the people—political speech must prevail against laws that would suppress it by design or inadvertence." The same reasoning applies to dollar limits placed upon individual and group contributions to federal candidates for public office. Individuals and groups should be permitted to contribute as much as they wish to their favored candidates.

It is true that individuals and organizations usually find ways to get around campaign finance laws anyway. The Supreme Court itself noted that "Political speech is so ingrained in this country's culture that speakers find ways around campaign finance laws." But there is no reason to evade these laws; they ought to be judged unconstitutional. "Restrictions on the amount of money a person or group can spend on political communication during a campaign . . . necessarily reduces the quantity of expression by restricting the number of issues discussed, the depth of their exploration, and the size of the audience reached."

The public's interest in combating corruption in politics can be satisfied by open disclosure laws—requiring candidates to disclose during the campaign the names of organizations and individuals that are contributing to their campaigns and the amounts of these contributions. Let the voters decide whether or not a candidate is supported by the "wrong" individuals or organizations, or whether or not a candidate is too heavily indebted to a particular contributor.

finance law that banned unions and corporations from paying for political ads 30 days before a presidential primary and 60 days before the general election.[54] The Court said, "Restrictions on the amount of money a person or group can spend on political communication during a campaign . . . necessarily reduces the quantity of expression by restricting the number of issues discussed, the depth of their exploration, and the size of the audience reached." However, the ruling did leave some important limits in place. Corporations and unions are still prohibited from giving money *directly* to federal candidates or national party committees; they may only spend unlimited amounts of their own money advocating *independently* for or against federal candidates.[55] And nonprofit groups like Citizens United that advocate for political candidates still must adhere to disclaimer and disclosure laws regarding donors.[56] Predictably, no sooner had the ruling been released than some in Congress began efforts to draft legislation that would effectively overturn the verdict. But some ardent free speech advocates have continued to press for eliminating campaign spending limits altogether. (See *Up Close: A Conflicting View: Eliminate Campaign Spending Limits.*)

These decisions not only affect federal campaign finance laws but also the laws of state and local jurisdictions. The *Citizens United* case affected laws in 24 states. At the time of the ruling, 1 state banned union political activity, 9 banned corporate political activity, and 14 banned both. These states had to adjust their laws to bring them into compliance with the Court's new interpretation of campaign finance laws.[57] The Court has also held in another case that a state law that places too low a limit on how much individuals can contribute to a candidate or party violates the First Amendment's guarantee of free speech. When Vermont placed a $200 limit on campaign contributions for offices in that state, the Court held that limits could not be so low as to prevent challengers from mounting effective campaigns. Vermont's limits were held to be "disproportionately severe."[58]

Do Campaign Finance Reforms Work?

It is not clear whether state campaign finance laws actually succeed in limiting overall spending in elections. Experience suggests that in reality "If you squeeze money out of one arena, it will ooze into another."[59] Reforms often squeeze money out of candidates' hands and into the hands of self-proclaimed voter education groups with narrow agendas and obscure memberships. These groups spend large amounts of money urging voters to support one candidate or another. Opponents of unrestricted independent spending by interest groups argue that the proliferation of SuperPACs is weakening the power of state political party committees by siphoning off funds that are essential to state party building. Many donors that used to give to state parties now prefer giving to independent groups.[60]

Note also that, under *Buckley,* any candidate can spend unlimited personal wealth on his or her own election campaign, and individuals can spend any amount to advertise their own personal views, as long as they do not spend their money through a party or campaign organization. If anything, the personal wealth of the candidate has become an even more important qualification for successful campaigning. And in states with spending limits tied to public funding of campaigns, more candidates are simply refusing public funds, which means they must raise even more money from donors.

The overall conclusion is one that affirms what many Americans have always believed: "Money always finds a way into the system. . . . Twenty years from now reformers will be screaming for something else. Stay tuned."[61]

CHAPTER HIGHLIGHTS

- The political party system, once regarded as the principal means for Americans to direct public policy and hold elected officials accountable (the responsible party model), has given way increasingly to candidate-centered campaigns in which individuals decide on their own to run for office and develop policy positions.

- State laws govern political party affairs, including what qualifies an organization to be a party and how to nominate candidates for public office. Most states have closed primaries (only party members can vote) and require that winners get at least a plurality (or majority, in some states) of votes. A few states have "top two" primaries where top two vote getters run against each other in the general election regardless of their party affiliation.

- During presidential election years, states hold primaries (or caucuses) to select candidates to be considered at the national convention for the party's official presidential nominee. Large diverse states are critical of Iowa and New Hampshire going first in the presidential nominating cycle.

- At the state level, a few full-time party activists, usually strong ideologues and potential or former political officials, manage party affairs. Leadership is through a state party chairperson and committee.

- At the county and city level, party officials are chosen locally. Consequently, authority is vested at the grassroots level, and local organizations are probably the most important building blocks of American party structure.

- The degree of party competitiveness in a state can be measured by the winning candidates' margins of victory, the existence of divided government (legislative and executive branches are controlled by different parties), party control of the state's top elected offices, and the percentages of voters that identify with each party.

- Public relations firms, rather than parties, manage political campaigns for top offices. These marketing and media experts may do everything from conducting public opinion polls and raising funds to developing the candidate's image and message through ads and media coverage.

- Polling can be statistically accurate or unrepresentative (often intentionally). Professional standards for the industry are set by the American Association of Public Opinion Research.

- Targeted mailings, frequent news coverage, negative ads, and interactive Web sites are effective campaign tools. The increase in negative ads has raised the question of whether they dampen turnout in key swing states barraged with TV ads.

- In addition to traditional fund-raising dinners and party coffers, campaign funding is increasingly supplemented by the candidate's own wealth and political action committees (PACs). Contributions reflect a state's economy but usually include lawyers, lobbyists, and real estate firms. Individual contributors are typically high on the socioeconomic ladder.

- Large campaign treasuries are most important at the beginning of a campaign, in contested primary elections, and in large jurisdictions. Television typically consumes three-quarters of a campaign's resources.

- Most states have enacted laws to bring greater "ethics" into political campaigning and reduce the importance of large campaign contributions, but the impact of such reforms is unclear.

- The U.S. Supreme Court has recognized that limitations on campaign *contributions* help prevent corruption but has been reluctant to allow limitations on campaign *expenditures* in the interest of free speech.

CHAPTER SIX

LEGISLATORS IN STATE POLITICS

LEARNING OBJECTIVES

6.1 Describe the lawmaking and other functions of state legislatures.

6.2 Compare the demographic characteristics of state legislators with those of ordinary citizens, and assess the extent to which state legislators are professionals or amateurs.

6.3 Analyze the extent to which women and racial or ethnic minorities comprise state legislatures, and trace how these patterns have changed over time.

6.4 Explain the prior political experience of state legislators and the process they endured to get to the state capital, including raising money for their campaigns and navigating the primary and general elections.

6.5 Examine the advantages of incumbency for winning reelection.

6.6 Assess how *Baker* v. *Carr* affected legislative apportionment, describe the processes used to draw district lines, and evaluate how this process can be used for political purposes.

6.7 Trace the typical lawmaking process in state legislatures, paying specific attention to the disorderliness of process and areas of frequent logjams.

6.8 Describe the institutionalization of state legislatures, and assess how increased professionalism has impacted legislative processes and outcomes.

6.9 Explain the functions and composition of legislative committees.

6.10 Examine the roles of legislative leaders and subject-matter experts, evaluate the extent to which legislators act as trustees and delegates, and assess the impact of terms limits in those states that have adopted them.

6.11 Analyze the influence of political parties in state legislatures.

6.12 Characterize the role of the media in the state legislative process.

6.13 Describe lobbying in state legislatures, assess which lobbying techniques are most effective, and evaluate the extent to which lobbying efforts are effectively regulated.

6.14 Determine whether citizens' critical assessments of state legislatures are well deserved.

FUNCTIONS OF STATE LEGISLATURES

Describe the lawmaking and other functions of state legislatures.

If you were to ask state legislators what the job of the legislature is, they typically say: "Our job is to pass laws," or "We have to help the people who live in the districts we represent," or "We have to make policy." All these answers are correct, but none by itself tells the whole story.

Enacting Laws

It is true that, from a *legal viewpoint,* the function of state legislatures is to "pass laws," that is, the enactment of statutory law. A legislature may enact more than a thousand laws in a single legislative session. The average legislator introduces 10 to 12 bills each year. Many are never expected to pass. They are introduced merely as a favor to a constituent or an interest group, or to get a headline in a newspaper back home, or to create awareness of an issue.

The nation's 50 state legislatures collectively consider more than 101,000 bills each session, and they pass nearly 19,000.[1] The range of subject matter of bills considered by a legislature is enormous. A legislature may consider authorization of $50 billion of state spending, or it may argue whether or not inscribing license plates with "The Poultry State" would cause the state to be called "Chicken." Obviously, these considerations range from the trivial to the vital.

Among the recent issues confronting state legislatures are budget shortfalls, jobs, environmental cleanup, the rising costs of prescription drugs for the poor and for seniors, identity theft, highway safety, student achievement tests, college tuition hikes, abandoned babies, the manufacture and use of methamphetamines, and the monitoring of sexual predators. Flurries of new state laws have dealt with children's safety seats, texting while driving, rising prison costs, crumbling infrastructure, public employee pensions, and use of red light cameras. A number of states have approved laws allowing young mothers to leave their babies at hospitals without fear of prosecution, an effort to save abandoned babies. Laws against identity theft—when someone's credit and personal information is misused—have passed in many states, as have laws requiring the whereabouts of sexual predators to be made known to citizens. And, of course, legislatures continue to address trivial matters: Kentucky made the Appalachian dulcimer the state's official musical instrument; Arkansas made the Dutch oven the official state cooking pot; Florida finally made the orange the Sunshine State's official fruit.

Considering Constitutional Amendments, Gubernatorial Appointments, and State Courts

In addition to the enactment of statutory law, legislatures share in the process of state constitutional revision (see "Constitutional Change in the States" in Chapter 2) and consider amendments to the U.S. Constitution (see "Battles in the States over Constitutional Amendments" in Chapter 3). Many governors' appointments to high state offices require legislative approval (see "Managerial Powers" in Chapter 7). The legislature also makes laws authorizing and funding the establishment of new courts and more judges as needed.

Approving Budgets

Perhaps their single most important function is the passage of the appropriation and tax measures in the state budget. No state monies may be spent without a legislative appropriation, and it is difficult to think of any governmental action that does not involve some financial expenditure. Potentially, a legislature can control any activity of the state government through its power over appropriations.

Serving Constituents

CONSTITUENTS
Residents of a legislator's district; the people who are represented by a legislator.

Legislators spend a great deal of time answering requests from **constituents**—"servicing the district." Many letters, e-mails, and phone calls come from interest groups in their districts—business, labor, agriculture, school teachers, and municipal employees. These communications may deal with specific bills or with items in the state budget. Other communications may come from citizens who want specific assistance or favors—help with getting a state job, help with permits or licenses, voicing an opinion about whom the state university should hire as a new football coach, or asking for state funding for a new road or museum in their community.

Overseeing State Agencies 𝗑

Legislators frequently challenge state administrators to explain why they are doing what they do. Frequently, committee hearings and budget hearings, in particular, provide opportunities for legislators to put administrators "through the wringer" about programs and expenditures via **legislative oversight**. Lately child welfare agency administrators in many states have been called to explain their agency's difficulty in curbing the rising incidences of runaway children and child abuse by foster parents. Often embarrassed administrators feel harassed at these meetings, but the true purpose is to remind state administrators that elected representatives of the people are the final legal authority.

Most states now have "**sunset" laws** that call for their legislatures to reenact programs every few years or else see them go out of existence (sunset). Few programs or agencies are ever sunseted, but such laws force periodic legislative reexamination and evaluation of agency performance.

LEGISLATIVE OVERSIGHT
The monitoring of activities of state agencies by the legislature and its committees.

SUNSET LAWS
Laws that fix termination dates for programs and agencies in order to force the legislature to renew them if the legislators wish the programs to continue.

MAKING OF A STATE LEGISLATOR

6.2

State legislators are not "representative" of the population of their states in the sense of being typical cross sections of them. On the contrary, the nation's 7,383 state legislators are generally selected from the better-educated, more prestigiously employed, upper-middle-class segments of the population.

Compare the demographic characteristics of state legislators with those of ordinary citizens, and assess the extent to which state legislators are professionals or amateurs.

Status

Legislators tend to come from the "upwardly mobile" sectors of the population. This places many of them among the "second-rung" elites in the status system rather than the established wealthy. Although the sons and daughters, grandsons and granddaughters of distinguished old families of great wealth frequently enter presidential and gubernatorial politics in the states, they seldom run for the state legislature. Legislators tend to be among the upper-middle-class status groups for whom politics is an avenue of upward mobility.

Occupation

Legislators must come from occupational groups with flexible work responsibility or from the ranks of retired persons. The lawyer, the farmer, or the business owner can adjust his or her work to the legislative schedule, but the office manager cannot. The overrepresented occupations are those involving extensive public contact. The lawyer, real estate agent, insurance agent, and merchant establish in their business the wide circle of friends necessary for political success. Physicians and educators interface with persons from all walks of life. In short, the legislator's occupation should provide free time, public contacts, and social respectability.

Education

State legislators are generally well educated. More than three-quarters of them are college educated, compared to only one-quarter of the general population.

Age 𝗑

The average age of a state legislator is 56. Legislators have gotten slightly older in recent years, thanks to the aging of the population and more retirees running for office. Retirees (12% of all state legislators) now make up the third largest occupation group (behind full-time legislators—over 16%—and lawyers—15%).[2] Retirees as a proportion of state legislators are higher in states with larger senior populations, such as Nevada.

Personal Wealth

Legislators frequently claim that public service is a financial burden. While this may be true, legislators are generally recruited from among the more affluent members of society, and they become even more affluent during their tenure. Indeed, there is evidence that (1) the average **net worth** of new legislators is increasing over time, and (2) the average legislator increases his or her net worth while serving in the legislature. (Net worth is the total value of all assets—houses, autos, stocks, bonds, and property—after subtracting the total value of all outstanding debts—such as mortgages and loans.) For example, in Florida, the average legislator more than *tripled* his or her net worth in 10 years of legislative service. Asked to explain these increases in personal wealth, one legislator said, "Maybe they do well because they're achievers. That's why they win when they run for office and that's why they make money."[3] But it's more likely that legislative service, and the public name recognition that comes with it, enhances one's legal practice, real estate or insurance business, as well as investment opportunities.

Lawyers

Attorneys no longer dominate most state legislatures, although most citizens still believe they do. According to the National Conference of State Legislatures, only about 15 percent of legislators are attorneys, down considerably from the 1970s when one-fourth of all legislators were lawyers.[4] However, lawyers are still overrepresented in legislative bodies at all levels of government relative to their proportional makeup in the population at large. It is sometimes argued that the lawyer brings a special kind of skill to politics. The lawyer's occupation is the representation of clients, so he or she moves to representing constituents in the legislature. Lawyers are trained to deal with public policy as it is reflected in the statute books, so they may be reasonably familiar with public policy before entering the legislature.

Service in the legislature offers many benefits to lawyers. It can help a lawyer's private practice through free public advertising and opportunities to make contacts with potential clients. It can also offer important institutional advantages—specifically, the availability of highly valued "lawyers-only" posts in state government, such as judge and prosecuting attorney. Lawyers are eligible for many elective and appointive public jobs from which nonlawyers are excluded. State legislative seats are viewed by lawyers as stepping-stones to these posts—appellate court judge, Supreme Court justice, attorney general, regulatory commissioner. The post-legislative careers of lawyers show that over half go on to other public offices, compared to less than one-third of the nonlawyer legislators.[5]

Do lawyers behave any differently from nonlawyers in the legislature? Lawyers do *not* vote any differently from nonlawyers on most issues; lawyers are neutral "contractors" for parties, interest groups, constituents, and others. Generally, they do not vote together as a bloc. However, lawyers do act together in legislatures to protect the legal profession. The opposition of trial lawyers to insurance reform, including "no-fault" insurance, and their opposition to "tort reform" (a **tort** is a civil wrong that results in damages) has kept both from passing in many state legislatures where reforms have been introduced. This, in turn, has prompted more doctors and small business owners to run for the state legislature.

Amateurs

Most state legislatures are still part-time bodies. There are constitutional limits to the length of legislative sessions in most states; the most common limit is 60 days per year. Legislators spend anywhere from 54 to 80 percent of their time on their legislative job, depending on the degree to which their state's legislature is professionalized.[6] It is true that interim committee meetings and other legislative responsibilities may add to their duties, and over the years sessions have grown longer. But most state legislators have other occupations, and few rely on their legislative compensation alone.[7]

In recent years, however, an increasing number of state legislators are **full-time legislators**. The "**citizen legislator**" who spends two months in the state capital and then returns home to his or her own business or profession still predominates in the states, but the proportion of full-time legislators is growing. Full-time legislators (those who have no other occupation) tend to be in large states with better-paid legislatures, such as California, New York, and Michigan. However, the line between full time and part time has been blurred. All legislators are spending more time on the job, whether their legislature is formally full time or not.[8] "No matter the length of session, state lawmakers' work is full time. When not in regular session, legislators are assisting constituents, doing interim committee work, studying up on issues, campaigning, giving speeches, attending luncheons, returning phone calls, and even riding in parades."[9]

MINORITIES AND WOMEN IN STATE LEGISLATURES

6.3

Analyze the extent to which women and racial or ethnic minorities comprise state legislatures, and trace how these patterns have changed over time.

Minorities and women have made impressive gains in American state legislatures in recent decades. Today, African Americans occupy about 9 percent of all state legislative seats in the nation, Hispanics about 3 percent, Asian Americans 1 percent, and Native Americans 1 percent. Women occupy about 24 percent of all seats.[10] (For state totals, see "*Rankings of the States:* African Americans, Hispanics, Asians, Native Americans, and Women in State Legislatures.")

African American Representation

Black voter mobilization, stemming initially from the Voting Rights Act of 1965 and later from federal court enforcement of amendments to that Act following the 1990 Census (see "Race, Ethnicity, and Political Participation" in Chapter 4), has resulted in the election of substantial numbers of African American state legislators. Most are elected from majority black districts. Southern states, with larger black populations, have the largest percentages of African American state legislators. Nonetheless, nationwide the percentage of African American state legislators (9%) is less than the percentage of African Americans in the voting-age population (12%).

Black legislators in the states have had a significant impact on public policy, especially as they have become committee chairs, majority leaders, speakers of the house, or presidents of the senate.[11] (Colorado's legislators, in 2008, were the first in the nation to choose African Americans as presiding officers in both the House and the Senate.) Their voting on civil rights and welfare issues is clearly distinguishable in southern states.[12] White legislators, even those with substantial numbers of black constituents, are not as strong in support of these issues as black legislators. The National Black Caucus of State Legislators (NBCSL), established

For the first time in 1966, California's State Legislature included five Black Assembly Members and its first Black Senator. In 1967, these legislators organized into the California Legislative Black Caucus, the first caucus of its kind in the nation. The Caucus produces an annual report on the State of Black California to guide their legislative objectives each year.

in 1977, has been instrumental in helping its members develop policy initiatives on a wide range of topics, from HIV/AIDS and education reform, to equity in home ownership.

Hispanic Representation

The largest Hispanic delegations are found in those states with large Hispanic populations—New Mexico, California, Texas, Arizona, Florida, and Nevada. However, Hispanic representation in state legislatures remains well below what we would expect given the growing Hispanic percentage of the nation's population. Nationwide, 3 percent of all state legislators are Hispanic but Latinos make up 14 percent of the voting-age population. When citizenship is considered, Hispanics or Latinos make up a smaller proportion (10%) of the citizen voting-age population. The current underrepresentation of Hispanics differs from state to state and is generally a product of the same forces that appear to reduce Hispanic political participation generally. (See "Race, Ethnicity, and Political Participation" in Chapter 4.)

Like African American legislators, Hispanic state legislators have their own association. The National Hispanic Caucus of State Legislators (NHCSL) was founded in 1989 to organize Latino state lawmakers and strengthen the voice of Hispanic America. Improving educational outcomes for Latino children is a top priority for the group.

Native American and Asian American Representation

Native American and Asian American representation in most states' legislatures is still quite low. Their representational levels are generally highest in the Far West states where each group makes up a larger share of the overall population. Native American state legislative representation is highest in Oklahoma, Alaska, Hawaii, Montana, and New Mexico. Asian Americans hold larger shares of legislative seats in Hawaii (where Asians are a majority of the state's population) and California.

The National Caucus of Native American State Legislators (formerly the National Council of Native American Legislators) was chartered in 1992. Today the Caucus consists of 72 members from 17 states whose goals include increasing communication among Native American legislators, creating greater awareness of the diverse Native American cultures in the United States, and promoting a better understanding of state-tribal issues among policymakers and the public at large. And a number of states have Asian legislative caucuses. California's Asian Pacific Islander (API) Legislative Caucus seeks to increase Asian Pacific Islander participation and representation in all levels of government and to ensure the API community has equal access to education, social services, health, mental health, and other government programs and services.

Women in State Legislatures

While women today occupy only about 24 percent of all state legislative seats in the nation, this is a significant increase over the scant 4 percent of female state legislators in 1969, although the percentages have flattened off. However, in New Hampshire in 2008 women candidates won a majority of the races for the Granite State's Senate, making it the first time in U.S. history that a legislative body had a majority of women members. Minority women comprise a little over 20 percent of all female legislators. Black, Latina, and Asian women legislators make up a higher proportion of their racial/ethnic group's legislative representation than white or Native American female legislators.[13]

Like their male counterparts, female legislators tend to come from politically active families, to have lived in their communities for a long time, to be representative of their district in race and ethnicity, and to enjoy higher social status than most of their constituents. Women are better represented in the New England and western states with less "professional" legislatures. The large urban industrial states with more "professional" legislatures have fewer female representatives.[14] Southern states also tend to have fewer female legislators.

African Americans, Hispanics, Asians, Native Americans, and Women in State Legislatures

African American State Legislators

Rank	State
1.	AL
2.	GA
3.	MS
4.	LA
4.	FL
6.	NY
7.	NC
7.	IL
9.	MD
9.	SC
11.	OH
12.	NV
12.	NJ
14.	VA
15.	AR
15.	MI
17.	MO
17.	CT
17.	DE
20.	IN
21.	PA
21.	TN
21.	WI
24.	CA
24.	KS
24.	NE
27.	OK
27.	CO
27.	IA
30.	KY
31.	MA
31.	RI
31.	TX
31.	VT
31.	AZ
31.	WA
37.	AK
37.	MN
37.	OR
37.	WV
41.	HI
41.	ID
41.	ME
41.	MT
41.	NM
41.	ND
41.	SD
41.	UT
41.	WY
41.	NH*

(axis: 0 5 10 15 20 25 30)

Note: Data accessed January 2013.
*Data for New Hampshire from 2009. Most current data available at time of publication.
Source: National Conference of State Legislatures, Legislator Demographic Map. Available at http://www.ncsl.org/legislatures-elections/legisdata/legislator-demographic-map.aspx.
© 2013 National Conference of State Legislatures.

Hispanic State Legislators

Rank	State
1.	NM
2.	TX
3.	CA
4.	AZ
5.	NV
6.	CO
6.	FL
8.	NY
8.	IL
9.	NJ
9.	UT
12.	CT
12.	RI
12.	HI
15.	KS
15.	MA
15.	DE
15.	MO
15.	OH
15.	WA
21.	WY
21.	GA
21.	IN
21.	LA
21.	MD
21.	MI
21.	MN
21.	NC
21.	OR
21.	TN
21.	VT
32.	WI
32.	AL
32.	AK
32.	AR
32.	ID
32.	IA
32.	KY
32.	ME
32.	MS
32.	MT
32.	NE
32.	ND
32.	OK
32.	PA
32.	SC
32.	SD
32.	VA
32.	WV
32.	NH*

(axis: 0 5 10 15 20 25 30 35 40 45)

Note: Data accessed January 2013.
*Data for New Hampshire from 2009. Most current data available at time of publication.
Source: National Conference of State Legislatures, Legislator Demographic Map. Available at http://www.ncsl.org/legislatures-elections/legisdata/legislator-demographic-map.aspx.
© 2013 National Conference of State Legislatures.

Asians in State Legislatures

Rank	State
1.	HI
2.	WA
3.	CA
3.	MI
3.	MN
3.	PA
7.	CT
7.	UT
7.	VA
7.	AL
7.	AK
7.	AZ
7.	AR
7.	CO
7.	DE
7.	FL
7.	GA
18.	ID
18.	IL
18.	IN
18.	IA
22.	KS
18.	KY
18.	LA
18.	ME
18.	MD
18.	MA
18.	MS
18.	MO
18.	MT
18.	NE
18.	NV
18.	NJ
18.	NM
18.	NY
18.	NC
18.	ND
18.	OH
18.	OK
18.	OR
18.	RI
18.	SC
18.	SD
18.	TN
18.	TX
18.	VT
18.	WV
18.	WI
18.	WY
18.	NH*

(axis: 0 10 20 30 40 50 60 70 80)

Note: Data accessed January 2013.
*Data for New Hampshire from 2009. Most recent data available at time of publication.
Source: National Conference of State Legislatures, Legislator Demographic Map. Available at http://www.ncsl.org/legislatures-elections/legisdata/legislator-demographic-map.aspx.
© 2013 National Conference of State Legislatures.

(continued)

Rankings of the States
Women and Minorities in State Legislatures *(continued)*

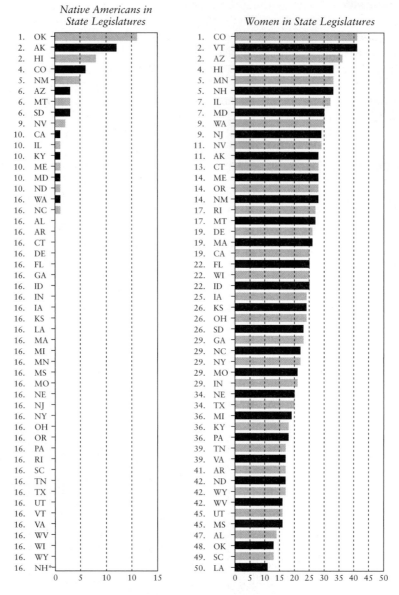

Native Americans in State Legislatures

1. OK
2. AK
2. HI
4. CO
5. NM
6. AZ
6. MT
6. SD
9. NV
10. CA
10. IL
10. KY
10. ME
10. MD
10. ND
16. WA
16. NC
16. AL
16. AR
16. CT
16. DE
16. FL
16. GA
16. ID
16. IN
16. IA
16. KS
16. LA
16. MA
16. MI
16. MN
16. MS
16. MO
16. NE
16. NJ
16. NY
16. OH
16. OR
16. PA
16. RI
16. SC
16. TN
16. TX
16. UT
16. VT
16. VA
16. WV
16. WI
16. WY
16. NH*

Women in State Legislatures

1. CO
2. VT
2. AZ
4. HI
5. MN
5. NH
7. IL
7. MD
9. WA
9. NJ
11. NV
11. AK
13. CT
14. ME
14. OR
14. NM
17. RI
17. MT
19. DE
19. MA
19. CA
22. FL
22. WI
22. ID
25. IA
26. KS
26. OH
26. SD
29. GA
29. NC
29. NY
29. MO
29. IN
34. NE
34. TX
36. MI
36. KY
36. PA
39. TN
39. VA
41. AR
42. ND
42. WY
42. WV
45. UT
45. MS
47. AL
48. OK
49. SC
50. LA

Note: Data accessed January 2013. *Data for New Hampshire from 2009. Most current data available at time of publication. *Source:* National Conference of State Legislatures, Legislator Demographic Map. Available at http://www.ncsl.org/legislatures-elections/legisdata/legislator-demographic-map.aspx. © 2013 National Conference of State Legislatures.

Note: Data are for 2013. *Source:* Center for American Women and Politics, "Women in State Legislatures 2013," January 2013. Available at http://www.cawp.rutgers.edu/fast_facts/levels_of_office/documents/stleg.pdf.

Among the factors associated with increased representation of women are the female percentage of the labor force and the proliferation of active women's organizations in the states.[15] Obstacles to their gaining political office include certain cultural forces in the states, notably religious fundamentalism.[16] Another "obstacle" is the growing attractiveness of city and county elective offices that pay better than the state legislature, are less likely to have term limits, and allow one to stay home rather than having to split time between one's hometown and the state capital.[17]

Women candidates are just as successful in primary and general elections as men.[18] Voters are *not* predisposed to cast ballots either for or against female candidates.[19] However, there is evidence that female turnout rates increase when women candidates run, in part because of their belief that women legislators would be more likely to protect their interests if threatened by legislative action.[20] Incumbency gives all officeholders an electoral advantage; since more males held office in the past, women challengers have faced the obstacle of incumbency. But women and men fare equally well in races for open seats, and there is no evidence they drop out of races any more often than male candidates.[21] So why are women underrepresented in state legislatures?

Fewer women than men run for state legislative seats. Scholars frequently cite women's traditional family roles of wife and mother as obstacles to a political career. Female legislative candidates with young children are rare; newly elected women legislators are four years older on the average than newly elected male legislators—a fact generally attributed to women waiting until their children are older.[22] Many women who confront conflicts between family life and political activity choose in favor of their families. One study found that more women serve in the legislatures of states whose capitals are located close to the major population centers than in the legislatures of states whose capitals are isolated and require long commutes from home.[23] Some researchers believe that gender-role attitudes about the "proper role" of women in politics vary among the states, and these attitudes independently affect the gender gap in state legislative representation.[24]

Women in Legislative Leadership Positions

Women continue to score a lot of "firsts" in the various states—first woman speaker of the house, first woman president of the senate, first woman majority or minority leader. Women who have gained leadership posts, however, believe that they had to work harder, study the issues more closely, and overcome more stereotyping than their male counterparts in order to win respect in their chambers.[25]

Women have also won their fair share of committee chairs; that is, in most states they occupy as many or more committee chairs than the percentage of women in the legislative body would indicate.[26] Indeed, they chair a disproportionate number of education, health, and human service committees, while at the same time, they chair a fair share of the key budget and taxation committees.

More women are ascending into state leadership posts. Democrat Therese Murray, President of the Massachusetts Senate, is the first woman to lead either house of the Massachusetts General Court (legislature).

Women have also ascended into major leadership posts in each chamber: presidents and president pro tems of the senate, speakers or speaker pro tems of the house, and majority leaders, minority leaders, floor leaders, and whips in each chamber.

The Effect of Electing Women to State Legislatures

Most of the evidence to date indicates that women exhibit unique priorities, particularly on women's issues.[27] Women legislators are more liberal in their policy attitudes, and they exhibit greater commitment to the pursuit of feminist initiatives and legislation incorporating issues of concern to women, including education, health, and welfare. In law enforcement, women are more likely to favor rehabilitative approaches, while men are more likely to prefer punishment. The growing presence of women's caucuses in state legislatures accentuates gender-based voting behavior by women legislators. Women are just as likely as men to secure the passage of legislation that they introduce.[28]

There is also evidence that women go about lawmaking differently than men. Traditionally, male legislative behavior (described as competitive, bargaining, logrolling, and confrontational) was regarded as the norm in legislative institutions. Some research suggests that women are slowly transforming legislative processes by emphasizing consensual, cooperative, and inclusive decision making.[29] But other research has found more differences among women or among men than differences *between* the sexes. One study of legislators in Arizona and California found that female representatives do not weigh the concerns, needs, or demands of their constituents more heavily than their male counterparts, nor do women devote any less time and energy to legislative duties and the policymaking process than men. But women legislators do forge closer ties to their female constituents.[30]

6.4

GETTING TO THE STATE CAPITOL

Explain the prior political experience of state legislators and the process they endured to get to the state capital, including raising money for their campaigns and navigating the primary and general elections.

The state legislature is a convenient starting place for a political career. About one-half of the state legislators in the nation never served in public office before their election to the legislature, and a greater percentage of new members are in the lower rather than upper chambers. The other half had only limited experience on city councils, county commissions, and school boards.

Getting into Politics

Why does a legislator decide to run for office in the first place? It is next to impossible to determine the real motivations of political office seekers—they seldom know themselves. Legislators will usually describe their motivations in highly idealistic terms: "I felt that I could do the community a service," or "I considered it a civic duty." Only seldom are reasons for candidacy expressed in personal terms: "Oh, I just think it's lots of fun." Gregariousness and the desire to socialize no doubt contribute to the reasons for some office seekers. Politics can have a special lure of its own: "It gets into your blood and you like it." That is often the perspective of those who got their start in politics serving as legislative aides or working in campaigns. Particular issues may also mobilize a political career. Activity in organizations that are deeply involved in politics also often leads to candidacy.

Political Experience

States with stronger parties are more likely to nominate people who have worked for the party in some previous appointed or elective office. States with weaker parties are more likely to elect "amateurs" with no previous political experience. The stronger the party organization, the more likely a legislative candidate will have to serve a political apprenticeship in some local or party offices. However, as party organizations weaken, the easier it becomes for individuals with little or no prior governmental experience, and with more personal wealth, to win legislative seats.

Raising Campaign Money

The first challenge that an aspiring legislator faces is raising money to finance his or her campaign. In some states with small legislative districts, nonprofessional legislatures, and largely rural constituencies, a state legislative race may cost less than $25,000.[31] But large urban state legislative races may cost upwards of several hundred thousand dollars, especially in competitive races. Senate contests cost more than house contests, and winners usually spend more than losers. Money allows a candidate to produce commercials, buy television and radio time, place ads on the Internet and in newspapers, travel around the district, and distribute bumper stickers, yard signs, and campaign buttons.

Some state legislative candidates employ expensive professional campaign management firms. Most state legislative campaigns are relatively amateurish, but they still cost money. When campaigns are relatively inexpensive, the candidate and his or her friends contribute most of the money. But in more expensive races, candidates may turn to PACs. Corporate, labor, environmental, and ideological PACs are becoming increasingly active in state capitals, particularly in the larger states. (See "Money in State Politics" in Chapter 5.) Perhaps as much as one-third of money for state legislative campaigns now comes from PAC contributions, most of which goes to incumbents. But a growing source of money is the "527" organization—an independent advocacy group that can spend money for or against a candidate with no limit.[32] In general, incumbents have an easier time raising money; so, too, do moderates as opposed to ideologically extreme candidates.[33]

Facing the Primaries

More than half of the nation's state legislators are *unopposed* for their party's nomination in **uncontested elections**. Many legislators who do face primary competition have only token opposition. Most primary competition occurs in a party's "**safe**" **districts**, some competition occurs in "**close**" **districts**, and there is a distinct shortage of candidates in districts where the party's chances are poor. In other words, primary competition is greater where the likelihood of victory in the general election is greater. Primary competition is also stiffer when there is an open seat and in states with more professional (full-time) legislatures.[34]

Some states require runoff elections when no candidate wins a majority in the first primary. (See Chapter 5.) Thus, some candidates face three elections on their way to the legislature—a first primary, a runoff primary, and the general election.

The General Election

The culmination of the recruitment process is in the general election, yet in many legislative constituencies one party is so entrenched that the voters have little real choice in the general election. In some districts, the minority party is so weak that it fails to run candidates for legislative seats. Overall about one-quarter of state legislative general elections are uncontested; that is, one or another of the major parties does not even field a candidate. Incumbents win over 90 percent of the uncontested general election races.[35]

"Competition" implies more than a name filed under the opposition party label. Generally a **competitive election** is one in which the winning candidate wins by something less than two to one. In light of this more realistic definition of competition, the absence of truly competitive politics in state legislative elections is striking. Overall, more than half of the nation's legislators are elected in *noncompetitive* general elections, where their opponents are either nonexistent or receive less than one-third of the vote. Even

UNCONTESTED ELECTION

An election in which a candidate has no opponent.

"SAFE" DISTRICTS

Districts in which there is little party competition, one party dominates.

"CLOSE" DISTRICTS

Competitive districts where electoral competition is great.

COMPETITION

In electoral politics, confronting an opponent or party that has a reasonable chance to win the election.

COMPETITIVE ELECTION

An election in which the loser receives at least one-third of the votes.

in competitive states, such as California, Michigan, Minnesota, New York, Pennsylvania, and Wisconsin, over half the state legislators face only token opposition in the general election.[36] Moreover, competition within legislative districts is *declining* over time, as more legislators are winning by lopsided margins.[37] Some blame this on the redistricting process whereby legislators draw themselves fairly "safe," noncompetitive districts. In 2012, following redistricting, nearly 40 percent of all state legislative seats were uncontested.[38] (More is said about this later in the chapter.) But others point to the growing financial advantage incumbents have over challengers and to the fact that "Americans are increasingly living in communities and neighborhoods whose residents share their values and they are increasingly voting for candidates who reflect those values."[39]

<table>
<tr><td>6.5</td></tr>
</table>

THE GREAT INCUMBENCY MACHINE

Examine the advantages of incumbency for winning reelection.

Legislators who choose to run for reelection (**incumbents**) are seldom defeated. Indeed, they are usually unopposed in the primary election, and sometimes unopposed in the general election. Potential challengers are discouraged by the record of success of incumbents.[40] Nearly 90 percent of incumbent state legislators who seek reelection are successful, however recently incumbents have had a slightly lower success rating. Aspiring newcomers in politics are advised to wait for incumbents to leave office voluntarily or until an incumbent is term limited and cannot run again. Redistricting also opens up legislative seats and occasionally forces incumbents to run against each other, but in most states that only happens every 10 years. Although there is some evidence that "**quality challengers**"—people who have won previous state or local elections and can raise campaign funds—have a better chance than newcomers to defeat incumbents, nonetheless, the likelihood of defeating an incumbent in either the primary or general election is low.[41] Even in states with term limits or public financing programs, the incumbency advantage remains strong.[42] Why is this so?

INCUMBENTS
Persons currently serving in elective or appointed positions in government.

QUALITY CHALLENGERS
People who have won previous state or local elections and can raise campaign funds.

Visibility

Incumbents enjoy greater visibility and name recognition in their districts: "The reason I get 93 percent victories is what I do back home. I stay highly visible. No grass grows under my feet. I show I haven't forgot from whence I came."[43] Incumbents spend a major portion of their time throughout their term of office campaigning for reelection: "I have the feeling that the most effective campaigning is done when no election is near. During the interval between elections you have to establish every personal contact you can." Legislators regularly appear at civic clubs, social and charitable events, churches, and many other gatherings: "Personally, I will speak on any subject. I talk on everything whether it deals with politics or not." Indeed, many legislators spend more time campaigning for reelection than lawmaking. Few challengers can afford to spend two or four years campaigning.

Resources of Office

As legislatures become more professional over time—employing large professional staffs; providing offices, expense accounts, and travel budgets to legislators; and increasing their pay—incumbents acquire greater resources to assist them in servicing constituents. **Constituents' services** or "**casework**" is growing in state legislatures; legislators are increasingly involved in assisting constituents in dealing with state agencies, providing information, and doing small favors at the capital. Over time this form of "retail" politics gradually builds a network of grateful voters.

CASEWORK
Services performed by legislators or their staffs for individual constituents.

Legislators in professional legislatures are given large sums to subsidize what are really campaign activities—printing and mailing of newsletters; press rooms and video studios; travel reimbursement; and aides, assistants, staffers, and interns who spend much of their time on constituent services.

Professional legislatures enjoy abundant resources, sometimes referred to as the five S's: space, salary, session length, staff, and structure. There is evidence that these resources contribute to incumbent reelection.[44] It is increasingly difficult for challengers to confront incumbents with these resources, and access to the five Ss encourages incumbents to remain in office.

Money

Finally, and perhaps most important, incumbents attract a lot more campaign contributions than challengers. Interest group contributions go overwhelmingly to incumbents. (See "Money in State Politics" in Chapter 5.) These groups are seeking access and influence with decision makers, so they direct their contributions to people in office. Moreover, group leaders know that incumbents are rarely defeated and they do not want to antagonize incumbents by contributing to challengers. Incumbents can build a "war chest" over time; often its size is enough to discourage potential challengers from entering races against them. When incumbent state legislators decide to run for Congress (often because they have been "termed out of office"[45] or are smart enough to run only in races that they are most likely to win), they are much better at attracting money, especially early on in primary battles, than their opponents.[46]

Professionalism and Careerism

Professionalism in state legislatures encourages **careerism**. It encourages people who view politics as a career to seek and win a seat in the state legislature. Higher pay makes the job more attractive and allows legislators to devote all their time to politics and policymaking.[47] Year-round sessions discourage people who cannot take leave from their business or profession. Greater resources available to legislators allow them to perform more casework for constituents and to build a personal organization devoted to keeping themselves in office. Additional resources make life at the state capital more comfortable, especially for party leaders.[48] There is less voluntary turnover in professional legislatures, and less likelihood that an incumbent will be defeated. Political scientist Alan Rosenthal writes, "One quality that distinguishes the new breed of full-time, professional politicians from the old breed of part-time, citizen legislators is ambition. The latter were content to spend a few years in legislative office and then return to private careers. The former, by contrast, would like to spend most of their careers in government and politics. They find public office appealing and the game of politics exhilarating."[49] Some state legislators have even gone on to be president. (See *Did You Know?* How Many State Legislators Later Became President?)

CAREERISM
In politics, the tendency of people to view running for and occupying elected public office as a full-time career.

APPORTIONMENT
The determination of how many residents should live in a representative's district; must be equal (one person, one vote).

LEGISLATIVE APPORTIONMENT AND DISTRICTING

6.6

Legislative **apportionment** refers to the allocation of seats to specific populations. When state legislative and congressional district boundary lines have to be redrawn after each census, several factors are taken into consideration: compliance with the "one-person, one-vote," adherence to federal Voting Rights Act requirements to protect minorities, and respect for a state's **traditional redistricting principles**—such as compactness, contiguity, maintaining communities of interest, and minimizing the splitting of counties, cities, and precincts. These factors have become more critical over the years, primarily through court rulings.[50]

Prior to 1962, malapportionment was common in American state legislatures. **Malapportionment** occurs when there are differing numbers of people in legislative districts that receive the same number of seats. Malapportionment creates inequality of representation: If one single-member district has twice the population of another, the value of a vote in the larger district is only half the value of a vote in the smaller district. Small minorities of the population could elect a majority of the house or senate or both in most of the states. Generally, it was the rural voters in a state who controlled a majority of legislative seats, and it was the urban voters who were discriminated against in the value of their vote. Finally, the U.S. Supreme Court intervened and the "one person, one vote" principle prevailed.

Assess how *Baker v. Carr* affected legislative apportionment, describe the processes used to draw district lines, and evaluate how this process can be used for political purposes.

TRADITIONAL REDISTRICTING PRINCIPLES
Compactness; contiguity; keeping communities of interest, counties, towns, and precincts together.

MALAPPORTIONMENT
Unequal numbers of people in legislative districts creating inequality of representation; declared unconstitutional by the U.S. Supreme Court.

How Many State Legislators Later Became President?

President	State Legislative Body	Served in Legislature
George Washington	Virginia House of Burgesses (Colonial Era)	1758–1774
John Adams	Massachusetts General Court (Colonial Era)	1768–1774
Thomas Jefferson	Virginia House of Burgesses (Colonial Era)	1769–1774
James Madison	Virginia House of Delegates (Colonial Era)	1776–1777
James Monroe	Virginia Assembly	1782–1783
John Quincy Adams	Massachusetts Senate	1802–1803
Martin Van Buren	New York Senate	1813–1820
William Henry Harrison	Ohio Senate	1819–1821
John Tyler	Virginia House of Delegates	1811–1816
James Polk	Tennessee House of Representatives	1823–1825
Millard Fillmore	New York Assembly	1829–1831
Franklin Pierce	New Hampshire House of Representatives	1829–1833
James Buchanan	Pennsylvania House of Representatives	1814–1816
Abraham Lincoln	Illinois House of Representatives	1834–1842
Andrew Johnson	Tennessee House of Representatives	1835–1837, 1839–1841
	Tennessee Senate	1841–1843
James Garfield	Ohio Senate	1859–1861
Theodore Roosevelt	New York Assembly	1882–1884
Warren G. Harding	Ohio Senate	1899–1903
Calvin Coolidge	Massachusetts House of Representatives	1907–1908
	Massachusetts Senate	1912–1915
Franklin Delano Roosevelt	New York Senate	1911–1913
Jimmy Carter	Georgia Senate	1963–1966
Barack Obama	Illinois Senate	1997–2004

Source: National Conference of State Legislatures, "Former State Legislators in the White House." Available at http://www.ncsl.org/legislatures-elections/state-federal/former-state-legislators-in-congress.aspx.

Supreme Court Intervention

After years of avoiding the issue of malapportionment, the U.S. Supreme Court acted in 1962 in the landmark case of *Baker v. Carr.*[51] This case involved the complaint of urban residents in Tennessee where the largest district in the lower house was 23 times larger than the smallest district. The Supreme Court decided that such inequalities in state apportionment laws denied voters "equal protection of the laws" guaranteed by the Fourteenth Amendment and that the federal courts should grant relief from these inequalities. The Supreme Court did not decide on any firm mathematical standard of correct apportionment, holding only that "as nearly as practicable, one man's vote should be equal to another's."[52] The Supreme Court required that *both* houses of the state legislature be apportioned on the basis of population; the Court rejected the federal analogy of a senate based on geographic units: "Legislators represent people, not trees or acres. Legislators are elected by voters, not farms or cities or economic interests."[53] State after state was forced to reapportion its legislature under the threat of judicial intervention.

In addition to requiring population equality in legislative districting, the U.S. Supreme Court also required population equality in congressional districting by state legislatures. The philosophy underlying these decisions was expressed by the Court: "The conception of political equality from the Declaration of Independence to Lincoln's Gettysburg Address, to the Fourteenth, Fifteenth, Seventeenth, and Nineteenth Amendments, can mean only one thing—one person, one vote."[54]

The Impact of Reapportionment

The reapportionment revolution of the 1960s significantly increased the representation afforded urban interests in state legislatures. Initially, reapportionment also seemed to bring younger, better-educated, more prestigiously employed people into state legislatures, many of whom were from urban areas. It also brought many "new" people into legislative politics—people who had little or no previous experience in public office.

Standards of Equality among Districts

Today, there is little inequality in the number of people in legislative districts in any state, and "one person, one vote" is the prevailing form of representation. But federal courts have not always been consistent or precise in determining exactly *how equal* congressional and state legislative districts must be. In several early cases, federal courts calculated an "ideal" district by dividing the total population of the state by the number of legislative seats and then comparing all district populations to this ideal district. Variations of more than 2 percent in any district from the ideal often led to federal court invalidation of a state's redistricting plan. Later the federal courts began calculating an "overall range" by adding the deviations of the largest district and the smallest district from the ideal, disregarding the plus and minus signs. (Thus if the largest district was 2% larger than the ideal, and the smallest district 1% smaller than the ideal, the "overall range" would be 3%.)

With regard to *congressional* districts, the U.S. Supreme Court has required strict standards of equality. Indeed, no population inequality that "could practicably be avoided" is permitted in congressional districts; a New Jersey plan with an overall range of 0.70 percent was struck down upon presentation of evidence that the legislature could have reduced the range to 0.45 percent.[55]

However, the U.S. Supreme Court has been more lenient in considering *state legislative* districting plans. The Court has refused to set any specific mathematical standards of equality for legislative districts. Nonetheless, districting plans with an overall range of more than 10 percent "create a prima facie case of discrimination and therefore must be justified by the state."[56] Federal courts will allow some deviations from absolute equality in order to recognize political subdivision (e.g., city, county) boundaries. Some citizens do not agree with this philosophy. Several states were sued about the population deviations in their post–2000 Census plans, most notably New York and Georgia. In Georgia, the federal court overturned the state's legislative plans.[57]

Districting: Partisan and Incumbent Gerrymandering

Districting refers to the drawing of boundary lines for legislative districts. While malapportionment refers to inequality in representation, **gerrymandering** refers to the drawing of district lines for political advantage. The population of districts can be equal, yet the districts drawn in such a fashion as to give advantage to one party or group over another. Consider a simple example:

For a city that is entitled to three representatives, the eastern third of the city is Republican while the western two-thirds are Democratic. If the Republicans draw the district lines, they will draw them along a north–south direction to allow them to win in one of the three districts; if Democrats draw the district lines, they will draw them along an east–west direction to allow them to win all three districts by diluting the Republican vote. Often, gerrymandering is not as neat as our example; district lines may twist and turn and create grotesque geographic patterns.

DISTRICTING
Drawing geographical boundaries of representatives' districts.

GERRYMANDERING
The drawing of electoral district boundary lines to grant political advantage to a particular party, candidate, or group.

SPLINTERING

In districting, dividing and diluting a strong minority to deny it the ability to elect a number of representatives comparable to its percentage of the population.

CRACKING

Splintering or dividing up a sizable minority group into several districts to deny it the power to elect a representative.

PACKING

Concentrating partisan voters in a single district in order to maximize the number of representatives that can be elected by the opposition in other districts.

PARTISAN GERRYMANDERING

The drawing of electoral district boundary lines to grant political power to a particular party, therefore increasing the number of winning candidates within that party.

Gerrymandering can be accomplished by the combined methods of splintering, cracking, and packing. **Splintering** involves dividing up and diluting a strong minority to deny it the power to elect a representative. **Cracking** involves splintering or dividing up a sizable minority group into several districts to deny it the power to elect a representative. **Packing** involves the concentration of partisan voters in a single district in order to "waste" their votes in large majorities for a single representative and thereby protect modest majorities in other districts (see "*Up Close:* The Original Gerrymander"). Some describe the redistricting process as "the most naked exercise of political power in the states."[58]

As long as districts are equal in population, **partisan gerrymandering** does *not* violate federal court standards for "equal protection" under the Fourteenth Amendment. There is no constitutional obligation to allocate seats "to the contending parties in proportion to what their anticipated statewide vote will be."[59] However, the federal courts may intervene in political gerrymandering if it "consistently degrades a voter's or a group of voters' influence on the political process as a whole." This vague standard set forth by the U.S. Supreme Court keeps the door open to judicial intervention in particularly grievous cases of political gerrymandering. But so far, the Court has continued to keep the door shut, much to the dismay of some.[60] A partisan gerrymandering–based legal challenge to Pennsylvania's redistricting was rejected by a 5–4 decision of the U.S. Supreme Court in *Vieth* v. *Jubelirer* (2004).[61] After years of trying to establish a standard for partisan gerrymandering, the Supreme Court gave up. It firmly rejected the notion that districting had to be "fair" to the parties. "'Fairness' is not a judicially manageable standard." They reaffirmed that partisan gerrymandering was a *nonjusticiable* issue—it could not be decided by courts. Frustration with the high court's failure to rule partisan gerrymandering unconstitutional has led some states to amend their constitutions to prohibit such action (Florida's Fair Districts amendment adopted by voters in 2010).

Incumbent gerrymandering sometimes supplements traditional partisan gerrymandering. The object of incumbent gerrymandering is to protect the seats of incumbents. Often if party control of state government is divided, thus preventing the passage of a partisan gerrymander, legislators will agree to protect themselves. This explains why some citizens refer to some redistricting maps as nothing more than "incumbency protection" plans, particularly if the legislators draw the lines.

The Seats–Votes Relationship

One way to determine whether partisan gerrymandering has shortchanged a party is to compare the total statewide vote compiled by all of the party's candidates with the proportion of legislative seats it won.[62] For example, if a party's candidates won 55 percent of the total votes cast in all legislative elections, but won only 45 percent of the seats, we might conclude that partisan gerrymandering was to blame. This comparison is not always valid, however, especially when it is understood that a party that wins a slight majority of votes would normally be expected to win a much larger proportion of seats. For example, a party that wins 52 percent of total votes cast in all legislative elections might win 65 percent of the seats; theoretically it could win 100 percent of the seats in the unlikely event that its 52 percent of the votes was spread evenly in every legislative district. The U.S. Supreme Court has held that "a mere lack of proportionality in results in one election" cannot prove an unconstitutional gerrymander; however, the Court said that it might intervene when there is "a history of disproportionate result."[63] It is important to remember that the United States does *not* employ proportional representation as do many European democracies. Hence we cannot expect proportionality in the seats–votes relationship. However, extreme and persistent differences in this relationship may signal the existence of partisan gerrymandering.

Affirmative Racial Gerrymandering

Gerrymandering designed to *dis*advantage blacks and language minorities is a violation of the Equal Protection Clause of the Fourteenth Amendment, and it is a violation of the

The term *gerrymander* immortalizes Governor Elbridge Gerry (1744–1814) of Massachusetts, who in 1812 redistricted the state legislature to favor Democrats over Federalists. A district north of Boston was designed to concentrate and thus waste Federalist votes. The district was portrayed in a political cartoon in the *Boston Gazette* on March 26, 1812, as a "gerrymander."

federal Voting Rights Act of 1965.[64] In 1982 Congress strengthened the Voting Rights Act by outlawing any electoral arrangements that had the *effect* of weakening minority voting power (see "Securing the Right to Vote" in Chapter 4). The U.S. Supreme Court obliged the states whenever possible to maximize opportunities for blacks and minority candidates to win election.[65] This apparent mandate for **affirmative racial gerrymandering** governed redistricting following the 1990 Census and resulted in a significant increase in black and minority representation in many state legislatures. However, the creation of some bizarre-shaped **majority-minority** congressional districts (see Figure 4–5 in Chapter 4) led the U.S. Supreme Court to express constitutional doubts about districts that appear designed exclusively to separate the races. In 2001, in *Hunt* v. *Cromartie,*[66] the Court ruled that while state legislatures can take racial considerations into account when redistricting, they cannot use race as the *predominant* factor. To do so violates the Equal Protection Clause of the Fourteenth Amendment.

The redistricting process in racially/ethnically diverse states can be difficult and divisive, often ending up in court.[67] Other perennial debates center on where prisoners and college students should be counted and how citizenship status should factor in when determining the racial/ethnic composition of a proposed district.

Multimember Districts

Multimember legislative districts (MMDs)—those that elect two or more members to a legislative body—were once common. (Seventeen states had multimember districts in at least one of their legislative chambers before 1990.) Today, only two states—Vermont and West Virginia—use MMDs to elect all their legislators. Four states still use them for their lower chamber (Arizona, New Jersey, South Dakota, and Washington). And several other states use them for a limited number of districts.[68] Proponents argue that MMDs increase collaboration among legislators more than single member districts.[69] But court challenges and complaints

AFFIRMATIVE RACIAL GERRYMANDERING

Drawing legislative district lines in order to maximize opportunities for minority candidates to win elections

MAJORITY-MINORITY DISTRICTS

Districts in which minorities make up the majority of the population.

MULTIMEMBER LEGISLATIVE DISTRICTS (MMDS)

Districts from which two or more members are elected to a legislative body; must meet equal population size criteria.

by minority parties and racial minorities have restricted the use of MMDs. The U.S. Supreme Court has never held multimember districts to be unconstitutional per se, as long as the population representation is equal.[70] A two-member district, for example, should have twice the **ideal district population** (calculated by dividing the total state population by the total number of districts in each legislative chamber). However, multimember district plans that discriminate against racial minorities are unconstitutional.[71] Single-member districts are strongly preferred by minorities—minority political parties as well as racial minorities.

IDEAL DISTRICT POPULATION

The ideal population within a district, calculated by dividing the total state population by the total number of districts in each legislative chamber.

District Size

State legislative districts, in both upper and lower chambers, are much smaller than congressional districts. Each of the 435 members of the U.S. House of Representatives serves about 710,767 constituents. (The only state legislative chambers in which members serve so many constituents are the California Senate, where 40 senators each serve 931,349 constituents, and the Texas Senate, where 31 senators each serve 811,147 constituents.) Some house districts in rural states have fewer than 10,000 constituents, while house districts in large urban states (Arizona, California, Florida, Illinois, New York, Ohio, and Texas) have more than 100,000 constituents. (New Hampshire, with 400 house members serving a total population of only 1.3 million, has the nation's smallest legislative constituencies—3,291 persons.) Senate districts across the nation regularly exceed 100,000 constituents.[72]

Who Draws the Lines?

Traditionally, legislatures drew up their own district lines. In most states this continues to be the case. Many legislatures employ private consultants to assist in the task, and computer mapping is now common. Legislatures generally try to protect incumbents, and the majority party frequently tries to maximize its advantages over the minority party. But in recent years, because of court challenges over apportionment (equality of population in districts) and racial gerrymandering, most legislative districting plans must be approved by courts. Reformers (Americans for Redistricting Reform, FairVote.org, Common Cause, National Municipal League, League of Women Voters) have urged state legislatures to turn over redistricting to appointed **independent nonpartisan redistricting commissions**, and some states have done so. (See Figure 6–1.) The creation of independent redistricting commissions (IRCs) generally requires a constitutional amendment.

INDEPENDENT NONPARTISAN REDISTRICTING COMMISSIONS

Bodies designed to, impartially and without political interference, redistrict in an effort to decrease political gerrymandering.

How Often to Redistrict?

Historically, most states have redrawn their legislative and congressional districts just once every 10 years—right after the release of new census figures. That pattern was disrupted in the early 2000s. Several state legislatures attempted to redraw districts created for the 2002 election cycle in time for the 2004 cycle. In each instance, litigation ensued. In Colorado, the State Supreme Court threw out the legislative new plan. In New Hampshire, the State Supreme Court upheld the legislative plan. And in Texas, after much litigation, the new congressional districts were upheld by the federal courts, which rejected plaintiffs' claims that the plan was both a racial and partisan gerrymander and a violation of the federal Voting Rights Act.[73]

6.7 LEGISLATIVE ORGANIZATION AND PROCEDURE

Trace the typical lawmaking process in state legislatures, paying specific attention to the disorderliness of process and areas of frequent logjams.

The formal rules and procedures by which state legislatures operate are primarily designed to make the legislative process fair and orderly. Without established customs, rules, and procedures, it would be impossible for fifty, one hundred, or two hundred people to arrive at a collective decision about the thousands of items submitted to them during a legislative session. State legislatures follow a fairly standard pattern in the formal process of making laws. Figure 6–2 provides a brief description of some of the more important procedural steps in lawmaking.

FIGURE 6–1 Independent Redistricting Commissions

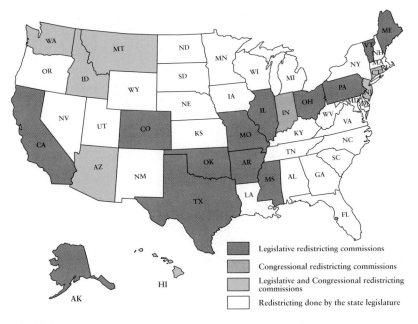

Note: Data are for 2010.
Source: National Conference of State Legislatures.

Procedures Have Consequences

What are the political consequences of the legislative procedures described in Figure 6–2? Obviously, the process for a bill to become a law is difficult—legislative procedures offer many opportunities to defeat legislation. Formal rules and procedures of state legislatures lend themselves easily to those who would delay or obstruct legislation. Figure 6–2 illustrates the deliberative function of legislatures and the consequent procedural advantages given to those who would defend the status quo. Moreover, these procedures imply that the legislature is structured for deliberation and delay in decision making, rather than speed and innovation. This suggests that the legislature functions as an arbiter, rather than an initiator, of public policy, since its procedures are designed to maximize deliberation, even at the expense of granting advantage to those who oppose change.

Disorderliness

As experienced legislators are fond of saying: "There are two things in the world you do not want to watch being made—sausages and laws." Lawmaking is a disorderly process, in spite of the formal procedures listed in Figure 6–2. Students often express shock and dismay when they spend time watching or working in their legislature. After studying the formal rules, they may be unprepared for the "actual" haste, disorganization, logrolling, informality, infighting, petty jealousies, vote trading, ignorance, and ineptitude that they encounter. There are times that legislators step over the bounds of acceptable behavior. In such a situation, it is up to the legislature to take action. In 2013, Nevada legislators removed one of their own from the state Assembly. Fearing their own safety from observing his actions and unwillingness to take a leave of absence to get professional help, they deemed him too dangerous to remain as a legislator.[74] The expulsion of a member from a state legislature is a fairly rare event. Only 19 legislators, including the one most recently-removed, have been expelled from state legislatures over the past 50 years.

FIGURE 6-2 How an Idea Becomes a Law—Bill Originating in the Florida Senate

THE FLORIDA SENATE — *HOW AN IDEA BECOMES A LAW*

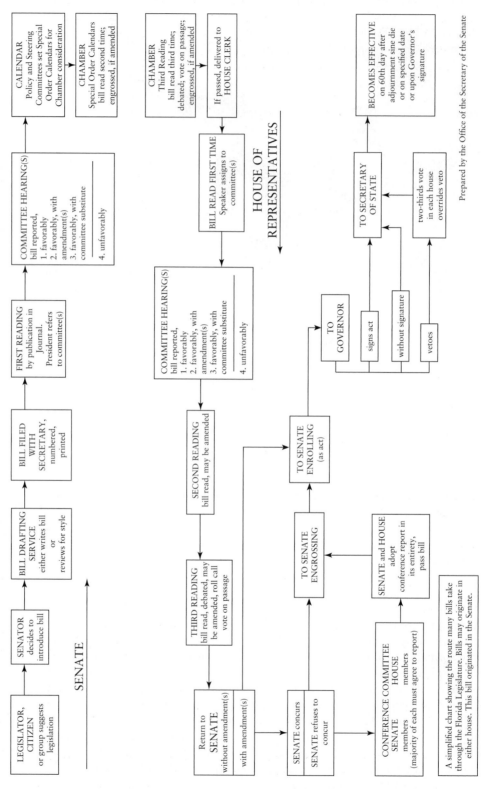

Source: Available at http://www.flsenate.gov/data/civics/idea_to_law_chart.pdf.

Workload

Fewer than one in four bills introduced in a legislative session actually makes its way through the whole process and becomes law. In large states such as California and Texas somewhere between 2,000 and 5,000 bills may be introduced in a single legislative session, and about 1,000 may be enacted into law. In smaller states, a typical legislative session may produce 100 to 400 new laws. Most bills die in committee. Many bills are introduced with no real expectation they will pass; legislators simply seek to "go on record" as working for a particular goal or to get discussion of an issue started, knowing full well it might take several sessions for it to capture the full attention of other legislators.

Logjams

The end-of-session **logjam** is typically the most disorderly phase of lawmaking. In the closing days of a legislative session, hasty efforts are made to win approval for many bills and amendments that are still languishing somewhere in the legislative process. Legislative chambers sometimes become scenes of noisy confusion, with legislators voting blindly on bills described only by number, often resembling a "**train**" because so many bills have been hooked together into one large omnibus bill. Most reformers condemn the end-of-session logjam as a source of inferior quality legislation. Other observers consider it an inevitable product of workload. For still others, the logjam is a strategy to enhance the power of legislative leaders. These leaders control the daily agenda and grant recognition to members seeking the floor; these decisions in a confused end-of-session logjam can determine whose bills get passed and whose do not. In some states in some sessions, over half of all the bills passed will be pushed through in the last few days of the session.[75]

Sessions

Traditionally, state constitutions limited legislative **sessions** to 30 or 60 days once every two years. These limits reflected the "citizen" nature of state legislatures, in contrast to the "professional" full-time congressional model of a legislature. Many observers still argue that the predominant occupation of members should *not* be "legislator," and that legislative sessions should be kept short so that citizens with other occupations can serve in the legislature. But the growing demands of legislative business have led to longer regular sessions.

Most states hold **annual legislative sessions;** only a few are limited to **biennial sessions** (see Table 6–1). Fourteen states place no limit on the length of sessions, while the rest have either constitutional limits (the most common) or statutory limits. The most common limit is 60 days; most legislatures convene in January and adjourn in March.

Frequently legislatures convene in "**special sessions**" in addition to those regularly scheduled. Special sessions may be called by the governor, or in some states by the legislative leadership, to consider special topics—for example, projected budget deficits, reapportionment, or a lawsuit facing the state unless preemptive action is taken. Usually these sessions are limited to the topic for which they were called.

We should remember that legislators have many duties between sessions; their work does not end when the session adjourns. Often legislative committees meet between sessions, and constituents continue to contact legislators for services.

LEGISLATIVE INSTITUTIONALIZATION

Over time political bodies develop their own rules, organizational structures, and patterns of behavior. Social scientists refer to this process as "**institutionalization.**" In legislative bodies, institutionalization is said to occur when (1) membership stabilizes and legislators come to look upon their service as a career; (2) staffs are added, salaries increased, and internal operations expanded; and (3) rules of procedure become more complex.[76]

LOGJAMS
In legislative affairs, the rush to pass a large number of bills at the end of the session.

TRAIN
A number of bills are combined into a single bill that legislators must vote up or down.

SESSIONS
The meetings of elected legislative bodies from their initial convening to their official adjournment.

ANNUAL LEGISLATIVE SESSIONS
Legislative sessions that take place every year.

BIENNIAL SESSIONS
Legislative sessions that take place every two years.

SPECIAL SESSION
Legislative sessions that may be called by the governor, or in some states by the legislative leadership, to consider special topics.

6.8

Describe the institutionalization of state legislatures, and assess how increased professionalism has impacted legislative processes and outcomes.

INSTITUTIONALIZATION
The development of rules and
procedures, organizational
structures, and standard
patterns of behavior in political
bodies.

State legislatures have gradually become more institutionalized. Overall, membership turn-over has diminished over time (except where there are legislative term limits; see Table 2–6 in Chapter 2), legislative salaries and perks have risen, and incumbents have enjoyed a heavy advantage in seeking reelection. More legislators are coming to see their jobs as full-time occupations.

Professionalism

PROFESSIONALISM
In legislatures, the extent to
which members are devoted
full time to their legislative jobs
and have the assistance of staffs
and other legislative support
services.

Some state legislatures are highly professional, while others are not. By **professionalism** we mean that in some legislatures the members are well paid and tend to think of their jobs as full-time ones; members and committees are well staffed and have good informational services available to them; and a variety of legislative services, such as bill drafting and statutory revision, are well supported and maintained. In other legislatures, members are poorly paid and regard their legislative work as part-time; there is little in the way of staff for legislators or committees; and little is provided in legislative assistance and services. Figure 6–3 groups the states by the professionalism of their legislatures.

Effects of Professionalization

Professionalization of state legislatures includes the development of large **staffs** for the leadership and for committees, as well as the provision of aides and assistants to individual members; the provision of offices, expense accounts, travel budgets, and other perks; assistance in communication with constituents, including printing and mailing of newsletters, press rooms and television studios, and Web site development and maintenance; and, of course, higher salaries that allow legislators to spend more time both legislating and politicking.[77]

STAFF
In legislatures, aides employed
to assist individual members or
committees in their work.

All of these elements of professionalization combine to allow legislators to do more individual "casework" for constituents (often by contacting state agencies[78]), to devote more time pursuing their districts' interests, and, in effect, aiding them in campaign-type activities during their tenure in office. Knowing this, the press often focuses on the expense reimbursement requests filed by legislators, especially during an election year.

As the level of professionalism in a legislature increases, its members' probability of winning reelection rises. Legislative tenure increases. State legislative elections become more insulated from political and economic developments in the nation and interstate. In other words, political and economic changes in the nation or in a state have their strongest effects on the probability that incumbents will win reelection when professionalism is low. "Coattail" effects—legislators gaining electoral support when running with a popular gubernatorial, U.S. senatorial, or presidential candidate of the same party—are diminished by professionalism. That is to say, professionalism tends to "insulate" legislative elections.[79]

"COATTAIL" EFFECTS
Legislators gaining electoral
support when running with
a popular gubernatorial, U.S.
senatorial, or presidential
candidate of the same party.

Professionalism and Public Policy

Does it make any difference in public policy whether a legislature is "professional" or not? Reformers often *assume* that "professionalism" will result in legislatures that are "generally innovative in many different areas of public policy, generous in welfare and educational spending and services, and 'interventionist' in the sense of having powers and responsibilities of broad scope."[80] Does legislative reform, however, *really* have any policy consequences? Unfortunately, there is little systematic evidence that legislative professionalism has any *direct* effect on public policy. A state's income, urbanization, and education better explain policy outcomes than legislative professionalism.

Legislative Staffing

Years ago, state legislatures employed only a few clerks and secretaries to handle the clerical chores and a few lawyers in a small "legislative reference service" to draft bills at the request of lawmakers. Today, the movement toward professionalism in state legislatures has created large professional staffs to serve the needs of the leadership and the standing committees. Some more "professional" legislatures have full-time professional staffs—lawyers, researchers, speechwriters, press liaisons, as well as secretarial assistants—for the house speaker, senate

TABLE 6-1 The State Legislatures

State	Official Name	Senate Number	Senate Term	House Number	House Term	Salaries	Regular Sessions
Alabama	Legislature	35	4	105	4	Per diem+	Annual
Alaska	Legislature	20	4	40	2	50,400+	Annual
Arizona	Legislature	30	2	60	2	24,000+	Annual
Arkansas	General Assembly	35	4	100	2	15,869+	Annual
California	Legislature	40	4	80	2	95,291+	Biennium*
Colorado	General Assembly	35	4	65	2	30,000+	Annual
Connecticut	General Assembly	36	2	151	2	28,000	Annual
Delaware	General Assembly	21	4	41	2	42,750+	Annual
Florida	Legislature	40	4	120	2	29,687+	Annual
Georgia	General Assembly	56	2	180	2	17,342+	Annual
Hawaii	Legislature	25	4	51	2	46,273+	Annual
Idaho	Legislature	35	2	70	2	16,116+	Annual
Illinois	General Assembly	59	(a)	118	2	67,836+	Annual
Indiana	General Assembly	50	4	100	2	22,616+	Annual
Iowa	General Assembly	50	4	100	2	25,000+	Annual
Kansas	Legislature	40	4	125	2	Per diem+	Annual
Kentucky	General Assembly	38	4	100	2	Per diem+	Annual
Louisiana	Legislature	39	4	105	4	16,800+	Annual
Maine	Legislature	35	2	151	2	13,852+	Annual*
Maryland	General Assembly	47	4	141	4	43,500+	Annual
Massachusetts	General Court	40	2	160	2	61,300+	Biennium
Michigan	Legislature	38	4	110	2	71,865+	Annual
Minnesota	Legislature	67	4	134	2	31,141+	Biennium
Mississippi	Legislature	52	4	122	4	10,000+	Annual
Missouri	General Assembly	34	4	163	2	35,915+	Annual
Montana	Legislature	50	4	100	2	Per diem+	Biennial-odd year
Nebraska	Legislature	49	4	N/A	N/A	12,000+	Annual
Nevada	Legislature	21	4	42	2	Per diem+	Biennial-odd year
New Hampshire	General Court	24	2	400	2	200	Annual
New Jersey	Legislature	40	4[a]	80	2	49,000	Biennium
New Mexico	Legislature	42	4	70	2	No salary+	Annual
New York	Legislature	63	2	150	2	79,500+	Annual
North Carolina	General Assembly	50	2	120	2	13,951+	Annual*
North Dakota	Legislative Assembly	47	4	94	4	Per diem+	Biennial-odd
Ohio	General Assembly	33	4	99	2	60,584	Biennium
Oklahoma	Legislature	48	4	101	2	38,400+	Annual
Oregon	Legislative Assembly	30	4	60	2	21,936+	Biennial-odd year
Pennsylvania	General Assembly	50	4	203	2	82,026+	Biennium*
Rhode Island	General Assembly	38	2	75	2	14,186	Annual
South Carolina	General Assembly	46	4	124	2	10,400+	Biennium
South Dakota	Legislature	35	2	70	2	12,000+	Annual
Tennessee	General Assembly	33	4	99	2	19,009+	Biennium
Texas	Legislature	31	4	150	2	7,200+	Biennial-odd year

		Senate		House			
State	**Official Name**	**Number**	**Term**	**Number**	**Term**	**Salaries**	**Regular Sessions**
Utah	Legislature	29	4	75	2	Per diem+	Annual
Vermont	General Assembly	30	2	150	2	605/week+	Annual
Virginia	General Assembly	40	4	100	2	18,000+[b]	Annual
Washington	Legislature	49	4	98	2	42,106+	Annual
West Virginia	Legislature	34	4	100	2	20,000+	Annual
Wisconsin	Legislature	33	4	99	2	49,943+	Biennium
Wyoming	Legislature	30	4	60	2	Per diem+	Biennium

TABLE 6–1   The State Legislatures (Continued)

Note: + means legislator gets per diem living expenses in addition to his or her legislative salary; * means that session length varies.

[a]Term length varies by year.

[b]Virginia House and Senate are paid differently. The House only makes $17,640 (plus per diem living expenses).

Source: Book of States, 2012, Vol. 44, various tables, pp. 113, 114, 118–119, 129–132. Printed with permission from the Council of State Governments.

president, majority and minority leaders, and all standing committees; and many states now even provide full-time, year-round staff for each house and senate member. Only the less "professional" rural, small-state legislatures still depend on a small legislative reference service to serve all legislators in drafting bills and doing research.

For years, legislative staffs grew rapidly, making this new "legislative bureaucracy" an important political force. Often "staffers" are young, yet they exercise a great deal of influence in policymaking.[81] And in spite of the fact that it is a tough, grueling job, with frequent cuts or freezes in pay and benefits, many young staffers love the job. Said one, "My Legislature is . . . one of the most interesting places to work, like being a university with all the intellectual stimulation and variety of high-energy people, but without exams, registration, tuition or GPAs to worry about."[82]

Staff members are political appointees, and they are supposed to reflect the political views of their legislator-bosses in their work. However, some "staffers" become so knowledgeable about state government, or about the state budget, or about their aspects of legislative work that they are kept on in their jobs even when their original sponsor leaves the capital.

The staffs are expected to research issues, find out what other states are doing, assist in analyzing the budget, schedule legislative hearings, line up experts and interest groups to testify, keep abreast of the status of bills and appropriation items as they move through the legislature, maintain contact with state agencies and the governor's staff, make coffee and fetch doughnuts, write and rewrite bills, and perform other assorted chores and errands. As legislators come to rely on trusted "staffers," the "staffers" themselves become more powerful.[83] Their advice may kill a bill or an appropriation item, or their work may amend a bill or alter an appropriation, without the legislator becoming directly involved.

Staffers also have a good vantage point from which to assess who is most effective at influencing public policy outcomes. Majority party leaders are rated highest, minority party leaders the lowest. But the senate, the house, the governor, and committee chairs are ranked so closely they can almost be considered equal.

Turnover Rates & Newcomer Challenges

TURNOVER RATE

In legislatures, the percentage of members replaced in each legislative session.

In states *without* term limits, the overall **turnover rate** (the percentage of legislators replaced each session) is roughly 25 percent. This means that about one-quarter of all state legislators are newcomers at any legislative session. (The turnover rate is higher—around 30%—in the election following redistricting). These new members have taken the seats of members who do not return to the state house because of a career change, a run for higher office, retirement, illness or death, or, in relatively rare instances, defeat in their bid for

FIGURE 6–3 Professionalism in State Legislatures

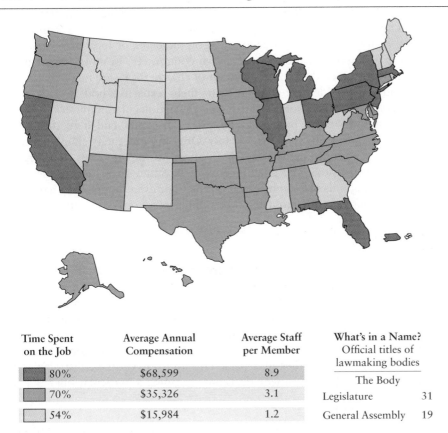

Time Spent on the Job	Average Annual Compensation	Average Staff per Member	What's in a Name? Official titles of lawmaking bodies	
			The Body	
80%	$68,599	8.9		
70%	$35,326	3.1	Legislature	31
54%	$15,984	1.2	General Assembly	19

Note: Data are for 2013
Source: National Conference of State Legislatures, "STATESTATS," State Legislatures, Vol. 39, Issue 1, January 2013, p. 5. © 2013 National Conference of State Legislatures.

reelection. Tips on how to be an effective legislator are often distributed to newcomers to help them avoid "amateur" mistakes early in their legislative careers.

High turnover rates cause some to worry about the loss of some "**institutional memory**"— the observations and insights of veteran legislators about how issues were handled in the past. Interestingly, it is *not* party competition that increases turnover; far more legislators voluntarily quit than are defeated for reelection. There is *less* turnover in the larger states, which have longer legislative sessions and pay their legislators more money. In other words, more "professional" legislatures have lower turnover rates than the "amateur" legislatures. This helps explain why turnover rates vary by state; however, recently turnover rates have been high across the majority of states, with the 2012 election turnover rate around 30 percent of all seats.[84]

"INSTITUTIONAL MEMORY"

The knowledge of veteran legislators about how issues were handled in the past.

LEGISLATIVE COMMITTEES

While it is most convenient to study legislative decision making by observing floor actions, particularly the division of ayes and nays, the floor is not the only locus of important legislative decisions.[85] Committee work is essential to the legislative process. It is here that public hearings are held, lobbyists plead their case, policies are debated, legislation amended and compromised, and bills rushed to the floor or "**pigeonholed**" (ignored). The function of the committee system is to reduce legislative work to manageable proportions by providing for a division of labor among legislators. However, by so doing the committees themselves often come to exercise considerable influence over the outcome of legislation. Another opportunity is provided for delay and obstruction by less than the majority of legislators, sometimes by a single committee chairperson.

6.9

Explain the functions and composition of legislative committees.

"PIGEONHOLED"

A bill is ignored, never reported out of committee.

Functions

A typical legislative chamber will have between 20 and 30 **standing committees** that consider all bills in a particular area, such as revenue (often referred to as "ways and means"), appropriations, highways, welfare, education, labor, judiciary, or local government. Typically, a legislator will serve on three, four, or five committees. In most state legislatures, committee assignments, including the assignment of chairpersons, are made by the speaker of the house and the president of the senate in their respective bodies. This power of appointment gives these leaders some control over the actions of committees.

Committees may decide to hold early hearings on a bill, send it to the floor with little or no revision, and recommend it favorably. Or committees may simply ignore a bill ("pigeonholing"), fail to schedule hearings on it, allow hostile witnesses to testify against it, or write extensive revisions and amendments to it. Some states reduce the power of committees by allowing bills to be considered on the floor even though they have not been reported out of committee, or by requiring that all bills be reported out either favorably or unfavorably.

Personnel

Committee assignments in most legislatures are made by the leadership. Occupational background frequently determines a legislator's initial committee assignments. Thus, lawyers are frequently assigned to committees on the judiciary and civil and criminal law, educators to education committees, farmers to agricultural committees, and bankers to banking committees. The effect of these assignments is to further strengthen the power of special interests in the legislative process. Legislators with occupational ties to a particular legislative committee—either of a personal nature or via their district's economic interests—may influence the committee's decisions regarding a particular bill.[86]

Committee Preferences

Overall, committees generally reflect the preferences of the legislative chambers from which they are drawn. This is especially true where the house speaker and the senate president control **bill referrals**—the assignment of bills to specific committees. One study reports that only about 5 percent of committees can be labeled as "outliers"—committees likely to defy the preferences of their parent chambers. And these are usually issue-specific committees, such as water resources, oil and gas, and labor relations, rather than key committees such as appropriations, ways and means, and rules.[87] Party leadership in most state legislative chambers prevents committees from becoming independent "fiefdoms," although some states have more powerful committee systems than others.[88]

6.10   LEADERSHIP AND ROLE-PLAYING IN LEGISLATURES

Roles are expectations about the kind of behavior people ought to exhibit. Expectations are placed upon a legislator by fellow legislators, the legislator's party, the opposition party, the governor, constituents, interest groups, and friends, as well as by the legislators themselves.

Leadership Roles

Perhaps the most distinctive roles in the legislative process are those of the leadership. A typical legislative chamber has a **presiding officer** (usually a **speaker of the house** and a **president of the senate**), a majority and a minority floor leader, a number of committee chairpersons, and a steering committee. These leaders perform functions similar to the functions of rules. First of all, leaders are expected to help make the legislative system stable and manageable. They are expected to maintain order, to know the rules and procedures, to follow the rules, and to show fairness and impartiality. Leaders are also expected to help focus the issues and resolve conflict by presenting issues clearly, narrowing the alternatives, organizing public hearings, and promoting the party or administrative point of view on bills. The **majority leader** is supposed to "get the administrative program through," while the **minority leader** develops a "constructive opposition."

Leaders are also expected to administer the legislature and expedite business. This includes "promoting teamwork," "being accessible," starting the sessions on time, keeping them on schedule, and distributing the workload. It involves communication, coordination, and liaison with the governor, the administrative departments, and the other chamber.

Members' Expectations of Leaders

From the members' perspective, successful leaders are those who assist them in achieving their personal political goals. Most legislators possess a desire for reelection, as well as power and policy influence within the legislature. The relative importance of these goals will vary for each individual member. A freshman lawmaker who feels electorally insecure will have different priorities than a senior legislator from a safe district. The key to effective leadership is to understand the particular needs and goals of individual members and to respond as necessary.[89]

Leaders' Legislative Priorities

Leaders face a difficult challenge in balancing competing priorities with limited resources. In recent years the top priorities identified by state legislative leaders across the country have been in the areas of education—K–12 and higher education, school reform, Medicaid, health care reform, criminal justice, homeland security and disaster management, budgets, taxes, job creation, public pensions, energy, the environment, and transportation.[90] And, of course, they want fewer unfunded federal mandates to the states and greater control over federal programs in their state (see Chapter 3).

Expert Roles

Another set of legislative roles that are commonly encountered and make important contributions to the legislative process are the "**subject-matter experts.**" Unlike leadership roles, the roles of subject-matter experts are not embodied in formal offices. The committee system introduces specialization into the legislature, and the seniority system places at the head of the committee those persons longest exposed to the information about the committee's subject matter. Thus, subject-matter experts emerge among legislators in the fields of law, finance, education, agriculture, natural resources, local government, labor, and transportation.

Trustees, Delegates, and Politicos

Another way of describing roles in a legislature is to discover the legislators' orientations toward the expectations of constituents. Legislators can be classified as trustees (those who are guided in legislative affairs solely by their personal conscience) and delegates (those who are guided by the instructions or wishes of their constituents). One study has found that more legislators see themselves as trustees than delegates, especially where there are term limits in place or multimember legislative districts.[91]

A classic dilemma of representative government is whether the legislator should vote his or her own conscience—"the trustee"—or vote the constituency's wishes—"the delegate." Good philosophical arguments can be found to support either of these guiding principles. Nearly two hundred years ago English political philosopher Edmund Burke confronted this question directly and urged representatives to vote their own conscience about what is right for society. Burke believed that the voters should elect wise and virtuous representatives to govern *for* them—to use their own judgment in deciding issues regardless of popular demands. Even today the term **Burkean representation** refers to the

SPEAKER OF THE HOUSE
The presiding officer of the lower house of a legislature.

PRESIDENT OF THE SENATE
The presiding officer of the upper house of a legislature.

MAJORITY LEADER
A leader in the controlling party who is supposed to "get the administrative program through."

MINORITY LEADER
The leader of the minority party who is supposed to develop a "constructive opposition" against the policies of the controlling party.

SUBJECT-MATTER EXPERTS
Legislators who gain a reputation for having in-depth knowledge of a particular issue.

TRUSTEE
A role that representatives adopt when they decide to vote their conscience and use their best personal judgment, rather than catering to the narrow interests of their constituents.

DELEGATE
A legislator votes on bills based on the priorities of the constituents back home rather than on his or her personal views.

BURKEAN REPRESENTATION
The belief that legislators should use their own best judgment about what is good for their state or nation, rather than conforming to their constituents' narrow interests.

willingness of a representative to ignore public opinion and decide public issues on the basis of one's own best judgment about what is right for society.

Other political philosophers stress responsiveness of representatives to the views of their constituents. Consider, for example, philosopher Hanna Pitkin's definition of representation: "Representation means acting in the interest of the represented, in a manner responsive to them."[92] **Responsiveness** connotes a deliberate effort by legislators to match their votes on public policy issues to their constituencies' preferences. However, to be "responsive" to one's constituents, two conditions must be met: (1) the legislator must correctly perceive the constituents' views on the issues, and (2) the legislator must act in accord with these views.

Do legislators know the views of their constituents on public issues and how often do they vote on bills before them accordingly? Unfortunately, the evidence is mixed. When Iowa legislators were asked to predict whether their own district would vote for or against some proposed constitutional amendments, the resulting predictions were good on some issues but poor on others.[93] Interestingly, the poorest predictions came from legislators from poor districts, suggesting that legislators have less understanding of the views of poor constituents than affluent ones. In contrast, when Florida legislators were asked to predict how both their state and district would vote on referenda on school busing and school prayer, nearly all of them made accurate predictions for both their district and the state.[94]

Perhaps one explanation for these apparently conflicting findings is that legislators know their constituents' views on well-publicized, controversial, emotionally charged issues, but that legislators are poor predictors of constituent opinion on other kinds of issues. This scenario has generated a third legislative orientation—that of the "**politico,**" which refers to a legislator who plays both the delegate and trustee roles, but at different times. Legislators in this category vote as a delegate on hot-button issues that are high priorities back home in the district but as a trustee on low-key issues. Today, legislators turn to multiple sources to gauge public opinion back home. Attending public events, carefully reviewing personalized messages from constituents, and holding town hall meetings are the most common means of determining constituent preferences on key issues. (See Figure 6–4.)

Term Limits

Legislative behavior is affected by the imposition of term limits. In the 15 states with term limits (see Table 2.6 in Chapter 2), studies show the following:

- The power of the governor over legislation increases; the influence of majority party leaders and committee chairs is weakened.[95]
- Power is shifted to the upper chamber; the power of party caucus leaders is reduced; contributions to incumbents decline somewhat.[96]
- Bipartisanship and consensus-building are more difficult.[97]
- Overall legislative policy knowledge is reduced, especially in part-time legislatures with small staffs.[98] Legislative inexperience results in poorly constructed fiscal policies.[99]
- Term-limited legislators are more likely to be motivated by issues than non-term-limited legislators and are also more likely to possess progressive ambition—to run for higher offices.[100]
- Some ambitious legislators resign before their term is up to run for another legislative post when there is an open seat—the "anticipatory effect."[101]
- Some "careerist" termed-out legislators run for offices once seen as "less valuable" than the one they hold (e.g., a senator running for the house or for a local office).[102]
- Legislators in states with term limits often favor eliminating them or increasing the number of terms one can serve before being "termed out." To date, term limits have been repealed in six states by either legislative or state supreme court action—never by a vote of the people.[103] Term limits remain more popular with the public at-large than with legislators.

There is also little evidence that adopting term limits has increased the representation of women and minorities in the legislature.[104] But there is evidence that term limits shorten the length of time legislators serve in leadership posts, with the average now at around five years.

RESPONSIVENESS

The extent to which legislators appear to reflect the views of their constituents in their lawmaking.

"POLITICO"

A legislator who plays both the delegate and trustee roles, but at different times, depending on how "hot" the issue is back home in the district.

FIGURE 6–4 Legislators' Sources for Gauging Public Opinion

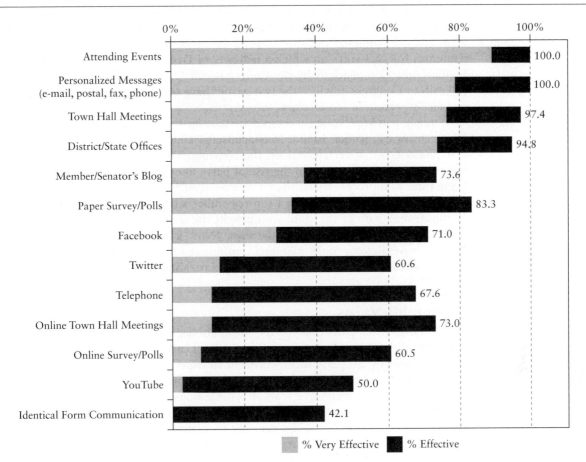

Source: Kevin Cate Communications, Inc., 2012 Survey of Florida Legislative Aides. Used with permission. Available at http://www.catecomm.com/communicating-with-the-florida-legislature.

Ethical Behavior

Legislators must establish the rules spelling out what is ethical behavior on their part and what is not. The National Conference of State Legislatures Ethics Center has identified seven major categories of ethics-related activities or situations that are regulated by various states:[105] gift-giving and receiving, honorariums (payments for speeches, articles, or personal appearances), nepotism (hiring relatives), legislators lobbying government after they leave office (revolving-door scenarios), conflict of interest (representing others before government, contracting with government, voting on an issue in which one has some formal role), personal financial disclosures, and legislative interaction with lobbyists. Forty-one states have state ethics commissions, which watch over legislators and state staff as well.[106] And there is always the capitol press corps whose job it is to play a watchdog role. The press is particularly on the lookout for legislators or staffers who use state time or state resources for political purposes (campaigning).[107]

PARTY POLITICS IN STATE LEGISLATURES

While the influence of parties varies from state to state, parties are perhaps the single most important influence over legislative behavior.

Analyze the influence of political parties in state legislatures.

Two-Party Competitive States: More Straight Party-Line Votes

As the parties have become more competitive in the states, party divisions on legislative roll-call votes have become more frequent than any other divisions, including rural–urban divisions. One common measure of party influence on voting is the percentage of nonunanimous roll-call votes on which a majority of Democrats voted against the majority of Republicans. Compilations by the *Congressional Quarterly* show that the proportion of roll calls in Congress in which the two parties have been in opposition has ranged from 60 to over 70 percent in recent years.

Straight party-line voting in competitive state legislatures such as New York, Pennsylvania, Ohio, Delaware, Rhode Island, Massachusetts, and Michigan may be even higher than it is in Congress; it certainly is on the upswing. The nation's longest serving legislator (first elected in 1956) has seen the rise of party line voting in his state: "The [Wisconsin] Legislature is more polarized than I've ever seen it. There are more straight party-line votes than there have ever been. I can remember when the rurals would fight the urbans or the eastern part of the state would fight the western part or the north would fight south. But now it isn't that way," he says. "Now it's Democrats versus Republicans."[108] The executive director of the National Conference of State Legislatures acknowledges that "We do see within states the same kind of polarization or split that we see at the national level."[109]

Leadership Votes

Voting along strict party lines is the norm for legislative leadership posts, notably for speaker of the house and president of the senate. Leaders are initially selected in the majority party's caucus; all party members are then expected to support their party's choice in the official house vote that follows. Indeed, real difficulties have emerged where parties have evenly divided legislative seats in a state house. (The Indiana house once resolved the issue by agreeing to "co-speakers" who would preside on alternate days; the Florida senate once resolved the issue by agreeing to switch presidents each year of the session.) Rarely do legislators break party lines in voting on leadership posts, although considerable pressure may be placed upon some to do so where the parties are evenly or almost evenly divided. One side effect of term limits has been to speed up legislators' campaigns for leadership posts in each chamber. Some freshmen start campaigning among their peers to become president of the senate or speaker of the house almost as soon as they take the oath of office.

Party Issues

Parties usually display the greatest cohesion on issues involving taxation and appropriations, welfare, moral issues, and regulation of business and labor—in short, the major social and economic controversies that divide the national parties. Minor bills involving the licensing of water well drillers, cosmetologists, or barbers do not usually become the subject matter of party votes, and only infrequently will the parties divide over such matters as the designation of an official state bird. Party influence in budgetary matters is particularly apparent, since the budget often involves issues of social welfare and class interest on which parties in many states are split. In addition, the budget is clearly identified as the product of the governor and carries the label of the party of the governor.

Another type of bill that is often the subject of party voting is one involving the party as an interest group. Parties often exhibit an interest in bills proposing to transfer powers from an office controlled by one party to an office controlled by the other, or bills proposing to create or abolish noncivil service jobs. Parties display considerable interest in bills affecting the organization of local government, state administration, the civil service, registration and election laws, and legislative procedure. And during an election year session, both parties are intent on establishing voting records that legislators can take with them on the campaign trail back home.

Sources of Party Voting

What factors distinguish those states in which the party substantially influences legislative decision making from those states in which it does not?

Party cohesion is strongest in those urban industrial states in which the parties represent separate socioeconomic constituencies. Party voting occurs in those competitive states in which Democratic legislators represent central-city, low-income, ethnic, and racial constituencies, and Republican legislators represent middle-class, suburban, small-town, and rural constituencies. Party cohesion is weak in states where party alignments do not coincide with socioeconomic divisions of constituencies.

It is this division of constituencies that is the basis of party cohesion and influence in the legislature. Even within each party, members from districts typical of their party in socioeconomic attributes support the party position more often than members from districts atypical of the party. Constituency characteristics, then, help to explain not only the outcome of elections but also the behavior of the elected.

PARTY VOTING

In legislatures, voting in which a majority of one party's members vote in opposition to a majority of the other party's members.

THE GROWING ROLE OF THE MEDIA IN THE LEGISLATIVE PROCESS

6.12

Characterize the role of the media in the state legislative process.

Constituents learn about their legislators via the media and the legislators know it! Some have become quite adept at getting good media coverage—writing clever press releases, staging a press conference at a time virtually guaranteeing that it will be covered on the evening news, and appearing on popular radio and television news magazine shows. But a legislator's use of the media is not just to influence the voters back home. It is often aimed at fellow legislators or even the governor, the motive being to improve the odds that the legislator's bills may pass.

The growing media savvy of state legislators has prompted scholars to ask whether legislators now regard use of the media as a more common, and effective,

CAPITOL, OR STATEHOUSE, PRESS CORPS

Reporters from various news outlets who are assigned to cover state government full time. The capitol press corps usually expands while the legislature is in session.

way of accomplishing policy successes than the traditional tactics (such as personally contacting other legislators, the governor, or executive agency officials; meeting with lobbyists). One study of state legislators from California, Georgia, and Iowa found that while legislators still use traditional legislative tactics more often, they generally believe that media tactics are more effective.[110]

At the same time legislators acknowledge the media can be helpful to them, they are wary of members of the **capitol, or statehouse, press corps**. (These are reporters from various news outlets across the state who are assigned to cover state government full time. The capitol press corps usually expands while the legislature is in session.) The "wariness" feeling is mutual. The reporters are on guard for legislators trying to "spin" them.

The capitol press corps is composed of reporters from various news outlets across a state who are assigned to cover state government full time. The media and state legislators are a bit wary of each other, but generally each acknowledges they need the other to get their own job done.

A Web-based survey designed to compare the views of legislators and capitol reporters found that "reporters question legislators' honesty and understanding of how the media operates. And legislators question reporters' coverage choices and objectivity."[111] However, both acknowledge they need each other. In the words of one Pennsylvania state representative who is a former reporter: "It's a parasitic relationship. Each person in the relationship has a need that the other person can fill. For the reporter, the need is information. And for the legislator, the need is free publicity. . . . We each have a job to do."[112] The job is becoming more difficult for state public affairs networks (PANs) that provide live or taped coverage of legislative deliberations. Expensive new technologies and public funding cutbacks have forced some PANS to reduce coverage at precisely the same time citizens are clamoring for more transparency and openness in government operations.[113]

<table>
<tr><td>**6.13**</td><td></td></tr>
</table>

Describe lobbying in state legislatures, assess which lobbying techniques are most effective, and evaluate the extent to which lobbying efforts are effectively regulated.

LOBBYING IN STATE LEGISLATURES

The influence of organized interest groups in the legislative process varies from state to state. Earlier in Chapter 5 we discussed interest groups in the 50 states and their involvement in public relations, campaign financing, and lobbying. We define lobbying as any communication by someone acting on behalf of a group directed at a government decision maker with the hope of influencing decisions. Lobbying is done not only by professionals but also by average constituents. In fact, many interest groups encourage their members to lobby legislators via personal visits to their district or state capitol offices, e-mail, personal letters, or phone calls because they know that "the best lobbyist is a constituent residing—and voting—in a representative's district."[114] In general, direct contacts are much more effective forms of citizen lobbying than form letters. (See Figure 6–5.)

Constituent lobbying of state legislators is easier than citizen lobbying of U.S. Congress members because (1) there are fewer members in a state legislature than in the U.S. Congress; (2) members of a state legislature are, in most cases, more accessible—they spend more time in their home district, making it easier for citizens to have personal contact with them; (3) there is less interference from state legislative staffs than from congressional staffs; and (4) there is less emphasis placed on campaign contributions as a means of accessing the state legislator.[115]

CONSTITUENT LOBBYING

Individual citizens letting their representatives know how they feel about key issues before the legislature; these constituents are therefore lobbying their representatives.

Narrow Issues

On what kinds of decisions are interest groups more likely to exercise influence? Party and constituency interests are most apparent on broad social and economic issues. On narrower issues voters are less likely to have either an interest or an opinion. The legislator is, therefore, freer to respond to the pleas of organized groups on highly specialized topics than on major issues of public interest.

Economic interests seeking to use the law to improve their competitive position are a major source of group pressure on these specialized topics. Particularly active in lobbying are the businesses subject to extensive government regulation. The truckers, railroads, insurance companies, and gaming, tobacco, liquor, and restaurant interests are consistently found to be among the most highly organized and active lobbyists in state capitals. Organized pressure also comes from associations of governments and associations of government employees. State chapters of the National Education Association are persistent in presenting the demands of educational administrators and occasionally the demands of the dues-paying teachers as well.

Information Exchange

Legislators depend on lobbyists for much of their information on public issues. Legislators are aware of the potential bias in information given them by lobbyists. But the constant

FIGURE 6–5 Most Effective Lobbying Strategies

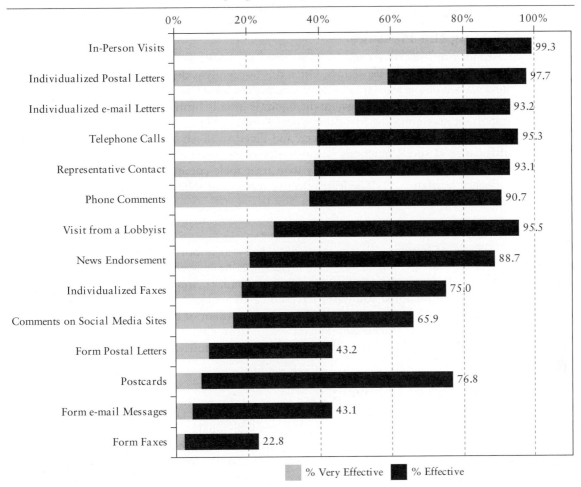

Legend:
- % Very Effective
- % Effective

Strategy	Value
In-Person Visits	99.3
Individualized Postal Letters	97.7
Individualized e-mail Letters	93.2
Telephone Calls	95.3
Representative Contact	93.1
Phone Comments	90.7
Visit from a Lobbyist	95.5
News Endorsement	88.7
Individualized Faxes	75.0
Comments on Social Media Sites	65.9
Form Postal Letters	43.2
Postcards	76.8
Form e-mail Messages	43.1
Form Faxes	22.8

Note: The portion of a full-time job spent on legislative work includes time in session, constituent service, interim committee work and election campaigns. The estimated compensation includes salary, per diem and unvouchered expense payments. And the ratio of all staff to all legislators does not indicate how many staff work directly for each legislator.
Source: Kevin Cate Communications, Inc., 2012 Survey of Florida Legislative Aides. Used with permission. Available at http://www.catecomm .com/communicating-with-the-florida-legislature.

proximity of lobbyists to legislators facilitates information exchange.[116] Legislators *use* lobbyists, just as lobbyists use legislators:

> Typically, legislators utilize lobbyists as sources of influence in three ways: by calling upon lobbyists to influence other legislators, by calling upon lobbyists to help amass public opinion in favor of the legislator's position, and by including lobbyists in planning strategy in an effort to negotiate a bill through the legislature.[117]

Threats and Unsolicited Campaign Contributions

It is unwise for lobbyists to threaten legislators, for example, by vowing to defeat them in the next election. This is the tactic of an amateur lobbyist, not a professional. It usually produces a defensive response by the legislator. As one lobbyist put it: "Once you have closed the door you have no further access to the individual. Once you've threatened an individual, there is no possibility of winning in the future."[118] Legislators also do not appreciate unsolicited campaign contributions from lobbyists. "Even if you don't ask for it, they'll send you money—if they think you're going to win," complained one legislator who intentionally funded his own campaign to avoid being painted by the media as dependent on special interest money.[119]

Getting the Message

Testimony at legislative committee hearings is a common form of information exchange between lobbyists and legislators. Often this testimony is the legislators' primary source of information about legislation. Direct meetings in legislators' offices are also frequent and effective. Social gatherings (where the liquor is usually furnished by the lobbyist) are more important in establishing friendships; professional lobbyists seldom bring up "business" on such occasions. Legislators are wined and dined so much during legislative sessions that attendance at social functions is sometimes viewed as a chore. (One recent study found that women lobbyists are less likely than their male counterparts to use social events to influence legislators.[120]) The least effective method of lobbying is the submission of long letters or reports.

Lobbying the Staff

One form of lobbying that is growing rapidly in importance is communication with legislative *staff* personnel. As state legislatures have acquired more full-time staff for their standing committees, house and senate leaders, and majority and minority party caucuses, professional lobbyists have come to recognize that these staff people can have as much or more to do with the specific content of bills as legislators themselves. Many of the more "professional" state legislatures rely heavily on the advice of professional staffs. The wise lobbyist in these states cultivates friendships among staff personnel.

Regulation of Lobbying

The U.S. Constitution guarantees the right "to petition the government for redress of grievances." This First Amendment right protects individuals and groups in their attempts to communicate with and influence their lawmakers. Nonetheless, lobbying is regulated in some fashion in all of the states. Most state laws require lobbyists ("anyone receiving compensation to influence legislative action") to (1) register with the clerk or secretary of the house or senate, and (2) file periodic reports of direct expenditures for lobbying activity. These regulations have relatively little impact on lobbying activity; many organizations claim that they are educational or religious in nature and not really lobbies, and they do not register. Many lobbies do not report all of their educational and public relations expenditures, but only a small portion, which they attribute directly to lobbying. Campaign contributions usually must be reported under state election laws. Of course, bribery and conspiracy may be prosecuted under criminal laws.

State legislatures and agencies charged with enforcement of lobbying regulations have traditionally been notorious for their neglect of their responsibilities. An analysis of state lobbyist disclosure laws by the Center for Public Integrity gave just nine states a satisfactory score; 27 failed outright.[121] However, increasing professionalization of state legislatures appears to increase both their capacity and willingness to regulate lobbying.[122] So, too, does a major scandal which gets massive media attention and generates citizens' demands to "throw the rascals out."[123]

Ex-Legislators as Lobbyists

Some legislators choose to become lobbyists after they leave office. Special interests (public, private, nonprofit) hire them for their knowledge of the legislative process, personal connections with legislators, and their subject-matter expertise. One study found that former legislators often turn out to be powerful, well-connected lobbyists.[124]

STATE LEGISLATURES: A CRITICAL ASSESSMENT

Determine whether citizens' critical assessments of state legislatures are well deserved.

State legislatures are not popular with the American people. Over 40 years ago political scientist William Keefe wrote: "It is very possibly true that no American political institution has ever had so many detractors, so few defenders, or such a wide array of charges levied against it. . . . Legislatures are located on the outskirts of public esteem and affection."[125] And despite institutional reforms of the past decades—higher salaries, more professional legislators, longer sessions, increased staff, better resources—it does not appear that state legislatures have improved their standing with the American people. Indeed, the strong support of term limits wherever they have appeared on the ballot suggests that Americans continue to hold state legislatures in low esteem. In a well-titled book, *The Decline of Representative Democracy,* political scientist Alan Rosenthal describes the general public's growing preference for direct democracy—voting on referendum issues themselves—over representative democracy.[126]

It is likely that the public's disdain of state legislatures is part of the popular cynicism for politics generally. About two-thirds of the American public say that government "is pretty much run by a few big interests looking out for themselves" rather than "run for the benefit of all people."

- State legislatures enact laws, consider U.S. constitutional amendments for ratification, approve governor-appointed nominees for high office, provide services and information to individual constituents, oversee state agencies, and, most important, appropriate money for public programs and levy taxes to pay for them.

- Legislators tend to be "upwardly mobile" with college educations and professional careers. The proportion of lawyers, who once dominated legislative bodies, has dropped from 25 to 15 percent since the 1970s.

- Women and minorities have made significant gains in legislative seats and leadership since the 1960s. However, female membership has hit a plateau at one-quarter of state legislative seats. Compared to men, women are more concerned with education, health, and welfare issues and use a more cooperative style in decision making.

- Legislators who run for reelection are seldom defeated because of the visibility they gain in office, the resources they enjoy while holding office, and the money they can attract from interest groups.

- In *Baker* v. *Carr*, the U.S. Supreme Court in 1962 declared the "one person, one vote" principle to guide the drawing of election district lines. By requiring districts to have equal populations, the decision transferred political power from rural to urban districts.

- Legislatures typically redraw district boundaries after every 10-year census. Boundaries often favor incumbents and the majority party.

- Racial gerrymandering is easier to challenge in court than partisan gerrymandering.

- Fewer than one in four bills introduced in a legislative session actually becomes law.

- Most legislatures meet annually. The trend is toward greater professionalism, with career legislators and full-time staffs. Where there is more professionalism, there is less turnover in membership and greater political influence from staff.

- Legislative turnover is highest in states with term limits and in the first election following redistricting.

- Legislators do much of their work in committees where they gather information, hear debates, haggle over bill provisions, and decide on a bill's fate.

- Legislative leaders (house speaker or senate president, floor leaders, committee chairs) appoint members to committees, maintain order, focus policy issues, resolve conflict, and invite public input.

- The imposition of term limits in some states has increased the power of the governor and the staff, made consensus building more difficult, reduced members' knowledge of lawmaking, and accelerated career-building strategies of ambitious members.

- Legislators get their best "reads" of public opinion by attending public events, reviewing personalized messages from constituents, and holding town hall meetings.

- Political party membership is perhaps the single most important influence over legislative behavior. There has been an increase in straight party-line voting in legislatures.

- To influence each other and constituents, legislators have increasingly used media coverage. But media coverage of state legislatures is not as extensive as it once was due to budget cutbacks.

- Lobbyists are important to legislators and legislators to lobbyists. Lobbyists provide information and legislators use it to craft bills or decide how to vote on key proposals. Direct contacts are the most effective way for citizens to lobby legislators.

CHAPTER SEVEN

GOVERNORS IN STATE POLITICS

LEARNING OBJECTIVES

 7.1 Outline the various gubernatorial roles arising from his or her formal and informal powers.

7.2 Describe the background, political experience, and demographic characteristics of governors.

 7.3 Assess which gubernatorial candidates and campaign strategies are most likely to be successful.

7.4 Compare the powers of weak and strong governors.

 7.5 Describe the role of the governor in the legislative process, and assess the governor's ability to impact legislative outcomes.

7.6 Analyze how divided government affects the relationship between the governor and the legislature.

7.7 Assess the effectiveness of various checks on the power of the governor.

 7.8 Evaluate how well governors are able to harness their informal powers to be effective political leaders.

7.9 Outline the roles of the lieutenant governor and other executive officers.

THE MANY ROLES OF A GOVERNOR

Governors are central figures in American state politics. "A governor is the most visible political actor in a state and is viewed by many citizens as the personification of the state itself. . . . The state legislature, bureaucracy, press, politics, and policies [in a state] all bear the imprint of the governor."[1]

Governors bring industry and jobs into their states, prevent prison riots, raise teachers' salaries, keep taxes low, see that the state gets its fair share of grant money from Washington, provide disaster relief, and bring tourists into the state. Governors offer reassurance to citizens during crises and disasters—everything from floods, hurricanes, fires, and droughts, to toxic waste spills, nuclear plant accidents, and acts of terrorism. These public expectations far exceed the **formal powers** of governors spelled out in the state constitution or in state statutes.

FORMAL POWERS

Gubernatorial authority established in state statutes or a state constitution; a governor's tenure potential, appointment, budget and veto powers, and party control.

INFORMAL POWERS

A governor's strength stemming from personal attributes or unusual circumstances.

Formal powers are just one-half of the formula to gauge gubernatorial power. **Informal powers** are the other half. They are a bit more difficult to measure because they are more intangible and are uniquely personal. A governor's popularity, charisma, ability to generate positive media attention, path-breaker status (gender, race/ethnicity, age, party), unusual occupation, atypical political career progression, famous relatives, designation as a potential presidential candidate, or the crisis situation under which he or she took office are but a few sources of informal power. And of course, what voters in one state find appealing and enduring may have the opposite effect in another because the states are so different in their makeup and politics. For example, South Carolinians could identify with *their* governor when he "carried two squealing piglets into the Statehouse to make a point against pork" and "brought a horse and buggy to the Statehouse entrance to argue against South Carolina's outmoded system of governance."[2] But it is doubtful that New Yorkers would have reacted the same way if *their* governor had used similar tactics! Political scientists agree that "the dynamics of gubernatorial approval are highly idiosyncratic."[3]

In many ways, the expectations placed upon the governor resemble those placed upon the president, which isn't all that surprising since both are elected chief executives. Like the president, governors are expected to be their state's chief administrator, chief legislator, leader of their party, ceremonial head of their government, chief ambassador to other governments, leader of public opinion, and chief crisis manager.

Chief Administrator

The governor must coordinate the state's bureaucracy, oversee the preparation of the state's budget, and supervise major state programs. Governors must resolve conflicts within their administrations and troubleshoot where difficulties arise. If a scandal occurs, governors must act decisively to eliminate it. The public will hold them responsible for any scandal in their administration, whether they were a party to it or not. The public will hold them responsible for the financial structure of the state, whether it was they or their predecessors who were responsible for the state's fiscal troubles. And the voters will blame the governor if an appointee has to be removed as head of an agency for incompetence or corruption.

Yet, as we shall see in this chapter, the formal administrative powers of a governor are limited. Many of the governor's administrative agencies are headed by elected officials or independent boards or commissions, over which the governor has little or no control. Governors' powers of appointment and removal are severely restricted by state constitutions. Governors do not have control over their administration commensurate with their responsibility for it.

Chief Legislator

The governor is responsible for initiating major statewide legislative programs. There is a general public expectation that every governor will put forward some sort of legislative program. By sending bills to the legislature, governors are cast in the role of the "initiator" of public policy decisions. If they want to see their legislative proposals enacted into law, they must also persuade legislators to support them. In other words, they must involve themselves directly in legislative decisions.

The **veto power** gives the governor bargaining power with the legislature. Few vetoes are overridden; in most states a two-thirds majority vote in both houses is required to override a veto. This means a governor needs only one-third plus one in either house to sustain his or her veto. So even the *threat* of a veto can force changes in a bill under consideration in the legislature. Moreover, in most states, the governor possesses the line-item veto, allowing the governor to veto specific items in an appropriations bill, including legislators' home district **"pork" or "turkeys."** The threat of vetoing these vote-winning projects gives the governor additional bargaining power with legislators. A governor can also call special sessions of the legislature, allowing the governor to spotlight specific issues and pressure the legislature to do something about them.

Party Leader

Traditionally governors were regarded as the head of their party in the state.[4] But governors do not have the power to deny party nominations to recalcitrant legislators of their own party. Party nominations are won independently by legislators in primary elections held in their own districts. Governors have no formal disciplinary powers over members of their own party. And governors may choose to emphasize their own independence from their national party to further their own electoral ambitions.

However, within the legislature, parties still count. Governors usually receive greater support for their programs from members of their own party. Legislators who run for office under the same party label as the governor have a stake in his or her success. Since all who run under the party's label share its common fortunes, and since its fortunes are often governed by the strength of its gubernatorial candidate, there will always be a tendency for loyal party members to support their governor.

The organization of the legislature along party lines reinforces the party role of the governor. Legislative leaders of the governor's party—whether in the majority or minority—are expected to support the governor's program. (When they don't, it makes big news and the governor is cast as "weak," even though these leaders may have their eyes on the governor's chair. This happens most when governors are lame ducks.)

Ceremonial Head

Ceremonial duties occupy a great deal of a governor's time—signing bills, welcoming delegates, attending professional association conventions held in their state, meeting with schoolchildren visiting the state capitol, and, of course, representing their state at important events held nationally and internationally. A governor may not be able to mobilize the symbolic and ceremonial power of the office on behalf of state goals in the same way that the president can mobilize the power of that office on behalf of national goals. Nonetheless, the skillful use of symbols and ceremonies can add to a governor's prestige and popularity. These assets can in turn contribute to political power.

Chief Negotiator

Governors must negotiate with their local governments on the division of state and local responsibilities for public programs, and with other state governments over coordinating highway development, water pollution, resource conservation, and reciprocity in state laws. Governors must undertake responsibility for negotiation with the national government as well. The governor shares responsibility with the state's congressional delegation in seeing to it that the state receives a "fair share" of federal contracts, highway monies, educational monies, and poverty funds, and doesn't lose key military bases when the Pentagon proposes to close bases.

VETO POWER

Rejection of proposed legislation by the chief executive (governor), usually subject to legislative override by a two-thirds vote of both houses.

"PORK" OR "TURKEYS"

Pet projects in the budget that will benefit an individual legislator's district but not any others; often vetoed by a governor.

Opinion Leader

Governors are the most visible of state officials. Their comments on public affairs make news, and they are sought after for television, radio, and public appearances. They are able to focus public opinion on issues they deem important. They may not always be able to win public opinion to their side, but at least they will be seen and heard.

Crisis Manager

Finally, governors may be called upon to *manage crises* in their states—hurricanes, floods, droughts, oil spills, mudslides, tornadoes, blizzards, civil disorders, mass murders, collapsing infrastructure, and other disasters. Indeed, a governor's performance in a crisis may determine his or her standing with the public. Governors often call upon the National Guard units in their state to help in crisis situations.

The recent Great Recession thrust governors into a new kind of crisis management role—one stemming from a major economic crisis. Many governors were forced to do everything possible to bring jobs to their states, diversify their economies, and bolster their businesses, including reaching out to other countries through international trade missions. Now, many governors routinely lead delegations of state officials, business leaders, and academics on international trade missions designed to develop ties with potential trading partners. In the words of the governor of Nevada, "We have to recognize that it's now a global economy and our state has to be a player in that."

| 7.2 | THE MAKING OF A GOVERNOR |

Describe the background, political experience, and demographic characteristics of governors.

As the central position in American state politics, the governorship is a much sought-after office. The prestige of being called "governor" for the rest of one's life, and the opportunity to use the office as a stepping-stone to the U.S. Senate, or even the presidency or vice-presidency of the United States, is extremely attractive to people of ambition in American politics.

Varieties of Background

Historically, many governors were the sons of families of great wealth, who chose public service as an outlet for their energies—the Roosevelts, the Harrimans, the Rockefellers, the Scrantons, and, more recently, the Bushes.

Governors have been movie actors (Ronald Reagan of California), restaurant owners (Lester Maddox of Georgia), truck drivers (Harold Hughes of Iowa), country music singers (Jimmie Davis of Louisiana, who wrote "You Are My Sunshine"), and wrestlers (Jesse "The Body" Ventura of Minnesota). However, the majority of governors have been *lawyers* by profession.

The occupations of twenty-first century women governors, while equally diverse, are not as colorful. For women, their occupations are far less interesting or unique than their "*path-breaker*" status: first woman to be elected governor in their state. Minority women who achieve the "first" status receive a lot of attention not only in their home states but nationally. (See *People in Politics:* "First-time Women Governors: Minority Pathbreakers Rise on the National Political Stage.") Republicans Susana Martinez (New Mexico) and Nikki Haley (South Carolina) became the first female governors in their states as part of the Republican wave that swept across many states in the 2010 midterm election. They were given speaking roles at the 2012 Republican National Convention, and then mentioned as possible presidential candidates in 2016.

The first independent candidate to win a governorship in modern history was James B. Longley of Maine; he has been followed by independent mavericks Walter Hickel of Alaska, Lowell Weicker of Connecticut, Angus King of Maine, Jesse Ventura of Minnesota, and Lincoln Chaffee of Rhode Island. Independent and third-party candidates are most likely to enter a governor's race when they perceive there is little difference ideologically or on issues between the major party candidates.[5]

Age

Television has accented youth and good looks among state governors. In this highly visual society, it helps one's image to be tall, slim, attractive, fashionable, and smiling. Bill Clinton became the nation's youngest modern day governor when he won that post in Arkansas in 1978 at age 32. (The youngest governor in the nation's history was actually Stephens T. Mason who was elected Michigan's first governor in 1813 at age 23 but that was before Michigan had actually achieved statehood.[6]) More recently, Louisiana governor Bobby Jindal was 36 when he won his initial race; Nikki Haley, governor of South Carolina, was 38. Most current governors, on average, are in their late-fifties, with the oldest being California's Jerry Brown who is in his mid-seventies.

Race/Ethnicity

Until Democrat Douglas Wilder's successful run for the Virginia statehouse in 1989, no state had ever elected a black governor. Democrat Deval Patrick became the nation's second African American governor when elected by Massachusetts voters in 2006. Democrat David Paterson became the third when as lieutenant governor, he ascended to the post in 2008 after New York's Governor Elliot Spitzer resigned following a scandal. Several Hispanics have been elected governor: Democrat Jerry Abodaca of New Mexico, Democrat Raul Castro of Arizona, Democrat Toney Anaya of New Mexico, Republican Bob Martinez of Florida, and, more recently, Democrat Bill Richardson of New Mexico followed by Republican Susana Martinez, and Republican Brian Sandoval of Nevada. Three Asian Americans have served as governor, the first being Chinese-American Democrat Gary Locke, who served as Washington's governor from 1997 to 2005. More recently, two Indian Americans, both Republicans, have been elected governor—Bobby Jindal of Louisiana and Nikki Haley of South Carolina. (For a list of African Americans, Hispanics, and Asian Americans elected governor, see Figure 7–1.)

Gender

Over 30 women have served as governor or acting governor in U.S. history. (See Figure 7–1.) Prior to 1974, only three women had *ever* served as governor of a U.S. state, and all three succeeded their husbands in office—Nellie Ross of Wyoming and Miriam "Ma" Ferguson of Texas in the 1920s, and Lurleen Wallace of Alabama in the 1960s. In 1974, Ella T. Grasso of Connecticut became the first woman governor whose husband had not previously held the office. Later that same year, Dixy Lee Ray of Washington accomplished the same feat.

Since then, the number of women running for and winning the state's top executive post has been climbing as more women hold positions that are seen as excellent training grounds. Over half of the states have had a women governor; Arizona has had four.[7] Political scientists have found that the public is impressed with governors who have experience in local elective offices, statewide executive posts, agency administration, and law enforcement.[8] A sizeable number of the current women governors have been mayors or county commissioners, state agency directors, lieutenant governors, attorneys

Governors are getting younger. Louisiana Governor Bobby Jindal (R), the state's first Asian American governor, was 36 when first elected. In college, he double majored in biology and public policy, both of which have helped him govern a state periodically ravaged by storms that wreak havoc on the state's environment, economy, and citizens.

FIGURE 7–1   States with Female and Minority Governors 1872 to 2013

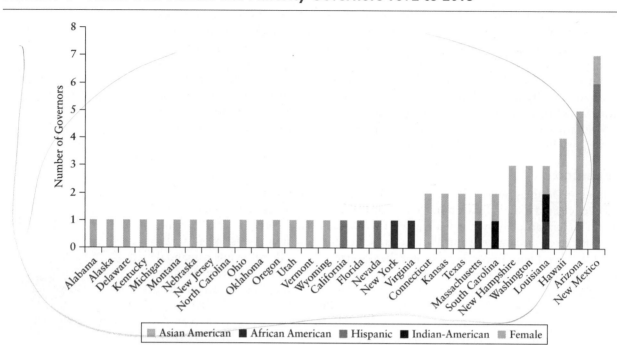

Notes: Data are from 1872 to 2013. Over half the states have had at least one female governor; six have elected more than one. Two minority women have been elected governor (South Carolina; New Mexico). Twelve states have had a minority governor: five have elected an Hispanic, four an African American, two an Indian American, and two an Asian American. One state, New Mexico, has had three Hispanic governors. Another (Hawaii) has elected four Asian-American governors.

Source: Based on National Archives State Archives accessed at http://www.archives.gov/research/alic/reference/state-archives.html.

general, and/or chairs of statewide boards and commissions. As New Hampshire governor Maggie Hassan (D) has noted: "[W]omen, once they participate in the political process and run for office, can do very well in it." When asked how to get more women to run, she has advised current women officeholders to keep "reaching out to other women and let them understand that running for office can fit into their lives and that they can be good at it."[9]

Political Experience

Governors usually come to their office with considerable experience in public affairs. Only about 14 percent come into the governor's chair without prior office holding. The number has escalated as more independently wealthy candidates make a run, often promising to make government run more like a business and to wrest state government from the hands of the "professional politicians." But the more common, well-worn paths are from a statewide elective office—lieutenant governor and attorney general, especially—or from a state legislative office.

More Congress members (U.S. senators and U.S. representatives) are choosing to come back home to run for governor, especially those from the South and Northeast.[10] Many interviews with current and past governors all seem to come to the same conclusion: they believe the governor's job is the best one in politics—an indication of the power and prestige of the office of governor more than the salary. Some, like Florida's Rick Scott and Alabama's Robert Bentley, do not accept their salaries; others take a reduced or token salary (Michigan governor Rick Snyder accepts $1 per year). Pennsylvania's governor is the highest paid at $183,255; the lowest is Maine's at $70,000. But it often takes millions to win the office.

First-time Women Governors: Minority Pathbreakers Rise on the National Political Stage

Until the 1980s and 1990s, it was rare for women to be elected governor. Today the number is still small: only about one state in 10 has a woman governor. When women are elected, they are often the state's first. That was true in 2010 for Nikki Haley in South Carolina and for Susana Martinez in New Mexico. Martinez enjoys another milestone as the first woman Hispanic governor in the nation. For these two, becoming the first was neither easy nor swift, but their journeys were similar and remarkable in many ways.

Both women came from families that had immigrated to America: Haley's parents from India, and Martinez's grandparents from Mexico. Both had jobs as teenagers working for the family business: Haley kept books for the family's clothing store, and Martinez patrolled parking lots at bingo games for the family's security firm.

Both women pulled themselves up by their own bootstraps, although each chose a different career route. Haley earned an accounting degree and worked as a corporate accountant before returning to the family business, helping it grow into a multimillion-dollar company. Martinez's degrees in criminal justice and law set the stage for her 20-year career as a public prosecutor. Haley entered politics as a state representative; Martinez as a county district attorney. Both women are Republicans,

although Martinez was a Democrat before making her first run for office.

Both faced formidable opponents in their first races: Martinez ran against her former boss; Haley, against an entrenched state legislator. Martinez, who grew up in El Paso, was chided for being too Texan to lead New Mexico. She also had to admit that her father's father, like many immigrants in the early 1900s, had come into the United States illegally. Haley, who had been raised in the Sikh religion, met public doubts about her adult conversion to the Methodist Church. In the governor's race, opponents alleged that she had had two extramarital affairs, which she denied. In addition, one detractor called her a "raghead," referring to her Indian heritage, a remark for which he later apologized.

"The fact that I happen to be an Indian female, of course that brings a new dynamic," she was quoted as saying (*Newsweek*, June 2010). "But what I hope it does is cause a conversation in the state where we no longer live by layers, but we live by philosophies."

As governors, both women have pushed conservative agendas. On the fiscal side, they pledged to cut waste in government spending, keep taxes low, create jobs, and make government more accountable. On social issues, they urged education reform, stricter enforcement of immigration laws, and opposition to Obamacare.

In the 2012 election, both were mentioned as possible running mates for Mitt Romney, a clear sign that the political frontiers for women and ethnic/racial minorities have advanced. In that advancement, however, both women in their speeches at the Republican National Convention hailed the basics. "My parents taught me to never give up and to always believe that my future could be what I dreamt it to be," Martinez said. "Success, they taught me, is built on the foundation of courage, hard work and individual responsibility."

How Many Governors Later Became President?

President	State	Served as Governor
Thomas Jefferson	Virginia	1779–1781
James Monroe	Virginia	1799–1802
Martin Van Buren	New York	1828–1829
John Tyler	Virginia	1825–1827
James Polk	Tennessee	1839–1841
Andrew Johnson	Tennessee	1853–1857
Rutherford B. Hayes	Ohio	1867–1871, 1875–1877
Grover Cleveland	New York	1882–1884
William McKinley	Ohio	1892–1896
Theodore Roosevelt	New York	1898–1900
Woodrow Wilson	New Jersey	1911–1912
Calvin Coolidge	Massachusetts	1918–1920
Franklin D. Roosevelt	New York	1929–1933
Jimmy Carter	Georgia	1971–1975
Ronald Reagan	California	1967–1975
Bill Clinton	Arkansas	1979–1981, 1983–1992
George W. Bush	Texas	1994–2000

7.3 GUBERNATORIAL POLITICS

Assess which gubernatorial candidates and campaign strategies are most likely to be successful.

State governors appear to be gaining political strength within their states and in national politics. Governors are receiving more media attention, undertaking more initiatives in policies and programs, winning more legislative battles, and even acquiring more national political clout. More governors have ascended to the presidency than U.S. senators (see "*Did You Know?: How Many Governors Later Became President?*"). Consequently, the national media are always interested in covering "governors who might become president."

Competition

Competition is usually strong, both in primary and general elections, for the governorship. Indeed, competition for the job has been increasing over time, especially in the southern states where Republican candidates now have an equal chance of winning. Yet traditionally the Democratic Party has dominated state gubernatorial politics. In 1994, for the first time in 30 years, Republican governors (30) outnumbered Democratic governors (19), and Republican governors continued to outnumber Democratic governors until 2006. (See Figure 5–3 in Chapter 5.) In 2010, Republicans won back the majority and continued to expand their number in 2012. Some Democratic strategists believe that the nation's changing racial/ethnic makeup and generational voting patterns (see Chapter 5) may help them win back some state governorships, especially in some of the nation's largest states.

Getting Elected

What forces influence the outcome of gubernatorial elections? Are gubernatorial elections affected by national voting trends—"**coattails**"? Or are they more affected by conditions within the states, especially the performance of the state's economy? Or are gubernatorial elections primarily "**candidate centered**"—influenced mostly by the personal qualities of the candidates, their handling of state issues, the strength of their own political organizations, and their success in fundraising and campaigning?

Gubernatorial Vote Choice

If voters are asked "What mattered most in voting for governor?" they cite personal leadership qualities of the candidate more often than anything else. Party affiliation and agreement on issues follow in importance. Negative voting—dislike of the opponent—also plays a significant role in gubernatorial voting.

Governors are better known to the voters than any other state officials or even U.S. senators and representatives. Governors receive more media attention than any other state official. However, this does not always guarantee that governors will be liked better than other elected officeholders.

Voters do not usually hold a governor solely responsible for economic problems confronting the state, unless they perceive the problems were caused by specific taxing or spending decisions recommended by the governor. Most voters recognize that state economic conditions depend more on national market factors, or on the actions of the national government, including the president, than on the governor.[11] Yet state (or local) officials may be held responsible for actions that make an already weak economy worse; voters may expect a governor to do all that he or she can to ameliorate hard times. And there is some evidence that the popularity of governors is linked to unemployment rates in their states, even though there is little that governors can do to reduce unemployment.[12] It is true that governors emphasize economic, or "**pocketbook,**" **issues** more than twice as much as social issues in their annual State of the State addresses to their citizens.[13] Three costly pocketbook issues mentioned a lot by governors during the Great Recession were Medicaid, public pensions, and mental health funding. (See Figure 7–2.)

Coattail Effects

Gubernatorial candidates running on the same party ticket as popular presidential candidates enjoy a significant advantage. But most gubernatorial elections are held in "off years"—years

COATTAILS

In politics, a reference to the effect that a party's leader may have on voting for that party's candidates for other offices.

CANDIDATE-CENTERED ELECTION

Refers to an election primarily focusing on the personal qualities of the candidates.

POCKETBOOK ISSUES

Those affecting a voter's wallet; economic issues.

FIGURE 7–2 Governors' Priorities: Topics Emphasized in State of the State Addresses

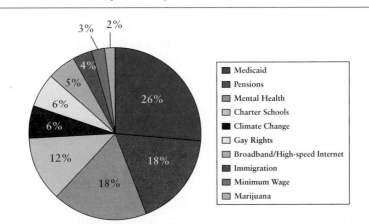

Source: Governing, "State of the State Addresses: What Are Governors' Priorities," March 11, 2013, posted by Mike Maciag. Available at http://www.governing.com/blogs/by-the-numbers/gov-state-of-the-state-speeches-summary.html.

OFF-YEAR ELECTIONS

Usually refers to an election not held in the same year as a presidential election.

in which the nation is not electing a president. **Off-year elections** are deliberately designed to minimize the effects of presidential voting trends on state governors' elections. Nonetheless, there is some evidence that the electoral fate of gubernatorial candidates is affected by the popularity of the president. Gubernatorial candidates of the president's party attract more votes when the president's popularity in opinion polls is high. This is true whether the candidates are incumbents or challengers.[14] Conversely, gubernatorial candidates of the president's party suffer when the president's popularity is low. Insofar as a president's popularity is affected by national economic trends, gubernatorial candidates of the president's party can suffer from national recessions and benefit from national prosperity.

Candidate Effects

Despite these coattail effects, gubernatorial elections are mostly candidate centered. The outcome of gubernatorial elections depends more on the personal qualities of the candidates, their ability to associate themselves with popular issues, the strength of their personal political organizations, their ability to raise campaign funds, and their skills in campaigning.

The popularity of the incumbent governor has a significant effect on voters' decisions, not only with respect to reelecting the incumbent but also electing the candidate of the incumbent's party when the incumbent is not running for reelection.[15] Unpopular lame duck governors often spell trouble for their party's gubernatorial candidate in the general election. Nothing makes a governor more unpopular than people out of jobs. Some scholars have found that a state's unemployment rate is a better gauge of gubernatorial popularity than more political matters.[16]

Campaign Issues

Even though most gubernatorial elections are candidate centered, the candidates are obliged to talk about issues. Campaigns consciously seek to highlight issues on which the candidate is well positioned (or the opponent is poorly positioned) relative to the voters' preferences. Setting the campaign issue agenda is often the key to victory.[17] Debates and candidate forums play a big part in forcing the candidates to constantly fine-tune their positions or reprioritize their issues. A high proportion of voters now say televised debates play a big role in their ultimate decision as to which candidate to support for governor.

Reelection

Incumbent governors who seek reelection are usually successful. In primary elections, incumbent governors usually face *little* serious opposition.[18] In recent years the overall success rate for incumbent governors seeking reelection has averaged about 75 percent.[19] However, governors are more vulnerable to defeat than U.S. senators or U.S. House members whose reelection rates are closer to 90 percent. Occasionally governors are defeated, more often in the general election than in their own party primary, and it is interesting to try to understand these failures.

Political folklore includes the belief that any governor who raises taxes during his or her term will be defeated for reelection. But a careful study of this notion shows only a weak connection between tax increases and electoral defeat for governors.[20] Most governors who raise taxes and then seek reelection are successful, especially if they are on tobacco products! Frequently, however, those who are defeated *blame* their loss on raising taxes. But more often than not, when taxes are the key issue bringing down an incumbent, it is because of the governor's refusal to get rid of an unpopular fee or tax (like a car tag tax) or tax loopholes that appear to the voter to benefit narrow, but powerful, special interests.

It is not always fiscal issues that lead to an incumbent governor's defeat. Scandals, corruption, or personal weaknesses, including moral shortcomings, can end a governor's tenure in that position or in any other elective post. So, too, can a poor performance by an unpopular president of your own party or a major shift in the party preferences of voters in a state (partisan realignment). And as with presidential candidates, some gubernatorial candidates are simply not very good at campaigning. One study of why incumbent governors are not reelected lists "poor campaign skills" as one of the reasons.[21]

Campaigning

Modern gubernatorial campaigns usually involve high-powered public relations organizations, experienced mass media and television advertising firms, professional polling and political consultants, and sophisticated direct mail and fundraising techniques. (See "Professional Media Campaigns" in Chapter 5.) Until recently, party organizations and amateur volunteers have played a limited role in most gubernatorial campaigns in the states. Now state-level campaigns are patterned after presidential campaigns. Of course, campaign themes and candidate "images" must be tailored to a state's political culture and tradition. For example, running on a gun control platform may be a good strategy in a liberal state, but ill-advised in a more rural conservative state.

Money

Today a typical gubernatorial campaign can cost $5–10 million in small states. (See Table 7–1.) But it can be over $200 million in big states with lots of expensive media markets. Television advertising, polling, and precisely targeted direct mail (micro-targeting) are the major reasons for increased costs, not to mention population growth. But so is greater competition at both the primary and general election stages. Candidates for governor have spent anywhere from $4 to over $30 *per vote*. Costs per vote seem to be highest when there is an open seat (no incumbent running) or when an unpopular incumbent is running for reelection (and loses)—high turnout scenarios. "Hotly contested, high-spending" gubernatorial campaigns can increase voter turnout.[22]

TABLE 7–1	Gubernatorial Races Are Expensive				
2010 Gubernatorial Campaign Spending					
State	**Number of Candidates**	**Total Spent ($)**	**Total Primary Vote**	**Total General Election Vote**	**Cost per Vote ($)**
CA	8	219,802,866	3,429,424	10,094,839	21.77
TX	12	97,399,214	2,165,090	4,979,870	19.56
PA	6	67,880,692	1,885,638	3,987,551	17.02
CT	5	34,056,201	301,097	1,145,781	29.72
FL	7	22,199,829	2,165,773	5,359,735	4.14
ID	11	3,208,692	190,523	452,535	7.09
AK	10	2,781,674	154,409	256,192	10.86
NE	4	1,389,992	227,553	487,988	2.85
2011 Gubernatorial Campaign Spending					
State	**Number of Candidates**	**Total Spent ($)**	**Total Primary Vote**	**Total General Election Vote**	**Cost per Vote ($)**
KY	5	15,060,810	142,108	833,139	18.08
LA	10	6,615,023	1,023,163	Election decided in the primary[a]	6.46
MS	9	8,801,588	702,318	893,468	9.85

Note: Table includes a sample of the most and least expensive races from 2010. There were 27 total governor's races in 2010.

[a]Incumbent Republican Bobby Jindal captured more than 50% of the vote in the blanket primary, winning the election outright

Source: Thad Beyle, "Gubernatorial Elections, Campaign Costs, and Winning Governors," *Book of the States: 2012*, Volume 44, Table C, p. 208; number of candidates and total votes from each state's election information website.[24] Printed with permission from the Council of State Governments.

Although money cannot buy a governorship, it is important to realize that (1) no one can mount a serious gubernatorial campaign without either personal wealth or strong financial backing by others, and (2) the heavier-spending candidate wins in two out of three elections. Most states require public reporting of campaign contributions and expenditures, and most states place limits on contributions by individuals and groups (although research shows these limits do not hold down overall spending).[23] Nonetheless, individuals and independent advocacy groups ("527s") can spend what they wish in order to express their personal political preferences separate from official campaigns; fundraising political action committees (PACs) can multiply in number; and wealthy candidates can spend as much of their own money as they wish on their own campaigns. (See Chapter 5.)

Political Ambitions

About one-third of the nation's presidents have been chosen from among the ranks of America's state governors, particularly the governors of the larger states. (See *Did You Know?:* How Many Governors Later Became President?) Governors tend to be associated with domestic rather than foreign policy questions. So in periods when foreign policy issues dominate a presidential campaign, Americans tend to elect Congress members to the nation's highest office rather than governors. That was the case during the Cold War and again in the 2012 election when former U.S. senator Barack Obama defeated Governor Mitt Romney to win reelection in 2012. But the growing distrust of "the government in Washington" and the low esteem of Congress in the eyes of the general public have some analysts speculating that the presidential fortunes of governors seeking the White House may improve in 2016.

7.4 · EXECUTIVE POWER IN STATE GOVERNMENT

Compare the powers of weak and strong governors.

Frequently we speak of "strong" and "weak" governors. Yet it is difficult to compare the power of one governor with that of another. To do so, one must examine their *formal, or institutional, powers*—the constitutional position of governors relative to others, their powers of appointment and removal over state officials, their ability or inability to succeed themselves, their powers over the state budget, their veto powers, and their position in their own party and its position in state politics. (See "*Rankings of the States:* Institutional (Formal) Powers of Governors.")

Governors, Weak and Strong

In many ways the organization of American state government resembles political thinking of earlier historical eras. Jacksonian "popular democracy" brought with it the idea that the way to ensure popular control of state government was to elect separately as many state officials as possible. The Reform movement of the late nineteenth and early twentieth centuries led to merit systems and civil service boards, which further curtailed the governor's power of appointment. Many important state offices are governed by boards or commissions whose members may be appointed by the governor with the consent of the state senate but for long overlapping terms, which reduces the governor's influence over members of these boards and commissions. Not all of these trends were experienced uniformly by all 50 states, and there are considerable variations from state to state in the powers that governors have over the state executive branch. Today there are nearly three hundred separately elected executive branch officials in the 50 states. 10 states also elect members of various other multimember boards, commissions, or councils.[25] Only Maine, New Hampshire, New Jersey, and Tennessee have a single statewide elected official, the governor. The others must share at least some executive authority with other elected officials, effectively diluting some of their executive authority. (See Table 7–2.)

Institutional Powers of Governors

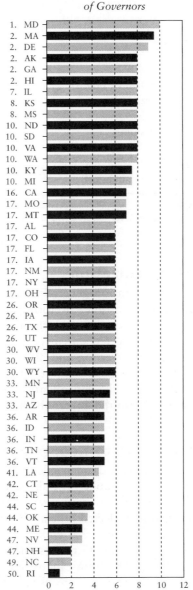

*Institutional Powers
of Governors*

1.	MD
2.	MA
2.	DE
2.	AK
2.	GA
2.	HI
7.	IL
8.	KS
8.	MS
10.	ND
10.	SD
10.	VA
10.	WA
10.	KY
10.	MI
16.	CA
17.	MO
17.	MT
17.	AL
17.	CO
17.	FL
17.	IA
17.	NM
17.	NY
17.	OH
26.	OR
26.	PA
26.	TX
26.	UT
30.	WV
30.	WI
30.	WY
33.	MN
33.	NJ
33.	AZ
36.	AR
36.	ID
36.	IN
36.	TN
36.	VT
41.	LA
42.	CT
42.	NE
44.	SC
44.	OK
44.	ME
47.	NV
47.	NH
49.	NC
50.	RI

0   2   4   6   8   10   12

Note: Data are for 2012. Rankings based on comparisons of tenure potential, appointment power, budget power, and veto power.
Source: The Book of the States: 2012, Volume 44, Table 4.4, pp. 219–220. Printed with permission from the Council of State Governments.

TABLE 7–2 Elected Executive Officials in the States	
Office	**Number of States Electing**
Governor	50
Lieutenant governor	43
Attorney general	43
Treasurer	36
Secretary of state	34
Auditor	23
Comptroller	11
Education (superintendent or board)	14
Secretary of agriculture	13
Insurance commissioner	11
Public utilities commissioner	6
Labor commissioner	4
Chief financial officer	1
Adjutant general (National Guard)	1

Note: Data are for 2012.
Source: Book of the States: 2012, Vol. 44, pp. 231–233. Printed with permission from the Council of State Governments.

Executive Reorganization

Modern public administration generally recommends a stronger governor and a more centralized state executive branch. Reform and reorganization proposals usually call for (1) four-year terms for governors with the ability to succeed themselves; (2) the elimination of many separately elected state executive officials and limiting the statewide ballot to governor, lieutenant governor, and attorney general; (3) elimination of boards and commissions as heads of agencies and their replacement by single, removable gubernatorial appointees; and (4) the consolidation of many state agencies into larger departments reporting directly to the governor. However, states have been slow to adopt these reforms.

Political Opposition to Reorganization

Separately elected officials and independent boards and officials will be around for a long time. Political parties and public officials develop a stake in the continued existence of these elected offices. Moreover, many interest groups prefer to be governed by boards and commissions or separately elected officials. They feel they have more influence over these independent offices than those that come directly under a governor's authority. Interest groups, from educational administrators and teachers' unions, to the agriculture, insurance, real estate, and public utility industries, prefer to have direct access to executive officials. Incumbent officeholders are usually able to rally their client groups to defeat reorganization proposals that threaten their office.

Tenure Power

TENURE POWER
The length of time an elected official can serve in office.

Another component of a governor's influence is self-succession in office. Governors with the highest "**tenure power**" are those who are elected for a four-year term and are permitted to succeed themselves indefinitely—no term limits. Governors with the lowest "tenure power" are those who have only two-year terms (New Hampshire and Vermont). The Twenty-second Amendment to the U.S. Constitution restricts executive tenure at the presidential level to two terms, and most states have similar restrictions on their governors.

Managerial Powers

Governors are chief executives; they are supposed to manage state governmental bureaucracies. But aside from intervening occasionally in response to a crisis, governors generally turn over their management chores to others. Governors downplay their managerial role and avoid expending energy and power on management because "greater rewards derive from the pursuit of other functions—formulating policy, building popularity and support among the public, helping develop the state economy."[26]

Executive Orders

Managing state agencies is generally left to the governor's staff and department heads (see Chapter 8). But from time to time governors directly intervene in well-publicized, politically sensitive executive decisions. Governors may do so by **executive order**—a special directive issued by the governor to one or more executive agencies. Executive orders must be based on state constitutional powers given governors or on powers delegated to them by state laws. Executive orders are often issued to deal with public emergencies or disasters, or political messes that require the suspension or removal of a public official.

EXECUTIVE ORDER
A directive issued by a chief executive to administrative agencies.

Appointment Powers

Perhaps the most important managerial power is the **power to appoint** subordinate officials. Appointment of subordinates does not guarantee their responsiveness, but there is a greater likelihood that an official appointed by a governor will have values that coincide with the governor's. If an agency head is separately elected by the people (as are most attorneys general, treasurers, and secretaries of state), then the governor has little direct control over them. If the governor can appoint an agency head *without* the need for legislative approval, we can say that the governor has stronger appointive powers than if legislative confirmation of appointment is required. Indeed, agency heads tend to evaluate the governor's influence largely in terms of the ability to appoint them to office.[27] (There is an old saying that to understand who has power or influence over someone, just identify who can hire and fire that person.)

APPOINTMENT POWER
Authority to choose officials to head agencies and sit on various boards and commission.

State Cabinets

State **cabinets**, composed of the heads of the major executive departments, advise the governors in most of the states. Indeed, in a few states the cabinet is recognized in the state constitution and given more than just advisory powers. Cabinets range in size from less than 10 members to more than 25. Most cabinets meet at the governor's discretion and function more or less in the fashion of the president's cabinet in the national government. In a few states they function as a body of equals on certain issues, such as granting pardons and purchasing environmentally sensitive land, but that is not the norm.

CABINET
The heads of executive departments of a government.

Removal Powers

Restrictions on governors' powers of appointment are further complicated by restrictions on their powers of removal. A common statutory or constitutional provision dealing with governors' **removal powers** states that removal must be **"for cause only"**; that is, governors must provide a clear-cut statement of charges and an opportunity for an open hearing to the employee they are trying to oust. This process is often unpleasant, and governors seek to avoid it unless they have strong evidence of incompetence, fraud, or mismanagement. It is especially painful and politically embarrassing when the person to be removed is one of the governor's appointees. Such a situation is guaranteed to generate big headlines. That is why governors have become more careful in "vetting" (checking the credentials of) a potential appointee.

When a governor's removal powers are limited to "for cause only," it is next to impossible to remove a subordinate for policy differences. As a final resort, a determined

REMOVAL POWER
Authority to force an official to step down from his or her position.

"FOR CAUSE ONLY"
Governors must provide a clear-cut statement of charges and an opportunity for an open hearing to the employee they are trying to oust.

governor with influence in the legislature can always oust an official by a legislative act, which abolishes the office or agency the official heads and replaces it with another; this device is sometimes called a "**ripper bill**."

Fiscal Power

Governors are generally responsible for preparing the state budget for consideration by the legislature. The state budget is the single most important policy document in state government. Although the legislature must enact the state budget into law, and no state monies may be spent without the passage of an appropriations act by the legislature, in practice the governor exercises considerable influence over state spending in the preparation of the state budget. Research shows that governors with greater power over the budget process are more effective at influencing public policy.[28] However, in general, governors are more effective at influencing the state's budget than specific state policies.[29] It is always a big media day when a governor formally announces his or her proposed budget and sends it to the legislature. Governors are aided by their budget offices in preparation of each fiscal year's "Budget Recommendations" to the legislature (see Chapter 8).

7.5

THE GOVERNOR'S LEGISLATIVE POWERS

Describe the role of the governor in the legislative process, and assess the governor's ability to impact legislative outcomes.

The responsibility for initiating major statewide legislative programs falls upon the governor. The governor's programs are presented to the legislature in various speeches, reports, and the budget. While these instruments are only recommendations, the governor can set the agenda for policy debate with them. "**Agenda setting**" is an important power.

Setting Priorities

Governors are well advised to limit their policy agenda to a few priority issues each year, rather than sending the legislature a smorgasbord of items without any unifying goal or theme. (They usually unveil these issues in their annual "State of the State" speeches.[30]) (See Figure 7–2.) A governor wants to develop a **strong "batting average"**—a reputation for getting a high percentage of his or her recommendations enacted by the legislature. Submitting only a few high-visibility proposals, and concentrating energy and power on securing their passage, usually increases the ratio of bills passed to bills submitted. But it is often difficult for governors to select their priority issues from the host of recommendations that come to them from interest groups and executive agencies. Governors can expand their policy agenda in good economic times when there are more revenues to pay for new initiatives. But in recessionary times, governors are constrained to few if any new initiatives. In fact, during the most recent major economic downturn (the Great Recession), two thirds or more of the nation's governors focused most of their efforts on economic development (job creation) and education.[31]

Providing Leadership

"What does the governor want?" is a frequent question heard in legislative debate. Leadership requires the governor to do more than simply propose legislation. The governor must also "make it happen." Governors must rally public support, packaging their proposals in a way that people will understand and support. They must make speeches and public appearances and prepare news releases highlighting their proposals.

This "outside" strategy must be integrated with an "inside" strategy to persuade legislators to support the program. Governors must carefully steer their proposals through the legislative process—the committee system, floor proceedings, votes on amendments, conference committees, and final passage. They must develop good working relationships with the legislative leadership and with as many rank-and-file members as possible. They must mobilize the support of interest groups behind their proposals. Finally, governors must be willing to compromise—to take "half a loaf" and declare victory. Governors must be flexible, accepting legislative amendments when necessary to preserve the major thrust of their program.

Special Sessions

Governors can increase pressure on legislatures to act on particular recommendations by calling special sessions. The governor can specify the topics that should be considered in the special session. This device can be particularly effective if the legislature has buried one of the governor's favorite programs in the regular session. Legislators do not like to be called back from their businesses to the state capital for a special session, so even the threat of one may force them to pass the governor's program in the regular session. Of course, legislatures can defeat a governor's program even in special session, but their actions will be spotlighted.

Vetoes

The **governor's veto** power is a major source of power within the legislature. Only in North Carolina does the governor have no veto power at all. In some states, the veto power is restricted by giving the governor only a short time to consider a bill after it has passed the legislature, by permitting a simple majority of legislative members to override the veto, or by requiring vetoed bills to reappear at the next legislative session. In other states, governors are given longer periods of time to consider a bill, and a two-thirds vote of both houses of the legislature is required to override a veto, rather than a simple majority.

The veto is often the governor's principal source of bargaining power in the legislature. A **veto override** by a legislature is rare. Only about 5 percent of bills passed by state legislatures are vetoed by governors, and governors are overridden on less than 10 percent of their vetoes. Of course, vetoes and veto overrides are more common when a governor faces a legislature controlled by the opposition party—a situation referred to as "power split" or divided control.[32]

Occasionally legislatures may challenge governors to veto bills. This is more likely to occur with divided party control of state government—one party controls the legislature with a governor from the opposition party. The legislature can pass a popular bill opposed by the governor and then dare the governor to veto it. Even if the governor's veto is sustained, the majority party leaders in the legislature may feel they have created an issue for the next gubernatorial election.

Line-Item Veto

Most governors also have the power to veto particular items in larger appropriations bills. This allows them to pick out particular legislative spending proposals (frequently labeled "turkeys" by unsympathetic governors) and veto those proposals without jeopardizing the entire budget. In states *without* the line-item veto, governors may be forced to accept many legislative spending proposals in order to get a budget passed.

The **line-item veto** can be a powerful weapon in the governor's arsenal. It allows the governor to take legislators' pet budget items as hostage for their support on other unrelated legislation favored by the governor. Legislators who fail to support the governor risk losing their "turkeys." Trade-offs need not be explicit. Legislators who consistently oppose the governor's programs throughout the legislative session risk losing "pork" for their district when the governor goes through the appropriations acts line by line.

Governor–Legislature Relations

For most governors, working with the legislature is considered the most difficult and demanding part of their job. "Practically all governors regard their legislature as a problem and are happy when the legislature leaves town."[33] About half of all governors

GOVERNOR'S VETO
Formal rejection of proposed legislation by governors.

VETO OVERRIDE
Legislative power to enact a law over a veto by the governor, usually requiring a two-thirds vote of both houses.

LINE-ITEM VETO
The power of a governor to reject certain portions of a legislative appropriations bill without killing the entire bill.

Governors routinely say working with the state legislature is the most difficult and demanding part of their job even when each chamber is controlled by the governor's own party.

have had some legislative experience before becoming governor. They may have some friends and acquaintances left over from their legislature days. And they may have greater respect for the legislative branch and greater empathy with the concerns of legislators. But many governors have little sympathy or patience with the slow and complicated legislative process.

What works with the legislature? Governors should:

Stand tall. This entails not only the appearance of strength and decisiveness but a willingness to punish one's enemies.

Consult members. Inform legislators of plans and programs and listen to their concerns.

Talk turkey. Communicate in legislators' language of patronage and deals, give and take, and reciprocity.

Rub elbows. Stay in personal contact with legislators on a regular basis.

Massage egos. Legislators like to share center stage with the governor, to be seen at bill signings, to be invited to dinner at the governor's mansion, and to have the governor praise them in public.[34]

7.6 DIVIDED GOVERNMENT: GOVERNOR VERSUS THE LEGISLATURE

Analyze how divided government affects the relationship between the governor and the legislature.

DIVIDED GOVERNMENT (POWER SPLIT)

A government in which one party controls the governor's office while another party controls one or both houses of the legislature.

Some level of **divided government**, where one party either controls one or both houses of the legislature and the other party controls the governorship, is increasingly a fact of life in American state politics. (It is also referred to as a "**power split**.") In recent years over half of the states experienced divided party control. Much of this was attributed to the election of Republican governors in southern states with heavily Democratic legislatures, as well as an increased tendency of voters everywhere to split their tickets.

In 2012, the trend toward divided control was reversed. In 46 states, the same party controlled both houses of the state legislature—the highest since World War II. And in 38 of those states (25 Republican, 13 Democrat), the same ruling party controlled the governor's mansion (25 Republican, 13 Democrat). In the states where the governor and the legislature are not controlled by the same party, Republican governors are slightly more likely to face Democratic-controlled legislatures than the reverse.[35] But divided government has a major impact on executive–legislative relations.

Partisanship Cuts Both Ways

Party works to the advantage of governors when their party has a majority in the legislature. The governor and a legislature controlled by the same party have an incentive to produce results. There is still institutional rivalry, wherein governors compete with legislatures for policy leadership. But both have an interest in compiling a record of success that the voters can attribute to everyone running under the party's label in the next election.[36] But when partisan differences are added to institutional rivalry, conflict rather than cooperation is more likely to characterize relations between the governor and legislature.

Confronting Gridlock

A governor confronting opposition party control of the legislature must spend a great deal of time bargaining and compromising with legislative leaders of the opposition party. Governors must ensure that they keep their own party's legislators behind their proposals and then either work out accommodations with the opposition leadership or chip off enough votes from less loyal opposition members to win passage of their proposals.[37] Neither is an easy task. Party activists, including legislators, differ on ideological grounds and policy issues. Moreover, the opposing party looks forward to defeating the governor in the next election. Only a very able governor can avoid gridlock with divided party control of state government. Sometimes it just boils down to the interpersonal skills of the governor.

IMPEACHMENTS, INVESTIGATIONS, AND RECALLS

7.7

Assess the effectiveness of various checks on the power of the governor.

Impeachment is a political process, not a legal process. While state constitutions, like the U.S. Constitution, usually define an impeachable offense as "treason, bribery, or other high crimes and misdemeanors," the *political* errors of impeached officials are usually more important than their legal offenses.

Impeachment, Trial, and Removal

All state constitutions, except Oregon's, provide for the impeachment of elected state officials by the legislature. Impeachment proceedings are initiated in the lower houses of forty-eight states, in the unicameral legislature of Nebraska, and the upper house in Alaska. Impeachment trials are held in the upper houses in 47 states, in a special court of impeachment in Nebraska, in the lower house in Alaska, and in a special commission in Missouri. Most states require a two-thirds vote to convict and remove an official.

These impeachment provisions are rarely used. There appear to have been only 17 gubernatorial impeachments and seven trial convictions since the nation's birth. When Arizona governor Evan Mecham (R) was impeached and convicted by the state legislature in 1988 for fiscal improprieties; it was the first such event in nearly 60 years. In January 2009, Illinois governor Rod Blagojevich (D) was impeached and removed from office by a 59–0 vote of the Illinois Senate after accusations of trying to sell the U.S. Senate seat vacated by Barack Obama. (See "*Up Close:* Three Scandal-Ridden Governors Embarrass Their States.")

IMPEACHMENT
The power of legislatures to remove executive and judicial officers from office for good cause; generally the lower house must first vote for impeachment, then the upper house must hold a trial and vote for removal.

Criminal Investigations

Criminal investigations have led to the demise of a number of other governors over the years. Some were convicted, while others were acquitted of criminal charges, but all were finished politically; no miraculous comebacks were possible. For example, former Illinois governor George Ryan (R) was convicted of racketeering, fraud, obstructing the Internal Revenue Service, and lying to the FBI. The corruption scandal ended his political career. The same year, former Alabama governor Don Siegelman (D) was convicted of a "pay-to-play" scheme—trading government favors for campaign donations when he was governor and, before that, lieutenant governor. At the time he was attempting to make a comeback by running for the Democratic nomination for governor. The voters said "No" loud and clear.

Recall

Nineteen states allow citizens to recall the governor, but vary in how the new governor is selected. (The **recall process**, initiated by a citizen petition, allows a vote on whether

RECALL PROCESS
Initiated by a citizen petition, it allows a vote on whether to remove an elected official from office before his or her term is completed.

---

to remove an elected official from office before his or her term is completed.) The most famous recall took place in 2003 when California voters tossed out Governor Gray Davis (D) for his handling of an electricity crisis and a recession. They voted in Governor Arnold Schwarzenegger (R). Prior to that, North Dakota governor Lynn Frazier (R) was recalled in 1921 during his third term for issues related to state-owned industries. Several other governors had recall petitions certified during their tenure but left office before the recall election could be held. In 2012, Wisconsin governor Scott Walker (R) became the third governor to face a recall election; he was the first to beat back the removal effort.[38]

7.8 THE GOVERNOR AS POLITICAL LEADER

Evaluate how well governors are able to harness their informal powers to be effective political leaders.

The formal powers of governors can take them only so far. Their personal (informal) powers, or "political clout," are often essential to helping them gain control of public policy, legislative output, and state agency performance. Their *personal, or informal, powers* are measured by their margin of victory over their opponent, political career progression, personal ambitions, and influence over public opinion in the state.[39] A landslide election that carries the governor's party into control of both houses of the legislature can overcome many formal weaknesses in a governor's powers. A politically resourceful governor enjoying widespread public popularity who can skillfully employ the media to his or her advantage can overcome many constitutional weaknesses in the office. A young, up-and-coming governor from a big state with lots of Electoral College votes can gain a spot on the national stage, which catches people's attention at home.

Governors spend more time meeting the general public, attending ceremonial functions, and working with the press and television than they do managing state government and working with the legislature. They focus on these public relations tasks not only to improve their chances for reelection, but also to give themselves the political clout to achieve their goals for state government. All 50 governors have press secretaries or public information offices, some with large staffs. Press conferences, policy announcements, and other media events are carefully orchestrated for maximum coverage in the nightly news and morning papers. Increasingly, state legislatures are creating their own media offices, but media coverage of state legislatures has traditionally been sparse, mostly because many do not meet year-round, as Congress does.

Media Access

Governors are the most visible figures in state politics. An attractive governor who is skillful in public relations can command support from administrators, legislators, local officials, and party leaders through public appeals to their constituents. Politicians must respect the governor's greater access to the communications media and hence to the minds of their constituents. Effective governors not only understand the broad range of issues facing their states but also are able to speak clearly and persuasively about them. Many have their press conferences video-streamed on the Web, can "friend" constituents on their Facebook page or tweet them (and the media) via their own Twitter account. Stellar photo images of events attended by the governor, infrastructure projects underway in the state, or citizens using state services can be posted via Pinterest. Governors in the twenty-first century have to be social media savvy.

State Media Coverage

Press coverage of state government has declined in recent years, mostly due to cutbacks in the capitol press corps, especially newspaper reporters. However, the media still pays close attention to the governor. Regular updates (scorecards) are done on how many of his or her campaign promises have been kept (or not yet kept). And reporters are always on the lookout for official misconduct by the governor or anyone else in his or her administration. However, with fewer reporters, it is becoming more difficult to conduct thorough investigations of suspected misconduct. A Pew Research Center Project for Excellence in Journalism study has found that "the news industry is more undermanned and unprepared to uncover stories, dig deep into emerging ones or to question information put into its hands."[40]

Overall, reporters lean more heavily Democratic than Republican in their own politics. A survey of 1,149 print, radio, and television journalists found that in American newsrooms, Democrats outnumber Republicans by two-to-one (37 to 18%), with one-third saying they are independents.[41] This is nothing new. Similar patterns have been observed since the 1980s when a pathbreaking study by S. Robert Lichter first observed the partisan leanings of the press.[42] Thus, it is not surprising that there is a general perception among political analysts that Democratic governors tend to get more positive coverage than Republican governors.

But "**media savvy**"—skill in working with the media—is more important than partisan affiliation in winning good media coverage. A governor who "knows what's newsworthy," puts ideas across in brief "sound bites," makes timely use of widely reported events to get into the news, "hangs around the press area in the state capitol building," and cultivates good relationships with reporters is far more likely to garner favorable media stories than a governor who is "media shy," "tongue-tied," "standoffish," self-conscious, or who "hates the press," "blames the media," and thereby encourages an adversarial relationship with them.[43]

MEDIA SAVVY
Knowledge of how to use the press to get one's message across to the public.

Popularity

Media access and the visibility it produces provide governors with the opportunity to promote their personal popularity with the citizens of the state. The legislature is seldom as popular as the governor. Even if individual legislators are popular in their districts, the legislature as an institution is not. Statewide opinion polls do not track governors' popularity as closely as national polls track the president of the United States. But opinion in most large states is regularly surveyed by private, university, and newspaper polls.

All governors have press secretaries whose responsibility it is to develop and maintain a favorable media image for the governor. Many governors devote a great deal of their personal attention to this task—massaging the capitol press, organizing media events, holding town meetings or "virtual" townhall meetings, personally answering their e-mail or going into official chat rooms, and traveling about the state. There may be some tendency for legislators and interest groups to avoid direct confrontations with a popular governor. Certainly a popular governor is in a better position to advance his or her program than an *un*popular governor. But the real challenge for many governors is turning personal popularity into political power.

Leadership

Governors' reputations as leaders stem not only from what they say but also from what they do. Their reputations must include a capacity to decide issues and to persist in the decision once it is made. A reputation for backing down, for avoiding situations that involve them in public conflict, or for wavering in the face of momentary pressures invites the governors' adversaries to ignore or oppose them. A sense of insecurity or weakness can damage a governor's power more than any constitutional limitation. Governors can also increase their influence by developing a reputation for punishing their adversaries and rewarding their supporters. Once the reputation as an effective leader is established, cooperation is often forthcoming in anticipation of the governor's reaction.

Party

Governors are also the recognized leaders of their state parties. In a majority of states, it is the governor who picks the state party chairperson and who is consulted on questions of party platform, campaign tactics, nominations for party office, and party finances. The

Three Scandal-Ridden Governors Embarrass Their States

The Impeachment of Rod Blagojevich

Rod Blagojevich is the first governor in Illinois history to be impeached and removed from office. He was impeached in January 2009 by the state House of Representatives on a 114–1 vote and convicted by the state Senate on a 59–0 vote. The Illinois legislature also voted to ban him from ever again seeking public office in the state.

Blagojevich was arrested by federal authorities in December 2008 on charges of "corrupt use" of his office for "personal gain." He allegedly attempted to auction off appointment to the vacant U.S. Senate seat of Barack Obama in exchange for campaign contributions. He made numerous appearances on national television to deny the charges.

Blagojevich is the son of a Serbian immigrant laborer. He was raised in Chicago and graduated from Northwestern University in 1979 with a degree in history. He obtained a

Former Ilinois Governor Rod Blagojevich (D).

law degree in 1983 from Pepperdine University in Malibu, California. He married the daughter of a powerful Chicago city alderman who helped him win a job as a Cook County state prosecutor. In 1992 he won election to the Illinois House of Representatives. He was never very popular with either Democrats or Republicans in the state legislature. One legislator described him as a "devious, cynical, crass, and corrupt politician." But in 1996, he won election to the U.S. House seat from Chicago, a seat once held by Dan Rostenkowski (D) who himself was indicted and convicted on federal corruption charges. "Blago" served three terms in Washington. In 2002, he won a close Democratic primary election for Illinois governor. In the general election he faced Republican Illinois Attorney General Jim Ryan. Blagojevich won with 52 percent of the vote and in 2006, with the support of U.S. Senator Barack Obama, won reelection.

As governor, Blagojevich ruffled feathers in both his own administration and in the Democratic-controlled legislature. He argued often with his own lieutenant governor, the attorney general, the comptroller, and the treasurer—all Democrats. He gradually lost the support of Obama and members of his team. Chicago mayor Richard M. Daley called him a "cuckoo." Polls recorded his approval rating as the lowest of any governor in the nation at the time he was removed from office.

In 2011, he was sentenced to 14 years in prison on 18 counts of criminal corruption.

Mark Sanford, Redemption or Rejection?

Mark Sanford was once a popular Republican governor of South Carolina, chairman of the Republican Governors Association, and potential vice presidential candidate. But in a stunning reversal of fortunes, he was cited by the State Ethics Commission for using public funds to pursue an affair with his Argentine mistress. In a bizarre twist to the affair, Sanford had disappeared from the statehouse for five days, leaving no traces of his whereabouts.

Sanford is the son of a prominent physician and owner of a 3,000-acre plantation in Beaufort, South Carolina. He graduated from Furman University in 1983 and earned an MBA at the University of Virginia. He ran for Congress in 1994 having never run for office before. He served three terms in the House of Representatives as a staunch Republican conservative. He did not run for reelection in 2000 in keeping with a promise to limit his terms in office.

He set his political sights on the governorship in 2002. He won the Republican primary against the incumbent lieutenant governor, and then won the general election against the Democratic incumbent governor. He was reelected with 55 percent of the vote in 2006 and was mentioned as John McCain's running mate in 2008.

But in June 2009 Sanford appeared to vanish from office, garnering national news coverage as the missing governor. He told his staff that he would be hiking on the Appalachian Trail, but he did not return calls from his office or his family. When he finally reappeared, he tearfully confessed that he had been visiting his Argentine girlfriend whom he described as his "soulmate." The State Ethics Commission brought a series of charges against him for using state-funded commercial and private aircraft to pursue his extramarital affair. His wife promptly divorced him. The South Carolina House of Representatives considered impeachment charges but ultimately decided against his

Former South Carolina Governor, now Congressman, Mark Sanford (R).

Spitzer was raised in the Bronx, the son of a Jewish real estate tycoon. He was educated at Princeton University, majoring in public and international affairs. He graduated in 1981 and went on to Harvard Law School where he served as an editor of the prestigious *Harvard Law Review*. He served as an assistant district attorney in Manhattan investigating labor racketeering and organized crime. He won recognition in 1992 by successfully prosecuting the Gambino crime family.

He sought to parlay his reputation as a crime fighter into an election bid for attorney general of New York in 1994. But despite heavy funding from his own family, he lost the Democratic nomination. He returned to the fray in 1998, won the Democratic primary, and went on to defeat incumbent Republican Dennis C. Vacco in a close vote. As attorney general, Spitzer investigated and prosecuted Wall Street corporate rip offs. The "Sheriff of Wall Street" was reelected in 2002 with an impressive 66 percent of the vote, and by 2006 was heralded as "the future of the Democratic Party." He easily won the Democratic nomination for governor and went on to win the general election with a record 70 percent of the vote. He selected state senate leader David Paterson as his lieutenant governor and running mate.

His stunning political downfall was triggered by a *New York Times* report in March 2008 that federal investigators had linked him to a prostitution ring catering to wealthy men. According to published reports he had paid up to $80,000 for prostitutes over several years, including one payment of $4,300 for a meeting at the Mayflower Hotel in Washington, DC. He was identified in recorded telephone conversations as "client nine" and nicknamed by the press as the "Luv Gov."

He was not charged with a crime, but he announced his resignation in the wake of the revelations. "I cannot allow my private failings to disrupt the people's work."

Like Sanford, Spitzer let time pass, then jumped back into the political arena. In 2013, he filed to run for New York City Comptroller but lost in the race to secure the Democratic Party nomination. For Spitzer, the vote spelled rejection, not redemption.

removal. He refused to resign but agreed to pay $74,000 in fines to resolve the ethics charges. He denounced "the media circus" that surrounded his escapades.

That was not the end of Governor Sanford's political career. Banking on the fact that South Carolinians, like other Americans, are willing to forget past sins, Sanford declared his candidacy for a vacant U.S. Congressional seat in 2013. He survived the Republican primary only to face the Democratic sister of political satirist Stephen Colbert, Elizabeth Colbert Busch. He defeated her in a special election and became a U.S. Congressman representing South Carolina's 1st Congressional District. Said one supporter, "Following his heart as he did was foolish but it happens." For Sanford, it was redemption!

Eliot Spitzer: A Prostitute's "Client Nine"

Eliot Spitzer reached the governorship of New York on the strength of his reputation as a crusader against crime and corruption. Yet he was obliged to resign following revelations naming him as "client nine" in a high-priced prostitution ring.

Former New York Governor, Eliot Spitzer (D).

amount of power that a governor derives from the position of party leader varies from state to state according to the strength, cohesion, and discipline of the state parties.

But there are limitations to the power that governors derive from their role as party leader. First of all, a governor cannot deny party renomination to disloyal members. Nominations are acquired in primary elections. Legislators must first consider the demands of their own constituents, not the voice of the governor. Second, the frequency of divided control, where governors face legislatures dominated by the opposition party, requires them to bargain with individuals and groups in the opposition party. If they have acquired a reputation for being too "partisan" in their approach to state programs, they will find it difficult to win over the necessary support of opposition party members. Finally, the use of patronage may make as many enemies as friends. There is an old political saying: "For every one patronage appointment, you make nine enemies and one ingrate."

7.9 | OTHER EXECUTIVE OFFICES

Outline the roles of the lieutenant governor and other executive officers.

Lieutenant Governor

The lieutenant governor's formal duties are comparable to those of the vice president of the United States; in other words, lieutenant governors have relatively few formal powers. The two basic functions of the office are to serve in direct line of succession to the governor and replace him or her in the event of a vacancy in that office, and to be the presiding officer of the state senate, or secretary of state in a handful of states. Vacancies can occur because of death, incapacity, impeachment and removal, recall, or resignation. The likelihood of a vacancy has increased considerably over the past decade.[44] Since 2000, some 20 gubernatorial successions have occurred following the death, resignation, or criminal conviction of a sitting governor. In 43 states the lieutenant governor is next in line to be governor; in four states, it is the president of the state senate; in three others, it is the secretary of state.[45] In 26 states, the governor and the lieutenant governor run on the same ticket, much as the president and vice president. In 19 others, the lieutenant governor position is separately elected. (Five states have no lieutenant governor.)

One in four lieutenant governors who run for governor win. Nebraska's governor David Eugene "Dave" Heineman (far left) did just that, although he was first appointed to the position when the state's governor resigned to become U.S. secretary of agriculture.

In states where gubernatorial candidates select their running mates, a great deal of attention is paid to whether that running mate will boost the ticket. One question that often surfaces is whether putting a woman on the ticket will help. One study has found that it often does.[46]

Regardless of how the lieutenant governor is selected, the lieutenant governor's office in many states is looked upon as a platform to campaign for the governorship. In fact, a study by the National Lieutenant Governors Association found that lieutenant governors are more successful at being elected governor than any other local, state, or congressional office. Lieutenant governors are said to have a head start for the top job. Approximately one in every four governors over the past 100 years first served as lieutenant government. Consequently, lieutenant governors generally have political ambitions of their own.

The most ambitious seldom make good "assistant governors" who will submerge their own interests for the success of the governor's administration. Friction between a governor and lieutenant governor is often most noticeable in states where they are separately elected and of different political parties.

For many years, lieutenant governors had little to do. One candidate for the office in Wisconsin went so far as to run a campaign ad "detailing" what the position entailed in his state: "You just stand around and wait for the governor to die. It's a plum job."[47] More recently, efforts have been made by governors to give more responsibilities to lieutenant governors by assigning them membership on various boards and commissions, tasking them with a wider range of policy functions, or using them as a liaison to the legislature. This approach is helpful in recruiting lieutenant governors. Maryland's lieutenant governor's first conversation with the governor who selected him as a running mate went like this: "I told him that this needed to be more than calling the governor's house every morning and asking if the governor is still with us. This needed to be a meaningful opportunity."[48]

Attorney General

The office of attorney general has more real powers and responsibilities than that of the lieutenant governor. Attorneys general are elected in 43 states, and appointed in the other states, usually by the governor. Attorneys general (AGs) are the chief legal counsel for their states. They represent the state in any suits to which it is a party. They act as legal counsel for the governor and for other state officials. The legal business of state agencies is subject to their supervision. The source of the attorney general's power comes from the quasi-judicial duty of rendering formal written opinions in response to requests from the governor, state agencies, or other public officials regarding the legality and constitutionality of their activities. These opinions have the power of law in state affairs unless they are successfully challenged in court. The governor and other officials are generally obliged to conform to the attorney general's legal opinion until a court specifies otherwise. Attorneys general render authoritative interpretations of state constitutions, laws, city ordinances, and administrative rulings.

The attorney general also has substantial law enforcement powers. Most states allow attorneys general to initiate criminal proceedings on their own motion, and nearly all states assign them responsibility for handling criminal cases on appeal to higher state courts or to federal courts. In some states the attorney general has supervisory powers over law enforcement throughout the state.

The state AGs, through the National Association of Attorneys General, have become more powerful politically by jointly suing companies for consumer fraud and using the settlement monies (in the billions) to fund important consumer protection activities in their respective states. The association routinely monitors issues such as antitrust, bankruptcy, civil rights, cyber crime, end-of-life health care, the environment, Medicaid fraud, and violence against women. The association also prepares thorough analyses of newly emerging issues. Recently, it completed studies of school safety, online privacy, and human trafficking.[49] The growing clout and visibility of state attorneys general have led some to conclude that of all the statewide elected offices, it is the one that has undergone the most change in recent years.

Treasurers, Auditors, and Comptrollers

Most states have elected *treasurers*, but treasurers in other states are appointed by either the governor or the legislature. Treasurers are the trustees of the public purse. They are the state "*money managers*," custodians of state funds: collecting taxes, acting as paymaster for the state, managing trust funds (like the tobacco settlement monies in 24 states), and administering the investment of state funds. (States invest billions of dollars annually.) The principal job of the treasurer is to make payments on departmental requisitions for payrolls and for checks to be issued to those who have furnished the state with goods and services. Generally, the department's requests for checks must be accompanied by a voucher showing the proper legislative authority for such payment. Requests for payment usually are accompanied by a statement from the auditor's or the comptroller's office that legislative appropriations are available for such payment.

The primary duty of the state *comptroller* is to ensure that a prospective departmental expenditure is in accordance with the law and does not exceed the appropriations made by the legislature. This "**pre-audit**" occurs before any expenditure is made by the treasurer.

The principal duty of the state *auditor* is that of assuring the legislature that expenditures and investment of state funds have been made in accordance with the law. This function is known as a "**post-audit**" and occurs after state expenditures have been made.

Public administration experts consider the comptroller's job of pre-audit to be an executive function, and they urge that the comptroller be appointed by the governor. On the other hand, the job of post-audit is essentially a legislative check on the executive, and students of public administration generally feel that the auditor should be elected or appointed by the legislature. However, there is still some confusion in state organizations about the separate functions of auditors and comptrollers—some auditors do "pre-auditing" and some comptrollers do "post-auditing."

The National Association of State Auditors, Comptrollers, and Treasurers has become more active of late, bringing state financial officers together to tackle such big issues as the financial soundness of state retirement systems and prepaid college savings plans, regulation of the municipal bond market, the security of the state's financial system in the event of natural disasters or terrorist attacks, investment fraud, and identity theft. The Association also keeps a close watch on federal grants-in-aid programs and regulations attached to them. Federal requirements attached to the American Recovery and Reinvestment Act of 2009 (the economic stimulus plan) mandated that states be more transparent and timely in the reporting of their spending of these funds to prevent and detect waste, fraud, and abuse and to increase accountability to the taxpayers.[50]

Secretary of State

Thirty-five states elect secretaries of state. These officials are the chief custodians of state records and, in the case of several states, "keepers of the great seal of the commonwealth." They are also the state's chief elections officer. It is this function, more than the record-keeping function, that puts secretaries of state in the news. When there are close, contested elections (Florida, 2000) secretaries of state become the focal point of massive media attention and lawsuits. Secretaries of state are responsible for supervising the preparation of ballots and certifying election results for the state. Their Web sites typically report historical and current voter registration and turnout data, candidate filings, campaign contributions and spending, and include links to local election officials. Secretaries of state, who belong to the National Association of Secretaries of State, have been given more important roles in election administration by the Help America Vote Act of 2002.

In their less visible record-keeping function, they register corporations, trademarks, and trade names; publish state administrative codes and registers; handle business and occupational licensing; and administer the uniform commercial code. They also register lobbyists, record all laws, and publish the state constitution. Beginning with the Great Recession, the business-related activities of secretaries of state have expanded a lot and been more focused on making processes in their offices less bureaucratic. Specifically, they are "making efforts to ensure that state filing and licensing officers are business-friendly and streamlined for success through business one-stops, fee reductions, and other incentives" to encourage economic growth and stability.[51]

PRE-AUDIT

The state comptroller's duty; it involves making sure that a prospective departmental expenditure is in accordance with the law and does not exceed the appropriations made by the legislature before any expenditure is made by the treasurer.

POST-AUDIT

An auditor's duty; it involves making sure that expenditures and investment of state funds have been made in accordance with the law; done after expenditure is made.

Personal Staff

All governors are permitted to maintain a small group of loyal, dedicated personal aides—the governor's staff. Many staff members previously worked in the governor's political campaign. Most work long hours in small offices for relatively low pay. Most are young. Most envision some sort of political career for themselves in the future; they believe the experience they are acquiring in the governor's office, and the contacts they are making, will help in their careers. The governor may have a chief of staff, an appointments secretary, a press secretary, a legal counsel, several speechwriters, one or more legislative aides, and advisors in key policy areas—education, welfare, highways, health, homeland security, economic development, and the environment. As the policymaking role of governors has expanded and policies have become more complex, governors have added more policy analyst positions to their staffs and hired more professionals to fill them. No one on the governor's staff is a civil service employee; their jobs depend directly on their value to the governor. Without a doubt, the smooth operation of a governor's office is heavily dependent upon the staff.

The Best Job!

With all the stresses of the office, it is interesting to note that many governors who have held other elected offices, even in Washington, still describe being governor as "the best job they ever had." For many, it was the job they said allowed them to have the greatest influence over key public policies that had long-lasting effects on their state and its voters.

CHAPTER HIGHLIGHTS

- The governor is the best known, most recognizable politician in any state.

- Governors are gaining greater political power within their states and in national politics.

- A governor functions as the state's chief administrator, chief legislator, party leader, ceremonial head, chief negotiator, opinion leader, and crisis manager.

- Most governors have come to the office with considerable experience in public affairs, usually from state and local government. By profession, the majority of governors have been lawyers.

- The number of women and minority governors, while still small, is on the upswing.

- The outcome of gubernatorial elections depends mostly on the personal qualities of the candidates, their ability to associate themselves with popular issues, the strength of their personal political organizations, their ability to raise campaign funds, and their skills in campaigning.

- In presidential-year elections, gubernatorial candidates of the president's party can suffer from national recessions and benefit from national prosperity.

- The formal powers of governors are measured by their appointment, budget, and veto powers and by their tenure potential. Reformers recommend strengthening the governorship by having terms last four years (with provisions for self-succession) and having the governor appoint state agency heads without having to secure legislative approval.

- A governor's State of the State address is given to state legislators and broadcast to the public, usually at the beginning of the year. The address signals the governor's priorities.

- Governors exercise considerable influence over state affairs by preparing the state budget and setting the policy agenda. They must work with legislators on passing preferred bills, often bargaining and compromising with the opposing party.

- Governors can exert pressure on the legislature by threatening to veto legislation in whole or by item and by threatening to call a special session. Most governors can veto specific lines in the legislature's appropriation bill (budget).

- A governor's performance depends heavily on his or her informal powers—public popularity, positive media coverage, and reputation for leadership among legislators and party officials.

- In 49 states, governors accused of wrongdoing can be impeached by their legislatures, although the threat of impeachment or the possibility of criminal investigation is often enough to force resignation. Voters in 18 states can remove their governors by recall.

- Press coverage of governors is more extensive than of state legislatures.

- Lieutenant governors have become more visible in recent years. A slight majority run on the same ticket as the governor. The rest are separately elected. Five states do not have one. Their roles beyond succession vary but nearly all would like to be governor themselves at some point.

- Governors in a number of states must share executive power with other statewide elected officials like the attorney general, secretary of state, auditor, treasurer, or comptroller. These positions have also become more visible and seen as stepping stones to being governor.

CHAPTER EIGHT

BUREAUCRATIC POLITICS IN STATES AND COMMUNITIES

LEARNING OBJECTIVES

8.1 Assess the need for a bureaucracy.

8.2 Outline how bureaucracies exercise power over the policymaking process.

8.3 Enumerate the reasons for bureaucratic growth.

8.4 Describe the structure of state bureaucracies, and compare bureaucratization across states.

8.5 Analyze state and local bureaucracies to determine the extent to which they are democratic, representative, and responsive to the people.

8.6 Evaluate the benefits of labor unions for public employees and for the public as a whole.

8.7 Assess the ability of state and local governments to regulate public policy.

8.8 Describe and evaluate the effectiveness of efforts to reform government through mechanisms that include privatization and entrepreneurial approaches that "reinvent government."

8.9 Explain the process by which states determine their budgets, and assess the influence of state agencies in the process.

8.10 Outline how political factors such as incrementalism, earmarks, and uncontrollable expenses affect the budget, and assess efforts to ensure that public funds are allocated appropriately.

GOVERNMENT AND BUREAUCRACY

Political conflict does not necessarily end after the state legislature passes a law or the city council enacts an ordinance. Eighty-seven percent of all government employees work for state and local governments. These workers come under a lot of scrutiny from citizens, interest groups, the press, and politicians primarily because they are responsible for implementing laws passed by state and local legislative bodies. Dedicated opponents of a law not only regroup to fight for repeal by the legislative body, but they also turn their attention to the bureaucracy, hoping to delay, modify, or even cripple the implementation of the law. Dedicated supporters of the law must also turn to the bureaucracy to ensure the law's prompt implementation and strict enforcement. State and local government employees are pressured from all sides. Over time, bureaucrats come to exercise considerable power in state and local politics.

In popular conversation, "**bureaucracy**" has come to mean red tape, needless paperwork, waste and inefficiency, senseless regulations, impersonality, and unresponsiveness to the needs of people. And indeed bureaucracy is all of that (although certainly not all government employees act in such a manner). But the true meaning of bureaucracy is simply a "rational" way for an organization to go about carrying out its tasks. Bureaucracies may be governmental or corporate or military. They are the administrative structures of any organization, public or private. All that is required for an organization to be a bureaucracy is

BUREAUCRACY

Departments, agencies, bureaus, and offices that perform the functions of government.

- A chain of command in which authority flows downward;
- A division of labor in which workers specialize in their tasks;
- Clear lines of responsibility;
- Specific organizational goals; and
- Impersonal treatment of all persons equally and according to rules.

In the public sector, a "bureaucrat" is someone working in a bureaucracy—a non-elected person who is employed by government.

Overall, there are approximately 19 million employees of state and local governments. However, if all of the people employed under state contracts to outside organizations were counted as public employees, the numbers of "public" employees would be much higher.

SOURCES OF BUREAUCRATIC POWER

In theory, government bureaucracies, whether at the federal, state, or local level, do *not* make policy. Rather, they are created to *implement* policies passed by legislative bodies. But in practice, government bureaucracies do engage in policymaking as they go about their tasks. How do bureaucrats exercise power and why has their power grown over the years?

Implementation

IMPLEMENTATION

The development by executive bureaucracies of procedures and activities to carry out policies enacted by the legislature.

Implementation is the development of procedures and activities to carry out policies enacted by the legislative body. It may involve creating new agencies or bureaus or assigning new responsibilities to old agencies. It often requires bureaucracies to translate laws into operational rules and regulations and usually to allocate resources—money, personnel, offices, supplies—to the new function. All of these tasks involve decisions by bureaucrats—decisions that drive how the law will actually affect society.

Regulation

REGULATION

The development by the bureaucracy of formal rules for implementing legislation.

Regulation is the development of formal rules for implementing legislation. State agencies charged with the task of regulating various activities—for example, environmental protection, business and professional codes, banking and insurance regulations, consumer affairs, and public utilities—must develop and publish specific (and sometimes lengthy) sets of rules. Most states require that proposed new regulations be published in advance of any action, that hearings be held to allow individuals and groups to comment on the proposed new regulations, and that new regulations be formally published prior to implementation. This process is designed to allow all interested parties the chance to help shape the actual rules that set policy.

Adjudication

Adjudication is bureaucratic decision making about individual cases. While regulation resembles the legislative process, adjudication resembles the judicial process. In adjudication, bureaucrats must decide whether an individual or firm is failing to comply with laws or regulations and, if so, what penalties or corrective actions are to be applied. Bureaucrats can decide to hold individuals strictly accountable to rules, to impose heavy penalties, or to mandate expensive corrective actions. Alternatively, they can interpret the rules loosely and allow individuals or firms that violate rules to get off lightly.

ADJUDICATION
Decision making by bureaucracies on whether an individual or organization has complied with or violated government laws and/or regulations.

Discretion

Bureaucrats almost always have some discretion in performing even the most routine tasks. Discretion is greatest in cases that do not exactly fit established rules, or when more than one rule might be applied to the same case, resulting in different outcomes. Bureaucrats may be courteous, helpful, and accommodating to citizens; or alternatively, impersonal, unhelpful, and even downright frustrating. Increasingly governments are conducting citizen surveys to determine how well citizens believe employees of a particular agency treat them.

Bureaucratic Goals

Bureaucrats generally believe strongly in the value of their programs and the importance of their tasks. But beyond these public-spirited motives, bureaucrats, like everyone else, seek added power and prestige for themselves. These public and private motives converge to inspire them to seek to expand their authority, functions, and budgets. (Rarely do bureaucrats request a reduction in their authority, the elimination of the program under their direction, or a decrease in their agency's budget.) Rather, over time, bureaucrats help to expand governmental functions and increase governmental spending, although the process slows during recessions.

THE GROWTH OF BUREAUCRATIC POWER

8.3

Enumerate the reasons for bureaucratic growth.

Bureaucracies at all levels of government—federal, state, and local—have grown over time. Several explanations have been offered for this growth.

First, elected officials cannot be expected to deal with the myriad details of environmental protection, insurance and banking regulations, law enforcement, highway planning and construction, university governance, and school curricula. They must, therefore, create bureaucracies, appropriate money to run them, and authorize them to draw the rules and regulations that actually govern us. Increasingly they are hiring better-educated employees with expertise in specific policy areas and with advanced technical skills. Second, bureaucrats must give practical meaning to the symbolic measures passed by politicians. Third, bureaucrats themselves have both public and personal motives to expand their own authority, increase the amount of money they can spend, and augment the number of employees under their supervision. Finally, bureaucracies expand because governmental decision making is **incremental**. By that we mean that each year bureaucrats and elected officials focus on proposed *new* programs and policies and *increases* in budgets and personnel. Existing policies, programs, agencies, or expenditures are seldom reviewed as a whole each year. Doing so would require far too much time and energy, simply to confirm decisions

INCREMENTALISM
In government budget making, the tendency of bureaucrats and elected officials to focus on new programs and increases in spending, while seldom reviewing existing programs or previous levels of spending.

that had been made in previous years. Over time the effect of incremental decision making is to expand the size of bureaucracies, as new programs and new spending are authorized while old programs and previous spending levels are seldom reconsidered.

There are times such as following the Great Recession that bureaucratic expansion slows down. But even when economic downturns (recessions) require spending and personnel reductions, the cutbacks are more likely to be made across the board rather than by eliminating programs—a situation often referred to as a **decremental** approach to program reduction.

STATE BUREAUCRACIES

Describe the structure of state bureaucracies, and compare bureaucratization across states.

State governments in America spend most of their money on education, public welfare, highways, health and hospitals, government administration, and corrections. State departments and agencies responsible for these functions are usually the largest bureaucracies at the state capital. However, the authoritative *Book of the States* lists nearly 50 separate bureaucratic functions in state governments, although not all states have separate agencies for each of these functions and many functions are combined in larger departments.

Overall, the largest share of state and local government employees are teachers, aides, and support staff working in elementary education, followed by protective services (police officers, fire fighters, and correctional officers), higher education, health care, and transportation.[1]

Organizational Disarray

The executive branches of virtually all state governments in the United States are fragmented, complex, and unwieldy. These organizational problems arise, first of all, as a result of the separate election of many statewide officials—for example, attorney general, secretary of state, treasurer, comptroller, superintendent of education, and others (see Table 7–2 in Chapter 7). There are nearly 300 separately elected executive branch officials in all the states. Only four states—Maine, New Hampshire, New Jersey, and Tennessee—have a single statewide elected executive, the governor, who heads the executive branch of government.

Organizational problems also arise as a result of the extensive use of boards and commissions throughout the states to head executive departments. Appointments to these boards and commissions are often for long terms and members cannot be removed except for "cause"—proven misconduct in office. The proliferation of separately elected executive officers in the states as well as independent boards and commissions creates messy organizational charts for state governments. To see this clearly, contrast the organizational chart for Mississippi's executive branch—which is composed of the *governor* heading 12 departments, 9 *separately elected executive officials,* and 16 *independent agencies and institutions*—with that of Michigan whose governor is shown at the top of the chain of command for 19 departments (including the State Department headed by a separately elected secretary of state and the Attorney General Department headed by a separately elected attorney general). There are no separate independent boards or commissions on the chart. (See Figure 8–1, Mississippi, and Figure 8–2, Michigan.)

Organizational disarray, particularly the lack of clear lines of authority, makes it far more difficult to coordinate responses to disasters, hold the right officials accountable when things go wrong or don't happen at all, or react to changing technologies that have the potential to harm the public. Nothing better demonstrates the technological challenges facing today's public administrators than the growing threat of cybersecurity breaches. While public employees may be linked via networks, they may be denied access to critically important information generated by other departments on the grounds that it is "classified." The situation raises up the age-old debate about how to make government operations

FIGURE 8-1 State of Mississippi Organization Chart (Very Fragmented Executive Branch)

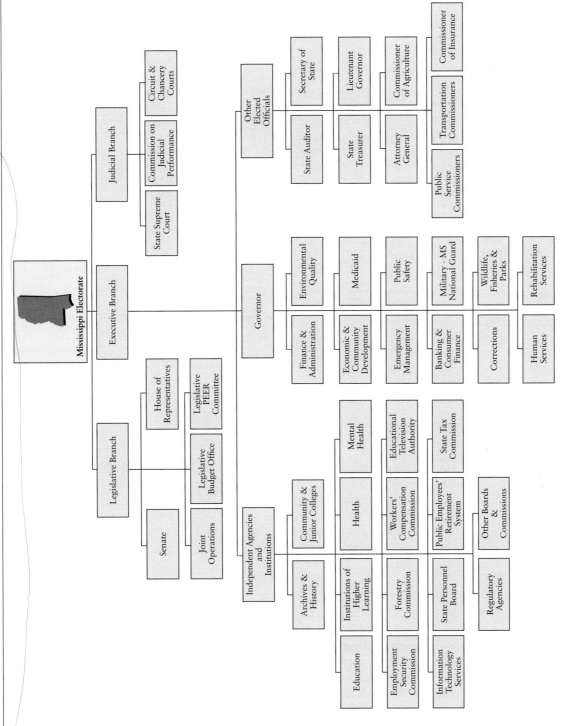

Source: Mississippi Department of Finance and Administration; https://merlin.state.ms.us/Web_Archives/SAASWA.nsf/626e6035eadbb4cd8525649900 6b15a6/29d05b0c1b1c12bd86256e5300 4c596f/$FILE/orgchart.pdf

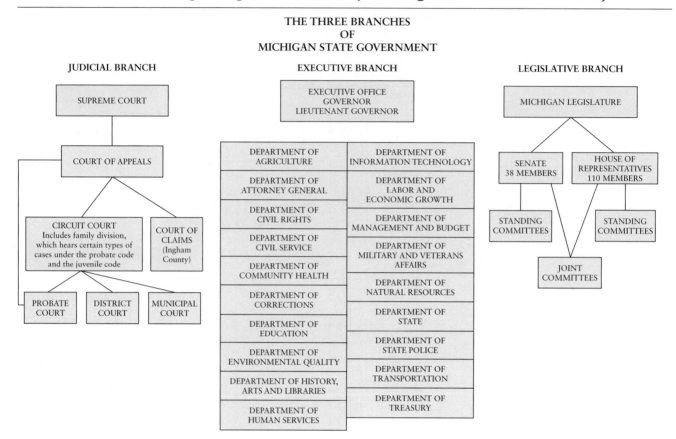

THE THREE BRANCHES
OF
MICHIGAN STATE GOVERNMENT

JUDICIAL BRANCH — EXECUTIVE BRANCH — LEGISLATIVE BRANCH

Note: The Michigan Department of State is headed by a separately elected secretary of state; the Department of Attorney General is headed by a separately elected attorney general.
Source: http://www.legislature.mi.gov/documents/publications/citizensguide.pdf.

and information transparent while protecting individual privacy rights. The issue garnered a lot of attention when personal and financial data, including Social Security numbers, were posted on the Internet for First Lady Michelle Obama, Vice President Joe Biden, former secretary of state Hillary Clinton, and Los Angeles Police chief Charlie Beck. Another issue that has surfaced is how governments and private industry should share information about cybersecurity threats, particularly to critical infrastructure like dams, water systems, and power plants.

Executive Reorganization

Modern public administration generally recommends a stronger governor and a more centralized state executive branch. Reform and reorganization proposals usually recommend (1) the elimination of many separately elected state executive officials and limiting the statewide ballot to governor, lieutenant governor, and attorney general; (2) eliminating boards and commissions as heads of agencies, and their replacement by single, removable gubernatorial appointees; and (3) consolidating many state agencies into larger departments, and making these agency and department heads report directly to the governor. While states have been slow to adopt these reforms, there has been some movement in this direction, but only marginally, as noted in Chapter 7. Reorganization, especially agency consolidation, is also often touted as a cost-saving mechanism. But the evidence is mixed as to whether it really saves money or not.

Variations in Bureaucracy among the States

Bureaucracies are frequently measured by how much money they spend and how many people they employ. As we would expect, states with larger populations spend more money and employ more people than states with smaller populations. Perhaps **"bureaucratization"** might be better measured by state and local spending per capita and the percent of a state's workers that are employed by state and local governments. These measures control for population size and tell us how large a part state and local government spending and employment play relative to the population of each state (see *"Rankings of the States: Government Spending and Employment"*).

Populous states require big bureaucracies. It is no surprise that California, New York, Texas, and Florida, the nation's four largest states in population, employ more people and spend more money than other states. However, when population size is controlled, it turns out that the largest states are not necessarily the biggest spenders. In per capita (per person) spending, New York ranks 3rd, California ranks 5th, while Texas is 35th, and Florida 36th.

Nor are these states necessarily the most "bureaucratized" in government employment in relation to their populations (percent of adult population employed by government). Using this measure, Alaska, Hawaii, and West Virginia rank as the most bureaucratized states in state and local government employees combined, while New York ranks 5th, California 32nd, Florida 35th, and Texas 45th. State and local government employment was hit harder than federal government employment by the recession.

BUREAUCRATIZATION

A general reference to the size of government, often measured by spending per capita and percent of adults employed by government.

BUREAUCRACY, DEMOCRACY, REPRESENTATIVENESS, AND RESPONSIVENESS

8.5

Analyze state and local bureaucracies to determine the extent to which they are democratic, representative, and responsive to the people.

Certain questions repeatedly get asked about government bureaucracies and their employees. The questions are raised by both citizens and politicians who want government to operate differently in a representative democracy. How can we overcome the "bankruptcy of bureaucracy"—the waste, inefficiency, impersonality, and unresponsiveness of large government organizations? How can democratic governments overcome the "routine tendency to protect turf, to resist change, to build empires, to enlarge one's spheres of control, to protect programs regardless of whether or not they are any longer needed?"[2] Should governments be staffed by people politically loyal and responsive to elected officials? Or should governments be staffed by nonpartisan people selected on the basis of merit and protected from political influence?

The Patronage System

Historically, government employment in states, counties, and cities was allocated by the **patronage system**. Jobs were handed out on the basis of party loyalty, electoral support, political influence, personal friendships, family ties, and financial contributions, rather than on the basis of job-related qualifications.

Although widely condemned by reformers, the traditional patronage system helped to strengthen political parties. It helped organize voters and motivated them to go to the polls. It maintained discipline within a party's ranks. Patronage was a central component of political "machines" and a source of power for political "bosses" (see "Old-Style Machine Politics" in Chapter 11).

Patronage was also a major source of power for state governors. As late as the 1960s, almost half of all state jobs were filled by the governor or the governor's patronage advisors from the ranks of "deserving" party workers. Patronage was especially widespread in the older, two-party states of the East and Midwest.

PATRONAGE SYSTEM

Selection of employees for government agencies on the basis of political loyalty and electoral support.

The Merit System

The **merit system**—government employment based on competence, neutrality, and protection from partisanship—was introduced at the federal level in the Pendleton Act of 1883.

MERIT SYSTEM

Selection of employees for government agencies on the basis of competence, with no consideration of an individual's political loyalties or support.

RANKINGS
OF THE STATES

Government Spending and Employment

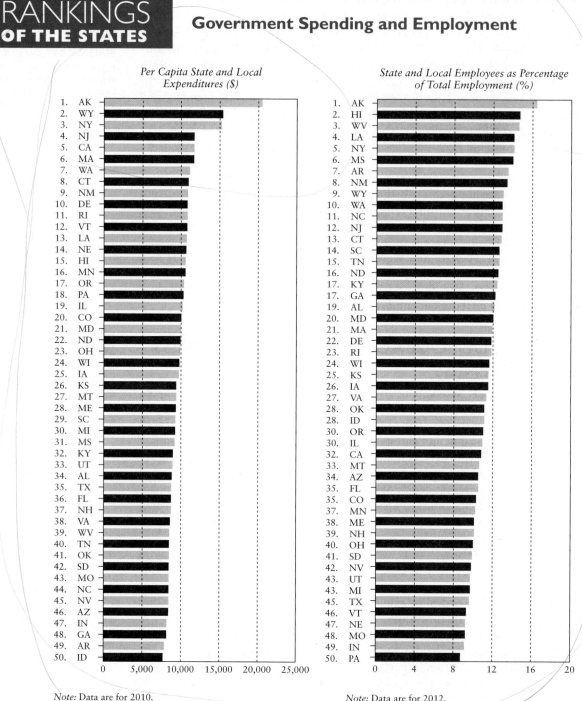

Per Capita State and Local Expenditures ($)

1. AK
2. WY
3. NY
4. NJ
5. CA
6. MA
7. WA
8. CT
9. NM
10. DE
11. RI
12. VT
13. LA
14. NE
15. HI
16. MN
17. OR
18. PA
19. IL
20. CO
21. MD
22. ND
23. OH
24. WI
25. IA
26. KS
27. MT
28. ME
29. SC
30. MI
31. MS
32. KY
33. UT
34. AL
35. TX
36. FL
37. NH
38. VA
39. WV
40. TN
41. OK
42. SD
43. MO
44. NC
45. NV
46. AZ
47. IN
48. GA
49. AR
50. ID

0   5,000   10,000   15,000   20,000   25,000

Note: Data are for 2010.
Source: U.S. Census Bureau, "State and Local Government Finances." Available at http://www.census.gov/govs/estimate/.

State and Local Employees as Percentage of Total Employment (%)

1. AK
2. HI
3. WV
4. LA
5. NY
6. MS
7. AR
8. NM
9. WY
10. WA
11. NC
12. NJ
13. CT
14. SC
15. TN
16. ND
17. KY
17. GA
19. AL
20. MD
21. MA
22. DE
23. RI
24. WI
25. KS
26. IA
27. VA
28. OK
28. ID
30. OR
30. IL
32. CA
33. MT
34. AZ
35. FL
35. CO
37. MN
38. ME
39. NH
40. OH
41. SD
42. NV
43. UT
43. MI
45. TX
46. VT
47. NE
48. MO
49. IN
50. PA

0   4   8   12   16   20

Note: Data are for 2012.
Source: Gallup, Inc. "Alaska, Hawaii Follow D.C. in Highest Government Employment," February 11, 2013. Available at http://www.gallup.com/poll/160337/alaska-hawaii-follow-highest-gov-employment.aspx#1. Copyright © 2013 Gallup, Inc. All rights reserved. The content is used with permission; however, Gallup retains all rights of republication.

This act created the federal Civil Service Commission (now called the Office of Personnel Management) for selecting government personnel based on merit. That same year New York became the first state to enact a merit system. Yet for many years only a few states adopted merit systems, and even in those states only a small proportion of government employees came under civil service protection.

But over time the merit system came to replace patronage as the principal means of staffing state and local government. In 1939, Congress amended the Social Security Act of 1935 to require states to set up merit systems in welfare and unemployment compensation agencies that received federal grants-in-aid. Gradually the states expanded their merit systems to encompass most of their employees. Reform governors capitalized on the public's image of patronage as corrupt, and the federal courts began to strike at patronage systems with decisions preventing governments from firing their employees for partisan political reasons.[3]

Bureaucratic "Cultures"

Bureaucracies often develop their own "cultures," usually in strong support of the function they serve, their client interest group, and of course, their own pay, perks, and job security. Government agencies become dominated by people who have worked there for most of their lives. They believe that their work is important, and they resist efforts by governors, legislators, mayors, and council members to reduce the authority, size, or budget of their agency. Change comes hard. Even when organizational charts are redrawn, new management philosophies are put in place, and new leaders get installed at the top, changing the **bureaucratic culture** will not be automatic. Success is often dependent on the degree to which persons at the lower levels of the organization are involved and can see potential personal benefits from shaking up business as usual.

> **BUREAUCRATIC "CULTURE"**
> Support within an agency for its own function and for its clients and the pay, perks, and security of its employees.

The Problem of Productivity

Another troublesome problem in federal, state, and local bureaucracies is that of ensuring **productivity**—producing desired results at the least possible cost to taxpayers. Government executives often find it difficult to improve productivity because of the obstacles to rewarding or punishing public employees. Seldom can good performance be rewarded with raises or bonuses as in private employment. And, at the same time, poor performance often goes unpunished. Firing a public employee is difficult (see "*Up Close:* Firing a Public Employee").

> **PRODUCTIVITY**
> In government, performing functions and producing desired results at the least possible cost to taxpayers.

The Problem of Representativeness

Democratic governments generally seek to ensure a **representative bureaucracy**. This means the recruitment and employment of a workforce that closely reflects the social composition of the population being served. It is believed that a representative workforce will reflect the values and interests of the people it serves and will be responsive to their problems and concerns. Moreover, a representative workforce provides symbolic evidence of a government "of the people, by the people, and for the people."

Protection against discrimination based on race, gender, age, disability, and other factors unrelated to job performance is embodied in the Civil Rights Act of 1964, the Age Discrimination Act of 1973, and the Americans with Disabilities Act of 1990, as well as the Fourteenth Amendment to the U.S. Constitution. But how can state and local governments go about ensuring representativeness of their workforces without compromising the merit principle? Should state and local governments extend preferential treatment to minority job applicants in order to achieve a representative workforce?

Affirmative action programs were initially developed in the federal government. **Affirmative action programs** seek to achieve minority and gender representativeness in the workforce through preferential hiring and promotion tactics designed to redress perceived imbalances. Virtually all state and local governments in the United States today have affirmative action programs.

> **REPRESENTATIVENESS**
> As applied to public bureaucracies, the extent to which their workforces generally reflect the social characteristics of the citizens they serve.

> **AFFIRMATIVE ACTION PROGRAMS**
> In government agencies, efforts to achieve minority and gender representativeness in the workforce through preferential hiring and promotion.

I t is not impossible to fire a poorly performing state employee. But it takes a lot of managerial skill and tenacity.

It is a common perception that public employees cannot be fired for incompetence, that civil service protections, union contracts, court decisions, and smart lawyers can keep even the worst state and city employee on the public payroll. And, indeed, it is true that the involuntary discharge rate for public employees is estimated at well below 1 percent, compared to 10 percent for privately employed service workers. But if government executives follow specific processes for firing a truly poorly performing employee, they can do so. This means successfully negotiating myriad legal constraints, contract provisions, published regulations, appeals, and other assorted hoops and hurdles. For example, typically the following steps are required:

1. The employee is given a notice of disciplinary termination.
2. The employee has 15 to 30 days to respond.

3. If the employee responds, the agency must schedule a hearing before a disinterested officer.
4. The decision of the hearing officer following the hearing may be appealed by the employee to the personnel or civil service board.
5. The employee is entitled to legal counsel during all phases of the process. Unionized employees are often provided free counsel by their union.
6. Personnel boards frequently have lengthy backlogs. They review written appeals, hold hearings, listen to testimony, and often delay their final decisions for many months. Normally the employee remains on the public payroll during this time.
7. The decisions of the personnel board may be appealed to state or federal courts, which may under some circumstances issue an injunction against firing the employee until after the case is fully resolved.

A common problem in firing a public employee is the manager's failure to maintain a written record of poor performance. Or worse, the manager may have previously provided regular satisfactory job evaluations. Having checked "satisfactory" on previous standardized forms, perhaps in haste or to avoid conflict, the manager is in a poor position to later fire an employee for unsatisfactory performance. Government managers must carefully document poor job performance over time, logging in absences, tardiness, insubordination, and incompetence each time these offenses occur. Managers must communicate with errant employees after each and every offense and give them some opportunity to improve their performance. Most important, managers must carefully follow all procedural rules and regulations set forth in state laws, city ordinances, personnel manuals, and union contracts.

The constitutional question posed by affirmative action programs is whether they discriminate against nonminorities in violation of the Equal Protection Clause of the Fourteenth Amendment. (We explore this topic in more detail in Chapter 15, "Politics and Civil Rights.") The Supreme Court has generally approved of affirmative action programs when there is evidence of past discriminatory employment practices. However, the Court has also held that race-based actions by government—any differences in treatment of the races by public agencies—must be found necessary to remedy past proven discrimination, or to further clearly identified, compelling, and legitimate government objectives. Moreover, race-based actions must be "narrowly tailored" so as not to adversely affect the rights of nonminority individuals.

Many state and local governments have affirmative action plans that go beyond federal equal opportunity requirements, which help explain why women and minorities comprise a larger share of public than private sector employees. Women make up nearly 60 percent of state and local government employees compared to 47 percent of private sector workers. African Americans also make up a larger share of state and local government employees (13%) compared to 10 percent in the private sector. The pattern is similar among Hispanics: 16 percent of state and local public sector employees, 11 percent of private sector employees.[4] Today, African Americans and Hispanics are fairly well represented nationwide among firefighters, police officers, correctional guards, and technicians, and among support, service, and maintenance jobs.

Women and minorities are still underrepresented among top-ranked policymaking administrators at the state level (heads of departments, agencies, boards, commissions, and authorities; top staff advisors with policy-influencing responsibility in governors' offices).[5] African American women have made the greatest strides in gaining these top policy positions. Nevertheless, women and minority employment at all levels of state and local government exceeds that in the private sector workforce.

THE POWER OF PUBLIC EMPLOYEE UNIONS

8.6

Evaluate the benefits of labor unions for public employees and for the public as a whole.

Unions among public employees further complicate executive control of the bureaucracy. Today, over one-third of all state and local government employees are unionized. The largest public employee union in the states is the American Federation of State, County, and Municipal Employees (AFSCME). **Collective bargaining** agreements between state and local governments and public employee unions usually stipulate salaries and wages, pensions and benefits, grievance procedures, and seniority. These restrict executive authority over dismissals, layoffs, reorganization, elimination of positions, merit and incentive pay plans, and other actions affecting public employees. (See "*Up Close:* A Showdown over Public Employee Union Power.")

COLLECTIVE BARGAINING

The determination of wages, benefits, and working conditions through bargaining with unions that represent employees.

Collective Bargaining

Most state laws today recognize the right of public employees to organize unions and bargain collectively with state and local governments over wages, hours, and conditions of work. Only a handful of states continue to resist collective bargaining with public employees. (State Right-to-Work laws allow unions, but do not allow dues to be mandatory for employees of unionized workplaces, see Figure 8–3.) However, in the early 2010s, a number of other states sought to restrict collective bargaining to help balance their strained budgets. Public employees everywhere have a constitutional right to *join* a union, but governments are not required by federal laws or the U.S. Constitution to *bargain* with them.

ARBITRATION

Submission of disputes between parties to a neutral third party for resolution.

Strikes

In contrast to *private* employees, *public* employees are generally prohibited by law from striking. Instead, most state laws stipulate that public employee labor disputes are to go to **arbitration**—that is, be submitted to neutral third parties for decision. Decisions of arbitrators (or arbitration boards consisting of equal representation from employees and employers, together with neutral members) may or may not be binding on both the city and union, depending on specific provisions of each state's laws. However, many public employee unions throughout the country have rendered "no-strike" laws practically useless in a heated labor dispute. Police, firefighters, teachers, sanitation workers, and others have struck in many large cities, and there have been statewide strikes as well. Unions can nullify no-strike laws by simply adding another demand—no

The largest *public* employee union in the states is the American Federation of State, County, and Municipal Employees (AFSCME). Government employee unions fight vigorously against any sort of privatization because it means lost jobs for their members. The nation's largest *private* sector union is the Teamsters.

A Showdown over Public Employee Union Power

Government workers took to the streets of Madison, Wisconsin, in 2011 to protest a series of reforms proposed by Republican Governor Scott Walker. To close a gaping hole in the state budget, the governor proposed that state workers, including schoolteachers, contribute more to their pension and health care benefits. He also proposed that pensions and benefits be taken off of the collective bargaining table, limiting collective bargaining to wages only. And he proposed that union dues be voluntary. These direct challenges to union power inspired mass demonstrations at the capitol and a walkout of Democratic state legislators.

Traditionally public employee unions justified generous benefit levels on the grounds that government wages were modest in comparison to the private sector. But in recent years government wage levels have increased significantly, and public health, pension and other benefits now far exceed those in private employment.[a] And public employees are far more secure in their jobs than private sector workers.

Public employee unions have been growing in size and power, even while union membership in the private sector has been declining. The percentage of the private workforce belonging to unions has declined from about 37 percent in the 1950s to no more than 8 percent today. In contrast, unions of government employees—for example, the American Federation of State County and Municipal Employees (AFSCME), the National Education Association (NEA), the American Federation of Teachers (AFT), as well as the Teamsters Union and the Service Employees International Union (SEIU) that organize public workers in transportation and sanitation—have grown to encompass over half of all government workers. Union dues are a major source of political campaign funding.

Public employee unions are ranked among the top political campaign contributors, almost all of their money going to Democratic candidates. This gives public employee unions a huge advantage at the bargaining table when sitting opposite Democratic officeholders who benefited from union support. Politicians frequently succumb to union demands that private employers would resist, especially when it comes to health and pension benefits. It is no coincidence that it was a Republican governor and a Republican-controlled legislature in Wisconsin that precipitated the showdown with public employee unions.

Efforts to limit collective bargaining for public employees spread to other states. Ohio Republican Governor John Kasich signed legislation viewed as tougher than the Wisconsin bill. But these efforts have energized unions and their liberal allies to take the battle from the streets to the courts, challenging the legality of these measures. And unions have promised political retribution against Republican legislators and governors who support limits on public employee collective bargaining.

[a]Bureau of Labor Statistics, www.bls.gov, as reported in *USA Today*, March 4, 2010.

legal prosecution of strikers or union leaders—as a condition of going back to work, although the public is far less sympathetic to these workers' demands during recessions.

Wages and Benefits

State and local employees, who for generations were paid wages below those for comparable jobs in private enterprise, now match or even exceed private employees in salaries, benefits, pensions, and so on for many government jobs. Unions in the *private* sector of the American economy have been in steep decline in recent decades; today only about 7 percent of the private workforce is unionized. But unions in the *public* sector have grown dramatically, although lately they, too, have experienced a slight decline in membership. However, the unionization rate of public sector workers (36%) is still considerably higher than that of private sector workers. Most of AFSCME's membership is concentrated in ten states—New York, Ohio, Pennsylvania, Michigan, Illinois, Wisconsin, Massachusetts, Minnesota, Connecticut, and Hawaii.

Political Clout

CLOUT

Informal power in the world of politics; usually infers someone who can get things done in the political process.

Public sector unions, notably AFSCME and state chapters of the National Education Association (NEA) and the American Federation of Teachers (AFT), are regularly ranked among the most effective lobbying groups in state capitals. And public employee union PACs regularly rank among the largest campaign contributors in state gubernatorial and legislative elections; the vast majority of their donations go to Democratic candidates.

FIGURE 8–3 Right-to-Work Laws

☐ States with right-to-work laws

☐ States where employees at unionized workplaces are required to pay dues.

Source: U.S. Department of Labor, Wage & Hour Division, "State Right-to-Work Laws," 2009. Available at http://www.dol.gov/whd/state/righttowork.htm.

Public employees and their families turn out on Election Day far more frequently than the average voter.

Public Employee Views of Unions

The vast majority of public service employees trust labor *unions* more than the governments they work for to provide good wages and benefits (72%), provide accurate information about workplace issues (72%), provide safe working conditions (65%), and provide steady employment (61%). But 67 percent say they trust *government*, not unions, to increase employee productivity, and 44 percent believe that unions tend to oppose management when it comes to improving production goals and work rules.[6] Overall, gung-ho public sector union members are less likely to see red tape in their agency and to have a higher level of job satisfaction than nonunion members. One reason for their seeing less red tape may be "because they are afforded the opportunity to participate in rule creation through the collective bargaining process."[7]

Public Employee Benefits and Pensions under Attack

Government employee benefits and pensions tend to come under attack when the economy worsens. The common perception is that during economic downturns "government workers" keep their jobs, benefits, and pensions while others lose theirs. Opposition to public employee pensions strengthened in the early 2010s as large states such as California, New York, and Illinois were on the verge of bankruptcy. Some of the opposition came from within the ranks of lower-level government employees who worried about being laid off or were forced to work part time while high-salaried administrators retired with full benefits and big pensions. But it was Wisconsin governor Scott Walker's successful crusade to reform the state's public pension system that prompted a number of other states and localities to reexamine the structure and payouts of their public employee pension systems. Where successful, reformers have tapped into feelings of resentment among private sector workers toward public sector employees. (See *People in Politics:* Scott Walker Tackles Public Employee Unions.)

The most controversial reform is changing the structure of a pension system from a defined-benefit to a defined-contribution plan. Under a **defined-benefit plan,** a state or local government "promises a salary-like stream of retirement income based on an employee's longevity and end-of-career earnings,"[8] and covers the cost of providing it, even when the pension fund may be underfunded. (Severely underfunded pension systems may be paying out more in retiree benefits than in pay to current employees.) In contrast, under a **defined-contribution** system, the government "provides employees with some fixed amount toward their retirement while they are working, allowing them to invest the money on their own."[9] This system places the responsibility for managing public employees' retirement savings on the employees themselves, not the state or local government's taxpayers.

DEFINED-BENEFIT PLAN

A benefit plan that promises retirement income in a salary-like method; traditional pension plan.

DEFINED-CONTRIBUTION PLAN

A benefit plan that provides employees with a fixed amount of retirement money while working that employees can invest on their own.

STATE REGULATORY POLICY

Assess the ability of state and local governments to regulate public policy.

The emergence of new regulations often tracks closely with intense media coverage of a problem—an outbreak of food poisoning, child pornography on a teacher's computer at work, the death of an infant in a day care facility, a faulty roof job on an elderly person's home following a hurricane, or an identity theft scam that led to ruined lives. Other times regulations get put in place when one level of government is attempting to "control" another or when interest groups seek to maintain or expand control over a process, profession, or product. The evolution of regulatory policy closely parallels the evolution of federal–state–local relations. However, most Americans see the regulatory maze as federalism at its worst, rather than federalism at its finest.

Regulatory power in the United States has accumulated over time at the federal level. The Federal Reserve Board exercises great power over the banking industry; the National Labor Relations Board protects unions and prohibits "unfair labor practices"; the National Transportation Safety Board oversees safety in automobiles, trucks, and buses; the Federal Trade Commission oversees product labeling; the Equal Employment Opportunity Commission investigates complaints about racial and sexual discrimination in jobs; the Consumer Product Safety Commission reviews the safety of marketed products; the Federal Communications Commission regulates radio and television broadcasting; the Food and Drug Administration determines when drugs are "safe and effective";

Federal–state battles over regulatory authority, particularly with regard to energy policy, are often intense. The federal Environmental Protection Agency is concerned about the environmental impacts of wind power, while state economic development agencies see the new energy source as important to the state's economic growth and competitiveness.

Scott Walker, Republican governor of Wisconsin, became a national figure by signing a bill that significantly changed the collective bargaining process for most public employee unions in his state. His controversial action launched a state recall election that Walker won decisively. He is the first governor in history to win a recall election

Scott Walker is a native of Wisconsin who attended Marquette University in Milwaukee for four years but never graduated. Instead, at age 22 he ran for a seat in the Wisconsin State Assembly, winning the GOP nomination but losing the general election. It was the only losing election in his political career. He moved to a predominantly Republican district in Wauwatosa, won the Assembly seat, and was reelected four times. He compiled a record of fiscal and social conservatism.

In 2002 Walker won a special election for Milwaukee County Executive. He was easily reelected to that post in 2004 and 2008. Pursuing a fiscally conservative agenda, he kept property taxes low, cut the county's workforce, and reduced the county's debt load. He even returned half of his salary to the county treasury. In 2010 he won the Republican nomination for governor, receiving 59 percent of the primary vote. He stressed his fiscal conservatism in the general election campaign and won with 52 percent of the vote.

As governor, Walker succeeded in getting the Republican-controlled state legislature to pass a "Wisconsin budget repair bill." It required state workers to increase their health care contributions, and most importantly it eliminated many collective bargaining topics, including pensions. Only wages would be subject to collective bargaining. Moreover, under the bill, public employee unions would have to win yearly representational votes, and they could no longer have dues automatically deducted from workers' paychecks. Police and firefighters were excluded.

Boisterous demonstrations at the state capitol followed the introduction of the bill. Some Democratic state senators boycotted, hoping to deny the Senate a quorum. (Reportedly they hid in Illinois in order to avoid arrest by the sergeant at arms.) Walker's negotiations with the Democrats faltered, and the Republican Senate passed the bill by a simple majority. A state judge struck down the bill, but the state supreme court upheld it.

Opponents of Walker's action launched a recall petition, with the strong support of the state's labor unions and the Democratic Party. The petition succeeded and the recall election was held June 5, 2012. But the recall was unsuccessful; 53 percent voted to keep Governor Walker in office.

Walker's victory projected him onto the Republican national scene. He is prominently mentioned for the GOP presidential nomination 2016.

the Department of Agriculture inspects agricultural products; the Occupational Safety and Health Administration inspects the workplace; and the Environmental Protection Agency has broad powers over virtually every aspect of American life. It is difficult to find an activity in public or private life that is *not* regulated at the federal level.

However, states exercise considerable regulatory power and authority in fields *not pre-empted* by federal law and regulation. For example, *state* regulatory agencies exercise principal powers over public utilities, including electric and gas, corporate chartering, insurance, alcoholic beverages, occupational licensing, health and hospitals, the real estate industry, and motor vehicles.

Understanding Regulatory Policy

Regulations usually do not involve large amounts of direct government expenditures. Instead, regulatory policy allows governments to shift costs to private firms and individuals by directing them to spend money and resources to comply with regulations. Indeed, often a regulatory approach to public problems is preferred by politicians precisely *because* it does not involve the direct expenditure of tax monies. For example, state governments do not appropriate money for power plants, but their regulatory agencies can impose costs on private electric utilities by mandating safety regulations, employment rules, and even the rates they are permitted to charge customers. However, if a state's regulatory environment becomes too burdensome, it may become more difficult to attract new jobs and industries. Economic development groups routinely publish rankings of state business climates; regulations are one of the key factors used to calculate those rankings.

8.8

Describe and evaluate the effectiveness of efforts to reform government through mechanisms that include privatization and entrepreneurial approaches that "reinvent government."

REFORM, PRIVATIZATION, AND "REINVENTING GOVERNMENT"

Polls repeatedly show that people believe governments are spending more but delivering less; they are frustrated with bureaucracies over which they have little control and tired of politicians who raise taxes and cut services. Specifically, a majority believes that elected officials do not care what the average citizen thinks and that government bureaucracies have become "too powerful." Less than half of the populace believe that government is run for the benefit of all people. A sizable majority believe that when government does something, it is usually inefficient and wasteful. They also are convinced that government regulation of business usually does more harm than good. (See Table 8–1.) But they would rather have governments closer to home in charge than the federal government.

Privatization as Reform

Political conservatives have mounted a reform movement in state and local government, centering on the notion of the "privatization" of public services. In the broadest sense, **privatization** includes the shifting of many responsibilities *from* government *to* the private marketplace. "**Load shedding**" implies that government should sell off many of its enterprises—for example, housing projects, airports, and stadiums—to private individuals or firms that would operate them more efficiently and effectively. But privatization has also generally come to mean greater reliance on private and not-for-profit providers of governmental services functioning in a competitive marketplace and giving individuals greater choice in services.

Privatization recognizes a distinction between government provision of a service and government production of a service. Governments may decide to *provide* citizens with certain goods and services—for example, schools, police and fire protection, garbage collection, bus transportation, and street maintenance—but not necessarily *produce* these services directly through government entities—public schools, municipal police and fire departments, municipal garbage collection, city-owned buses, and city street maintenance departments. Rather, a variety of other methods of "service delivery" are available that rely more on private or not-for-profit, competitive producers, and individual choice.

PRIVATIZATION

Shifting the production of government services from public bureaucracies to private firms.

"LOAD SHEDDING"

Government selling off many of its enterprises—for example, housing projects, airports, stadiums—to private individuals or firms who might operate them more efficiently and effectively.

TABLE 8–1 Citizen Views on Government Responsiveness, Effectiveness, and Efficiency			
View	Agree (%)	Disagree (%)	Don't Know (%)
Most elected officials care what people like me think.	35	62	2
People like me don't have any say about what the government does.	55	43	2
Government regulation of business usually does more harm than good.	57	37	5
Elected officials in Washington lose touch with the people pretty quickly.	81	16	2
When something is run by the government, it is usually inefficient and wasteful.	59	37	4
The government is really run for the benefit of all the people.	41	57	3

Source: Pew Research Center, "Trends in American Values: 1987–2012," June 2012. Available at http://www.people-press.org/files/legacy-pdf/06-04-12%20 Values%20Release.pdf.

The following are among the most common methods of privatizing the provision of government services:

- *Contracting:* Governments contract with private or not-for-profit organizations to provide a publicly funded service. These firms compete to win and keep the contracts by providing quality services at low costs.

- *Franchising:* Governments grant exclusive contracts for a certain period of time to a private firm to provide a monopoly service—for example, cable television or garbage collection. The private firm collects fees directly from citizens under contractual terms agreed to by the government. The franchise firm may pay a fee to the government for the privilege. Government may terminate the franchise for poor performance or excessive fees charged to citizens.

- *Grants:* Governments provide direct grants of money to private firms or nonprofit organizations conditioned on their providing low-cost services to citizens. Grants are typically made to hospitals and health facilities, libraries and cultural centers, and low-cost housing projects, among others.

- *Vouchers:* Vouchers are given directly to citizens who qualify for them, allowing these citizens to exercise free choice in selecting the producers of the service. Unlike grants, in which the government chooses the producers of the service, vouchers give citizens the power to choose the producer. Producers compete to attract citizens who have vouchers; the vouchers are later turned in to the government by producers for cash. For example, rent vouchers to the poor or homeless allow them to select housing of their choice; grants to public housing organizations oblige the poor and homeless to seek shelter in specific projects. Education vouchers (see Chapter 16) would allow parents to choose any school, public or private, for their children. Schools would compete to attract pupils, cashing in their accumulated vouchers.

Surveys show that at the state level, the most commonly privatized (contracted out) programs and services are in the corrections, education, health and human services, transportation, and personnel areas. At the local level, they are (in descending order):[10] vehicle towing and storage; commercial and residential solid waste disposal; day care facilities; street light operation; traffic signal installation/maintenance; street repairs; bus system operation; ambulance service; airport operation; and hospital operations/management. A few cities and counties have even privatized jail operations, building and grounds maintenance, data processing, tax billing, delinquent tax collection, and other functions traditionally performed by government employees. Regardless of whether it is at the state or local level, public officials find privatization decisions difficult and often politically charged. (See "*Up Close:* Privatizing Prisons: The Pros and Cons").

The Pros and Cons of Privatization

Privatization is usually defended as a cost-saving measure—a way of reducing the waste, inefficiency, and unresponsiveness of "bloated bureaucracies." It is argued that private contractors, operating in a competitive marketplace, can provide the same services at much lower costs than government. Privatization advocates also believe that businesses and nonprofits have a greater propensity to be innovative and have more "resources in computer technology, high volume processing equipment, and specialized personnel, plus the flexibility to assign [workers] wherever they are needed most."[11] At the same time, privatization is seen as strengthening private enterprise.

But privatization is usually opposed by powerful political groups—especially municipal employees and their unions and teachers' unions and public school administrators. They argue that the cost savings of privatization are often exaggerated and that the savings come at the price of reduced quality and/or a failure to serve all of the people. From the government employees' perspective, "privatization threatens job security, pay and benefits, working conditions, and career opportunities."[12] Some critics worry about the loss of public control of services and argue that government contractors and franchises can become at least as arrogant and unresponsive as government bureaucracies. For example, some prison reformers argue that privatizing corrections facilities treats offenders as

A common argument for privatizing prisons is that it can save the state a lot of money because the private sector can operate prisons more efficiently than the public sector. But comparing the private-versus- public approach is enormously complicated, warned a 2008 National Institute of Justice study. An earlier study by the Bureau of Justice Assistance flatly stated that the promised cost savings of privatization have not materialized. So who is right?

The real question may be who can operate prisons more efficiently for the right purpose.

The purpose of imprisonment, some say, is punishment. According to this view, offenders will spend their time behind bars repenting their behavior and missing loved ones. Others believe the purpose is rehabilitation. That is, offenders will get treatment for alcohol and drug addiction, improve literacy skills, and acquire job skills.

With purpose clearly in mind, one can consider quality issues, such as the following:

- Programs and curriculum: What kinds of education and therapy programs are offered to inmates? How effective are the activities in modifying behavior and preparing a return to society?

- Safety: How safe are inmates and staff from violence? How safe is the surrounding community from possible escapes or riots?
- Quality of life: How nutritious is the food? What are the opportunities for physical exercise? How sanitary are living conditions? Is housing overcrowded?
- Health care: How prompt and adequate is medical care? What kind of mental health services are available?
- Employees: What training and experience is required of guards, administrators, and other staff, including volunteers? How do wages and benefits compare to that of workers with similar training and experience in other fields?
- Justice: How are human rights respected? Who makes decisions about discipline, conditions of confinement, and parole? What access do inmates have to a law library?

In the context of quality, neither the private nor the public approach is perfect. But careful consideration of the purpose and quality issues can help guide decisions about how best to improve the criminal justice system.

"commodities" instead of human beings. These latter problems, the loss of accountability and compassion, become big concerns when governments do not properly audit contractors and subcontractors, as was the case with post-Katrina rebuilding in New Orleans.[13]

"Reinventing Government"

Reformers have also argued that "Our fundamental problem today is not too much government or too little government . . . [but] the wrong kind of government." Rather than rely exclusively on either bureaucratization or privatization, they call for an "entrepreneurial" government that "searches for efficient and effective ways of managing."

How is the "entrepreneurial spirit" to be encouraged in government? By **reinventing government**. A widely read and cited book, *Reinventing Government*, sets out ten principles of government entrepreneurialship:

"REINVENTING GOVERNMENT"

A reform movement that encourages government agencies to be more entrepreneurial, mission-driven, results-oriented, decentralized, and responsive to citizens' needs.

- *Steer rather than row.* Separate policy decisions (steering) from service delivery (rowing). Government should focus on steering while relying more on private firms to deliver services. Government should be a catalyst.

- *Empower people rather than simply deliver services.* Governments should encourage communities and neighborhoods to undertake ownership and control of public services. Government should be community owned.

- *Inject competition into service delivery.* Competition between public and private agencies, among private contractors, or between different governments encourages efficiency, innovation, and responsiveness. Government should be competitive.

- *Make government organizations mission driven rather than rule driven.* Do not prescribe how government organizations should go about doing things by prescribing rules, procedures, and regulations but, rather, set goals and encourage government organizations to find the best ways to achieve them. Government should be mission driven.

- *Encourage governments to be results oriented.* Government bureaucracies should be measured by their results, not their size, numbers, or services. Government should fund outcomes, not inputs.

Did YOU KNOW?

Bureaucrats Challenged to "Write It Simple!"

Citizens constantly complain that there is too much jargon in government documents. Florida's Agency for Health Care Administration (AHCA) has implemented a "Plain Language Program." When employees log on to their computers, they see a big "splash screen" that pulls a wordy policy statement from an agency document and challenges the worker to rewrite it. The following day, the workers receive another e-mail showing the statement rewritten in plain language. Here are some examples:

First day: the challenge

Plain Language
The art of clear and concise communication

Change the words below to plain language.

Pursuant to Section 409.913(3), Florida Statutes, the Agency for Health Care Administration has determined that a prepayment review be conducted on your Medicaid claims. This action is effective for those claims currently in the system for processing as well as claims submitted after this date. These claims will be suspended by the Agency for review prior to processing.

AHCA
American Health Care Association

Following day: the challenge and the answer

question: **Pursuant to Section 409.913(3), Florida Statutes, the Agency for Health Care Administration has determined that a prepayment review be conducted on your Medicaid claims. This action is effective for those claims currently in the system for processing as well as claims submitted after this date. These claims will be suspended by the Agency for review prior to processing.**

answer: **Under Section 409.913(3), Florida Statutes, the Agency for Health Care Administration will conduct a review of your Medicaid claims prior to processing them. This action affects claims currently in the system as well as future claims.**

Source: *Palm Beach Post.* Available at http://www.palmbeachpost.com/politics/content/local_news/slideshows/plain_language/.

- *Focus on the needs of customers, not the bureaucracy.* Governments should treat citizens as if they were customers, responding to their needs, "putting them in the driver's seat." Government should be customer driven. (See "*Did You Know? Bureaucrats Challenged to Write It Simple!*")

- *Encourage governments to earn money through user charges.* Charging the users of government services, whenever possible, is fair; it raises revenues and balances demands for services. Governments should be enterprising.

- *Practice prevention rather than cure.* Problems from fires to ill health are cheaper to address through prevention than services. Government should be anticipatory.

- *Decentralize government organizations.* Decentralization increases flexibility, effectiveness, innovation, morale, and commitment. Government should be decentralized.

- *Use market incentives to bring about change rather than command and control.* Market mechanisms are preferred over regulations. Government should be market oriented.[14]

Note that these are guiding principles, rather than recommendations for changes in the structure of state and local government. Unlike earlier reformers who focused on structural changes, today's reformers are more concerned about *how* governments go about their tasks.

The search for new ways of doing things is ongoing. Pick up any public administration text and you can read about a multitude of past efforts, including management by objectives (MBOs), **zero-based budgeting** (ZBB), total quality management (TQM), performance-based management (PBM), **balanced scorecard** (BSC), and best practices (BP), to name a few. Some long-time public employees are frustrated with "this constant cycle of reform by acronym."[15] But it's no different in government than in the business world, where new books on "how to be a success in corporate America" are constantly being released in the wake of new technologies or on the heels of management scandals.

Public administration experts are always in search of ways to increase the odds that a reform will succeed on its own merits and not be stymied by changes in political leaders. Three widely cited pieces of advice are (1) Codify reforms in law. If it is in the law that agencies have to produce performance reports—it can't be completely ignored by the next

ZERO-BASED BUDGETING

A method of budgeting that demands justification for the entire budget request of an agency, not just its requested increase in funding.

BALANCED SCORECARD

A management system that considers both human capital and financial capital costs in making decisions.

governor or mayor; (2) Make reforms quietly and gently. It helps to avoid calling a reform a reform and to use words like "progressive" so that a new administration will not associate it with previous administration; and (3) Do not try to make too many changes at the same time. When too much change occurs simultaneously, the organization doesn't have time to learn from it and employees get "reform fatigue."[16]

Reforming the Bureaucracy during Economic Downturns

A common perception is that government employees keep their jobs during tough economic times while workers in the private sector lose theirs. In fact, that perception fuels antigovernment sentiments among the public at large. The reality is that major downturns in the economy affect governments too and require them to make difficult cost-cutting decisions regarding their employees. This is necessary because personnel costs are a large part of every government's budget (people provide services). During the Great Recession of the 2000s, 71 percent of all the nation's cities made personnel-related cuts ranging from hiring freezes, layoffs, and furloughs to major reductions in employee health care and pension benefits.[17] Counties took similar actions. A number also entered into regional cooperative service agreements and privatized county services to cut personnel costs. (See Figure 8–4.) The need to "reinvent" and reform government is always urgent and difficult when fiscal stress is most intense. But sometimes that urgency can be a catalyst for changing inefficient and ineffective bureaucratic organizations, particularly those top-heavy with administrators or with histories of costly unethical behavior.

New Emphasis on Ethics and Codes of Conduct

Many governments have established ethics commissions or committees and require all employees to engage in some form of ethical conduct training as a condition of employment. Most often ethics codes prohibit employees from engaging in political activities at work, soliciting or accepting gifts from certain types of persons (e.g., contractors doing business with the government, lobbyists, someone seeking an official action from the employee or their agency), asking for or taking bribes, using one's position to get special favors for a family member or business associate, or revealing confidential information to an unauthorized person for personal gain or benefit.

Some state and local governments have ethics specialists in their personnel and legal offices to develop training materials, conduct training, and advise employees on ethics

FIGURE 8–4 How U.S. Counties Lowered Personnel Costs during the Great Recession

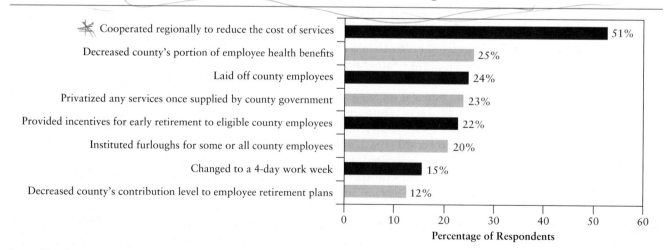

Source: How U.S. Counties Lowered Personnel Costs during the Great Recession 2010; in National Center for the Study of Counties, "National Survey of County Elected Officials 2010," p. 12. Reprinted with Permission © 2010 National Association of Counties Research Foundation Inc. Washington D.C.

matters. All 50 states have whistle-blower protection laws protecting an employee from retaliation when he or she reports someone for illegal or unethical conduct.[18] Many employees belong to professional associations, such as the American Society for Public Administration, that have developed their own ethics codes of conduct.

The Quality of State Bureaucracies: States Get Grades!

Despite the many criticisms heaped upon state government agencies, there is evidence that many are performing reasonably well, certainly better than in years past. An extensive evaluation of state government administrative performance by a team of experts from the Pew Center on the States and *Governing* magazine and some university professors graded states in four areas: money, people, infrastructure, and information. Most states got Bs and Cs. There were only a handful of As but no Fs.[19]

More recent analyses have focused on how states have used new technology to improve performance and enhance accountability. Every two years, the Center for Digital Government grades states on their use of digital technologies, using five broad criteria: (1) adoption of new technologies designed to improve operations or services, (2) quantifiable hard and soft-dollar savings or benefits, (3) progress over the last two years, (4) innovative solutions or approaches, and (5) effective collaboration. The most recent evaluation gave 8 A grades, 22 Bs, 18 Cs, and 2 Ds.[20]

Another study by the U.S. Public Interest Research Group, a consumer advocacy group, graded states on the extent to which they have websites providing an easily accessible and searchable detailed expenditure database that enables citizens to see exactly how the state spends taxpayer dollars. Most states got Bs and Cs for their online transparency and seven states got As. The five states that received Fs lacked detailed data. The transparency scores represent a marked improvement. The study's co-author put it in context: "Fifteen years ago, a state being transparent meant that if you went to the right office and knew exactly what form to ask for you might get what you wanted a few weeks later."[21] The improvements are mostly attributable to better technology and greater citizen demands for access to government information.

THE BUDGETARY PROCESS

8.9
Explain the process by which states determine their budgets, and assess the influence of state agencies in the process.

Too often we think of budgeting as the dull province of clerks and statisticians. Nothing could be more wrong. **Budgets** are political documents that record the struggles over "who gets what." The budget is the single most important policy statement of any government. It is prepared by the executive branch but must be approved by the legislative body. There are few government activities or programs that do not require an expenditure of funds, and no public funds may be spent without budgetary authorization. The budget sets forth government programs, with price tags attached. The size and shape of the budget is a matter of serious contention in the political life of any state or community. Governors, mayors, administrators, legislators, interest groups, and citizens all compete to have their policy preferences recorded in the budget. The budget lies at the heart of the political process. (See Figure 8–5.)

BUDGET

A document prepared by the executive branch of government that estimates next year's revenue and proposes programs and the objects of expenditures; must be approved by the legislature.

The Executive Budget

The budgetary process begins with the governor or mayor's budget office sending to each governmental agency and department a budget request form, accompanied by broad policy directives to agency and department heads about the size and shape of their requests. Often these budget requests must be made 6 to 12 months prior to the beginning of the **fiscal year** for which the requests are made; state and local governmental fiscal years usually run from July 1 to June 30.[22] After all requests have been submitted to the budget office, the serious task of consolidating these many requests begins. Individual department requests

FISCAL YEAR

The yearly government accounting period, not necessarily the same as the calendar year; most state and local governments' fiscal years begin July 1 and end June 30.

FIGURE 8–5 The Budgetary Process in the States

GOVERNOR/ BUDGET OFFICE	DEPARTMENTS AGENCIES	GOVERNOR/ BUDGET OFFICE	LEGISLATURE	GOVERNOR
▪ Provide Budget Instruction to Departments ▪ Estimate Revenue	▪ Prepare Strategic Plans ▪ Prepare Legislative Budget Request ▪ Prepare Capital Improvement Plan	▪ Review/Analyze Agency Legislative Request, Strategic Plan, Capital Improvement Plan, Information Resource Plan ▪ Hold Public Hearings ▪ Develop Recommendations Based on Governor's Priorities and Available Revenues	▪ Prepare Appropriations Act Review Governor's Recommendations Review/Analyze/ Revise Budget ▪ Appropriations Act Passed by Both Houses	▪ Review/Analyze Changes Governor May Line-Item Veto Specific Appropriations ▪ Governor Signs into Law

are reviewed, revised, and generally scaled down; often departments are given more or less formal hearings on their budget request by the budget director. The budget agency must also make revenue estimates based on information it obtains from the tax department.

Governors or mayors must decide the overall size and scope of their budget; whether particular departmental requests should be increased or reduced, in view of the programs and promises important to their administrations; whether economies should involve overall "belt tightening" by every agency or merely the elimination of particular programs; or finally, whether they should recommend the raising of new taxes or the incurring of additional debt. These decisions may be the most important that mayors or governors make in their terms of office, and they generally consult both political and financial advisors— budget and tax experts, party officials, interest group representatives, and legislative leaders. Ordinarily, these difficult decisions must be made before governors or mayors present their budget message to the legislature. This budget message explains and defends the final budget presented by the chief executive to the legislative branch.

Budget Making at the State Level

Budget making involves bringing together the requests of all existing state agencies, calculating the costs of new state programs, estimating the probable income of the state, and evaluating these costs and income estimates in light of program and policy objectives. The final budget document is submitted to the legislature for its adoption as an appropriations bill. No state monies can be spent without a legislative **appropriation**, and the legislature can make any alterations in the state budget that it sees fit. Potentially, then, a legislature can control any activity of the state government through its power over appropriations, but as a practical matter, the legislature seldom reviews every item of the governor's budget. In practice, budgets tend to reflect the views of those responsible for their preparation, namely the governor.

The most common budgetary behaviors in the states are as follows:

▪ Agency heads consistently request higher funds.

▪ Governors' budget staffers consistently reduce agency requests.

▪ The governor consistently pursues a balanced budget at higher expenditure levels than the previous year.

▪ Legislatures approve higher appropriations but try to blame the governor if higher taxes are required.

APPROPRIATION

An act of the legislature that authorizes executive agencies to spend a specific amount of money.

Agency Pressure

The pressure for budget increases comes from the requests of agency officials. Most agency officials feel compelled to ask for more money each year. Requesting an increase in funds affirms the significance and protects the status of agency employees, and it assures clientele groups that new and higher standards of service are being pursued aggressively. Requested increases also give the governor's office and the legislature something to cut that will not affect existing programs. The governor's budget staff generally recognizes the built-in pressure to expand budgets. The budget staff sees itself as "cutters." Agencies press for budgetary

Cuts to local police department budgets prompt protests from officers and citizens alike who worry that such cuts will result in higher crime rates.

expansion with better programs in mind, while the governor's budget staff tries to reduce expenditures with cost cutting in mind (see "*Up Close:* How to Win at the Budget Game").

The Legislative Appropriation

The governor's budget generally appears in the legislature as an appropriations bill, and it follows the normal path of any bill. It is assigned to an appropriations committee, which often holds hearings on the bill and occasionally reshapes and revises the executive budget. The fate of the governor's budget in the legislature generally depends on his or her general political power, public reactions to recommendations, the degree of support he or she receives from department heads (who are often called to testify at legislative budget hearings), his or her relationships with key legislative leaders, and the effectiveness of interest groups that favor or oppose particular expenditures.

After it is passed in identical form by both houses, the final appropriations measure is sent to the governor for signature. If the governor has an item veto, he or she can still make significant changes in the budget at that time.

THE POLITICS OF BUDGETING

8.10

Budgeting is *political*. It is often described as a **zero sum game**—"for every dollar spent on *x,* there is one less dollar to spend on *y.*" Being a good politician involves (1) the cultivation of a good base of support for one's requests among the public at large and among people served by the agency; (2) the development of interest, enthusiasm, and support for one's program among top political figures and legislative leaders; and (3) skill in following strategies that exploit one's opportunities to the maximum. Informing the public and one's clientele of the full benefit of the services they receive from the agency may increase the intensity with which they will support the agency's request. If possible, the agency should inspire its clientele to contact governors, mayors, legislators, and council members and help work for the agency's request. This is much more effective than the agency's promoting its own requests. However, a mistake that many citizen groups who want to influence the budget process make is to wait to get involved until the budget is being considered for *approval* by the legislative body. Often, a more effective strategy is to become proactive during the budget *formation* stage—in agency deliberations or when it is still in the hands of the governor or mayor.

Outline how political factors such as incrementalism, earmarks, and uncontrollable expenses affect the budget, and assess efforts to ensure that public funds are allocated appropriately.

ZERO SUM GAME
The theory that for someone to win, someone must lose.

Experienced bureaucrats have learned a number of strategies that help them "maximize" their budgets.

Spend it all. Spend all of your current year's appropriation. A failure to use up an appropriation indicates that the full amount was unnecessary in the first place, which in turn implies that your budget should be cut next year.

Ask for more, not less. Never request a sum less than your current appropriation. It is easier to find ways to spend up to current appropriation levels than it is to explain why you want a reduction. Besides, a reduction indicates your program is not growing and this is an embarrassing admission to most government administrators.

Hide new programs in the base. Put top priority programs into the base, that is, that part of the budget that is within current appropriation levels. Budget offices, governors and mayors, and legislative bodies will seldom challenge programs that appear to be part of existing operations.

Make changes appear incremental. Increases that are desired should be made to appear small and should appear to grow out of existing operations. The appearance of a fundamental change in a budget should be avoided.

Give them something to cut. Give the budget office, chief executive, and the legislature something to cut. Normally it is desirable to submit requests for substantial increases in existing programs and many requests for new programs, in order to give higher political authorities something to cut. This enables them to "save" the public untold millions of dollars and justify their claim to promoting "economy" in government. Giving them something to cut also diverts attention from the basic budget with its vital programs.

Make cuts hurt. If confronted with a real budget cut—that is, a reduction from last year's appropriation—announce reductions in, or elimination of, your agency's most popular program. Never acknowledge that cuts might be accommodated without reducing needed services.

"Incrementalism" in Budgeting

What forces are actually involved in the budget-making process? Invariably, the forms provided by the budget office require departments to prepare budget requests alongside the previous year's expenditures. Decision makers generally consider the last year's expenditures as a base (a starting point). Consequently, active consideration of budget proposals is generally narrowed to new items or requested increases over the last year's base. The attention of governors and legislators, and mayors and councils, is focused on a narrow range of increases or decreases in a budget. A budget is almost never reviewed as a whole every year, in the sense of reconsidering the value of existing programs. Departments are seldom required to defend or explain budget requests that do *not* exceed current appropriations; but requested increases in appropriations require extensive explanation, and they are most subject to downward revision by higher political officials. Consequently, "padding" in existing budget lines is far less obvious than in proposed new lines of spending or in lines featuring big increases over the previous budget year. A sizable portion of the proposed spending is "untouchable" due to earmarking and other uncontrollable expenses.

EARMARKING

In government budgeting, the practice of allocating specific revenue sources to specific programs, such as gasoline taxes to highways.

"Earmarking"

Chief executives have little influence over many items of state and local government spending. Over 50 percent of state finances come from specially **earmarked** (dedicated) funds. It is common to earmark in state constitutions and laws certain funds for particular purposes, such as gasoline taxes for highways or lottery funds for education. The earmarking device provides certain agencies with an independent source of income, thus reducing the chief executive's control over operations. What is left, "general fund expenditures," is also largely committed to existing state programs, particularly welfare and education.

"UNCONTROLLABLES"

In government spending, increases that cannot be easily limited because of prior commitments to existing programs, federal mandates, or court rulings.

"Uncontrollables"

Politicians typically campaign on platforms stressing both increased service and lower taxes. Once in office, however, they typically find it impossible to accomplish both and difficult to accomplish either one. Often new programs planned by a governor must be put aside because of "uncontrollable" growth in existing programs. For example, additional money may be required to educate more students who are entitled to an education under existing programs; or money must be found to pay the welfare benefits of additional clients or the Medicaid costs of additional patients "entitled" to care under existing laws. These *entitlement programs* constitute over three-quarters of state general fund appropriations. Another **uncontrollable expense** occurs when the federal government issues "*mandates*" requiring state and local governments to spend money to meet certain legislatively dictated criteria. Lawsuits and *litigation* are a third, and growing, uncontrollable expense.

Nonprogrammatic Budgeting

Finally, in some jurisdictions—usually smaller ones—the budget format is primarily *nonprogrammatic*. Specific expenditure items, or "lines," are listed under broad categories such as "personnel services," "contractual services," "travel," "supplies," or "equipment." (This is known as a line-item, object-of-expenditure format.) Needless to say, it is impossible to tell from such a listing exactly what programs the agency is spending its money on, which is why many governments no longer exclusively use this budget format. Even if these categories are broken down into line items (e.g., under "personnel services," the line-item budget might say, "John Doaks, Assistant Administrator, $35,000"), it is still next to impossible to identify the costs of various programs. It is also impossible to determine whether the program efficiently, effectively, or equitably achieved what lawmakers had in mind when they funded it.

Program and Performance-Oriented Budget Reforms

Over the years, reform-oriented administrators have favored expanding the amount of information included in budgets—making them more useful as management tools, not just as accounting tools, although financial control is still a major function of budgets. Reforms over the years have attempted to tie inputs (spending) to outcomes (results)—**performance budgeting**. Since many governments are in a "perpetual fiscal crisis," they are always in search of ways to "do more with less" . . . and, at the same time, to do it better.[23] Reformers have also emphasized putting budgetary information in more "citizen-friendly" or "customer-friendly" formats and making the process more accessible to citizen input in response to growing taxpayer demands for more accountability. They have also adopted the practice of comparing their jurisdiction's budget and performance with other effective and efficient jurisdictions—**benchmarking**.

That doesn't mean that all agency heads or public employees automatically or enthusiastically buy in to the latest budget reform. Often it's not that they are resisting change as much as it is that their staff is already stretched thin. New budgeting systems, like new technology, are often perceived by managers as having steep start-up costs whether they are in the form of staff training, new data entry requirements, or organizational restructuring. Overall, however, experts agree that the *cumulative* effect of these reform efforts over the years has been to make government more accountable for its spending.

The "incremental" nature of budgetary politics—and reforms—helps reduce political conflict and maintains stability in governmental programs. As bruising as budgetary battles may be in state capitols and city halls, they would be much worse if governments tried to review the value of *all* existing expenditures and programs each year. Comprehensive budgetary review would "overload the system" with political conflict by refighting every policy battle every year.

Balancing the Budget

Unlike the federal government, most state budgets must be balanced. The same is true for most cities, counties, and school districts. This means that chief executives must submit to the legislature a budget in which projected revenues are equal to recommended expenditures. And the legislature must not appropriate funds in excess of projected revenues. There are, of course, many accounting devices that allow governors and mayors and legislatures and councils to get around the balanced budget limitation—devices known as "blue smoke and mirrors." These include "off-budget" special funds, separate state authorities, and capital budgets (see Chapter 14).

PERFORMANCE BUDGETING

Instead of focusing on an organizational unit, a budget is done by program or activity and includes performance to tie expenditures for each program to specific goals established for that program.

BENCHMARKING

Comparing a jurisdiction's budget and performance data against those of other high-performing state or local governments.

REVENUE SHORTFALLS
Revenues that fall below those estimated in the budget and force spending cuts during a fiscal year.

Nonetheless, balanced budget requirements are a major restraint on state and local government spending. Indeed, often **revenue "shortfalls"**—revenues that fall below those estimated for the year in the budget—force painful mid-year spending cuts. Only a few states allow deficits to be carried over into the next fiscal year. And these carryover deficits force governors and legislatures to be more conservative in their spending plans for the following year.[24]

State and local government agencies and employees are constantly reacting to changes in the political and economic climate—and often catching flak for their responses from some citizens, but praise from others. Such is life in the bureaucracy.

CHAPTER HIGHLIGHTS

- The term "bureaucracy," typically applied to government agencies, refers to organizations that operate with a top-down chain of command and carry out prescribed tasks in an impersonal way. Bureaucracies exist in many large organizations, including corporations, the military, churches, and educational institutions.

- In theory, government bureaucracies do not make policy; they only implement it. In reality, they wield a great deal of power by establishing regulations for mandated programs and determining compliance.

- Historically, the number of government employees working for state and local governments steadily increased until the Great Recession, when the trend was reversed—at least temporarily. Where and when it occurs, bureaucratic growth can be attributed to an increasingly complex society, bureaucrats' own ambitions, and the authorization of new programs.

- The executive branch of virtually all state governments is fragmented, complex, and unwieldy because of the many separately elected public officials and extensive use of boards and commissions.

- Patronage, once the principal means of hiring state and local government employees, has gradually been replaced by the merit system (civil service). Patronage today is limited to boards, commissioners, policymaking offices, university trusteeships, and some judicial posts. A civil service job is more permanent than a patronage job. Civil service employees are very hard to fire—which has generated a lot of criticism from disgruntled citizens.

- Tensions between public and private sector workers are increasing, stemming from private sector workers' belief that government workers have more job security, better pensions, and superior health benefits.

- Virtually all state and local governments have affirmative action programs to make the workforce representative of the population, especially of women and minorities. Protection against discrimination based on race, gender, age, disability, and other factors unrelated to job performance is embodied in federal laws and the Fourteenth Amendment.

- Over one-third of all state and local government employees are unionized. Public employee unions are required to submit their disputes to arbitration rather than go on strike.

- Regulatory policy is complicated by the expertise required to carry out laws, the influence that the regulated eventually gain over their regulators, and the natural tendency of bureaucrats to expand their own programs.

- Polls repeatedly show that people believe governments are spending more but delivering less. One hotly debated solution, privatization, shifts some government services to the private and nonprofit sectors through contracts, franchises, grants, and vouchers.

- A movement to "reinvent government" seeks to incorporate entrepreneurial principles such as competition, customer focus, results measurement, and prevention rather than cure.

- The newest trend is for various groups to issue state "report cards" assigning each state a grade for agency transparency, use of digital technology to improve performance and accountability, and accessible financial databases that permit citizen input into the budget process.

- Budgets are political documents that record the conflict over "who gets what." They are prepared by the executive branch but must be approved by the legislative body. Unlike the federal budget, state and local government budgets must be balanced.

CHAPTER NINE

COURTS, CRIME, AND CORRECTIONAL POLICY

RICHARD F. TOOHEY
JUDGE

LEARNING OBJECTIVES

9.1 Outline the role of the courts in the policymaking process, and describe how the policymaking style of the courts is distinct from those of the legislative and the executive branches.

9.2 Explain the litigious nature of the United States, and assess efforts at tort reform.

9.3 Discuss the gradual expansion of individual rights, and compare the roles of the national and state judicial systems in protecting individual rights.

9.4 Describe the structure of the state court systems.

9.5 Compare and contrast the five methods used for selecting judges in the states; describe their status, race, gender, and party affiliation; and explain the processes for disciplining state judges.

9.6 Explain how judicial decisions are made in both state trial and supreme courts, and compare judicial activism and judicial restraint.

9.7 Trace crime rates in the states over time, compare crime rates across states, and describe juvenile and hate crimes.

9.8 Examine the various law enforcement agencies that operate in our states and communities.

9.9 Describe the law enforcement, peacekeeping, and service provider functions of law enforcement; compare the proactive and reactive approaches to police activity; and assess the role of the citizen in law enforcement.

9.10 Explain the role of the prosecutor in the judicial system, evaluate whether prosecutorial discretion and plea bargaining yield desirable outcomes, and assess the effectiveness of grand juries as a check on prosecutors.

9.11 Examine the extent to which the American population is jailed or otherwise under the supervision of the judicial system; explain differences in incarceration rates among states; assess the effectiveness of deterrence, rehabilitation, parole, and probation; and analyze the causes and consequences of prison overcrowding.

9.12 Trace the history of the death penalty in the United States, compare capital punishment across the states, and analyze whether the United States should continue to have the death penalty.

POLITICS AND THE JUDICIAL PROCESS

Courts are "political" institutions because they attempt to resolve conflicts in society. Like legislative and executive institutions, courts make public policy in the process of resolving conflicts. Some of the nation's most important policy decisions have been made by courts rather than legislative or executive bodies at both the federal and state levels. Federal courts have taken the lead in eliminating racial segregation, ensuring the separation of church and state, defining the rights of criminal defendants, guaranteeing individual voters an equal voice in government, and establishing the right of women to obtain abortions. These are just a few of the important policy decisions made by courts—policy decisions that are just as significant to all Americans as those made by Congress or the president. Courts, then, are deeply involved in policymaking, and they are an important part of the political system in America. Sooner or later in American politics, most important policy questions reach the courts.

Whether a case is filed in a federal or state court depends on whether the infraction involves a federal or state law. While each court system is responsible for hearing certain types of cases, neither is completely independent of the other, and the systems often interact, particularly on cases involving interpretations and implementation of principles laid out in the U.S. Constitution's Bill of Rights and Fourteenth Amendment.

State courts mostly handle the types of cases that the individual citizen is most likely to be involved in—robberies, traffic violations, broken contracts, divorces, child custody, and other family disputes. Over 100 million cases are filed in state courts annually. State courts hear 98 percent of all the nation's cases.[1]

The Judicial Style of Decision Making

In resolving conflict and deciding about public policy, courts function very much like other government agencies. However, the *style* of judicial decision making differs significantly from legislative or executive decision making. Let us try to distinguish between courts as policymaking institutions and other legislative and executive agencies.

- A *"passive" appearance:* First of all, courts rarely initiate policy decisions. Rather, they wait until a case involving a policy question they must decide is brought to them. The vast majority of cases brought before courts do not involve important policy issues. Much court activity involves the enforcement of existing public policy. Courts punish criminals, enforce contracts, and award damages to the victims of injuries. Most of these decisions are based on established law. Only occasionally are important policy questions brought to the court.

- *Special rules of access:* Access to courts is through "cases." (Only rarely do state courts render advisory opinions to governors or legislatures.) A "**case**" requires two disputing parties, one of which must have suffered some damages or faces some penalties as a result of the action or inaction of the other. The accused party is the "**defendant**"; the accusing party is the "**plaintiff**" (**prosecutor** when the state brings a suit against a defendant).

- *Legal procedures:* The procedures under which judges and other participants in the judicial process operate are also quite different from procedures in legislative or executive branches of government. Facts and arguments must be presented to the courts in specified forms—writs, motions, written briefs, and oral arguments that meet the technical specifications of the courts. While an interest group may hire lobbyists to pressure a legislature, they must hire a law firm to put their arguments into a legal context.

- *Decisions in specific cases:* Courts must limit their decisions to specific cases. Rarely do the courts announce a comprehensive policy in the way the legislature does when it enacts a law. Of course, the implication of a court's decision in a particular case is that future cases of the same nature will be decided the same way. This implication amounts to a policy statement; however, it is not as comprehensive as a legislative policy pronouncement, because future cases with only slightly different circumstances might be decided differently. (It is true that higher appeals courts, like state supreme courts, may decide to hear a case knowing that the decision will have a far-reaching impact beyond just the case at hand.)

CASE
A court matter involving two disputing parties.

DEFENDANT
The accused party in court.

PLAINTIFF
The accusing party in court.

PROSECUTOR
The attorney acting on behalf of the government in a criminal case.

- *Appearance of objectivity:* Perhaps the most important distinction between judicial decision making and decision making in other branches of government is that judges must not appear to permit political considerations to affect their decisions. Judges must not appear to base their decisions on partisan considerations, to bargain, or to compromise in decision making. The *appearance of objectivity* in judicial decision making gives courts a measure of prestige that other governmental institutions lack. Court decisions appear more legitimate to the public if they believe that the courts have dispensed unbiased justice. Unfortunately, the highly partisan battle over the confirmation of *federal* court judges has made Americans somewhat less confident about the objectivity of judges at all levels.

Foundation of Common Law

Legal traditions are influential in court decisions. English common law has affected the law of all of our states except Louisiana, which was influenced by the French Napoleonic Code. English common law developed in the thirteenth century through the decisions of judges who applied their notions of justice to specific cases. This body of judge-made law grew over the centuries and is still the foundation of our legal system today. However, **statutory law**—laws passed by legislatures—take precedence over common law. The **common law** is only applied by the courts when no statutory provisions are relevant or when statutory law must be interpreted. The degree to which statutory law has replaced common law varies among the states according to the comprehensiveness of state statutes and codes. Common law covers both criminal and civil law, although the common law of crimes has been replaced by comprehensive criminal codes in the states.

STATUTORY LAW
Laws passed by legislatures.

COMMON LAW
Legal traditions developed through court cases going back to England.

THE LAWYERING OF AMERICA

9.2

Explain the litigious nature of the United States, and assess efforts at tort reform.

The United States is the most litigious society in the world. We are threatening to drown ourselves in a sea of lawsuits. The rise in the number of lawsuits in the United States corresponds to a rise in the number of lawyers. There were 285,000 practicing lawyers in the nation in 1960; by 2012, this figure had grown to over 1.2 million (compared to 835,000 licensed physicians). The continuing search for legal fees by these bright professional people has brought an avalanche of **civil cases** in federal and state courts—about 15 million per year. An analysis by the Bureau of Justice Statistics finds that cases involving the highest estimated median damage awards are medical malpractice and product **liability** lawsuits. Lawsuits may involve:

CIVIL CASES
Disputes between individuals or organizations that do *not* involve law-breaking.

LIABILITY
Legal responsibility for damages caused by civil wrongdoing.

- *Expanded liability.* Virtually any accident involving a commercial product can inspire a product liability suit. An individual who gets cut opening a can of peas can sue the canning company. Manufacturers must pay large insurance premiums to insure themselves against such suits and pass on the costs of the insurance in the price of the product. Municipal and state governments, once generally protected from lawsuits by citizens, have now lost most of their "immunity" and must purchase liability insurance for activities as diverse as recreation, street maintenance, waste collection, and police and fire protection. Real estate brokers may be sued by unhappy buyers and sellers. Homeowners and bar owners may be sued by persons injured by their guests. Hotels have paid damages to persons raped in their rooms. Coastal cities with beaches have been successfully sued by relatives of persons who drowned themselves in the ocean.

- *Contingency fees.* Many of these lawsuits are initiated by lawyers who charge fees on a **contingency** basis; the plaintiff pays nothing unless the attorney wins an award. Up to half of that award may go to the attorney in expenses and fees. Trial attorneys argue that many people could not afford to bring civil cases to court without a contingency fee contract.

- *Third-party suits.* Defendants in civil cases are not necessarily the parties directly responsible for damages to the plaintiff. Instead, wealthier third parties with "**deep pockets**," who may indirectly contribute to an accident, are favorite targets of lawsuits. For example, if a drunk driver injures a pedestrian, but the driver has only limited insurance and small personal wealth, a shrewd attorney will sue the bar that sold the driver the drinks instead of the driver.

CONTINGENCY FEES
A plaintiff pays nothing in attorney fees unless the attorney wins an award.

DEEP POCKETS
A party to a lawsuit with an abundance of financial resources.

For this reason, insurance premiums have risen sharply for physicians seeking malpractice insurance, as have premiums for recreation facilities, nurseries and day care centers, nursing homes, motels, and restaurants.

■ *"Pain and suffering" and "punitive" awards.* Awards in liability cases, sometimes running into tens of millions of dollars, cover much more than the doctor bills, lost wages, and cost of future care for injured parties. Most large damage awards are for pain and suffering. **Pain and suffering awards** are *added* compensation for the victim, beyond actual costs for medical care and lost wages. So also are **punitive damage awards**, multiples of the actual damages designed to deter and punish persons or firms found to be at fault.

■ *"Joint and several" liability.* Moreover, a legal rule known as **joint and several liability** allows a plaintiff to collect the entire award from any party that contributed in any way to the accident, if other defendants cannot pay. So if a drunk driver crosses a median strip and crashes into another car leaving its driver disabled, the victim may sue the city for not placing a guard railing in the median strip. The rule encourages trial lawyers to sue the party "with the deepest pockets," that is, the wealthiest party rather than the party most responsible for the accident. Unsophisticated juries can be emotionally manipulated into granting huge damage awards, especially against businesses, municipalities, and insurance companies.

■ *Alternative dispute resolution.* A less controversial approach, and one that is now found in most states, is alternative dispute resolution, that is, the use of mediation or arbitration in order to settle civil suits without a formal trial. Over 60 percent of the conflicts that end up in arbitration are contract and personal injury disputes.[2] Often third-party mediators are retired judges or attorneys who try to get the parties to voluntarily agree to a binding resolution of their case. The parties get a quick settlement, usually some compromise, and the courts reduce their backlogs. Most are very satisfied with the arbitrator's performance, the confidentiality of the process, and its length. Persons who have used the arbitration process rate it as faster, simpler, and cheaper than going to court. Two-thirds said they would be likely to use arbitration again.[3]

Tort Reform

A **tort** is a civil wrong or injury case involving private parties. The role of the court in such cases is to provide a remedy in the form of damages. Reforming the nation's liability laws is a major challenge confronting the nation's state governments. The most common reform proposals seek to cap the dollar amount of awards for "pain and suffering"; eliminate punitive damage awards; restrict the fees that lawyers can subtract from a victim's award; and end the rule of "joint and several" liability. Perhaps the simplest reform is a **"loser pays" law**—a requirement that the losing party in a civil suit pay the legal fees of the winner. This would discourage frivolous suits that are often designed to force innocent parties to pay damages rather than incur even higher costs of defending themselves. The reform movement has been heavily supported by some traditionally powerful groups—insurance companies, product manufacturers, physicians and hospitals, and even municipal governments.

On the other side are the trial lawyers, who are disproportionately represented in state legislatures and very willing to continue to fund fights against tort reform (see Chapter 6). The American Trial Lawyers Association is bitterly opposed to tort reform, believing that such initiatives will limit the average citizen's access to the courts and stop people from suing who have been harmed.

PAIN AND SUFFERING AWARDS
Added compensation for the victim of a crime, beyond actual costs for medical care and lost wages.

PUNITIVE DAMAGE AWARDS
Multiples of the actual damages found; designed to deter and punish persons or firms found to be at fault.

JOINT AND SEVERAL LIABILITY
Legal responsibility for full damages regardless of the degree of contribution to harm.

TORT
A legal harm caused by civil wrongdoing.

LOSER PAYS LAW
Requirement that the losing party in a civil suit pay the legal fees of the winning party.

9.3 JUDICIAL FEDERALISM

Discuss the gradual expansion of individual rights, and compare the roles of the national and state judicial systems in protecting individual rights.

The Supremacy Clause of the U.S. Constitution (Article VI) ensures that the federal constitution supersedes state constitutions and binds the judges in every state. State constitutions cannot deny rights granted by the U.S. Constitution, and state courts may not limit federal constitutional guarantees. But state constitutions cover many topics that are not addressed in the U.S. Constitution. More importantly, state constitutions may add individual rights that are not found in the U.S. Constitution, and state courts may interpret state constitutional language to expand individual rights beyond federal constitutional guarantees.

We might think of the U.S. Constitution as a floor, providing minimum protection of individual rights for all persons in the nation. But state constitutions can build on that floor, adding individual protections for persons within their state.

Judicial Federalism

Judicial federalism refers to state courts' exercise of their authority to interpret their own state constitutions to guarantee protections of individual rights beyond those protected by the U.S. Constitution. While this authority has always existed under the American federal system, it was seldom exercised in the past. Historically, the remedy to civil rights violations was to be found in federal court if it was to be found at all. Civil rights attorneys almost always turned to federal courts and the U.S. Constitution to seek protection for their clients. But the new activism of state courts in interpreting their own states' constitutional guarantees has begun to change this pattern. "**Court, or forum, shopping**" is a common strategy of lawyers; it involves the search for a court that will be most favorably disposed to one's argument. In the past, federal courts were almost always the forum of choice for civil rights claims. But recently state courts have become the forums of choice for some claims. Probably the highest profile case that ended up being tossed between the state and federal courts for years was the Terri Schiavo case pitting her husband against her parents in a heart-wrenching right-to-live versus right-to-die battle that was only resolved by her death.

Many state constitutions contain rights not explicitly found in the U.S. Constitution. For example, various state constitutions guarantee rights to privacy, rights of political participation, rights of victims of crime, rights to public information, rights to work, rights to free public education, and equal gender rights (state ERAs).

Nationalizing the Bill of Rights

The Bill of Rights in the U.S. Constitution begins with the words "*Congress* shall make no law . . .," indicating that it was originally intended to limit only the powers of the federal government. The Bill of Rights was added to the Constitution because of fear that the *federal* government might become too powerful and encroach on individual liberty. But what about encroachments by state and local governments and their officials? The Fourteenth Amendment to the U.S. Constitution includes the words "No State shall . . ."; its provisions are directed specifically at states. Initially, the U.S. Supreme Court rejected the argument that the Fourteenth Amendment's Privileges or Immunities Clause and the Due Process Clause incorporated the Bill of Rights. But beginning in the 1920s, the Court handed down a long series of decisions that gradually brought about the "*incorporation*" of almost all of the protections of the Bill of Rights into the "liberty" guaranteed against state actions by the Due Process Clause of the Fourteenth Amendment. In *Gitlow* v. *New York* (1925), the Court ruled that "freedom of speech and of the press—which are protected by the First Amendment from abridgment by Congress—are among the fundamental personal rights and liberties protected by the due process clause of the Fourteenth Amendment from impairment by the states."[4] Over time, the Court applied the same reasoning in incorporating almost all provisions of the Bill of Rights into the Fourteenth Amendment's Due Process Clause. (See Table 9–1.) States and all of their subdivisions—cities, counties, townships, school districts, and so on—are bound by the Bill of Rights.

Extending Personal Liberties

Several state supreme courts have taken the lead in extending personal liberties under their own state constitutions, even when the U.S. Supreme Court has declined to incorporate these same liberties within the U.S. Constitution. Some examples include:

- The Florida Supreme Court decided that the state constitutional guarantee of the right of privacy struck down laws restricting abortion, although the U.S. Supreme Court had earlier upheld similar restrictions as permissible under the U.S. Constitution (*Webster* v. *Reproductive Health Services*, 1989).

JUDICIAL FEDERALISM
State courts' authority to interpret their own states' constitutional guarantees to expand upon those in the U.S. Constitution.

COURT, OR FORUM, SHOPPING
Common strategy of lawyers; it involves the search for a court that will be most favorably disposed to one's argument.

TABLE 9–1 Incorporating the U.S. Constitution's Bill of Rights into the Fourteenth Amendment

Year	Issue	Amendment Involved	Court Case
1925	Freedom of speech	I	*Gitlow* v. *New York*, 268 U.S. 652.
1931	Freedom of the press	I	*Near* v. *Minnesota*, 283 U.S. 697
1932	Right to a lawyer in capital punishment cases	VI	*Powell* v. *Alabama*, 287 U.S. 45
1937	Freedom of assembly and right to petition	I	*De Jonge* v. *Oregon*, 299 U.S. 353
1940	Freedom of religion	I	*Cantwell* v. *Connecticut*, 310 U.S. 296
1947	Separation of church and state	I	*Everson* v. *Board of Education*, 330 U.S. 1
1948	Right to public trial	VI	*In re Oliver*, 333 U.S. 257
1949	No unreasonable searches and seizures	IV	*Wolf* v. *Colorado*, 338 U.S. 25
1961	Exclusionary rule	IV	*Mapp* v. *Ohio*, 367 U.S. 643
1962	No cruel and unusual punishment	VIII	*Robinson* v. *California*, 370 U.S. 660
1963	Right to a lawyer in all criminal felony cases	VI	*Gideon* v. *Wainwright*, 372 U.S. 335
1964	No compulsory self-incrimination	V	*Malloy* v. *Hogan*, 378 U.S. 335
1965	Right to privacy	I, III, IV, V, IX	*Griswold* v. *Connecticut*, 381 U.S. 363
1966	Right to an impartial jury	VI	*Parker* v. *Gladden*, 385 U.S. 363
1967	Right to speedy trial	VI	*Klopfer* v. *North Carolina*, 386 U.S. 213
1969	No double jeopardy	V	*Benton* v. *Maryland*, 395 U.S. 784

Source: Supreme Court of the United States, Washington, DC.

■ The Texas Supreme Court (and several other states' high courts) held that the state's constitutional guarantee of equality in public education required the system of local school finance to be replaced with statewide financing that equalized educational spending throughout the state. Years earlier, the U.S. Supreme Court had decided that the U.S. Constitution did *not* include a right to equal educational funding across school districts (*San Antonio Independent School District* v. *Rodriguez*, 1973).

■ New York and Pennsylvania Supreme Courts were the first to strike down state sodomy laws (anal sexual penetration) under privacy provisions of their state constitution, although the U.S. Supreme Court had upheld a Georgia sodomy statute ruling that "there is no constitutional right to commit sodomy" (*Bowers* v. *Hardwick*, 1986).

■ California's Supreme Court ruled that the state's constitution compelled the state to pay for abortions for poor women, although the U.S. Supreme Court ruled that there was no requirement in the U.S. Constitution that states fund abortions (*Harris* v. *McRae*, 1980).

■ The Massachusetts Supreme Court ruled that nude go-go dancing is a protected form of free expression under the state's constitution, even though the U.S. Supreme Court had ruled that it is *not* protected by the First Amendment (*Barnes* v. *Glen Theatre Inc.*, 1991).

AMICUS CURIAE

"Friends of the court"—persons or groups not directly involved in a case who submit written arguments to the court.

Judicial activism by state supreme courts encourages interest groups to bring cases and **amicus curiae** briefs (written arguments submitted by "friends of the court") to state "forums." Of course, the state strategy has significant drawbacks compared to winning at the U.S. Supreme Court level; interest groups must proceed from state to state instead of dealing with the issue once and for all in the nation's highest court.[5]

Judicial Policy Divergence

While civil rights organizations generally applaud the new judicial federalism, others have expressed concern over increased divergence between U.S. Supreme Court policy and the policies of state courts. A stable and predictable system of law is essential for democracy. Judicial federalism seems to open the law to diversity between federal and state law as well as to the "Balkanization" of law from state to state. Judicial policy diversity opens the nation's court system to intensified interest group activity and perhaps greater partisan political influence.[6] The good news is that in some states, their supreme courts often make decisions with an eye as to what the U.S. Supreme Court might do in a pending case.[7]

THE STRUCTURE OF COURT SYSTEMS

State courts are generally organized into a hierarchy similar to that shown in Figure 9–1. The courts of a state constitute a single, integrated judicial system; even city courts, traffic courts, and justices of the peace are part of the state judicial system. According to the National Center for State Courts, over half the states now have **unified court systems**. Unified court systems are more streamlined; they treat the courts in a state as a single administrative unit. The administrative tasks of the court are handled by professional court administrators who are trained in management. Sophisticated and integrated data management and budgeting systems are in place in unified systems and each court's jurisdictional authority is clearly spelled out. States whose courts are not unified may have as many as nine different trial courts combined with many appellate courts (e.g., Georgia, Indiana).[8] **Trial courts** are those that first hear the facts of a case and reach a verdict. **Appellate courts** review the decision of a trial court to determine whether errors were made (primarily legal errors rather than factual errors).

Describe the structure of the state court systems.

UNIFIED COURT SYSTEM
All courts in a state are part of a single administrative unit.

TRIAL COURTS
Courts that originally hear the facts of a case and deliver a verdict

APPELLATE COURTS
Courts that review the decisions of trial courts to determine whether errors were made.

TRIAL COURTS OF LIMITED JURISDICTION
Courts that are concerned principally with traffic cases, small claims, divorces and child custody, juvenile offenses, and misdemeanors, although they may hold preliminary hearings to determine whether a person accused of a felony shall be held in jail or placed under bond.

Minor Trial Courts

At the lowest level are minor trial courts, often referred to as "**trial courts of limited jurisdiction**." These may be municipal courts, magistrate courts, police courts, traffic courts, family courts, and small claims courts. They are presided over by justices of the peace, magistrates, or police judges, not all of whom are trained in the law. These courts are concerned principally with traffic cases, small claims, divorces and child custody,

FIGURE 9–1 The Structure of State and Local Courts

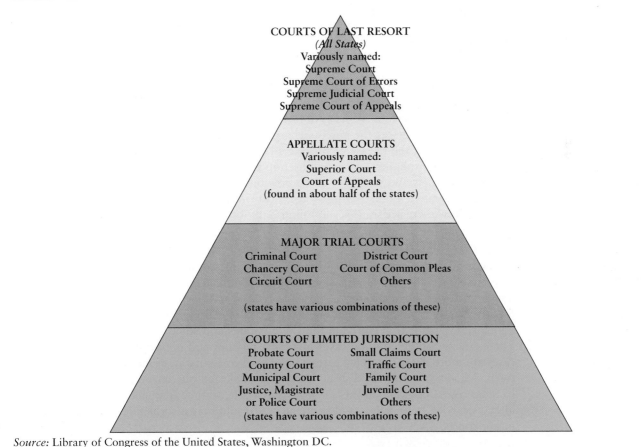

Source: Library of Congress of the United States, Washington DC.

Court rooms are often quite small, crowded, and noisy. Not much space separates the attorneys and the accused from the public at large.

juvenile offenses, and misdemeanors, although they may hold preliminary hearings to determine whether a person accused of a felony shall be held in jail or placed under bond. (A **felony** is a crime punishable by at least a year's imprisonment; a **misdemeanor** is a crime punishable by a fine or less than a year's imprisonment.) Rarely are these cases heard by juries; mostly the judge decides guilt or innocence and the sentence.

In many cities, municipal courts dispense justice in a "production line" style. Courtrooms are old, crowded, noisy, and confusing; witnesses, defendants, friends, and relatives all wait for hours for their cases to be called. Most cases are handled informally at the bench in discussions with the judge (a **bench trial**). Leniency is the rule with most judges, unless the face of the defendant is very familiar to the judge; then 30-, 60-, or 90-day sentences may be imposed very quickly. Rarely are juries involved in misdemeanor, or minor, court cases. Usually when a **jury trial** is used, the jury decides guilt or innocence and the judge determines the sentence.

The trend is toward specialized courts, particularly in large, diverse metropolitan areas with heavy caseloads. The growth of **small claims courts** throughout the country has helped millions of people who could not afford an attorney to bring a civil claim into the court with simplicity and low cost. Television shows, including *Judge Judy*, have popularized the functioning of small claims courts. Proceedings in these courts are very informal: Both sides simply "tell it to the judge." Buyers and sellers, landlords and tenants, creditors and debtors can get a resolution to their case quickly and easily. Plaintiffs usually prevail in small claims courts, often because the defendant never shows. The biggest problem for the winner, however, is actually collecting the money the court has ruled they are owed.

The newer specialty ("boutique") courts that have sprung up in some states are often called "**problem-solving courts**": drug courts (adult, juvenile, family), mental health courts, community courts, veterans courts, domestic violence courts, dependency courts (substance abuse treatment services for parents charged with child abuse and neglect), and reentry courts (overseeing the release of prisoners back into society). In general, problem-solving courts "impose probation and rehabilitation rather than incarceration on defendants facing minor charges and with few or no previous convictions."[9] Miami–Dade County was the first to create a County Drug Court. Problem-solving courts have proved to be quite popular. Now there are some several thousand of them across the states.

Major Trial Courts

Major **trial courts of general jurisdiction**—sometimes called district courts, circuit courts, superior courts, chancery courts, county courts, criminal courts, or common pleas courts—handle major civil and criminal cases arising out of statutes, common law, and state constitutions. The geographic jurisdiction of these courts is usually the county or city; there are about 1,500 major trial courts in the United States and some 30,000 trial court judges.[10] These courts handle criminal cases involving felonies and important civil suits. Criminal cases are more likely than civil cases to be heard by a jury. In **criminal cases,** the prosecutor is the state attorney or district attorney—an elected official. Almost all cases decided by state courts originate in these major trial courts; trial courts make the initial decisions in cases carried to appellate and supreme courts and may also handle some appeals from minor courts.

FELONY

A serious violation of criminal law that can bring a penalty of one year or more in prison.

MISDEMEANOR

A crime that is punishable by a fine or less than one year in jail.

BENCH TRIAL

Cases that are handled informally at the bench in discussions with the judge.

JURY TRIAL

A case where a jury decides guilt or innocence and the judge usually determines the sentence.

SMALL CLAIMS COURT

Court in which two parties simply "tell it to the judge," without the need for lawyers.

PROBLEM-SOLVING COURT

Specialty courts that deal with defendants facing minor charges, such as county drug courts and domestic violence courts.

TRIAL COURTS OF GENERAL JURISDICTION

Courts that handle major civil and criminal cases arising out of statutes, common law, and state constitutions. The geographic jurisdiction of these courts is usually the county or city.

Juries: Trial (Petit) and Grand

There are two types of juries: trial (petit) and grand. **Petit juries** seated to hear cases in trial courts determine the guilt or innocence of the accused. **Grand juries,** ranging in size from 12 to 23 jurors, have two primary functions: investigation and indictment. While grand jury investigations usually involve crimes, in some states, the focus may be on the misconduct of public officials, corruption, prisons, public records, public offices, or public facilities. The proceedings are secret to protect the accused.[11] Historically, *petit juries* have been composed of 12 citizens, plus a couple of alternate jurors ready to step in should a regular juror become unable to serve. However, several states allow smaller juries (six or eight members) in non–capital felony criminal cases while most states permit smaller juries in civil cases. Smaller juries are seen as saving time and money, although some have criticized them for their lack of diversity. Some states do not require unanimous verdicts if the jury is large (12 members) or for civil cases. But unanimous verdicts are mandatory in a death penalty case (except in Florida).

The racial/ethnic makeup of juries assigned to hear death penalty cases has gotten the attention of the U.S. Supreme Court. In 2005, it instructed lower courts and prosecutors against removing potential jurors on the basis of their race, thereby creating racial bias in jury selection. The Court ordered new trials for two black murder defendants (one in Texas, one in California) after hearing their appeals claiming that they faced juries made up of white jurors unfairly selected.[12] The 2005 ruling strengthened the Court's 1986 decision in *Batson* v. *Kentucky,*[13] which set standards for proving claims of prosecutorial bias in the use of "**peremptory challenges (strikes),**" or automatic objections to potential jurors for which no reason must be given.[14]

States differ in how they select potential jurors. Many randomly select jurors from sources such as driver's license lists, motor vehicle registration lists, or voter registration rolls. Usually jurors must be residents and age 18 or older, although the age requirement is higher in two states (Mississippi and Missouri). States also differ in the maximum time they expect a juror to serve. Most states allow some persons to be exempt from jury duty—the sick, the mentally handicapped, teachers, doctors, and other professionals. But with the growing technical complexity of issues and evidence, states are beginning to eliminate some of these exemptions. While some Americans try to avoid jury duty, studies show that those who serve end up feeling more positive about the court system than their fellow citizens who do not serve.[15]

Selecting jurors who are impartial has become a bigger challenge in the social media age. According to the National Center for State Courts, "Internet-based technologies now make it possible for jurors to access virtually any piece of published information about pending cases in minutes, regardless of when or where published." Even during a trial, jurors' normal use of smartphones to contact family and friends might introduce them to "evidence" not introduced into the courtroom. Consequently, "judges and lawyers can no longer be confident either that a sufficient number of prospective jurors on any given panel will meet the traditional definition of impartiality or that the jurors selected for trial will remain so for the entire trial."[16]

The Public Defender

If arrested, people who cannot afford an attorney must be provided one by the state. So ruled the U.S. Supreme Court in *Gideon* v. *Wainwright* (1963)[17] and *Argersinger* v. *Hamlin* (1972).[18] The right to legal counsel stems from the Sixth Amendment to the U.S. Constitution: "In all criminal prosecutions, the accused shall enjoy the right to have the assistance of counsel for his defense." States vary on how lawyers defending the indigent are selected. (Even in the same state, the method may differ across counties.) They may rely on **public defenders,** who are usually county elected officials. They may turn to nonprofit agencies that specialize in public defense cases. The state may contract with individual attorneys or

CRIMINAL CASES

Cases brought by government prosecutors against persons or organizations charged with law-breaking.

PETIT JURIES

A jury that determines the guilt or innocence of criminal defendants.

GRAND JURIES

Juries that have two primary functions: investigation and indictment.

PEREMPTORY CHALLENGE (STRIKE)

Lawyer blocks a potential juror without having to give cause.

PUBLIC DEFENDER

Attorneys provided by the state to those who could not otherwise afford an attorney.

law firms to handle court-appointed cases. Or the state may rely on an assigned-counsel system in which an attorney is appointed off of a list and paid by the case or by the hour.[19] Groups such as the American Bar Association, the National Association of Criminal Defense Lawyers, and the National Legal Aid and Defenders Association constantly monitor the quality of lawyers assigned to represent the poor and the fairness of the assignment process. Inadequate representation can be grounds for an appeal.

Appellate Courts: District Courts and State Supreme Courts

Every state has a court of last resort, which is generally called the supreme court. These courts consist of three to nine judges, and most of their work is devoted to cases on appeal from major trial courts, although some states grant original jurisdiction to supreme courts in special types of cases. Since they consider questions of law rather than questions of fact, they sit without a jury. **State supreme courts** are the most important and visible judicial bodies in the states. Their decisions are written, published, and distributed like the decisions of the U.S. Supreme Court. Judges can express their views in majority opinions, dissenting opinions, or concurring opinions. These courts get the most controversial cases and those with the most at stake, since these cases are most likely to be appealed all the way to the state's highest court.

To relieve state supreme courts of heavy case burdens, many of the more populous states maintain intermediate courts of appeal between trial courts and courts of last resort. (Only 11 states do not have an intermediate appellate court.) Intermediate appellate courts range in size from 3 judges (Alaska and North Dakota) to 105 judges (California). Often appellate courts are divided into regions or districts. To help move the caseload along, several appellate judges (a **panel**) in a district may be assigned to hear a case rather than the entire body of appellate court judges (**en banc**) in that district. State appellate courts also differ in the type of jurisdiction they have: discretionary or mandatory. (**Discretionary jurisdiction** means that they pick which trial court cases they will hear on appeal; **mandatory jurisdiction** means that state law dictates which cases they must hear on appeal from the lower trial court.) State intermediate appellate courts tend to hear more mandatory appeals whereas state supreme courts hear more discretionary appeals. Appeals court judges hear arguments of law rather than arguments about the facts of a case. There are no juries in appellate courts.

All state supreme courts stand atop their own state's judicial system. In 39 states, the state supreme court has considerable discretionary jurisdiction, typically turning down some 90 percent of the appeals.[20] Some have mandatory jurisdiction over certain types of cases—death penalty appeals, interjurisdictional disputes among state agencies and branches or between local governments, the constitutionality of a state law, or complaints involving judges. Some state supreme courts enjoy national reputations. Their decisions on points of law are often cited by other state supreme courts as well as by federal courts. Indeed, it is possible to identify judicial leadership among state courts by examining the number of times they are cited by other courts.[21] Supreme courts in California, New York, New Jersey, Massachusetts, and Pennsylvania enjoy superior reputations, followed by those in Illinois, Wisconsin, Washington, Michigan, Iowa, Colorado, and Minnesota.

Appeals to the U.S. Supreme Court

Appeals from the state supreme courts may go directly to the U.S. Supreme Court on federal constitutional grounds. State supreme courts have the final word in the interpretation of *state* constitutions and laws. But many cases also raise federal constitutional questions, especially under the broad meaning of the "due process" clause and "equal protection" clause of the Fourteenth Amendment. So while most judicial appeals will end in state courts, the U.S. Supreme Court exercises general oversight through its power to accept appeals based on federal questions.

STATE SUPREME COURTS
The highest courts of appeal in the states.

PANEL
A few judges assigned to a particular court hear and decide a case.

EN BANC
All judges assigned to a particular court hear and decide a case.

DISCRETIONARY JURISDICTION
An appellate court chooses which cases they will hear on appeal.

MANDATORY JURISDICTION
State law dictates types of cases appellate courts must hear on appeal.

THE MAKING OF A JUDGE

Political debate over methods of selecting judges in the states has been going on for many years. In writing the federal Constitution, the Founding Fathers reflected conservative views in establishing an independent federal judiciary, whose members were appointed by the president for life terms and were not subject to direct popular control. Jacksonian views of popular election were strong in the states, however, and today a majority of state judges are directly elected by the people on partisan or nonpartisan ballots. Proponents argue that elections "inject state courts with enhanced institutional legitimacy" because "when people know they have the power to turn out judges who perform poorly, they are more willing to accept the decisions of those judges."[22] In contrast, opponents are convinced that by having to raise money to run, judges who win are unduly influenced by special interest groups, including lawyers, that contributed to their campaign and are less objective in their decision making.

Five different methods of selecting judges are found in the 50 states: *partisan election, nonpartisan election, appointment by the governor, legislative selection,* and the *appointment–retention election plan.* Many states use more than one method. (See Table 9–2 for the method used to select state supreme court justices and major trial court judges.) Twenty-three states elect their supreme court justices, either in partisan elections (8) or in nonpartisan elections (15) in which candidates for the bench do not carry party labels. In two states, judges are chosen by their legislatures, and in nine states, they are appointed by the governor, often with approval required by other bodies. Sixteen states have adopted the **appointment–retention judicial election plan** (initially called the Missouri plan), in which

Compare and contrast the five methods used for selecting judges in the states; describe their status, race, gender, and party affiliation; and explain the processes for disciplining state judges.

APPOINTMENT–RETENTION JUDICIAL ELECTION PLAN (MISSOURI PLAN)

A method of judicial selection in which a nominating committee sends names to the governor, who then makes the appointment; appointees must win a retention vote in the next election.

TABLE 9–2 Methods of Selecting State Court Justices and Judges

State Supreme Court (Appellate)

Election		Appointment		Combination
Partisan Election (Run with a Political Party Label)	**Nonpartisan Election (Do Not Run with a Political Party Label)**	**Selection by Legislature**	**Governor Appointment**	**Appointment–Retention Election**
Alabama	Arkansas	South Carolina	Connecticut[b]	Alaska
Illinois	Georgia	Virginia	Delaware[b]	Arizona
Louisiana	Idaho		Hawaii[a]	California[b]
New Mexico[a]	Kentucky		Maine[b]	Colorado
New York[a]	Michigan[a]		Massachusetts[b]	Florida
Pennsylvania[a]	Minnesota		New Hampshire[b]	Indiana
Texas	Mississippi		New Jersey[b]	Iowa
West Virginia	Montana		Rhode Island[b]	Kansas
	Nevada		Vermont[b]	Maryland[b]
	North Carolina			Missouri
	North Dakota			Nebraska
	Ohio[a]			Oklahoma
	Oregon			South Dakota
	Washington			Tennessee
	Wisconsin			Utah[b]
				Wyoming

(continued)

TABLE 9–2 Methods of Selecting State Court Justices and Judges (Continued)

Major State Trial Court					
Election		**Appointment**		**Combination**	
Partisan Election (Run with a Political Party Label)	Nonpartisan Election (Do Not Run with a Political Party Label)	Selection by Legislature	Governor Appointment	Appointment–Retention Election	Method of Selection Varies within the State
Alabama	Arkansas	South Carolina	Connecticut[b]	Alaska	Arizona
Illinois[a]	California	Virginia	Delaware[b]	Colorado	Kansas
Indiana	Florida		Hawaii[a]	Illinois[a]	Maryland
Louisiana	Maryland		Maine[b]	Iowa	Missouri
New Mexico[a]	Georgia		Massachusetts[b]	Nebraska	
New York	Missouri		New Hampshire[b]	New Mexico[a]	
Pennsylvania[a]	Idaho		New Jersey[b]	Pennsylvania[a]	
Tennessee	Kentucky		Rhode Island[b]	Utah[b]	
Texas	Michigan		Vermont[b]	Wyoming	
West Virginia	Minnesota				
	Mississippi				
	Montana				
	Nevada				
	North Carolina				
	North Dakota				
	Ohio[a]				
	Oklahoma				
	Oregon				
	South Dakota				
	Washington				
	Wisconsin				

[a] These states have very unique and complex methods of selecting justices and judges. For specific information on the state, see: "Methods of Judicial Selection," Available http://www.judicialselection.us/judicial_selection/methods/selection_of_judges.cfm?state=.

[b] The State Senate, State Legislature, or a separate committee must confirm the governor's appointee.

Source: American Judicature Society, "Judicial Selection in the States," February 25, 2013. Available at http://www.judicialselection.us/judicial_selection/methods/selection_of_judges.cfm?state=.

governors appoint judges on the recommendation of a select committee, and after the judge has been in office for a year or more, the voters are given the opportunity to retain or oust the appointed judge via a **retention election**.

RETENTION ELECTION
A judicial election in which voters choose between keeping or ousting an incumbent judge.

Appointment

The argument for selecting judges by appointment rests upon the value of judicial independence and isolation from direct political involvement. Critics of the elective method feel that it forces judges into political relationships and compromises their independence on the bench. This is particularly true if judicial elections are held on a partisan rather than a nonpartisan ballot, where judges must secure nomination with the support of party leaders. Moreover, it is argued that voters are not able to evaluate "legal" qualifications—knowledge of the law, judicial temperament, skill in the courtroom, and so on. Hence, judges should be appointed, rather than elected by voters. Attorneys, bar associations, and judges themselves prefer an appointive method in which they are given the opportunity to screen candidates and evaluate legal qualifications prior to appointment.

Actually it is not possible to "take judges out of politics." Selection by appointment removes the selection of judges from *party* politics but simply places the selection in different political hands. Instead of party leaders, the governor or the bar association become the principal actors in judicial selection. It is not clear which system leads to "better" judges, or whether "better" judges are those more sensitive to community values or more trained in legal procedures.

Interim Appointment

In practice many judges come to the bench in elective states through the appointment procedure. The apparent paradox comes about because even in elective states, governors generally have the power to make **interim appointments** when a judgeship is vacant because of the retirement or death of a judge between elections. Interim-appointed judges must seek election at the next regular election, but by that time they have acquired the prestige and status of a judge, and they are unlikely to be defeated by an outsider. Many members of the judiciary in elective states deliberately resign before the end of their term, if they are not seeking reelection, in order to give the governor the opportunity to fill the post by appointment. It is interesting to note that over half of the supreme court justices in states that elect their judiciary come to the bench initially by means of appointment. In practice, then, the elective system of judicial selection is greatly compromised by the appointment of judges to fill unexpired terms.

INTERIM APPOINTMENT
In government, appointment to a vacancy created by death or resignation prior to the expiration of an elected term.

Election

Few incumbent judges are ever defeated in running for reelection. The majority of judges seeking reelection are unopposed by anyone on the ballot, and very few judges seeking reelection are ever defeated. Voter interest in judicial elections is quite low.[23] Given a lack of information and interest in these elections, incumbent judges have an enormous advantage. They have the prestigious title "Judge" in front of their names and some name recognition. In states with partisan elections, judges are occasionally defeated if their party loses badly.[24] But even in these partisan elections judges enjoy more stability and independence from popular control than do legislators or governors, although judicial elections can be very expensive and contentious.

Very few voters know anything about judicial candidates, although that may be changing. One study suggests that fewer than 15 percent of voters *coming from the polls* remembered the name of one candidate for the state supreme court, and fewer than 5 percent could remember the name of one candidate for county court.[25] An estimated 10–15 percent of the voters just skip over the judicial contests altogether. Part of the problem is that historically many states have greatly restricted how judicial candidates may campaign in order to maintain the perception of objectivity in the judiciary. Consequently, candidates for judicial posts were often limited in the kind of statements they may make in their ads and campaign literature. But in 2002, a 5–4 U.S. Supreme Court ruling (*Republican Party of Minnesota* v. *White*) based on the First Amendment (freedom of speech) prevents government from prohibiting candidates from communicating relevant information to voters during an election.[26]

Following that ruling, judicial candidates in the states that elect judges began spending large sums on campaigns. (See Table 9–3.) To some in the legal community and to the public at large, the politicization of the judiciary was (and is) highly disturbing, particularly the infusion of out-of-state money into trial court races. In the words of California's chief justice, "If the judiciary becomes politicized, then the rule of law is in jeopardy." Several years later (2009), the U.S. Supreme Court ruled 5–4 in *Caperton* v. *Massey Coal Company* that an elected judge could be made to step aside in a particular case based on campaign spending in state judicial races. The case involved a West Virginia judge who had refused to recuse himself from a lawsuit involving an executive who spent $3 million to elect the judge (more than all other contributions to the judge's election combined). At that very time the judge was considering the executive's case.[27] The Court ruled that given the "serious risk of actual bias," the Constitution's due-process clause required him to excuse himself from the case.

TABLE 9-3   Top Six Economic Sectors Giving to Judicial Campaigns, 2009–2010

Sector	High Court Candidates ($)	Appellate Court Candidates ($)	Total	Percentage of Overall Total
Lawyers, Lobbyists, and Law Firms	8,366,950	6,352,163	14,719,113	33
Self-Financed Candidates	1,320,047	3,452,486	4,772,533	11
Political Party Committees	3,486,599	876,904	4,363,503	10
General Business	2,215,769	517,587	2,733,356	6
Organized Labor	2,212,591	504,278	2,716,869	6
Finance, Insurance, and Real Estate	1,493,448	627,754	2,121,202	5
Total	19,095,404	12,331,172	31,426,076	70

Note: Data are for 2010.

Source: National Institute on Money in State Politics, "Money in Judicial Elections, 2009-2010." Available at http://www.followthemoney.org/press/ReportView.phtml?r=485.

Appointment–Retention Judicial Election Plan

Appointment by the governor followed by a retention election combines the elective and appointive systems of selection. Under this Missouri plan, a select committee of judges, attorneys, and laypeople make nominations for judicial vacancies. (In various states these nominating committees are called the Judicial Nominating Commission, the Judicial Council, the Commission on Court Appointments, etc.) The governor appoints one of the committee's nominees to office. After the judge has served a specified time period (usually one year), the judge's name is placed on a nonpartisan ballot without any other name in opposition. "Shall judge (the name of the judge is inserted) of the (the name of the court is inserted) be retained in office? Yes_____No_____." If voters vote yes, the judge is then entitled to a full term of office. If the voters vote no, the governor must select another name from those submitted by the nominating committee and repeat the whole process.

In practice, a judge is hardly ever defeated in a retention election, in part for the same reasons that make it difficult to defeat an incumbent judge (see preceding discussion). Moreover, since "you can't beat somebody with nobody," running in a judicial retention election is the equivalent of being unopposed. The effect is to place judicial selection in the hands of the judges or attorneys who compose the nominating committee and the governor, with only a semblance of voter participation. Reformers argue that the plan removes judges from politics and spares the electorate the problem of voting on judicial candidates when they know little about their professional qualifications. While less than 2 percent of judges are voted out of office in retention elections,[28] it *can* happen and did in Iowa in 2010. Three Iowa Supreme Court justices ruled a state statute defining marriage exclusively as the union between one man and one woman as unconstitutional. This ruling mobilized voters opposed to same sex marriage to campaign against the justices' retention; they were soundly defeated.

Status

Judges are rarely recruited from among the most prestigious high-paying law firms. Judges at the trial level may earn $100,000 to over $180,000 per year, and appellate and supreme court judges in excess of $200,000 or more (chief justice). These incomes exceed those of the average attorney, but they are lower than salaries of senior partners at elite law firms. Moreover, judges are restricted in investments and opportunities for outside income by judicial ethics codes. While a judge enjoys status in his or her courtroom, much of the work at the trial court level is tedious and repetitive. Finally, many elite lawyers do not relish the political tasks required to secure a judgeship—garnering the support of the bar association's judicial selection panel, or attracting the nod of the governor, or worse, campaigning for the office in an election.

**Candy VanDercar Knows Courtroom Experience Counts...
Because the Courtroom is the Extension of the Judge**

The St. Petersburg Times

"...VanDercar has the most diversified resume.

...VanDercar's trial experience sets her apart from the rest of the field.... Voters should give her the chance..."

Editorial - August 21, 2006

Experience

Jury Trials	32 jury trials
Courtroom experience	Has handled *over 3500* judicial cases
Legal Experience	Family law & criminal litigation

The VanDercar Record

- Graduate of Stetson Law School
- 17 years as a school psychologist
- Masters Degree in School Psychology
- Past President and Founding Member Pasco County League of Women Voters
- Past Council Member, Florida KIDS COUNT
- Trained as a Guardian ad Litem
- Florida Supreme Court Certified Mediator in: family, county and dependency issues

VOTE CANDY *for* **County Court Judge Group 7** **VANDERCAR**

Judicial candidates' ads stress experience, law school credentials, and community involvement but do not include information on how candidates would rule from the bench once elected. But citizens often want to know whether the person would be tough on criminals or would be more inclined to rule for rehabilitation or probation. Consequently, citizens complain they cannot get the type of information they would really like to have about judicial candidates. However, laws limiting such information are designed to maintain the perception that once judges are elected, they will be objective, rather than partisan, in their rulings.

Gender and Race

The United States is more diverse than ever, but its state judges are not, regardless of whether it is an appointed or elected system.[29] Women and minorities are underrepresented on courts at all levels. Things are improving, albeit slowly, as more women and minorities graduate from law school. According to the National Association of Women Judges, 27 percent of all state court judges are female. They comprise 32 percent of state supreme justices, 32 percent of intermediate appellate courts, 25 percent of general trial courts, and 31 percent of limited and special jurisdiction courts.[30] Judges of color make up some 10 percent of the nation's state supreme court and intermediate appellate court judges, 10 percent of the general trial court judges, and 7 percent of limited jurisdiction trial court judges. African Americans make up 4 percent of all state court judges, Latinos 3 percent, Asian/Pacific Islanders less than 1 percent, and Native Americans even fewer.[31] The lack of racial/ethnic diversity on the bench is cited as one reason for distrust of the legal system in minority communities.[32]

Party Affiliation

Traditionally, Republicans did proportionately better in winning judgeships than in winning legislative seats or governorships when they were the minority party. Most of the judges selected in nonpartisan elections refuse to identify themselves with a political party, as do nearly all the judges selected under the appointment–retention election plans, although the media and challengers may try their best to "paint" a judge as a Democrat or a Republican based on his or her past voter registration information, which is public information. Judges selected in partisan elections, of course, usually do not hesitate to identify themselves as Republicans or Democrats.

✳ Disciplining and Removing Judges

Usually state constitutions spell out the methods to be used to remove state judges. The most common method of removal is by **judicial conduct commissions,** in combination with state supreme courts. All states have some type of judicial disciplinary body, often made up of judges, lawyers, and citizens, with the authority to hold hearings and make recommendations regarding members of the judiciary. They may recommend a judge be suspended, fined, censured, involuntarily retired, or removed, but the supreme court makes the final determination.[33] Nationally in one year alone, 12 judges were removed from office, 22 resigned or retired, and 82 were publicly sanctioned.

Almost all states have constitutional provisions for removing state judges by impeachment. The decision about whether to formally charge or indict a judge is made by the state House of Representatives; the actual trial takes place in the state Senate. The Senate determines guilt or innocence. Grounds for impeachment include "malfeasance," "misfeasance," "gross misconduct," "gross immorality," "high crimes," "habitual intemperance," and "maladministration."[34] Of course, state laws define what each of those terms means. Historically, impeachment rarely happened. Today, more judges are being threatened with impeachment as citizens and watchdog groups alike have honed in on the ethics of judges or their judicial rulings.

Sixteen states have a provision for **legislative address**—a procedure that allows the state legislature, often with the governor's consent, to vote to remove a judge from the bench. But it has rarely been used until recently, when 14 bills to remove judges were introduced in seven states. These judges were deemed "judicial activists" by legislators wanting them removed. None of these removal attempts were successful.[35] The **recall procedure** has not been used very often either, primarily because only a few states allow recall elections for judges. Even where judges are elected, few are ever tossed out of office by voters using the recall process.

JUDICIAL CONDUCT COMMISSIONS

Judicial disciplinary body, often made up of judges, lawyers, and citizens, with the authority to hold hearings and make recommendations regarding members of the judiciary.

LEGISLATIVE ADDRESS

Procedure that allows the state legislature, often with the governor's consent, to vote to remove a judge from the bench.

RECALL PROCEDURE

The process by which citizens may instigate a vote for the recall of a member of the judiciary, usually through the petition process.

Competition in Judicial Elections

Historically, judicial elections have produced very little competition. From 1986 through 2008, only about one-third of state supreme court justices seeking reelection faced any real competition.[36] (In *retention* elections judges can only be challenged by a "No" vote.) Incumbent state supreme court justices running for retention or reelection are seldom defeated. A careful study of judicial elections in the states over the 12-year period revealed that only 2 percent of all state supreme court justices voted upon for retention were defeated. In nonpartisan elections 7 percent of incumbent justices were defeated, and in partisan elections 26 percent of incumbent justices were defeated.[37]

In the 2010s, state judicial elections have become much more competitive. Some attribute this shift to the fact that judicial candidates are less restricted in how they may campaign. (The U.S. Supreme Court in *Republican Party of Minnesota* v. *White* ruled that limiting a judicial candidate's right to express his or her views on political issues likely to come before the court was unconstitutional.) New studies of state judicial elections are finding that judicial campaigns resemble campaigns for any other office, filled with fundraising and television advertising by both the candidates and 527s. Judicial elections are more closely contested: where there are lots of lawyers or a new judge; when they are partisan, involve an open seat, and are held in a presidential election year; and in a state where justices have longer terms, can determine whether citizen initiatives get on the ballot, and decide a high number of tort cases.[38]

| 9.6 | JUDICIAL DECISION MAKING |

Explain how judicial decisions are made in both state trial and supreme courts, and compare judicial activism and judicial restraint.

Social scientists know more about the behavior of U.S. Supreme Court justices and federal court judges than they know about the thousands of state and local judges throughout the nation. This is largely because the decisions of federal courts are very visible and closely watched by lawyers and scholars.

Trial Courts

The actions of trial judges do not appear, at first glance, to have broad political impact. Nevertheless, trial court judges have enormous discretion in both civil and criminal cases. Perhaps the most dramatic and visible area of trial judge discretion is **sentencing**. Trial court judges display great disparities in the sentences they give out in identical cases. As most good attorneys know, as well as many defendants with long criminal records, it matters a great deal who sits as the judge in your case. The outcome of *most* criminal cases is decided in "**plea bargaining**" between prosecuting attorneys and defense attorneys, where defendants agree to plead guilty to a lesser offense and the prosecution agrees not to press more serious charges or ask for stiffer penalties. However, the bargain must be approved by the judge. Wise attorneys know in advance what kinds of bargains different judges are likely to accept. It is *not* the determination of guilt or innocence that concerns judges, so much as the processing of cases, the acceptance of pleas, and sentencing. One study presented 48 trial judges in Wisconsin with the same hypothetical case: breaking and entering, one count, in which the defendant was a 25-year-old, employed white male without any previous record. The sentences ranged from 11 months in jail to 30 days of unsupervised probation.[39]

SENTENCING
A judge's decision as to the punishment to be given to a person convicted of a crime.

PLEA BARGAIN *agreement*
An agreement by a criminal defendant to plead guilty to lesser charges with lighter penalties in order to avoid a jury trial.

Supreme Courts

Criminal appeals account for less than one-third of the workload of state supreme courts. The largest proportion of state supreme court decision making involves economic interests. (Those opposed to judicial elections point to the large campaign contributions to judicial candidates coming from key economic sectors.) (See Figure 9–3.) The large number of cases involving economic interests results from the important role of the states in the allocation of economic resources. All states regulate public utilities, including water and electric, gas, and public transportation companies. The insurance industry is state regulated. Labor relations and worker's compensation cases are frequently found in state courts. Litigation over natural resources, real estate, small-business regulations, gas, oil, lumber and mining, alcoholic beverage control, racing, and gambling reflects the importance of state regulation in these fields.

There is a correlation between the kinds of economic litigation decided by state supreme courts and the socioeconomic environment of the state. Supreme courts in poorer, rural states spend more time on private economic litigation (wills, trusts, estates, contracts, titles, and so on), while courts in urban industrial states wrestle with corporate law and governmental regulation of large economic interests. Justices are also called upon to make decisions in political controversies—disputes over elections, appointments to government positions, and jurisdictional squabbles between governments.

Partisanship in State Courts

What is the impact of the party affiliation of the judges in court decision making? Party affiliation probably has little impact on decisions in lower trial courts, where much of the litigation has little to do with policymaking. However, several early studies showed that party affiliation tended to correlate with state supreme court decision making.[40] Democratic judges tended to decide more frequently for (1) the administrative agency in business regulation cases, (2) the claimant in unemployment compensation, (3) the government in tax cases, (4) the tenant in landlord–tenant cases, (5) the consumer in sale-of-goods cases, and (6) the employee in employee injury cases. And a more recent study showed that Democratic judges, especially those appointed rather than elected and those serving for long terms, were more likely to oppose the death penalty than Republican judges.[41] Even among the lawyer ranks, there is a general partisan divide: "Plaintiff's lawyers (often Democrats) represent individuals who sue insurance companies, hospitals, and other businesses and organizations for injuries or other damages, and defendants' lawyers (often Republicans) defend these organizations from lawsuits."[42]

The Federalist Society is an organization of conservative lawyers and law students seeking to challenge the prevailing liberal judicial activism in most law schools. It began at Yale Law School, Harvard Law School, and the University of Chicago Law School in 1982 "to promote the principles that the state exists to preserve freedom, that the separation of governmental powers is central to our Constitution, and that it is emphatically the duty of the judiciary to say what the law is, not what it should be."

The Society is committed to the strict construction of the Constitution and its interpretation according to the original intent of the Founders. It frequently cites Alexander Hamilton in Federalist 78 arguing the virtue of judicial restraint: "It can be of no weight to say that the courts, under pretense of a repugnancy, may substitute their own pleasure to the constitutional intentions of the legislature."

The Society sponsors speakers and debates on constitutional issues and public policy questions. Funding comes from member dues and grants from conservative foundations. The logo of the Society features James Madison, although Madison later identified himself as a "Democratic Republican" in opposition to the Federalist Party. The membership of the Society has included Supreme Court Chief Justice John Roberts and Associate Justices Antonin Scalia and Samuel Alito.

Judicial Activism versus Restraint

Great legal scholars have argued the merits of activism versus self-restraint in judicial decision making for more than a century.[43] (See *Up Close*: The Federalist Society: Proponents of Judicial Restraint.) The traditional restraint of state courts has been increasingly challenged in recent years by activism on the part of some state courts. As noted earlier, some state supreme courts have decided to go beyond the U.S. Supreme Court in finding new constitutional rights for citizens. And several state supreme courts have insisted on protections for criminal defendants that go beyond those provided by the U.S. Supreme Court.[44]

Liberals, Conservatives, and Judicial Activism

JUDICIAL ACTIVISM

The making of new laws through judicial interpretation of laws and constitutions.

JUDICIAL RESTRAINT

Self-imposed limits on courts to defer to legislative intent or to previous court decisions.

Theoretically, activist and the more restrained views of the judicial role are independent of liberal or conservative ideology. That is, **judicial activism** could be used in support of either liberal or conservative goals; or alternatively, **judicial restraint** could limit the lawmaking of judges disposed to either liberal or conservative ideas. However, there appears to be a tendency for liberal judges to be more activist than conservative judges. But the major impact of ideology is *through* the role orientation of judges. Self-restraint reduces the impact of ideology on judges' decisions. Activism greatly increases the impact of judges' ideologies. Activist judges are overtly ideological in reactions to criminal appeals—activist liberal judges vote for the defendant far more frequently than activist conservative judges who tend to support the prosecution.[45] Although modified by role orientation, liberal and conservative ideology can be influential in state supreme court decision making.

A careful study of the ideological predispositions of supreme courts in the 50 states produced a ranking from liberal to conservative. Among the most liberal state supreme courts were Hawaii, Rhode Island, Maryland, Massachusetts, New York, Connecticut, and California. Among the most conservative were Arizona, Mississippi, New Hampshire, Iowa, Kansas, Nebraska, Idaho, Indiana, Nevada, and Texas.[46] And another study of state supreme court justices concluded that their religious affiliation also affected their decision making: evangelical justices were found to be significantly more conservative than mainline Protestant, Catholic, and Jewish justices in death penalty, gender discrimination, and obscenity cases.[47]

CRIME IN THE STATES

Crime rates are the subject of a great deal of popular discussion. Crime rates are based on the Federal Bureau of Investigation's *Uniform Crime Reports,* but the FBI reports are compiled from figures supplied by state and local police agencies. (See Figure 9–2.) The FBI has established a uniform classification of the number of serious crimes per 100,000 people that are known to the police: **violent crimes** (crimes committed against persons)—murder and non-negligent manslaughter, forcible rape, robbery, and aggravated assault and **property crimes** (crimes committed against property)—burglary, larceny, arson, and theft, including auto theft. However, one should be cautious in interpreting official crime rates. They are really a function of several factors: the tendencies of victims to report crimes to police, the accuracy of police departments in tabulating crime, and the amount of crime itself.

CRIME RATE

The number of serious offenses reported to police per 100,000 population, as tabulated by the FBI.

VIOLENT CRIME

Crimes against persons, including murder and non-negligent manslaughter, forcible rape, robbery, and aggravated assault.

PROPERTY CRIME

Crimes against property, including burglary, larceny, arson, and theft.

Trends in Crime Rates

From 1960 to 1980 the national crime rate rose dramatically, and "law and order" became an important political issue. But in the early 1980s crime rates leveled off and even declined slightly from their record years. It was widely believed that the early rapid increase and later moderation was a product of age group changes in the population: The early baby boom had expanded the size of the "crime-prone" age group in the population, people age 15 to 24; later, crime rates leveled off when this age group was no longer increasing as a percentage of the population. In the early 1980s many analysts were looking forward to gradual decreases in crime rates based on smaller crime-prone age groups. But by 1990 crime rates had soared upward again. The new factor in the crime rate equation appeared to be the introduction of relatively cheap "crack" cocaine and later methamphetamine ("meth"). Now, it is prescription drugs. Approximately 4.7 million people used prescription drugs nonmedically for the first time in 2008.[48] Perhaps as many as one-half of all crimes today are drug related.

FIGURE 9–2 Crime Rates in the United States

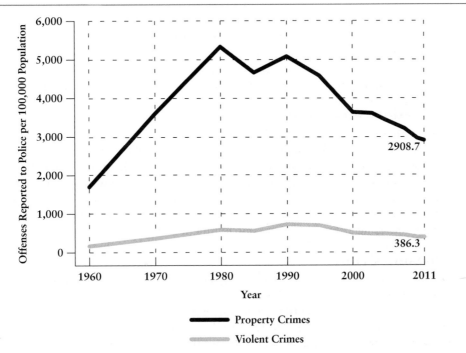

Source: Federal Crime Bureau of Investigation, "Crime in the United States, Uniform Crime Reports 2011," Table 1. Available at http://www. fbi.gov/about-us/cjis/ucr/crime-in-the-u.s/2011/crime-in-the-u.s.-2011/tables/table-1.

Many crimes committed today are drug-related. Law enforcement officials in Oregon and elsewhere frequently use dope sniffing dogs to detect drugs in suspicious-looking vehicles stopped for traffic violations.

Since peaking in the early 1990s, crime rates have been on a steady decline nationally. There are multiple explanations for this decline. Some attribute declining crime rates to the "**get-tough movement**" characterized by police "crackdowns," longer minimum sentences for violent criminals, longer prison sentences for repeat offenders, including "three strikes you're out" laws, determinate (absolute) sentences, more extensive use of surveillance cameras, more officers on the street, more targeted policing of high-crime areas, and more prisons.[49] The focus of the get-tough movement is more on punishment and deterrence than on rehabilitation.

Others attribute falling crime rates to increased efforts to rehabilitate offenders. They point to successes related to community outreach programs aimed at young offenders, in-prison education, mental health, substance abuse assistance, spiritually focused programs, intensive supervised probation, electronic monitoring, housing offenders in community residential centers rather than in prisons, programs aimed at helping offenders reintegrate into the community after release from prison, and even decriminalization of certain crimes.

"GET-TOUGH MOVEMENT"

Reaction to crime rates characterized by a focus on punishment and deterrence than on rehabilitation.

Demographic and economic theories for why crime rates have fallen also abound. Demographers believe the aging of the population has been a factor. Younger people now make up a smaller proportion of the population and it is young people (men more than women) who commit the most crime. Some criminologists credit the recession, specifically high unemployment rates, for the drop in residential burglaries. More people at home, with fewer cash and valuables on hand, makes a home a less-attractive target.[50]

Variations among the States

Crime rates in some states (e.g., South Carolina, Louisiana) are double those in other states (e.g., South Dakota, North Dakota). (See "*Rankings of the States:* Crime Rate and Incarceration Rate.") Generally crime rates are higher in border and coastal states, with more mobile populations and wider wealth gaps between the rich and the poor. Crime rates are also higher in cities that have lost population, like Flint, Detroit, New Orleans, Newark, Oakland, and Cleveland. Police chiefs in these cities also point to high levels of poverty, drugs, and gang crimes as major contributing factors.[51]

Juvenile Crime

The juvenile system is not designed for deterrence. Children are not held personally responsible for their actions, in the belief that they do not possess the ability to understand the nature or consequences of their behavior or its rightness or wrongness. Yet juvenile crime, most of which is committed by 15- to 17-year-olds, accounts for about 16 percent of the nation's overall crime rate. Research shows that juvenile crime, including violent offenses, peaks between 3:00 and 6:00 p.m., generally right after school lets out. Increasingly some occurs at school. During the average school year, there are hundreds of school crimes,

Crime Rate and Incarceration Rate

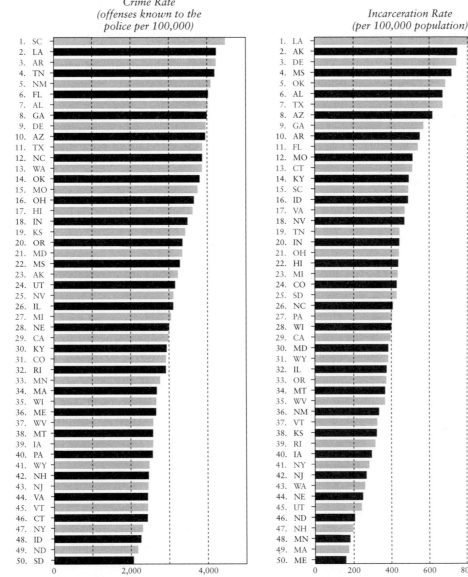

Crime Rate
(offenses known to the
police per 100,000)

1.	SC
2.	LA
3.	AR
4.	TN
5.	NM
6.	FL
7.	AL
8.	GA
9.	DE
10.	AZ
11.	TX
12.	NC
13.	WA
14.	OK
15.	MO
16.	OH
17.	HI
18.	IN
19.	KS
20.	OR
21.	MD
22.	MS
23.	AK
24.	UT
25.	NV
26.	IL
27.	MI
28.	NE
29.	CA
30.	KY
31.	CO
32.	RI
33.	MN
34.	MA
35.	WI
36.	ME
37.	WV
38.	MT
39.	IA
40.	PA
41.	WY
42.	NH
43.	NJ
44.	VA
45.	VT
46.	CT
47.	NY
48.	ID
49.	ND
50.	SD

0   2,000   4,000

Note: Data are for 2011.
Source: Federal Bureau of Investigation, Crime in the United States, Uniform Crime Reports 2011. Available at http://www.fbi.gov/about-us/cjis/ucr/crime-in-the-u.s/2011/crime-in-the-u.s.-2011/tables/table-5.

Incarceration Rate
(per 100,000 population)

1.	LA
2.	AK
3.	DE
4.	MS
5.	OK
6.	AL
7.	TX
8.	AZ
9.	GA
10.	AR
11.	FL
12.	MO
13.	CT
14.	KY
15.	SC
16.	ID
17.	VA
18.	NV
19.	TN
20.	IN
21.	OH
22.	HI
23.	MI
24.	CO
25.	SD
26.	NC
27.	PA
28.	WI
29.	CA
30.	MD
31.	WY
32.	IL
33.	OR
34.	MT
35.	WV
36.	NM
37.	VT
38.	KS
39.	RI
40.	IA
41.	NY
42.	NJ
43.	WA
44.	NE
45.	UT
46.	ND
47.	NH
48.	MN
49.	MA
50.	ME

0   200   400   600   800   1,000

Note: Data are for 2011.
Source: U.S. Department of Justice, Bureau of Justice Statistics, "Prisoners in 2011," E. Ann Carson and William J. Sabol, Dec. 2012. Available at http://bjs.ojp.usdoj.gov/content/pub/pdf/p11.pdf.

violence, and crisis incidents reported—shootings, suicides, murder-suicides, fighting, and stabbings.[52] The most horrific mass murder occurred at Sandy Hook Elementary School in Newtown, CT. A mentally ill 20-year-old male walked into the school and killed 20 children and 6 adult staffers, prompting major gun control efforts in a number of states and communities across the United States.

Offenders under 18 years of age are usually processed in a separate juvenile court system, regardless of the seriousness of their crime. Only about 5 percent of all young violent offenders are tried as adults. Very few juveniles are sentenced to detention facilities for very long. Their names are withheld from publication, eliminating the social stigma associated with their crimes. Their juvenile criminal records are expunged when they become adults, so that they can begin adulthood with "clean" records.

States differ in their approach to reforming the juvenile criminal justice system. Some have taken "get tougher" steps: more detention facilities, "boot camps" with intensive disciplinary training, and transfers of older youths who commit violent crimes to the adult justice system. Other states have moved more in the direction of rehabilitation and community-based intervention programs, especially with the overcrowding of detention facilities. So, too, has the U.S. Supreme Court which ruled in *Miller* v. *Alabama* (2012) that state laws requiring life imprisonment without parole for juveniles committing a homicide were unconstitutional. The Court cited new research showing that "the less-formed brains of the young make them less morally culpable and more capable of change [rehabilitation] later."[53] Whatever the merits of the juvenile system in the treatment of young children, it is clear that the absence of deterrence via intervention of some sort contributes to criminal behavior among *older* youths—15-, 16-, and 17-year-olds. Indeed these years are among the most crime-prone ages.

Hate Crimes

In 1990, Congress passed the Hate Crime Statistics Act, which required the Attorney General to collect data "about crimes that manifest evidence of prejudice based on race, religion, sexual orientation, or ethnicity." The Attorney General, in turn, delegated the responsibilities for compiling and publishing annual statistics on **hate crimes** to the FBI. Congress later expanded the definition of a hate crime to include bias against persons with disabilities (the Violent Crime Control and Law Enforcement Act of 1994), and crimes against a particular gender and gender identity, as well as against juveniles (Matthew Shepard and James Byrd, Jr. Hate Crime Prevention Act of 2009).[54] Hate crimes reported by the police are confirmed incidents of bias-motivated acts when the offender used hate language or left behind hate symbols.

An extensive study of hate crime victimization over an eight-year period found that on average, there are 260,000 hate crimes annually—just over 1 percent of all crimes. Violent hate crimes (rape/sexual assault, robbery, aggravated assault) are on the upswing and make up 92 percent of all hate crime victimizations, while property hate crimes (burglary, theft) make up 8 percent.[55] The offender had a weapon in at least 25 percent of the violent crime victimizations; the victim sustained an injury in about 17 percent. Nearly one-third of the incidents occurred at or near the victim's home; another 25 percent occurred in public places (parking lots, on the street, on public transportation), and 19 percent occurred at a school. Two-thirds of all hate crimes are not reported to the police. The two most common reasons for a victim's failure to report the crime are a belief that police could not or would not help (35%) or that it was dealt with in another way or the victim considered it a private or personal matter (23%).

Where such crimes take place, FBI reports show that nearly two-thirds are motivated by racial prejudice, although whites, blacks, and Hispanics had similar rates of violent hate crime victimization. The greatest increase in hate crimes has been on the basis of the victim's religion. Hate crimes based on religion are most prevalent against persons of the Jewish faith, followed by those of Islamic faith. Hate crimes based on sexual orientation are primarily against gay males.

𝗑 **HATE CRIMES**
Offenses committed against individuals on the basis of their race/ethnicity, religion, and sexual orientation.

Victimization

Official crime rates understate the real amount of crime. Citizens do not report many crimes to police. "Victimization" surveys regularly ask a national sample of individuals whether they or any member of their household has been a victim of crime during the past year, and are used to calculate **victimization rates**.[56] These surveys reveal that the actual amount of crime is greater than that reported to the FBI. The highest percentages of unreported crimes are for household theft (67%) and rape or sexual assault (65%). The lowest rate is for motor vehicle theft (17%), indicating that most people call the police when their cars are stolen.

Interviewees give a variety of reasons for their failure to report crime to the police. The most common reason is the feeling that police could not be effective in dealing with the crime. Other reasons include the feeling that the crime was a "private matter," that the offender was a member of the family, or that the victim did not want to harm the offender. Fear of reprisal is mentioned much less frequently, usually in cases of assaults and family crimes. Data collected by the FBI routinely show that the victims of violent crimes (not just of violent hate crimes) are most likely to be disproportionately young, male (except in the case of rape/sexual assault), poor, single, and a racial/ethnic minority.

Judicial Officials under Attack

A growing number of judges, prosecutors, law enforcement and corrections officers, and court employees are victims of violent crime. (See "Total Law Enforcement and Corrections Officers Deaths" in *Rankings of the States*: Police Protection and Death Rates of Law Enforcement and Corrections Officers" and "*Did You Know?* Disturbing Trend: Criminal Attacks on Judicial Officials.") Some of these occur in courtrooms across the United States. The Center for Judicial and Executive Security reports that since 2005, there have been over 400 "court-targeted-acts-of-violence incidents against court personnel including shootings, bombings, arson attacks and incidents of knifings, assaults, murder-for-hire and bomb plots, suicides, and other violence."[57] At risk are court personnel and the public at large. The situation has worsened in recent years, prompting the Conference of Chief Justices and Conference of State Court Administrators to circulate the "Ten Essential Elements for Court Security and Emergency Preparedness." Some states and localities now have court-security coordinators and officers specifically focused on making the courts safer.

VICTIMIZATION RATE
In law enforcement, the number of people who in surveys say they were victims of crime, in comparison to the population as a whole.

POLICE PROTECTION IN THE STATES

9.8

Examine the various law enforcement agencies that operate in our states and communities.

State, county, and municipal governments are all directly involved in law enforcement. Every state has a central law enforcement agency, sometimes called the state police, state troopers, state highway patrol, or even Texas Rangers. At one time, state governors had only the National Guard at their disposal to back up local law enforcement efforts, but the coming of the automobile and intercity highway traffic led to the establishment in every state of a centralized police system. In addition to patrolling the state's highways, these centralized agencies now provide expert aid and service for local police officers and strengthen law enforcement in sparsely populated regions.

Most of the states have given their central police agencies full law enforcement authority in addition to highway duties. They may cooperate with local authorities in the apprehension of criminals, or even intervene when local authorities are unable or unwilling to enforce the law. The size and influence of these agencies vary from state to state. On the whole, however, state police forces constitute a very small proportion of the total law enforcement effort in America. About 9 percent of all state and local law enforcement officers are state police, 31 percent are county officers (sheriffs and deputies), and 60 percent are city police officers. Law enforcement in the nation is principally a local responsibility. The size of a local police force is often best explained by the extent to which there have been racial disorders in the community in the past and to a lesser extent by the violent

Police Protection and Death Rates of Law Enforcement and Corrections Officers

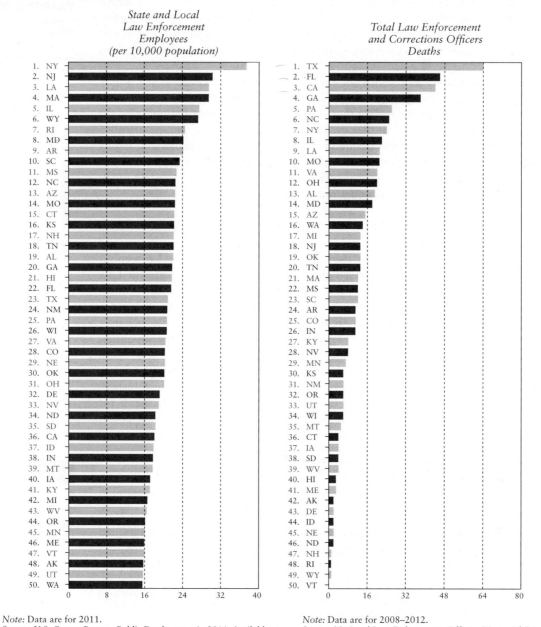

State and Local
Law Enforcement
Employees
(per 10,000 population)

1.	NY
2.	NJ
3.	LA
4.	MA
5.	IL
6.	WY
7.	RI
8.	MD
9.	AR
10.	SC
11.	MS
12.	NC
13.	AZ
14.	MO
15.	CT
16.	KS
17.	NH
18.	TN
19.	AL
20.	GA
21.	HI
22.	FL
23.	TX
24.	NM
25.	PA
26.	WI
27.	VA
28.	CO
29.	NE
30.	OK
31.	OH
32.	DE
33.	NV
34.	ND
35.	SD
36.	CA
37.	ID
38.	IN
39.	MT
40.	IA
41.	KY
42.	MI
43.	WV
44.	OR
45.	MN
46.	ME
47.	VT
48.	AK
49.	UT
50.	WA

0   8   16   24   32   40

Total Law Enforcement
and Corrections Officers
Deaths

1.	TX
2.	FL
3.	CA
4.	GA
5.	PA
6.	NC
7.	NY
8.	IL
9.	LA
10.	MO
11.	VA
12.	OH
13.	AL
14.	MD
15.	AZ
16.	WA
17.	MI
18.	NJ
19.	OK
20.	TN
21.	MA
22.	MS
23.	SC
24.	AR
25.	CO
26.	IN
27.	KY
28.	NV
29.	MN
30.	KS
31.	NM
32.	OR
33.	UT
34.	WI
35.	MT
36.	CT
37.	IA
38.	SD
39.	WV
40.	HI
41.	ME
42.	AK
43.	DE
44.	ID
45.	NE
46.	ND
47.	NH
48.	RI
49.	WY
50.	VT

0   16   32   48   64   80

Note: Data are for 2011.
Source: U.S. Census Bureau, Public Employment in 2011. Available at http://www.census.gov/govs/apes/.

Note: Data are for 2008–2012.
Source: National Law Enforcement Officers Memorial Fund. Available at http://www.nleomf.org/facts/officer-fatalities-data/officer-fatality-data.html.

crime rate and the size of the minority population.[58] However, attitudes toward the police are not the sole function of race or class; they are also affected by a resident's perceptions of the community's social capital.[59]

The County Sheriff

There are 3,083 sheriffs in the United States. Historically, the county sheriff has been the keystone of law enforcement in the United States. Sheriffs and their deputies are still the principal enforcement and arresting officers in rural counties and in the unincorporated fringe areas of many urban counties. (Three states—Alaska, Connecticut, and Hawaii—do not have sheriff's offices at the county level.) In addition, the sheriff serves as an executive agent for county and state courts in both civil and criminal matters, and maintains the county jail for the retention of persons whose trials or sentences are pending or who are serving short sentences. The sheriff's office is a political one; in every state with county sheriffs (except Rhode Island), the sheriff is an elected official. Sheriffs are elected to four-year terms in 41 states, two-year terms in 3 states, a three-year term in 1 state, and a six-year term in 1 state.[60]

Prior to 9/11, heavier reliance upon the sheriff's office for law enforcement was more characteristic of rural states. In the more urbanized states, city police forces played the larger role. However, since 9/11, federal and state laws dictate that sheriffs must play a major role in homeland security preparedness, regardless of whether the county is rural or urban. That mandate plus the growing number of drug-related incidents, street gangs, identity theft rings, and hate crimes have thrust urban sheriffs into more active roles, often working in partnership with city police chiefs.

City Police

Urban police departments are the most important instruments of law enforcement and public safety in the nation today. Nationwide, there are around 13,000 local police departments. City police officers vastly outnumber all other state and county law enforcement officers combined. The urban police department does more than merely enforce the law; it engages in a wide range of activities for social control. In large police departments, officers usually are assigned to a specific type of duty. Some are uniformed patrol officers who are assigned to patrol a specific geographic area. During their shift, they may identify, pursue, and arrest suspected criminals; resolve problems within the community; and enforce traffic laws. Other police officers specialize in such diverse fields as chemical and microscopic analysis, training and firearms instruction, or handwriting and fingerprint identification. Some cities may have special police units such as horseback, bicycle, motorcycle, or harbor patrol; canine corps; or special weapons and tactics (SWAT) or emergency response teams. A few local and special law enforcement officers primarily perform jail-related duties or work in courts.[61]

Police and Crime

The total number of full-time sworn police officers nationwide has grown to more than 800,000. This figure includes all city, county, state, federal, and specialized law enforcement agencies. But police protection varies considerably among the 50 states, with some states having nearly 40 law enforcement personnel per 10,000 population, and other states with fewer than 20 (see Police Protection in "*Rankings of the States:* Police Protection and Death Rates of Law Enforcement and Corrections Officers"). But the number of officers has *not* kept abreast of crime. On the contrary, the number of police officers relative to the number of reported crimes has declined steadily. This decline is unique to police personnel, as growth in the number of other state and local employees has generally exceeded the growth of their workload, with some exceptions during the Great Recession.

<table>
<tr><td>9.9</td><td></td></tr>
</table>

Describe the law enforcement, peacekeeping, and service provider functions of law enforcement; compare the proactive and reactive approaches to police activity; and assess the role of the citizen in law enforcement.

POLICE AND LAW ENFORCEMENT

Police perform at least three important functions in urban society—law enforcement, keeping the peace, and furnishing services. Actually, law enforcement may take up only a small portion of a police officer's daily activity, perhaps only 10 percent. The service function is far more common—attending accidents, directing traffic, escorting crowds, assisting stranded motorists, and so on. The function of peacekeeping is also very common—breaking up fights, quieting noisy parties, handling domestic or neighborhood quarrels, and the like. It is in this function that police exercise the greatest discretion in the application of the law. In most of these incidents blame is difficult to determine, participants are reluctant to file charges, and police must use personal discretion in handling each case.

Police are on the front line of society's efforts to resolve conflict. Indeed, instead of a legal or law enforcement role, the police are more likely to adopt a peacekeeping role. Police are usually lenient in their arrest practices; that is, they use their arrest power less often than the law allows. Rather than arresting people, the police prefer first to reestablish order. Of course, the decision to be more or less lenient in enforcing the law gives the police a great deal of discretion. But the growing tendency of Americans to sue police officers makes them more prone to "go by the book" in arresting individuals. Some departments now even put video cams in police cars to permit officers to record interactions with arrestees in the event they are sued.

Police "Culture"

What factors influence police decision making? Probably the first factor to influence police behavior is the attitude of the other people involved in police encounters. If people adopt a cooperative attitude, display deference and respect for the officers, and conform to police expectations, they are much less likely to be arrested than those who show disrespect or use abusive language toward police. Formal police training emphasizes self-control and caution in dealing with the public, but on-the-job experiences probably reinforce predispositions toward distrust of others. The element of danger in police work makes police officers naturally suspicious of others. They see many of the "worst kind" of people, and they see even the "best kind" at their worst.

Police and Crime Reduction

Does increased police protection significantly reduce crime? The common assumption is that increased numbers of police officers and increased police expenditures can significantly reduce crime in cities. However, unfortunately, it is very difficult to produce firm evidence to support this assumption. So many other factors may affect crime rates in cities—size, density, youth, unemployment, race, poverty, and so on—that police activity appears insignificant.

Community Policing

Most police activity is "reactive": typically two officers in a patrol car responding to a radio dispatcher who is forwarding reports of incidents. Police agencies frequently evaluate themselves in terms of the number and frequency of patrols, the number of calls responded to, and the elapsed time between the call and the arrival of officers on the scene. But there is little evidence that any of these measures affect crime rates or even citizens' fear of crime or satisfaction with the police.

An alternative strategy is for police to become more "proactive": typically becoming more visible in the community by walking or bicycling the sidewalks of high crime areas; learning to recognize individuals on the streets and winning their confidence and respect; deterring or scaring away drug dealers, prostitutes, and their customers by a police presence. Proponents argue that where effective community policing is in place, citizens have a more favorable opinion of law enforcement in their neighborhood and believe it helps stop crime before it occurs. But this "**community policing**" is often expensive and potentially more dangerous for police officers.

Police Crackdowns

Police crackdowns—beefed-up police actions against juvenile gangs, prostitutes, and drug traffickers; the frisking of likely suspects on the street for guns and drugs; and arrests for (often ignored) public drinking, graffiti, and vandalism—can reduce crime only if supported by the community as well as prosecutors and judges. Crime rates, even murder rates, have been significantly reduced during periods of police crackdowns in major cities.[62] However, these efforts are often sporadic; enthusiasm ebbs as jails fill up and the workload of prosecutors and courts multiplies.

"Broken Windows"

New York City once ranked among the most crime-ridden of the nation's cities, but no longer. In 1993 the city's newly elected mayor Rudolph Giuliani began to implement what became known as the "**broken windows**" strategy in law

COMMUNITY POLICING
More active involvement of police with individuals and groups on streets and sidewalks.

"BROKEN WINDOWS" STRATEGY
The theory that overall crime rates can be reduced by strictly enforcing laws against petty offenses.

Horse mounted police are examples of special police units. In large cities, these units are often used for crowd control.

enforcement. The strategy is based on the notion that one neglected broken window in a building will soon lead to many other broken windows. In crime-fighting, this theory translates into more arrests for petty offenses (e.g., subway turnstile jumping, graffiti, vandalism, and aggressive panhandling, including unwanted automobile window washing) in order not only to improve the quality of life in the city but also to lead to the capture of suspects wanted for more serious crimes. This strategy was coupled with the use of the latest computer mapping technology to track crime statistics and pinpoint unusual activity in specific neighborhoods. Each police precinct was regularly evaluated on the number and types of crimes occurring in it.

The introduction of these hard-line tactics created more than a little controversy. Civil libertarians, as well as many minority-group leaders, complained that these police tactics fell disproportionately on minorities and the poor. It was alleged that Mayor Giuliani's hard-nosed attitude toward crime created an atmosphere that led to increased police brutality.

But the "broken windows" strategy appears to have made New York City a safer city. Over a five-year period following the introduction of Mayor Giuliani's tough policies, the city's overall crime rate fell by an unprecedented 50 percent, and murders fell by 70 percent. After decades of social malaise, New York City was no longer seen as "ungovernable," but rather as one of the nation's leading tourist destinations and the self-proclaimed "Capital of the World." It has remained so even after the 9/11 attack.

Citizen Surveillance: Safety versus Privacy

Technology advances, such as security cameras, red light cameras, and unmanned drones, have made citizen surveillance a key component of law enforcement strategies to combat crime. In a survey, over half of the respondents felt surveillance cameras were very important for helping law enforcement solve crimes and that surveillance and security cameras actually reduce crime, with over 70 percent favoring the use of security cameras in public places. However, over 20 percent of the respondents felt surveillance cameras have violated their privacy,[63] which highlights the public concern, and major argument against surveillance technology, that such surveillance devices can invade the individual's right to privacy.

The increased use of unmanned drones abroad has triggered discussion on using drones domestically for surveillance. Law enforcement and other supporters of domestic drone use say that drones can be used in situations where manned aircraft would be either too expensive or too dangerous, including search and rescue, manhunts, and missions where officers would benefit from a different vantage point. Public concern regarding privacy rights has led some states to pass legislation banning or restricting drone use.[64] While the majority of Americans support law enforcement use of surveillance cameras, they are much less sure about using drones domestically. Less than one-third of likely voters favor police agency use of drones in the United States and over half oppose drone use.[65] Law enforcement and public officials will need to find ways to balance the public safety with the public's right to privacy.

Citizen Action

Anticrime efforts by private citizens have risen dramatically over the last decade. Today, there are over 1 million private security guards overseeing businesses, banks, ports, airports, stores, hotels, and residential communities. (In effect, this force doubles the size of the nation's police force.) Improved security devices are now found in virtually all commercial establishments—from gas stations and neighborhood convenience stores to banks and schools. Millions of Americans live in communities with security gates and guards and millions more have installed security systems in their houses. Citizen patrol groups and "town watch" associations have multiplied. When budget cutbacks hit local police departments during the Great Recession, some neighborhood homeowners associations hired their own "force" but the move was not without controversy. Residents of poorer neighborhoods complained about unequal protection by their local government.

Police Efficiency

One commonly used measure of police efficiency is the clearance rate—a statistic generated by the FBI based on local police reports. Clearance rates are arrest rates, not conviction rates. Crimes least likely to be cleared are those which seldom produce eyewitnesses or other useful information, while those most likely to be cleared occur in cases in which the victim and perpetrators know each other. On average across the nation, police claim to solve about 13 percent of burglaries and 12 percent of auto thefts. Police have much higher clearance rates for murder and non-negligent manslaughter (65%), aggravated assault (57%), and forcible rape (41%).[66]

THE POLITICS OF PROSECUTION

9.10

Explain the role of the prosecutor in the judicial system, evaluate whether prosecutorial discretion and plea bargaining yield desirable outcomes, and assess the effectiveness of grand juries as a check on prosecutors.

Prosecution is also part of the political process. Legislatures and governors enact policy, but its enforcement depends on the decisions of prosecutors as well as judges. Political pressures are most obvious in the enforcement of controversial policies—gambling laws, Sunday closing laws, liquor rules, laws against prostitution, and other laws that are contrary to the interests of significant segments of the population. Prosecution also involves decision making about the allocation of law enforcement resources to different types of offenses—traffic violations, juvenile delinquency, auto theft, assault, burglary, larceny, and robbery. Decisions must be made about what sections of the city should be most vigorously protected and what segments of the population will be most closely watched. The public prosecutor, sometimes called the district attorney (D.A.) or state's attorney, is at the center of diverse pressures concerning law enforcement. According to the Bureau of Justice Statistics, 85 percent of all chief prosecutors reported they had been elected or appointed to a four-year term.[67]

The political nature of the prosecutor's job is suggested by the frequency with which this job leads to higher political office. Prosecuting attorney is often a stepping-stone to state and federal judgeships, congressional seats, and even the governorship. Ambitious D.A.s, concerned with their political future, may seek to build a reputation as a crusader against crime and vice, while at the same time maintaining the support and friendship of important interests in the community.

Prosecutor's Discretion

The political power of prosecutors stems from their discretion in deciding (1) whether or not to prosecute in criminal cases, and (2) whether prosecution will be on more serious or less serious charges. Prosecutors may decide simply to drop charges ("**nol-pros**") when they feel adequate proof is lacking, or when they feel that police have committed a procedural error that infringed on the defendant's rights, when they feel that the resources of their office would be better allocated by pursuing other cases. About half of all felony arrests result in dismissal of charges against the defendant. Prosecutors may also engage in "plea bargaining"—reducing the charges from more serious to less serious crimes in exchange for defendants' promises to plead guilty. Or prosecutors may reduce charges because they believe it will be easier in court to obtain a guilty verdict on the lesser charge.

NOL-PROS

A prosecutor's decision to simply drop charges.

The Role of Grand Juries

Are there any checks on the power of prosecutors? In principle, the grand jury is supposed to determine whether evidence presented to it by the prosecutor is sufficient to warrant the placing of a person on trial in a felony case. Ideally, the grand jury serves as a check against the overzealous district attorney, and as a protection for the citizen against unwarranted harassment. However, in practice, grand juries spend very little time deliberating on the vast majority of the cases.[68] A typical grand jury spends only 5 to 10 minutes per case, primarily listening to the prosecutor's recommendation as to how the case should be decided. Over 80 percent of the cases may be decided on an immediate vote, without discussion among jurors, and almost always with unanimous votes. Finally, and most importantly, grand juries follow the recommendations of prosecutors in over 98 percent of the cases presented to them. The prosecutor controls the information submitted to grand juries, instructs them in their duties, and is usually perceived by jurors as an expert and relied on for guidance. In short, there is no evidence that grand juries provide much of a check on the power of prosecutors.

Plea Bargaining

Most convictions are obtained by guilty pleas. Indeed, about 90 percent of the criminal cases brought to trial are disposed of by guilty pleas before a judge, not trial by jury. The Constitution guarantees defendants a trial by jury (Sixth Amendment), but guilty pleas outnumber jury trials by 10–1.

Plea bargaining, in which the prosecution either reduces the seriousness of the charges, drops some but not all charges, or agrees to recommend lighter penalties in exchange for a guilty plea by the defendant, is very common. Some critics of plea bargaining view it as another form of leniency in the criminal justice system that reduces its deterrent effects. Other critics view plea bargaining as a violation of the Constitution's protection against self-incrimination and guarantee of a fair jury trial. Prosecutors, they say, threaten defendants with serious charges and stiff penalties to force a guilty plea. Still other critics see plea bargaining as an under-the-table process that undermines respect for the criminal justice system and leads to different sentences for the same crime.

It is very fortunate for the nation's court system that most defendants plead guilty. The court system would quickly break down from overload if any substantial proportion of defendants insisted on jury trials.

9.11

Examine the extent to which the American population is jailed or otherwise under the supervision of the judicial system; explain differences in incarceration rates among states; assess the effectiveness of deterrence, rehabilitation, parole, and probation; and analyze the causes and consequences of prison overcrowding.

STATE PRISONS AND CORRECTIONAL POLICIES

The United States experienced an explosive growth in its **prison population** until 2009. (The decline parallels the drop in crime rates from 2009 to 2011.) Still, millions of Americans each year are brought to a jail, police station, or juvenile home or prison. The vast majority are released within hours or days. Nearly 7 million adult men and women are under federal, state, or local probation or parole jurisdiction. About 1 in every 34 adult residents (3%) in the United States is under some form of correctional supervision. Most (57%) are on **probation**, court-ordered community supervision of convicted offenders by a probation agency. Others (12%) are on **parole** supervision following a conditional release from prison. Twenty-two percent (over 1.5 million) are inmates in state and federal prisons in the United States, amounting to almost 500 for every 100,000 population. These prisoners are serving time for serious offenses, with sentences of more than one year. Ninety percent had a record of crime before they committed the act that led to their current imprisonment. An additional 736,000 persons (11%) are temporarily residing in city or county jails at any one time across the country.[69] The annual cost of prisons ranges from less than $100,000 in small rural states like New Hampshire to nearly $8 million in big heavily urbanized states like California.[70]

The **jail population** includes persons confined to a local jail awaiting trial or awaiting sentencing, as well as persons serving sentences of less than one year. Many counties have been forced to build new jails or jointly build larger regional jails, subcontract with another local jurisdiction with more jail space capacity, or even turn to privately operated prison facilities to house the growing number of inmates. (Over 8 percent of all prisoners are housed in private correctional facilities.)[71] Overcrowding has created other problems such as prison riots, viral outbreaks, and strained budgets stemming from the need to hire more corrections officers and pay more overtime.

Prisoners in the States

States differ a great deal in the number of prisoners and the proportion of their populations behind bars. (See "Incarceration Rate" in *Rankings of the States:* Crime Rate and Incarceration Rate.") As might be expected, prisoner populations generally reflect the crime rate in the states; higher crime rate states have larger proportions of their population in prison. In recent years, the growing numbers of violent offenders and drug offenders have swelled state prison populations. Another cause of increased prison populations in the states is an increase in the length of criminal sentences. As noted earlier, many states have attempted to "get tough on crime" by legislating longer sentences for particular crimes, specifying **mandatory minimum sentences** for crimes, eliminating judicial variation in sentences, adding years to the sentences given repeat or "habitual" criminals, and abolishing parole. Some judges resent the loss of their discretion and have begun to pressure state legislators to restore some of their flexibility in sentencing. But flexibility in sentencing sometimes leads to claims of injustice, particularly when statistics show differences by race and gender.[72]

The Great Recession prompted some changes in support levels for "get tough" sentencing policies even in the conservative-leaning states with more punishment-oriented approaches to crime control. The high costs of prison construction, along with a rising number of inmates with special needs requiring additional resources or programs during incarceration (elderly, drug offenders, mentally ill, extremely violent offenders, individuals with infectious diseases such as HIV). Consequently, some of these fiscally strapped states with high levels of inmate crowding (California, Florida, Georgia, Ohio) have moved toward community alternatives to incarceration.[73] In one year alone, 15 states passed significant sentencing reform legislation; Democrats and Republicans were equally determined to cut prison populations.[74]

The Failure (and Rebirth) of Rehabilitation

Beginning in the 1970s with the explosion in urban violence and increased drug use and continuing into the 1980s and 1990s, the prevailing philosophy toward corrections in many states was punishment. Rapidly escalating crime rates and high recidivism rates raised doubts about the effectiveness of rehabilitation. Over 80 percent of all felonies were committed by repeaters—individuals who have had prior contact with the criminal justice system and were not corrected by it. Within three years of release from prison, 67 percent of the released had been rearrested and 52 percent were returned to prison. Of the "recidivists"—people returned to prison for new crimes—almost half had three or more prior prison sentences.[75]

In the 2010s, it appears that in some states, the pendulum is swinging more toward rehabilitation, partly because of costs, but also due to younger, more liberal voters who have become a larger share of the electorates. Rehabilitation-focused policies give judges more freedom to consider not only the crime, but personal characteristics of the defendant in deciding sentences. Moreover, judges in these states have the option of imposing "indeterminate" sentences (e.g., not less than one or more than five years) and leaving the decision concerning how long a prisoner will serve to parole boards. While in prison, individuals are afforded more and better opportunities to "rehabilitate" or "correct" themselves. Reformers generally recommend more education and job training, more and better facilities, smaller prisons, halfway houses where offenders can adjust to civilian life before parole, more parole officers, and greater contact between prisoners and their families and friends. While many remain skeptical that these investments can significantly reduce what criminologists call **recidivism,"** the offenders' return to crime, for the moment they are reducing the cost of keeping criminals incarcerated for long periods of time.

Prison life does little to encourage good behavior. For the most part, many inmates spend their days in idleness—watching television, weightlifting, walking, and talking in the yard. "Meaningful educational, vocational, and counseling programs are rare. Strong

JAIL POPULATION
Persons convicted of a crime and sentenced to serve a term of less than a year, or those awaiting sentencing.

MANDATORY MINIMUM SENTENCES
Minimum sentences for various crimes enacted into law by state legislatures.

RECIDIVISM
The likelihood of a former convict returning to prison for new crimes.

Prison overcrowding is a growing problem for states. When a federal court orders a state to remedy the situation, the ruling is based on the U.S. Constitution's Eighth Amendment prohibition against "cruel and unusual punishment."

inmates are permitted to pressure weaker prisoners for sex, drugs, and money. Gangs organized along racial and ethnic lines are often the real 'sovereign of the cellblocks.'"[76] Most state prison systems, like the Federal Bureau of Prisons, operate **maximum-security institutions** for high-risk inmates who have proven too violent to mix with the general prison population.

Sentencing

Clearly, indeterminate sentencing and discretion given parole boards do *not* serve the goal of deterrence. Rather, deterrence is served by making prison sentences predictable (certain) and long (severe). Potential lawbreakers are supposed to say to themselves, "If you can't serve the time, don't do the crime." Throughout the 1980s states enacted amendments to their criminal codes specifying **determinate sentences** for various crimes. The discretion of judges was restricted. Variation in sentencing was reduced (although not eliminated); judges were obliged by law to mete out sentences based on the crime and the number of previous convictions amassed by the defendant. Greater uniformity of sentencing also served the goal of reducing arbitrary, unfair, and discriminatory sentencing. For many crimes, deterrence was also strengthened by long mandatory minimum sentences. For example, many states enacted mandatory one-, two-, or three-year prison terms for the use of a gun in the commission of a felony. Now some states are rethinking strict mandatory sentencing laws, particularly for drug offenders and nonviolent offenders, due to prison overcrowding.

Prison Overcrowding

The effect of longer sentences, combined with higher crime rates and more prisoners, has been to create mammoth prison overcrowding. Overcrowding contributes directly to unsanitary and dangerous prison living conditions; it is associated with assaults, rapes, homicides, suicides, and riots. Prison staff are also placed at risk by overcrowding and the violence it produces. Lawsuits against the prison system are brought by inmates and prison personnel alike.

Federal courts have determined that prison overcrowding is a violation of the U.S. Constitution's Eighth Amendment prohibition against "cruel and unusual punishments." (Simple crowding per se is not unconstitutional; federal courts must also find evidence of adverse effects of overcrowding.) Virtually all of the states confront federal court orders to reduce prison overcrowding at one or more of their prisons or their entire prison system. Most state prison systems are near, at, or over their capacity to house prisoners. In the landmark 2011 *Brown* v. *California* decision, the U.S. Supreme Court ruled 5–4 that California had to reduce its prison population by more than 30,000 inmates. The severe overcrowding kept the state's prison system from providing help to prisoners with serious medical and mental health problems and produced "needless suffering and death"—a clear violation of the Eighth Amendment's prohibition of "cruel and unusual punishment."

Early Releases

As a result of overcrowding, most states have had to resort to **early release programs**. Sentences of prisoners are automatically reduced and those near the end of their terms are let go first. Some states deny early release to certain violent offenders, while granting it to drug offenders who have been overcrowding prisons. Nonetheless, violent criminals on the average serve less than half of their sentences, and nonviolent offenders less than one-third of their sentences. In some states, due to prison overcrowding, inmates serve only one-quarter of their sentences.[77] Early release programs are often subject to revision, even reversal, by elected officials if a high profile heinous crime is committed by a prisoner who was released early. In such a situation, the political costs may outweigh the economic costs.

The 85 Percent Solution

Media reports of **"avertable crimes"**—crimes committed by persons who would still have been imprisoned based on earlier convictions if they had served their full sentence—has placed heavy pressure on state legislatures to end early releases. In order to stem the tide of early releases, many state legislatures initially turned to the **"85 percent solution"**—mandating that all convicted felons serve at least 85 percent of the length of their sentences. These **"truth in sentencing"** laws, adopted in some form by 39 states, have effectively lengthened the average time served by prisoners. (Courts have held that prisoners convicted prior to the passage of such laws cannot be held to the new standard.) In recent years, prosecutors have been pressing for longer sentences and judges have been imposing them. This trend, together with a mandated serving of 85 percent of sentences, has added to the need for more prison space.

It is not just the need for more prison space that has prompted some states to reexamine their 85 percent laws. It is also the rising costs of providing health care for sick elderly inmates. At least 16 states already provide special housing units for geriatric inmates; more than two dozen states operate hospice facilities inside prisons to provide end-of-life care. An Arizona study found that "Prison inmates age even faster than people on the outside. A lifetime of poor diets, drug and alcohol abuse and violence, coupled with the stress of prison, triggers the earlier onset of chronic and geriatric ailments. Often, an inmate's physiological age is 10 years older than his chronological age. As a result, 55 is considered elderly in prison."[78] This situation has caused some states to consider creating early release programs for elderly prisoners who are chronically or terminally ill. Spending on medical care for prisoners costs over $335 million annually.[79]

Building More Prisons

States have been compelled to build more prisons in recent years. But taxpayers are understandably upset with the prospects of spending on average over $31,000 per prisoner each year to keep him or her behind bars.[80] But if the costs of incarceration are weighed against its benefits, taxpayers may feel better about prison construction and maintenance. A prisoner's "rap sheet" may list only three or four convictions and a dozen arrests. But interviews with offenders suggest the typical convict has committed hundreds of crimes. Various studies have attempted to estimate the dollars lost to society in the crimes committed by the typical convict in a year. Estimates run from $41,000 (car break-in), $336,000 (armed robbery), $449,000 (rape), to over $17 million for a murder.[81] These estimates include direct costs (damaged property, lost careers, prison upkeep, lawyer fees) and intangible societal costs (such as more frequent police patrols, more complicated alarm systems, more expensive life-insurance plans). This means that a year of crime may be considerably more costly to society than a year of incarceration.

EARLY RELEASE PROGRAMS

In an effort to relieve overcrowding, sentences of prisoners are automatically reduced and those near the end of their terms are let go first.

AVERTABLE CRIMES

Crimes committed by persons who would still have been imprisoned based on earlier convictions if they had served their full sentence.

85 PERCENT SOLUTION

Mandating that all convicted felons serve at least 85 percent of the length of their sentences.

"TRUTH IN SENTENCING"

Definitive punishments that leave judges no flexibility in assessing penalties.

"Three Strikes You're Out"

The "revolving-door" syndrome, with its heavy toll in crimes committed by persons previously convicted of crimes, has led to a nationwide movement to impose minimum 25-years-to-life sentences on criminals convicted of a third felony or third violent felony crime. A California citizens' initiative in 1994, Three Strikes You're Out, illustrates the popularity of this crackdown with voters; it passed 72 to 28 percent. Twenty-four states have passed similar legislation. The California initiative was begun by a father whose 18-year-old daughter had been murdered by a parolee. Some of these initiatives are broadly written to include *all* felony convictions and therefore often encompass drug offenders, bad-check writers, and other nonviolent criminals. Other initiatives specify three *violent* felony convictions and thus target a smaller population of repeat criminals. In 1995, Congress mandated life sentences for federal defendants convicted of their third violent felony.

Like the 85 percent rule, "three strikes and you're out" rules have increased the prison population and put pressure on state budgets, causing several states to alter their rules. For example, the Indiana State Legislature repealed mandatory minimum sentences in many drug cases; Louisiana amended its "three strikes" law to read that the first two "strikes" refer only to violent crimes.[82]

In general, states with tough sentencing laws are keeping them. Public opinion polls in many of those states have repeatedly shown that a majority of their citizens do not want criminals released early. But prison reformers favoring more rehabilitative approaches have continued to fight against "three strikes you're out" laws. "Instead of dealing with problems like poverty, drug abuse and mental illness, we increasingly just removed them all from view by putting them in jail. It's not an accident that so many of the most ridiculous Three Strikes cases are semi coherent homeless people or people with drug problems who came from broken homes."[83]

Probation and Parole: Effective or Not?

Probation and parole are examples of community-based corrections. Each allows a criminal offender to live in a community rather than in a jail or prison but with supervision. State officials see these alternatives to prison as big cost savers, whereas prison reformers view them as promoting and enabling rehabilitation rather than punishment focused. Probation, often court-ordered, conditionally suspends a convicted person's sentence and places that person under supervision for a set period of time, subject to good behavior. Parole allows a prisoner to be released from prison or jail after a portion of the sentence has been served but before his or her sentence is completed, again subject to supervision and continued good behavior. The average length of stay on probation is about 22 months; on parole, it is 19 months.[84] Years ago, 15 states eliminated parole when they adopted definitive sentencing. How well do these programs reduce recidivism? One study examining the effect of states' reform of "hair-trigger" parole systems that send parolees back to prison for technical violations (like missing an appointment with a parole officer) found a slight reduction in the reincarceration rate from 36 to 32 percent.[85] But another concluded that there was no clear pattern; recidivism rate reductions are heavily contingent upon the ability of supervision agencies to detect violations and respond to them.[86]

9.12

THE DEATH PENALTY

Trace the history of the death penalty in the United States, compare capital punishment across the states, and analyze whether the United States should continue to have the death penalty.

Perhaps the most heated debate in criminal justice today concerns **capital punishment**. While a majority of Americans still favor the death penalty, support has slipped in recent years. (See Figure 9–3.) Opponents of the death penalty argue that it is "cruel and unusual punishment" in violation of the Eighth Amendment of the U.S. Constitution. They also argue that the death penalty is applied unequally. A large proportion

FIGURE 9–3 Changing Attitudes toward the Death Penalty

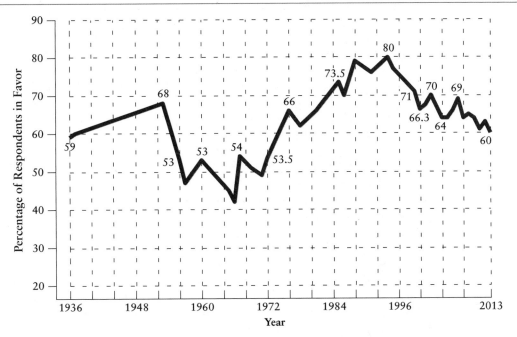

Note: Respondents were asked "Are you in favor of the death penalty for a person convicted of murder?"
Source: Gallup, Inc., "U.S. Death Penalty Support Lowest in More Than 40 Years," October 29, 2013. Available at http://www.gallup.com/poll/165626/death-penalty-support-lowest-years.aspx. Copyright © 2013 Gallup, Inc. All rights reserved. The content is used with permission; however, Gallup retains all rights of republication.

of those executed have been poor, uneducated, and nonwhite. Recognizing that in the past many indigents facing the death penalty did not have the best lawyers, Congress passed the Innocence Protection Act (formally the Justice for All Act of 2004, Public Law No. 108-405). Besides creating a DNA testing program, the Act authorizes a grant program, to be administered by the U.S. Attorney General, to improve the quality of prosecution and defense representation in capital cases. The grants may not be used to pay for lawyers in specific cases, but instead are to be used to establish, implement, or improve an effective system for providing competent legal representation to indigents charged with capital offenses or sentenced to death and seeking appellate review in state court.[87]

In contrast, there is a strong sense of justice among many Americans that demands retribution for heinous crimes—a life for a life. The death penalty dramatically signifies that society does not excuse or condone the taking of innocent lives. It symbolizes the value that society places on innocent lives. A mere jail sentence for murder devalues the life of the innocent victim. In most cases, a life sentence means less than 10 years in prison under the current parole and probation policies of most states. Convicted murderers have been set free, and some have killed again. Moreover, prison guards and other inmates are exposed to convicted murderers who have "a license to kill," because they are already serving life sentences and have nothing to lose by killing again.

Furman v. *Georgia* and Unfair Application

Prior to 1972, the death penalty was officially sanctioned by about one-half of the states. Federal law also retained the death penalty. However, no one had actually suffered the death penalty since 1967, because of numerous legal tangles and direct challenges to the constitutionality of capital punishment. In 1972, the Supreme Court ruled

CAPITAL PUNISHMENT
The death penalty. (The word *capital* is derived from the Latin word for "head"—*caput.* The Latin word for "punish" is *punire.* Combined, they mean "head punishment," that is, a cutting-off of one's head.)

that capital punishment as it was then imposed violated the Eighth and Fourteenth Amendment prohibitions against cruel and unusual punishment and due process of law.[88] The decision was made by a narrow 5–4 vote of the justices, and the reasoning in the case is very complex. Only two justices—Brennan and Marshall—declared that capital punishment itself is cruel and unusual. The other three justices in the majority—Douglas, White, and Stewart—felt that death sentences had been applied unfairly: A few individuals were receiving the death penalty for crimes for which many others were receiving much lighter sentences. These justices left open the possibility that capital punishment would be constitutional if it was specific for certain kinds of crime and applied uniformly.

The Death Penalty Reinstated

After *Furman* v. *Georgia*, most states rewrote their death penalty laws to try to ensure fairness and uniformity of application. Generally, these laws mandate the death penalty for murders committed during rape or robbery, hijacking, or kidnapping; murders of prison guards; murder with torture; multiple murders; and so on. Two trials are held: one to determine guilt or innocence and another to determine the penalty. At the second trial, evidence of "**aggravating**" and "**mitigating**" **factors** are presented; if there are aggravating factors but no mitigating factors, the death penalty is mandatory. Aggravating factors are those that make a juror more likely to impose the death penalty. Examples would be a defendant's past criminal record and the degree to which the murder was heinous, atrocious, cruel, or depraved. Mitigating factors, such as whether the murder was committed due to the extreme duress of being dominated by another person or having a serious emotional disorder, may make a juror less likely to impose the death penalty.

In 1976, in *Gregg* v. *Georgia*, the U.S. Supreme Court upheld state laws that were carefully written to ensure fairness and due process in the application of the death penalty.[89] The Court declared that capital punishment itself was not "cruel or unusual" within the meaning of the Eighth Amendment; that the authors of the Constitution did not consider it cruel or unusual; and that the reenactment of the death penalty by so many state legislatures was evidence that the death penalty was not considered cruel or unusual by contemporary state lawmakers. Today, over half the states have the death penalty. (See Figure 9–4.)

No Death Penalty for the Mentally Handicapped or Juveniles

The U.S. Supreme Court has upheld the death penalty but ruled that it is unconstitutional when ordered for a mentally handicapped person or a juvenile (a person who was under the age of 18 at the time they committed a crime punishable by death). In both instances, the Court said that putting those persons to death would be "cruel and unusual punishment" in violation of the Eighth Amendment to the U.S. Constitution. In 2002, by a 6–3 vote in *Atkins* v. *Virginia*,[90] the Court barred the execution of Daryl Renard Atkins, who was sentenced to death for the 1996 murder of a U.S.

AGGRAVATING FACTORS

Factors and circumstances of a crime that would cause a juror to favor imposing the harshest sentence available.

MITIGATING FACTORS

Characteristics of a defendant and the circumstances of a crime that would cause a juror to favor imposing a lesser sentence.

Opposition to the death penalty stems from religious beliefs, incidences of wrongful convictions, and concerns about racial inequalities in sentencing.

FIGURE 9–4 Death Penalty Laws in the States

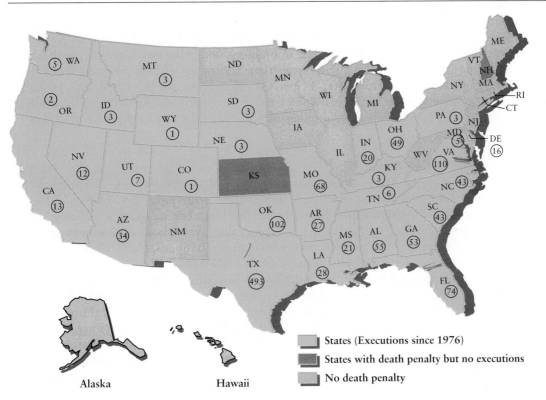

Legend:
- States (Executions since 1976)
- States with death penalty but no executions
- No death penalty

Alaska Hawaii

State execution numbers shown on map:
WA (5), OR (2), ID (3), MT (3), WY (1), ND, SD (3), NE (3), MN, WI, MI, NV (12), UT (7), CO (1), KS, IA, IL, IN (20), OH (49), CA (13), AZ (34), NM, OK (102), MO (68), KY (3), WV, VA (110), NC (43), TN (6), AR (27), MS (21), AL (55), GA (53), SC (43), TX (493), LA (28), FL (74), PA (3), NJ, MD (5), DE (16), NY, CT, RI, MA, NH, VT, ME

Note: Data are through March 1, 2013.
Source: Death Penalty Information Center. Available at http://www.deathpenaltyinfo.org.

airman in Virginia for beer money. Atkins has an IQ of 59, a score classified by the American Association of Mental Retardation as mild retardation. In 2005, by a 5–4 vote, the U.S. Supreme Court in *Roper* v. *Simmons*[91] upheld a ruling by the Missouri State Supreme Court outlawing the death penalty for juveniles. "Comprehensive neuropsychiatric and psychosocial assessments of death-row inmates and imaging studies exploring brain maturation in adolescents" played a key role in the decision.[92]

Few Executions

In recent years, fewer executions have been carried out. Slightly over 3,100 prisoners are currently awaiting execution on "death row." In any single year, 40–50 will be executed. California has had the highest number of prisoners on **death row** (724 in 2012); it carried out only 13 executions between 1976 and 2012. Southern states generally lead the nation in executions; Texas has carried out more than four times as many executions as any other state since 1976.

With only about 2 percent of death sentences actually carried out over the past decade, the death penalty cannot possibly be a deterrent to murder. Respect for the court system is eroded when the decisions of juries and judges are frustrated by convicted murderers. As trial judges and juries continue to impose the death penalty, and appellate courts continue to grant stays of execution, the number of prisoners on death row grows. The few who have been executed have averaged 10 years' delay between trial and execution. This frustrates many citizens, but they do want to make sure someone is absolutely guilty.

DEATH ROW

Prison cells for inmates awaiting execution.

Who's on Death Row?

Much more attention is given to the racial makeup of those on death row than the gender composition. Minority rights groups rigorously track such statistics and use them as evidence of racial inequality in the criminal justice system. And Gallup Polls over the years have shown a big racial divide in opinions about the death penalty, with blacks opposing it at considerably higher rates than whites. As of 2012, 43 percent of those awaiting execution were white, 42 percent African American, 12 percent Hispanic, and 3 percent were other races. Women make up a very small percentage of those on death row (2%); however, the number of females in the criminal justice system is on the upswing.

Methods of Execution

Although there are five methods of execution, all states but one (Nebraska) that have the death penalty use lethal injection as their primary method of execution. The other little-used methods are electrocution, gas chamber, hanging, and firing squad; where these methods still exist, the law generally gives a convicted person the right to choose them over lethal injection, which rarely happens. Since 1976, 87 percent of all executions have been by lethal injection. (Nebraska is the only state to solely use electrocution.) Recently, even the lethal injection method has been vigorously debated in state legislatures and in the courts. The tough questions are "About how much pain the condemned feel as they die and what role, if any, medical professionals should play in executions?"[93] Critics argue that medical practitioners are better able to administer the fatal dose than correctional officers who, in some instances, have not done the job properly, leading to legal claims of "cruel and unusual punishment." Some death penalty states have found themselves facing a new lethal injection-related problem. The Illinois drug company that once produced the anesthetic used in the injections quit making it in 2011, sending the states scrambling to find new sources of the drug or alternatives.

Moratoriums, Abandonments, and Reinstatements

The potential for wrongful executions has always worried Americans. With the emergence of better evidence (DNA), pro-active civil rights lawyers, and more cautious judges, convicted persons have been removed from death row because of trial errors, attorney incompetence, evidence withheld by the prosecution, new DNA evidence, and the like. (Since 1973, over 130 people have been released from death row based on new evidence of their innocence.) In 2000, the Illinois governor declared a moratorium on executions in that state, citing the many trial errors that were reported to him and the possibility that an innocent person might be put to death. He commuted the death sentences of all 167 inmates on death row, citing a state investigation that uncovered police corruption and racial bias in the state's capital punishment system. Several other states followed suit. In 2006, the U.S. Supreme Court ruled in *House v. Bell*[94] that a Tennessee death row inmate be given a new trial based on new DNA evidence, establishing that as precedent. In that same year, a number of states imposed temporary halts to executions because of questions over the administration of lethal injections.

In 2004, death penalty statutes in New York and Kansas were ruled unconstitutional by those states' high courts. (In 2006, the U.S. Supreme Court reinstated Kansas' death penalty law in *Kansas v. Marsh*.) In 2005, New York's State Assembly voted against reinstating it, making New York the first state to abandon the death penalty since the U.S. Supreme Court reinstated it in 1976. (New York was followed by New Jersey in 2007, New Mexico in 2009, Illinois in 2011, Connecticut in 2012, and Maryland in 2013.) Several other states have since considered removing the death penalty. But in 2012, California's voters rejected a proposal to eliminate the death penalty.

On the other hand, bills to reinstate the death penalty have been introduced in some of the states that do not have it. Prosecutors, victims' advocates, and a sizable portion of the public in those states believe it is an effective crime-fighting tool and righteous punishment for heinous crimes. Aware of the concerns of putting an innocent person to death, some of these states contemplating adopting the death penalty are looking at more stringent ways to safeguard against wrongful convictions. Being considered are stricter requirements for scientific evidence, such as DNA and fingerprints, and raising the bar for a death penalty sentence from the normal legal standard of guilt "beyond a reasonable doubt" to a finding of "no doubt about the defendant's guilt."[95]

CHAPTER HIGHLIGHTS

- Judicial decision making differs significantly from legislative or executive decision making in its passive role, access, legal procedures, and appearance of objectivity.

- The rise in the number of lawsuits nationally corresponds to a rise in the number of lawyers and the expansion of liability for accidents and injury.

- State courts are organized in a hierarchy, going from courts of limited jurisdiction (traffic, small claims) at the bottom to trial courts, appellate courts, and supreme courts. A case cannot go up to the U.S. Supreme Court unless it involves a federal constitutional question. The Fourteenth Amendment is the most common path.

- Judges are selected by one of five methods: partisan election, nonpartisan election, appointment by the governor, legislative selection, and the appointment–retention election plan (or Missouri plan). The two most common are nonpartisan and appointment–retention.

- The largest proportion of state supreme court decision making involves economic interests, and judges' decisions often correlate with party affiliation.

- Citizen watchdog groups monitor judges' behavior more than in the past. In states where judges are elected, campaigns have become more competitive and expensive.

- Conservatives and liberals disagree over whether the proper role of judges in deciding a case should be judicial restraint (conservatives) or judicial activism (liberals).

- There are two types of juries—trial (petit) and grand. Social media have made it more difficult to ensure juror impartiality throughout the entire trial.

- Violent crimes against judges, court officials, law enforcement officers, and corrections personnel are on the upswing.

- Crime rates as calculated by the FBI have declined in the 2000s. Crime rates in the states tend to be related to growing population, increasing urbanization, and economic decline.

- Over half of all crimes are related to drugs. Most crimes are never solved.

- City police officers vastly outnumber all other state and county law enforcement officers combined. Private security forces effectively double the size of the nation's police force.

- In addition to enforcing laws, police keep the peace (handle disturbances) and provide services such as controlling traffic and crowds. New strategies include becoming proactive in the community, cracking down on specific activities, and maintaining a well-ordered environment ("broken windows").

- Public prosecutors (district attorneys) play a central role in law enforcement by deciding which crimes to bring to the grand jury for indictment and how to handle the case (plea bargain, evidence).

- Although the Constitution guarantees trial by jury (Sixth Amendment), defendants choose guilty pleas over jury trials by a ratio of 10 to 1.

- State prison populations have exploded in recent years because of a rise in violent and drug-related crimes as well as get-tough-on-crime policies such as longer sentences and "three strikes you're out" laws.

- To relieve overcrowding, states have constructed new prisons at enormous, and unsustainable, costs. A number of states are looking at cost-reduction options, such as adopting alternative consequences for low-level crimes.

- The guiding principle of most correctional systems is punishment, not rehabilitation. Some states are experimenting with restorative justice programs and considering preventive approaches that begin in early childhood.

- Despite the Supreme Court's ruling that capital punishment is not "cruel and unusual punishment" as defined by the Eighth Amendment, a number of states have halted executions and several states have abandoned it altogether. Public support for the death penalty has slipped a bit in recent years. Younger, more liberal voters are stronger proponents of rehabilitation than punishment.

CHAPTER TEN

GOVERNING AMERICA'S COMMUNITIES

LEARNING OBJECTIVES

 10.1 Explain the challenges local governments face because of their diversity in population size, square miles, and socioeconomic composition.

 10.2 Analyze the structure and functions of the system comprised of 89,000 local governments.

10.3 Describe the diversity of county governments.

10.4 Compare and contrast county commission, county administrator, and county executive governmental structures. Describe the duties of county officials, and discuss how home rule charters, townships, and New England towns are organized.

10.5 Analyze the various types of city charters, and discuss the limits of such charters.

 10.6 Examine the mayor-council and council-manager forms of city government; outline the commission, town meeting, and representative town meeting forms of city government; and describe which forms of city government are most prevalent.

 10.7 Evaluate how successfully nonpartisan elections have taken the "politics" out of local government and raised the caliber of candidates for elected office.

 10.8 Compare at-large and district electoral systems, and how the electoral system affects which candidates are most likely to be victorious.

 10.9 Describe special-purpose local governments known as special districts, and list the various purposes for which these districts were created.

10.1

Explain the challenges local
governments face because of
their diversity in population
size, square miles, and
socioeconomic composition.

SO MANY LOCAL GOVERNMENTS, SO MUCH CONFUSION

A bomb threat is called in to a local television station. An explosion occurs at a nearby oil refinery. A neighborhood panics when its drinking water suddenly has a suspicious color and odor. Several gunmen go on a shooting rampage at a local pharmaceutical company's research lab. Dangerous microorganisms are missing. A stranger hops onto a school bus en route to the local high school and terrifies the students who use their cell phones to call their parents. In each instance, the first question that will be raised in the minds of many citizens is likely to be: "Are terrorists to blame?" followed by an even more critical question: "Whose responsibility is it to take charge of the situation?" Soon thereafter, the community's residents will begin asking whether the response of the local government(s) in charge has been efficient, effective, and conducted fairly. Initially, most citizens will not know whether it is the county, the city, a town, township, some special district government (the hospital district, school district), or some combination thereof that must react because most Americans do not have a clear idea of which local government does what even in noncrisis situations. If they do know which local government is responsible, they may not know which official within that government has the authority to act.

America's communities are incredibly diverse—in population size, square miles, and socioeconomic composition. Our communities are governed in vastly different ways. To put it simply—there is no "one size fits all" local governance structure. Even within the same state, there is likely to be considerable variation in what form of local government has been adopted, the powers and responsibilities of local officials, and the method of electing local officials.

Generalizing about community politics is perhaps even more difficult than generalizing about American state politics. There are over 89,000 local governments in the United States. These include municipalities, townships, counties, and a host of other school districts and special districts. (See Table 10–1.) Nearly two-thirds of the American people live in urban units of local government known as "municipalities," including "cities," "boroughs," "villages," or "towns." Other Americans are served by county or township governments. Moreover, there are 365 metropolitan areas in the United States; these are clusterings of people and governments around a core city of 50,000 or more residents. These metropolitan areas range in size from the Carson City, Nevada, area population of 55,000 up to the New York City area, which has 600 local governments and nearly 19 million people.

TABLE 10–1 Local Governments in the United States	
General Purpose	
Counties	3,031
Municipalities	19,522
Townships	16,364
Total	**38,917**
Special Purpose	
School Districts	12,884
Special Districts	37,203
Total	50,087
Total Local Governments	**89,004**

Note: Data are for 2012.
Source: U.S. Census Bureau, 2012 Census of Governments, Table 2. Available at http://www2.census.gov/govs/cog/2012/formatted_prelim_counts_23jul2012_2.pdf.

Within the same geographical area, a multitude of local governments coexist to provide citizens with a wide array of services, activities, and infrastructures. These range from public safety, mosquito control, water, sewers, sports stadiums, and schools to ports, hospitals, and libraries, depending on where you live. The local government arena is incredibly complex, fragmented, and often confusing to Americans who tend to move around a lot. Local governments vary significantly in their functions, the titles and responsibilities they give to their elected officials, and in how and when they conduct local elections.

Creating a "Sense of Community"

One of the biggest challenges facing local governments in the twenty-first century, especially in light of America's highly mobile population, is how to define and create a "**sense of community**" among an area's residents. Community ties are stronger where friends and neighbors frequently interact with each other socially, voluntarism rates are high, communication channels between government and citizens are open, citizens are satisfied with local services, local governments cooperate with each other more than they conflict, and turnout in local elections is high.[1] In such places, a higher proportion of residents say they are proud to live there. Studies have found that "strong, engaged communities are desirable places to live because they offer residents a sense of belonging and a feeling of efficacy."[2] That doesn't necessarily mean that everyone agrees on what their local officials should do. In general, however, citizens consistently rate local government more favorably than either the federal or state government. (See Figure 10–1.)

SENSE OF COMMUNITY
Friends and neighbors frequently interact with each other socially, voluntarism rates are high, and communication channels between government and citizens are open.

FIGURE 10–1 Government Favorability by Level: Local Government Rated Highest

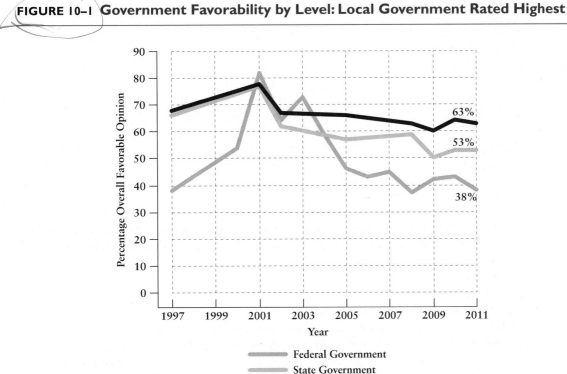

Note: Respondents were asked the question, "Just in general . . . Is your overall opinion of [THE FEDERAL GOVERNMENT IN WASHINGTON/YOUR STATE GOVERNMENT/YOUR LOCAL GOVERNMENT] very favorable, mostly favorable, mostly unfavorable, or very unfavorable?"
Source: Pew Research Center, "Changing Views of Federal Spending: Fewer Want Spending to Grow, but Most Cuts Remain Unpopular," February 10, 2011. Available at http://www.people-press.org/files/2011/02/702.pdf.

People feel more of a sense of community when friends and neighbors interact with each other socially, often by volunteering to do something to improve their community.

Providing Services and Managing Conflict

Community political systems serve two principal functions. One is that of supplying goods and services—for example, police protection or sewage disposal—that are not supplied by private enterprise. This is the **"service" function**. The other function is the **"political" function**, that of *managing conflict* over public policy. Of course, the "political" and the "service" functions of local governments are often indistinguishable in practice. A mayor who intervenes in a dispute about the location of a park is managing a local government service, namely recreation, at the same time that he or she is managing political conflict about whose neighborhood should get the most benefit from the new park.

Sources of Community Conflict

Human diversity is the source of all political conflict—differences among people in wealth, occupation, education, ethnicity, race, religion, and style of living. In the United States, there are many rural communities, small towns and cities, and compact suburbs with relatively homogeneous populations. In these communities, there are fewer differences among citizens and fewer permanent lines of cleavage. Some conflicts occur in these communities, of course, but groupings of forces are usually temporary. In contrast, in most large cities and metropolitan areas there are many different kinds of people living closely together, and there are more lasting cleavages, or "fault lines," which tend to open when controversial issues arise. These cleavages are readily recognized in disputes among upper-, middle-, and lower-income groups; ethnic groups; property owners and nonproperty owners; renters and homeowners; families with children and those without; old timers and newcomers; young and old; suburbanites and city dwellers; and traditional political party divisions.[3]

Increasingly in America's large cities, racial and ethnic conflicts are becoming more intense as the population makeup of urban areas is becoming more diverse. These conflicts are not always between minority groups and white residents. In some multiracial communities, the fiercest conflicts may be between several minority groups fighting with each other for resources and representation.

Coping with Dissatisfaction

If you are dissatisfied with the way things are going in your community, you have three choices: (1) resign yourself to the situation, do nothing, and just tolerate it; (2) move away and find a community that provides more satisfaction; (3) stay and make an attempt to change things. Political scientists tend to focus their attention on the people who try to change things, implying that this is the only way to respond rationally to community problems. However, economists have developed theories of residential mobility that focus on the individual's choice of community based on a rational calculation of personal costs and benefits.[4] (The theory is most applicable to metropolitan areas where many different kinds of communities are available.)

There are recognized negative **"push"** factors—crime, congestion, noise, overcrowding, racial conflict—and positive **"pull"** factors—more space, larger houses, better schools, "nice" playmates for the children—both of which affect decisions to move. One might move to the suburbs "for the kids," or move to the city to be close to good restaurants, fine entertainment, cultural events, and specialty shops, or to reduce the trip to work. In short, economists emphasize rational calculations and freedom of choice, which they assume most citizens possess.

How do people actually respond to community dissatisfactions? There is some evidence to suggest that, in the face of community problems:[5]

When city residents see their own children drawing pictures focusing on crime, it often pushes them to move to the suburbs.

- Higher-status whites tend either to become politically active or to move out, with political activity somewhat more common.
- Lower-status whites tend to move out rather than become politically active.
- In the past, blacks have been more likely to become politically active in city politics rather than to move out, probably because of the increased difficulties most blacks face in residential relocation. Now many middle- and upper-class black professionals move to the suburbs rather than stay in the city and fight.[6]
- City residents are more likely to move out, whereas suburbanites are more likely to become politically active.
- Newly arrived immigrants are likely to stay put in the city but stay out of politics; it is the second or third generation of immigrants who become politically engaged.
- People who have been generally satisfied with the past performance of their local government, as well as people who have invested in home ownership or local businesses, are more likely to become politically active to solve a current problem, rather than to move out or do nothing.
- Dissatisfied affluent residents may choose to "privatize" the community services that distress them. The most common example is the choice of private schools over the public school system, but occasionally residents and businesses also turn to private police protection, security services, garbage collection, and other services.

PUSH FACTORS

Negative aspects within a community that can cause that community to be undesirable.

PULL FACTORS

Positive aspects within a community that can cause that community to be desirable.

EIGHTY-NINE THOUSAND GOVERNMENTS

10.2

Analyze the structure and functions of the system comprised of 89,000 local governments.

Local government is not mentioned in the U.S. Constitution. Although we regard the American federal system as a mixture of federal, state, and *local* governments, from a constitutional point of view, local governments are really parts of state governments. Communities have no right to self-government in the U.S. Constitution. All of their governmental powers legally flow from state laws and constitutions. Local governments—cities, townships, counties, special districts, and school districts—are creatures of the state, subject to the obligations, privileges, powers, and restrictions that state governments impose upon them. The state may create or destroy any or all units of local government. To the extent that local governments can collect taxes, regulate their citizens, and provide services, they are actually exercising *state* powers delegated to them by the state in either its constitution or its laws.

Why Should You Care about the Structure of Local Government?

Most citizens see little need to understand the structure of the local governments that serve them—until there's a crisis or pressing need in our own neighborhood or a concern that touches members of our own household. Is there a pothole in the middle of

Do you know who to call if your house or apartment caught fire? Many citizens do not know which local government to contact when a crisis hits their own home. The poor understanding of which local government has what functional responsibility also makes it difficult to hold public officials accountable at election time.

the street that has been there for weeks? Who is to blame for the change in zoning that allowed a Super Wal-Mart to be built two blocks from our home? Why have public swimming pools been built in every neighborhood except ours? How many more people have to be killed or injured before a traffic light is installed at the corner where we turn to go to work? Why has our community been judged to be "less-than-ready" for responding to a possible bioterrorism attack?

The answers to these typical questions differ considerably depending on the structure of the local governments in our community. The bottom line is that we do not know whom to hold accountable for action—or inaction—unless we understand which official has the formal authority to deal with an issue or problem. Each state determines which type of local government shall bear the major responsibility for providing major services and functions. The assignment of responsibility often differs across the states and even within the same state.

What does this complex local government landscape mean for the average citizen who moves several times in his or her lifetime? It means that we must make an effort to educate ourselves about which local governments and which officials do what within our community. If we don't make this effort, then we may place blame on the wrong local officials—and become frustrated and cynical when nothing happens.

What Should Citizens Focus on at the Local Level?

As a citizen, it is important to know who "hires and fires" various types of local officials. In the case of elected officials, we the citizens "hire and fire" them at the ballot box. In communities with a city, county, or town manager, the elected commissioners usually hire and fire the manager. Depending on the type of local government in place, department heads and their deputies may be hired and fired by the mayor, the manager, the commission or council, or several acting together.

It is equally important to know who has the major responsibility for preparing or drafting the budget and then approving it. After all, the budget is the single best statement about a government's priorities. No pothole will be filled, no swimming pool will be built, and no traffic light can be purchased and installed without funds being budgeted.

Another key to understanding a local government's modus operandi is determining the degree to which a local government's structure provides for separation of powers (checks and balances). Are the executive and legislative branches separate or do the same officials act as both branches? How much power does the chief executive have over the budget? In the hiring and firing of department heads? To veto the actions of the legislative body?

We also need to know who elects each of the commissioners. Do only voters living in his or her district elect a commissioner or is the commissioner elected by a citywide or countywide vote? Within your community, are some commissioners elected from districts while others run at large? Why should this matter? An individual council member's or commissioner's priorities may differ considerably depending on his or her constituency base. The bottom line is that how local officials are elected affects their approach to policymaking and problem solving.

Local Government Functions Differ by State

Counties, cities, and townships are referred to as **general-purpose governments**. They provide a wide range of services, from law enforcement to parks and recreation, human services, roads, and public works. Special districts and school districts are known as **special-purpose governments**. They are much more limited in the number of functions they perform for the public.

Different units of government are assigned different responsibilities by each of the states, so it is difficult to generalize about what each of these types of local governments is supposed to do. Indeed, even in the same state, there may be overlapping functions and responsibilities assigned to cities, counties, school districts, and special districts. Nevertheless, let us make some generalizations about what each of these types of government does, realizing of course that in any specific location the pattern of governmental activity may be slightly different:

COUNTIES

—*Rural:* keep records of deeds, mortgages, births, marriages; assess and levy property taxes; maintain local roads; administer elections and certify election results to state; provide law enforcement through sheriff; maintain criminal court; maintain a local jail; administer state welfare programs. **Rural county government** provides an arena for a folksy, provincial, individualistic, "friends and neighbors" type of politics. Contrary to conventional wisdom that rural residents feel isolated and physically detached, surveys show that rural residents are more likely to feel connected to their small communities than urban residents. They are also quite content with "small-town" county politics.[7]

—*Urban:* provide most of same functions as rural counties (except police and court systems, which often become city functions), together with planning and control of new subdivisions; mental health; public health maintenance and public hospitals; care of the aged; recreation, including parks, stadiums, and convention centers; and perhaps some city functions, such as fire protection, water, sewers, and libraries to the unincorporated areas of the county, that is, to the areas not within the boundaries of cities. In large metropolitan areas, **urban counties** are increasingly providing more facilities and services that benefit an entire region, such as mass transit, convention centers, airports, sports stadiums, and pollution control.[8]

CITIES

—Provide the "common functions" of police, fire, streets, sewage, sanitation, and parks; over half of the nation's large cities also provide welfare services and public education. (In other cities welfare is handled by county governments or directly by state agencies, and education is handled by separate school districts.)

TOWNS AND TOWNSHIPS

—*Midwestern townships:* generally subdivisions of counties with the same responsibilities as their county; perform many of the functions of county governments at a grassroots level—elections, road repair, tax administration, fire protection, and even law enforcement through local justices of the peace.

New England towns: deliver extensive services similar to those provided by municipalities.[9]

SCHOOL DISTRICTS

—Organized specifically to provide public elementary and secondary education; community colleges may be operated by county governments or by special districts with or without state support. Most school districts are **independent,** but some are "**dependent**" because other governments (state, county, municipality, town, or township) are responsible for the administration and operation of the public school system.

GENERAL-PURPOSE GOVERNMENT

A government that provides a wide range of services, such as a county or city or township.

SPECIAL-PURPOSE GOVERNMENT

A government that performs a very specific function, such as a school district or a mosquito control district.

RURAL COUNTY GOVERNMENT

The traditional administrative subdivision of state government. It is responsible for law enforcement, courts, roads, elections, and the recording of legal documents.

URBAN COUNTY

County governments that perform all of the services of traditional rural counties together with many contemporary urban services.

INDEPENDENT SCHOOL DISTRICT

School districts that are not directly run by another governmental entity.

DEPENDENT SCHOOL DISTRICT

School districts that are run or overseen by another governmental body that they must report to.

SPECIAL DISTRICTS

—Provide specific services that are not being supplied by existing general-purpose governments; most (92%) perform a **single function,** such as fire protection, mass transit, soil conservation, libraries, water and irrigation, mosquito control, sewage disposal, airports, sports, and convention centers; some **multi-function special districts** provide several related types of services such as water supply and sewerage services.

The 50 states vary a great deal in the numbers and types of local governments they authorize. (See "*Rankings of the States:* General-Purpose Local Governments" and "*Rankings of the States:* Special-Purpose Local Governments.") Hawaii is the nation's most centralized state: There are only 21 local governments in the Aloha State; 17 of these are special districts without taxing power; 3 are counties; and 1 is the city of Honolulu. In contrast, there are 6,968 local governments in Illinois, including 1,298 cities, 102 counties, 1,431 townships, 905 school districts, and 3,232 special districts.

COUNTY GOVERNMENTS: RURAL AND URBAN

All states, with the exception of Connecticut and Rhode Island, have organized *county* governments. In Louisiana, counties are called "parishes," and in Alaska they are called "boroughs." Historically, states created counties as their administrative arms, which is why counties are often described as legal subdivisions of the state. It is difficult to generalize about the powers of the nation's 3,031 counties. The legal powers, organization, and officers of counties vary a great deal.

Counties range in area from 67 square kilometers (Arlington, Virginia) to 227,559 square kilometers (North Slope Borough, Alaska). The number of county governments per state also differs widely, from the Texas total of 254 down to fewer than 20 in several states.

THE STRUCTURE OF COUNTY GOVERNMENT

Although county governments may differ markedly in their organization, they generally have (1) a governing body, variously called the "**county commissioners,**" "county board," "board of supervisors," or even "judges," which is composed of anywhere from three to 50 elected members, either elected by district or countywide; (2) a number of separately elected officials with countywide jurisdictions, such as sheriff, county attorney, auditor, recorder, coroner, assessor, judge, and treasurer; (3) a large number of special boards or commissions that have authority over various functions, whose members may be elected or appointed by the county commissioners or may even include the county commissioners in an ex officio capacity; and (4) an appointed county bureaucracy in planning, transportation, health, welfare, libraries, and parks. Larger, more urban counties may also have an elected chief executive and/or an appointed county administrator or manager.

Traditional County Commission Structure

Traditionally, county governments have been organized around the commission structure (see top of Figure 10–2). Over one-third of the nation's counties still operate under this structure. In a **traditional county commission structure,** typically there are three or five county commissioners, elected for overlapping four-year terms, and a large number of separately elected county officials. There is no single person responsible for administration of county functions. The commissioners may supervise some functions themselves and share supervision of other functions with other elected officials. Thus, for example, both the elected sheriff and the county commissioners share responsibility for the county jail, with the sheriff supervising day-to-day operations, but the commissioners deciding on its construction, repair, and financing. The commissioners usually decide on the **property tax ("millage") rate,** with one mill equal to one-tenth of a percent or $1 per $1,000 of assessed property value to be imposed on property owners (subject to maximums usually set by the

General-Purpose Local Governments

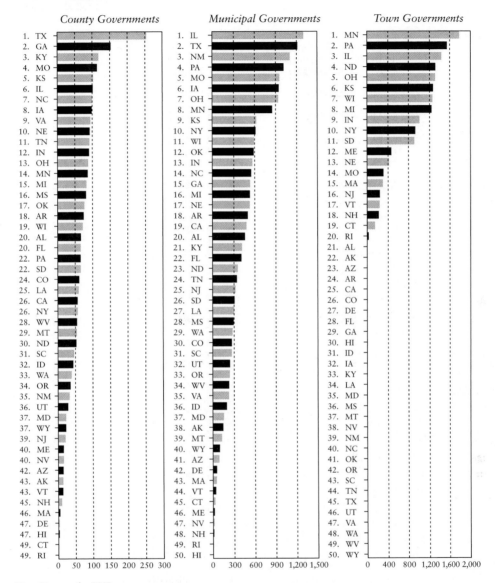

County Governments

1. TX
2. GA
3. KY
4. MO
5. KS
6. IL
7. NC
8. IA
9. VA
10. NE
11. TN
12. IN
13. OH
14. MN
15. MI
16. MS
17. OK
18. AR
19. WI
20. AL
20. FL
22. PA
22. SD
24. CO
25. LA
26. CA
26. NY
28. WV
29. MT
30. ND
31. SC
32. ID
33. WA
34. OR
35. NM
36. UT
37. MD
37. WY
39. NJ
40. ME
40. NV
42. AZ
43. AK
43. VT
45. NH
46. MA
47. DE
47. HI
49. CT
49. RI

0 50 100 150 200 250 300

Municipal Governments

1. IL
2. TX
3. NM
4. PA
5. MO
6. IA
7. OH
8. MN
9. KS
10. NY
11. WI
12. OK
13. IN
14. NC
15. GA
16. MI
17. NE
18. AR
19. CA
20. AL
21. KY
22. FL
23. ND
24. TN
25. NJ
26. SD
27. LA
28. MS
29. WA
30. CO
31. SC
32. UT
33. OR
34. WV
35. VA
36. ID
37. MD
38. AK
39. MT
40. WY
41. AZ
42. DE
43. MA
44. VT
45. CT
46. ME
47. NV
48. NH
49. RI
50. HI

0 300 600 900 1,200 1,500

Town Governments

1. MN
2. PA
3. IL
4. ND
5. OH
6. KS
7. WI
8. MI
9. IN
10. NY
11. SD
12. ME
13. NE
14. MO
15. MA
16. NJ
17. VT
18. NH
19. CT
20. RI
21. AL
22. AK
23. AZ
24. AR
25. CA
26. CO
27. DE
28. FL
29. GA
30. HI
31. ID
32. IA
33. KY
34. LA
35. MD
36. MS
37. MT
38. NV
39. NM
40. NC
41. OK
42. OR
43. SC
44. TN
45. TX
46. UT
47. VA
48. WA
49. WV
50. WY

0 400 800 1,200 1,600 2,000

Note: Data are for 2012.
Source: U.S. Census Bureau, "2012 Census of Governments," Table 2. Available at http://www2.census.gov/govs/cog/2012/formatted_prelim_counts_23jul2012_2.pdf.

Note: Data are for 2012.
Source: U.S. Census Bureau, "2012 Census of Governments," Table 2. Available at http://www2.census.gov/govs/cog/2012/formatted_prelim_counts_23jul2012_2.pdf.

Note: Data are for 2012.
Source: U.S. Census Bureau, "2012 Census of Governments, Table 2." Available at http://www2.census.gov/govs/cog/2012/formatted_prelim_counts_23jul2012_2.pdf.

Special-Purpose Local Governments

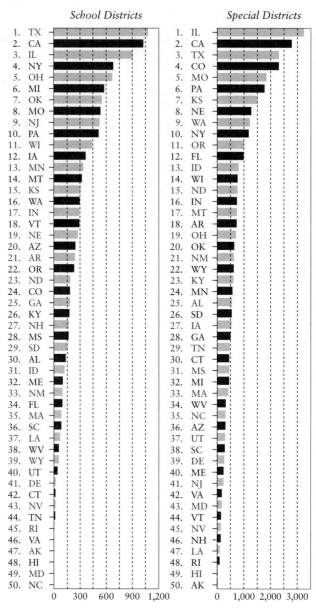

School Districts

1. TX
2. CA
3. IL
4. NY
5. OH
6. MI
7. OK
8. MO
9. NJ
10. PA
11. WI
12. IA
13. MN
14. MT
15. KS
16. WA
17. IN
18. VT
19. NE
20. AZ
21. AR
22. OR
23. ND
24. CO
25. GA
26. KY
27. NH
28. MS
29. SD
30. AL
31. ID
32. ME
33. NM
34. FL
35. MA
36. SC
37. LA
38. WV
39. WY
40. UT
41. DE
42. CT
43. NV
44. TN
45. RI
46. VA
47. AK
48. HI
49. MD
50. NC

0   300   600   900   1,200

Special Districts

1. IL
2. CA
3. TX
4. CO
5. MO
6. PA
7. KS
8. NE
9. WA
10. NY
11. OR
12. FL
13. ID
14. WI
15. ND
16. IN
17. MT
18. AR
19. OH
20. OK
21. NM
22. WY
23. KY
24. MN
25. AL
26. SD
27. IA
28. GA
29. TN
30. CT
31. MS
32. MI
33. MA
34. WV
35. NC
36. AZ
37. UT
38. SC
39. DE
40. ME
41. NJ
42. VA
43. MD
44. VT
45. NV
46. NH
47. LA
48. RI
49. HI
50. AK

0   1,000   2,000   3,000

Note: Data are for 2012.
Source: U.S. Census Bureau, "2012 Census of Governments," Table 2. Available at http://www2.census.gov/govs/cog/2012/formatted_pre-lim_counts_23jul2012_2.pdf.

Note: Data are for 2012.
Source: U.S. Census Bureau, "2012 Census of Governments," Table 2. Available at http://www2.census.gov/govs/cog/2012/formatted_prelim_counts_23jul2012_2.pdf.

state legislature). But the tax *assessor* determines the value of each parcel of property in the county against which the rate is to be applied. And in some counties a separate tax *collector* actually sends out the tax bills and undertakes to collect the revenue. A separate *treasurer* may maintain the county's financial accounts and write the checks. Thus, responsibility for county government is fragmented and dispersed. Reformers view this traditional structure of county government as lacking in efficiency and accountability.

County Administrator Structure

Urbanization and the proliferation of county functions usually result in demands for more professional administration of county government. When county commissioners find that they cannot cope with the volume and complexity of county business, they often seek professional assistance. The **county administrator (or county manager) structure** of government offers a solution. (See middle of Figure 10–2.) It is based on the council-manager form of city government (see "Forms of City Government" later in this chapter). An appointed county administrator, responsible to the county commission, is placed in charge of the various county departments and agencies. The commission makes policy and appoints the administrator to *implement* policy. The administrator prepares the budget for the commission's approval and then implements it; the administrator hires and fires department heads and reports back regularly to the commission on county business. It seldom works out as neatly as it appears on the organization chart, but the use of the county administrator plan has grown rapidly throughout the United States in recent years. More than half of all U.S. counties are governed by such a structure. (See Figure 10–3.)

COUNTY ADMINISTRATOR STRUCTURE The organization of county government in which the elected commission appoints an administrator/manager who supervises county functions.

Elected County Executive/County Mayor Structure ✕

In recent years, more counties in the United States have adopted a governmental structure that features an elected "county executive" or countymayor. Voters elect both a county commission and a separate county executive officer, who exercises formal responsibility over county departments. (See bottom of Figure 10–2.) The elected county executive usually appoints the county administrator subject to approval of the commission. The **elected county executive (county mayor)** structure envisions the separation of legislative and executive powers, much like American state and national governments. The elected county executive, like the county administrator, has won approval in many urban counties over recent years. Urban counties often experience more crises and emergencies and need a strong executive with the authority to act in such situations. Today, 13 percent of U.S. counties elect a county executive.

ELECTED COUNTY EXECUTIVE (COUNTY MAYOR) The organization of county government in which a chief executive officer is elected separately from the county commission.

County Officials ✕

Typically, county officials have the following duties:

Commissioners: elected governing body with general responsibility for all county functions; most commissions have three to seven members (larger counties) with election by the county's voters at large.

Sheriff: maintains jail; furnishes law enforcement in unincorporated areas; carries out orders of the county court.

Coroner: conducts medical investigations to determine cause of death; maintains county morgue.

County or district attorney: serves as chief prosecuting attorney; conducts criminal investigations and prosecutes law violators.

Clerk: registers and records legal documents including deeds, mortgages, subdivision plots, marriages, divorces, births; certifies election returns.

Tax assessor: determines value of all taxable property in the county.

Tax collector: collects taxes.

Treasurer: maintains and disperses county funds; makes county fiscal reports.

Auditor: maintains financial records; authorizes payment of county obligations.

FIGURE 10–2 Structures of County Government

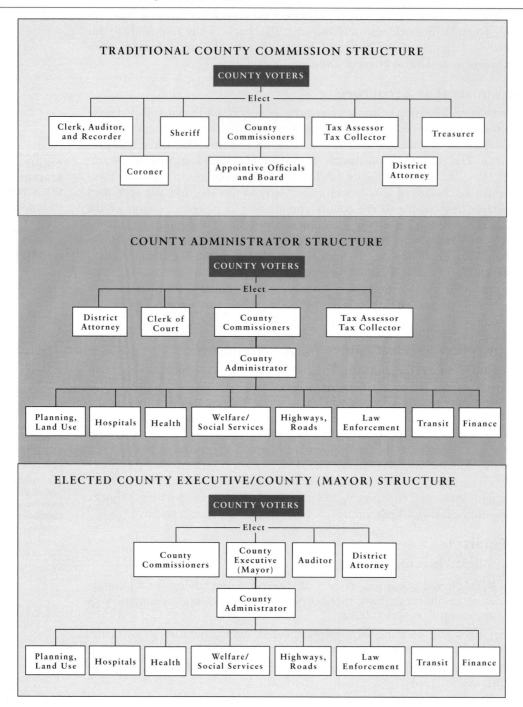

FIGURE 10–3 Forms of County Government

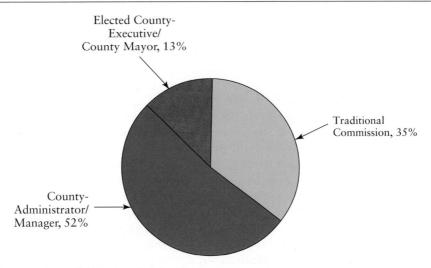

Elected County-Executive/County Mayor, 13%

Traditional Commission, 35%

County-Administrator/Manager, 52%

Note: Data are for 2007. Most recent data available at time of publication.
Source: Adapted/Reprinted with permission of the International City/County Management Association, 777 North Capitol Street, NE, Suite 500, Washington, DC 20002. All rights reserved.

The many separately elected county officials are generally considered an obstacle to the emergence of strong executive leadership at the county level. The ability of county governments to assume more important functions and responsibilities, particularly in urban areas, probably hinges on a reorganization of county government to provide for stronger executive leadership.

Home Rule Charter Counties

Most counties in America are still heavily dependent upon the state legislature to define their functions and cannot do anything that is not explicitly spelled out in state law (**Dillon's rule**). In its history of county government, the National Association of County Officials describes the legal status of most county governments: "Counties [have] to have specific enabling legislation to authorize whatever functions they might fulfill at the local level, and to respond to the changing needs of their citizens, they [have] to petition the [state] legislature for additional authority, which might or might not be granted."[10] The trend in county governance is for states to pass legislation allowing counties to operate under a home rule charter. (A **county charter** is like a state constitution; it lays out the structure and powers of the local government for which it is written. It must be adopted by a majority of the county's voters.) A **home rule charter** grants a county more local control, greater policymaking authority, and more self-government than it is given by the state constitution or state statutes. California was the first state to allow home rule for its counties; Los Angeles County became the first county in the United States with a home rule charter. Today, 37 states permit some form of home rule for at least some of their counties, usually the most populous counties. However, just 9 percent of all counties are home rule charter counties.

Townships

"**Township government**" is found in 20 states—the northern states from New England to the Midwest. Southern and western states have made little use of this unit of government. Most townships are unincorporated, which means they do not have charters from state governments guaranteeing their political independence or authorizing them to provide many municipal services. However, some states, such as Michigan, grant townships a charter under certain conditions. The jurisdiction of townships may extend over many square

DILLON'S RULE
The legal doctrine that local governments possess only those powers expressly granted in their charter.

COUNTY CHARTER
Like a state constitution, it lays out the structure and powers of the local government for which it is written. It must be adopted by a majority of the county's voters.

HOME RULE CHARTER
A charter that authorizes a city or a county to exercise all powers not specifically prohibited by law or by charter.

TOWNSHIP GOVERNMENT
The traditional administrative subdivision of county government, mostly in the unincorporated areas in northeastern and midwestern states.

miles of sparsely populated rural territory. More than 55 million people, or one-fifth of the U.S. population, live under township governments today. They are usually governed by an elected board of supervisors, trustees, or commissioners who oversee township operations; the structure is much like the traditional commission form of county government, although some have professional township managers. Some townships also elect other officials, such as a clerk or a constable.

The New England Town

TOWN MEETING GOVERNMENT

A form of local government in which the entire citizenry meets periodically to govern the community.

In the New England states (Connecticut, Maine, Massachusetts, New Hampshire, Rhode Island, and Vermont), the "town" is a significant unit of local government, with long traditions and deep roots in the political philosophy of the people of the region. In fact, the New England "town meeting" is often cited by political philosophers as the ideal form of *direct* democracy as distinguished from *representative* democracy. For the **town meeting** was, and to some extent still is, the central institution of "town" government. The town meeting is open to all eligible voters; it is generally an important social as well as political event. The town meeting levies taxes, makes appropriations, determines policy, and elects officers for the year. Between town meetings, a board of selected officials supervises the activities of the town—such as schools, health, roads, and care of the poor. Other officers include town clerks, tax assessors and collectors, justices of the peace, constables, road commissioners, and school board members.

REPRESENTATIVE TOWN MEETING GOVERNMENT

Town meeting members are elected prior to a town meeting.

Although the ideal of direct democracy is still alive in many smaller New England towns, in the large towns, the pure democracy of the town meeting has given way to a representative system (**representative town meeting government**), in which town meeting members are elected prior to the town meeting. Moreover, much of the determination of the towns' financial affairs, previously decided at town meetings, has now been given over to elected officials, and many towns have appointed town managers to supervise the day-to-day administration of town services.

10.5 CITIES AS "MUNICIPAL CORPORATIONS"

Analyze the various types of city charters, and discuss the limits of such charters.

MUNICIPAL CORPORATION

A city government chartered by the state government.

CITY CHARTER

The document that grants powers to, and determines the structure of, a city government.

Legally speaking, cities are "**municipal corporations**" that have received charters from state governments setting forth their boundaries, governmental powers and functions, structure and organization, methods of finance, and powers to elect and appoint officers and employees. In some ways, a charter may be thought of as a license to operate as a city granted to a community by the state. The **city charter** is intended to grant the powers of local self-government to a community. In this sense, a city charter is similar to a state constitution in that it establishes the city's structure and governing processes. Of course, the powers of self-government granted by a municipal charter are not unlimited. A state can change its charter or take it away altogether as it sees fit. Cities, like other local governments, have only the powers that state laws and constitutions grant them.

Perhaps the most serious limitation on the powers of cities is the fact that American courts have insisted upon interpreting the powers granted in charters very narrowly. The classic statement of this principle was made by John F. Dillon many years ago and is now well known as "Dillon's rule":

> It is a general and undisputed proposition of law that a municipal corporation possesses and can exercise the following powers, and no others: first, those granted in express words; second, those necessarily or fairly implied in or incident to the powers expressly granted; third, those essential to the accomplishment of the declared objects and purposes of the corporation—not simply convenient, but indispensable. Any fair, reasonable, substantial doubt concerning the existence of power is resolved by the courts against a corporation, and the power is denied.[11]

The restrictive interpretation of the powers of cities leads to lengthy city charters, since nearly everything a city does must have specific legal authorization in the charter. The city charter of New York, for example, is several hundred pages long. City charters must cover in detail such matters as boundaries, structure of government, ordinance-making powers, finances, contracts, purchasing, bonds, courts, municipal elections, property assessments, zoning laws and building codes, licenses, franchises, law enforcement, education, health, streets, parks, public utilities, and on and on. Since any proposed change in the powers, organization, or responsibilities of cities requires an act of a state legislature amending the city's charter, state legislatures are intimately involved in local legislation.

Types of Municipal Charters

1. *Special Act Charters* State legislative control over cities is most firmly entrenched in **special act charters**. These charters are specially drawn for the cities named in them. Cities under special act charters remain directly under legislative control, and specific legislative approval for that city and that city alone must be obtained for any change in its government or service activities. Under special act charters, laws that apply to one city do not necessarily apply to others.

2. *General Act Charters* In contrast, **general act charters** usually classify cities according to their size and then apply municipal laws to all cities in each size classification. Thus, a state's municipal law may apply to all cities of fewer than 10,000 people, another law to all cities with populations of 10,000–24,999, another to cities with 25,000–49,999 people, and so on. These general act charters make it difficult to interfere in the activities of a particular city without affecting the activities of all cities of a similar size category.

3. *Optional Charters* **Optional charter** laws provide cities with some choice in the structure and organization of their governments. Such laws generally offer a choice of governmental forms: strong mayor and weak council, weak mayor and strong council, commission, city manager, or some modification of these.

4. *Home Rule* Municipal home rule charters, like county home rule charters, are designed to give cities the power to adopt governmental forms and provide municipal services, as they see fit, without state legislative interference. Home rule charters may be given to cities by state constitutions or by legislative enactments; legislative home rule is considered less secure, since a legislature could retract the grant if it wished to do so. Beginning with Missouri in 1875, more than half the states have included in their constitutions provisions for the issuance of home rule charters. About two-thirds of the nation's cities with populations over 200,000 have some form of home rule. Any change in the charter must be approved by a majority of the voters.

The intended effect of home rule is to reverse "Dillon's rule" and enable cities to "exercise all legislative powers not prohibited by law or by charter." In other words, instead of preventing a city from doing anything not specifically authorized, home rule permits the city to do anything not specifically prohibited. The theory of home rule grants sweeping powers to cities; however, in practice, home rule has not brought self-government to cities.

Courts Restrict Local Powers

Courts figure prominently in municipal politics. This is because of the subordinate position of the municipal corporation in the hierarchy of governments, and legal traditions, such as Dillon's rule, which narrowly interpret the power of local governments. The power of courts over municipal affairs grants leverage to defenders of the status quo in any political battle at the local level. Proponents of a new municipal law or municipal service not only must win the battle over whether a city *ought* to pass the new law or provide the new service but also must win the legal battle over whether the city *can* pass the law or provide the service. Limitations and uncertainties abound about the validity of local enactments. Legal challenges to the authority of the city to pass new regulations or provide new services are frequent. The city attorney becomes a key official because he or she must advise the city about what it can or cannot do. Not only must the city obey the

SPECIAL ACT CHARTER
A charter granted by the state to a particular city.

GENERAL ACT CHARTER
A charter granted by the state to all cities in a specified size classification.

OPTIONAL CHARTER
Provides cities with some choice in the structure and organization of their governments and offers a choice of governmental forms.

federal constitution (and adhere to federal mandates and strings attached to federal aid), but it is also subject to the restraints of the state constitution, state laws, its municipal charter, and of course, Dillon's rule. The result is to greatly strengthen courts, attorneys, and defenders of the status quo.

10.6 FORMS OF CITY GOVERNMENT

Examine the mayor-council and council-manager forms of city government; outline the commission, town meeting, and representative town meeting forms of city government; and describe which forms of city government are most prevalent.

American city government comes in various structural packages (see Figure 10–4). There are some adaptations and variations from city to city, but generally one can classify the form of city government as mayor-council (strong mayor or weak mayor), commission, council-manager, town meeting, or representative town meeting. Over half of American cities now operate under council-manager governments (see Figure 10–5).

Commission

COMMISSION FORM OF CITY GOVERNMENT

The traditional form of city government in which legislative and executive powers are combined in an elected commission that directly supervises city departments.

The traditional **commission form of city government** gives both legislative and executive powers to a small body, usually consisting of five members. The commission form originated at the beginning of the century as a reform movement designed to end a system of divided responsibility between mayor and council. One of the commission members is nominally the mayor, but he or she has no more formal powers than the other commissioners. The board of commissioners is directly responsible for the operation of city departments and agencies. In practice, one commission member may take on responsibility for the management of a specific department, such as finance, public works, or public safety. As long as the council members are in agreement over policy, there are few problems; but when commissioners differ among themselves and develop separate spheres of influence, city government becomes a multiheaded monster, lacking in coordination. The results of a commission form of government were generally so disastrous that the reform movement abandoned its early support of this form of government in favor of the council-manager plan. Today, less than 1 percent of U.S. cities, mostly those with populations below 25,000, are still governed by the commission form.

Council-Manager

COUNCIL-MANAGER FORM OF GOVERNMENT

The form of city government in which the elected council or commission appoints a manager to supervise city departments.

The **council-manager form of government** revived the distinction between legislative "policymaking" and executive "administration" in city government. Policymaking responsibility is vested in an elected council, and administration is assigned to an appointed professional administrator known as a manager. The council chooses the manager who is responsible to it. All departments of the city government operate under the direction of the manager, who has the power to hire and fire personnel within the limits set by the merit system. The council's role in administration is limited to selecting and dismissing the city manager. The plan is based on the idea that policymaking and administration are separate functions, and that the principal task of city government is to provide the highest level of services at the lowest possible costs—utilities, streets, fire and police protection, health, welfare, and recreation. Hence, a professionally trained, career-oriented administrator is given direct control over city departments. The manager even prepares the budget. Today, it is used by 59 percent of all U.S. cities.

Elected Mayor (Hybrid Mayor-Manager Form of Government)

HYBRID MAYOR-MANAGER FORM OF GOVERNMENT

A city manager who is hired and fired by a city council functions as the chief executive but voters also separately elect a mayor.

A **hybrid mayor-manager form of government** has emerged over the years.[12] The manager who is hired and fired by the council still functions as the chief executive but the voters also separately elect a mayor. Mayors in council-manager cities play two major roles. They are consensus builders and they guide the development and implementation of policies that improve community service delivery. By the late 2000s, 67 percent of all council-manager communities separately elected their mayor.[13]

FIGURE 10–4 **Forms of City Government**

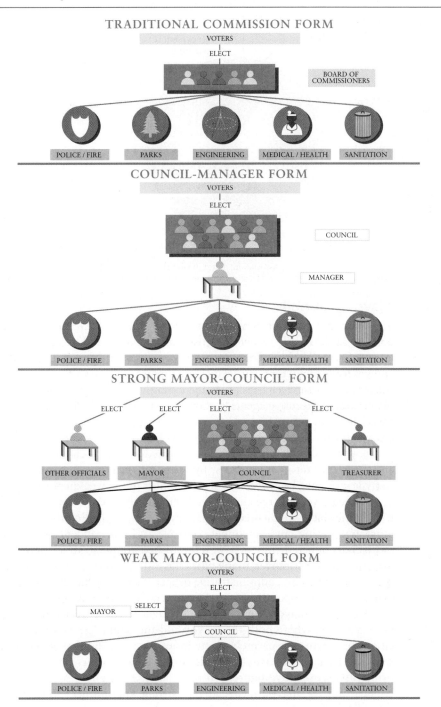

FIGURE 10–5 American Cities: Forms of Government

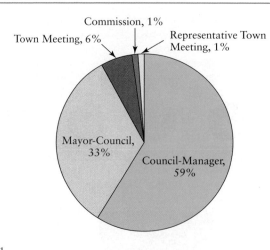

Note: Data are for 2011.
Source: International City/County Management Association "Form of Government Survey 2011." Statistics calculated from data set provided to Susan A. MacManus by ICMA.

Mayor-Council

STRONG MAYOR-COUNCIL FORM OF GOVERNMENT

The form of city government in which legislative power is exercised by an elected council, and city departments are supervised by a separately elected mayor.

There are two types of mayor-council government: strong mayor-council and weak mayor-council. (See "*People in Politics:* Just Call Me Mayor: Young Politicians on the Rise, One 'Strong,' One 'Weak'.") The nation's largest cities tend to function under the "**strong mayor-council form of government**." This structure is designed in the American tradition of separation of powers between legislature and executive. A strong mayor is one who is the undisputed master of the executive agencies of city government and who has substantial legislative powers in the form of budget making, vetoes, and opportunity to propose legislation. Only a few cities make the mayor the sole elected official among city executive officers; it is common for the mayor to share powers with other elected officials—city attorney, treasurer, tax assessor, auditor, clerk. Yet many mayors, by virtue of their prestige, persuasive abilities, or role as party leader, have been able to overcome most of the weaknesses of their formal office.

In recent years, large cities have been adding to the formal powers of their chief executives. Cities have augmented the mayors' role by providing them with direction over budgeting, purchasing, and personnel controls; and independent boards and commissions and individual council members have relinquished administrative control over city departments in many cities. Moreover, many cities have strengthened their mayors' position by providing them with a **chief administrative officer (CAO)** to handle important staff and administrative duties of supervising city departments and providing central management services.

CHIEF ADMINISTRATIVE OFFICER (CAO)

(CAO) In a strong mayor-council form of government, an official who functions as a city manager; is appointed by the mayor not the council.

WEAK MAYOR-COUNCIL FORM OF GOVERNMENT

The form of city government in which legislative and executive powers lie with an elected council and the mayor is primarily a figurehead who presides at council meetings and signs official papers.

The "**weak mayor-council**" **form of government** is most common in cities under 10,000 in population, where both the mayor and the council serve on a part-time basis. In some cities the mayor is separately elected, but in most, the mayor is a member of the council who has been chosen mayor by his or her council peers. In both situations, the mayor is primarily an executive figurehead responsible for signing papers and cutting ribbons. The council, not the mayor, has relatively strong appointment, budget, policy initiation, and management powers, although the powers of mayors even in this weak system are being expanded. Even so, such councils typically meet only once or twice a month because the issues they must deal with are not as complex or pressing as those facing big city councils.[14]

Town Meeting and Representative Town Meeting

Town-meeting and representative town-meeting governments are currently found in Connecticut, Maine, Massachusetts, New Hampshire, and Vermont. Most town meetings are held in response to the issuance of a warrant (agenda) by an elected town clerk and/or

Just Call Me Mayor: Young Politicians on the Rise, One "Strong," One "Weak"

"I didn't honestly expect to win," said Tashua Allman, mayor of Glenville, West Virginia. "I just wanted the experience and to get my name out there." Svante Myrick, mayor of Ithaca, New York, drew inspiration from Barack Obama (like the President, he is biracial). If a "guy with that name and those ears can do it, then a guy with this name and these ears can do it," he said.

Allman and Myrick were elected mayor shortly after graduating from college. They reflect diverse backgrounds and discharge different duties (one is a "strong" mayor, the other a "weak" mayor), but they bring energy and audacity to their public roles. Allman presides over a town of 1,500 people in the Mountain Lakes region of West Virginia; Myrick governs a city of 30,000 in central New York state. In both towns, education is a major industry. Glenville is home to Glenville State College (GSC); Ithaca, to Cornell University as well as two small colleges.

Allman showed an interest in politics as an undergraduate at GSC, serving as student body president and president of College Democrats. In 2009, with no job in sight and graduation looming, she ran for mayor as a write-in candidate. She beat the former mayor by one vote: 56–55. At age 21, Allman became the youngest mayor in West Virginia history. She was reelected in 2011 with no opposition.

Myrick was a junior at Cornell when a friendly alderman persuaded him to run for his seat in 2007. He won the race and managed to graduate, along with working odd jobs and tutoring as a volunteer. He announced his bid for mayor in 2011, annoying local Democratic leaders who thought he was too young and resented his professional campaign tactics. He won the primary with 46 percent of the vote and then the general election with 54 percent. At 24, he became the youngest mayor in the town's history.

Both Glenville and Ithaca operate under a mayor-council form of government. Glenville's mayor is considered "weak" because the mayor and council share administrative authority. Ithaca's mayor, on the other hand, is "strong." The mayor can appoint committees, veto actions of the city council, execute contracts, and propose budgets.

Salaries reflect mayoral duties. Allman draws $10,000 a year as a part-time mayor, so she works full-time counseling GSC students at risk of dropping out. Myrick earns $53,561 a year as a full-time mayor, and actually spends closer to 80 hours a week on the job.

Although a "weak mayor," Allman used her symbolic authority to revitalize the downtown and increase voluntarism in city improvement efforts. She started the volunteer "Street Gang" to help clean up the downtown and promoted events that combine fun and charity, such as the Zombie Walk Food Drive.

Myrick likewise came in with new ideas. Not owning a car, he had city workers turn the mayor's parking space into a mini park where he hosted occasional forums with residents. But he was not averse to using old ideas either. Faced with a $3 million budget deficit, he cut expenses and raised revenues, something his single mother did continuously in raising four children. "When you grow up in a household without enough money to make ends meet," he said, "you have to make difficult, and within the family, unpopular decisions."

The two mayors, although serving in cities with different forms of government, both reflect a commitment to search for innovative solutions to local problems. *Governing* magazine reports that across the United States, young elected officials are bringing new energy to local governance.

---

by the elected town council. The town meeting is open to all residents and it possesses full legislative authority. A town meeting may be called once or twice a year. In most town meetings, the passage of the annual budget is the most important item of business.

Town meetings usually choose a board to oversee business between meetings. Voters separately elect a town clerk, treasurer, assessor, constable, school board, and other officers. The town meeting may also elect a finance committee to prepare the budget.

While the town meeting has been celebrated by many political philosophers as "pure democracy," the reality is much less than full participatory democracy. Attendance at town meetings is usually less than 10 percent of the town's voters. In larger towns, the participation rate may be only 1 or 2 percent of the voters. The idealized town meeting democracy is really governance by a small group of political activists. Of course, attendance increases when controversial items are on the agenda. And in many town-meeting governments, a decision can be overturned by citizen initiative and referendum.[15]

Representative town-meeting (RTM) government is a hybrid political institution that seeks to combine features of the open town meeting with representative government. In RTM the voters elect a relatively large number of persons to vote at meetings, yet voters retain the right to attend and speak at town meetings. However, in practice the number of candidates for town-meeting members is frequently equal to or even smaller than the number of town-meeting members to be elected. Town clerks often must recruit people to become town-meeting members. In theory, representative town-meeting members should be more attentive than townspeople because they accepted the responsibility of public office. But attendance is also a problem in RTM government.

Changing City Charters: The Trend toward Hybrid Forms

It is not uncommon for citizens to want to change some aspect of their city charter. Over the years, a number of mayor-council cities have adopted some elements of council-manager governments (e.g., professional administrator, civil service) and some council-manager governments have adopted several elements of the strong-mayor-council form (e.g., separately elected mayor with veto power). "Fewer cities are now either distinctly mayor-council or council-manager in form, and most cities are structurally less distinct, constituting a newly merged or hybrid model of local government."[16] What prompts a city's voters to support changing the city charter? Often it is rapid growth, but any sharp shift in local conditions such as economic decline, government corruption, and/or rising crime rates may prompt change. Politically savvy community activists are often the catalysts for successful charter change movements. But in general, getting voters to support structural changes is a difficult task; many efforts fail. (See Table 10–2.)

10.7

Evaluate how successfully nonpartisan elections have taken the "politics" out of local government and raised the caliber of candidates for elected office.

NONPARTISAN ELECTIONS

Elections in which candidates' names appear on a ballot without listing their party affiliation.

NONPARTISAN ELECTIONS

Most of America's cities use the nonpartisan ballot to elect local officials. Reformers believed that **nonpartisan elections** would take the "politics" out of local government and raise the caliber of candidates for elected offices (see Chapter 11). They believed that nonpartisanship would restrict local campaigning to local issues and thereby rule out extraneous state or national issues from local elections. They also believed that by eliminating party labels, local campaigns would emphasize the qualifications of the individual candidates rather than their party affiliations.

Nonpartisanship is found in both large and small cities. Nonpartisanship is even more widespread than council-manager government. However, there is a tendency for these two forms to be related: 85 percent of all council-manager cities have nonpartisan ballots, while only 65 percent of all mayor-council cities are nonpartisan. Party politics is still the prevailing style of local elections in eastern cities, except for New England. Elsewhere in the nation, nonpartisanship prevails. The nonpartisan ballot is more likely to be adopted in homogeneous middle-class cities, where there is less social cleavage and smaller proportions of working-class and ethnic group members.

Do nonpartisan elections remove politics? To what extent has nonpartisanship succeeded in removing "politics" from local government? Of course, if "politics" is defined as conflict over public policy, then "politics" has certainly not disappeared with the elimination of party labels. First of all, in some nonpartisan cities, parties continue to operate effectively behind the scenes in local affairs. *Disguised party politics* is most likely to be found in big cities of the Northeast and Midwest, in states where political parties are strong and competitive. In these cities, persons who are known Democratic and Republican candidates run in officially "nonpartisan" elections.

Another type of nonpartisan political system is one in which the major parties are inactive, but clear *coalitions* of socioeconomic groups emerge that resemble the national Democratic and Republican parties. These opposing coalitions may involve liberal, labor, Catholic, and minority groups on one side and conservative, business, Protestant, and middle-class groups on the other.

Nonpartisan systems may feature the activities of independent community *groups* and organizations. Frequently, these groups are civic associations led by newspapers, chambers of commerce, or neighborhood associations. These organizations may "slate" candidates, manage their campaigns, and even exercise some influence over them while they are in

TABLE 10–2 Voters Don't Always Approve Structural Changes

Proposed Change	Percentage Approved
Election Method	
From at-large to single-member district (ward) elections	17
From single-member district (ward) to at-large elections	14
To a mixed (combination) system with some at-large and some single-member district seats	19
The mix between the number of council members elected at large and the number elected by single-member district (ward)	11
The method of electing the mayor	20
Powers of Mayor/Chief Elected Official	
Increase powers/authorities	29
Decrease powers/authorities	26
Size of City Council	
Increase the number of council members	31
Decrease the number of council members	17
City Manager/Chief Appointed Professional Administrator	
Add the position of professional administrator or manager	48
Eliminate the position of administrator or manager	10

Source: Adapted from International City/County Management Association, "Municipal Form of Government Survey 2011." Data are for changes that occurred between 2006 and 2011. Available at http://icma.org/en/icma/knowledge_network/documents/kn/Document/303954/ICMA_Municipal_Form_of_Government_Survey_2011_Summary.

office. These organizations are not usually as permanent as parties, but they may operate as clearly identifiable political entities over the years.

In still another type of nonpartisan political system, neither parties, nor coalitions, nor groups play any significant role, and there are no local slate-making associations. Individual candidates select themselves, collect their own money, and create their own temporary campaign organizations. Voting does not correlate with issues, or party identification, or socioeconomic groups, but instead tends to follow a *friends and neighbors* pattern. Indeed, voting in local nonpartisan elections often depends on factors such as incumbency, name recognition, position on the ballot (the first name on the list gets more votes), and brief personal contacts (a handshake at the office or factory, a door-to-door canvass, or even a telephone call).

Does nonpartisanship increase Republican influence in city government? It is sometimes argued that the removal of party designations from local elections hurts Democrats by disengaging their traditional support from urban voters—the low-income, labor, ethnic, and black groups that traditionally vote the Democratic ticket. Moreover, the well-educated, high-income groups and interests that are normally Republican have a natural edge in organization, communication, and prestige in the absence of parties. Republicans also have better turnout records in nonpartisan elections. Surveys of local officials elected under partisan and nonpartisan systems tend to confirm that nonpartisanship results in the election of more Republicans. However, this Republican advantage in nonpartisan elections is modest; it appears to be limited to smaller cities and cities that are dominated by Democrats.[17]

Does nonpartisanship result in better-qualified candidates winning public office? Of course, the answer to this question depends on one's definition of "better qualified." Nonpartisanship means that recruitment of candidates will be left to civic associations, or ad hoc groups of one kind or another, rather than to Democratic or Republican Party organizations. This difference in recruitment and endorsement practices tends to give an advantage to middle-class candidates. Working-class candidates seldom have the organizational ties or memberships that would bring them to the attention of civic associations that recruit in nonpartisan elections.

Incumbent Advantage

Nonpartisanship appears to contribute to the reelection of incumbent council members, particularly when nonpartisanship is combined with at-large elections. Incumbent council members are reelected on the average about 80 percent of the time. When incumbents *are* defeated, they tend to suffer defeat in a group as a result of intense community conflict.[18] Incumbents are more likely to have a name that is known to the voters. Incumbent council members in partisan cities are not reelected as often as incumbents in nonpartisan cities. This suggests that it is difficult to hold public officials accountable in nonpartisan elections.

10.8

LOCAL ELECTION SYSTEMS: AT LARGE, DISTRICT, AND COMBINATION

Compare at-large and district electoral systems, and how the electoral system affects which candidates are most likely to be victorious.

Local elected legislative officials—county commissioners, city council members, town and township board members, school board members, and special district board members—are usually elected one of two ways. The first is *at large*—by the entire electorate (e.g., citywide, countywide, school districtwide). The second is *from a district.*

Some local governments elect all legislative officials at large; others elect all from single-member districts; but a growing number elect some officials at large, but others from single-member districts (a combination, or mixed, system). Today, roughly 66 percent of American cities elect their council members at large, about 17 percent by districts, and 17 percent by a combination of at-large and district constituencies.[19] Indeed, there are many hybrid local election systems used across the United States, which is confusing to those who move from one community to another.

Types of At-Large Systems

The city council has been selected as the local legislative body used to illustrate how different types of at-large electoral systems work. (They work the same for county commission, town board, township board of trustees, school board, or special district board elections.)

Under an at-large system, all council members run citywide and are voted on by all the voters in the city.[20] Under a **pure at-large electoral system**, if there are six seats up for election, each voter can vote for up to six candidates. The six candidates receiving the highest number of votes are elected. But there are other forms of at-large systems. In some cities, a person runs for a numerically or alphabetically labeled seat but is elected citywide (an **at-large by position electoral system**). A person must decide whether he or she wants to run for Council Seat No. 1, or A, or Council Seat No. 2, or B, and so forth. The council seat, regardless of how it is labeled, has no geographical basis. On Election Day, all voters in the city can select the candidates they prefer for each nongeographically defined seat up for election. If there are six seats up for election, each voter may cast six votes—one for each seat.

There is yet a third type of at-large election called the **at-large from residency district electoral system**. The city is divided into equally populated, geographically defined districts. A candidate runs to represent the district in which he or she lives (e.g., District 1), but all voters in the city get to vote on who shall represent that district. If there are six districts, each voter casts a ballot for a preferred candidate from each district. The intent of this type of system is to guarantee broader representation of geographical areas, while requiring candidates to take a citywide perspective.

Traditionally, reformers believed that district elections encourage parochial views, neighborhood interest, "logrolling," and other characteristics of "ward politics." These "undesirable" characteristics occur because council members are responsible to local majorities in the particular sections or wards from which they are elected. In contrast, council members elected at large are responsible to citywide majorities; this should encourage impartial, communitywide attitudes. Moreover, in council-manager cities, it is argued that the manager can be more effective in serving the "general good" of the whole community if the manager is responsible to council members elected at large rather than by districts. (Of manager

PURE AT-LARGE ELECTORAL SYSTEM

Elections in which candidates are chosen by all of the voters in a community; the number of seats up for election are won by the highest vote-getters.

AT-LARGE BY POSITION ELECTORAL SYSTEM

A person runs for a numerically or alphabetically labeled seat but is elected citywide.

AT-LARGE FROM RESIDENCY DISTRICT ELECTORAL SYSTEM

A candidate runs to represent the district he or she lives in, but all voters in the city get to vote on who shall represent that district.

cities, 70% elect council members at large, compared to only 50% of mayor-council cities. Council-manager cities also tend to have more racially/ethnically homogeneous populations. Racial and ethnic groups have pressed for single-member district election systems.)

Single-Member District Systems

A **single-member district electoral system** limits each voter's choice to a single contest. A voter must choose among the candidates who have filed to represent the district (sometimes called a "ward") in which the candidate and the voter both reside. (See Choctaw, Oklahoma, in Figure 10–6.)

SINGLE-MEMBER DISTRICT ELECTORAL SYSTEM
Elections in which candidates are chosen by voters in separate geographically defined districts.

Minority spokespersons frequently argue that minority candidates have a better chance of winning when they run from districts, especially when they make up less than a majority of the city's voting-age population but live in a residentially concentrated area. In such settings, switching to a district-based electoral system permits the drawing of a district in which minorities make up a majority of the electorate. District-based elections are also alleged to increase voter turnout rates and reduce campaign spending costs, although the data are clearly mixed on those counts. For example, there is some evidence that minority voter turnout declines once a minority candidate is elected and becomes an entrenched incumbent.

For racial/ethnic minorities, district-based elections have been shown to promote slightly higher levels of representation depending on the size of the group, their geographic concentration, their political cohesiveness, and their ability to coalesce with other groups. However, there is considerable evidence that the size of the minority electorate within a community is a far more powerful predictor of a group's proportional representation on city council than the electoral system itself.[21] For example, one summary of this literature notes: "As black populations have grown, especially in large central cities, as black political participation rates (registration and turnout) have equaled or exceeded those of whites, and as successful black candidates have paved the way for others, the independent effect of electoral structure on black council representation levels has waned in certain parts of the country."[22] There is less evidence that the type of election system independently affects Hispanic or Asian representational levels.

Even the importance of minority group size is beginning to weaken as more minorities capture at-large posts in big cities such as Houston and Kansas City or win seats in districts with less than majority-minority populations. This trend is expected to accelerate as more Americans begin to label themselves biracial or multiracial and cities become more multiethnic in composition.

Combination Election Systems

Voters in cities using a **combination (mixed) electoral system** to choose council members can vote for all the at-large positions but for only one of the district-based council seats. For example, if a city has two at-large seats and four single-member district seats, each voter can cast three ballots (for the two at-large seats and for one district-based seat—the one in which he or she resides. See Houston, Texas, in Figure 10–6.)

COMBINATION (MIXED) ELECTORAL SYSTEM
Some officials are elected at large; others are elected from single-member districts.

Proponents of mixed systems promote them precisely because they retain some council members who bring a citywide perspective to matters before the council but allow other council members to represent more narrow neighborhood or group perspectives. Minority groups (racial or partisan) who comprise a sizable portion of the population but are not concentrated in a specific neighborhood often prefer at least some at-large seats. This makes it possible for them to elect a candidate of their choice, or serve as the swing vote, if they vote as a bloc. Term-limited district-based minority council members also favor having some at-large seats for which they can run once the district seat term limits kick in. Increasingly, minorities are winning these at-large seats in combination systems.

Civil Rights Tests

The use of at-large elections to discriminate against racial minorities in their ability to participate in the political process and elect candidates of their own choice clearly violates

FIGURE 10–6 Comparing Single-Member District and Mixed (Combination) Election Systems

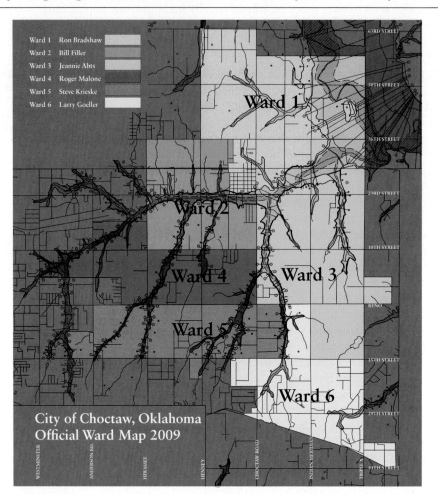

Ward 1   Ron Bradshaw
Ward 2   Bill Filler
Ward 3   Jeannie Abts
Ward 4   Roger Malone
Ward 5   Steve Krieske
Ward 6   Larry Goeller

City of Choctaw, Oklahoma
Official Ward Map 2009

Note: The City of Choctaw, Oklahoma, elects its city council members using a single-member district election system, also referred to as a ward system. A citizen may vote in only one council race—the one featuring candidates running from the district in which the voter lives.
Source: City of Choctaw, OK http://www.ok.gov/choctaw/documents/City%20of%20Choctaw%20ward%20Map%202009.11.12.pdf.

**VOTING RIGHTS
ACT OF 1982**

Established a "totality of circumstances" test to be used in deciding whether the at-large elections resulted in racial discrimination.

the Equal Protection Clause of the Fourteenth Amendment and the federal Voting Rights Act. The U.S. Supreme Court in *Mobile* v. *Bolden* (1980) held that at-large elections are *not* unconstitutional in the absence of any evidence of discriminatory intent.[23] However, Congress amended the **Voting Rights Act of 1982** to substitute a *results test* for the more difficult to prove *intent test* in assessing discrimination. But Congress stopped short of declaring all at-large elections discriminatory and illegal. Instead, Congress established a "totality of circumstances" test to be used in deciding whether the at-large elections resulted in racial discrimination. The elements to be considered by the federal courts are:[24]

- A history of official discrimination. (This test applies primarily to southern states.)
- A record of racial polarization in voting.
- Unusually large election districts.
- The existence of candidate slating by parties or groups, and whether minority members have been slated.
- The extent to which minorities have been adversely affected by local government decisions.
- Whether political campaigns have been characterized by racial appeals.
- The extent to which minority group members have been elected to office.

FIGURE 10–6   Continued

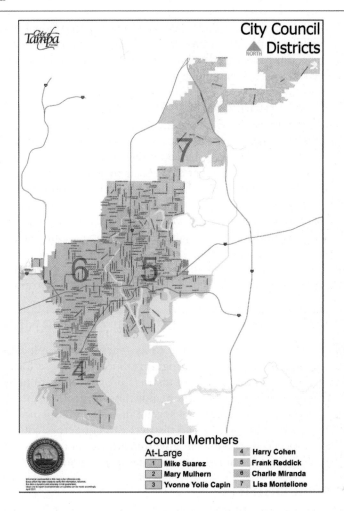

Note: The City of Tampa, Florida, elects its city council members using a mixed, or combination, election system. Three members are elected citywide; four are elected from single-member districts. A citizen may vote in four council races—all three of the at-large races, and one district race (the one in which the voter resides).
Source: City of Tampa, FL http://www.tampagov.net/dept_geographic_information_systems/files/City_of_Tampa_Maps/Council_Districts_ALL_D.pdf.

The federal courts are prepared to evaluate the use of at-large elections in each community by these tests.[25]

Federal Court Intervention

Federal court cases in recent years involving at-large elections suggest that it is becoming increasingly difficult for cities, counties, and even school districts to defend exclusive reliance on at-large elections. Civil rights groups have effectively utilized the "totality of circumstances" test to invalidate at-large elections across the country and especially in southern states. In some cases federal courts have ordered district elections for all officials, and in other cases federal courts have accepted combination plans—some council members elected by district and some at large.

Some federal courts have even ordered other election systems put in place. **Cumulative voting** has been adopted in over 40 localities to resolve federal voting rights cases, including Alamogordo, New Mexico; Amarillo, Texas; Peoria, Illinois; and Chilton County, Alabama.[26] Cumulative voting is actually a variation of at-large voting. "Candidates run in multimember districts. Voters have as many votes as there are seats. Voters cast their votes for individual candidates and the winners are the ones with the most votes. Voters may 'cumulate' or combine their votes on one or more candidates instead of having to cast one

CUMULATIVE VOTING
Variation of at-large voting. Candidates run in multi-member districts. Voters have as many votes as there are seats. Voters cast their votes for individual candidates and the winners are the ones with the most votes. Voters may also "cumulate" or combine their votes on one or more candidates.

vote for each candidate."[27] Supporters believe it enhances the chances of minority election and increases voter turnout slightly.[28]

The U.S. Supreme Court does *not* require **proportional representation** for minorities, that is, a council that is 20 percent black if the city's population is 20 percent black. However, lower federal courts have tended to compare the black proportion of the council with the black proportion of residents in determining whether the "totality of circumstances" suggests discrimination.

Minority Representation

Until recently, blacks were significantly *underrepresented* on city councils that elected their members at large. In the 1970s several studies reported that blacks won fewer than 50 percent of the seats they deserved (based on their percentage of a city's population) in *at-large* cities, compared to 85–100 percent of the seats they deserved in cities that elected council members *by districts*.[29] However, by the late 1980s, black representation on city councils throughout the nation had increased dramatically, and it no longer made much difference in black representation whether councils were elected at large or by district.[30] For cities with more than 10 percent and less than 50 percent black population, black representation on city councils is only slightly below black population percentages, and the difference between at-large and district elections is minuscule. For cities with black populations over 50 percent, "then it is whites who need district representation to obtain their proportional share of council seats."[31]

10.9

SPECIAL-PURPOSE LOCAL GOVERNMENTS

Counties and cities are referred to as general-purpose local governments. They provide a wide range of services and programs. Special-purpose local governments have narrower service responsibilities. School districts provide education. Special districts are formed for functions such as transportation, mosquito control, hospitals, or parks, to name a few. The geographical area covered by special districts often is not the same as that covered by a county or city. In fact, special districts can cut across county lines. An **authority**, another type of special-purpose local government, can cut across county and state lines (e.g., the New York Port Authority that includes territory in New York and New Jersey).

School Districts

There are nearly 14,000 public school districts in the United States today that serve over 50 million students. Local school districts are governed by an elected **school board** (legislative body) and an elected or appointed **school superintendent** (chief executive). In some school districts, board members are appointed rather than elected, usually by city councils, county commissions, mayors, or even judges. (For a more detailed description of school system responsibilities and powers, see Chapter 16.)

The vast majority of school boards have either five or seven members. Few school districts (less than 10%) have term limits for school board members. Being a school board member is generally a part-time position. A majority receive no pay for serving and spend less than five hours per week on school board–related issues. However, in larger, more diverse school districts, board members are paid and spend a lot more time on the job. Regardless of the size of the district, those who serve on school boards are regarded by both teachers and school superintendents as being influential in the community in which they serve.[32]

There are fewer minorities and females on school boards than on other local governing bodies. A recent survey by the National School Boards Association found 81 percent of all school board members are white, 12 percent are African American, and 3 percent are Hispanic; 44 percent are women.[33] Minority and female representation levels are higher in larger school districts, which are typically more diverse. Several factors deter minorities from running for school board posts: income, time commitment required, and lack of experience in holding leadership posts. In some districts, at-large elections may make it more difficult as well. Today, 57 percent of all school board members are elected at large, while 41 percent are elected by single-member district. The rest are appointed. Most of those elected to office run without a political party label (nonpartisan elections).

Most school superintendents are appointed. Only three states permit the election of school superintendents—Alabama, Florida, and Mississippi.[34] In 12 states, some school superintendents are paid more than the governor.[35] (See Figure 10–7.) The profile of school superintendents is even more white and male. A national survey of school superintendents[36] finds that 76 percent of school superintendents are male. Only 4 percent are black and 2 percent are Hispanic. White males still dominate in positions that are seen as pathways to becoming a superintendent (high school principal; business manager). Female school administrators in similar positions who have been passed over for a superintendency blame school board members who make the appointment as prejudiced by myths and stereotypes of women as inadequate administrators.[37]

In most states, local school board members are elected. Minority and female representation levels are higher in large school districts, which are typically more diverse. Issues brought before school boards are often highly contentious, ranging from sex education, school uniforms, and religious holidays, to teacher–student relationships.

Special Districts

There are over 37,000 special district governments across the United States. Many are governed by a quasi-independent board or commission. Most of these board members or

FIGURE 10–7 Some School Boards Pay School Superintendents More than the Governor Makes

States highlighted are states that pay a superintendent more than the Governor. Pay includes salary, compensation and bonuses.

Note: States highlighted are states that pay a superintendent more than the Governor. Pay includes salary, compensation and bonuses.
Sources: Governors' salaries (2013) from the Pew Center on the States, "How much does your governor make?;" http://www.pewstates.org/projects/stateline/headlines/governors-salaries-range-from-70000-to-187256-85899486281, June 26, 2013; School superintendent pay data from individual state public records.

commissioners are appointed by governors, legislators, and/or local elected officials such as mayors or county commissioners. Some board members serve by virtue of the fact that they hold another elective position. There is no national association of special districts so it is difficult to generalize about their structure or their diversity. Special districts are the least understood of all the types of local government, yet they frequently control multimillion-dollar budgets. In a nutshell, there is little accountability to the general public. The news media rarely covers special district activities unless there is a major crisis. (For a more detailed description of special district functions and responsibilities, see Chapter 12.)

Most citizens find discussions of local government structures and governance documents (charters) to be boring—and confusing. But when they want something done or they want to vote someone out of office whom they feel has been inept, irresponsible, or unresponsive, they soon recognize the importance of understanding which local government and public official has the authority to deal with their concern.

CHAPTER HIGHLIGHTS

- One of the biggest challenges facing local governments, especially in light of America's highly mobile population, is how to define and create a "sense of community" among an area's residents.
- Citizens unhappy with community problems can (1) become politically involved in change, (2) just live with it, or (3) move to another community. The choice can depend on one's education and income level as well as other factors.
- Because local government powers vary so widely across the country, citizens wanting change need to know who hires and fires local officials, who prepares the budget, and how local officials are selected.
- County governments generally have (1) a governing body often called the "county commission," (2) a number of separately elected officials such as sheriff and county attorney, (3) a large number of special boards with authority over various functions, and (4) an appointed county bureaucracy to carry out various functions.
- A number of states have granted counties and cities "home rule," which allows greater self-governance than ordinarily provided by the state constitution or state statutes. Home rule is more often granted to larger cities and counties with broader tax bases.
- Northern states from New England to the Midwest use the township, a governmental unit smaller than a county that performs many county government functions, like road maintenance, at a grassroots level.
- Cities are "municipal corporations" that have received a charter from the state to operate as a self-governing unit. "Dillon's rule" limits that self-governance to only those powers expressly granted in the charter.
- Over half of American cities operate under the council-manager form of government. Other forms include mayor-council (strong or weak mayor), commission, town meeting, and representative town meeting. Strong mayor-council forms are more common in large cities.
- Nonpartisan local elections tend to benefit Republicans more than Democrats and incumbents more than first-time candidates.
- Local governments elect legislative officials at large, from single-member districts, or using a combination of the two. Because of civil rights challenges to at-large elections, Congress has instituted a "totality of circumstances" test to determine if at-large election systems are discriminatory.
- Local school districts are generally governed by an elected school board (legislative) and an elected or appointed school superintendent (executive); appointed superintendents are more common. Some superintendents in large, diverse school districts are paid more than the governor.
- Special districts are the most common type of local government in most states and the least familiar to citizens, primarily because governing boards are usually appointed rather than elected. They frequently control multimillion-dollar budgets.

CHAPTER ELEVEN

PARTICIPATION IN COMMUNITY POLITICS

LEARNING OBJECTIVES

 11.1 Describe the different ways that citizens participate in community politics, and compare the frequency of citizen participation at the local and national levels.

 11.2 Analyze the roles played by political parties in big-city politics, and assess the relative successes of the Democratic and Republican Parties in urban areas.

 11.3 Explain the tools used by old-style political machines to dominate big-city politics.

11.4 Discuss the reforms sought by the progressive movement, and assess their success in bringing about the reforms and weakening political machines.

11.5 Outline efforts by local governments to increase the involvement of citizens in the decision-making process through e-government and policy elections.

 11.6 Describe those who are likely to run for local office, and outline how the professionalization of local politics has influenced who chooses to run.

 11.7 Explain the role of city council members in shaping public policy, and assess the ability of citizens to hold elected local officials accountable for their decisions.

 11.8 Discuss the role that city managers play in local policymaking, and evaluate whether or not city managers should shun politics.

 11.9 Outline the powers and limitations of mayors.

 11.10 Describe the extent to which minorities and women participate in local politics, and assess the extent of their influence over public policy.

 11.11 List the types of interest groups that are active in community politics, and analyze their ability to influence local government decisions.

CITIZEN PARTICIPATION

Describe the different ways that citizens participate in community politics, and compare the frequency of citizen participation at the local and national levels.

A local business owner applies for a permit to build an adult business featuring "lap dancing." A police officer is arrested for selling drugs to high school students. The mayor proposes raising residential property tax rates by 10 percent during an economic downturn. A huge pothole causes a driver, swerving to miss it, to kill a dog beloved by an entire neighborhood. A weed-infested vacant lot has turned into a ready-made dump. A young girl is molested by a neighbor who is a registered sex offender. A city council passes an ordinance outlawing "Satan" (this really happened).[1] What do each of these happenings have in common? Wherever they occur, they are likely to prompt citizens to get involved in local community affairs when they otherwise would not. At the community level, it's the little things that matter most—the things that directly affect someone's daily quality of life. Local politics is often said to be centered on police, potholes, porno, property, pets, pollution, "problem" neighbors, citizens' pocketbooks, and, of course, "politicians."

Ideally, democracy inspires widespread citizen participation in government—as voters, community activists, neighborhood association and interest group members, party workers, and candidates for public office. But in fact, rarely do many citizens participate actively in community politics.

A "**communitarian**" **view** praises the many values of direct citizen participation in community affairs, not just by voting, but perhaps more importantly, by participating in groups and forums, working with neighbors to solve the problems of the community. This view asserts that where neighbors talk about community affairs in face-to-face meetings, they learn from one another, become more tolerant of different people with different views, create bonds of friendship, and look to common solutions to their problems.

In reality relatively few people are interested in community political affairs. They are busy at their jobs and professions, concerned with raising their children, and more interested in watching reality shows or sports on television than broadcasts of city council meetings. And it may be naïve to believe that community political activism always engenders tolerance, respect, and common efforts to resolve problems. Often, increased participation inspires rancorous conflict, intolerant popular policy initiatives, and even violence. Indeed, a surge of participation, with resulting conflicting claims upon a government that cannot satisfy everyone, may simply engender cynicism and disrespect toward government. Citizen activists are not always well informed even on the issue on which they are most vociferous. Activism—particularly neighborhood NIMBY activity ("not in my backyard" opposition to community projects)—may paralyze local government, preventing it from effectively addressing community-wide problems.[2]

COMMUNITARIAN VIEW
Praises the many values of direct citizen participation in community affairs, not just by voting, but perhaps more importantly, by participating in groups and forums, working with neighbors to solve the problems of the community.

Volunteering as Civic Participation

Many believe that "Americans are sitting in their homes and offices isolated from their communities and neighbors, shunning civic activities, and unwilling to get involved."[3] But surveys by groups like the Pew Partnership for Civic Change have reported that Americans are volunteering more than ever before and are helping neighbors to solve problems. Many citizens, especially younger ones, do not

Volunteering by citizens of all ages is a form of activism that helps build a sense of community.

think of volunteering as a form of community participation. But volunteering for soup kitchens, domestic violence shelters, mentoring programs, and the like is a critical component of building a sense of community. Civic engagement is not limited to voting or joining organizations, although both are measures of a community's civic health.

Voters in Local Elections

Voter turnout in local elections is substantially lower than in state or national elections. While 55–60 percent of the nation's eligible voters may cast ballots in a presidential election, voter turnouts of 25–35 percent are typical in local elections. Local elections differ from national and state elections in several important ways. In *local* (county, city, town, township, and school board) elections[4]:

- Turnout is usually lower.
- Political parties and party allegiance play a less influential role, especially in smaller jurisdictions; 80 percent of all local governments have nonpartisan elections.
- Group identities and group interests (racial, ethnic, religious, union) are more important voting cues than political party identification.
- Campaigns focus more on "who gets what and at the expense of whom?"—the outputs of government (police and fire protection, garbage collection, parks and recreational facilities, the quality of roads and public schools, health care programs). The "zero sum" nature of resource allocation is "front and center" in campaign debates.
- Issues are smaller in number, less complicated, but more personally relevant to individual voters.
- Certain types of issues, especially moral and fiscal, can be more important at promoting turnout than a candidate's personality or party, but usually personality and party dominate.
- The politics of "place" is more prevalent (eastside vs. westside, north vs. south, downtown business district vs. residential areas).
- A wider variety of candidates run for office (candidate heterogeneity). It is easier to find someone of your own race, ethnicity, religion, social class, gender, or political ideology to vote for.
- Candidate and group get-out-the-vote (GOTV) strategies are typically narrowly targeted and group specific.
- Electoral coalitions are often the key to winning, but are constantly shifting as a community's demographic makeup changes. This is most common in fast-growing, increasingly diverse communities.
- The timing (when the election is held) can drastically affect turnout. Local election turnout is lowest in nonpresidential election years (off-cycle).
- Media coverage, especially by television, of local campaigns is far less extensive. (See "*Did You Know?:* Broadcast Television Coverage of Local Campaigns Is Limited.") Mayoral races get far more coverage than county commission, city council, or school board races, even in local newspapers.

Nonpartisanship in local elections depresses voter turnout substantially. Voter turnout for municipal elections in nonpartisan cities averages closer to 25 percent, compared to over 35 percent for cities with partisan elections. Partisan campaigns heighten voter turnout, in part because of the greater interest they generate and in part because of the role of party workers in getting out the vote. However, most local governments, especially municipalities, have nonpartisan elections.

Voter participation in local government can be further reduced by holding municipal elections at odd times of the year when no other state or national elections are being held. Approximately 60 percent of the nation's cities hold municipal elections that are completely independent of state or national elections. Yet studies show that the voting rate in local election contests is 36 percent higher when they are held at the same time as the presidential election.[5] A common rationale for holding municipal elections at times other than state or national elections is to separate local issues from state or national questions, but the real effect of scheduling local elections independently is to reduce voter turnout

Broadcast Television Coverage of Local Campaigns Is Limited

The portion of a typical local TV news broadcast that is devoted to politics and government has slipped from 7 percent in 2005 to just 3 percent. Local television stations do not devote a lot of time to local government in general, let alone local election races. So it is no wonder that candidates running for local offices complain about the lack of local election coverage by the media.

Coverage of *local* contests is especially limited during a presidential or gubernatorial election year. A national study of local election coverage during a presidential election year found that only a very small percentage of the political stories were focused on a *local* candidate's race. The average campaign story was just 86 seconds long. Candidate sound bites featuring a candidate in his or her own words appeared in just 28 percent of the stories; the average sound bite was 12 seconds long.

Some local stations have reacted to criticism about local political race coverage by expanding content and videos posted on their Web sites or in social media.

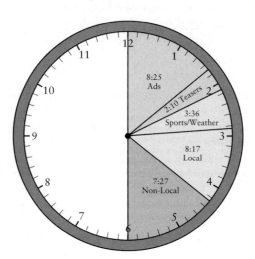

The Changing Make-up of Local News

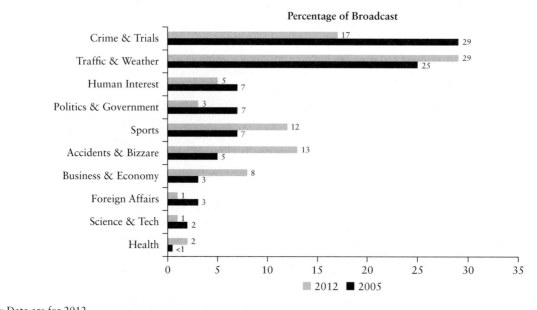

Percentage of Broadcast

Category	2012	2005
Crime & Trials	17	29
Traffic & Weather	29	25
Human Interest	5	7
Politics & Government	3	7
Sports	12	7
Accidents & Bizzare	13	5
Business & Economy	8	3
Foreign Affairs	1	3
Science & Tech	1	2
Health	2	<1

■ 2012　■ 2005

Note: Data are for 2012.
Sources: The Pew Research Center's Project for Excellence in Journalism, *The State of the News Media 2013*. Available at http://stateofthemedia.org/2013/overview-5/overview-infographic/.

and to increase the influence of groups who vote more regularly, especially senior voters. Consequently, more local governments are shifting to "on-cycle" elections to boost voter turnout rates and to save money. (Elections are expensive to conduct.)

Voter turnout in large cities with a strong mayor-council form of government and with partisan elections is higher than in smaller cities with a council-manager plan and nonpartisan elections. In summary, nonpartisanship, council-manager government, and separate municipal elections—all part of the municipal "reform" movement—operate to reduce voter turnout and probably strengthen the influence of middle-class and older voters at the polls.

Voter turnout in municipal elections is also affected by the social character of cities. Social cleavages, especially race, increase voter turnout. Mayoral elections in which the racial or ethnic backgrounds of the candidates are well publicized inspire heavy voter turnout.[6] Latino and African American turnout rates often exceed white turnout rates in such elections. Minority group turnout rates increase sharply when a candidate from that group stands a good chance of being elected and would be the first member of that group to hold local office. Social homogeneity, on the other hand, is associated with lower voter interest.

Turnout is also affected by the presence of a local issue on the ballot (permissible in states allowing local governments to utilize the tools of direct democracy—initiative, referendum, and recall). Having a "hot issue" on the ballot increases turnout by 4 percent or so.[7]

In summary, voter turnout in municipal elections can be described as follows:

Lower voter turnout is expected with	Higher voter turnout is expected with
Nonpartisan electoral systems	Partisan elections with competitive parties
Council-manager form of government	Strong mayor form of government
City elections held separately from state and national elections	City elections held concurrently with state and national elections
Small or middle-sized cities	Large cities
Middle-class, homogeneous cities	Ethnic, heterogeneous cities
No hot issue on the ballot	Hot issue on the ballot

Local Referenda Voters

In most states, citizens are given at least some tools to "take local government into their own hands" through the initiative, referendum, and recall processes.[8] The initiative process is an option in over 50 percent of all cities. By collecting a required number of signatures on a petition, citizens can place a change to the structure of local government (charter, ordinance, home rule) or policy changes on the ballot for voter approval. The recall process, in which voters can remove an elected official before his or her term is completed, is also available in over 50 percent of the cities. The process typically begins with the circulation of a petition among registered voters asking for a recall election to be held, naming the official(s) to be recalled, and identifying the cause for removal. The most common causes are misuse of the office or failure to perform duties. Occasionally a recall effort centers on an official's "unusual" behavior or demeanor.[9]

The referendum is even more widely available, with 70 percent of American cities having this method in their charters. It gives voters the final say about the disposition of some issue or proposal put on the ballot by a county commission or city council. There are several different forms: binding, nonbinding, and petition or protest (to delay). **Referenda voting** is an important aspect of local politics—an aspect not found at the national level. City charters frequently require that referenda be held on all proposals to increase indebtedness, increase property taxation, or amend the charter.

Many voters in local referenda will weigh the benefits that will come to them from a bond issue against the amount of the tax that will fall on them as a result of the expenditure. Non–property owners, having nothing to lose by the expenditure and something to gain,

REFERENDA VOTING
Voters deciding whether to approve an issue or proposal put on the ballot by a local government.

however small, can be expected to favor the passage of bond and expenditure referenda. (Renters seldom realize that landlords will pass the tax increase on to them in higher rent.) Homeowners are more likely to oppose public expenditures that are financed from property taxes than nonhomeowners. Among homeowners, support for local public expenditures often *increases* with education, wealth, and income. This tendency of upper-class, liberal voters to support recreational, cultural, and environmental projects (e.g., parks, museums, stadiums, libraries, art centers) was once labeled "**public-regardingness.**"[10]

The types of issues that end up on local ballots for voter approval, whether through a referendum or initiative procedure, are as diverse as local governments. A sample of the wide range of issues placed before voters in the 2000s and their resolution included:

- In Greenfield, Massachusetts, voters overwhelmingly rejected the city's involvement in a proposed 47-megawatt wood-burning "biomass" power plant. Specifically, voters disapproved of the town's sale of its treated wastewater to the proposed plant for cooling or other purposes.
- In Miami Beach, Florida, voters said the city should provide employee benefits to gay and heterosexual domestic partners.
- In Plymouth, California (population 1,090), voters recalled the mayor and two city council members for supporting efforts by the Mikok Indian tribe to purchase 200 acres to build a casino inside the city limits.

Issues put on local ballots for voter approval, if controversial and high profile, may increase voter turnout. Campaign ads are likely to be run on both sides of the issue.

Campaign Contributors

Money is playing an increasingly influential role in politics at all levels of government.[11] The costs of campaigning, especially the costs of television advertising, are rising rapidly. Earlier we observed that it is not uncommon for candidates for governor in large states to raise and spend millions in an election, and campaigns for highly competitive state legislative seats in large states often require upwards of hundreds of thousands of dollars (see "Money in State Politics" in Chapter 5). Tracking the amount of money raised by a candidate and those who are contributing to the campaign is a common way the media gauges the momentum of a local race.[12]

In local politics it is still possible to run a low-budget, door-to-door "shoe leather" campaign, especially in suburbs and small towns. It is still possible for many candidates for city council and county commission to rely on small contributions from friends, neighbors, and relatives, or on their own pocketbooks, to pay for signs, brochures, and newspaper ads.[13]

But in big cities, candidates for mayor, as well as city council and county commission, must raise substantial campaign money. Mayoral campaigns in America's big cities may cost millions of dollars, and even city council campaigns can be quite expensive. There has been an upswing in wealthy individuals like New York City's Michael Bloomberg choosing to finance their own campaigns and to spend whatever is necessary to win. But a more common reason for the rising costs of local elections is the nationalization of local politics. When broad issues like gay rights, pension reform, global warming, or health care become part of a local contest, *out-of-state* donors or SuperPACs interested in those topics may pour money into those races.[14]

Who *locally* contributes to candidates for local office? A careful inspection of candidate campaign contributors offers great insights into the range of individuals and interest groups involved in any community's political process. Traditionally the largest sources of campaign contributions for city and county offices have come from business interests with direct contacts with these governments—real estate developers, builders, contractors, professional service providers (law, accounting, public relations/advertising), and nonprofit human service agencies.[15] They seek to "invest" in winners in order to establish access and goodwill among the officials who will be deciding on contracts for a variety of goods and services, zoning and land-use questions, building and construction codes, environmental regulations, and various "**growth management**" policies (see Chapter 13, "Community Power, Land Use, and the Environment"). Aside from the possibility of getting a government contract, more local business owners began contributing to local campaigns during the Great Recession in hopes of getting more "business-friendly" local officials in office—those committed to regulatory relief and economic development.

It is difficult to say whether money "buys" local elections. **Incumbents** raise and spend much more money than challengers, and incumbents almost always win reelection. A more serious question is whether campaign contributions to a winning candidate "buy" influence and a favorable vote on an issue of high priority to the contributor. State laws and local ordinances spell out rules governing the link between campaign contributors, gifts, lobbyists, and elected officials, although in many cases the rules are not explicit. Elections commissions and/or ethics commissions investigate complaints and impose penalties unless the allegation is a criminal offense, in which case it would be investigated by state or federal prosecutors. Defeated opponents and citizen watchdog groups are most often the source of official complaints. But local newspapers often play a key role in publicizing perceived wrongdoings. The "political" rule of thumb is that even if a link between a contributor and an elected official is legal, if it doesn't pass the "smell test" it may be perceived by the public as unethical.

GROWTH MANAGEMENT
In local government, efforts to limit or restrict population growth and commercial and industrial development.

INCUMBENT
The person currently serving in a public office.

PARTIES IN BIG-CITY POLITICS

11.2

Analyze the roles played by political parties in big-city politics, and assess the relative successes of the Democratic and Republican Parties in urban areas.

While political parties play less of a role in local politics than national or state politics, their presence in big-city politics is still observable. This is true whether a city elects its mayor and council members via partisan (e.g., New York, Chicago, Philadelphia, Boston) or nonpartisan (e.g., Los Angeles, Detroit, San Antonio, Miami) elections. Traditionally, Democrats have dominated politics in the nation's large central cities, even while their surrounding suburbs have usually been governed by Republicans. Social groups that normally vote Democratic—white ethnic groups, Catholics and Jews, African Americans, Latinos (excluding Cubans in Miami), union members, low-income families—tend to be concentrated in big cities. Since the formation of the modern "New Deal" Democratic Party coalition under President Franklin D. Roosevelt in the 1930s, most big cities in the United States have been governed by Democrats. This has been true whether the city's electoral system has been officially partisan or nonpartisan.

Party identification patterns of the various ethnic groups in cities are diverse. African Americans are the most solidly Democratic.[16] Hispanics and Asians, while often voting Democratic, are somewhat more likely to identify themselves as independents than as Democrats. However, party identification is not always the best predictor of policy positions. Even within each group, there are differences of opinion, often depending on how long an individual has been in the United States. Immigrants tend to be more conservative than native-born residents, with the exception of Asians. It is also important to recognize that because many minorities are recent immigrants and not yet citizens, they are not registered voters. This is particularly true of Hispanic and Asian immigrants.[17]

Splits among Urban Democrats

Political cleavages within the Democratic Party have been a driving force in big-city politics over the years. Political conflict in many of America's largest cities has centered on differences between working-class, Catholic, white ethnic (especially Irish, Italian, and Polish) Democrats versus upper-class, white, liberal Protestants and Jews, allied with black and Latino Democratic voters. These factions within the Democratic Party have frequently battled over such issues as affirmative action hiring in city government, busing in schools to achieve racial balance, and the behavior of police and prosecutors in crime control.

And they have often differed over the burdens of public spending for welfare, health, and public housing—with working-class white ethnics, who are often homeowners and property tax payers, opposed to higher taxes and spending for these services; and upper-class liberals and blacks, many of whom are renters whose property taxes are hidden in rent payments, supporting these expenditures (see "Minorities and Women in Local Politics" later in this chapter).

Occasionally, Democratic Party organizations have been strong enough to hold these diverse Democratic groups together. Traditional party "**machines**" would slate candidates for city office with an eye to racial and ethnic group balance. But as these party machines lost influence over time, intraparty factional conflict—especially between working-class white ethnics and minorities—intensified in many cities.[18]

The growing Hispanic vote in many of America's largest cities adds another potentially unstable element to the Democratic Party coalition. Both African Americans and Hispanics have suffered discrimination in a predominantly white, "Anglo" society, and both have higher-than-average rates of poverty and unemployment and lower median family incomes. But a number of studies have shown this coalition to be unstable, occasionally engaging in competition over city jobs, language issues, and representation (e.g., as in Chicago, Denver, Miami, Houston, and Los Angeles).[19]

Republican Big-City Resurgence?

Splits among urban Democrats, combined with continuing big-city ills—huge deficits, violent crime, racial and ethnic conflicts—have opened up new opportunities for Republican candidates. Despite overwhelming Democratic registration, big-city voters have elected a number of Republican mayors to cope with urban problems. Republican prosecuting attorney Rudolph Giuliani was first elected mayor of New York in 1994, the first Republican to govern that city in over twenty years. Richard Riordan, a multimillionaire lawyer-businessman, was elected mayor of Los Angeles in 1993, the first Republican to hold that office in twenty years. Since that time, other Republicans (Michael Bloomberg in New York City[20] who later became an independent), and some conservative Democrats have won unexpected victories in heavily Democratic cities. When Republicans began winning in Democratic-dominated areas, certain common themes dominated their campaigns: a crackdown on crime, cutting the size of the city bureaucracy, reducing city deficits, easing tax burdens, and stimulating the city's economy. Republicans also heavily targeted the Hispanic vote, especially in cities with sizable black and Hispanic populations where there was friction between the two groups. Initially, it was not clear whether these Republican inroads in big-city politics were temporary responses to voter frustration or a more permanent resurgence of Republican strength. More recently, Republican victories in big-city mayoral contests have largely been in municipalities located in Republican-dominated states or metropolitan areas.

MACHINE

In politics, a tightly disciplined political organization, historically centered in big cities, which traded patronage jobs, public contracts, services, and favors for votes.

11.3 OLD-STYLE MACHINE POLITICS

Explain the tools used by old-style political machines to dominate big-city politics.

Machine politics has gone out of style. Machines—tightly disciplined party organizations, held together and motivated by a desire for tangible benefits rather than by principle or ideology and run by professional politicians—emerged in the nation's large cities early in the nineteenth century. This style of city politics has historical importance. Between the Civil War and the New Deal, every big city had a machine at one time or another, and it is sometimes easier to understand the character of city politics today by knowing what went on in years past. A more important reason for examining the machine style of politics is to understand the style of political organization that employs personal and material rewards to achieve power. These kinds of rewards will always be important in politics, and the big-city machine serves as a prototype of a style of politics in which ideologies and issues are secondary and personal friendships, favors, and jobs are primary.

The **political machine** was essentially a large brokerage organization. Its business was to get votes and control elections by trading off social services, patronage, and petty favors to the urban masses, particularly the poor and the recent immigrants. To get the money to pay for these social services and favors, it traded off city contracts, protection, and privileges to business interests, which paid off in cash. Like other brokerage organizations, a great many middlemen came between the cash paid for a franchise for a trolley line or a construction contract and a Christmas turkey sent by the ward chairman to the Widow O'Leary. However, the machine worked. It performed many important social functions for the city.

POLITICAL MACHINE

A political organization that employs personal and material rewards (friendships, favors, jobs) to achieve power.

Personal Attention

The machine personalized government. With keen social intuition, the machine recognized the voter as a person, generally living in a neighborhood, who had specific problems and wants. The machine provided individual attention and recognition. As Tammany Hall **boss** George Washington Plunkitt, the philosopher king of old-style machine politics, explained: "I don't trouble them with political arguments. I just study human nature and act accordin'."[21] The machine also performed the functions of a welfare agency. According to Plunkitt, "What tells in holdin' your grip on your district is to go right down among the poor families and help them in the different ways they need help."[22] In the absence of government unemployment insurance or a federal employment service, **patronage** was an effective political tool, particularly in hard times. Not only were city jobs at the disposal of the machine, but the machine also had its many business contacts. Yet it was not so much the petty favors and patronage that won votes among urban dwellers as it was the sense of friendship and humanity that characterized the "machine" and its "boss."[23]

BOSS

The acknowledged leader of a political machine, who may or may not occupy a public office.

PATRONAGE

Rewards granted by government officeholders to political supporters in the form of government jobs or contracts.

Assimilation

The machine also played an important role in educating recent immigrants and assimilating them into American life.[24] Machine politics provided a means of upward social mobility for ethnic group members, which was not open to them in businesses or professions. City machines sometimes met immigrants at dockside and led them in groups through naturalization and voter registration procedures. Machines did not keep out people with "funny"-sounding names but instead went out of the way to put these names on ballots. Politics became a way "up" for the bright sons of Irish and Italian immigrants.

"Getting Things Done"

Finally, for businesses, and particularly for public utilities and construction companies with government contracts, the machine provided the necessary franchises, rights of way, contracts, and privileges. As Lincoln Steffens wrote: "You cannot build or operate a railroad, or a street railway, gas, water, or power company, develop and operate a mine, or cut forests or timber on a large scale, or run any privileged business, without corrupting or joining in the **corruption** of government."[25] The machine also provided the essential protection from police interference, which is required by illicit businesses, particularly gambling. In short, the machine helped to centralize power in large cities. It could "get things done at city hall."

CORRUPTION

In politics, the use of public office for private gain, including bribery, conflict of interest, and the misuse and abuse of power.

REFORMERS AND DO-GOODERS

A reform style of politics appeared in the United States shortly after the Civil War to battle the "bosses." Beginning in 1869, scathing editorials in the *New York Times* and cartoons by Thomas Nast in *Harper's Weekly* attacked the "Tammany Society" in New York City, a political organization that controlled the local Democratic Party. William M. Tweed was president of the board of supervisors of New York County and undisputed

Discuss the reforms sought by the progressive movement, and assess their success in bringing about the reforms and weakening political machines.

boss of "Tammany Hall," as the New York County Democratic committee was called, after its old meeting place on Fourteenth Street. This early reform movement achieved temporary success under the brilliant leadership of Samuel J. Tilden, who succeeded in driving the "Tweed Ring" out of office and went on in 1876 to run for president, win a majority of popular votes, and then be denied the presidency through the operation of the Electoral College.

Early municipal reform is closely linked to the Progressive movement in American politics. Leaders such as Robert M. La Follette of Wisconsin, Hiram Johnson of California, Gifford Pinchot of Pennsylvania, and Charles Evans Hughes of New York backed municipal reform at the local level as well as the direct primary and direct election of senators and woman's suffrage at the national level.[26] In 1912, social worker Jane Addams, who labored in slums and settlement houses, sang "Onward Christian Soldiers" at the Progressive Party convention that nominated Teddy Roosevelt for president. Lincoln Steffens wrote in *The Shame of the Cities,* "St. Louis exemplified boodle; Minneapolis, police graft; Pittsburgh, a political industrial machine; and Philadelphia (the worst city in the country), general civic corruption."[27]

Social Bases of Reform

From its beginning, the **municipal reform movement** was strongly supported by the upper-class, Anglo-Saxon, Protestant, longtime residents of cities whose political ethos was different from that which the new immigrants brought with them. The immigrant, the machine that relied upon his or her vote, and the businessperson who relied upon the machine for street railway and other utility franchises had formed an alliance in the nineteenth century that had displaced the native, old family, Yankee elite that had traditionally dominated northern cities. This upper-class elite fought to recapture control of local government through the municipal reform movement.

Machine politicians catered to ethnic groups, organized labor, blue-collar workers, and other white working-class elements of the city. The reform politician appealed to the upper- and middle-class affluent Americans who were well educated and public-service minded. Reform was popular among liberals, newspaper reporters, college professors, and others who considered themselves "intellectuals."

Reform Goals

Reform politics included a belief that there was a "public interest" that should prevail over competing, partial interests in a city. The idea of balancing competing interests or compromising public policy was not part of the reformers' view of political life. Rather, the reform ethos included a belief that "politics" was distasteful. Enlightened people should agree on the public interest; municipal government is a technical and administrative problem rather than a political one. City government should be placed in the hands of those who are best qualified—by training, ability, and devotion to public service—to manage public business. These best-qualified people can decide on policy and then leave administration to professional experts. Any interference by special interests in the politics or administration of the best-qualified people should be viewed as corruption.

The objectives of early reform movements were:

- *Eliminate corruption.* The elimination of corruption in public office, and the recruitment of "good people" (educated, upper-income individuals who were successful in private business or professions) to replace "politicians" (who were no more successful than their constituents in private life and who were dependent upon public office for their principal source of income).
- *Nonpartisanship.* The elimination of parties from local politics by nonpartisan elections.
- *Manager government.* The establishment of the council-manager form of government, and the separation of "politics" from the "business" of municipal government.

Rahm Emanuel: Coming Home to Run Chicago: A Tougher-than-Expected Job

Prior to running for mayor of Chicago, Rahm Emanuel was White House Chief of Staff under President Barack Obama. Reported to be the most powerful Chief of Staff in recent history, Emanuel was responsible for orchestrating Obama's extensive policy agenda. According to Emanuel: "Never let a crisis go to waste. Crises are opportunities to do big things." At the White House, "big things" included bailing out the nation's financial institutions, stimulating the nation's economy, increasing federal spending and deficit levels, making the tax structure more progressive, and transforming the nation's health care system. The big question was whether Emanuel could shift gears from national policy issues to municipal demands for speedy garbage collection and rapid snow removal.

Emanuel entered the Chicago mayor's race well-suited for the rough-and-tumble of Chicago politics, with a reputation for being a prodigious campaigner, rising early to stand at El stops and shake the hands of riders. He was also an awesome fund-raiser with a national profile and unmatched connections from his White House days. He convinced the Illinois Supreme Court to declare him a Chicago resident, reversing a lower court ruling that he had lived in Washington too long. He quickly amassed the largest campaign fund in the city's history, dwarfing the combined total of his six rivals. On the campaign trail he held in check his famous temper and acid tongue.

Emanuel replaced the retiring Mayor Richard M. Daley, Chicago's longest serving mayor, who surpassed the long tenure of his father, Richard J. Daley. Together the Daleys had dominated Chicago politics for a half-century. They were the last vestiges of old big-city machine politics. The family name carried a lot of weight in national Democratic politics. Mayor Richard M. Daley's younger brother William took Emanuel's place as President Obama's White House Chief of Staff.

Emanuel's first name, Rahm, means "high" or "lofty" in Hebrew. Emanuel was born and raised in Chicago; he and his brothers went to summer camp in Israel. He attended the Evanston School of Ballet and later graduated from Sarah Lawrence College in 1981. During the first Gulf War he served with the Israeli Defense Forces as a civilian volunteer. He began his political career as a public interest organizer for Illinois Public Action. But his real strength was in political fund-raising: he served as chief fund-raiser for Mayor Richard M. Daley and later as chairman of Bill Clinton's campaign finance committee in the presidential election of 1992. Following this campaign, Emanuel became a senior adviser in the Clinton White House. He left his first White House job in 1998 to become an investment banker in Chicago.

Emanuel resigned his investment banker post to run for the U.S. House of Representatives in 2002, for the Chicago seat vacated by Rod Blagojevich, who had just won the Illinois governorship. Emanuel defeated seven other candidates in the Democratic primary and went on to easily win the general election. In Congress, he gained a reputation as a highly partisan, Chicago-style, combative liberal. When Barack Obama won the presidency, he needed a well-connected powerbroker to oversee his vast policy agenda and tapped Emanuel as his Chief of Staff.

Being mayor turned out to be a much bigger challenge than Emanuel thought it would be when he took office in the middle of the Great Recession. The realities of having to deal with budget problems, city pension woes, a wave of murders, and declining city schools required him to make tough decisions that were quite unpopular. Emanuel's approval ratings plunged. At one point, just 2 percent of Chicagoans strongly approved of his performance as mayor. Even then, few were willing to bet against his reelection in 2015. One *Washington Post* blogger has even mentioned him as a potential presidential candidate in 2016—if Hillary Clinton does not enter the race.

- *At-large districts.* The establishment of at-large citywide constituencies in municipal elections in lieu of "district" constituencies in order to ensure that an elected official would consider the welfare of the entire city in public decision making and not merely his or her own neighborhood or "ward."

- *Short ballot.* The reorganization of local government to eliminate many separately elected offices (the "short-ballot" movement) in order to simplify the voters' task and focus responsibility for the conduct of public affairs on a small number of top elected officials.

- *Strong executive.* The strengthening of executive leadership in city government—longer terms for mayors, subordination of departments and commissions to a chief executive, and an executive budget combined with modern financial practices.

- *Merit system.* The replacement of patronage appointments with the merit system of civil service.

- *Home rule.* The separation of local politics from state and national politics by home-rule charters and the holding of local elections at times when there were no state and national elections.

All these objectives were interrelated. Ideally, a "reformed city" would be one with the manager form of government, nonpartisan election for mayor and council, a home-rule charter, a short ballot, at-large constituencies, a strong executive, a merit service personnel system, and honest people at the helm. Later, the reform movement added comprehensive city planning to its list of objectives—official planning agencies with professional planners authorized to prepare a master plan of future development for the city. The National Municipal League (now the National League of Cities) incorporated its program of reform into a **Model City Charter**, which continues today to be the standard manual of municipal reform.[28]

MODEL CITY CHARTER

A guide for cities to use when writing or revising their charters, written by the National Civic League, a good government reform-minded organization.

Reasons for the Machine's Decline

Parties in general are losing their appeal to many Americans. Increasing proportions of voters are identifying themselves as "independents," rather than as Democrats or Republicans. (See Chapter 5.) Party offices (precinct committee, ward chairperson, county committee) are vacant in many cities and counties. The general decline in parties has contributed to the decline of machine politics. Several additional factors might be cited as contributing to the decline of machine politics:

- *The decline in European immigration* and the gradual assimilation of white ethnic groups—Irish, Italians, Germans, Poles, Slavs.

- *Federal social welfare programs,* which undercut the machine's role in welfare work—unemployment insurance, workers' compensation, Social Security, and public assistance.

- *Rising levels of prosperity* and higher educational levels, which make the traditional rewards of the machine less attractive.

- *The spread of middle-class values* about honesty, efficiency, and good government, which inhibit party organizations in purchases, contracts, and vote buying, and other cruder forms of municipal corruption.

- *New avenues of upward social mobility* that have opened up to the sons and daughters of working-class families, and higher education, which has allowed many to join the ranks of professionals, corporate executives, educators, and other white-collar workers so that the party machine is no longer the only way "up" for persons at the bottom of the social ladder.

- *Structural reforms* such as nonpartisanship, better voting procedures, city-manager government, and—most important of all—civil service, which have weakened the party's role in municipal elections and administration.

- *The rise of self-financed candidates* who no longer need a political party's blessing or endorsement to enter an electoral contest or to mount a formidable campaign.

- *The emergence of television as the best way to get a candidate's message out to the voters,* rather than through party volunteers. Fewer Americans have time to volunteer for party "get out the vote" efforts.

Today's local politics might be characterized as less party and more politician.

The New Personalized Machines

Some big-city mayors have been successful in building personal political organizations centered on the mayor's office. They have expanded their supply of patronage jobs by enlarging the mayoral office staff and creating public authorities and agencies that are directly responsible to the mayor's office. Many of these bureaucracies are federally funded and their top posts can be filled by an astute mayor using "creative" personnel practices. In many large cities, elements of the old ward politics survive in particular neighborhoods. It still matters to many voters that their representative grew up in the neighborhood, still lives there, can be contacted day or night, knows their names, and gives personal attention to their problems. It also matters that a twenty-first century big-city mayor still takes pride in promoting "our town" and opts for a local over a national political career. (See "*People in Politics:* Rahm Emanuel: Coming Home to Run Chicago: A Tougher-than-Expected Job.")

If we define **patronage** to include a wide range of tangible benefits—construction contracts, insurance policies, printing and office supplies, architectural services, and other government contracts for goods or services—then patronage is still important in many communities. Competitive bidding by potential government contractors is required in most states and cities, but it is not difficult to "rig" the process. The fact that the firms that do much of their business with government are also the largest contributors to political campaigns cannot be a coincidence.[29] Another source of patronage is the power of courts to appoint referees, appraisers, receivers in bankruptcies, and trustees and executors of estates; these plums require little work and produce high fees for attorneys who are "well connected."

Ethics: The Never-Ending Battle to Combat Corruption

Reformers continue to fight against unethical and corrupt behavior of local officials. "**Public or political corruption** occurs when government officials use their public office for private gain or benefit."[30] Some localities have long histories of rampant political corruption, like Cook County, Illinois, often referred to as "Crook County." An in-depth study by researchers at the University of Illinois at Chicago identified more than 150 politicians and government officials who have been convicted of outright theft and bribery, as well as endemic patronage, nepotism, and cronyism. They found that the graft and corruption is widespread across multiple local governmental units. While not all localities have such deep-seeded, long histories of fraudulent and unethical behavior, claims of such behaviors do surface elsewhere, although on a more isolated basis. (See "*Up Close:* Exposing Political Corruption.") But corruption wherever and whenever it occurs reduces citizens' trust and confidence in their government and in people generally.[31]

The result has been more attention to public service ethics and required ethics training for public employees as well as elected officials. (See Figure 11–1.) Some localities now have ethics codes and ethics commissions, often in response to state mandates. Ethics training covers such topics as personal financial disclosure laws, perk issues (compensation, use of public resources and gifts), transparency laws, conflict of interest laws, use of staff on campaigns, and competitive bidding requirements.[32] Ethics reform efforts have been most successful in cities and counties with strong good government organizations, especially those that are well-established coalitions composed of multiple groups that have deep roots and connections in the community, and are nonpartisan.[33]

PUBLIC OR POLITICAL CORRUPTION
When government officials use their public office or position for personal gain or benefit.

FIGURE 11–1 Local Government Ethics Code Coverage

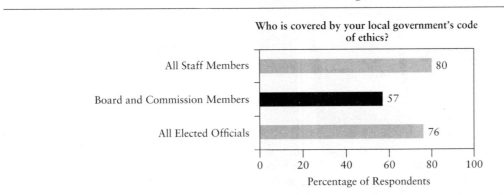

Who is covered by your local government's code of ethics?

Category	Percentage
All Staff Members	80
Board and Commission Members	57
All Elected Officials	76

Percentage of Respondents

Source: International City/County Management Association, "ICMA State of the Profession Survey, 2009." Available at http://transformgov.org/ Documents/Document/Document/100267. Adapted/Reprinted with permission of the International City/County Management Association, 777 North Capitol Street, NE, Suite 500, Washington, DC 20002. All rights reserved. Most recent data available at time of publication.

NEW CONNECTIONS WITH CITIZENS

Outline efforts by local governments to increase the involvement of citizens in the decision-making process through e-government and policy elections.

In today's high-tech society, governments are constantly in search of ways to improve their contact with the citizenry through the Internet and other interactive mechanisms. As one communications expert puts it: "Governments are shifting their view of citizens as consumers, and allowing citizens to become contributors in the development of government."[34] Changing technology, specifically the rise of social media, has greatly altered the way local government officials communicate professionally with each other and directly with their constituents. The most popular vehicles are LinkedIn and the ICMA Knowledge Network.

Increasingly popular ways to make local government information more accessible and transparent to citizens and to solicit their input on key issues are[35]:

- *Interactive Web sites* that allow citizens to "talk" to elected officials in online chat sessions, respond to surveys, register complaints, purchase licenses and permits online, pay parking and other fines online, bid on government contracts, and watch local government hearings via streamed video. Effective Web sites are mobile friendly, with location awareness (mapping capabilities), notification services, and chat windows allowing contact with a live government employee.[36]

- *Social networks, YouTube, Twitter, text messaging.* Use of Facebook, Twitter, text messaging, and videos via YouTube are being used to build a better sense of community, connect neighborhoods and individual citizens, and promote active civic engagement in local activities and programs. However, their use is hampered by the lack of access of Web managers to social media tools because of legal issues related to cybersecurity and the protection of individual rights.[37]

- *Mobile "Apps" for everything.* With a majority of Americans now owning smartphones, smart local governments are developing apps to better inform citizens about a wide range of services, from public transportation, public safety, and recreation, to housing, health, and garbage pickup. Some apps also allow citizens to inform their local government about problems ranging from blight, graffiti, and other code enforcement violations to potholes and street flooding (often by sending photos taken with their cell phone camera).[38]

- Challenge.gov *(Crowdsourcing).* Crowdsourcing is a new and popular way to invite the public to participate in solving problems. A government presents a problem plaguing it to a broad online audience, asks for solutions from the interested public, then examines its feasibility for possible adoption.[39]

- *Citywide "wireless" zones or Wi-Fi "hot spots."* Communities see being on the leading edge of the broadband revolution as critical to maintaining and expanding strong residential and commercial sectors.

- *Targeting constituents/neighborhoods using GIS.* Geographic Information System (GIS) is a software system that enables the plotting of data geographically. It enables a local government to visually show citizens where funds are being spent, who is being served by government programs, and where government-owned infrastructure (buildings, facilities) is located. GIS systems are also seen as a way to distribute technical and scientific knowledge to citizens and, in turn, to get feedback on complex issues traditionally viewed as "too difficult" or "too sensitive" for citizens to grasp.[40]

The widespread use of smartphones and tablets has prompted local governments to use various forms of social media and "apps" to better connect with their constituents.

orruption is an ever-present theme in American political life. We all know that "politics is corrupt," but with the exception of some well-publicized cases we really do not know *how* much corruption takes place. Corruption may be more widespread in state and local politics than in national politics, because state and local officials avoid the spotlight of the national news media. One major problem in studying corruption is defining the term. What is "corrupt" to one observer may be "just politics" to another or merely "an embarrassment" to someone else.

For example, here is a list of hypothetical acts that state senators in 24 states were asked to rate as more or less corrupt, together with the percentage of senators who viewed each act as corrupt[a]:

- ■ The driveway of the mayor's home being paved by the city crew—95.9 percent.
- ■ A public official using public funds for personal travel—95.2 percent.
- ■ A state assembly member, while chairman of the public roads committee, authorizing the purchase of land he or she had recently acquired—95.1 percent.
- ■ A legislator accepting a large campaign contribution in return for voting "the right way" on a legislative bill—91.9 percent.
- ■ A judge with $50,000 worth of stock in a corporation hearing a case concerning that firm—78.8 percent.
- ■ A presidential candidate promising an ambassadorship in exchange for campaign contributions—71.1 percent.
- ■ A secretary of defense owning $50,000 in stock in a company with which the Department of Defense has a million-dollar contract—58.3 percent.
- ■ A member of Congress who holds a large amount of stock (about $50,000 worth) in Exxon working to maintain the oil depletion allowance—54.9 percent.
- ■ A member of Congress using seniority to obtain a weapons contract for a firm in his or her district—31.6 percent.
- ■ A public official using influence to get a friend or relative admitted to law school—23.7 percent.

The line between unethical behavior and criminal activity is a fuzzy one. Unethical behavior includes lying and misrepresentation; favoritism toward relatives, friends, and constituents; and conflicts of interest, in which public officials decide issues in which they have a personal financial interest. Not all unethical behavior is criminal conduct. But bribery—soliciting or receiving anything of value in exchange for the performance of a governmental duty—is a criminal offense.

Reports from the U.S. Justice Department indicate that over 1,200 public officials are indicted and convicted of criminal activity each year.

While investigating and prosecuting state and local government officials for corrupt activity was once the exclusive responsibility of the state attorney general's office using state laws, today U.S. attorneys have largely taken over this responsibility. Acting under broad federal statutes—dealing with mail fraud, tax fraud, and the RICO Act (Racketeer Influenced and Corrupt Organizations)—federal prosecutors have largely displaced state prosecutors in dealing with official corruption Federal prosecutors have the vast resources of the FBI, the Internal Revenue Service, the Postal Inspection Service, and myriad other federal agencies to assist them in investigations.

Journalists also play a major role in exposing the misdeeds of elected officials. The biggest prizes in the field of both print and electronic journalism (Pulitzers—newspapers; Edward R. Murrows—television and radio) are usually given for stories that result in public officials being booted from office for corruption.

Even when politicians are exposed, voters don't always punish officials for corrupt activities. Voters sometimes reelect officials who have been convicted of criminal offenses. The reasons vary.[b] First of all, *charges* of corruption are so frequent in election campaigns that voters disregard information about improprieties in office. Or voters may perceive both candidates as more or less corrupt and simply make their voting choices on other factors. Second, if voters believe that officials' corrupt acts were designed to benefit their district or their race or their ethnic group, they may support them despite (or even because of) their corrupt acts. Third, corrupt politicians may be popular with their constituents, whether personally or because of their stand on issues; constituents may knowingly ignore corruption because they value the representation more.

A strategy of some disgraced officeholders today is to publicly acknowledge one's past errors, claim personal redemption, go on television talk shows, and ask voters to accept a restored and chastised candidate. Others just take the punishment, serve the time, and fade away from public life.

[a]John G. Peters and Susan Welch, "Political Corruption in America: A Search for Definitions and a Theory," *American Political Science Review* 72 (September 1978): 974–984.

[b]For tests about voter reaction to corruption, see Barry S. Rundquist, Gerald S. Strom, and John G. Peters, "Corrupt Politicians and Their Electoral Support," *American Political Science Review* 71 (September 1977): 954–963.

- *Keypad polling at public town hall meetings and forums.* Audience response systems (ARS), or keypad polling, relies on a combination of handheld devices, computers, a receiver, and a projector. This technology allows public officials to ask meeting participants to answer multiple choice–type questions with a clicker and to immediately display the responses for everyone to see. The technology can make meetings more productive, educational, and participatory if used properly.[41]

- *Citizen satisfaction surveys.* These allow the concerns and policy preferences of average citizens to reach elected officials rather than just the views of the noisy few who can attend city council, county commission, or school board meetings.[42] Some local governments routinely use these surveys to find out how to better communicate with their citizens.

- *Government access cable television stations.* Citizens can watch public meetings, political debates, and forums, as well as learn about upcoming community events.

- *Appearances by local officials on television and radio.* Call-in talk and news magazine (public affairs) shows.

- *Citizen academies.* Small groups of citizens of all ages and backgrounds meet once a week or so to learn about government operations firsthand; they attend council or commission hearings, meet department heads, observe how the government delivers its services, and thereby gain a better understanding of how citizens can make a difference at city hall. Citizen academies are a form of civic capacity building that contributes to more citizen engagement and collaboration.[43]

- *Active volunteer recruitment programs.* Virtually every department, from parks and recreation to health and hospitals, has stepped up its recruitment of volunteers from the community, knowing that such voluntarism increases civic engagement and political participation.[44]

- *Kiosks at malls.* Interactive computers let citizens send a message directly to city hall, on issues ranging from potholes to budget priorities; new voting technologies, such as touch-screen voting machines, are often put in malls to allow citizens to test them out before Election Day.

- *Better use of diverse communication skills.* Greater use of "signers" to reach hearing-impaired citizens, Braille to reach the sight-impaired, and multilingual communicators to interact with non-English-speaking residents.

- *Annual performance reports e-mailed or mailed to each household.* Borrowing an idea from the corporate world, citizens (community shareholders) are sent an annual report highlighting services provided, facilities constructed, and the bottom line (the budget). A comment card is included soliciting citizen reaction to the government's "report card."

- *Call centers.* Nearly half of all local governments have implemented centralized customer service systems, also known as 311 call systems.[45] They are designed to handle nonemergency requests, taking pressure off of 911 systems. "One-stop" call centers that blend phone, Web, and e-mail route citizen requests for services or information, along with complaints, comments, and suggestions, to the correct place through a central call center. The "calls" are recorded to more easily permit follow-ups. Data generated allow local officials to improve their response rates to citizen requests and increase productivity. Call centers can also be used to call citizens and invite them to attend civic meetings; invitation phone calls have been found to increase attendance.[46]

Another trend in recent years has been for city councils to let voters make the final decision on highly explosive and divisive issues. Fiscal issues (taxing, spending, and borrowing) and moral issues (e.g., abortion, gay rights, gambling) top the list of issues typically laid in the laps of city voters by nervous council members. The bottom line is that efforts to involve citizens in decision making, whether via the ballot box or e-government, improve transparency and trust in government.[47]

11.6   RECRUITING CITY COUNCIL MEMBERS

Describe those who are likely to run for local office, and outline how the professionalization of local politics has influenced who chooses to run.

Political ambition is the most distinguishing characteristic of elected officeholders at all levels of government. The people who run for and win public office are not necessarily the most intelligent, best-informed, wealthiest, or most successful business or professional people. At all levels of the political system, from presidential candidates, members of Congress, governors, and state legislators, to city council and school board members, it is the most politically ambitious people who are willing to sacrifice time, family and private life, and energy and effort for the power and celebrity that comes with public office.

Most politicians publicly deny that personal ambition is their real motivation for seeking public office. Rather, they describe their motives in highly idealistic terms—"civic duty," "service to community," "reform the government," "protect the environment." These responses reflect the norms of our political culture: People are not supposed to enter politics to satisfy *personal* ambitions, but rather to achieve *public* purposes. Many politicians do not really recognize their own drive for power—the drive to shape their community according to their own beliefs and values. But if there were no personal rewards in politics, no one would run for office.

There are some gender-based differences in characteristics of those who ultimately run for local office. Men are more likely to become interested through being active in college government, while women began their activism in high school government. Men who run have more political acquaintances, are married, and have preschoolers at home. Women who run are more likely to have experienced gender bias and see themselves as leaders.[48]

Professionalization

Politics is becoming increasingly professionalized. "**Citizen politicians**"—people with business or professional careers who get into politics part time or for short periods—are being driven out of political life by **career politicians**—people who enter politics early in life as a full-time occupation and expect to make it their career. Politics is increasingly demanding of time and energy. At all levels of government, from city council to state legislatures to the U.S. Congress, political work is becoming full time and year round. It is not only more demanding to *hold* office than it was a generation ago, but also far more demanding to *run* for office. Campaigning has become more time-consuming, more technically sophisticated, and much more costly over time.

CITIZEN POLITICIAN
People with business or professional careers who get into politics part time or for short periods.

CAREER POLITICIAN
People who enter politics early in life as a full-time occupation and expect to make it their career.

Traditionally, city council members and county commissioners were local businesspeople who were respected in the community and active in civic organizations. They were likely to own small businesses and to have many contacts among constituents—retail merchants, real estate brokers, insurance agents. (Seldom do executives of large corporations concern themselves with local affairs, although they may encourage lower-management personnel to do so.) The part-time nature of traditional community governance, combined with only nominal pay and few perks of office, made local office-holding a "community service." It attracted people whose business brought them into close contact with the life of the community and allowed them spare time to attend to community affairs.

These civic-minded small businesspeople are still politically dominant in many small towns and rural counties throughout the nation. But they are gradually being replaced by lawyers, government employees, teachers, and professional officeholders in medium to large cities. In these cities, council pay is higher, the work is more time-consuming, celebrity status is greater (a council member can expect television interviews, newspaper stories, deference, and respect), and greater opportunities exist for political advancement.

Why Run for City Council?

Few Americans ever take the bold step of running for city council. To them, council salaries are too low, citizen expectations are unrealistic, politicians are held in low regard, and the media scrutiny of candidates is too intense.

The formal qualifications for city council members are actually minimal. Most cities require that a candidate for council be a registered voter, a U.S. citizen, and a resident of the community for a certain period of time (usually a year or less). Persons convicted of a felony offense and those formally certified as mental incompetents generally are prohibited from running unless they petition to have their voting rights restored (most states have provisions for this).[49]

POLITICOS

Those who run because they enjoy politics and hope to move on to another office.

SELF-REGARDERS

Those who enter city politics intent on personal enrichment.

COMMUNITY-REGARDERS

People who run for office to serve the whole community and seek no personal gain.

LOCALS

Citizens who run primarily to help friends and neighbors, not parties (*partisans*) or single-issue interest groups.

So why *do* people choose to run for city council? One widely cited study classifies council members according to the reason they say they ran.[50] **Politicos** say they ran because they enjoy politics and hope to move on to another office. **Self-regarders** enter city politics intent on personal enrichment. **Community-regarders** run to serve the whole community and seek no personal gain. **Locals** run primarily to help friends and neighbors, not parties (*partisans*) or single-issue interest groups. **Particularists** run because of an overriding concern for a specific issue or issues; they tend to be outsiders—minorities or members of groups long underrepresented in government—and one-termers. Regardless of why someone decides to run, there are some basic questions each potential candidate should ask first, ranging from "Is my family on board?" to "Is the timing right?" (See Table 11–1.)

Motivations for running differ across age groups. Older voters, many of whom are retirees, report they initially decided to run because they finally had the time and resources to do so. Younger candidates are more likely to say they ran because no one else would or because it would give them experience in office before running for a higher office.[51] However, fewer young people are entering politics at the local level, choosing instead to make their first run for office for a state legislative seat.

Some council members choose not to run again after serving just a few terms, and the number is growing, especially those serving in big cities. The greatest source of frustration is conflict among council members, cited by 55 percent.[52] Conflict seems to be worse

---

TABLE 11–1 10 Questions to Ask Yourself before Running for Office

1. Is my family on board?

If you have any doubts as to whether your family is behind your campaign, or can withstand the scrutiny, you shouldn't be running.

2. Are my finances sound?

Calculate the personal financial cost of running for the office you're considering, and make sure you have a candid discussion about it with your family

3. Do I have the stomach to ask for the cash?

Don't delude yourself into thinking money will come easily. If you're not willing to spend the next year or more prodding people to open up their checkbooks, this might not be for you.

4. Do I have the stomach to go negative?

Winning in politics doesn't necessarily mean playing dirty, but these days most campaigns tend to get ugly. Before you commit, consider whether you have the stomach for contrast.

5. Do I understand my own values?

A candidate who is able to articulate his or her value set, and connect those values to issues important to the electorate, stands to make fewer mistakes on the campaign trail and avoid the traps that will be set by opponents or ideological groups.

6. Do I understand my constituency?

Even if you think you already do, spend some time really getting to know the geographic and demographic makeup of the area you want to represent.

7. Can I really win support?

Never allow yourself to say, "I've got those voters in the bag."

8. What if my opponent finds out about . . .?

If you have a skeleton in the closet, assume that it will come to light over the course of a hard-fought campaign.

9. Can I trust a campaign manager?

Be honest with yourself about how you work best and the types of people you are most comfortable around.

10. Is the timing right?

Plenty of candidates who look great on paper seal their electoral fate by choosing the wrong time to run.

Source: Dave Nyczepir and Shane D'Apile, "10 Questions Consultants Wish You Would Ask before Deciding to Run," *Campaigns & Elections* (315) (January/ February 2013): 30–32.

when councilors are elected from single-member districts with sharply divergent constituency profiles, creating "a sense of parochialism and feudalism" among them. "There are councils where bickering and infighting are so intense that the entire body acquires an image of irresponsible flakiness."[53] Today, the median length of service on city council is just five years.

City Councils: Terms and Elections

In most American cities, especially those with nonpartisan elections, getting elected to city council is a do-it-yourself project. Most party organizations and civic associations are unreliable as sources of money and workers. Candidates must mobilize their own resources and create their own organizations. Challenging an incumbent can be risky. Historically, over 80 percent of all incumbent council members seeking reelection have been returned to office,[54] although the reelection rate has declined slightly in cities experiencing significant demographic and socioeconomic change. When a vacancy occurs creating an open seat, there are likely to be many candidates in the race. Since local races lack the visibility of national or statewide races, most focus on the personality, style, or image of the candidate. Even when local issues divide the candidates, most voters in local elections will be unaware of the candidates' stands on these issues.

In this fluid setting, electoral success depends on (1) the social acceptability of candidates relative to the community (especially their race and ethnic background); (2) their personal recognition in the community (name recognition, contacts from business, church, civic activity); and (3) their political resources (endorsements by newspapers and civic associations, access to political contributors, people willing to serve as volunteer workers). These factors are especially important for first-time candidates.[55] In subsequent campaigns, candidates develop more stable political followings.

Most city councils have 5 or 7 members, but large city councils with up to 52 members (New York City) are found in the larger, older cities of the Northeast and Midwest. Four-year terms for council members are most frequent, but some council members are elected for two- or three-year terms. In most cities, council member terms overlap, so that some council seats are filled at every municipal election. Presumably overlapping terms ensure continuity in the deliberations of the council. Although term limits for council members are growing in popularity, as yet only about 10 percent of cities have adopted them.

Friends at City Hall

A surprising number of council members are initially *appointed* to their office to fill the unexpired terms of resigning members. Those appointees are likely to be personal friends of council members or to have held some other city job. Voluntary retirement is the most common exit from community politics.

PARTICULARISTS

Those who run because of an overriding concern for a specific issue or issues; they tend to be outsiders—minorities or members of groups long underrepresented in government—and one-termers.

COUNCIL MEMBERS: RESPONSIBLE POLICYMAKERS?

11.7

The typical city council member represents, legislates, oversees city management (checks the chief executive, city departments, and employees), and judges the fairness of government operations.

> Members of the city council . . . speak for and make decisions on behalf of the citizens of the community [their representation role], engage in "*lawmaking*"—policy leadership, enactment of ordinances and resolutions, debate, criticism, and investigation [their legislative role], . . . respond to problems their constituents have with administrative agencies by seeking to bring about corrective action . . . and oversee the *execution of policy* in order to insure that the purpose of their lawmaking is accomplished [their executive oversight role], . . . and fill a *judicial function* either in the informal sense that they serve as the "court of last resort" for certain kinds of appeals from citizens who feel they have been harmed by city government, or in the more formal sense, in a few cases, of following strict procedures to adjudicate regulations or settle legal disputes.[56]

Explain the role of city council members in shaping public policy, and assess the ability of citizens to hold elected local officials accountable for their decisions.

The policymaking role of council members varies a great deal from city to city. Council members have more formal power in commission or weak-mayor forms of government, where the council sometimes appoints officials, prepares the budget, supervises departments, and performs other administrative tasks. However, in other cities—particularly strong mayor or manager cities—the council merely oversees city affairs. In these cities, the function of the council may be principally the representation of the interests of local constituents—forwarding complaints, making inquiries, and pushing for new sidewalks or streetlights.

The typical city council member represents, legislates, oversees city departments and administrators, and judges the fairness of government operations. Citizens expect their elected officials to be responsive to voter demands.

Accountability

Most constituents cannot even name their council member(s). The question is: How can citizens hold a council member accountable if they do not even know who represents them?[57] The problem of political **accountability** in local politics is aggravated by several factors:

> **ACCOUNTABILITY**
>
> In politics, the extent to which an elected official must answer to his or her constituents.

1. *The frequency of appointment to elected office.* It is probable that as many as one-quarter of the nation's council members initially come into office by appointment rather than election. They are appointed, usually by the mayor, to fill unexpired terms.

2. *The effective constituency is small.* Given the low turnout in municipal elections, and the small constituencies served by a council member, only a few votes may elect a person to office. A council member's personal friends, immediate neighbors, business associates, fellow church members, and acquaintances at the Rotary Club may be enough for election.

3. *Limited contact with citizens.* Few citizens know how to contact city officials, and even fewer citizens actually do so. Moreover, citizen-initiated contacts are closely related to socioeconomic status, with higher-status individuals far more likely to contact city officials about a problem than middle- or lower-status persons.

4. *The infrequency of electoral defeat.* Incumbents running for reelection are hardly ever defeated. When they are defeated, it is frequently in groups, when several incumbents are turned out of office at once owing to a specific community controversy.

5. *The frequency of voluntary retirement from elected office.* The vast majority of council members voluntarily retire from office, over half of them after two terms. Officeholders simply conclude that the obligations of office exceed the rewards.

All these factors, together with the attitude of voluntarism, tend to distance municipal government from direct citizen control.

Representation

Despite this evidence of a lack of electoral accountability in local politics, some factors may compel council members to reflect the will of their constituents in policymaking. Moreover, council members tend to reflect, in their own socioeconomic background, the characteristics of their constituents. This does not *ensure* that council members share the same attitudes as their constituents on all matters; indeed, the experience of being a public official itself can help to shape a council member's views and give a different perspective on public affairs than those of constituents. However, if council members have deep roots in their communities (many social contacts and group memberships; shared socioeconomic, ethnic, racial, and religious characteristics with their constituents), they may reflect these in their policymaking, whether they are consciously aware of these "constituency influences" or not.

CITY MANAGERS IN MUNICIPAL POLITICS

When council-manager government was first introduced as part of the municipal reform movement, managers were expressly admonished not to participate in community "politics." Early supporters of manager government believed in the separation of "politics" from "administration."[58] Politics, not only *party* politics but *policy*making as well, should be the exclusive domain of the elected city council. The **city manager** was hired by the council to carry out its policy directives, and the manager could be removed by the council by majority vote at any time. This belief in the separation of policymaking from administration was intended to produce "nonpolitical," efficient, and economical government, which middle-class supporters of the reform movement valued so highly. Popular control of government was to be guaranteed by making the manager's tenure completely dependent upon the will of the elected council.

CITY MANAGER
The chief executive of a city government, who is appointed by the city council and responsible to it.

However, after a few years of experience with manager government in America, it became increasingly apparent to the managers themselves that they could not escape responsibility for policy recommendations. It turned out to be difficult in practice to separate policymaking from administration. The first code of ethics of the International City Managers' Association (ICMA) stated flatly that "no manager should take an active part in politics." Managers agreed that they should stay out of partisan politics and election campaigns, but there was a great deal of debate about the role of managers in community policymaking. In 1938, the ICMA revised its code of ethics to recognize the positive role of managers in policy leadership.[59] Even with the change, one of the toughest jobs managers have always had is meeting the expectations of both the politicians (city council) and the professionals in city government (the staff).

Manager Role Orientations

Today, we are likely to find varying role orientations among city managers. Some see themselves as "**policy managers**," providing community leadership through their recommendations to their councils on a wide variety of matters. They believe they should innovate and lead on policy matters. Others see themselves as "**administrative managers**," restricting themselves to the supervision of the municipal bureaucracy and avoiding innovative policy recommendations, particularly in controversial areas. Ambivalent about innovation and leadership on policy matters, these managers avoid involvement in community issues.

POLICY MANAGERS
City managers who provide community leadership through their recommendations to their city councils on a wide variety of matters.

ADMINISTRATIVE MANAGERS
City managers who restrict themselves to the supervision of the municipal bureaucracy and avoid innovative policy recommendations, particularly in controversial areas.

A majority of professionally trained city managers see themselves as "policy managers." However, managers without professional training in city administration or those with engineering degrees, who have lived most of their lives in their own communities and who expect to remain there, are more likely to accept a fairly narrow administrative role.[60]

Prudent managers will not wish to *appear* to be policymakers even when they are. Their dependence upon the council for their jobs prevents them from being too extreme in policy promotion. Managers can push their councils, but they can seldom fight them with any success. Open disputes between the manager and the council are usually resolved by the dismissal of the manager. Managers who assume strong policy leadership roles have shorter tenures than those who do not.

Nevertheless, the manager is the most important policy initiator in most council-manager cities. Most managers determine the agenda for city council meetings. This permits them to determine the kinds of issues to be raised and the policy options to be considered. The council may not accept everything recommended by the manager, but the manager's recommendations will be given serious consideration. The city manager is the major source of information for most council members. The manager prepares the city budget; writes formal reports on city problems, defining the problems and proposing solutions; and advises and educates the council privately as well as publicly.

How Council Members View Managers

What kind of managers do mayors and council members want? Certainly some mayors and council members want to retain a larger policy role for themselves and resent a manager who wants to run the show. These elected officials might try to recruit "administrative managers" by avoiding applicants with forceful personalities, high professional qualifications, and experience in other cities. However, we have already suggested that many council members are "volunteers" who prefer a passive role in policymaking—approving or disapproving proposals brought before them by the manager and others. A weak manager can lengthen council meetings and significantly increase the council's workload. So we should not be surprised to find many council members welcoming policy leadership from the manager (as long as the manager avoids the appearance of dominating the council). Indeed, one study indicates that a majority of council members "expect the manager to take the lead" in budget decisions, hiring and firing personnel, reorganization of city departments, wage and salary negotiations, community improvements, and cooperative proposals with other communities.[61] Only in planning and zoning do council members say they want to retain leadership.

Professionalism

A high percentage of today's city managers are white males under 50 years of age, although the number of women and minorities in city manager positions is on the upswing. Most city managers are professionals who have been trained in university graduate programs in public administration. They are familiar with budgeting and fiscal administration, public personnel management, municipal law, and planning. They tend to move from city to city as they advance in their professional careers. They may begin their careers as a staff assistant to a city official and then move to assistant city manager, then manager of a small town, and later perhaps of a larger city. About three-quarters of all city manager appointments are made from outside the city, and only about one-quarter are local residents, which indicates the professionalism of city management.

The average tenure of managers who resigned or were removed from office has been about five years.[62] One in ten managers reports having been fired at least once. Most of these found another job within six months but reported using up their savings or severance pay to survive between jobs. The three principal reasons given for having been fired were "poor working relationship with council," "politics," and "change in the council." All of these reasons might be termed political.[63] However, other managers move on

Jay Williams, the first black mayor of Youngstown, Ohio, is the first independent to win the position in 80 years. Williams (far left) often speaks to groups across the country on the special problems facing small and midsize industrial communities. *Governing* magazine selected him as one of its eight Public Officials of the Year for developing "an aggressive [comprehensive redevelopment] plan to create a Youngstown that will be smaller, but better." "We always have to make sure we remind people," he says, "that the transformation into a smaller community doesn't mean we're going to be an inferior community."

because they have been offered more attractive professional opportunities. Most managers love their career choice, regardless of how long they serve in one place. They say they get the most satisfaction from having made specific significant contributions to the communities in which they have served.[64]

MAYORS IN CITY POLITICS

11.9

Outline the powers and limitations of mayors.

Today, more than ever before, the nation's cities need forceful, imaginative political leadership. The nation's major domestic problems—race relations, poverty, violence, congestion, poor schools, and fiscal crisis—are concentrated in cities. Mayors are in the "hot seat" of American politics; they must deal directly with these pressing issues. No other elected official in the American federal system must deal face-to-face, eyeball-to-eyeball with these problems. Mayoral races are often hard-fought campaigns, particularly in large cities. (See Table 11–2.)

Limited Powers

The challenges facing big-city mayors are enormous; however, their powers to deal with these challenges are restricted on every side. Executive power in major cities is often fragmented among a variety of elected officials—city treasurer, city clerk, city comptroller, district attorney. The mayor may also be required to share power over municipal affairs with

TABLE 11–2 Competitiveness of Big-City Mayoral Contests: A Single-Year Snapshot

City	State	Winner	Race	%	Population
Miami-Dade	FL	Carlos A. Gimenez[a]	H	54	2,496 ,435
San Diego	CA	Bob Filner	W	52	1,307,402
Austin	TX	Lee Leffingwell[a]	W	52	790,390
Milwaukee	WI	Thomas "Tom" Barrett[a]	W	70	597,867
Portland	OR	Charlie Hales	W	61	583,776
Fresno	CA	Ashley Swearengin[a]	W	75	494,665
Sacramento	CA	Kevin Johnson[a]	B	59	466,488
Virginia Beach	VA	William D. Sessoms, Jr.[a]	W	69	437,994
Bakersfield	CA	Harvey L. Hall[a]	W	93	347,483
Honolulu	HI	Kirk Caldwell	W	53	337,256
Santa Ana	CA	Miguel A. Pulido[a]	H	48	324,528
Corpus Christi	TX	Nelda Martinez	H	53	305,215
Riverside	CA	Rusty Bailey	W	33	303,871
Anchorage	AK	Dan Sullivan[a]	W	59	291,826
Stockton	CA	Anthony Silva	W	59	291,707
Orlando	FL	Buddy Dyer[a]	W	58	238,300
Lubbock	TX	Glen Robertson	W	65	229,573
Baton Rouge	LA	Melvin L. "Kip" Holden[a]	B	60	229,493
Glendale	AZ	Jerry Weiers	W	46	226,721
Chesapeake	VA	Dr. Alan P. Krasnoff[a]	W	74	222,209
Scottsdale	AZ	W.J. "Jim" Lane[a]	W	55	217,385
Fremont	CA	Bill Harrison	W	34	214,089
Irvine	CA	Steven S. Choi, Ph.D.	A	46	212,375
Richmond	VA	Dwight C. Jones[a]	B	72	204,214

Note: Results are from 2012 Mayoral Elections.
[a]Incumbent; W = white, B = black, H = Hispanic, A = Asian.
Source: U.S. Conference of Mayors: Mayoral Elections Center. Available at http://www.usmayors.org/elections/displayelections2012.asp.

county officials. Many city agencies and functions are outside the mayor's formal authority. Independent boards and commissions often govern important city departments—for example, the board of education, board of health, zoning appeals board, planning commission, civil service board, library board, park commission, and sewage and water board. Even if the mayor is permitted to appoint the members of the boards and commissions, they are often appointed for a fixed term, and the mayor cannot remove them.

The mayor's power over the affairs of the city may also be affected by the many special district governments and public authorities operating within the city, including public housing, urban renewal, sewage and water, mass transit, and port authority. Traditionally, school districts have been outside the authority of the mayor or city government except in the nation's oldest cities in the Northeast and Midwest. Mayors' powers over city finances may even be restricted—they may share budget-making powers with a board of estimate, and powers over expenditures with an elected comptroller or treasurer. Civil service regulations and independent civil service boards can greatly hamper mayors' control over their own bureaucrats. The activities of federal and state agencies in a city are largely beyond the mayor's control.

Selecting Mayors

The method of selecting mayors also influences their powers over city affairs. Mayors in cities with weak mayor-council, council-manager, or commission forms of government are often selected by their city councils or commissions and generally have little more power than other council members or commissioners. Their job is generally ceremonial: They crown beauty queens, dedicate parks, lay cornerstones, lead parades, and sign official papers. Larger cities, usually strong mayor-council cities, generally elect their mayors, although now over half of all council-manager cities do, too. Mayors may be elected for anything from one to five years, but two-year and four-year terms are most common in American cities. Some mayors run at a young age and win.

Legislative Powers

Mayors' legislative powers also vary widely. Of course, in all cities they have the right to submit messages to the council and to recommend policy. These recommendations will carry whatever prestige the mayor possesses in the community. Moreover, in council-manager and commission cities, mayors usually are themselves members of the council. In these cities where mayors are chosen by the council, they generally have voting power equal to that of other council members. In about one-third of mayor-council cities, the mayor also serves on the council; in about half of the mayor-council cities the mayor presides over meetings of the council and can cast a tie-breaking vote. In most cities where the mayor is *not* a member of the council, the mayor enjoys veto power over council-passed ordinances. The veto power helps distinguish between "strong-mayor" and "weak-mayor" cities.

Administrative Powers

Another distinction between "strong" and "weak" mayors is determined by their powers of administration. Weak mayors have limited appointing powers and even more limited removal powers. They have little control over separately elected boards and commissions or separately elected offices, such as clerk, treasurer, tax assessor, comptroller, and attorney. The council, rather than the mayor, often appoints the key administrative officers. No single individual has the complete responsibility for law enforcement or coordinating city administration.

Political Powers

In summary, a mayor's ability to provide strong leadership in many cities is limited by fragmented authority, multiple elected officials, limited jurisdiction over important urban services, civil service, state or federal interference, and constraints placed upon that power by "reform" and "good-government" arrangements. Nevertheless, even though it is recognized that mayors have few formal powers to deal with the enormous tasks facing them, it is frequently argued that mayors can and should exercise strong leadership as "political brokers"—mediating disputes, serving as a channel of communications, bringing conflicting groups together for reasonable discussions of their differences, and suggesting solutions that diverse groups can accept in coping with the city's problems. In other words, the "ideal" mayor overcomes limited formal powers by skill in persuasion, negotiation, and public relations.

But this "ideal" city leadership requires that the mayor possess certain minimum resources[65]:

- Sufficient financial and staff resources in the mayor's office and in city government generally.
- City jurisdiction over social-program areas—education, housing, urban renewal.
- Mayor's jurisdiction within city government over these areas.
- A salary that enables the mayor to spend full time on the job.
- Friendly newspapers or television stations supportive of the mayor and his or her goals.
- Political groups, including a political party, that the mayor can mobilize to attend meetings, march in parades, and distribute literature, on his or her behalf.

Successful mayors must rely chiefly upon their own personal qualities of leadership: their powers to persuade, to sell, to compromise, to bargain, and to "get things done."[66] Mayors are primarily promoters of public policy: Their role is to promote, publicize, organize, and finance the projects that others suggest. The money side of the job is usually the toughest and getting more so by the day. The former mayor of Indianapolis put it like this: All "mayors are being so squeezed they don't have time for anything except to make ends meet. Their noses are so close to the grindstone that nobody can see their faces."[67]

MINORITIES AND WOMEN IN LOCAL POLITICS

11.10

Describe the extent to which minorities and women participate in local politics, and assess the extent of their influence over public policy.

Local politics is the entry level in the American political system for minorities as well as women. Currently about half of the 100 largest cities in the United States have minority or women mayors. All but a few of these cities have had minority or women mayors in the recent past. As the nation's minority population has grown and become less geographically concentrated, more Asians, African Americans, and Hispanics have won elective office in medium-size and smaller counties, cities, and school districts across the United States.

Minority Mayors

African Americans have served as mayors in many cities with majority white populations, including New York, Chicago, Los Angeles, and Philadelphia, as well as cities with majority black populations, including Detroit, Washington, DC, New Orleans, and Atlanta. In fact, by 1999, almost one-third of all cities with over 200,000 population had elected black or Hispanic mayors.[68] States with the most black mayors are Mississippi, Alabama, Texas, Louisiana, Arkansas, Georgia, and North Carolina.[69] Black mayors are most likely to be elected in cities where there is a large black population, black representation on city council, a more educated black population, and reformed governments.[70] States with the largest number of local Hispanic elected officials are Texas, California, New Mexico, Arizona, Colorado, Florida, New York, Illinois, and New Jersey.

The success of blacks and Hispanics in city politics, especially in majority white and Anglo cities, suggests that race is becoming less important as a criterion in voter choice for municipal leadership. However, voting patterns in city elections in which minority and white candidates face each other indicate a continuing residue of racial politics. Black and Hispanic voters continue to cast their votes solidly for black and Hispanic candidates

Burnsville, Minnesota, Mayor Elizabeth B. Kautz was elected president of the prestigious U.S. Conference of Mayors, making her the first female president from a small suburban city in the history of the organization. Reelected mayor multiple times, Kautz gets high marks from voters for having led an effort to revitalize Burnsville's downtown into a mixed-use, pedestrian-friendly downtown.

in these elections; white voters continue to give majority support to white candidates. The swing vote in these minority–white election confrontations usually rests with 30–40 percent of white voters who are prepared to support qualified minority candidates. Support patterns are more complex in multiracial/ethnic communities.

Successful black mayoral candidates in majority white cities have generally emphasized racial harmony and conciliation. They have stressed broad themes of concern to all voters—regardless of race. They have built coalitions that cut across racial, ethnic, and economic lines; many have worked their way up through the ranks of local organizations. They have avoided identification as "protest" candidates. However, in cities where blacks are a majority, black candidates favor a more highly racial campaign strategy.[71] In multiracial cities, race may play a major role in the candidate's first election, but job approval becomes more important when the minority candidate runs for reelection.[72] In general, blacks are less cohesive in local than national politics, often due to sizable socioeconomic differences within the black community.[73]

The strategies used by Hispanic mayoral candidates in areas where Latinos are in the minority are twofold. In more suburban areas where there are lots of middle- and upper-middle-class white homeowners, they campaign on platforms calling for preservation of property values, better schools, and tougher law enforcement. In urban areas, Hispanic candidates focus on building winning "biracial, multiracial, multiple issue, and labor–Latino alliances."[74] Hispanics that win landslide victories in large U.S. cities often catch the attention of national political parties, regardless of whether their city's elections are partisan or nonpartisan. (See "*People in Politics:* San Antonio Mayor Julian Castro: Nonpartisan on Ballot but Democrat in Practice.")

Across the United States, the trend is toward more racially pluralist cities, where no one racial or ethnic group makes up a majority of the population. Different, and shifting, electoral coalitions are more the rule in such cities. They vary as each racial and ethnic group changes in its relative group size, cohesion, resources, partisan makeup, residential concentration patterns, issue priorities, and candidates.

Minorities on Councils

In general, minority candidates for city council are the most successful in larger cities, with sizable, concentrated, cohesive minority populations and better-educated, liberal white populations willing to vote for minority candidates. Until recently, blacks were generally underrepresented on city councils across the country. That is to say, blacks held a smaller proportion of seats on city councils than the black percentages of city populations. But the steady rise in the number of black city council members and county commissioners over the last 30 years has brought black representation to rough proportionality in most American cities. In cities in which blacks constitute 10–50 percent of the population, black representation on city councils generally reflects the black population percentage. In cities in which the black population constitutes a majority (over 50%), black representation on city councils usually exceeds the black population percentage.[75]

San Antonio Mayor Julian Castro: Nonpartisan on Ballot but Democrat in Practice

San Antonio, America's seventh largest city with a population of 1.4 million, is like most large U.S. cities in that mayoral candidates are not identified by party on the ballot. Such nonpartisan elections tend to draw a large field of candidates. The 2009 election was no exception, with nine candidates squaring off against each other in the mayor's race. Julián Castro, then 34 and a former city councilman, won with a 56 percent majority.

His repeat victory in the 2011 election, by a whopping margin of 82 percent, and subsequent appearances on the national scene left no doubt about his party affiliation, reflecting a trend of partisanship seeping into nonpartisan races.

The son of a Chicana activist, Castro witnessed local politics early at committee meetings, strategy sessions, and rallies. By the time he ran for mayor, however, he had discerned the value of bringing together people in the street with people in the board room. His aim, "to create a brainpower community that is the liveliest city in the United States," fit as easily with Chamber of Commerce boosters as with middle-class voters. He envisioned twenty-first century jobs in information technology and security, new energy, and aerospace.

As mayor, he created SA2020, a community-wide effort to transform the city into a world-class metropolis by 2020. As part of that effort, Castro declared the years 2012–2022 the "Decade of Downtown," designed to make the urban core more hospitable to residents with the construction of housing, parks, walkable streets, and arts facilities, all of which would create jobs.

With the example of his own academic achievements (degrees from Stanford University and Harvard Law School), he championed educational opportunity. Under his leadership, the city in 2010 opened Café College, a program providing free college advice to all students in the area. In its first year, the program assisted 5,000 students. Convinced that college success starts in early childhood, he advocated a one-eighth-cent sales tax to fund full-day kindergarten for 22,000 San Antonio four-year-olds over eight years. Local CEOs and seven chambers of commerce lent their support, and voters approved the referendum in November 2012.

When President Barack Obama selected Castro to give the keynote address at the Democratic National Convention in September 2012, he was instantly dubbed "a rising star" in Democratic politics—along with twin brother Joaquin, a state legislator who won election to Congress the same year. In a state where 38 percent of citizens identify themselves as Hispanic, Democrats saw exciting possibilities: winning back the governorship and a U.S. Senate seat.

In contrast, Hispanic representation on city councils is significantly below the Hispanic population percentages.[76] Earlier we observed that Hispanic voter turnout was significantly lower than that for other social groups (see Chapter 4). Lower voter turnout among Hispanics is frequently attributed to cultural and language barriers and the resident alien status of many Hispanics. These factors, along with lower candidacy rates, less residential concentration, and some structural features of reform government, including at-large elections in some settings, continue to create barriers to the political mobilization of Hispanics.[77] Asian candidates are confronted with similar hurdles.[78]

Historically, Asian American elected officials, mostly Chinese and Japanese Americans, were concentrated in two states: Hawaii and California. But by 2000, over 300 Asian Americans had been elected to office, mostly at the local level, in 31 states. While Chinese and Japanese Americans still make up 67 percent, other Asian ethnic groups (e.g., Filipino, Korean, and Vietnamese) are being elected as well. Asian Americans are more likely to be elected from non-Asian majority districts that are either heavily white or multiracial. They "must rely on political strategies that have a mainstream platform or a multiracial platform focusing on both inter- and intraracial coalition building in order to be successful."[79]

Policy Consequences

What are the policy consequences of increasing minority representation on city councils? Perhaps the most obvious consequence is increased minority *employment* in city jobs. The single most important determinant of minority employment in administrative and professional positions is the proportion of blacks, Hispanics, and Asians elected to city councils.[80] The employment of minorities in service and maintenance jobs does not require political representation. However, to get important management-level jobs, minorities must first win political power.[81]

Urban police departments have long been a focus of concern for minorities. Police policies have come under scrutiny for contributing to racial tensions, triggering riots, blocking minority aspirations, and shaping minority perceptions of justice. Many black mayors have campaigned on explicit pledges to reform police departments and adopt policies designed to make police more responsive and sensitive to the concerns of minorities. The adoption of minority-oriented police policies, including increases in the number of minority police officers, has occurred with increases in black population percentages in cities, regardless of whether cities elect black mayors and council members. However, there is some evidence that the election of black mayors results in (1) the adoption of citizen review boards to oversee police actions,[82] (2) an increase in the share of the police force that is African American, and (3) a reduction in the size and payroll of the police department.[83]

Yet to date there is *no* evidence that cities with greater minority representation on city councils, or even cities with minority mayors, pursue significantly different taxing, spending, or service policies than do cities with little or no minority representation. This is really not surprising; African American, Latino, and other minority city leaders face the same problems as white city leaders in raising revenue, fighting crime, improving housing, reducing congestion, and removing garbage. It is possible, of course, that black neighborhoods receive better *delivery* of urban services under black leadership. However, the overall problems of cities may remain unaffected by substituting black leadership for white leadership. Research shows that while in office, black and white mayors are judged much more by their performance on the job than by their race. Performance in office accounts for 16–25 percent of the typical mayor's performance evaluation, race just 1–6 percent.[84]

The presence of minorities on city councils is important for city politics even if there is little impact on taxing and spending policies. Blacks, Hispanics, Asians, and gays and lesbians in city government improve the image of that government among each group's residents; it helps to link minorities to city hall, to provide role models, and to sensitize white officials to minority concerns. "When minorities talk to the city council now, council members nod their heads rather than yawn."[85]

Women in Local Politics

Women's participation in local politics has risen dramatically in recent years. Women occupy nearly 20 percent of mayors' offices across the country in cities with populations over 30,000.[86] Women mayors are more prevalent in larger cities with racially and ethnically diverse, and more affluent and better-educated, populations. In U.S. cities with populations over 100,000, about 15 percent have women mayors.

Likewise, women have made major gains in capturing city council, county commission, and school board seats. The number of women serving on city councils in cities with populations over 10,000 has gone from an estimated 4 percent in 1975 to 21 percent today.[87] Female county commissioners jumped from 3 percent in 1975 to 18 percent.[88] Women comprised 26 percent of all school board members in 1978 but 44 percent by 2011. The movement of women into politics generally is attributed to the movement of women into the workforce and the changing cultural values redefining women's role in American society. At the local level, women may find fewer obstacles to political office-holding than at the state or national level. Local offices do not require women to move away from their home communities to the state capital or to Washington. (Women candidates, unlike men, are seldom relieved of all of their home responsibilities when running for or occupying political office.[89]) Plus, local offices often have higher salaries than state- or national-level positions.

The number of women on city councils is on the upswing, often supported in their campaigns by women's groups who feel a female council member will be more pro-active in fighting discriminatory policies. Here New York City Council member Margaret Chin joins some of her female constituents in asking the New York City Police Department (NYPD) to abandon Stop-and-Frisk approaches the women regard as discriminatory.

Women (and men) who have been more active in civic and professional associations are more likely to get elected than those who have not. Winners of both sexes attribute at least part of their victory to this connection. Female city council candidates traditionally have received more support than have male candidates from neighborhood organizations, single-issue groups, and women's organizations. Male candidates still tend to get a marginally higher level of support from business groups, although this is changing, too.[90]

Some of the long-standing myths about the role of gender in city council elections have been refuted. We now know that when compared with male candidates, females win at the same rate, raise as much or more campaign money, are not disadvantaged by at-large elections, nonpartisan elections, runoff elections (second primaries), or newspaper or political party endorsements of male candidates, and are not deterred from running by steep filing fees. Media coverage of women candidates, relative to their male counterparts, has improved in frequency and content, although some women still complain that media coverage focuses too much on their clothing and appearance.

Age also is no longer much of a barrier. Formerly, younger and middle-aged professional women were the most likely to enter local politics, but that trend has changed considerably. Older women are running in record numbers, as the notion that politics is "a male thing" has rapidly eroded.

For years, black and Hispanic females did not run or win as often as did white females, even when they ran against minority males. For these minority women, gender was seen as a bigger barrier to their election to city councils than their race or ethnicity.[91] It still is for Latinas, although that is changing. But now, African American women are getting elected to office at a faster rate than black men, paralleling college graduation rates, which are higher among black women than black men.[92]

Today, there are few city councils with no female members. And it is increasingly common for female candidates to end up running against other females for the same position—a marked change from the past. Women opposing women is simply one more piece of evidence that women are not a politically monolithic group. Gender actually is a fairly weak voting cue compared to age, race, education, income, or religion.

Women are elected at the school board level at a higher rate than for other local offices. Few women (or men) run for school board thinking they will use the office as a stepping-stone to higher office, although some do. Virtually all school board members say they ran to make the community a better place. However, one study has found that men are more likely than women to say that a desire to apply their religious beliefs to policy and return schools to traditional values was important to their initial decision to seek a school board seat.[93]

What are the policy consequences of increased women's representation on city councils? Several studies have shown that women are more likely than men to favor greater representation of underrepresented groups and to put higher priorities on social issues. Female council members regard themselves as better prepared than their male counterparts, who believe women ask too many questions.[94]

11.11   # INTEREST GROUPS IN COMMUNITY POLITICS

List the types of interest groups that are active in community politics, and analyze their ability to influence local government decisions.

Interest group activity may be more influential in community politics than in state or national political affairs. Since the arena of local politics is smaller, the activities of organized interest groups may be more obvious at the local level. The types of groups that are active at the local level reflect the activities and services over which local governments have the most control.[95] Some services typically generate lower levels of citizen satisfaction (and more involvement) than others. (See Figure 11–2.)

Civic Associations

CIVIC ASSOCIATIONS

In local politics, an organization of citizens that works to further its own view of the best interest of the community.

At the local level, interest groups frequently assume the form of **civic associations**. Few communities are too small to have at least one or two associations devoted to civic well-being, and larger cities may have hundreds of these organizations. Council members usually name civic associations (service clubs, citizens' commissions, improvement associations) as the most influential groups or organizations that are active and appear before the council. Civic associations generally make their appeals in terms of the "welfare of the community," the "public interest," "civic responsibility," "making Janesville a better place to live." In other words, civic associations claim to be community-serving rather than self-serving. Members belong to these groups as a hobby because of the sense of prestige and civic participation they derive from membership. Occasionally, of course, participation in civic associations can be a stepping-stone to local office.

Taxpayer Groups

TAXPAYER GROUPS

Interest groups that generally stand for lower taxes and fewer governmental activities and services.

Organized **taxpayer groups** generally stand for lower taxes and fewer governmental activities and services. Their most enthusiastic support comes from the community's larger taxpayers, generally businesspeople with large investments in commercial or industrial property in the community. However, when the economy is in a downturn, middle-class citizens, especially homeowners, become active "anti-taxers."

Environmental and "Growth-Management" Groups

ENVIRONMENTAL "GROWTH MANAGEMENT" GROUPS

Interest groups that are generally opposed to community growth, highway construction, street widening, tree cutting, increased traffic, noise and pollution, and commercial or industrial development.

Environmental groups and opponents of residential and commercial development have become major forces in community politics throughout the nation. These groups are generally opposed to community growth, although they employ the terms "growth management" or "smart growth" to imply that they do not necessarily oppose all growth. But they are generally opposed to highway construction, street widening, tree cutting, increased traffic, noise and pollution, and commercial or industrial development. These groups generally reflect liberal reformist views of upper-middle-class residents who are secure in their own jobs and own their own homes. Often, **environmental "growth-management" groups** combine with neighborhood associations to oppose specific developmental projects.

FIGURE 11–2 Citizen Satisfaction with City Services

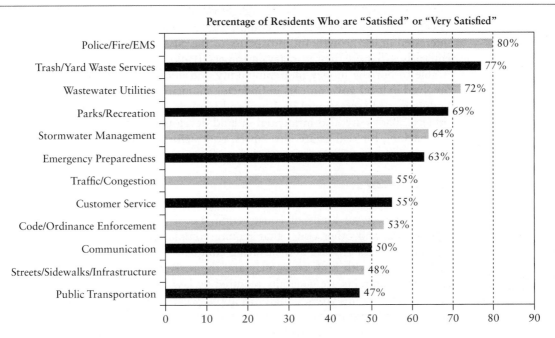

Percentage of Residents Who are "Satisfied" or "Very Satisfied"

Police/Fire/EMS — 80%
Trash/Yard Waste Services — 77%
Wastewater Utilities — 72%
Parks/Recreation — 69%
Stormwater Management — 64%
Emergency Preparedness — 63%
Traffic/Congestion — 55%
Customer Service — 55%
Code/Ordinance Enforcement — 53%
Communication — 50%
Streets/Sidewalks/Infrastructure — 48%
Public Transportation — 47%

Note: Data are for 2012.
Source: Governing, "Which Services Are Citizens Most, Least Satisfied With?," 2012 National Citizen Satisfaction Survey by ETC Institute. Available at http://www.governing.com/gov-data/other/government-satisfaction-surveys-statistics-national-averages.html.

Neighborhood Groups

Neighborhood associations frequently spring up when residents perceive a threat to their property values. They may be formed to oppose a rezoning that would allow new business and unwanted traffic in their neighborhood, or to oppose a new mobile home park, or to petition for traffic lights or sidewalks or pothole repairs. Sometimes neighborhood associations will fight to keep out "undesirables," whose presence they feel will reduce property values. Neighborhood groups may protest the location of low-income housing, halfway houses for parolees, or mental health facilities. Neighborhood associations may also lead the fight *against* development, where residents will be displaced or their lifestyle threatened. They may oppose road building, urban renewal, or industrial and commercial development in or near their neighborhood. The NIMBY (not in my backyard) forces may be closely identified with "growth-management" efforts to slow or halt development.

NEIGHBORHOOD ASSOCIATIONS

In local politics, an organization of the residents of a specific neighborhood that works to protect property values.

Business Groups

Business interests are represented in local politics by organized groups: The chamber of commerce and the junior chamber of commerce, or "Jaycees," are found in nearly every community, representing the general views of business. The program of the chamber of commerce is likely to be more general than the interests of particular sectors of the business community—banks, utilities, contractors, real estate developers, downtown merchants, or bar and club owners. The chamber or the Jaycees can be expected to support lower taxes and more economy and efficiency in government operations. They are also active "promoters" of community growth, business activity, and economic development. They can be expected to back civic improvements so long as it does not raise the tax rate too much. "Service to the community" creates a "favorable image," which the chamber and businesspeople are anxious to cultivate. The so-called service clubs—the Lions, Kiwanis, Rotarians, and others—are basically for businesspeople. Their interests are likely to be more social than political, but their service projects often involve them in political activity and their meetings provide an excellent opportunity for speechmaking by political candidates.

Banks

Banks often own, or hold the mortgages on, downtown business property. They have an interest in maintaining business, commercial, and industrial property values. Banks are also interested in the growth and prosperity of the city as a whole, particularly large business enterprises that are their primary customers. Banks are influential because they decide who is able to borrow money in a community and under what conditions. Banks are directly involved in local governments in financing municipal bond issues for public works, school buildings, and recreational facilities, and in pledging financial backing for urban renewal projects. Banks are also influential in land development, for they must provide the financial backing for real estate developers, contractors, businesses, and home buyers; hence, they are interested in business regulation, taxation, zoning, and housing.

Contractors

Contractors are vitally interested in city government because the city has the power of inspection over all kinds of construction. Local governments enforce building, plumbing, electric, and other codes that require compliance by contractors. Some contractors, particularly road-grading and surfacing companies, depend on public contracts, and they are concerned with both city policy and the personnel who administer this policy. While municipal contracts are generally required by law to be given to the "low bidder" among "responsible" contractors, definitions about what is or is not a "low bid" and who is or who is not a "responsible" contractor make it important for contractors to maintain close and friendly relationships with municipal officials. It is no accident that builders, contractors, and developers are a major source of campaign contributions for local office seekers.

Real Estate Developers

Real estate developers are particularly interested in planning, zoning, and subdivision control regulations and urban renewal programs. (These are discussed at length in Chapter 13.) Developers of residential, commercial, and industrial property must work closely with city government officials to coordinate the provision of public services—especially streets, sewage, water, and electricity. They must also satisfy city officials regarding planning and zoning regulations, building codes, fire and safety laws, and environmental regulations. Today, real estate developers must be highly skilled in governmental relations.

Newspapers, Television, and Radio

The media are an important force in community politics, especially newspapers that can engage in more investigative reporting. The influence of the press would be relatively minor if its opinions were limited to its editorial pages. The influence of the press arises from its power to decide what is "news," thereby focusing public attention on the events and issues it deems important. Newspaper writers must first decide what proportion of space in the paper will be devoted to local news in contrast to state, national, and international news. A big-city paper may give local news about the same amount of space that it gives to national or international news. Suburban or small-town papers, which operate within the circulation area of a large metropolitan daily, may give a greater proportion of the news space to local events than to national and international affairs. Crime and corruption in government are favorite targets for the press. Editors believe that civic crusades and the exposure of crime and corruption help sell newspapers. Moreover, many editors and writers believe they have a civic responsibility to use the power of the press to protect the public. (See "*Up Close:* Exposing Political Corruption.") In the absence of crime or corruption, newspapers may turn to crusades on behalf of civic improvements—such as a city auditorium or cultural center.

The role of local television news and news/talk radio should not be underestimated. (See Chapter 4.) Particularly in large metropolitan area markets, television and radio stations compete with each other for viewers and listeners. The most popular stations earn more advertising money. And nothing makes a better story to boost ratings than exposing some corrupt, inept, inefficient, or ridiculous action by a local public official.

Churches

Any listing of influential interest groups in local politics should include the community's churches and church-related organizations. Ministers, priests, rabbis, and leaders of religious lay groups are frequently participants in community decision making. Active church members feel less isolated from their community through involvement in social service–related activities.[96] A Catholic church and its many lay organizations, for example, may be vitally concerned with the operation of its parochial schools. Protestant ministerial associations in large cities may be concerned with public health, welfare, housing, and other social problems. Ministers and church congregations in small towns may be concerned with the enforcement of blue laws, limitations on

The faith communities may become quite involved in local politics, particularly when a moral issue surfaces. In such situations, members of the clergy often testify before city councils, county commissions, or school boards. When they do, they get the attention of elected officials, who are well aware that persons who attend a religious service are more likely to turn out to vote. However, most local churches are careful *not* to tell their members which candidates to vote for, fearing loss of their tax-exempt status with the Internal Revenue Service.

liquor sales, prohibitions on gambling, and other public policies relative to "vice" and public morality, ranging from free needle exchanges to gay rights ordinances. Morality politics is more prevalent at the local level than at the national or state levels.[97]

Municipal Employees

No one has a greater personal stake in municipal government than municipal employees—police, firefighters, street crews, transit employees, welfare workers, sanitation workers, clerks, and secretaries. (Over 70% of all state and local government employees in the nation are employees of cities, counties, school districts, and special districts.) Their rate of voter turnout in municipal elections is high, and they are politically influential in small towns and suburbs whether they are organized into unions or not.

Who Contributes the Most to Public Engagement? Local Officials' Ratings

A survey by the National League of Cities asked municipal officials across the United States to assess the degree to which local media, special interest groups, and community and civic groups help with creating a sense of community. Specifically, the officials were asked how well each set of local actors: (1) informed people about local public affairs with fair and balanced reporting, (2) contributed to constructive debate, and (3) involved people in deliberation and problem solving. City officials gave the highest marks to local community and civic groups for all three activities. Local media got their best marks for informing people and special interest groups for involving people in deliberation and problem solving.

Who Solves Community Problems Best? The Citizen Perspective

Americans believe that solutions to community problems come from a *variety* of sources—government, organizations, and individual citizens. When asked to identify the best problem solvers in their own community, they point to local police departments, religious institutions, nonprofit organizations, and friends and neighbors, as well as local governments and school boards[98]:

- Fifty-eight percent rate local police departments as crucial or important to problem solving. While whites are more likely than nonwhites to view the police in this strong role, even among nonwhites the police ranked extremely high compared with other institutions.

- Fifty-six percent say that local churches, synagogues, and mosques are important or crucial to finding solutions. African Americans (38%) are more likely than whites (29%) to rank religious institutions as crucial to local problem solving.

- Fifty-three percent say that nonprofit organizations such as the Salvation Army, Habitat for Humanity, and Goodwill Industries are crucial or very important to the solution of community problems.

- More than 50 percent say that friends and neighbors are problem solvers in their community. This holds true across race and income levels and it is even more evident among those age 65 and older. Nearly two-thirds of the seniors believe friends and neighbors are important problem solvers.

- Other problem solvers that received high marks as being crucial or very important are parent–teacher organizations (47%), local government officials (43%), local foundations and United Ways (39%), neighborhood organizations (39%), school boards (38%), and local businesses (36%).

At the local level, people usually get involved in politics when something promises to directly affect them, often at the urging of friends and neighbors and groups to which they belong. (See "*Did You Know?:* Americans Serve Their Communities by Volunteering.")

Americans Serve Their Communities by Volunteering

More than 61 million volunteers dedicate over 8 billion hours of service in communities across the United States. It is a measure of what is called a community's "social capital"—social connectedness or social networks. Voluntarism rates are higher in the suburbs and rural areas than in the more populous urban core. A higher proportion of women volunteer than men, and older persons more than younger or middle-age generations. Volunteering is more prevalent in areas with high home ownership rates, higher educational levels, and more organized nonprofit organizations. It is lower in areas with long commuting times. Volunteering often gets one involved in local politics as well and can be a launching pad for running for county, city, or school board offices—or even for a state-level position. Some states have a much higher incidence of voluntarism than others. (See *Rankings of the States: Citizen Voluntarism Rates.*)

Volunteer Efforts: Type of Organization

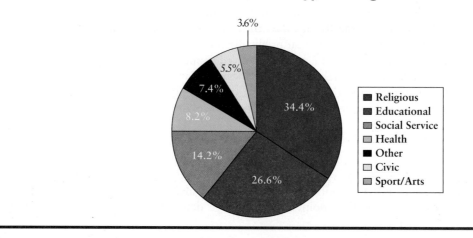

- Religious — 34.4%
- Educational — 26.6%
- Social Service — 14.2%
- Health — 8.2%
- Other — 7.4%
- Civic — 5.5%
- Sport/Arts — 3.6%

Citizen Voluntarism Rates

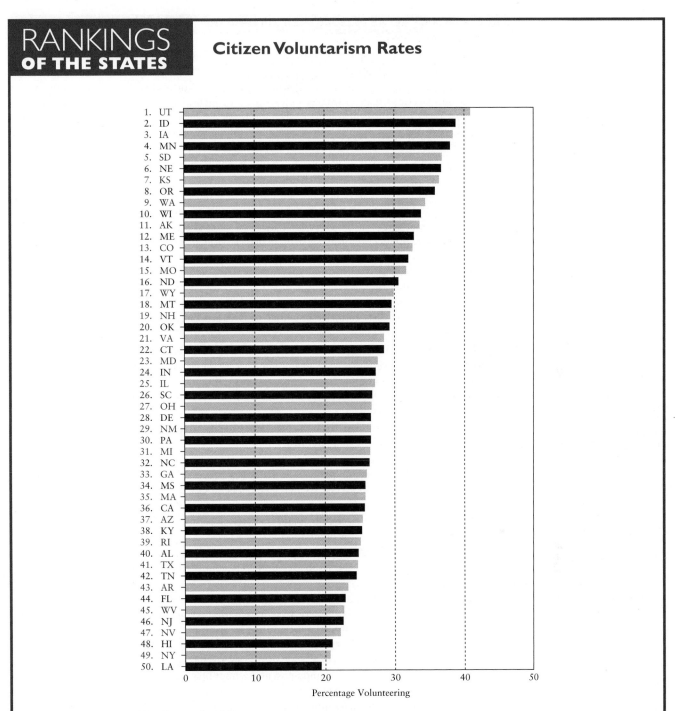

Percentage Volunteering

Note: Data are for 2011.
Source: Corporation for National & Community Service, Volunteering and Civic Life in America.
Available at http://www.volunteeringinamerica.gov/rankings.cfm.

- Ideally, democracy inspires widespread citizen participation in government—as voters, community activists, and political candidates—but in reality participation is low.

- Voter turnout is higher in large cities with a strong mayor-council form of government and partisan elections than in smaller cities with a council-manager plan and nonpartisan elections. Voter turnout is also higher when elections are held with state and national elections and when there are high profile issues and candidates on the ballot and media coverage is more extensive.

- Direct democracy tools—initiative, referendum, and recall—are more widely available to citizens at the local than at the state level.

- Elections in big cities have become "nationalized"—out-of-state donors and SuperPACs pour money into local contests when issues of national interest are a part of local races.

- Political "machines" in big cities have declined since the New Deal because of a decline in partisanship politics, reforms such as manager form of government and civil service, and social changes such as reduced European immigration and rising education and income levels. Reformers (progressives) favored government structures designed to "separate politics from administration."

- Corruption is a perennial problem at all levels of government. Corrupt politicians may be exposed by journalists and tried by public prosecutors but not always kicked out of office by voters.

- Ethics training is now required for most public employees and elected officials.

- State and local governments are encouraging greater citizen participation through such means as mobile apps, geographic information systems (GIS), interactive Web sites, social networks, keypad polling, Wi-Fi zones, mall kiosks, customer service call centers, public access TV, surveys, and citizen volunteers.

- At all levels of government, from the presidency to city councils, the people most likely to seek office are those with the most political ambition.

- Initially, city managers were urged to "stay out of politics" and focus on management duties. Today, more managers are involved in the policy process. Managers have a tough balancing act—having to please both city council members and city department heads and staff.

- Holding local public officials accountable is difficult because a significant proportion are appointed rather than elected, incumbents rarely lose, the number of active voters is small, and direct citizen contact is limited.

- Although mayors have few formal powers, they can exercise tremendous influence through persuasion, negotiation, and public relations. The number of women and minority mayors in big cities is on the rise.

- Black representation on city councils generally reflects the black population percentage of a city, but Hispanic and Asian American representation is lower than their population percentage. The presence of minorities in local office seems to make little or no difference in taxing, spending, and service policies, but it does with employment at city hall.

- Women's participation has risen dramatically in recent years, with major gains in mayoral seats, city councils, county commissions, and school boards. Women of color are running for office more frequently and winning.

- Interest groups may be more influential in community politics than in state or national political affairs. These groups include civic and neighborhood associations, taxpayer groups, environmental and "growth management" groups, chambers of commerce, banks, real estate developers and builders, churches, and the media.

- City officials give the highest marks to civic groups for contributing to constructive debates on issues and informing and involving citizens.

- Citizens rate local police departments, religious institutions, nonprofits, and friends and neighbors as the most effective community problem solvers.

CHAPTER TWELVE

METROPOLITICS: CONFLICT IN THE METROPOLIS

LEARNING OBJECTIVES

12.1 Describe the extent of metropolitization in the United States and the characteristics of metropolitan areas.

12.2 Compare cities with suburbs, trace the movement of people from cities to suburbs, and assess the extent to which the media has exaggerated urban problems.

12.3 Analyze the causes of suburban sprawl, and evaluate whether it is the root cause of inner-city problems.

12.4 Describe the characteristics of the metropolitan areas advocated for by new urbanists.

12.5 Compare regionalism and localism.

12.6 Discuss the purported benefits of metropolitan consolidation.

12.7 Analyze the purported benefits of maintaining the existing, fragmented system of metropolitan governments that emphasizes local control.

12.8 Evaluate whether current, fragmented metropolitan governments benefit the public by providing a marketplace in which citizens may select whichever community offers the services and taxes best suited to their needs.

12.9 Describe the tools used by metropolitan governments to coordinate activities throughout a region, and assess their effectiveness in addressing the problems of metropolitan areas.

THE METROPOLIS: SETTING FOR CONFLICT

Describe the extent of metropolitization in the United States and the characteristics of metropolitan areas.

Where will you live after you graduate? A big city? A suburb on the outskirts of a big city? A small town or some remote rural area? Will your choice of where you live be dictated by housing costs? Proximity to your job? The quality of local schools? Crime rates? Taxes? If faced with the choice of buying an affordable home on the outskirts of a large metropolitan area or living in an apartment or condo closer to where you work to reduce the long commute, which would you prefer? Are you moving to the Washington, DC, metropolitan area? If so, will you live in "the District"? In one of the northern Virginia suburbs such as Arlington, Alexandria, Manassas, Leesburg, or Woodbridge? Or in a southern Maryland suburban community such as Bethesda, Rockville, Beltsville, Columbia, or Frederick? (Democrats are more likely to choose Maryland; Republicans, Virginia!)

The U.S. Office of Budget and Management divides the nation's metropolitan area geographies into two categories: metropolitan (urban) and micropolitan (suburban). (See Figure 12–1.) One category represents the heavily urbanized core city area; the other category, the smaller, more newly urbanized, more suburban-like areas beyond the core. Together, they encompass many cities and counties and contain 93 percent of the U.S. population. The other 7 percent live in rural areas. We are indeed a metropolitan nation.

A "**metropolitan statistical area**" (MSA) is a core urban area of 50,000 or more people together with adjacent counties that have predominantly urban populations with close ties to the core urban area as measured by commuting patterns. Every state has at least one MSA; California has 26. (See *Rankings of the States*: Number of Metropolitan Statistical Areas in States.)

A **micropolitan statistical area** (M-PSA) has a population cluster of at least 10,000 but less than 50,000, plus adjacent territory that has a high degree of social and economic interconnectedness with the urban core.

METROPOLITAN STATISTICAL AREA

A core urban area of 50,000 or more people together with adjacent counties with predominantly urban populations and with close ties to the central city.

MICROPOLITAN STATISTICAL AREA

A smaller core urban area of 10,000–50,000 people with adjacent territory that has a high degree of social and economic interconnectedness with the urban core.

FIGURE 12–1 Metropolitan Statistical Areas

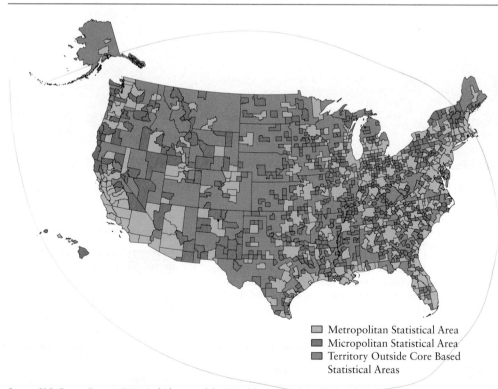

- Metropolitan Statistical Area
- Micropolitan Statistical Area
- Territory Outside Core Based Statistical Areas

Source: U.S. Census Bureau, *Statistical Abstract of the United States*, 2010. Available at http://www.census.gov/prod/2009pubs/10statab/app2.pdf.

Number of Metropolitan Statistical Areas in States

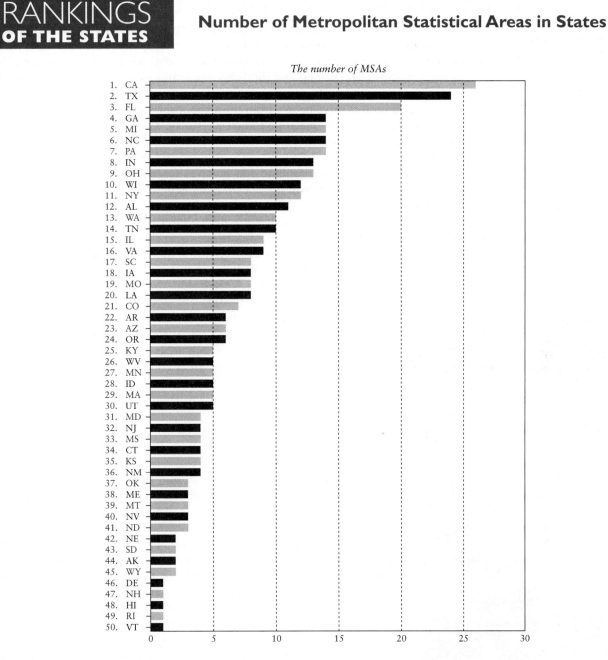

The number of MSAs

1. CA	
2. TX	
3. FL	
4. GA	
5. MI	
6. NC	
7. PA	
8. IN	
9. OH	
10. WI	
11. NY	
12. AL	
13. WA	
14. TN	
15. IL	
16. VA	
17. SC	
18. IA	
19. MO	
20. LA	
21. CO	
22. AR	
23. AZ	
24. OR	
25. KY	
26. WV	
27. MN	
28. ID	
29. MA	
30. UT	
31. MD	
32. NJ	
33. MS	
34. CT	
35. KS	
36. NM	
37. OK	
38. ME	
39. MT	
40. NV	
41. ND	
42. NE	
43. SD	
44. AK	
45. WY	
46. DE	
47. NH	
48. HI	
49. RI	
50. VT	

Note: Data are for 2012.

Source: Area Development Magazine Special Presentation, "Top States Doing Business 2013". Available at http://www.areadevelopment.com/Top-States-for-Doing-Business/Q3-2013/survey-results-landing-page-142378.shtml.

Some metropolitan areas adjoin each other, creating a continuous urban environment over an extended area. One such "**megalopolis**" is the New York–Northern New Jersey–Long Island area, encompassing parts of 4 states, 15 MSAs, and over 22 million people. While hundreds of local governments partition these metropolitan areas, people travel over these municipal boundaries often several times a day. Media markets—television, radio, newspapers—extend throughout these metropolitan areas. Most businesses depend on metropolitanwide markets for workers, suppliers, and customers. Cultural, restaurant, and entertainment centers serve people from throughout the metropolis.

The states have become "metropolitanized." Today, all 50 states have more than half of their populations concentrated in MSAs and M-PSAs; in 28 states, it is more than 90 percent.

The very definition of metropolitan life involves *large numbers* of *different* types of people living *close together* who are socially and economically *dependent* upon one another.[1] *Numbers, density, heterogeneity,* and *interdependence* are said to be distinguishing characteristics of metropolitan life. It is not difficult to envision a metropolitan area as a large number of people living together; we can see these characteristics in metropolitan life from a map or an airplane window. However, it is more difficult to understand the heterogeneity and interdependence of people living in metropolitan areas.

Growth Engines of the U.S. Economy

America's metropolitan areas make up a huge part of the nation's economy. The 10 largest metropolitan areas have economies larger than that of 36 states. The combined gross economic output of the U.S. metropolitan areas is greater than the combined output of 178 countries.[2] Even the smaller metro areas contribute billions of dollars to the economy.

Heterogeneity

The modern economic system of the metropolis is based on a highly specialized and complex division of labor. Highly specialized jobs account for much of the **heterogeneity** in urban populations. Different jobs produce different levels of income, dress, and styles of living. People's jobs shape the way they look at the world and their evaluations of social and political events. In acquiring their jobs, people attain a certain level and type of education that also distinguish them from those in other jobs with different educational requirements. There is a wide variation across MSAs in the proportion of adults who have a college degree, reflective of differences in their economic bases (e.g., high tech vs. manufacturing) and their non-English-speaking populations. (See Table 12–1.) Metropolitan living concentrates people with all these different economic, educational, and occupational characteristics in a few square miles. But America's metropolitan areas are as diverse as the nation itself. Some are magnets for the young, others for the old. Some are more "wired" than others. Do you like to go to live theater? Eat out? Travel? Buy electronics? Shop for clothes? Different metro areas rate better than others for these activities.

Ethnic and Racial Diversity

In the nineteenth and early twentieth centuries, opportunities for human betterment in the cities attracted immigrants from Ireland, Germany, Italy, Poland, and Russia, which is why some demographers have labeled these areas as "metro melting pots."[3] African Americans in search of opportunities migrated to cities from the rural South. Today, America's

It is not hard to imagine why residents of poor neighborhoods surrounding downtowns with shiny skyscrapers may view life as a conflict between the "haves" and the "have nots."

TABLE 12–1 Metro Area Variations in Proportion of Adults with a Bachelor's Degree

	Highest Rates				Lowest Rates		
Rank 2010	Rank 1990	Metro Area	Percentage with Bachelor's Degree	Rank 2010	Rank 1990	Metro Area	Percentage with Bachelor's Degree
1	1	Washington-Arlington-Alexandria, DC-VA-MD-WV	46.8	91	94	Las Vegas-Paradise, NV	21.6
2	4	San Jose-Sunnyvale-Santa Clara, CA	45.3	92	87	Fresno, CA	20.1
3	2	Bridgeport, CT	44	93	91	El Paso, TX	19.6
4	3	San Francisco-Oakland-Fremont, CA	43.4	94	92	Riverside-San Bernardino-Ontario, CA	19.5
5	5	Madison, WI	43.3	95	97	Youngstown, OH-PA	19.3
6	7	Boston-Cambridge, MA-NH	43	96	99	Lakeland, FL	17.9
7	8	Raleigh, NC	41	97	96	Stockton, CA	17.7
8	6	Austin, TX	39.4	98	98	Modesto, CA	16
9	9	Denver-Aurora, CO	38.2	99	100	McAllen, TX	15.8
10	11	Minneapolis-St. Paul, MN-WI	37.9	100	95	Bakersfield, CA	15

Note: Data are for 2010.

Source: Alan Berube, *Where the Grads Are: Degree Attainment in Metro Areas* (Washington DC: Metropolitan Policy Program, The Brookings Institution), May 31, 2012. Available at http://www.brookings.edu/blogs/the-avenue/posts/2012/05/31-educational-attainment-berube.

cities attract waves of immigrants from Mexico and other Latin American countries, Asia and the Philippines, and Haiti and other less-developed nations of the world. Newcomers to the metropolis bring with them different needs, attitudes, and ways of life. Today, a number of large MSAs have majority-minority populations. (See Figure 12–2.) The "melting pot" nature of MSAs tends to reduce some of this diversity over time, but the pot does not "melt" people immediately, and there always seem to be new arrivals.

Interdependence

Yet despite social and economic differences, urban dwellers are highly dependent upon one another in their daily activities. Suburbanites, for example, rely upon the central city for newspapers, entertainment, hospitalization, and a host of other modern needs. Many also rely upon the central city for employment opportunities. Conversely, the central city relies upon the suburbs to supply both employees and customers. This interdependence involves an intricate web of economic and social relationships, a high degree of communication, and a great deal of daily physical interchange among residents, groups, and firms in a metropolitan area.

Fragmented Government

However, another characteristic of metropolitan areas is **"fragmented" government**. Suburban development, spreading out from central cities, generally ignored governmental boundaries and engulfed counties, townships, towns, and smaller cities. Some

FRAGMENTED GOVERNMENT

Multiple governmental jurisdictions, including cities, townships, school districts, and special districts, all operating in a single metropolitan area.

FIGURE 12–2 Large Metro Areas with Majority-Minority Populations

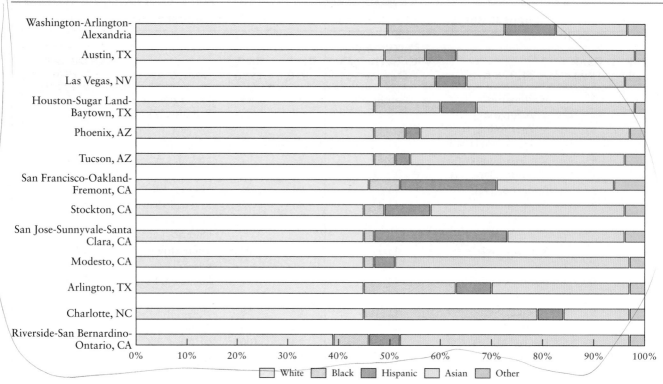

Source: Metropolitan Policy Program, *Melting Pot Cities and Suburbs: Racial and Ethnic Change in Metro America in the 2000s* (Washington DC: The Brookings Institute), May 2011. Available at http://www.brookings.edu/~/media/research/files/papers/2011/5/04%20census%20ethnicity%20frey/0504_census_ethnicity_frey.pdf.

metropolitan areas even spread across state lines, and four metropolitan areas of the United States—Detroit, San Diego, El Paso, and Laredo—adjoin urban territory in Canada or Mexico. This suburbanization has meant that hundreds of governments may be operating in a single metropolitan area. Thus, while metropolitan areas are characterized by social and economic interdependence, and consequently require coordinating mechanisms, metropolitan government is generally "fragmented" into many smaller jurisdictions, none of which is capable of governing the entire metropolitan area in a unified fashion.

Potential for Conflict

The metropolis presents a serious problem in *conflict* management. Because a metropolitan area consists of a large number of different kinds of people living closely together, the problem of regulating conflict and maintaining order assumes tremendous proportions. Persons with different occupations, incomes, and ethnic ties are known to have different views on public issues. People well equipped to compete for jobs and income in a free market view government housing and welfare programs differently than others not so well equipped. People at the bottom of the social ladder look at police—indeed, governmental authority in general—differently from the way those on higher rungs do. Homeowners and renters usually look at property taxation in a different light. Families with children and those without children have different ideas about school systems. And so it goes. Differences in the way people make their living, in their income levels, in the color of their skin, in the way they worship, in their style of living—all are at the roots of political life in a metropolis.

CITIES VERSUS SUBURBS

Suburbs account for most of the growth of America's metropolitan areas, although during economic recessions, the growth rate slows somewhat. New suburbs, most built since the 1970s on the outer fringes of metropolitan areas, are capturing increasing shares of both population and employment growth. Many central cities, especially in the Northeast and Midwest, actually lost people and jobs over the last two decades. These were mostly older industrial cities. These cities have had trouble transitioning from a manufacturing-based to a more knowledge-based economy.[4]

Compare cities with suburbs, trace the movement of people from cities to suburbs, and assess the extent to which the media has exaggerated urban problems.

Some central cities are showing signs of a second life. New waves of immigrants seeking welcoming populations; an aging Boomer population that prefers to be near top-notch hospitals and health care; young people delaying marriage, having fewer children, and choosing to live closer to colleges and universities; and environmentalists concerned about auto emission pollutants—all are trends that offer some promise of slowly revitalizing central cities.

Suburban growth patterns vary across the nation. While most suburbs (73 percent) have grown in size over the past few decades, some have not.[5] Declining suburbs are predominantly located in slow-growing metropolitan areas in the Northeast and Midwest; fast-growing suburbs are located in the South and West.

Suburbanization

America's suburbanization was a product of technological advances in transportation—the automobile and the expressway.[6] In the nineteenth century an industrial worker had to live within walking distance of his or her place of employment. This meant that the nineteenth-century American city crowded large masses of people into relatively small central areas, often in tenement houses and other high-density neighborhoods. However, modern modes of transportation—first the streetcar, then the private automobile, and then the expressway—eliminated the necessity of workers living close to their jobs. The same technology that led to the suburbanization of residences also influenced commercial and industrial location. Originally industry was tied to waterways or railroads for access to suppliers and markets. This dependence was reduced by the development of motor truck transportation, the highway system, and the greater mobility of the labor force. Many industries located in the suburbs, particularly light industries, which did not require extremely heavy bulk shipments that could be handled only by rail or water. When industry and people moved to the suburbs, commerce followed. Giant suburban shopping centers sprang up to compete with downtown stores. Thus, metropolitan areas become decentralized over time as people, business, and industry spread themselves over the suburban landscape. Today, 45 percent of all jobs in metropolitan areas are in places more than 10 miles away from the central business district (CBD), 34 percent are between 3 and 10 miles away. Just 21 percent are located within 33 miles from the CBD.[7] (Some refer to this as "**job sprawl.**")

JOB SPRAWL
The decentralization over time of people, businesses, and industry that spread themselves over the suburban landscape.

First Suburbs

One-fifth of Americans live in **first suburbs,** which are neither fully urban nor completely suburban. They are usually in the first ring of suburbs that sprang up around central cities right after World War II. They were the nation's first "bedroom communities." But today, they face a unique set of challenges: "concentrations of elderly and immigrant populations as well as outmoded housing and commercial buildings."[8] At the same time, they are home to some of the nation's wealthiest and most highly educated residents. First suburbs can be places where income, education, and racial divides are the widest in a metropolitan area.

FIRST SUBURBS
Communities that are neither fully urban nor completely suburban. They are usually in the first ring of suburbs that sprang up around central cities right after World War II.

"Boomburbs" and "Exurbs"

A **boomburb**[9] is a city with more than 100,000 residents located within a metropolitan area but that is *not* the central city and that has maintained a double-digit growth rate in recent years. Most are located in the Southwest. The Phoenix metropolitan area, for

BOOMBURB
A city with more than 100,000 residents located within a metropolitan area but that is *not* the central city and that has maintained a double-digit growth rate in recent years.

example, has seven boomburbs. These "burbs" typically contain a more economically and racially diverse population than smaller suburbs. While most are affluent, virtually all have low-income neighborhoods. But boomburbs are not just residential communities. They have vibrant commercial sectors as well. "These drive-by cities of highways, office parks, and shopping malls are much more horizontally built and less-pedestrian friendly than older suburbs."[10] At the same time, many are facing buildout by 2020 and competition from their "exurbs"—new suburbs that have sprung up beyond the boomburbs.

When Recessions Hit

The economy is cyclical. Population growth rates slow down during recessions. The slowdown often affects outlying suburbs (exurbs) more than central cities and suburban communities closer in. Recessions, with rising unemployment and housing foreclosure rates, make some people who might have moved out of the city into the "burbs" stay put. Such was the case during the Great Recession that began in 2007. During that time period, "the growth of primary city populations of the nation's 100 largest metropolitan areas accelerated at the same time that suburban population growth slowed."[11] The result was a narrowing of the growth rate differential between suburbs and cities, a pattern that continued as the recession wore on.

City–Suburban Differences

Social, economic, and racial conflict can be observed at all levels of government, but at the metropolitan level, it is most obvious in the conflict that occurs between central cities and their suburbs. At the heart of city–suburban conflict are the differences in the kinds of people who live in cities and suburbs. City–suburban conflict is at the center of **"the metropolitan problem"**; that is, the failure to achieve metropolitanwide consensus on public policy questions affecting the entire metropolitan area and the failure to develop metropolitan government institutions. Social, economic, and racial differences between cities and suburbs are major obstacles to the development of metropolitanwide policies and government institutions.[12]

Individual suburbs may be quite different from one another. There are, for example, industrial suburbs, residential suburbs, black suburbs, wealthy suburbs, and working-class suburbs.[13] There are declining "at-risk" first suburbs close in proximity to old central cities and fast-growing suburbs ("boomburbs" and "exurbs" or "edge cities") located at the outer extremities of metropolitan areas. Nevertheless, a clear perception of the social distance between cities and suburbs is important in understanding metropolitan politics, particularly why it is so hard to build city–suburban and regional coalitions.[14]

Life for a child growing up in an inner city is drastically different from that of children raised in the suburbs. The "social distance" between central-city and suburban residents is generally greater in larger metropolitan areas.

Social Class

Cities and suburbs can be differentiated, first of all, on the basis of **social class**—the occupation, income, and educational levels of their population. The cultured class of an earlier era established "country" living as a symbol of affluence; widespread prosperity has made possible mass imitation of the aristocracy by an upwardly mobile middle-class population. The suburbs house greater proportions of white-collar employees, college graduates, and affluent families than any other sector in American life.

Status differentials in favor of suburbs are more pronounced in larger metropolitan areas, although in some of the largest areas in California, Texas, and New York, class differences are beginning to shrink.[15] Status differentials in smaller metropolitan areas are not as great as in larger areas, and sometimes even favor the city rather than the suburbs. However, on the whole, suburban living still reflects middle-class values.

SOCIAL CLASS

The occupation, income, and educational levels of a population.

Familism

Cities and suburbs can also be differentiated on the basis of "**familism,**" or lifestyle. (See Figure 12–3.) Perhaps the most frequently mentioned reason for a move to the suburbs is "the kids." Family after family lists consideration of their young as the primary cause for their move to suburbia. A familistic, or child-centered, lifestyle can be identified in certain social statistics. In suburbia, by far the largest proportion of households with children is headed by married couples. While the same pattern is observable in cities, the incidence of children living with other types of families (unmarried, same-sex) is slightly higher. In general, there is a larger proportion of nontraditional households in cities than in suburbs, although that gap is narrowing.

"FAMILISM"

A reference to a child-centered lifestyle observed more frequently in suburbs than in central cities.

Race

Perhaps the most important difference between cities and suburbs is their contrasting *racial composition*. Overall, America's suburban population is still less diverse than the nation's overall central city population. However, suburbia has become more racially and ethnically diverse over the past decade, even in the newer exurbs farther away from the central city.[16] African Americans, Hispanics, and Asians have moved to the suburbs at a faster pace than whites.[17] The suburbs of virtually all metropolitan areas are more integrated today. Now, more than half of all racial and ethnic groups residing in the 100 largest MSAs

FIGURE 12–3 Suburbs versus Cities: More Traditional versus More Nontraditional Households

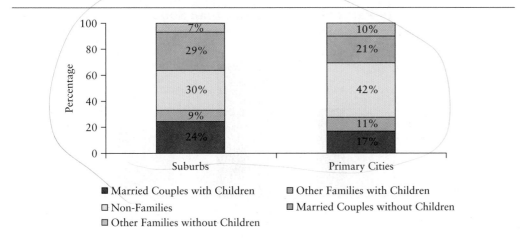

- ■ Married Couples with Children
- □ Non-Families
- □ Other Families without Children
- ▨ Other Families with Children
- ■ Married Couples without Children

Source: Metropolitan Policy Program, *State of Metropolitan America: On the Front Lines of Demographic Transformation* (Washington, DC: The Brookings Institution, 2010), p. 100.

live in the suburbs, countering the long-standing stereotype of "white" suburbs versus minority-dominated cities.[18] (See Figure 12–4.) "Melting pot metros"[19] (e.g., Los Angeles, Chicago, Washington, DC, Houston, and New York) have the largest minority suburban populations.

Poverty

Low-income, low-education, unskilled populations are concentrated in the central cities. Social problems are also concentrated in central cities—racial imbalance, crime, violence, inadequate education, poverty, slum housing. The poverty rate among central city residents is nearly twice that of suburbanites, although during a recession, suburban poverty rates increase more than those in the central cities. (See Figure 12–5) By moving to the suburbs, middle-class families not only separate themselves from poor people but also place physical distance between themselves and the major social problems that confront metropolitan areas. This permits them, for the time being, to avoid the problems associated with poverty, although in "first suburbs" there are growing numbers of poor neighborhoods.

FIGURE 12–4 A Majority of All Racial/Ethnic Groups in Major Metro Areas Now Live in the Suburbs

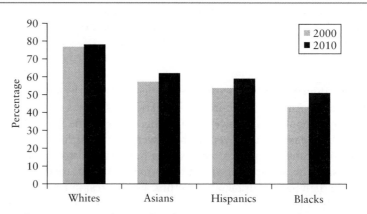

Source: Metropolitan Policy Program, *State of Metropolitan America: On the Front Lines of Demographic Transformation* (Washington, DC: The Brookings Institution, 2010), p. 60.

FIGURE 12–5 Poverty Rates Higher in Cities than Suburbs

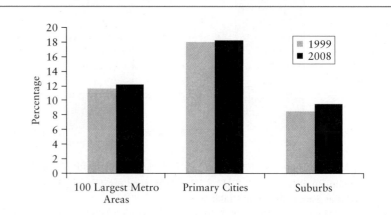

Source: Metropolitan Policy Program, *State of Metropolitan America: On the Front Lines of Demographic Transformation* (Washington, DC: The Brookings Institution, 2010), p. 139.

Parties

In general, large cities are much more Democratic than their suburban rings, which generally produce more Republican votes. While temporary shifts may occur from one election to another, this general pattern of Democratic cities and Republican suburbs is likely to prevail for the near future. As long as the national Democratic Party represents central-city, low-income, ethnic, labor, and racial constituencies, and the Republican Party represents middle-class, educated, managerial, white, Anglo-Saxon Protestant constituencies, the political coloration of cities and suburbs is likely to be different. Of course, the pattern of Democratic central cities and Republican suburbs is less evident in the "melting pot metros" where the suburbs house substantial minority populations.

Costs of Government

Large central cities show substantially higher operating expenditures per capita than their suburbs. The maintenance of a large physical plant for the entire metropolitan area requires city residents to make higher per capita operating expenditures than those required for suburbanites. In addition, many living costs in suburban communities are shifted from public to private spending (private septic tanks instead of public sewers, private instead of public recreation, for example). Differences in the public services provided by city and suburban governments are greatest in the area of police protection, recreation, and health. This reflects a concentration in the city of people who are likely to require these public services, in contrast to the suburbs.

Taxes

The tax bill in suburbs is only slightly lower than in central cities. Taxes had much to do with the migration of the "pioneer" suburbanites, those who moved to the suburbs in the 1930s and 1940s. At that time, suburban living offered a significant savings in property taxation over what were thought to be heavy city taxes. However, the tax advantage of the suburbs turned out partly to be a "self-denying prophecy": The more people fled to the suburbs to avoid heavy taxes, the greater the demand for public services in these new suburban communities, and the higher suburban taxes became to meet these new demands. Yet, the tax bill in most suburbs remains lower than in central cities. The difference in tax burden would be even greater if suburbanites did not choose to spend more per pupil in education than city residents, which produces higher school taxes in the suburbs. The suburbs also manage to limit their indebtedness more than cities, and most of the indebtedness incurred by the suburbs is for school rather than municipal purposes.

Is Bad News Coverage the Problem or the Solution?

Some urban scholars have concluded that the major media are at least partially to blame for reinforcing overly harsh and negative stereotypes of life in metropolitan America:

> The images from the nightly news, newsweeklies, and daily newspapers are an unrelenting story of social pathology—mounting crime, gangs, drug wars, racial tension, homelessness, teenage pregnancy, AIDS, inadequate schools, and slum housing. . . . Government programs are typically covered as well-intentioned but misguided, plagued by mismanagement, inefficiency, and, in some cases, corruption. . . . More important, the drumbeat of negativism has its political consequences. Many Americans have concluded that problems such as poverty and crime may be intractable.[20]

Others see the media as essential to the rebirth of urban areas—as necessary vehicles to promote economic development, civic pride, and cooperation. There is evidence that media coverage of the advantages of living in downtown areas has attracted people back to urban areas. They have been drawn by jobs, cultural, recreational, and social amenities, diversity, and higher levels of tolerance for different lifestyles.[21]

The debate over the causes and consequences of metropolitan conflict (or cooperation) is ongoing.

12.3

Analyze the causes of suburban sprawl, and evaluate whether it is the root cause of inner-city problems.

SUBURBAN "SPRAWL"

Suburban "sprawl" is often cited as the root cause of social, economic, and governmental problems in the nation's metropolitan areas. **"Sprawl"**—the outward extension of new low-density residential and commercial development from the core city—is seen by "smart growth" proponents as underlying many of the problems of **inner-city** life.

A number of central cities and older inter-ring suburbs have been left behind. They have lost millions of residents, particularly middle-class families who were the economic and social backbone of sustainable communities. Consequently these once-proud places now harbor higher and higher concentrations of the poor, particularly the minority poor, without the fiscal capacity to grapple with the consequences: joblessness, family fragmentation, failing schools, and deteriorating commercial districts.[22] However, sprawl is also seen as increasingly problematic for suburban residents themselves. Suburban sprawl is eating our open spaces, creating mind-boggling traffic jams, bestowing on us endless strip malls and housing developments, and consuming an ever-increasing share of our resources.[23]

"SPRAWL"

A negative reference to the outward extension of new low-density residential and commercial development from the central city.

INNER CITY

The area of the central city in which poverty, joblessness, crime, and social dependency are most prevalent.

Identifying Suburban "Sprawl"

It is argued that *not* all suburbanization can be castigated as "sprawl." Rather, *unwanted* "sprawl" can be identified by the following characteristics:

- Unlimited outward extension of new development
- Low-density residential and commercial settlements
- Leapfrog development jumping out beyond established settlements
- Fragmentation of powers over land use among many small localities
- Dominance of transportation by private automobiles
- Widespread development of commercial strips
- Great fiscal disparities among localities
- Reliance mainly on trickle-down to provide housing to low-income households[24]

Regardless of whether sprawl is wanted or unwanted, what we're seeing now is the urbanization of suburbia as the burbs continue to grow. In fact, suburban areas in large MSAs are no longer primarily bedroom communities. Today, 65 percent of major metropolitan area jobs are now in the suburbs, where 74 percent of workers live, meaning that there are only 11 percent fewer jobs in the suburbs than resident workers. In these large MSAs, the jobs–housing balance is nearing parity.[25]

The Causes of Sprawl

Suburban sprawl actually occurs because it is the preferred lifestyle of many Americans. Critics of sprawl—reformers, city planners, environmentalists—are reluctant to recognize the popular appeal of single-family homes on large lots with lawns, shrubs, and trees; open spaces for recreation; and quiet residential streets. Commercial businesses—supermarkets, shopping centers, malls—must follow their customers to the suburbs. And increasingly, industries, particularly financial, insurance, and other service companies, together with high-tech firms, want to be located nearer the homes of their middle-class employees and to enjoy pleasant working surroundings. More commuting now takes place from suburb to suburb than from suburb to central city.

It is true, of course, that government policies have facilitated suburban sprawl. Suburbanization was accelerated after the federal Interstate and Defense Highway Act of 1955 provided the financial support for the interstate "I Highway" system (see "Transportation Policy" in Chapter 13). Federal housing insurance—FHA (Federal Housing Administration) and VA (Veterans Administration) mortgages—enabled millions of American families to fulfill their dream of owning their own suburban home. Even the deductibility of home mortgage interest payments from federal income taxation is cited as a contributor to suburbanization.

Open land is easier and cheaper to build upon than downtown areas that must first be cleared of older buildings. Federal aid has long been available to city governments to assist in the redevelopment of blighted areas (see "Community Development and Revitalization Policy" in Chapter 13). But city bureaucracies have been slow and cumbersome in the implementation of urban redevelopment. City regulatory agencies frequently make the costs of complying with building codes, zoning regulations, and planning and environmental controls so high that builders and developers cannot produce affordable homes for middle-class residents, let alone the poor, in downtown areas. Finally, municipal governments in the suburbs contribute to sprawl when they themselves restrict growth, causing development to "leapfrog" to areas still farther from the central city, "the exurbs." Suburban residents use the tools of municipal government to exclude low-income housing and other "undesirable" development (see Chapter 13).

COMBATING SPRAWL WITH "SMART GROWTH"

12.4

Describe the characteristics of the metropolitan areas advocated for by new urbanists.

New urbanists ("smart growth" proponents) who favor more compact, livable communities, are disdainful of suburbs, which they describe as places "where the internal-combustion engine is king and the garage its castle, is seen by many land planners as a gas-wasting, fume-choked mess where the desolation is broken only by patches of high-maintenance grass and ornamental plants."[26] Urban planners, environmentalists, "growth management," and "smart growth" advocates (all sympathetic with the new urbanism movement) argue that sprawl increases the costs of highway building, water and sewer services, school busing, and other public infrastructure that must be extended over a wider area to accommodate low-density development. To them, "compactness" or high density is said to equal "efficiency." Environmentalists further argue that sprawl devours green spaces, increased automobile commuting fouls the air, paving over land adds to global warming, and that precious farmland is being lost.

NEW URBANIST

A person who favors more compact, livable communities rather than suburbs, which they see as contributing to pollution and environmental destruction.

Proponents of new urbanism strongly favor "**walkable urbanism**"—an approach to development that features pedestrian-oriented, mixed-use, and mixed-income areas within the same neighborhood. Their redevelopment plans for deteriorating downtown areas often favor commercial or high-income residential projects that promise to both beautify the city and add to its taxable property value. Indeed, "**gentrification**" of downtown residential areas—attracting upper-class residents and trendy high-priced restaurants and boutiques—is often the deliberate design. Lately, however, downtown developers in some metro areas have been successful at attracting less-affluent younger residents by turning abandoned offices into apartments within walkable distance of employment centers or with easy access to mass transit. The Millennial generation is more likely to favor renting rather than owning a home and having roommates with whom to share the rent. Many also prefer walking or riding mass transit to owning a car,[27] especially when commutes can be over an hour. (See "*Did You Know? Large Metro Areas Are Magnets for Mega-Commuters.*")

WALKABLE URBANISM

An approach to development that features pedestrian-oriented, mixed-use, and mixed-income areas within the same neighborhood.

"GENTRIFICATION"

The movement of upper-class residents and trendy high-priced restaurants and boutiques to downtown locations; revitalizes downtown areas.

Just as "smart growth" proponents see flaws with sprawl, supporters of suburbanization have raised serious questions about the feasibility and pragmatism of new urbanism. First, the automobile remains the near universal choice of Americans for transportation because of the freedom and flexibility it provides. Second, land is cheaper and housing more affordable farther away from the central city. Forcing more compact development in metropolitan areas may have negative impacts for low-income and minority populations. Third, higher population and housing densities (less sprawl) reduce the amount of park and recreational land, increase traffic congestion, and worsen air pollution in core cities. Finally, anti-sprawl efforts come "perilously close to a campaign against the American Dream" of many—living in a single-family home with a yard and play area in a quiet community.[28]

12.5 CONSOLIDATION OR FRAGMENTATION?

Compare regionalism and localism.

The brawl over sprawl has renewed the debate on how a metropolitan area can be governed most efficiently and effectively. Is it best to govern the area as a *regional* entity by centralizing or consolidating the common activities of existing local governments (**regionalism**)? Or is it better to continue governing via the existing decentralized and fragmented system of competing local governments (**localism**)? There are good arguments for each approach.[29]

12.6 THE CASE FOR METROPOLITAN CONSOLIDATION (REGIONALISM)

Discuss the purported benefits of metropolitan consolidation.

"Fragmented" government—that is, the proliferation of governments in metropolitan areas and the lack of coordination of public programs—adds to the metropolitan problem. The objective of the metropolitan reform movement of the last forty years has been to reorganize, consolidate, and enlarge government jurisdictions. The goal is to rid metropolitan areas of "ineffective multiple local jurisdictions" and "governments that do not coincide with the boundaries of the metropolis."[30] Some regionalists favor consolidating county and municipal *governments* but others propose combining certain *services* currently delivered independently by each local government. The latter approach is known as "**functional consolidation**" or "**service merger.**"

Public Services: Cost Reduction?

Many advantages are claimed for metropolitan governmental reorganization. First of all, the reorganization and consolidation of metropolitan governments is expected to bring about improved public services as a result of centralization. Consolidation of governments is expected to achieve many economies of large-scale operations and enable government to provide specialized public services, which "fragmented" units of government cannot provide. For example, larger water treatment plant facilities can deliver water at lower per gallon costs, and larger sewage disposal plants can handle sewage at a lower per gallon cost of disposal.[31]

REGIONALISM
Centralizing or combining activities of local governments in a metropolitan area; consolidation.

LOCALISM
Allowing individual local governments to provide services within their own communities; fragmentation.

FUNCTIONAL CONSOLIDATION ("SERVICE MERGER")
Several local governments jointly provide a service, such as emergency management.

The problem with this argument is that most studies show that larger municipal governments are *un*economic and fail to produce improved services. Only in small cities (populations under 25,000) can economies of scale be achieved by enlarging the scope of government. In cities of over 250,000, further increases in size appear to produce *dis*economies of scale and lower levels of public service per person. Thus, the outcomes of service mergers "are not automatically positive and will significantly vary based on the specific service under consideration and the process of negotiation and compromise" among the different governments involved.[32]

Coordination

Second, it is argued that metropolitan consolidation will provide the necessary *coordination of public services* for the metropolis. Study after study reports that crime, fire, traffic congestion, air

There is a growing urgency for better coordination among all local governments' first-responders in a metropolitan area. Responses to large-scale emergencies are dependent on effective intergovernmental communication. This responsibility often lies with county sheriffs' departments.

pollution, water pollution, and homeland security do not respect municipal boundary lines. In fact, technological advances and improved networking have even extended service demands beyond MSAs and heightened the call for more regionalism via collective networks linking governments, nonprofits, and private organizations.[33]

The transportation problem is the most common example of a coordination problem. Traffic experts have pleaded for the development of a balanced transportation system in which mass transit carries many of the passengers currently traveling in private automobiles. Yet mass transit requires decisive public action by the entire metropolitan area. Certainly, the city government is in a poor position to provide mass transit by itself without the support of the suburbanites. In the post-9/11 and post-Katrina eras, studies have shown the importance of coordination between first-responders of all local governments. Federal funding formulas have promoted metropolitanwide (regional) approaches to improve coordination.

Equality

The third major argument for metropolitan consolidation stresses the need to eliminate *inequalities in financial burdens* throughout the metropolitan area. Suburbanites who escaped many city taxes continue to add to the cities' traffic and parking problems, use city streets and parks, find employment in the cities, and use city hospitals and cultural facilities. By concentrating the poor, uneducated, unskilled minorities in central cities, we also saddle central cities with costly problems of public health and welfare, crime control, fire protection, slum clearance, and the like—all the social problems that are associated with poverty and discrimination. We concentrate these costly problems in cities at the same time that middle-class tax-paying individuals, tax-paying commercial enterprises, and tax-paying industries are moving into the suburbs. Thus, metropolitan-government fragmentation often succeeds in segregating financial needs from resources. The result is serious financial difficulty for many central cities.

Responsibility

It is also argued that metropolitan government will *clearly establish responsibility for metropolitanwide policy.* One of the consequences of "fragmented" government is the scattering of public authority and the decentralization of policymaking in the metropolis. This proliferation in the number of autonomous governmental units reduces the probability of developing a consensus on metropolitan policy. Each autonomous unit exercises a veto power over metropolitan policy within its jurisdiction; it is often impossible to secure the unanimity required to achieve metropolitan consensus on any metropolitanwide problem. Finally, citizens rarely know whom to hold accountable for inaction or obstruction when so many local governments are involved.

THE CASE FOR "FRAGMENTED" GOVERNMENT (LOCALISM)

12.7

Analyze the purported benefits of maintaining the existing, fragmented system of metropolitan governments that emphasizes local control.

Suburb "bashing" is a common theme among central-city politicians, city newspaper columnists, and many reform-minded scholars who would prefer centralized metropolitan government.[34] But the suburbs house well over half of the nation's population, and it is important to try to understand why so many suburbanites prefer "fragmented" government. Many citizens do not look upon the "optimum development of the metropolitan region" as a particularly compelling goal. Rather, there are a variety of social, political, and psychological values at stake in maintaining the existing "fragmented" system of local government.

Identity

First of all, the existence of separate and independent local governments for suburbs plays a vital role in developing and maintaining a sense of community *identity*. Suburbanites identify their residential community by reference to the local political unit. They do not think of themselves as residents of the "New York metropolitan region," but rather as residents of Scarsdale or Mineola. Even the existence of community problems, the existence of a governmental forum for their resolution, and the necessity to elect local officials heighten community involvement and identity. The suburban community, with a government small in scale and close to home, represents a partial escape from the anonymity of mass urban culture.

Access

The political advantages of a fragmented suburbia cannot easily be dismissed. The existence of many local governments provides *additional forums* for the airing of public grievances. People feel better when they can publicly voice their complaints against governments, regardless of the eventual outcome of their grievance. The additional points of access, pressure, and control provided by a decentralized system of local government give added assurance that political demands will be heard and perhaps even acted upon. Opportunities for individual participation in the making of public policy are expanded in a decentralized governmental system.

Effectiveness

Maintaining the suburb as an independent political community provides the individual with a sense of *personal effectiveness* in public affairs. A person can feel a greater sense of manageability over the affairs of a small community. A smaller community helps relieve feelings of frustration and apathy, which people often feel in their relations with larger bureaucracies. Suburbanites feel that their votes, their opinions, and their political activities count for more in a small community where they are more likely to know their local officials.[35] They cling to the idea of grassroots democracy in an organizational society.

Influence

Fragmented government clearly offers a larger number of groups the opportunity to *exercise influence* over government policy. Groups that would be minorities in the metropolitan area as a whole can avail themselves of government position and enact diverse public policies in smaller jurisdictions. Fragmented government creates within the metropolitan area a wide range of government policies. Communities that prefer, for example, higher standards in their school system at higher costs have the opportunity to implement this preference. Communities that prefer higher levels of public service or one set of services over another or stricter enforcement of particular standards can achieve their goals under a decentralized governmental system. Communities that wish to get along with reduced public services in order to maximize funds available for private spending may do so.

Schools

Racial imbalance and the plight of central-city schools are important forces in maintaining the political autonomy of suburban school systems in the nation's large metropolitan areas. Many suburbanites, whites and minorities alike, left the central city to find "a better place to raise the kids," and this means, among other things, better schools. Suburbs generally spend more on the education of each child than central cities. Moreover, the increasing concentration of minorities and newly arrived immigrants in central cities has resulted in racial imbalance in central-city schools. Efforts to end **de facto segregation** within the cities frequently involve busing schoolchildren into and out of ghetto schools in order to achieve racial balance. In Chapter 15 we will discuss de facto segregation in greater detail. However, it is important to note here that independent suburban school districts are viewed by many suburbanites as protection against the possibility that their children might be bused to inner-city schools. Autonomous suburban school districts lie outside the jurisdiction of city officials. While it is possible that federal courts may some day order suburban

DE FACTO SEGREGATION
Concentration of racial minorities in an area as a result of demographics or economics, not by law.

school districts to cooperate with cities in achieving racial balance in schools, the political independence of suburban schools helps to ensure that their children will not be used to achieve racial balance in city schools.

METROPOLITAN GOVERNMENT AS A MARKETPLACE

12.8

Evaluate whether current, fragmented metropolitan governments benefit the public by providing a marketplace in which citizens may select whichever community offers the services and taxes best suited to their needs.

Fragmented metropolitan government means many different mixes of municipal services, public schools, and tax levels in the same metropolitan area. So why can't people "shop around" among local communities and move into the community where the mix of services, schools, and taxes best suits their individual preferences?

The Tiebout Model

Economist Charles Tiebout argues that the existence of many local governments in the same area, all offering "public goods" (public schools, police and fire protection, water and sewer, refuse collection, streets and sidewalks) at various "prices" (taxes), provides a competitive and efficient government marketplace.[36] Families can choose for themselves what public goods they want at what price by simply moving to the community that best approximates their own preferences. The **Tiebout model** asserts that both families and businesses can "vote with their feet" for their preferred "bundle" of municipal services and taxes. Local governments must compete for residents and businesses by offering high-quality public services at the lowest possible tax rates. This encourages efficiency in local government.

TIEBOUT MODEL

An economic theory that asserts that families and businesses in metropolitan areas can maximize their preferences for services and taxes by choosing locations among multiple local governments.

Mobility?

The Tiebout model of efficient local government assumes that metropolitan residents have a high degree of *mobility,* that is, they can move anywhere in the metropolitan area anytime they wish. The major criticism of this model is that many metropolitan residents do not enjoy unlimited mobility. The poor are limited by meager financial resources from "shopping" for the best governmental services. And minorities often confront barriers to residential mobility regardless of their economic resources.

Equity?

Moreover, the Tiebout model in its original formulation ignores the interdependence of the metropolis. Many public services are metropolitanwide in scope—urban expressways, mass transit, clean air and water, public health and hospitals, and homeland security, for example. These services cannot be provided by small local governments. Suburbanites use public facilities and services of cities when they work in the city or go to the city for entertainment. If they do not share in the costs of these services and facilities, they become "**free riders**," unfairly benefiting from services paid for by others. The major social problems of the city—poverty, racial tension, poor housing, crime and delinquency—are really problems of the entire metropolis.[37]

FREE RIDERS

Those that unfairly benefit from services paid for by others.

Satisfaction?

Yet the Tiebout model is correct in asserting that there are a great variety of lifestyles, housing types, governmental services, and costs *within* large metropolitan areas, and that most families take this into account when choosing a place of residence. And judging by the subjective evaluations of residents, many different types of neighborhoods are judged satisfactory by the people living in them. Quality-of-life studies usually ask respondents how "satisfied" they are with their neighborhoods. These studies reveal that people living in *all* types of neighborhoods express satisfaction with them. Indeed, even lower-income people living in substandard housing or areas considered slums by outsiders report being satisfied. (However, attachment to friends and relatives is a major source of their satisfaction, rather than governmental services.[38])

MANAGING METROPOLITAN AREAS

Describe the tools used by metropolitan governments to coordinate activities throughout a region, and assess their effectiveness in addressing the problems of metropolitan areas.

In most of America's metropolitan areas, there are tremendous cross-pressures to coordinate governmental activity across a region, while at the same time protecting the values of suburban independence. A wide variety of approaches to accomplishing this difficult balancing act are used.

Annexation

ANNEXATION

The extension of city boundaries over adjacent territory in unincorporated areas; often requires voter approval.

The most obvious method of achieving some degree of governmental consolidation in the metropolitan areas would be for the central city to annex unincorporated suburban areas. **Annexation** continues to be the most popular integrating device in the nation's metropolitan areas. Not all cities, however, have been equally successful in annexation efforts. In some states, there are rather strong constraints on the annexation powers of local governments.[39] Opposition to central-city annexation is generally more intense in the larger metropolitan areas. The bigger the metropolis, the more one can expect that suburbanites will defend themselves against being "swallowed up" by the central city. While central cities expect fiscal gains from annexation, suburbanites often fear tax hikes. In reality, the pattern is mixed.[40]

Central cities in smaller urbanized areas experience more success in annexing adjacent land than cities in large urbanized areas. Yet size does not appear to be the most influential factor. Actually, the "age" of a city seems more influential than its size in determining the success of annexation efforts. Over three-fourths of the area and population annexed to central cities in the nation has been in newer cities of the West and South. City boundary lines in "older" metropolitan areas are relatively more fixed than in "newer" areas. Perhaps the immobility of boundaries is a product of sheer age. Over time, persons and organizations adjust themselves to circumstances as they find them. The longer these adjustments have been in existence, the greater the discomfort, expense, and fear of unanticipated consequences associated with change.[41] Annexation battles increasingly pit counties versus municipalities. Counties fear cities will "cherry-pick" wealthier residential and commercial unincorporated areas to annex, leaving the counties to deliver services to unincorporated areas with heavier concentrations of low-income residents and less lucrative tax bases.

City–County Consolidation

CITY–COUNTY CONSOLIDATION

The merger of a county and a city government into a single jurisdiction.

Three-quarters of the nation's metropolitan areas lie within single counties. From the standpoint of administration, there is much to be said for **city–county consolidation**. It would make sense administratively to endow county governments with the powers of cities and to organize them to exercise these powers effectively. Yet, important political problems—problems in the allocation of influence over public decision-making—remain formidable barriers to strong county government. Many central-city minorities oppose consolidation. They fear loss of political control and cultural identity.[42] Suburbanites are likely to fear that consolidation will give city residents a dominant voice in county affairs. Suburbanites may also fear that city–county consolidation may force them to pay higher taxes to help support the higher municipal costs of running the city. (Actually, county governments usually do provide more benefits to city than suburban residents, while receiving more tax revenues from suburbanites than city residents.[43]) Suburbanites with well-established, high-quality public school systems may be unenthusiastic about integrating their schools with city schools in a countywide system.

The track record for getting voters to approve city–county consolidation proposals is not good. Why? As one finance expert observed, it is because "consolidations are politically very difficult to pull off. Somebody has to give up power, and consolidations usually require a vote of the electorate in each of the combining jurisdictions."[44] Since 1921 nearly 170 city and county governments have attempted consolidation but just 41 have been successful, mostly relatively small jurisdictions in the South.[45] There was a flurry of passages

TABLE 12–2 City–County Consolidation Attempts: 2000–Present

2000	Hawkinsville/Pulaski County, Georgia	Fail
2000	**Louisville/Jefferson County, Kentucky**	**Pass**
2000	**Hartsville/Troosdale County, Tennessee**	**Pass**
2001	Fairbanks/Fairbanks Borough, Alaska	Fail
2001	Ketchikan/Ketchikan Borough, Alaska	Fail
2001	Gainesville/Hall County, Georgia	Fail
2001	Tullahoma/Coffee County, Indiana	Fail
2002	**Haines City/Haines Borough, Alaska**	**Pass**
2002	Campbellsville/Taylor County, Kentucky	Fail
2003	**Cusseta City/Chattahoochee County, Georgia**	**Pass**
2003	Albuquerque/Bernallilo County, New Mexico	Fail
2004	Des Moines/Polk County, Iowa	Fail
2004	Albuquerque/Bernallilo County, New Mexico	Fail
2004	Frankfort/Franklin County, Kentucky	Fail
2005	Topeka/Shawnee County, Kansas	Fail
2006	**Georgetown/Quitman County, Georgia**	**Pass**
2007	**Tribune/Greely County, Kansas**	**Pass**
2008	**Preston/Webster County, Georgia**	**Pass**
2008	**Statenville/Echols County, Georgia**	**Pass**
2010	Memphis/Shelby County, Tennessee	Fail
2012	Evansville/Vanderburgh County, Indiana	Fail
2012	**Macon/Bibb County, Georgia**	**Pass**

Source: National Association of Counties, "Reshaping County Government: A Look at City–County Consolidation," February 2012. Available at http://www.naco.org/newsroom/pubs/Documents/County Management and Structure/Reshaping County Government A Look at City–County Consolidation.pdf. © 2012 National Association of Counties. Reproduced with permission from the National Association of Counties.

in the 1960s and 1970s, then again in the 2000s. (See Table 12–2) The first to pass in the 2000s—the merger of the City of Louisville and Jefferson County, Kentucky—promised a different benefit to the voters: economic advantage:

> Merger will make us money. We'll vault from 65th largest U.S. city to 23rd. We'll be on the radar screen of major metropolises. We'll attract more jobs. Our young people won't have to go elsewhere for economic opportunity.[46]

Economic stress, specifically a major recession, was the driving force behind the others that consolidated their city–county governments in the late 2000s. These relatively small jurisdictions judged they were simply too small to "go it alone."

Has this approach been successful at managing the sprawl of cities into unincorporated areas of the county or at improving the efficiency of service delivery by eliminating duplication of services? Not entirely, primarily because these consolidations involve the central city and the county, but allow smaller cities in the county to opt out of the new structure. Thus, the city–county consolidation approach utilized so far has elements of both regionalism and localism.[47]

Sometimes, just changing the name of a county to include the major city helps create an image of a more coordinated areawide entity. For example, the county in which the City of Miami is located was formerly known as Dade County. But in 1997, voters approved renaming the county Miami–Dade County.

Special Districts

One of the more popular approaches to metropolitan integration is the creation of **special districts** or **authorities**. (See Chapter 10, "*Rankings of the States:* Special District Governments in the States.") These special-purpose governments are charged with administering a

SPECIAL DISTRICTS

Local governmental units usually charged with performing a single function; often overlap municipal and county boundaries.

AUTHORITIES:

Special purpose local governments similar in function to special districts but able to cross state lines.

particular function or service on a metropolitanwide or at least an intermunicipal level, such as a park, sewer system, water, parking, airport, planning, other district, or authority. Because the special district or authority leaves the social and governmental status quo relatively undisturbed, important integrative demands are met with a minimum of resistance with this device. The autonomy of suburban communities is not really threatened, loyalties are not disturbed, political jobs are not lost, and the existing tax structure is left relatively intact.

Special districts or authorities may be preferred by suburban political leaders when they believe it will lessen the pressure for annexation by the central city. Special districts or authorities may also be able to incur additional debt after existing units of government have already reached their tax and debt limits.[48] Thus, special districts or authorities may be able to operate in an area wider than that of existing units of governments and at the same time enable governments to evade tax or debt limits in financing a desired public service. The nation's largest special districts—New York's Metropolitan Transportation Authority, Boston's Massachusetts Bay Transportation Authority, Washington's Metro Area Transit Authority, the Los Angeles County Transportation Commission, and the Port Authority of New York and New Jersey—collect and spend billions of dollars each year.

Yet, experience in the cities that have relied heavily upon special districts or authorities has suggested that these devices may create as many problems as they solve. Many special districts and authorities are governed by a quasi-independent board or commission, which, once established, becomes largely immune from popular pressures for change. The structure of these districts and authorities usually confuses the voters and makes it difficult for the average citizen to hold officials of these agencies responsible for their decisions. Moreover, since these special districts and authorities are often created for a single purpose, they typically come to define the public interest in terms of the promotion of their own particular function—recreation, mass transit, water, parks—without regard for other metropolitan concerns. This "single-mindedness" can lead to competition and conflict between authorities and other governmental agencies in the region. Thus, even from the point of view of administrative efficiency, it is not clear whether the special district or authority, with its maze of divided responsibility, reduces or compounds the problem of governmental coordination in the metropolis in the long run.[49]

INTERJURISDICTIONAL AGREEMENTS
Voluntary contracts among local governments in a metropolitan area to perform services jointly or on behalf of each other.

Interjurisdictional Agreements

Voluntary cooperative agreements between governments in a metropolitan area are common. **Interjurisdictional agreements** may take the form of informal verbal understandings that might involve, for example, the exchange between welfare departments of information on cases, or cooperation among police departments in the apprehension of a lawbreaker, or agreements among local fire departments to come to the assistance of each other in the event of a major fire. Agreements may also be *formal* interjurisdictional agreements among governments, perhaps to build and operate a major facility such as a garbage incinerator or a sewage treatment plant. Interjurisdictional agreements may provide for (1) one government performing a service or providing a facility for one or more other governments on a contractual basis, (2) two or more governments performing a function

The Cowlitz-Wahkiakum Council of Governments (CWCOG) is one of nine councils of government and regional councils in Washington State. Its purpose is to provide a regional forum to address issues of mutual interest and concern (regional and local planning, transportation planning, community and economic development planning, technical assistance and information services, a wide array of contractual services, and substance abuse education and prevention strategies).

jointly or operating a facility on a joint basis, or (3) two or more local governments agreeing to assist and supply mutual aid to each other in emergency situations.

One of the attractions of interjurisdictional agreements is that they provide a means for dealing with metropolitan problems on a voluntary basis while retaining local determination and control. Interjurisdictional agreements do not threaten the existence of communities or governments. They do not threaten the jobs of incumbent public officials. Yet at the same time they enable governments to achieve the economies of scale and provide the specialized services that only a larger jurisdiction can make possible.[50] Local governments experiencing budget problems and political difficulties due to competition with other jurisdictions are often the most likely to search for ways to economize via interlocal agreements.[51]

Councils of Government

Metropolitan **councils of governments (COGs)** are associations of governments or government officials that provide an opportunity for study, discussion, and recommendations regarding common metropolitan problems. Not governments themselves, these councils of governments have no power to implement decisions but must rely instead upon compliance by member governments. Metropolitan councils provide an arena where officials of metropolitan governments can come together regularly, discuss problems, make recommendations, and, hopefully, coordinate their activities. Regional associations are the most successful when top-level local elected officials, rather than their staff, actively participate.

"Metro" Government

The American experience with federalism at the national level has prompted consideration of federated governmental structures for metropolitan areas. A **"metro" government** with authority to make metropolitanwide policy in selected fields might be combined with local control over functions that are "local" in character. Metropolitan federation, in one form or another and at one time or another, has been proposed for many major metropolitan regions in the nation. Yet, with the exception of Miami, and Nashville, proposals for metropolitan federation have been consistently rejected by both voters and political leaders. While metropolitan federation promises many of the advantages of governmental consolidation listed earlier—administrative efficiency, economy of large-scale operation, elimination of financial inequalities, and public accountability for metropolitanwide policy—it seriously threatens many of the social, political, and psychological values in the existing "fragmented" system of local government in the metropolis. Metropolitan federation also poses a problem discussed earlier, that of deciding what is a "metropolitan" problem. In order to

Law enforcement officers from many jurisdictions must work together in times of crisis in metropolitan areas, like they did in response to the bombings during the Boston Marathon in 2013 and the following investigation and manhunt.

allocate functions to a "metro" government in a federation arrangement, one must first determine what is a metropolitan problem for which all the citizens of the area have a responsibility.

Governance versus Government Structure

Can simply altering the structure of governments in metropolitan areas solve regional problems in fragmented areas? "No," say the urban scholars who have studied the impact of consolidating various cities and counties. Their research has shown: "There is no hard evidence that consolidated government will be a better, more honest, more efficient, more effective, or more democratic and responsive governmental structure."[52] Besides, "structure is really only a framework for how governance occurs and that structure is filtered through and colored by local political practices, historical patterns of behavior, and local civic cultures or ways of governance."[53] These scholars believe that voluntary cooperative efforts (governance) linking governmental and nongovernmental organizations are likely to be more effective than drastically altering existing governmental structures, which is often quite difficult. Examples of governance activities include "community visioning initiatives, collaborative planning processes, service integration efforts, community collaboratives, study circles, civic journalism projects, community disputes resolved through mediation, and multisectoral partnership."[54] The Internet, videoconferencing, government access cable television, and other telecommunication technologies have made it easier to "build an infrastructure for community collaboration."

Other scholars believe cooperative governance approaches can only go so far—but not far enough. To them, cooperation merely "serves to protect and preserve the status quo—governmental fragmentation, local government autonomy, and the absence of authoritative areawide decision making."[55] Why? Because it works only for highly local matters, not tough-to-solve metropolitanwide issues such as suburban sprawl or city–suburban fiscal and social disparities. As we have seen in this chapter, even with the greater emphasis on regional cooperation in certain areas,[56] metropolitics is a tough game to win.

Large Metro Areas Are Magnets for Mega-Commuters

Nothing proves the point that metropolitan areas are economically linked than the nearly 600,000 Americans who travel 90 or more minutes and 50 or more miles to work—the mega-commuters (1 in 122 of full-time workers).[a] Most depart for work before 6 a.m. The average travel time is 119 minutes; the average distance traveled is 166 miles. Over two-thirds (68 percent) drive alone, while 11 percent use public transportation and 14 percent carpool. Mega-commuters are more likely to be male (75 percent), older, married, high salaried, and with a spouse who does not work. For most, the long commute reflects employment and housing realities. In the words of a nine-year mega-commuter: "I can't afford to leave this job, and I can't afford to move. I have a good job, it's just 74 miles from home."[b] MSAs with the most mega-commuters are San Francisco-Oakland-Fremont, San Jose-Sunnyvale-Santa Clara, Washington-Arlington-Alexandria, and New York-Northern New Jersey-Long Island.

Metro Areas with the Most Mega-Commuters

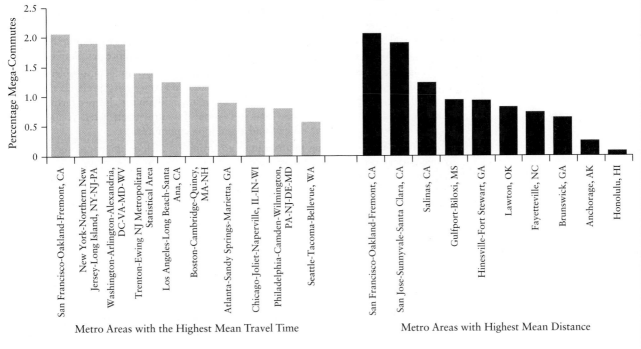

Note: Mega Commuters travel 90 or more minutes or 50 or more miles to work.
Sources: [a]U.S. Census Bureau, Melanie A. Rapino and Alison K. Fields, "Mega Commuting in the U.S.: Time and Distance in Defining Long Commutes Using the 2006-2010 American Community Survey." Available at http://www.census.gov/newsroom/releases/pdf/poster_megacommuting_in_the_u.s.pdf.

[b]James Joyner, "Rise of the Megacommuter," *Outside the Beltway,* March 5, 2013.

CHAPTER HIGHLIGHTS

- All 50 states have more than half of their populations concentrated in metropolitan statistical areas and micropolitan statistical areas. U.S. metropolitan areas combined have a larger economy than many countries.

- Metropolitan government is generally "fragmented" into many smaller jurisdictions, none of which has the legal authority to govern the entire metropolitan area as a single unit. Some prefer fragmentation, others favor more centralization.

- The growth of suburbs outward from central cities has been expedited by cars and highways.

- By moving to the suburbs, middle-class families not only separate themselves from poor people but also place physical distance between themselves and the major social problems that confront metropolitan areas. This makes it difficult to successfully craft metropolitanwide policies.

- Suburbs are not monolithic. The population makeup of older suburbs closer to the city differs a lot from newer suburbs on the edge of a metro area.

- Large cities are more Democratic than their suburban rings, which generally produce more Republican votes.

- Large central cities have substantially higher operating expenditures per capita than their suburbs, especially for police, recreation, and health. Suburbs spend more per pupil on education.

- Suburban sprawl has contributed to social, economic, and governmental problems, including increased pollution and decreased park and farmland, but Americans' preference for automobiles and single-family homes shows no sign of ending and land is cheaper farther out of the central city. However, during the Great Recession, downtowns attracted younger residents eager to ditch their cars, save on gas, and avoid long commutes.

- Arguments for consolidating metropolitan governments include improved services in small towns, better coordinated services such as transportation and firefighting across a region, elimination of financial inequalities among metropolitan residents, and clearly established responsibility for metropolitan policies.

- Arguments for maintaining fragmented governments include community identity, additional points of access to solve problems, a sense of greater personal effectiveness and influence in community matters, and political independence over suburban schools.

- According to the Tiebout marketplace model, families can choose the public services they want at what price (taxes) by simply moving to the community fitting their preferences. But this model ignores the immobility of some citizens and the "free ride" that some citizens get for services paid for by others.

- Methods to consolidate government activity include annexation, city–county mergers, special-purpose districts, interjurisdictional agreements, councils of government, and a federated metro structure.

CHAPTER THIRTEEN

COMMUNITY POWER, LAND USE, AND THE ENVIRONMENT

LEARNING OBJECTIVES

13.1 List the various public policies that are affected by land-use decisions made by local governments.

13.2 Compare and contrast the elite and pluralist models of community power.

13.3 Explain why there is a near-consensus among economic elites who benefit directly when land is used in a way that promotes economic development.

13.4 Trace the shift of local political influence from economic elites to political elites, and contrast the priorities of these two groups of elites.

13.5 Trace the growth of planning, assess the influence of planners, outline the opposition to planning, and describe the zoning process.

13.6 Detail the various innovative alternatives to strict land-use policies.

13.7 Explain the circumstances under which governments can take possession of or restrict the use of private land.

13.8 Analyze the effectiveness of the various urban renewal policies.

13.9 Discuss the transportation policies that affect local communities, compare the roles of the national and state governments in transportation policy, and compare transportation policies aimed at cars versus those aimed at other modes of transportation.

13.10 Describe the various environmental policies that affect states and communities, and assess the extent to which governments have been able to address these problems.

List the various public policies that are affected by land-use decisions made by local governments.

LAND USE, ECONOMICS, AND COMMUNITY POLITICS INTERTWINED

All local governments operate within specific geographical boundaries. How land is used within those boundaries greatly affects the economic and personal well-being of the citizens who live there and the finances and politics of the local governments that serve them. Land-use rules and regulations affect the quantity and type of housing units (single-family homes, condos, townhomes, mobile homes, apartments) permitted in an area, the number and type of jobs available, the types of business establishments in existence and the conditions under which they operate, and the proportion of the land area that is used for public purposes (e.g., roads, mass transit systems, parks, water and sewer lines, convention centers, sports stadiums, and public housing). Land-use decisions also affect the type of transportation system that will take residents to and from their jobs (cars, buses, subways, rail, air, water). And land-use decisions can greatly affect the environment.

A careful analysis of which individuals and groups are involved in local debates over land use–related issues—housing, planning, zoning, permitting, economic development and redevelopment, transportation, the environment—is one way to get a good glimpse of the political and economic power structures within a community.

Compare and contrast the elite and pluralist models of community power.

MODELS OF COMMUNITY POWER

Who runs this town? Do the elected public officials actually make the important decisions? Or is there a "power structure" in this community that really runs things? If so, who is in the power structure? Are public officials "go-fers" who carry out the orders of powerful individuals who operate "behind the scenes"? Or are community affairs decided by democratically elected officials acting openly in response to the wishes of many different individuals and groups? Is city government of the people, by the people, and for the people? Or is it a government run by a small "elite," with the "masses" of people largely apathetic and uninfluential in public affairs?

Social scientists have differed over the answers to these questions. Some social scientists posit an **elite model of community power**—that power in American communities is concentrated in the hands of relatively few people, usually top business and financial leaders. They believe that this "elite" is subject to relatively little influence from the "masses" of people. Other social scientists posit a *pluralist model* of community power—that power is widely shared in American communities among many leadership groups who represent segments of the community and who are held responsible by the people through elections and group participation. Interestingly, both elitist and pluralist models seem to agree that decisions are made by small minorities in the community. Direct, widespread, individual citizen participation in community decision making is more of an ideal than a reality. The *elite model describes a monolithic structure of power,* with a single leadership group making decisions on a variety of issues. The **pluralist model of community power** *describes a polycentric structure of power,* with different leaders active in different issues and a great deal of competition, bargaining, and sharing of power among them.

Most "real" communities will probably fall somewhere in between—that is, along a continuum from the monolithic elite model of power to a diffused and polycentric pluralist model. Many social scientists are neither confirmed "elitists" nor "pluralists," but they are aware that different structures and power may exist in different communities. Yet these ideal models of community power may be helpful in understanding the different ways in which community power can be structured.

ELITE MODEL OF COMMUNITY POWER

In community politics, the theory that power is concentrated in the hands of relatively few people, usually top business and financial leaders.

PLURALIST MODEL OF COMMUNITY POWER

In community politics, the theory that power is widely dispersed with different leaders in different issue areas responding to the wishes of various interest groups as well as voters.

The Elite Model

European social theory has long been at odds with democratic political writers about the existence and necessity of elites. Italian political theorist Gaetano Mosca, in his book *The*

Ruling Class, wrote, "In all societies . . . two classes of people appear—a class that rules and a class that is ruled."[1] For Mosca, elitism is explained by the nature of social organization. Organization inevitably results in the concentration of political power in the hands of a few. Organized power cannot be resisted by an unorganized majority in which each individual ". . . stands alone before the totality of the organized minority. A hundred men acting uniformly in concert, with a common understanding, will triumph over a thousand men who are not in accord and can therefore be dealt with one by one."[2] Since organized power will prevail over individual effort in politics, sooner or later, organizations will come to be the more important actors in political life. And organizations cannot function without leaders. In the words of European sociologist Robert Michels, "He who says organization, says oligarchy."[3]

Power in "Middletown"

One of the earliest studies of American communities, the classic study of Middletown, conducted by sociologists Robert and Helen Lynd in the mid-1920s and again in the mid-1930s, confirmed a great deal of elitist thinking about community power.[4] The Lynds found in Muncie, Indiana, a monolithic power structure dominated by the owners of the town's largest industry. Community power was firmly entrenched in the hands of the business class, centering on, but not limited to, the "X family."[5] The power of this group was based on its control over the economic life in the city, particularly its ability to control the extension of credit. The city was run by a "small top group" of "wealthy local manufacturers, bankers, the local head managers of . . . national corporations with units in Middletown, and . . . one or two outstanding lawyers." Democratic procedures and governmental institutions were window dressing for business control. The Lynds described the typical city official as a "man of meager calibre" and as "a man whom the inner business control group ignores economically and socially and uses politically."

Perhaps the most influential elitist study of community politics was sociologist Floyd Hunter's *Community Power Structure,* a study of Atlanta, Georgia. According to Hunter, no one person or family or business dominated "Regional City" (a synonym for Atlanta), as might be true in a smaller town.[6] Instead, Hunter described several tiers of community influentials, with business leaders dominating the top tier. The top decision makers were not formally organized but frequently met informally and passed down decisions to government leaders, city organizations, and other "figureheads."

The Pluralist Model

Modern pluralism does not mean a commitment to "pure democracy," where all citizens participate directly in decision making. The underlying value of individual dignity continues to motivate contemporary pluralist thought, but it is generally recognized that the town-meeting type of pure democracy is not really possible in an urban industrial society. To modern pluralists, individual participation has come to mean membership in *organized groups.* Interest groups become the means by which individuals gain access to the political system. Government is held responsible, not directly by individuals, but by organized interest groups and political parties. Pluralists believe that competition between parties and organized groups, representing the interests of their citizen members, can protect the dignity of the individual and offer a viable alternative to individual participation in decision-making.

The pluralist model of community power stresses the fragmentation of authority, the influence of elected public officials, the importance of organized group activity, and the role of public opinion and elections in determining public policy. Who rules in the pluralist community? "Different small groups of interested and active citizens in different issue areas with some overlap, if any, by public officials, and occasional intervention by a large number of people at the polls."[7]

Power in New Haven

Perhaps the most influential of the pluralist community studies was Robert A. Dahl's *Who Governs?*, a detailed analysis of decision making in New Haven, Connecticut. Dahl chose to examine 16 major decisions on redevelopment and public education in New Haven and on nominations for mayor in both political parties for seven elections. Dahl found a polycentric and dispersed system of community power in New Haven, in contrast to Hunter's highly monolithic and centralized power structure. Influence was exercised from time to time by many individuals, each exercising power over some issue but not over others. When the issue was one of urban renewal, one set of individuals was influential; in public education, a different group of leaders was involved. Business elites, who were said by Hunter to control Atlanta, were only one of many different influential groups in New Haven. The mayor of New Haven was the only decision maker who was influential in most of the issue areas studied, and his degree of influence varied from issue to issue.

13.3

Explain why there is a near-consensus among economic elites who benefit directly when land is used in a way that promotes economic development.

ECONOMIC ELITES IN COMMUNITIES

Great power derives from control of economic resources. Most of the nation's economic resources are controlled by national institutions—industrial corporations, banks, utilities, insurance companies, investment firms, and the national government. Most of the forces shaping life in American communities arise outside of these communities; community leaders cannot make war or peace, or cause inflation or recession, or determine interest rates or the money supply. But there is one economic resource—land—that *is* controlled by communities. Land is a valuable resource: Capital investment, labor and management, and production must be placed somewhere.

Local Control of Land Use

Traditionally, community power structures were composed primarily of economic elites whose goals were to maximize land values, real estate commissions, builders' profits, rent payments, and mortgage interest, as well as to increase revenues to commercial enterprises serving the community. Communities were traditionally dominated by mortgage-lending banks, real estate developers, builders, and landowners. They were joined by owners or managers of local utilities, department stores, attorneys and title companies, and others whose wealth was affected by land use. Local bankers who financed the real estate developers and builders were often at the center of the elite structure in communities. Unquestionably these community elites competed among themselves for wealth, profit, power, and preeminence. But they shared a consensus about intensifying the use of land. Corporate plants and offices, federal and state office buildings, and universities and colleges all contributed to the increased land values, not only on the parcels used by these facilities but also on neighboring parcels.

Growth as Shared Elite Value

Growth is the shared elite value. The community elite is indeed a "growth machine."[8] Economic growth expands the workforce and disposable income within the community. It stimulates housing development, retail stores, and other commercial activity. The economic elite understand that they all benefit, albeit to varying degrees, when economic growth occurs within the community. Not only must a community compete for new investments, but it must also endeavor to prevent relocation of investments it already has.

Attracting investors requires the provision of good transportation facilities—highways, streets, rail access, and water and airport facilities. It requires the provision of utilities—water, gas and electrical power, solid waste disposal, and sewage treatment. It requires the provision of good municipal services, especially fire and police protection; the elimination of harassing business regulations and the reduction of taxes on new investments to the lowest feasible levels; the provision of a capable and cooperative labor force, educated for the needs of productive capital and motivated to work; and finally, the provision of sufficient amenities—cultural, recreational, aesthetic—to provide the corporate managers with a desirable lifestyle.

Elites Striving for Consensus

Community economic elites usually strive for consensus. They believe that community economic growth—increased capital investment, more jobs, and improved business conditions—benefit the entire community. According to Paul E. Peterson, community residents share a common interest in the economic well-being of the city:

> Policies and programs can be said to be in the interest of cities whenever the policies maintain or enhance the economic position, social prestige, or political power of the city as a whole.[9]

When major land-use changes are proposed, fights between pro-development and anti-development forces often become intense.

Community economic elites would doubtlessly agree with Peterson. He adds that the interests of the city as a whole are closely bound to its export industries. These industries add net wealth to the community at large, while support and service industries merely transfer wealth within the community.

> Whatever helps them prosper rebounds to the benefit of the community as a whole—perhaps four or five times over. It is just such an economic analysis (of the multiplier effect of export industries) that has influenced many local government policies. Especially the smaller towns and cities may provide free land, tax concessions, and favorable utility rates to incoming industries.[10]

The less economically developed a community, the more persuasive the argument on behalf of export industries.

Growth as Good Politics

Economic elites expect local government officials to share in the growth consensus. Economic prosperity is necessary for protecting the fiscal base of local government. Growth in local budgets and public employment, as well as governmental services, depends on growth in the local economy. Governmental growth expands the power, prestige, and status of government officials. Moreover, economic growth is usually good politics. Growth-oriented candidates for public office generally have larger campaign treasuries than anti-growth candidates, unless they are running in an area that has become "anti-growth." Growth-oriented candidates routinely solicit contributions from the local community power structure. Finally, according to Peterson, most local politicians have a "sense of community responsibility." They know that if the economy of the community declines, "local business will suffer, workers will lose employment opportunities, cultural life will decline, and city land values will fall."[11] If that happens, they are sure to be defeated at the ballot box.

POLITICAL ELITES IN COMMUNITIES

 13.4

Trace the shift of local political influence from economic elites to political elites, and contrast the priorities of these two groups of elites.

Today, in many American communities, older economic elites have been replaced by newer political elites. Many of the old economic elites sold their businesses to national corporations and vacated their positions of community leadership. Locally owned stores and factories became manager-directed plants and chain stores. The result was a weakening of community loyalties in the business sector. The new corporate managers could easily decide, in response to national economic conditions, to close the local plant or store with minimal concern for the impact on the community. Local banks were merged into national banking corporations and local bankers were replaced by banking executives with few community ties. City newspapers that were once independently owned by families who lived in the communities were bought up by giant newspaper and publication chains. Instead of editors and reporters who expected to live the lives of their communities, city newspapers came to be staffed with people who hoped to move up in the corporate hierarchy—people who strived primarily to advance their own careers, not the interests of the local community.

Professional politicians have moved into this vacuum in city after city, largely replacing the local bankers, real estate developers, chambers of commerce, and old-style newspaper editors who had dominated community politics for generations. The earlier economic elites were only part-time politicians who used local government to promote their economic interests. The new professional political elites work full time at local politics. They are drawn primarily by personal ambition, not so much for the wealth as for the power and celebrity that accompany running for and winning public office. They are not "screened" by economic elites or political parties, but rather they nominate themselves, raise their own funds, organize their own campaigns, and create their own publicity.

Some Political Elites Opposed to Growth

Consensus on behalf of economic growth is sometimes challenged by political elites in communities. However much the economic elite may strive for consensus, some people do not like growth, and they are willing to use political power to stop it. Indeed, it has become fashionable in upper middle-class circles today to complain loudly about the problems created by growth—congestion, pollution, noise, unsightly development, or the replacement of green spaces with concrete slabs. People who already own their houses and do not intend to sell them, people whose jobs are secure in government bureaucracies or tenured professorships, people who may be displaced from their homes and neighborhoods by new facilities, people who see no direct benefit to themselves from growth, and businesses or industries who fear the new competition that growth may bring to the community, all combine to form potentially powerful political alliances.[12]

Not all of the opposition to growth is upper middle class in character. Students of community power have described the struggle of blacks and low-income neighborhood groups in opposing urban renewal and downtown city development. (Minorities and the poor fear being displaced by redevelopment.) In the past, community elites were likely to be successful against this kind of opposition because minorities and low-income residents had little political clout. But this has changed. Cities have become more diverse. More minorities are being elected to governing bodies. Federal aid programs require recipient governments to solicit citizen input from minorities in order to receive redevelopment funding. Thus, today's elites can no longer ignore the voices of minorities and the poor when they oppose growth because it threatens their homes and neighborhoods.

No-growth movements are *not* mass movements. They do *not* express the aspirations of workers for jobs or renters for their own homes. Instead, they reflect upper-middle-class lifestyle preferences of educated, affluent, articulate homeowners. They see growth as bringing ugly factories, cheap commercial outlets, hamburger stands, fried chicken franchises, and "undesirable" residents. Even if new business or industry would help hold down local taxes, these affluent citizens would still oppose it. They would rather pay the higher taxes associated with no growth than change the appearance or lifestyle of their community. They have secure jobs themselves and own their homes; they are relatively unconcerned about creating jobs or building homes for less affluent citizens.

No-growth political movements have challenged traditional economic elites in many large and growing cities in the West and South. The no-growth leaders may themselves have been beneficiaries of community growth only 5 or 10 years ago, but they quickly perceive their own interest in slowing or halting additional growth. Now that they have climbed the ladder to their own success, they are prepared to knock the ladder down to preserve their own style of living. They often ignore the fact that America's population is growing and that people must have somewhere to live. As an international observer of urban growth explains: "Urban populations and commercial activities can only grow in four directions: *in* (by crowding), *up* (as in Manhattan's skyscrapers), *down* (as in Tokyo's 700 subterranean mah-jongg parlors), and *out* (as on the peripheries of cities nearly everywhere except Gibraltar)."[13]

The NIMBY Syndrome

Opponents of growth can usually count on help from community residents who will be directly inconvenienced by specific projects. Even people who would otherwise support new commercial or housing developments or new public facilities may voice the protest, "Not in my backyard!" earning them the **NIMBY** label. Many Americans want growth; they just do not want it near them.[14]

NIMBY
An acronym for "not in my backyard," referring to residents who oppose nearby public or private projects or developments.

NIMBYs may be the noisiest of protest groups. They are the homeowners and voters who are most directly affected by a proposed private or public project. (And virtually every project inspires NIMBY opposition.) NIMBYs are particularly active regarding waste disposal sites, incinerators, highways, prisons, halfway houses, mental health facilities, low-income public housing projects, power plants, pipelines, airports, and factories. NIMBYs are formidable opponents. While they may constitute only a small portion of the community, they have a large stake in defeating a project. They have a strong motivation to become active participants—meeting, organizing, petitioning, parading, and demonstrating against a project, while seeking and attracting media attention. The majority of the community may benefit from the project, but because each person has only a small stake in its completion, no one has the same strong motivation to participate as the NIMBYs. Government agencies and private corporations seeking to locate projects in communities are well advised to conduct professional public relations campaigns well in advance of groundbreaking. When the power of the NIMBYs is added to that of "no-growth" forces, economic development can be stalemated, just as it can by "restricted growthers."

Restricted Growthers (The "Smart Growth" Movement)

Persons who favor the "right kind of growth" like to describe themselves as proponents of "growth management" or "**smart growth.**" Their major premise is that by dictating the right kind of growth, more livable communities can be created. (More will be said about livable communities later in the chapter.) Smart growth proponents argue restricted, directed growth "preserves community character, protects open space and the environment, strengthens the local economy, and uses taxpayer dollars efficiently."[15] Growth management supporters favor restricting growth through zoning laws, subdivision control restrictions, utility regulations, building permits, environmental regulations, and even municipal land purchases. Zoning laws can rule out multifamily dwellings or specify only large, expensive lot sizes for homes. Zoning laws can exclude heavy or "dirty" industrial development, or restrict "strip" commercial development along highways. Opposition to street widening, road building, or tree cutting can slow or halt development. Public utilities needed for development—water lines, sewage disposal, firehouses—can be postponed indefinitely. High development fees, utility hookup charges, or building permit costs can all be used to discourage growth. Unrealistic antipollution laws can also discourage growth. If all else fails, a community can buy up vacant land itself or make it a "wildlife refuge."

SMART GROWTH
Promotion of higher density growth so more livable communities can be created.

"Smart-growthers" have become influential in many large and growing cities—for example, Austin, Denver, Phoenix, San Francisco, San Jose, and Tucson. But they are also politically powerful in *many upper middle-class suburban communities* (even those in metropolitan areas with declining core cities) that view growth restrictions as in their own interest. Smart growthers, like no-growthers and NIMBYs, are concentrated among well-educated, upper middle-class, white residents who own their own homes. Within these households, it is women who first adopt no-growth attitudes.[16]

The Unintended Consequences of Growth Restrictions

Restricting land-use changes in such communities often inflates the prices of existing homes (and thereby limits the amount of affordable housing in the community). Hence it is in the economic interest of homeowners, once they have acquired their own homes, to oppose further development. Note that the burden of these policies falls not only on builders and developers (who are the most influential opponents of "no-growth" policies), but also on the poor, the working class, minorities, and non–property owners. These groups need the jobs that business and industry can bring to a community, and they need reasonably priced homes in which to live.

Land-use policies that restrict the supply of housing in a community increase its costs. Higher housing costs restrict access for minorities and the poor. Indeed, many "growth-management" policies do not limit population growth but rather discourage the movement of minorities and the poor into a community.[17]

When suburban communities restrict growth, they are often distributing population to other parts of the metropolitan area.[18] The people kept out do not cease to exist; they find housing elsewhere in the metropolitan area. They usually end up imposing greater costs on other municipalities—central cities or larger, close-in suburbs—which are less able to absorb these costs than the wealthier upper middle-class communities that succeeded in excluding them. What appears to be a local "growth" issue may be in reality a metropolitan "distribution" issue.

The bottom line is that more communities with highly restrictive housing policies are now facing "affordable housing" problems, which threaten to keep out teachers, nurses, firefighters, police officers, and other working families who are vital to the well-being of the community. Political activists fighting for government-imposed affordable housing policies argue, "If we don't keep fighting this fight, then those people we rely on—to teach our children, for example—won't be able to live in the communities in which they work and want to call home."[19] There is a widening gap between those who can afford to buy a home and those who cannot.

13.5 PLANNING AND ZONING

Trace the growth of planning, assess the influence of planners, outline the opposition to planning, and describe the zoning process.

CITY PLANNING
The original term for local government's role in determining the location of streets and other public facilities.

MASTER PLAN
A city map showing the location of present and future streets and public facilities.

City planning began in antiquity with the emergence of the first cities. Governing authorities have long determined the location of streets, squares, temples, walls, and fortresses. Most early American cities were planned as a gridiron of streets and squares in the fashion of William Penn's plan for Philadelphia in 1682. A notable exception to the gridiron pattern was Pierre L'Enfant's 1791 plan for Washington, DC, with radial streets slashing through the gridiron.[20] Until the early twentieth century, city planning was focused almost exclusively on the layout of streets and the location of public buildings and parks. A city's "**master plan**" was a map showing the location of present and future streets and public facilities. There was relatively little regulation of the use of private property.

Comprehensive Planning

But the reform movement of the early twentieth century (see "Reformers and Do-Gooders" in Chapter 11) brought with it a much broader definition of planning. "**Comprehensive planning**" involves not only the determination of the location of public facilities but also the control of private land uses.

Comprehensive planning involves the identification of community goals, the development of plans to implement these goals, and the use of governmental tools to influence and shape private and public decision making to serve these goals. Community goals are identified not only in land use and physical development policies, but also in those for population growth, health and safety, housing and welfare, education, transportation, economic development, culture, lifestyle and beautification, historic preservation, and environmental protection. According to the American Institute of Planners (AIP), planning is a "comprehensive, coordinated and continuing process, the purpose of which is to help public and private decision makers arrive at decisions which promote the common good of society."[21] Obviously this extended definition of planning plunges the planner deep into the political life of the community.

State laws authorize and often mandate that cities develop comprehensive plans. Traditionally, the comprehensive plan was prepared by semi-independent *planning commissions* composed of private citizens appointed by the mayor and approved by the city council. These commissions rely heavily on **professional planners** to prepare the comprehensive plan. Professional planners are mostly university graduates in city planning. They are organized into the American Institute of Planners (AIP), which publishes its own journal and grants professional credentials to planners. Over time, however, independent citizen planning commissions were gradually replaced with planning departments within city government that are directly responsible to the mayor and council. Federal (and many state) laws now mandate community and regional planning as conditions of fiscal assistance, especially for transportation.

Developing Political Support for Planning

Citizen planning commissions are still retained in many communities to facilitate citizen input into the planning process and to develop political support for the comprehensive plan. Planning commissions often hold public hearings on the comprehensive plans and proposed changes to it.

The decisions of professional planners and planning commissions are officially considered advisory. That is, the comprehensive plan must be enacted by the city council to become law. The recommendations of the planning commission can be overturned by the city council. But the advice of a prudent planning staff, with the support of influential private citizens on the planning commission, cannot be easily ignored.

Planners, like reformers generally, claim to represent the welfare of the community as a whole. They are usually hostile to what they perceive to be narrow, self-serving interests in the community, especially businesspeople, real estate developers, and property owners.

The Influence of Planners

While the formal role of planners is advisory, they can have a substantial influence on community policy. In smaller cities, planners may be preoccupied with the day-to-day administration of the zoning and subdivision control ordinances. They may have insufficient time or staff to engage in genuine long-range comprehensive planning. In large cities, the planning staff may be the only agency that has a comprehensive view of community development. Although they may not have the power to "decide" about public policy, they can "initiate" policy discussions through their plans, proposals, and recommendations. The planners can project the image of the city of the future and thereby establish the agenda of community decision making. Their plans can initiate public discussion over the goals and values to be implemented in the community. The current thrust of planning is to create **"livable" communities** by emphasizing the design and protection of neighborhoods and the environment. ("Conservation subdivisions" utilize the natural landscape of their design and have a common open space rather than individual backyards.[22]) Planning and the smart growth movement go hand-in-hand.

Opposition to Planning

There are, of course, some limitations on the influence of planners. First of all, many important decisions in community development are made by private enterprise rather than by government. Real estate interests, developers, builders, and property owners make many of the key decisions that shape the development of the community. Their actions are often determined by the economics of the marketplace. Property owners will try to find a way to make the most profitable use of their land, the ideas of the planners notwithstanding. Second, the planners can only advise policymakers; they are just one voice among many attempting to influence public decisions about land use and physical development.

Opponents of government planning and land-use control argue that the decisions of thousands of individual property owners result in a better allocation of land than the decisions of government bureaucrats. Decentralized marketplace decisions allow more rapid adjustment to change and satisfy the preferences of more people than centralized bureaucratic decision-making. Marketplace prices signal the most appropriate uses of land, just as they do the most appropriate uses of other resources.

Opponents also argue that requiring government permits for land uses—for new commercial, industrial, or residential developments and for new homes, buildings, or other structures—adds to the time and costs of development and the size of government bureaucracy. By adding to the costs of housing, planning places owning homes beyond the reach of many middle-class families. By adding to the costs of industry, or banning new industrial development altogether, planning limits the number of jobs created in a community. By empowering local officials to describe how land will be used, individual citizens are deprived of an important individual freedom.

Zoning

Planning agencies usually prepare the zoning ordinance for the approval of the city council. The **zoning** ordinance divides the community into districts for the purpose of regulating the use and development of land and buildings. Zoning originated as an attempt to separate residential areas from commercial and industrial activity, thereby protecting residential property values. The zoning ordinance divides the community into residential, commercial, and industrial zones, and perhaps subdivisions within each zone, such as "light industrial" and "heavy industrial," or "single-family residential" and "multifamily residential." Owners of land in each zone must use their land in conformity with the zoning ordinance; however, exceptions are made for people who have used the land in a certain way before the adoption of the zoning ordinance. An ordinance cannot prevent a person from using the land as they have done in the past; thus, zoning laws can influence land use only if they are passed prior to the development of a community. Many new and rapidly expanding communities pass zoning ordinances too late—after commercial and industrial establishments are strung out along highways, ideal industrial land is covered with houses, or good park and recreational land has been sold for other purposes.

Since the planning agency prepares the zoning ordinances as well as the comprehensive plan, the ordinance is expected to conform to the plan. In many communities, the role of the planning agency is strengthened by the requirement that a city council *must* submit all proposed changes in the zoning ordinance to the planning agency for its recommendation before any council action.

Changes in the zoning ordinance usually originate at the request of property owners. They may wish to change the zoning classification of their property to enhance its value—for example, to change it from single-family to multifamily residential, or from residential to commercial. Usually the planning agency will hold a public hearing on a proposed change before sending its findings and recommendation to the city council. The city council may also hold a public hearing before deciding on the change.

City councils can and sometimes do ignore the recommendations of their planning agencies when strong pressures are exerted by neighborhood groups or environmentalists opposed to rezoning, or by developers and property owners supporting it. However, the recommendations of planning agencies prevail in the vast majority of rezoning cases, indicating the power of the planners in community affairs.[23]

A zoning "variance" is a request for a limited and specific variation from the strict standards in a zoning ordinance as applied to a particular piece of property. Some cities create special boards to hear requests for zoning variances, and other cities allow their planning agency to grant variances. The zoning variance may be the most abused of all zoning procedures. It is not intended to encourage "spot" zoning, grant special privileges, or circumvent the interest of the zoning ordinance, but this is what happens frequently. Local zoning decisions may also conflict with regional planning efforts.[24]

ZONING VARIANCE
An exception to the zoning ordinance applied to a particular piece of property.

Subdivision Control

Another means of implementing the master plan is **subdivision regulations**, which govern the way in which land is divided into smaller lots and made ready for improvements. Subdivision regulations, together with the zoning ordinance, may specify the minimum size of lots, the standards to be followed by real estate developers in laying out new streets, and the improvements developers must provide, such as sewers, water mains, parks, playgrounds, and sidewalks. Often planning agencies are given direct responsibility for the enforcement of subdivision regulations. Builders and developers must submit their proposed "**plats**" for subdividing land and for improvements to the planning commission for approval before deeds can be recorded.

SUBDIVISION REGULATIONS
Regulations governing the dividing of land areas into lots.

PLATS
Plans for subdividing land and for improvements that must be submitted to a planning commission for approval before deeds can be recorded.

Official Map

The planning agency also prepares the **official map** of the city for enactment by the council. The official map shows proposed, as well as existing, streets, water mains, public utilities, and the like. Presumably, no one is permitted to build any structures on land that appears as a street or other public facility on the official map. Many cities require the council to submit to the planning agency for their recommendation any proposed action that affects the plan of streets or the subdivision plan and any proposed acquisition or sale of city real estate.

OFFICIAL MAP
Shows proposed and existing streets, water mains, public utilities, and other public facilities; must be approved by city council.

Building and Construction Codes

Most cities have **building codes** designed to ensure public health and safety. These codes are lengthy documents specifying everything from the thickness of building beams and the strength of trusses, to the type of furnaces, electric wiring, ventilation, fireproofing, and even earthquake resistance that must be incorporated into buildings. No construction may be undertaken without first obtaining a building permit, which must be prominently displayed at the building site. Building inspectors are then dispatched periodically to the site to see if work is progressing in conformance with the building codes. The planning agency does not usually administer the code (that is normally the function of a building or housing department), but the planners are usually consulted about proposed changes in the building code.

BUILDING CODES
Local government regulations requiring building permits and inspections of new construction to ensure compliance with detailed specifications.

Housing codes are designed to bring existing structures up to minimum standards. They set forth minimum requirements for fire safety, ventilation, plumbing, sanitation, and building condition. As with building codes, enforcement is the responsibility of city government, but the planning commission is normally consulted about changes in the code.

Capital Improvements

Non-structures

Comprehensive planning can also be implemented through a **capital improvement program**. This program is simply the planned schedule of public projects by the city—new public buildings, parks, and streets. Many larger cities instruct their planning agencies to prepare a long-range capital improvement program for a 5- or 10-year period. Of course, the council may choose to ignore the planning commission's long-range capital improvement program in its decisions about capital expenditures, but at least the planning commission will have expressed its opinions about major capital investments.

CAPITAL IMPROVEMENT PROGRAM (CIP)
The planned schedule of new public projects by a local government.

Environmental Regulations

Governments have increasingly turned to environmental laws and regulations to assert control over community development. State laws or local ordinances may designate "**areas of critical concern**" in an effort to halt development. Designation of such areas is usually subjective; they may be swamps, forests, waterfront, or wildlife habitats, or even historic, scenic, or archaeological sites. "Critical" may also refer to flood plains or steep hillsides or any other land on which governments wish to halt construction.

States and cities are increasingly requiring developers to prepare "**environmental impact statements**"—assessments of the environmental consequences of proposed construction or land-use change. These statements are usually prepared by professional consultants at added cost to builders and developers.

In most cities and counties, enforcement of environmental regulations is the responsibility of separate environmental departments. This means that landowners and developers usually must deal with two separate bureaucracies. Planning departments are generally consulted in the preparation of environmental regulations.

AREAS OF CRITICAL CONCERN

Land on which governments wish to halt construction.

ENVIRONMENTAL IMPACT STATEMENTS

Assessments of the environmental consequences of proposed construction or land-use change.

13.6

Detail the various innovative alternatives to strict land-use policies.

INNOVATIVE PLANNING PRACTICES: MORE DISCRETIONARY

The formal instruments of land-use control are often considered too inflexible for optimum planning. Local governments and private property owners frequently seek ways to avoid the rigidities of zoning and subdivision ordinances and construction codes.[25] These regulations, when applied strictly and uniformly, often limit the freedom of architects and developers, produce a sterile environment through separation of land uses, and lead to excessive court litigation. So planners have increasingly turned to a variety of practices intended to minimize some of the worst consequences of land-use regulation.

PUDs

One technique that has grown in popularity in recent years is **planned urban development** (**PUD**). PUD ordinances vary but typically they allow developers with a minimum number of acres (e.g., 10, 20, or more) to have the option of abiding by conventional zoning, subdivision, and building codes, or alternatively submitting an overall site plan for the approval of the planning agency and council. PUD designs usually incorporate mixed residential and commercial uses, perhaps with single-family homes and apartments or condominiums, retail shops, hotels and restaurants, parks and open spaces, all included. Planners and councils often exercise considerable discretion in approving or rejecting or forcing modifications in PUDs, depending on their own preferences.

PLANNED URBAN DEVELOPMENT (PUD)

Special ordinances, usually negotiated among developers and city officials, that approve a mixed-use—residential, commercial, and/or industrial—development plan.

Exactions and Impact Fees

Many communities require developers to pay substantial fees or give over land to local government in exchange for approval of their land-use plans.[26] This practice, known as "**exaction**," is often defended as a fee that pays the local government's costs in connection with the new development, for example, additional roads or sewers needed or additional schools or parks required for new residents. A closely related practice is that of charging developers "**impact fees**" that are supposed to compensate the community for increased costs imposed by the development *beyond* the added tax revenues that the development will generate when completed. But it is virtually impossible to accurately calculate impact costs, if indeed a development actually does impose more costs on a community than the revenues it produces. So impact fees become just another cost to developers that are passed on to homebuyers and (through commercial tenants) to consumers.

EXACTION

A fee that pays local government's costs in connection with new development. This charge can come in the form of money or land given to a local government in exchange for approval of land-use plans.

IMPACT FEES

Fees required from developers by local governments in exchange for approval of plans, presumably compensating for the increased governmental costs created by the new development.

Developer Agreements

Often, conflicts between local governments and developers are settled through *developer agreements*. Some states (e.g., California) specifically authorize municipalities to enter into such agreements, bypassing zoning, subdivision, and construction ordinances. In other states, often lawsuits, or the threat of lawsuits, by developers force municipalities into such agreements. The municipality benefits by being able to specify the details of a project. The developer benefits by obtaining a legally binding contract that cannot be changed later by the municipality as the project proceeds to completion.

Designing "Livable" Communities

The "New Urbanism" or "livable communities" movement began in the 1990s. It is a *design-oriented* approach to planning, initially developed by architects but now subscribed to by some demographers, sociologists, criminologists, political scientists, and community activists. "The basic unit of planning is the *neighborhood*, which is limited in physical size, has a well-defined edge, and has a focused center."[27]

The Urban Sustainability Movement

The International City/County Management Association has identified "the imperative to create more sustainable [enduring] communities" as the "greatest global challenge of the new century"[28] facing local officials. Providing for sustainable communities is contingent, at least in part, upon more resource- and cost-efficient energy. This will require more energy-efficient building codes, more mixed-use land, mixed income housing, more multimodal transit, more open space, more regional food production, and better air and water quality. Sustainable communities must also rely more on alternative energy sources: solar, wind, geothermal, hydroelectric, and tidal. Some states and communities are further along on this path than others.[29] Proponents argue that sustainability efforts, many based on land use, will help communities become more inclusive, improve social justice, result in better public policies and investments,[30] and attract the **"creative class."** Obviously the viability of achieving sustainability is greater in places with more financial resources, more permissive state laws, better city management, and greater citizen involvement.[31]

"Disaster-Proofing" Disaster-Prone Areas

Some communities are more vulnerable to major natural disasters (hurricanes, floods, fires, tornadoes, earthquakes) than others. There is now an effort in many places to develop housing-related policies and programs that reduce the likelihood of property damage and loss of life from such disasters. Housing advocacy groups are calling for stronger residential building codes, tax incentives to builders to construct more disaster-resistant homes, and rebates or tax credits to homeowners for making improvements that strengthen their homes. "Smarter and safer" construction practices that make a home more resistant to disasters include "increasing the structural integrity of roof attachments, creating water barriers and seals to prevent property flooding, safe room construction, elevation of electrical systems, and the addition of storm windows and shutters."[32]

NEW URBANISM
A design-oriented approach to planning that promotes walkable neighborhoods with diverse population, housing, and jobs and that celebrates local history and ecology.

LIVABLE COMMUNITIES
A design-oriented approach to planning in which neighborhoods enable all inhabitants to lead healthy and independent lives.

CREATIVE CLASS
Professionals who work in a wide range of knowledge-intensive industries.

EMINENT DOMAIN
The judicial process by which government can take private property for public use by providing fair (just) compensation.

JUST COMPENSATION
A fair price for land taken through eminent domain, as based on testimony from the owner, government, and impartial appraisers.

CONSTITUTIONAL CONCERNS: THE TAKINGS CLAUSE

13.7

Explain the circumstances under which governments can take possession of or restrict the use of private land.

How far can government go in regulating the use of property without depriving individuals of their property rights? The U.S. Constitution (Fifth Amendment) states clearly: "nor shall private property be taken for public use without just compensation." Taking land for highways, streets, and public buildings, even when the owners do not wish to sell, is known as **eminent domain**. A city or state must go to court and show that the land is needed for a legitimate public purpose; the court will then establish a fair price (**just compensation**) based on testimony from the owner, the city or state, and impartial appraisers. Eminent domain is a constitutional protection to American citizens against arbitrary government seizure of their land.

But what if a government does not "take" ownership of the property, but instead restricts the owner's use of it through regulation? Zoning ordinances, subdivision regulations, environmental regulations, or building and housing codes may reduce the value of the property to the owner. Should the owner be compensated for loss of use?

Courts have always recognized that governments can make laws to protect the health, safety, and general welfare of its citizens. Owners of property have never been entitled to any compensation for obeying laws or ordinances with a clear public purpose. But it was not clear that zoning restrictions were legitimate public purposes until 1926 when the U.S. Supreme Court upheld city-zoning ordinances as "a proper exercise of police powers."[33] Cities are *not* required to compensate owners for lost value as a result of zoning regulations. Yet it was still argued that some planning and zoning provisions, especially those designed for beauty and aesthetics, had no relation to public health, safety, and welfare. They simply enacted somebody's taste over that of their neighbor. But in 1954 the U.S. Supreme Court upheld a broad interpretation of the police power: "It is within the power of the legislature to determine that the community should be beautiful as well as healthy, spacious as well as clean, well-balanced as well as carefully patrolled."[34] So it is difficult to challenge the constitutionality of planning and zoning as a "taking" of private property without compensation.

"Takings"—When Cities Go Too Far

However, the U.S. Supreme Court has held that a regulation that denies a property owner *all* economically beneficial use of land (e.g., a state coastal zone management regulation preventing any construction on a beach lot) was a "taking" that required just compensation to the owner in order to be constitutional.[35] The **Takings Clause** of the Constitution's Fifth Amendment was designed to protect private property from unjust taking by government. Its purpose is "to bar Government from forcing some people alone to bear public burdens which, in all fairness and justice, should be borne by the public as a whole."[36] If a community wants open spaces, wildlife preserves, environmental havens, historic buildings, or other amenities, these should be paid for by all of the citizens of the community. Property should not be taken from private owners, even for public purposes, without compensation. All citizens should share in the costs of providing community amenities, not just the owners of particular properties.

The question remains, however, how far can government go in regulating land use without compensating property owners? Depriving landowners of *all* beneficial uses of their land without compensation is clearly unconstitutional. But what if their use of their land is devalued by 50 or 25 percent? Are governments constitutionally required to compensate them in proportion to their losses? In the past, federal courts have ruled that "mere diminution" in the value of property is

Local governments have the right to "take" privately owned property for public use (e.g., road, school) under their eminent domain power if they adequately compensate the property owner. But when local governments use their eminent domain power to take privately owned land for economic revitalization and turn it over to a private developer, citizens get up in arms. A number of state legislatures have passed laws prohibiting this practice.

not a "taking" within the meaning of the Fifth Amendment and hence does not require government to compensate landowners. However, in recent years both Congress and the federal courts, as well as some states, have undertaken to reconsider "how far" government can go in depriving property owners of valued uses of their land. Increasingly, regulatory devaluations of 50 percent or more are becoming highly suspect, and property owners have a reasonable chance of recovering compensation from governments.

"Takings" for Public Use (Economic Development)

Can governments use eminent domain to take privately owned land in order to turn it over to private developers to improve it and sell it for their own profit? Is this a "public use" under the Constitution, or a private use? The City of New London, Connecticut, exercised eminent domain in its "economic development" program to take private homes for a more expensive private development that would produce higher tax revenues for the city. Owners objected that this was not a "public use" such as highways, sewers, or schools but rather simply a means of forcibly transferring property from some private owners to other private owners who would build more expensive homes and sell them for a profit. The city would then collect higher taxes from the new owners. The U.S. Supreme Court, in a 5 to 4 decision, approved of this type of "taking" as a "public use," that is, economic development.[37] The ruling created an outcry from many citizens, prompting state legislators in a number of states to pass their own laws restricting their local governments' use of the eminent domain power.

COMMUNITY DEVELOPMENT AND REVITALIZATION POLICY

13.8

Analyze the effectiveness of the various urban renewal policies.

In the original Housing Act of 1937, the ideal of "**urban renewal**" was closely tied to public housing. Slums were to be torn down as public housing sites were constructed. Later in the Housing Act of 1949, the urban renewal program was separated from public housing, and the federal government undertook to support a broad program of urban redevelopment to help cities fight a loss in population and to reclaim the economic importance of the core cities. After World War II, the suburban exodus had progressed to the point where central cities faced slow decay and death if large public efforts were not undertaken. Urban renewal could not be undertaken by private enterprise because it was not profitable; suburban property was usually cheaper than downtown property, and it did not require large-scale clearance of obsolete buildings. Moreover, private enterprise did not possess the power of eminent domain, which enables the city to purchase the many separately owned small tracts of land needed to ensure an economically feasible new investment.

URBAN RENEWAL
The original term for federally aided programs carried out by local government agencies to rebuild blighted areas of central cities.

For many years, the federal government provided financial support for specific renewal projects in cities. By the early 1960s, it was obvious that federal urban renewal programs created by the Housing Act of 1949 were not working as intended. By the 1970s, the images of urban renewal were "of destruction and delay rather than renaissance and reconstruction." The National Commission on Urban Problems reported that the average urban renewal project took between 10 and 13 years to complete. In looking back at the lessons from the failure: "It was a valuable experiment that taught certain lessons necessary to later urban revitalization initiatives. It exposed the social and political costs of big bulldozer schemes and revealed the limitations inherent in federal policy."[38] It led to the adoption of federal block grant programs that gave localities funding with fewer strings attached than the old programs.

Community Development Block Grants

In the Housing and Community Development Act of 1974, federal development grants to cities were consolidated into the **Community Development Block Grant (CDBG)** program. Cities and counties were authorized to receive these grants to assist them in

COMMUNITY DEVELOPMENT BLOCK GRANT (CDBG)
Consolidated federal grants to cities for planning, redevelopment, and public housing.

eliminating slums; increasing the supply of low-income housing; conserving existing housing; improving health, safety, welfare, and public service; improving planning; and preserving property with special value. Today, local governments with 50,000 or more residents, central cities of metropolitan areas, and urban counties with populations of at least 200,000 are eligible for CDBG funds directly. (A state CDBG program provides funds to states, which they, in turn, allocate among localities that are not large enough to qualify for direct aid.) Each year, the grant funds available for entitlement communities are allocated according to relative need on the basis of the higher of two formulas—both of which have a housing component. The first considers the presence of overcrowded housing in the locality, its population, and the poverty rate. The second formula uses housing age, population growth lag, and poverty rate.[39] No local "matching" funds are required. Communities are required to submit an annual application that describes their housing and redevelopment needs, and a comprehensive strategy for meeting those needs.

To ensure that the CDBG program remains targeted on the poor, the legislation requires localities and states to certify that not less than 70 percent of their CDBG funds are spent on activities that benefit low- and moderate-income persons. Low- and moderate-income persons are defined as those persons whose income does not exceed 80 percent of the median income for the area.

Community development block grants can be used by local authorities to acquire blighted land, clear off or modernize obsolete or dilapidated structures, and make downtown sites available for new uses. When the sites are physically cleared of the old structures, they can be resold to private developers for residential, commercial, or industrial use, and the difference between the costs of acquisition and clearance and the income from the private sale to the developers is paid for by the federal government. In other words, local authorities sustain a loss in their redevelopment activities, and this loss is made up by federal grants.

No city is required to engage in redevelopment, but if cities wish federal financial backing, they must show in their applications that they have developed a comprehensive program for redevelopment and the prevention of future blight. They must demonstrate that they have adequate building and health codes, good zoning and subdivision control regulations, sufficient local financing and public support, and a comprehensive plan of development with provisions for relocating displaced persons.

HUD's CDBG program is one of the largest federal grant programs, serving nearly 1,000 of the largest localities in the nation, plus scores of smaller jurisdictions. While the rehabilitation of affordable housing has traditionally been the largest single use of CDBG funds, the program has increasingly become "an important catalyst for economic development activities that expand job and business opportunities for lower income persons and neighborhoods."[40]

Economics of Development

Urban redevelopment is best understood from an economic standpoint. The key to success is to encourage private developers to purchase the land and make a heavy investment in middle- or high-income housing or in commercial or industrial use. In fact, before undertaking a project, local authorities frequently "find a developer first, and then see what interests that developer." The city cannot afford to purchase land, thereby taking it off the tax rolls, invest in its clearance, and then be stuck without a buyer. A private developer must be encouraged to invest in the property and thus enhance the value of the central city. Over time a city can more than pay off its investment by increased tax returns from redeveloped property and hence make a "profit." Thus, many people can come out of a project feeling successful—the city increases its tax base and annual revenues, the private developer makes a profit, and mayors can point to the physical improvements in the city that occurred during their administrations.

Urban redevelopment in many cities has become the responsibility of semi-autonomous **community development corporations (CDCs) or authorities (CDAs)**. More than 4,000 of these now exist. They are located in all 50 states and in nearly every major city. Many were initially formed in the 1980s when federal aid to local governments declined, making it necessary to involve public, private, and nonprofit entities in the financing of urban redevelopment. Over time, CDC activity "has expanded beyond the traditional focus on housing and business development into human services, community empowerment, and building social capital."[41]

Enterprise Empowerment Zones

Beginning in the 1980s, the federal government offered assistance to communities for **enterprise zones**—federal grants, tax incentives, loans, and technical assistance to communities within areas of high unemployment and poverty to help them develop partnerships with businesses to revitalize distressed neighborhoods. Most states have also created their own enterprise zone programs. They differ considerably in the specific tax incentives offered, how they define an area eligible for zone status, and what eligibility criteria they use for businesses seeking tax breaks or subsidies. Do they work? The results are mixed, especially with regard to the effectiveness of tax incentives and job creation.[42] One of the reasons is that after the zones are adopted, political pressures take hold. Soon more zones are being created, which negates the initial targeting of areas of need.[43]

Relocation

Relocation is the most sensitive problem in redevelopment. Most people relocated by redevelopment are poor minorities. They have no interest in moving simply to make room for middle- or higher-income housing, or business or industry, or universities, hospitals, and other public facilities. Even though relocated families are frequently given priority for public housing, there is not nearly enough space in public housing to accommodate them all. They are simply moved from one slum to another. The slum landowner is paid a just price for the land, but the renter receives only a small moving allowance. Redevelopment officials assist relocated families in finding new housing and generally claim success in moving families to better housing. However, frequently the result is higher rents, and redevelopment may actually help to create new slums in other sections of the city. Small business owners are especially vulnerable to relocation. They often depend on a small, well-known neighborhood clientele, and they cannot compete successfully when forced to move to other sections of the city.

"Brownfields"

In the late 1990s and early 2000s, many advocates of urban redevelopment began focusing their attention—and hopes—on cleaning up "**brownfields**." "A brownfield is an abandoned, idle, or underused industrial or commercial property where more effective use is hindered by real or perceived contamination."[44] Brownfields, particularly those that are heavily polluted or contaminated, are the most problematic because they have a spillover effect.

Advocates of brownfield cleanup and development believe it will "generate jobs and tax revenues, revitalize neighborhoods, and control urban sprawl."[45] Others are less optimistic, in light of industry relocations to the suburbs (where the workers live) and minority concerns about relocation. At a minimum, both sides agree that brownfields and vacant land in declining inner cities tend to go hand-in-hand with crime, unemployment, health, and other social problems for areas surrounding them. This explains why so many federal agencies are currently involved in combating brownfields. The Environmental Protection Agency, HUD, the Department of Transportation, and the Economic Development Administration, along with many state and local agencies, have programs aimed at brownfield redevelopment. However, for some minority residents, brownfields have become a symbol of environmental injustice.[46]

Politics and Development

Political support for redevelopment has come from mayors who wish to make their reputation by engaging in large-scale renewal activities that produce impressive "before" and "after" pictures of the city. Business owners wishing to preserve downtown investments and developers wishing to acquire land in urban centers have provided a solid base of support for downtown renewal. Mayors, planners, the press, and the good-government forces have made urban redevelopment politically much more popular than public housing.

13.9

TRANSPORTATION POLICY

Discuss the transportation policies that affect local communities, compare the roles of the national and state governments in transportation policy, and compare transportation policies aimed at cars versus those aimed at other modes of transportation.

Roads take land. (And so do subways and light rail.) As we have seen, taking land creates conflicts. Yet transportation systems are critical to the economy and are to many citizens a measure of the quality of life in the area in which they live.

Cars, Cars, and More Cars

Few inventions have had such a far-reaching effect on the life of the American people as the automobile. Henry Ford built one of the first gasoline-driven carriages in America in 1893, and by 1900 there were 8,000 automobiles registered in the United States. The Model T was introduced in the autumn of 1908. By concentrating on a single unlovely but enduring model, and by introducing the assembly line process, the Ford Motor Company began producing automobiles for the masses. Today, there are over 250 million registered motor vehicles in the nation and nearly 4 million miles of roads. (Over three-quarters of Americans drive alone to work. See Figure 13–1.)

Highway Politics

Highway politics are of interest not only to the automotive industry and the driving public, but also to the oil industry, the American Road Builders Association, the railroads, the trucking industry, the farmers, the outdoor advertising industry, and the county commissioners, taxpayer associations, ecologists and conservationists, and neighborhood improvement associations. These political interests are concerned with the allocation of money for highway purposes, the sources of funds for highway revenue, the extent of gasoline and motor vehicle taxation, the regulation of traffic on the highways, the location of highways, the determination of construction policies, the division of responsibility among federal, state, and local governments for highway financing and administration, the division of highway funds between rural and urban areas, and many other important outcomes in highway politics.

Many federal, state, and local agencies are involved in cleaning up brownfields. A brownfield is an abandoned, idle, or underused property that is contaminated. Brownfield cleanup, like other forms of urban redevelopment, is often controversial. Some believe it will create jobs and generate tax revenues, while others believe it is a form of environmental injustice since such efforts may displace minorities or poor residents.

Early Federal Aid

It was in the Federal Aid Road Act of 1916 that the federal government first provided regular funds for highway construction under terms that gave the federal government considerable influence over state policy. For example, if states wanted to get federal money, they were required

FIGURE 13–1 How Americans Get to Work

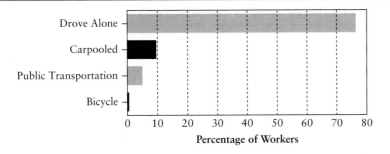

Source: U.S. Census Bureau, 2011 American Community Survey, "Means of Transportation to Work by Selected Characteristics for Workplace Geography." Available at http://factfinder2.census.gov/faces/tableservices/jsf/pages/productview.xhtml?pid=ACS_11_1YR_S0804&prodType=table.

to have a highway department, and to have their plans for highway construction approved by federal authorities. In 1921, federal aid was limited to a connected system of principal state highways, now called the "federal aid primary highway system." Uniform standards were prescribed and even a uniform numbering system was added, such as "US 1" or "US 30." The emphasis of the program was clearly rural. Later, the federal government also designated a federal aid "secondary" system of farm-to-market roads and provided for "urban extensions" of primary roads, in addition to the federal aid for the primary highway system.

The Interstate System

Congress authorized a national system of interstate and defense highways in 1956 ("I" highways). The interstate system is the most important feature of the federal highway policy. Costs are allocated on the basis of 90 percent federal and 10 percent state. The Federal Highway Act of 1956, as amended, authorized 46,000 miles of highway, designed to connect principal metropolitan areas and industrial centers and thereby shifted the emphasis of federal highway activity from rural to urban needs. Although the system constitutes less than 2 percent of the total surfaced roads in the nation, it carries over 25 percent of all highway traffic. The U.S. Department of Transportation has been given strong supervisory powers, including the selection of routes, but administration and execution of the Interstate Highway System are largely the responsibility of state highway departments. Federal monies are paid to the states, not to the contractors, as the work progresses. However, today the federal government spending on the interstate system averages less than 45 percent of all spending. States have to fund the rest of the costs associated with the maintenance, reconstruction, and expansion of the system, which collectively amounts to more than $25 billion per year according to the Federal Highway Administration. Transportation experts worry that the federal share will continue to decline over the next 50 years, leaving states in a big financial bind.[47]

Federal Highway Money

Revenue from the federal gasoline tax has long been "earmarked" for the Federal Highway Trust Fund. Since 1983, the Federal Highway Trust Fund has contained a highway account and a mass transit account. The current federal gasoline tax is 18.4 cents per gallon; the revenue from this tax alone is insufficient to repair and maintain the nation's highway system. Congress generally recognizes the need to rebuild the nation's highways and bridges. The real political fireworks center on requirements that Congress attaches to the receipt of federal highway funds. Even reauthorizing funding is getting more difficult. It took more than 1,000 days after the federal surface transportation law expired for Congress to finally pass the Moving Ahead for Progress in the 21st Century Act (MAP-21) reauthorizing funding for federal highway and transit programs. But it was only through September 2014.[48]

Road Mileage and Gasoline Taxes

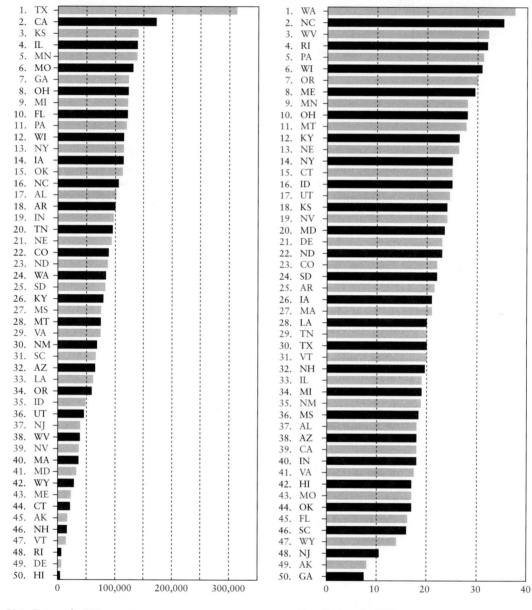

Total Road Mileage

1.	TX	
2.	CA	
3.	KS	
4.	IL	
5.	MN	
6.	MO	
7.	GA	
8.	OH	
9.	MI	
10.	FL	
11.	PA	
12.	WI	
13.	NY	
14.	IA	
15.	OK	
16.	NC	
17.	AL	
18.	AR	
19.	IN	
20.	TN	
21.	NE	
22.	CO	
23.	ND	
24.	WA	
25.	SD	
26.	KY	
27.	MS	
28.	MT	
29.	VA	
30.	NM	
31.	SC	
32.	AZ	
33.	LA	
34.	OR	
35.	ID	
36.	UT	
37.	NJ	
38.	WV	
39.	NV	
40.	MA	
41.	MD	
42.	WY	
43.	ME	
44.	CT	
45.	AK	
46.	NH	
47.	VT	
48.	RI	
49.	DE	
50.	HI	

0   100,000   200,000   300,000

Note: Data are for 2011.
Source: U.S. Department of Transportation, Federal Highway
Administration "Highway Statistics 2011," Table HM-20. Available
at http://www.fhwa.dot.gov/policyinformation/statistics/2011/pdf/
hm20.pdf.

Gasoline Tax Rate (cents per gallon)

1.	WA	
2.	NC	
3.	WV	
4.	RI	
5.	PA	
6.	WI	
7.	OR	
8.	ME	
9.	MN	
10.	OH	
11.	MT	
12.	KY	
13.	NE	
14.	NY	
15.	CT	
16.	ID	
17.	UT	
18.	KS	
19.	NV	
20.	MD	
21.	DE	
22.	ND	
23.	CO	
24.	SD	
25.	AR	
26.	IA	
27.	MA	
28.	LA	
29.	TN	
30.	TX	
31.	VT	
32.	NH	
33.	IL	
34.	MI	
35.	NM	
36.	MS	
37.	AL	
38.	AZ	
39.	CA	
40.	IN	
41.	VA	
42.	HI	
43.	MO	
44.	OK	
45.	FL	
46.	SC	
47.	WY	
48.	NJ	
49.	AK	
50.	GA	

0   10   20   30   40

Note: Data are for 2011.
Source: U.S. Department of Transportation, Federal
Highway Administration "Highway Statistics 2011,"
Table MF-121T. Available at http://www.fhwa.dot.gov/
policyinformation/statistics/2011/ mf121t.cfm.

Speed Limits

An example of the controversies generated by federal highway policy was the long battle over speed limits. Prior to 1974 most states had speed limits of 70 miles per hour on interstate highways. A national speed limit of 55 miles per hour was enacted by Congress that year as a means of saving gasoline. Congress mandated that a state be denied 10 percent of its federal highway aid if it failed to enact and enforce a 55-miles-per-hour speed limit. But truckers and others who drive a great deal, particularly over long open stretches of interstate highway in the western United States, lobbied hard to eliminate the 55-miles-per-hour national speed limit. They argued that the costs in billions of additional hours spent on the road were unreasonable, that the 55-miles-per-hour speed limit was widely ignored anyway, and that it eroded respect for the law.

The national speed limit was also seen as symbolic of federal intrusion in state affairs and a threat to American federalism. However, insurance companies and consumer safety groups lobbied hard to keep the 55-miles-per-hour speed limit. In 1987 Congress relented; the speed limit on rural portions of interstate highways was raised to 65 miles per hour.

Finally in 1995, 21 years after first imposing a national speed limit, Congress returned control of speed limits to the states. Arguments over speed and safety are now heard again in state capitals across the country. Proponents of lower limits argue that "speed kills" and that drivers will always exceed posted limits by 10 miles per hour. Opponents contend that most drivers exceed speed limits only when they are set too low, and that safety is more closely related to enforcement of drunk driving and seat belt laws, as well as with improved auto safety, than with speed limits. Most eastern states have retained the 65-miles-per-hour limit, but several Midwestern and western states have upped their limit to 70 or 75 miles per hour on rural interstates. Texas even allows speeds of up to 85 miles an hour on specified segments of rural interstates; in Utah, it is up to 80.

The 21-Year-Old Drinking Age

Currently, federal law also mandates that the Department of Transportation withhold 10 percent of a state's highway funds if it fails to enact a 21-year-old minimum age for the purchase of alcoholic beverages.

Auto Insurance

All states currently require drivers to have automobile liability insurance. Minimum amounts of coverage vary across the states. Most states require proof of insurance for annual automobile registration and authorize police to demand proof of insurance as well as driver's licenses when stopping motorists. Auto insurance rates are regulated in most states. Insurance rates and regulations inspire a near-constant political conflict in state capitols.

Traffic Safety

States have the responsibility for licensing drivers and vehicles and enforcing traffic laws. Prominent state efforts to improve traffic safety include mandatory seat belt laws and stronger enforcement of laws prohibiting driving under the influence of alcohol (DUI). Mandatory seat belt laws have been shown to more than double seat belt usage; usage is higher in states where a violation is considered primary (where a driver can be ticketed for nonusage alone) rather than secondary (where a driver can be ticketed for seat belt violation only if stopped for another reason).[49] Studies have generally found that increased seat belt usage (as well as air bags) have resulted in lower traffic fatality rates. Stepped-up enforcement of DUI laws has also been shown to reduce fatalities.[50]

Another growing problem is the incidence of accidents caused by motorists running red lights. Twenty-one states and the District of Columbia have laws permitting automated enforcement of traffic laws (red-light or speed cameras).[51] Ten states expressly outlaw use of such technology. Another 25 states have passed no laws addressing the issue and in most of those states, such camera programs are being used. Red-light cameras have generated a lot of controversy. Some see them as an effective safety device while others see the motive as money rather than safety.

Helmet Laws

The growing popularity of bicycles and motorcycles has generated helmet laws in many states and communities. Beginning in the 1960s, the U.S. Department of Transportation required states to enact motorcycle helmet laws in order to receive federal highway funds. DOT eliminated the requirement in 1976 but many states initially kept them in place. Proponents of motorcycle helmet laws cite statistics showing that motorcyclists experience more fatalities per 100 million vehicle miles traveled than automobile drivers. Opponents see the issue as one of personal choice and political freedom, rather than public safety. Some states have recently bowed to pressures from baby boomer motorcyclists and repealed their helmet laws.

Driver Distraction

The newest safety issue is driver distraction. The National Highway Traffic Safety Administration estimates that driver distraction is involved in over one-third of all accidents.[52] Eating, drinking, smoking, programming a GPS system, moving objects in the car, adjusting climate control, and texting cause motorist distraction. New York was the first state to ban handheld phones while driving. Most of the others have considered cell phone restrictions in response to high-profile crashes involving cell phones, both handheld and hands-free.[53] New technological distractions are likely to emerge in the future.

Auto Safety

Under pressure from consumer lobbies and the U.S. Department of Transportation, auto manufacturers gradually improved the safety of their products. The traffic fatality rate in the United States (the number of deaths from motor vehicle accidents per 100 million miles traveled) was 4.7 in 1970. This rate has dropped dramatically over the years to 1.2 in 2012. This reduction in auto fatalities is primarily a result of manufacturers' safety improvements, including air bags.

State Gasoline Taxes

State motor fuels taxes pay over two-thirds of total highway costs; the remainder comes from federal highway funds. Every state adds to the federal gasoline tax of 18.4 cents per gallon. State gasoline taxes range from 7.5 to 37.5 cents per gallon. (See "*Rankings of the States:* Road Mileage and Gasoline Taxes.")

Automobile and highway interests make vigorous efforts in state capitals to separate gasoline taxes from general revenues and to ensure that these taxes are used exclusively for highways. They strongly oppose "raiding" state highway tax funds for other purposes. In contrast, environmentalists and metropolitan interests frequently seek to use gasoline tax revenues for mass transit—buses, trains, and subways.

Fuel Efficiency

CORPORATE AVERAGE FUEL EFFICIENCY (CAFE) STANDARDS

Averages calculated from highway miles-per-gallon figures from all models of cars and light trucks produced by each manufacturer.

The federal government requires automobile manufacturers to maintain **corporate average fuel efficiency (CAFE) standards** in the production of automobiles and light trucks. These averages are calculated from highway miles-per-gallon figures from all models of cars and light trucks produced by each manufacturer. For years, the CAFE standard for cars was 27.5 miles per gallon. For light trucks, vans, and sports utility vehicles, the CAFE standard was much lower—23.5 miles per gallon. In 2012, the Obama Administration issued new passenger vehicle fuel economy and greenhouse gas standards for vehicle model years 2017–2025. The combined new passenger car and light truck CAFE standards will rise to as much as 41 miles per gallon in 2021 and 49.7 in 2025. Determining CAFE standards engenders near constant political conflict in Washington, pitting auto manufacturers against environmental and consumer groups. The increased popularity of pickup trucks, mini vans, and sports utility vehicles in recent years has meant that overall fuel efficiency on the roads has improved at a very slow pace. Alternative fueled vehicles—cars powered entirely or in part by electricity, natural gas, hydrogen, or ethanol—have long offered the promise of significant numbers of buyers, yet they constitute less than 5 percent of new vehicle sales. Some states, such as California and Florida, have moved toward more stringent fuel efficiency standards than the national government.

The Highway Lobby

Traditionally, highway interests in the states sought to separate highway departments from general state government and to separate gasoline tax revenues from general state revenues. Highway interests believed that their road-building programs would fare better when organization and funding were not in competition with other state programs. They succeeded in most states in obtaining (1) the creation of separate highway boards and commissions, and (2) the establishment of separate highway trust funds to receive gasoline tax revenues "earmarked" for highway construction and maintenance. Indeed, some states passed constitutional amendments preventing the "diversion" of gasoline taxes for nonhighway purposes. These policies guaranteed a continual flow of road-building funds and gave highways preferential treatment over other public programs. Today, some southern and western states retain these special organizational and funding arrangements for highways.

Infrastructure Investment and Economic Growth

Highway construction, and infrastructure development generally, is widely recognized as a key component of economic development. Nonetheless, while overall government spending has skyrocketed in recent decades, spending for public infrastructure (highways, bridges, ports, airports, and sewers) has not kept pace with growth. Despite evidence that spending for highways is linked to economic development,[54] state and local government spending for highway construction and maintenance has steadily declined. Not only is the nation failing to invest in *new* public infrastructure, but its older existing highways, bridges, sewers, and water mains are deteriorating as well. Every four years beginning in 1998, the American Society of Civil Engineers has graded the nation and individual states on current infrastructure conditions and needs. The grades have been near failing, averaging only Ds, mostly due to delayed maintenance and underinvestment. However, in 2013 there was a slight improvement in grades for roads, bridges, and rail but no improvement for aviation, ports, inland waterways, or transit.[55]

The Mass Transportation Movement

An alliance of environmentalists, social equity activists, bicycling advocates, transit supporters, architects, planners, community groups, the elderly, and others has recently emerged to oppose highway building in favor of mass transportation. The coalition has pushed for changes in U.S. transportation policy: "more equitable transportation outcomes, better environmental quality, improved public health and safety, stronger communities, and a thriving economy."[56]

"Anti-sprawlists" believe that transportation reform is necessary to stop sprawl. To get people out of their cars, they favor creating convenient, walkable neighborhoods that are served by public transit. Pedestrian and bicycle-friendly places will, in their judgment, improve residents' health and safety, while saving the environment. Most metropolitan areas are not bicycle or pedestrian friendly. One reform organization has labeled many large metro areas as "dangerous" places to walk. "The riskiest places are characterized by spread-out growth and wide, high-speed streets that often lack sidewalks and crosswalks."[57]

Metropolitan Transportation

City planners, urban reformers, and transportation specialists argue that the only way to relieve traffic congestion and preserve central cities is to get people out of private automobiles and onto public transit, that is, "to move people, not cars." Automobiles on expressways can move about 2,000 people per lane per hour; buses can move between 6,000 and 9,000; rail systems can carry up to 60,000 people per hour. In other words, one rail line is estimated to be equal to twenty or thirty expressway lanes of automobiles in its ability to move people.

Nationwide, approximately two-thirds of all commutes last less than 30 minutes and just 17 percent are 45 minutes or longer.[58] More time is spent commuting in the largest metropolitan areas such as Los Angeles, Dallas, Houston, and Washington, DC. (See *"Did You Know?:* Large Metro Areas Are Magnets for Mega-Commuters" in Chapter 12.)

The average citizen has a large investment in the automobile. Few Americans want to see their financial investment sit in a garage all day. Americans clearly prefer private automobile transportation and costly expressways to mass transit, regardless of the arguments of transportation experts. Only about 5 percent of Americans use buses or trains to commute to work. The result is that mass transit facilities generally lose money.

Almost all cities now experience heavy expressway congestion at rush hour and a resulting increase in time and cost to the average automobile commuter. (See Table 13–1.) But predictions about future expressway "gridlock" may prove inaccurate. The proportion of daily commuters who drive from the suburbs to work in central cities is gradually decreasing as more businesses move to the suburbs. Intersuburban commuting is increasing over time; circumferential expressways circling cities now carry more traffic than expressways leading into central cities. Rail-based mass transit facilities are usually designed for city–suburban commuting. As the central city fades as a center for employment and shopping, and more people travel from suburb to suburb, the ridership for mass transit decreases. But when gas prices go up, ridership increases.

The expense of rail-based transit and public opposition to paying higher taxes for it has prompted several cities and transit authorities to focus their efforts on transforming

TABLE 13–1 The Most Congested Urban Areas	
Urban Area	**Per Person Annual Hours of Delay**
Chicago, IL	44
Washington, DC	41
Los Angeles, CA	40
Houston, TX	37
Denver, CO	33
Baltimore, MD	33
Dallas, TX	32
San Francisco, CA	30
Boston, MA	28
Atlanta, GA	27
Seattle, WA	27
Orlando, FL	27
Minneapolis, MN	27
Philadelphia, PA	26
Miami, FL	26
U.S. Average	**25**

Note: Data are for 2009. Most recent data available at time of publication.
Source: U.S. Census Bureau, *Statistical Abstract of the United States, 2012,* Table 1099. Available at http://www.census.gov/prod/2011pubs/12statab/trans.pdf.

their standard bus systems into bus rapid transit (BRT)—an approach that has worked well in Cleveland, Ohio, with its HealthLine. The goal of BRT is to speed up rides with more frequent runs during rush hour, dedicated bus lanes, advance ticketing, and better traffic light coordination.[59]

The Case for Subsidies

It is necessary to provide public subsidies to commuter-rail companies or to have governments operate these facilities at a loss if commuter service is to be maintained. Only a small portion of the costs of public transit come from the fares charged riders. However, it is argued that the cost of mass transit subsidies is small in comparison to the cost of building and maintaining expressways. Thus, mass transit is considered cost-effective for many cities, even if fares do not meet operating expenses. Moreover, new, speedier, more comfortable, air-conditioned, high-capacity trains with fewer stops and more frequent trips may lure many riders back to public transportation.

Federal Mass Transit Aid

For many years the federal government has subsidized the building of highways, particularly the interstate highways, where the federal government assumed 90 percent of the costs. It was not until the 1970s that the federal government showed any comparable interest in mass transit. (Indeed, the *interstate* highway system, despite its name, has carried a major share of *intra*metropolitan city–suburban traffic.) The energy crisis accelerated federal efforts in mass transit. In the Urban Mass Transit Act of 1974, the U.S. Department of Transportation was authorized to make grants to cities for both construction and operation of mass transit systems. In many cities, this simply meant the creation of a local mass transit authority and the purchase of buses. However, in some cities, massive new mass transit programs were developed with federal funds.

Among the most striking efforts in mass transit were San Francisco's BART (Bay Area Rapid Transit), Washington, DC's METRO, and Atlanta's MARTA (Metropolitan Atlanta Rapid Transit Authority). These are large projects into which the cities and the federal government pumped hundreds of millions of dollars. They incorporated all of the latest features of modern, pleasant, rapid, convenient, and efficient mass transit. Nonetheless, ridership cannot pay for continuing operating costs, let alone the enormous costs of construction. Perhaps the worst example of federally subsidized mass transit is Miami's Metrorail. The costs were so great and the ridership so small that critics estimated it would have been cheaper for the federal government to buy every regular rider a Rolls Royce.

The battle for mass transit is filled with trade-off decisions. Certainly one goal of mass transit is to reduce the number of cars on the road in metropolitan areas and thereby reduce air pollution. But as with roads, it is often necessary to "take" land to construct rail systems and that is never an easy fight, particularly when it may involve relocating residents living in the inner city.

A New High-Speed Rail System?

Under the Obama administration, the debate about mass transit broadened to include high-speed rail. The administration put forth a proposal calling for "an efficient, high-speed passenger rail network of 100- to 600-mile intercity corridors that connect communities across America."[60] (See Figure 13–2.) The proposal was promoted on the grounds that it will foster more livable communities connected by safe, efficient modes of travel. The federal government initially budgeted $8 billion out of the American Recovery and Reinvestment Act but made it well known that it will take years to complete and will require major investments of money and land from both the federal and state levels and strong new partnerships between states and localities. Battles are most certainly to be fought over which corridors are to be built first, and at the local level, where stops will be located.

FIGURE 13–2 Proposed High-Speed Rail System

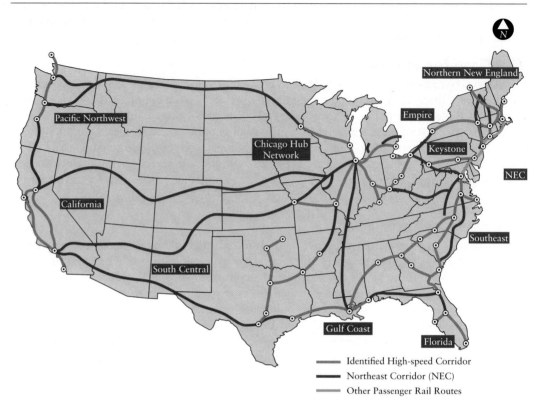

Source: U.S. Department of Transportation, Federal Railroad Administration, "Vision for High-Speed Rail in America," The High-Speed Rail Strategic Plan, The American Recovery and Reinvestment Act, April 2009.

Federal Support for Transportation Alternatives

The federal MAP-21 Act passed in 2012 created a new Transportation Alternatives Program. States are now required to spend 2 percent of their federal highway monies to support improvements benefitting nonmotorists. A wide range of potential improvements were listed in the legislation: bicycle and pedestrian trails, conversion of abandoned railroad corridors to bicycle/pedestrian and other nonmotorized transportation facilities, traffic calming techniques (to slow down motorists), lighting and other safety infrastructure, assistance for Americans with disabilities, safe routes for nondrivers, turnout, overlook and viewing area construction, community improvement activities, and environmental mitigation, including storm water runoff and vehicle-wildlife accidents.[61]

13.10

Describe the various environmental policies that affect states and communities, and assess the extent to which governments have been able to address these problems.

ENVIRONMENTAL PROTECTION

Historically, the principal responsibility for the protection of the environment rested with local governments—removing and disposing of trash, maintaining sewers and treating sewage, providing drinkable water, cleaning streets, and maintaining parks and recreation facilities. But over time, the national government has assumed ever-greater responsibilities in environmental protection. Federal environmental policymaking began in earnest in 1970 with the creation of the Environmental Protection Agency (EPA) and the subsequent passage of clean air and water acts. Potentially the EPA is the most powerful and far-reaching bureaucracy in Washington, with legal authority over any activity in the nation that affects the air, water, or ground.

The air and water in the United States are far cleaner today than in previous decades. This is true despite growth in population and an even greater growth in waste products. Nonetheless, genuine concern for the environment centers on the disposal of solid waste (especially hazardous waste), water pollution, and air pollution.

Solid Waste Disposal

The average American produces over four pounds of solid waste *each day*. (See Table 13–2.) There are essentially three methods of disposing of solid waste: landfills, incineration, and recycling. Modern landfills have replaced town dumps nearly everywhere. Landfills are usually lined with clay so that wastes do not seep into the water system. In addition, hazardous wastes are separated from those that are not hazardous and handled separately. Contrary to popular rhetoric, there is no "landfill crisis"; the nation is not "running out of land." However, both government agencies and private waste disposal firms are being stymied by the powerful organized NIMBYs. Landfill sites are plentiful in most areas, but local opposition is strong in every area.

Another alternative is to burn the garbage. Modern incinerators are special plants, usually equipped with machinery to separate the garbage into different types, with scrubbers to reduce air pollution from the burning. They may be sited alongside electric generation plants that can be powered by the heat from the garbage fire. One problem with this method is that the substances emitted from the chimney of the incinerator pollute the air. Another problem: the garbage separated during the screening phase still has to be disposed of; the need for landfill sites is only reduced, not eliminated.

A third method of reducing the amount of solid waste is recycling. Recycling is the conversion of waste into useful products. Newspapers are recycled into cardboard, insulation, and cat litter, and some of it is recycled into newsprint. Automobile batteries are the product recycled at the highest rate in the United States. (See Figure 13–3.) Overall, over one-third of all solid waste in the United States is recycled for reuse. This is a notable achievement over the mere 10 percent that was recycled some years ago.[62]

Toxic Waste

Toxic or hazardous wastes are those that pose a significant threat to public health or the environment because of their "quantity, concentration, or physical, chemical, or infectious characteristics."[63] The EPA has the authority to determine which substances are toxic, and to establish separate rules for toxic waste disposal. Hazardous wastes from old sites also constitute an environmental problem. The EPA is committed to clean up such sites under the **Superfund laws**. The EPA has developed a National Priority List of sites based on a hazard ranking system. Since 1983, nearly 1,700 hazardous waste sites have been listed but relatively few (360) have undergone complete cleanup to date, often causing state and local officials to get quite angry at Washington.

SUPERFUND LAWS

Laws that regulate the clean up of toxic waste. The EPA has developed a National Priority List of toxic waste sites that need to be cleaned up.

TABLE 13–2 Growth in Solid Wastes							
Waste Measure	**1960**	**1970**	**1980**	**1990**	**2000**	**2005**	**2009**
Gross waste (millions of tons)	87.5	120.5	151.6	205.2	242.6	252.4	243
Waste per person per day (lb)	2.65	3.22	3.7	4.5	4.7	4.7	4.3
Percentage recycled	NA	NA	9.6	16.2	29.7	31.6	33.8

Note: Most current data.
Source: U.S. Census Bureau, *Statistical Abstract of the United States, 2012*, Table 378. Available at http://www.census.gov/prod/2011pubs/12statab/geo.pdf.

FIGURE 13-3 Recycling Rates of Selected Products

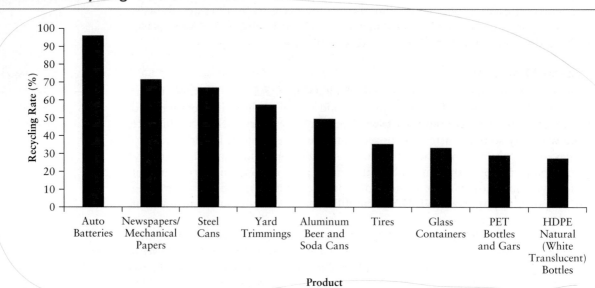

Note: Data are for 2010. Mechanical papers include directories, newspaper inserts, and some advertisement and direct mail printing.
Source: Environmental Protection Agency, "Municipal Solid Waste," Figure 3, November 15, 2012. Available at http://www.epa.gov/epawaste/nonhaz/municipal/.

Water Pollution

Water pollution comes from domestic sewage, industrial waste, agricultural runoff of fertilizers and pesticides, and silt deposits and sedimentation that may be caused by nearby construction. **Primary sewage treatment**—which uses screens and settling chambers, where filth falls out of the water and sludge—is fairly common. **Secondary sewage treatment** removes organic wastes, usually by trickling water through a bed of rocks 3 to 10 feet deep, where bacteria consume the organic matter. Remaining bacteria are killed by chlorination. **Tertiary sewage treatment** uses chemical filtration processes to remove almost all contaminants from water. Federal water pollution abatement goals call for the establishment of secondary treatment in all American communities. Tertiary treatment is expensive, costing two or three times as much to build and operate as a secondary treatment plant.

The federal government has provided financial assistance to states and cities to build sewage treatment plants ever since the 1930s. The Water Pollution Control Act of 1972 sets a "national goal" for the elimination of all pollutants from navigable waters; it requires industries and municipalities to install "the best available technology." The Act gave the EPA authority to initiate legal actions against pollution caused by private firms or governments. The EPA was authorized by the Safe Drinking Water Act of 1974 to set minimum standards for water quality throughout the nation. Water quality has improved significantly over the last 30 years.

Air Pollution

The air we breathe is about one-fifth oxygen and a little less than four-fifths nitrogen, with traces of other gases, water vapor, and waste products. Most air pollution is caused by the gasoline-powered internal combustion engines of cars, trucks, and buses. Motor vehicles account for more than 60 percent of the carbon monoxide emissions sent into the atmosphere every year. The largest industrial polluters are petroleum refineries, smelters, and foundries. Electrical power plants also contribute to total air pollution by burning coal or oil for electric power. Home heating is also a source of pollution, as is the incineration of garbage, trash, and other refuse by governments and industries.

PRIMARY SEWAGE TREATMENT

Screens and settling chambers, where filth falls out of sewage water and sludge.

SECONDARY SEWAGE TREATMENT

Removal of organic wastes, usually by trickling water through a bed of rocks 3 to 10 feet deep, where bacteria consume organic matter. Remaining bacteria are killed by chlorination.

TERTIARY SEWAGE TREATMENT

Expensive chemical filtration processes to remove almost all contaminants from water.

The EPA sets limits on fine particulate matter (silt, dust) in the air. But many large cities, Los Angeles, for example, regularly exceed these limits. Nonetheless, the air we breathe is significantly cleaner today than thirty years ago. The Environmental Protection Agency claims that the Clean Air Act of 1970 and subsequent amendments to it have resulted in an overall reduction in principal pollutants of 48 percent over 30 years.[64] This improvement in air quality has come about despite increases in the gross domestic product (economic growth), vehicle miles traveled, energy consumption, and population. However, the political reality is that environmentalists have become much more powerful in state and local politics and are increasingly effective at pressuring state and local governments to become more "green."

Environmental Politics

Everyone is opposed to pollution. Environmental groups begin with a psychological and political advantage: they are "clean" and their opponents are "dirty." Environmental groups, the news media, Congress, and executive agencies can be moved to support environmental protection measures with relatively little consideration of their costs—and job loss, price increases, and increased dependence on foreign sources of energy. Opponents—notably the electric power companies, oil and gas companies, chemical companies, and coal companies—must fight a rearguard action, continually seeking delays, amendments, and adjustments to federal standards. But these industries are suspect; environmentalists can charge that industry opposition to environmental protection is motivated by greed for higher profits. And the charge is partially true, although most of the cost of antipollution efforts is passed on to the consumer in the form of higher prices.

The environmental movement is generally supported by upper middle-class or upper-class individuals whose income and wealth are secure. Their aesthetic preferences for a no-growth, clean, unpolluted environment take precedence over jobs and income. Workers and small business people whose jobs and income depend on energy production, oil refining, forestry, mining, smelting, or manufacturing are unlikely to be ardent environmentalists. Minority opinion is split; some minority interests argue that minorities live closer to the sources of pollution and environmental degradation and therefore should support regulation; yet minorities are generally more concerned with jobs than with a clean environment.[65] Indeed, environmentalism is sometimes seen as a **white phenomenon.** Overall, public opinion supports environmental measures when they are posed in the abstract, but public opinion is divided when environmental concerns are matched against economic growth. The proposed Keystone XL pipeline is a good example of the tug-of-war between the two principles. (The Keystone XL pipeline is a proposed 1,700-mile, $7 billion project that would transport 700,000 barrels of oil per day from Alberta, Canada, to refineries on the Gulf Coast.[66])

Environmental groups have powerful allies in the nation's NIMBYs. Even people who otherwise recognize the general need for new commercial or industrial developments, highways, power plants (electric and nuclear), pipelines, and waste disposal sites voice loud opposition when any of these are planned for placement in their neighborhoods. (See *Up Close*: A Radioactive Waste Dump Proposal Divides a Small Town.)

Greening of the States and Cities

Since the creation of the Environmental Protection Agency in 1970, environmental protection has been a national responsibility. However, states and communities have undertaken important initiatives in the field, in addition to their traditional responsibilities for solid waste disposal, sewage treatment, and the provision of safe drinking water. State initiatives are encouraged by federal partial standard preemptions that permit states to regulate activities in a field already regulated by the federal government as long as state regulatory standards are at least as strict as those of the federal government. To receive such a

WHITE PHENOMENON
The perception that the environmental movement is a higher priority for whites than for racial minorities.

UP CLOSE

A Radioactive Waste Dump Proposal Divides a Small Town

It began innocently enough: a community seeking to enhance its economy. But the effort has fanned a heated and ongoing controversy.

In the 1980s, civic and business leaders in Andrews, Texas, a town of 10,000 on the flat West Texas prairie, began recruiting industry to diversify its economy. Up to that time, most residents in the county made a living in the boom-or-bust oil business or in cattle ranching. When Waste Control Specialists offered to build a hazardous waste landfill 31 miles west of town near the Texas-New Mexico state line, the Chamber of Commerce welcomed the company with open arms. The local newspaper publisher lauded the prospect of jobs and money and downplayed the hazard: "What it is, neighbor, is dirt—dirt that is cleaned up by professionals, in a safe secure manner and monitored six ways to Sunday by inspectors."

Waste Control Specialists, owned by Dallas billionaire Harold Simmons, opened the landfill in 1997. Recognizing a growing need for disposal of radioactive waste—and the potential for huge profits—the company in 2004 applied for state licensing to bury canisters of uranium and heavy metal waste materials. But environmental studies by state geologists revealed the presence of major aquifers, all connected, below the surface of Andrews County, raising the likelihood that waste could leak into the groundwater and contaminate drinking water for 2 million people as well as millions of acres of farmland.

At a local meeting to gather public input, 400 citizens showed up to voice their support. Feeling pressure despite their objections, three members of the application review team resigned. Officials, appointed by the governor (who had received major campaign contributions from Simmons), of the Texas Commission on Environmental Quality granted the license in 2008. The Sierra Club sued to overturn the decision, asking for a contested case hearing on behalf of at least two concerned residents. A year later the state regulatory agency approved yet another license, this one to dispose of low-level radioactive waste.

It soon became clear that the company saw itself as a "national solution" for nuclear waste accumulating in other states. In 2011 the government agency that had been formed as a compact between Texas and Vermont to oversee hazardous waste disposal for the two states adopted a rule that allowed the Andrews County site to accept radioactive waste from as many as 36 states and perhaps even foreign countries.

Critics expressed outrage. Public Citizen Texas questioned whether the site had adequate long-term capacity and declared the term "low level" misleading because, if the waste is measured by bulk amount, "low-level waste can be even more radioactive than 'high-level' by its sheer volume." The group further pointed to the risks of groundwater contamination, truck transport accidents, and possible security and terrorism threats.

The Texas Sunset Advisory Commission, which regularly assesses the need for a state agency to exist, warned that should an accident or leakage occur as geologists expect, the state would bear the ultimate liability. In other words, the taxpayers of Texas—not the licensee—would pay the untold millions to clean it up, and the radioactivity would linger for thousands of years.

Meanwhile the Sierra Club continued its legal battle in the courts, only to be sued by Andrews County in an attempt to end the club's claims. According to the county judge, the company had complained that it was losing money because of the Sierra Club's actions. In 2013 in further support for economic interests, a West Texas state senator filed a bill that would block New Mexico residents from challenging the dump.

A New Mexico claimant in the Sierra Club lawsuit, Ms. Rose Gardner, has followed the controversy closely. A resident of Eunice, only five miles from the 15,000-acre landfill, she ruefully remarked that the dump has been described as a "remote location," adding: "Remote from Dallas? OK. Remote from New York? OK. But it's right here. It's close to my town."

Source: Laray Polk, "Harold Simmons is Dallas' Most Evil Genius," *D Magazine,* February 2010. Available at http://www.dmagazine.com/Home/D_Magazine/2010/February/Harold_Simmons_Is_Dallas_Most_Evil_Genius.aspx?page=1.

Public Citizen, "Andrews County Low-Level Radioactive Waste Disposal," April 2011. Available at http://texasnuclearsafety.org/downloads/radioactive_waste_disposal_report.pdf.

Josh Harkinson, "A Texas-Sized Plan for Nuclear Waste," *Mother Jones,* March 29, 2011. Available at http://www.motherjones.com/environment/2011/03/texas-nuclear-waste-dump.

Nick Swartsell, "Sierra Club Fight Over Radioactive Waste Heats Up," *The New York Times,* October 20, 2012. Available at http://www.nytimes.com/2012/10/21/us/sierra-club-fight-over-radioactive-waste-in-texas-heats-up.html?pagewanted=all&_r=0.

Wesley Burnett, "2008: When Events Matured Toward Diversification," *Andrews County News,* January 8, 2009. Available at http://www.texassolution.com/documents/2008_historic_year.pdf.

preemption or waiver for an environmental protection initiative, states must usually submit their regulations to the EPA for approval.

Environmental groups often feel that the federal government has not gone far enough in mandating restrictions on air pollution. (An international Rio Treaty in 1992 and its follow-up Kyoto Protocol in 1998 set national goals for reducing greenhouse gases below 1990 levels. The United States failed to adopt the treaty citing the economic dislocations required to fully comply with it.) Environmentalists have increasingly turned to the states and cities to enact a wide variety of measures to reduce air and water pollution.

In the mid-2000s, California Governor Arnold Schwarzenegger committed his state to automobile fuel emission standards well beyond those of the federal government. He even threatened to sue the EPA if it failed to grant California a partial standard preemption to implement these tougher standards. Schwarzenegger also established a "Green Buildings" program, ordering all state buildings to be designed and reengineered to make them more energy efficient. New York City ordered its fleet of 13,000 taxis to go green over five years by substituting smaller hybrid-fueled cabs for larger gas-guzzling taxis. Dozens of other states and cities have initiated pollution control programs. The competition to be "the greenest," most environmentally friendly, less fossil fuel–dependent community has become intense in many parts of the country. (See Table 13–3.)

Land-use battles continue to be fierce in many communities—reflective of major power struggles for control of a scarce resource.

Environmental activists are more likely to be upper-middle-class or upper-class individuals whose income and wealth are secure. Poorer individuals whose jobs may be eliminated do not have the time to attend protest rallies and are often outnumbered at protest events.

TABLE 13–3	States on the Cutting Edge of Green Technology	
Highest Recycling Rates	**States with Best Solar Incentives**	**Total Power Capacities for Wind**
1. Minnesota	1. Louisiana	1. Texas
2. Washington	2. Oregon	2. Iowa
3. New Jersey	3. Connecticut	3. California
4. Maine	4. Massachusetts	4. Washington
5. Wisconsin	5. New York	5. Minnesota
6. Oregon	6. Hawaii	6. Oregon
7. Massachusetts	7. North Carolina	7. Illinois
8. Pennsylvania	8. Wisconsin	8. New York
9. Vermont	9. Illinois	9. Colorado
10. Maryland	10. Minnesota	10. North Carolina

Source: The Council of State Governments, "By the Book: Does Energy Efficiency Affect States' Carbon Footprints?" June 2010. Available at http://www.csg.org/pubs/capitolideas/may_june_2010/bythebook.aspx. Printed with permission from the Council of State Governments.

- In most communities the ruling power lies somewhere on a continuum between a monolithic elite and a diffused and polycentric pluralist model.
- National institutions control most of the nation's economic resources, but communities control the land.
- In many communities, older economic elites have been replaced by newer political elites.
- Economic growth (housing, manufacturing, transportation) is often challenged by no-growth advocates opposed to lifestyle changes, NIMBYs opposed to undesirable projects nearby, and "smart growth" proponents wanting "the right kind of growth."
- Heavy growth restrictions lessen affordable housing and thus keep out working families.
- Community governments control land use through recommendations of city planners and citizen planning commissions, zoning ordinances, subdivision regulations, building codes, and environmental laws and regulations. New planning practices include planned use developments (PUDs), exaction and impact fees, developer agreements, and disaster-proofing regulations. Neighborhoods are designed as livable communities in sync with new urbanism, or walkable city, principles and the urban sustainability movement.
- The Takings Clause of the Fifth Amendment aims to prevent government from taking private property without just compensation, but recent government actions have raised questions about how far government can go in using its eminent domain power.
- The federal government has helped communities with housing by backing FHA and VA mortgage loans and providing grants to build public housing. Federal grants for urban renewal projects, enterprise zones, and brownfield cleanup were designed to revitalize distressed neighborhoods.
- The federal government's control of transportation policy ranges from car safety and fuel efficiency design to linking highway funding to state speed limits and legal drinking age. Most recently, federal funds have helped local areas support projects benefitting nonmotorists (bicyclists, pedestrians).
- All states require drivers to purchase liability insurance, and many states require seat belt use and set limits for blood alcohol/drug levels. Local communities have created controversy over use of red-light cameras, bike helmets, and cell phones (texting).
- Even though highway spending is linked to economic development, state and local government spending for highway construction and maintenance has declined dramatically, and infrastructure is deteriorating.
- Despite concerns about pollution, traffic congestion, and long commutes, the mass transit movement has failed to catch on in many cities. Some cities have re-focused their efforts on buses, specifically on creating bus rapid transit systems.
- Because of federal laws such as the Clean Air Act of 1970, the nation's air and water are vastly cleaner than they once were. Toxic or hazardous waste disposal remains a big problem.
- Public opinion tends to support environmental measures in the abstract but is often divided when environmental concerns are matched against jobs, consumer prices, and other economic factors.

CHAPTER FOURTEEN

THE POLITICS OF TAXATION AND FINANCE

LEARNING OBJECTIVES

 14.1 Describe how much money federal and state governments spend, discuss the extent to which spending has increased over time, and compare spending patterns between local and state governments.

14.2 Compare and contrast state and local property taxes, sales taxes, excise taxes, and income taxes; evaluate whether each of these taxes is progressive, regressive, or proportional; and describe other revenue sources for state and local governments.

14.3 Discuss the differences in tax policy among the states, and explain what accounts for these differences.

 14.4 Describe Americans' attitudes about taxes, various mechanisms that are sometimes used to limit taxes, and the impact of such tax limits.

14.5 Outline the sources of fiscal stress in state and local governments, and assess how efforts to relieve this fiscal stress impact citizens.

14.6 Describe legal restraints on state and local government debt; explain how state and local governments can undertake capital projects nonetheless by issuing bonds; compare and contrast general obligation, revenue, and industrial development bonds; and discuss how the federal tax code treats income from different types of bonds.

 14.7 Describe what happens when a local government faces bankruptcy, and assess the financial health of U.S. cities in the wake of the Great Recession.

AN OVERVIEW OF GOVERNMENT FINANCES

Describe how much money federal and state governments spend, discuss the extent to which spending has increased over time, and compare spending patterns between local and state governments.

GROSS DOMESTIC PRODUCT (GDP)

The total value of all the goods and services produced in the United States in a year; a measure of the size of the U.S. economy.

Dollar figures in government budgets are often mind-boggling. The federal government spends over $3.5 *trillion* each year, and all state and local governments combined spend an additional $1.6 *trillion*. To better understand what these dollar figures mean, it is helpful to view them in relation to the nation's **gross domestic product (GDP)**, the sum of all the goods and services produced in the United States in a year.

Growth of Government Spending

In 1929 total governmental spending—federal, state, and local combined—amounted to only about 10 percent of the GDP. Today, total governmental spending amounts to about 34 percent of the GDP. (See Figure 14–1.) *Federal* spending accounts for about 22 percent of the GDP, and spending by all *state and local* governments adds another 11 percent. Federal government spending mushroomed, both in total dollar amounts and percentage of the GDP, in the administration of President Barack Obama.

State and Local Government Spending

State and local governments direct most of their spending toward education, social services (welfare and health), public safety (police and fire), and transportation. Spending patterns are different between states and local governments, primarily because they differ in the functions for which they have primary financial and service delivery responsibilities. (See Figure 14–2.)

TYPES OF TAXES AND TAX POLITICS

Compare and contrast state and local property taxes, sales taxes, excise taxes, and income taxes; evaluate whether each of these taxes is progressive, regressive, or proportional; and describe other revenue sources for state and local governments.

State and local governments in the United States derive revenue from a variety of sources. Of course, taxes are the largest source of revenue. The politics of taxation often center on the question of who actually bears the greatest **tax burden,** that is, which income groups must devote the largest proportion of their income to taxes. Taxes that require high-income groups to pay a larger percentage of their incomes in taxes than low-income groups are said to be **progressive,** while taxes that take a larger share of the income of low-income groups are said to be **regressive.** Taxation at equal percentage rates, regardless of income level, is said to be **proportional.**

FIGURE 14–1 Government Expenditures as a Percentage of GDP

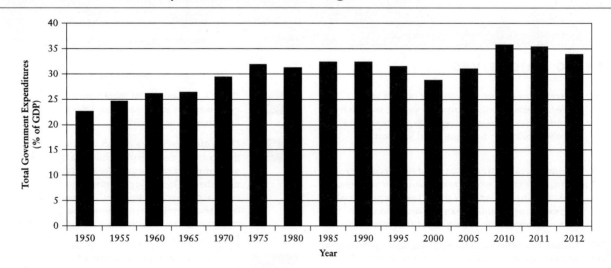

Source: White House, Office of Management and Budget, "Total Government Expenditures as Percentages of GDP: 1948–2012," Table 15.3. Available at http://www.whitehouse.gov/omb/budget/Historicals/.

FIGURE 14–2 Revenues and Expenditures: States versus Localities

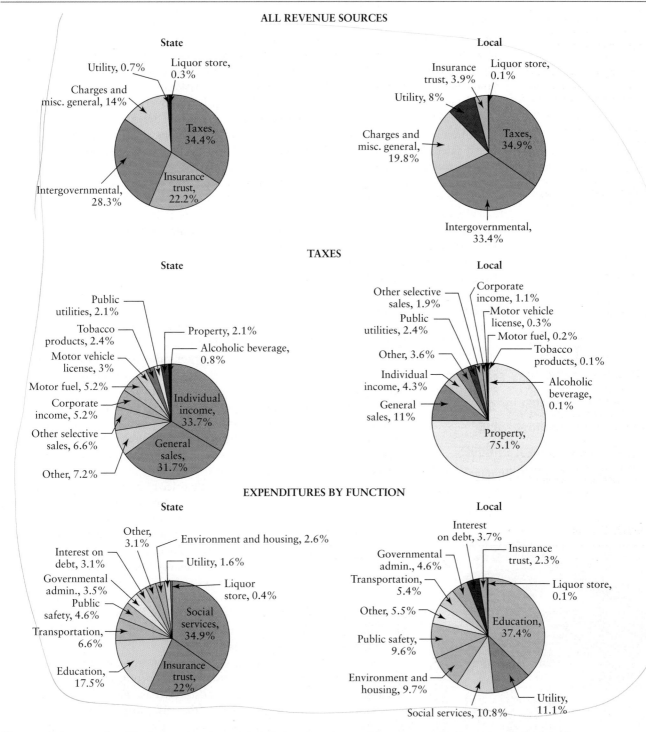

ALL REVENUE SOURCES

State

- Utility, 0.7%
- Liquor store, 0.3%
- Charges and misc. general, 14%
- Taxes, 34.4%
- Intergovernmental, 28.3%
- Insurance trust, 22.2%

Local

- Insurance trust, 3.9%
- Liquor store, 0.1%
- Utility, 8%
- Charges and misc. general, 19.8%
- Taxes, 34.9%
- Intergovernmental, 33.4%

TAXES

State

- Public utilities, 2.1%
- Tobacco products, 2.4%
- Motor vehicle license, 3%
- Motor fuel, 5.2%
- Corporate income, 5.2%
- Other selective sales, 6.6%
- Other, 7.2%
- Property, 2.1%
- Alcoholic beverage, 0.8%
- Individual income, 33.7%
- General sales, 31.7%

Local

- Other selective sales, 1.9%
- Corporate income, 1.1%
- Public utilities, 2.4%
- Motor vehicle license, 0.3%
- Motor fuel, 0.2%
- Other, 3.6%
- Tobacco products, 0.1%
- Individual income, 4.3%
- Alcoholic beverage, 0.1%
- General sales, 11%
- Property, 75.1%

EXPENDITURES BY FUNCTION

State

- Other, 3.1%
- Environment and housing, 2.6%
- Interest on debt, 3.1%
- Utility, 1.6%
- Governmental admin., 3.5%
- Liquor store, 0.4%
- Public safety, 4.6%
- Social services, 34.9%
- Transportation, 6.6%
- Education, 17.5%
- Insurance trust, 22%

Local

- Interest on debt, 3.7%
- Insurance trust, 2.3%
- Governmental admin., 4.6%
- Transportation, 5.4%
- Liquor store, 0.1%
- Other, 5.5%
- Education, 37.4%
- Public safety, 9.6%
- Environment and housing, 9.7%
- Utility, 11.1%
- Social services, 10.8%

Charges and misc.: = user fees: Miscellaneous general revenue includes interest earnings, special assessments, sale of property, and other general revenue.
Public utility: water, electric power, gas supply, and transit.
Insurance trust: unemployment compensation, employee retirement, workers' compensation, and other insurance trust revenue.
Note: Data are for 2010.
Source: U.S. Census Bureau, "State and Local Government Finances by Level of Government and by State: 2009–10," Table 1. Available at http://www.census.gov/govs/estimate/.

Local Property Taxes

Property taxes are the largest source of revenue for *local* governments in the United States. (See Figure 14–2.) However, property taxes are usually regressive. This conclusion is based on the assumption that renters actually pay their property taxes through increased rentals levied by the landlord, and the further assumption that high-income groups have more wealth in untaxed forms of property (stocks, bonds, mutual funds). Since the property tax is the foundation of local tax structures in every state, it is reasonable to conclude that states that rely largely upon local governments for taxes and services are relying more upon regressive tax structures. Yet, in defense of property taxation, it is often argued that no other form of taxation is really feasible for local governments. Local sales and income taxes force individuals and businesses to leave the communities levying them; real estate, on the other hand, is less easy to move about and hide from local tax assessors. Real estate taxes are the only type of taxes that can be effectively collected by local tax officials.

Revenues from property taxation depend on the property wealth of a community. Dependence upon property taxation means that wealthier communities will be able to raise more funds with less burden on taxpayers than communities without much property wealth. In other words, reliance on property taxation results in inequalities in burdens and benefits between wealthier and poorer communities.

The burden of property taxes depends on (1) the ratio of **assessed value** of property to the fair **market value** of the property; (2) the rate at which assessed property is taxed, which is usually expressed in **mills** or tenths of a percent; and finally, (3) the nature and extent of tax exemptions and reductions for certain types of property. The ratio of assessed value to full market value may vary from one community to the next, even in states with laws requiring uniform assessment ratios throughout the state. The failure of communities to have periodic professional and computer-generated tax evaluation means that taxes continue to be levied on old assessment figures, even while market values go up. The result, over time, is a considerable lowering of assessment ratios, and therefore taxes, on older homes and businesses and industries.

Tax assessors usually know the sale price of houses of newer residents, who must pay higher taxes than those paid by older residents. There are few communities in which a suggestion of a reevaluation will not set off a heated debate between those who are enjoying a low assessment and those who are not. If new tax revenues are needed, it is much easier to simply increase the millage rate to be applied against the assessed value of property. Many communities face state restrictions on maximum tax rates, or they are required to submit any proposed increase in tax rates to the voters in a referendum. These restrictions are usually favored by low-tax forces, which have succeeded in obtaining legislation at the state level that impairs the taxing abilities of local governments.

Some categories of property are exempt from taxation; these usually include properties that are used for nonprofit, charitable, religious, educational, and other public purposes. Occasionally, such **exemptions** are attacked by those who feel that they are, in effect, subsidies to the exempted organizations; this is particularly true regarding exemptions for religious property. Exemptions for educational or public properties sometimes work a hardship on communities in which large public facilities or educational institutions are located. However, the exemptions that arouse the greatest controversy are usually those given by state and local governments to new business and industry, in an effort to induce them to locate in the state or community granting the exemption.

Candidates from both parties often run on a platform promising to lower homeowners' property taxes. This clever ad was a very effective one for the candidate to hand to potential supporters as he campaigned door-to-door through neighborhoods.

State Sales Taxes

While the property tax is the most important source of revenue for local communities, the general sales tax is the most important source of tax revenue for *state* governments. Consumers are a notoriously weak pressure group. It is difficult for them to count pennies dribbled away five or six at a time; the tax does not involve obvious payroll deductions, as in income taxation, or year-end bills, as in property taxation. Only five states do *not* impose a general sales tax (Alaska, Delaware, Montana, New Hampshire, and Oregon). Some states get over half of their revenue from sales taxes.

State and local sales taxes are often considered regressive, that is, the poor are believed to devote a larger percentage of their income to paying these taxes than the wealthy. The regressivity of sales taxation is based on the assumption that low-income groups must use most, if not all, of their income for purchases, while high-income groups devote larger shares of their income to savings. However, many states exclude some of the necessities of life from sales taxation, such as packaged food, rent, and medical expenses, in order to reduce the burden of sales taxation on the poor. Because of these exclusions, sales taxes in many states are not really that regressive.

States generally rely more heavily on sales taxation than on income taxation. However, reliance upon one or the other type of tax varies from state to state. The decision to place primary reliance upon sales or income taxation is one of the most important policy choices facing state government. The yield from both types of taxation can be quite large.

There are several arguments on behalf of sales taxation in the states. The first is that sales taxation is the only major source of revenue left to the states—local governments must rely on property taxes, and the federal government has placed such a heavy tax burden on incomes that taxpayers will not countenance an additional state bite out of their paychecks. Moreover, sales taxes are not as visible as income or property taxes, since sales taxes are paid pennies at a time. Generally, the customer considers the sales tax as part of the price of an item. Taxpayers never add up the total they have paid in sales taxes, so sales taxation appears to be a relatively "painless" form of taxation. In addition, sales taxes ensure that low-income groups who benefit from public services will share in the costs of government. Actual hardships for the poor from sales taxes can be reduced by excluding food and other necessities from taxation, but the poor will pay taxes when purchasing luxury items. Finally, sales taxes are useful in reaching mobile populations, that is, tourists, commuters, and transients—people who derive benefits from a host state but who would not otherwise help pay for these benefits.

Selective Sales (Excise) Taxes: Cigarette, Alcohol, and Gas

States vary considerably in the sales taxes they place on certain selected items. Two of these selective sales taxes are sometimes referred to as "sin taxes" (cigarettes and alcohol). Few people object to raising either tax, unless they use or produce the product. Often these sorts of taxes are earmarked to specific programs—for example, cigarette taxes to help pay for indigent health care; alcohol taxes to fund domestic

MARKET VALUE

The estimated value of a property if sold on the open market.

MILL

A dollar per thousand dollars of assessed value of property; used to calculate a property owner's tax bill.

EXEMPTIONS

Categories of property that are not subject to taxation.

A proposal to levy a 10-cent-per-cup tax on espresso was roundly defeated by voters in Seattle, Washington—birthplace of the Starbucks Corporation. Opponents argued the tax would negatively impact small businesses (coffeehouses) and their employees. Proponents who signed petitions to get the issue on the ballot saw the consumption tax as a way to raise money for underfunded early childhood education programs.

violence shelters and other programs. A majority of states have tax rates over $1.00 per pack. Thirteen states charge $2.00 per pack or more, and New York's $4.35 rate is the highest in the nation. Alcohol tax rates differ by type of booze—wine, beer, hard liquor. Gasoline taxes, too, are often earmarked; they must be used on roads. But gas taxes are a lot more political than cigarette or alcohol taxes because gas is a necessity for most people.

State Income Taxes

PROGRESSIVE STATE INCOME TAX

Income tax rates rise with increases in income.

"ABILITY TO PAY" PRINCIPLE

Wealthier individuals pay a higher tax rate than poorer individuals.

SIXTEENTH AMENDMENT

Created the federal income tax, a progressive tax based on ability to pay.

FLAT RATE TAX

Income tax rate stays the same, regardless of taxable income.

Today, all but seven states tax individual income. Two others (Tennessee and New Hampshire) have a very limited personal income tax; they tax only dividend, interest, and capital gains income. (See Table 14–1.) Connecticut was the most recent state to enact an income tax in 1991. Fiscal pressures on state governments continue to stir debate in the non–income tax states over the adoption of the tax. At the same time, several states with income taxes have discussed eliminating them to better compete with neighboring states without them.

Progressive state income taxes—income taxes with rates that rise with increases in income—are usually defended on the **"Ability to pay" principle**; that is, the theory that high-income groups can afford to pay a larger percentage of their income into taxation at no more of a sacrifice than that required of low-income groups who devote a smaller proportion of their income to taxation. The principle of a graduated (progressive) income tax based on ability to pay, a principle accepted at the federal level in 1913 with the passage of the **Sixteenth Amendment**, together with the convenience, economy, and efficiency of income taxes, is generally cited by proponents of income taxation.

State income taxes in several states are **"flat rate"** taxes on personal income; for example, 5 percent in Illinois, 3.07 percent in Pennsylvania, 4.63 percent in Colorado, and

TABLE 14–1 Income Taxation in the States

States without an Individual Income Tax

Alaska	South Dakota	Wyoming
Florida	Texas	
Nevada	Washington	

State Individual Income Tax Rates (rate ranges in parentheses)

Alabama (2.0–5.0)	Louisiana (2.0–6.0)	North Carolina (6.0–7.75)
Arizona (2.59–4.54)	Maine (2.0–8.5)	North Dakota (1.51–3.99)
Arkansas (1.0–7.0)	Maryland (2.0–5.75)	Ohio (0.587–5.925)
California (1.0–9.3)	Massachusetts[a] (5.25)	Oklahoma (0.5–5.25)
Colorado (4.63)	Michigan (4.35)	Oregon (5.0–9.9)
Connecticut (3.0–6.7)	Minnesota (5.35–7.85)	Pennsylvania (3.07)
Delaware (2.2–6.75)	Mississippi (3.0–5.0)	Rhode Island (3.75–5.99)
Georgia (1.0–6.0)	Missouri (1.5–6.0)	South Carolina (3.0–7.0)
Hawaii (1.4–11.0)	Montana (1.0–6.9)	*Tennessee*[b]
Idaho (1.6–7.4)	Nebraska (2.56–6.84)	Utah (5.0)
Illinois (5.0)	*New Hampshire*[b]	Vermont (3.55–8.95)
Indiana (3.4)	New Jersey (1.4–8.97)	Virginia (2.0–5.75)
Iowa (0.36–8.98)	New Mexico (1.7–4.9)	West Virginia (3.0–6.5)
Kansas (3.5–6.45)	New York (4.0–8.82)	Wisconsin (4.6–7.75)
Kentucky (2.0–6.0)		

Note: Data are for 2012.
[a]Flat tax on wages and salaries (5.25), short-term capital gains (12), and other classes of capital gains income (5.30).
[b]State income tax is limited to dividends, interest, and capital gains only.
Source: National Conference of State Legislatures, "State and Personal Income Taxes, 2012." Available at http://www.ncsl.org/issues-research/budget/state-personal-income-taxes-2012.aspx. © 2012 National Conference of State Legislatures.

5.25 percent in Massachusetts. In other income tax states, the rates are "progressive"—rising from 1 or 2 percent, to 7 or 8 percent or more, with increases in income levels. Most states also have their own systems of exemptions.[1]

Corporate Taxes

In addition to property taxes paid to local governments, corporations in 44 states pay a state **corporate income tax**. (Nevada, South Dakota, Texas, Washington, Ohio, and Wyoming do not tax corporate income.) These taxes range from a 4.63 percent flat rate to sliding scales of 1 to 12 percent of net profits. Raising corporate taxes is popular with voters; however, while individuals do not pay corporate taxes directly, these taxes may be passed along to consumers in higher prices. The greatest barrier to higher state corporate taxes is the possibility that such taxes will cause corporations to locate in another state. It is difficult for a state to maintain a "good business climate" if its corporate taxes are high. Most studies find that industrial-location decisions are influenced by many factors other than taxes—for example, access to markets, raw materials, skilled labor, and energy. However, businesses expect their taxes to be kept in line with those of their competitors. In addition to corporate profits taxes, business looks at **unemployment compensation** and **workers' compensation "premiums"** (taxes) and the costs of environmental regulations.

Lottery and Gambling Revenue

Most states now have public lotteries as a means of raising money. However, lotteries bring in just over 2 percent of all state–local government revenue. The administrative costs, including prize money, take over 50 percent of the gross revenue. This compares unfavorably with the estimated 5 percent cost of collecting income taxes, and with the only slightly higher cost of collecting sales taxes. Some states also receive income from horse racing, dog racing, casino gambling, and video gaming devices. Nevada leads the way with 12.5 percent of its own-source general revenue coming directly from gambling taxes. At one time, most states restricted gambling to pari-mutuel betting on the racetrack. But in 2011, the U.S. Department of Justice gave states the right to allow purchase of lottery tickets and online gambling (online poker, roulette, blackjack, and other casino games), as long as the actual betting takes place within the state's boundaries.[2] Opponents of gambling-based revenue sources complain that they are regressive forms of taxation, while supporters say they are a "voluntary" tax—no one has to play. States downplay lottery and gambling as revenue sources, choosing instead to promote them as entertainment. From a player's perspective, the odds are pretty bad.

User Charges

User charges are currently the fastest-growing source of state and local government revenue. Today, charges and miscellaneous revenues constitute nearly 25 percent of state–local revenue. (This figure is really a combination of user charges, utility and liquor store revenues, and miscellaneous revenues.) **User charges** directly link the benefits and costs of public goods in the fashion of the marketplace. Only those persons who actually use the government service pay for it. User charges include charges for water and sewage, garbage collection, electricity supplied by municipalities, transit fares, toll

Lotteries have big jackpots but actually raise less than 2 percent of all state and local government revenue. Administrative costs, including payouts, take over half of the gross revenue.

CORPORATE INCOME TAX

Tax on the net profits of corporations.

UNEMPLOYMENT COMPENSATION

Payment received by unemployed workers who become unemployed through no fault of their own.

WORKERS' COMPENSATION "PREMIUMS"

A form of insurance held by employers that provides medical care and compensation for employees who are injured in the course of employment.

USER CHARGES

A major source of revenue; charges levied on specific users by a government agency for the services they use.

roads, airport landing fees, space rentals, parking meters, stadium fees, and admissions to parks, zoos, and swimming pools. States and localities have gotten creative in getting much-needed revenue from user fees.

14.3 EXPLAINING STATE TAX SYSTEMS

Discuss the differences in tax policy among the states, and explain what accounts for these differences.

What accounts for differences in tax policy among the states? Total state–local *tax revenues* per capita vary from a high of $8,684 per person in Alaska, to a low of $2,769 in Idaho (see "*Rankings of the States:* Per Capita State and Local Government Tax Revenue (Levels) and Tax Burdens"). This means that per capita tax levels of some states are twice as high as those of other states. While Alaska's tax *level* ranks highest, it receives most of its tax revenues from severance taxes on oil and gas. Therefore its *tax burden* does not fall directly on its population.

TAX BURDEN

Taxes as a percent of a person's income; the larger the proportion of the income paid in taxes, the larger the tax burden.

Tax burdens, that is, taxes in relation to personal income, also vary considerably among the states. The concept of tax *burden* generally refers to taxes paid in relation to personal income. Because of differences among the states in income levels, states with the highest per capita *levels of taxation* are not necessarily the same states with the highest *tax burdens*. Alaska has the lowest tax burden. (See "*Rankings of the States:* Per Capita State and Local Government Tax Revenue (Levels) and Tax Burdens," right column.) The state–local tax burden averages about 10 percent of personal income in the United States.

Progressivity and Regressivity

It is difficult to evaluate the overall progressivity or regressivity of state tax systems. It is generally believed that overall state and local government taxes are regressive.[3] This regressivity is largely attributed to state and local government reliance on sales and property taxation, rather than progressive income taxation. However, this belief fails to consider the many types of exemptions to sales taxes found in various states (food, rent, medical care); these exemptions make sales taxes less regressive. It also fails to consider property tax exemptions (**"homestead" exemptions**) found in many states that offer relief to owners of less expensive homes. Nevertheless, it is generally argued that states that rely more on income taxes (especially those states with progressive rate structures rather than flat rates) have more progressive tax systems.[4] Progressivity increases with higher levels of state income. It appears to be easier to make tax systems more progressive when the economic pie is expanding.[5]

HOMESTEAD EXEMPTION

Excludes a certain portion of the value of owner-occupied homes from property taxes.

14.4 REVOLTING AGAINST TAXES AND SPENDING

Describe Americans' attitudes about taxes, various mechanisms that are sometimes used to limit taxes, and the impact of such tax limits.

The United States is the land of tax revolts. The national tradition of revolting against taxes includes the Boston Tea Party in 1773, a leading event in the movement toward independence; Shays' Rebellion in 1786, an important stimulus to creating the Constitution of the United States; the Whisky Rebellion of 1794, forcefully extinguished by President George Washington; and the recent Tea Party protests. The political culture of the nation has always reflected a distrust of government power. The total tax burden in the United States is less than most other advanced industrialized nations of the world. Yet opinion polls regularly show that many Americans believe their taxes are "too high."

Popular Opposition to Rising Taxes

Voters are sensitive to levels of state and local taxation. That is to say, popular dislike of taxes rises with increases in real levels of taxation. (This is not as obvious a conclusion as it might seem; state and local taxes are not as visible to most people as federal taxes, and few people are informed or attentive to state and local matters.) Indeed, as state income taxes rise above 4 percent, levels of dislike begin to rise exponentially.[6] Likewise, when sales tax

Per Capita State and Local Government Tax Revenue (Levels) and Tax Burdens

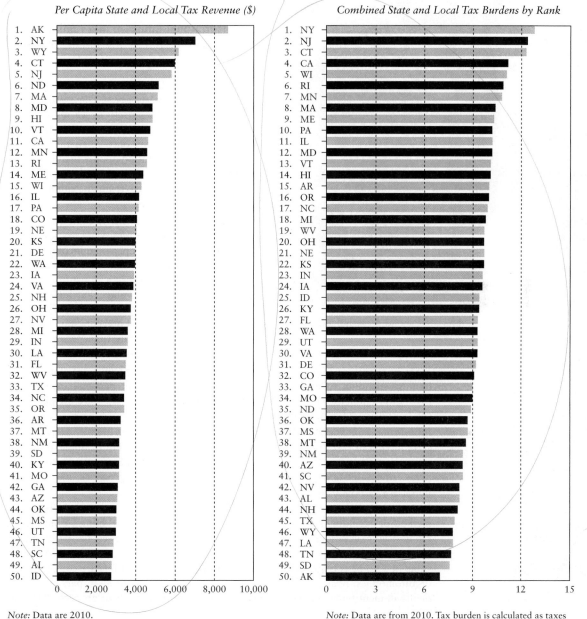

Per Capita State and Local Tax Revenue ($)

Rank	State
1.	AK
2.	NY
3.	WY
4.	CT
5.	NJ
6.	ND
7.	MA
8.	MD
9.	HI
10.	VT
11.	CA
12.	MN
13.	RI
14.	ME
15.	WI
16.	IL
17.	PA
18.	CO
19.	NE
20.	KS
21.	DE
22.	WA
23.	IA
24.	VA
25.	NH
26.	OH
27.	NV
28.	MI
29.	IN
30.	LA
31.	FL
32.	WV
33.	TX
34.	NC
35.	OR
36.	AR
37.	MT
38.	NM
39.	SD
40.	KY
41.	MO
42.	GA
43.	AZ
44.	OK
45.	MS
46.	UT
47.	TN
48.	SC
49.	AL
50.	ID

x-axis: 0, 2,000, 4,000, 6,000, 8,000, 10,000

Combined State and Local Tax Burdens by Rank

Rank	State
1.	NY
2.	NJ
3.	CT
4.	CA
5.	WI
6.	RI
7.	MN
8.	MA
9.	ME
10.	PA
11.	IL
12.	MD
13.	VT
14.	HI
15.	AR
16.	OR
17.	NC
18.	MI
19.	WV
20.	OH
21.	NE
22.	KS
23.	IN
24.	IA
25.	ID
26.	KY
27.	FL
28.	WA
29.	UT
30.	VA
31.	DE
32.	CO
33.	GA
34.	MO
35.	ND
36.	OK
37.	MS
38.	MT
39.	NM
40.	AZ
41.	SC
42.	NV
43.	AL
44.	NH
45.	TX
46.	WY
47.	LA
48.	TN
49.	SD
50.	AK

x-axis: 0, 3, 6, 9, 12, 15

Note: Data are 2010.
Source: U.S. Census Bureau, Governments Division, "State and Local Government Finances: 2009-2010." Available online at http://www.census.gov/govs/estimate/.

Note: Data are from 2010. Tax burden is calculated as taxes as a percent of personal income.
Source: Bureau of Economic Analysis, Department of Commerce, and Tax Foundation calculations. Available at http://taxfoundation.org/sites/taxfoundation.org/files/docs/BP65_2010_Burdens_Report.pdf.

Americans have a long history of protesting against taxes and government spending, especially during recessions.

levels rise above 5 percent, opposition increases rapidly. Homeowners are much more likely to object to property taxation than renters, while renters are more likely to object to sales taxes than homeowners.

Tax Limitations

State constitutional limits on taxes fall into several general categories. Of course, any specific plan may vary in details from the outlines described here.

■ *Property Tax Limits.* Some limitations are specifically directed at property taxes. These proposals may limit allowable tax rates to 10 or 15 mills of full value of property, limit annual assessment increases, and/or allow reassessments only when the property is sold. This form of limitation applies mainly to local governments and school districts and may actually increase state taxes if state governments simply take over local services.

■ *Personal Income Limits.* A somewhat more complex scheme promises to limit state taxes to a certain percentage of the state's personal income. For example, if state taxes currently amount to 7 percent of a state's total personal income, a constitutional amendment could be offered to voters that limits all future state and local taxes to a total of no more than 7 percent of personal income. This prevents state government from growing at a faster rate than personal income, but it does allow tax revenues to rise.

■ *State Expenditure Limits.* Similar restrictions can be placed on total state *expenditures*— limiting spending to a certain percentage of a state's total personal income. Presumably expenditure limits would hold down taxes over the long run, and therefore expenditure limits can be considered as an indirect form of tax limitation.

■ *Prohibitions on Specific Taxes.* State constitutions can be written or amended to prohibit certain types of taxes or require specific types of exemptions. For example, if the state constitution bars an income tax, this is an effective tax limitation. States may also exempt specific items from sales taxes; some common exemptions include groceries, medicines, rents, and purchases by religious, educational, or charitable organizations.

■ *Exemptions and Special Treatments.* The homestead exemption is an increasingly popular method of excluding some part of the value of owner-occupied homes from property taxes. Homestead exemptions go only to homeowners, not to businesses; these exemptions may be expressed in dollar amounts of assessed value (where the first $10,000 or $25,000 of assessed value of a home is nontaxable). **Personal property** tax exemptions are common—exemptions of automobiles, boats, furniture, stocks and bonds, and the like—in part because of the difficulty in identifying and assessing the true value of these types of property. Some states have adopted **circuit breaker programs** that exempt property from taxation for individuals who are poor, aged, or disabled.

Impact of Limits

What impacts have **tax limits** had on the state and local government operations? The consequences of tax limits have been greater for local than for state governments. Constitutional provisions limiting state government taxing or spending have generally failed to have any discernible effect on state taxing or spending levels.[7] However, local property tax limits have had the effect of increasing reliance of local governments on state aid as well as fees and charges.[8]

WHEN SPENDING CUTS ARE NECESSARY: CUTBACK MANAGEMENT

Fiscal stress does *not* refer to the annual struggle to balance the budget without raising taxes or cutting services. This struggle occurs in almost every state, city, county, and school district. **Fiscal stress** refers to a financial condition so unfavorable as to impair borrowing ability, require reduction of services, pose a threat to public health and safety, and thus diminish the quality and satisfaction of life.[9] Fiscal stress occurs when states and localities have large payrolls, large socially dependent populations, and heavy tax burdens, yet an eroding tax base, a weak or declining economy, and population loss.

Outline the sources of fiscal stress in state and local governments, and assess how efforts to relieve this fiscal stress impact citizens.

CIRCUIT BREAKER PROGRAM

Limits the proportion of an individual's income that is used to pay property taxes; designed to protect poor property owners from losing their home as property values escalate.

Fiscal Stress in the States

When the economy slows down, it triggers high levels of fiscal stress in many states. Unemployment rolls rise, consumer spending slows down, corporate earnings decline, housing values drop, people and businesses exit the state, and pressure to help the needy escalates. Balancing budgets becomes a nightmare. The Great Recession of the late 2000s hit a lot of states hard. As the economy slowed, states were forced to cut billions from their budgets. States that rely heavily on residential construction and real estate (property) taxes, including Arizona, Florida, and Nevada, felt the economic downturn earlier than most. But no state was hit harder than California. (See *Up Close*: The Decline of the Golden State.) The situation was so bad that then Governor Arnold Schwarzenegger declared the state on the brink of "financial armageddon."[10] When states find themselves in dire economic circumstances, elected officials have little choice but to make some substantial budget cuts—never an easy decision politically. By the time that level of crisis ensues, most states will already have exhausted most of their "easier" options—hiring freezes, travel cutbacks, delays in **capital spending**, smaller cuts, and as many tax or fee increases as could be done without sparking a citizen revolt.

FISCAL STRESS

Unfavorable financial conditions that impair borrowing ability, require the reduction of services, and may threaten public health and safety.

CAPITAL SPENDING

Spending on buildings, facilities, machinery—expensive items with a multiple-year lifespan.

Fiscal Stress at the Local Level

Fiscal stress has widespread impact at the local level as well.[11] As a city tries to solve its budget problems, it raises taxes; imposes fees; reduces its workforce; cuts back on maintenance of streets, bridges, buildings, and parks; and postpones capital construction projects. These measures further hurt the local economy. Businesses move away and cancel plans to expand. Unemployment increases, and so do demands for help from government. As a city's deficits grow, its bonds become hard to sell to banks and investors. This forces up interest costs that further hurt the city's budget.

Fiscal stress imposes new administrative tasks for mayors and managers. These tasks have been labeled as "**cutback management.**" Managing organizational decline—cutting back on spending and organizational activity, deciding who will be let go, which programs will be scaled down or terminated, and which citizens will be asked to make sacrifices—is not as much fun as managing an expanding organization.

CUTBACK MANAGEMENT

Deciding how to reduce spending and services in order to relieve fiscal stress.

Difficult Decisions

Cutback management presents a host of problems for government officials. These include the following considerations:

- *Resist cutting or smooth the decline.* Should officials resist cutting by claiming it cannot be done without great injury to the city? Should they cut vital and popular programs first in order to stir opposition to the cut? By taking police and firefighters off the streets or closing the schools? By refusing to cut back until paydays are missed and loans are defaulted? Or should officials try to smooth the cutback by cutting low-prestige programs, administrative personnel, social programs, and less vital services?

UP CLOSE   The Decline of the Golden State

California was once a prosperous, industrial, high-tech powerhouse, and a magnet for people across the country. Today it is a heavily taxed, high-spending, highly regulated, chronically broke welfare state that is fast losing its population as well as business and industry.

Since 1990 California has lost over 3.5 million residents, most leaving for Texas, Nevada, and Arizona. Out-migrants are largely middle-class Americans. The very rich and the very poor stay, along with the 1.8 million public employees who collect some of the highest government paychecks in the nation. California's population decline would be even greater if not for legal and illegal immigration, chiefly from Mexico.[a]

Each year California incurs budget deficits of billions of dollars. To cover these deficits, California regularly issues general obligation bonds, borrowing the money to close the gap between revenues and expenditures. As revenues stagnate and spending mushrooms, California goes deeper into debt each year. The result is that California now has the worst credit rating in the nation. Several of its cities, including Stockton, San Bernardino, and Vallejo, have declared bankruptcy. Others are likely to follow. The largest contributing cause to the state's fiscal ruin is the extravagant pension plans enjoyed by public sector employees.

Governor Jerry Brown's solution: a referendum, Proposition 30 in November 2012 that raised state taxes even higher. The sales tax was raised from 7.25 to 7.50 percent, and the top marginal income tax rate was raised from 10.55 to 13.30 percent. Voters approved Proposition 30 by a convincing 56 to 44 percent, following a $40-million public employee union campaign led by the California Teachers Association. At the same time, voters rejected a proposition which would have prevented unions from using automatic payroll deductions to fund political campaigns.

In addition to high taxes and burdensome debt, California ranks near the bottom on indices that measure business climate. Layers of costly regulation, a huge government bureaucracy, union power with compulsory dues paying, combined to drive out existing business and prevent new businesses from forming.

Today California is virtually a one-party state. Democrats hold all statewide offices and enjoy super majorities in both houses of the state legislature. The last Republican Governor, Arnold Schwarzenegger, tried unsuccessfully to limit union power in 2005 by backing four separate initiatives in a special election. One would have required unions to obtain their members consent to use dues for political purposes. A second would have lengthened the time for teachers to receive tenure (it is currently only two years). A third would have slowed the rate of state spending and a fourth would have established an independent commission to draw state and Congressional legislative districts (reducing Democratic advantages). All four were defeated in a union-led $225 million campaign. Schwarzenegger won reelection in 2006 but was virtually powerless for the rest of his time in office.

Recently other states—including Indiana, Wisconsin, and Michigan—have won victories against public-sector unions. Critics of union power argue that taxpayers are subsidizing bloated government workforces that typically enjoy higher pay, lifetime job security, and guaranteed pensions, far in excess of anything in the private sector. But the ruling Democratic Party in California is heavily indebted to public employee and teacher unions.

Is California's decline reversible? As taxes rise, regulations proliferate, and deficits accumulate, middle-class tax-paying residents, as well as businesses, flee the state, further deepening the hole the state has dug for itself. Breaking this cycle will require political leadership and an informed electorate that so far has yet to emerge in the Golden State.

[a]Tom Gray and Robert Scardamalia, *The Great California Exodus* (New York: Manhattan Institute, 2012).

DECREMENTS

Cutbacks made a little at a time, over time.

"ACROSS THE BOARD" CUTS

Every agency or program is cut back by the same percentage during economic downturns.

TARGETED CUTS

Larger spending cuts in some agencies or programs than in others; established by prioritization.

■ *Take one deep gouge or a series of decrements.* Should officials try to improve city finances with a single very difficult year by making one set of deep cuts in the budget? Or should they plan a series of smaller cuts over several years to minimize the impact of the cuts and hope that the financial condition of the city may turn around and the cutting can stop?

■ *Share the pain or target the cuts.* Should city officials cut all programs "**across the board**" in order to minimize pain, avoid conflict, maintain morale, and build team spirit in the organization? Or should they make hard decisions about which programs are not really necessary? **Targeting cuts** requires officials to identify and rank priorities; it generates intense political conflict and tends to be avoided until things get very bad and across-the-board cuts are no longer feasible.

■ *Promote efficiency or equity.* Should city officials favor the most efficient programs, usually police and fire protection and streets and sanitation, over the more costly social-service programs? Or should city officials act to protect the most dependent elements of the population?

Cutback (Retrenchment) Strategies

What strategies can be employed by local governments facing retrenchment? We have attempted to summarize some general strategies available to governments in confronting cutbacks:[12]

▪ *The no-change strategy: across-the-board cuts, seniority retention, and hiring freezes.* Across-the-board cuts appear to be popular. They distribute the pain of budget reductions equally across agencies and among services. However, eventually across-the-board strategies must be abandoned "as officials become aware that the reductions are permanent . . . that equal cuts are not fair, as some programs are more important than others."[13] A hiring freeze is also a convenient and popular short-run strategy to minimize the pain of cutbacks. Hiring freezes rely on "**natural attrition**" through resignations and retirements to cut down the size of the workforce. It does not require politically difficult decisions about which employees are most essential. If natural attrition does not occur fast enough to meet budget deficits, the next strategy is seniority retention. A **"last-in–first-out" rule** in layoffs may be viewed by most employees as fair, although it may result in disproportionate harm to women and minorities if they were recruited to government more recently.

▪ *A hierarchy of community-needs strategy.* An alternative strategy is for cities to set priorities for essential services. Decisions about which services are essential may differ from city to city, but in general we can expect a ranking (from most essential to least essential): public safety (police and fire), public works (streets, sewers, sanitation), administrative services, human services, and leisure services.

▪ *A "privatizing" strategy.* Some city services are "priceable"—users can be charged for them. Cities can charge users for garbage collection, water supply, ambulance service, special police services, transit, licensing, libraries, and recreation. So one retrenchment strategy is to increase the number and types of user charges for city services. A related strategy is to transfer these services to private enterprise (**privatization**) to save money. User charges are politically popular because citizens can "see" what they are buying and they are not forced to buy anything they do not want.

▪ *A reduction in capital spending strategy.* When tough times hit, one of the first responses is to cut back on capital spending—canceling or postponing new equipment purchases, new construction, and major repairs. There are short-term advantages to this strategy; city employees can keep their jobs and service levels can be maintained. But over the longer term, this strategy can produce costly results, as streets, bridges, buildings, and equipment fail. Some capital investments can save money over the long run if they improve productivity and reduce labor costs.

▪ *A reduction in labor strategy.* Cities may finally confront the necessity to reduce personnel costs—hiring freezes, layoffs, renegotiated labor contracts. The most labor-intensive city functions are police and fire protection, together with hospitals and schools in those cities that have these responsibilities. Cutbacks in police and fire personnel are politically unpopular. Indeed, city officials may threaten such cutbacks to force a reconsideration of the rollbacks, but that can backfire if taxpayers feel the government has been wasteful.

EFFICIENCY
Getting the biggest bang for the buck.

EQUITY
Fairness in spending; can be defined in terms of people or geography.

NATURAL ATTRITION
The elimination of jobs due to death, retirement, resignation, transfers, or moving.

"LAST-IN–FIRST-OUT" RULE
When cutbacks have to be made, the last person hired is the first person that has to go.

PRIVATIZATION
Transfer of services to private enterprise, on the premise that a service will be delivered more cheaply than if delivered by government.

OPERATING BUDGET
A plan detailing how much money will be raised from specific revenue sources and what it will be spent on; excludes spending on capital (multi-year) projects.

WHEN ENDS DON'T MEET: STATE AND LOCAL DEBT

14.6

Describe legal restraints on state and local government debt; explain how state and local governments can undertake capital projects nonetheless by issuing bonds; compare and contrast general obligation, revenue, and industrial development bonds; and discuss how the federal tax code treats income from different types of bonds.

What happens when revenues fail to match expenditures in state and local government budgets? Most state constitutions require the operating budget of the state government, and those of local governments as well, to be balanced. In other words, most state constitutions prohibit deficits in **operating budgets**. Revenue estimates must match authorized expenditures in the appropriation act. If actual revenues fail to meet the estimates during the fiscal year, expenditures must be cut so that no deficit occurs at the end of the year.

Capital Financing

However, state constitutions generally permit state and local governments to borrow funds for capital improvements, with provisions for repayment of the debt during the useful life of the project. State and local governments may sell bonds to finance traditional

Spending and Borrowing

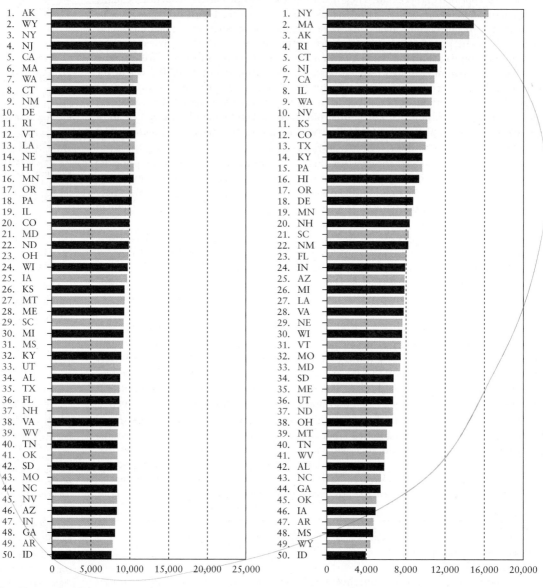

Per Capita State and Local Total Expenditures

1. AK
2. WY
3. NY
4. NJ
5. CA
6. MA
7. WA
8. CT
9. NM
10. DE
11. RI
12. VT
13. LA
14. NE
15. HI
16. MN
17. OR
18. PA
19. IL
20. CO
21. MD
22. ND
23. OH
24. WI
25. IA
26. KS
27. MT
28. ME
29. SC
30. MI
31. MS
32. KY
33. UT
34. AL
35. TX
36. FL
37. NH
38. VA
39. WV
40. TN
41. OK
42. SD
43. MO
44. NC
45. NV
46. AZ
47. IN
48. GA
49. AR
50. ID

0   5,000   10,000   15,000   20,000   25,000

Per Capita State and Local Debt Outstanding

1. NY
2. MA
3. AK
4. RI
5. CT
6. NJ
7. CA
8. IL
9. WA
10. NV
11. KS
12. CO
13. TX
14. KY
15. PA
16. HI
17. OR
18. DE
19. MN
20. NH
21. SC
22. NM
23. FL
24. IN
25. AZ
26. MI
27. LA
28. VA
29. NE
30. WI
31. VT
32. MO
33. MD
34. SD
35. ME
36. UT
37. ND
38. OH
39. MT
40. TN
41. WV
42. AL
43. NC
44. GA
45. OK
46. IA
47. AR
48. MS
49. WY
50. ID

0   4,000   8,000   12,000   16,000   20,000

Note: Data are for 2010.
Source: U.S. Census Bureau, Governments Division, "State and Local Government Finances: 2009-2010." Available online at http://www.census.gov/govs/estimate/.

Note: Data are for 2011.
Source: Tax Foundation, "Facts & Figures: How Does Your State Compare?," 2013, Table 38. Available at http://taxfoundation.org/sites/taxfoundation.org/files/docs/ff2013.pdf.

"essential functions"—roads, schools, parks, libraries, prisons, and government office buildings. These governments may also sell bonds to finance water and sewage systems, airports, ports, mass transportation facilities, solid waste disposal plants, hazardous waste disposal, single- and multifamily housing projects, and hospitals. In the world of municipal finance, these are referred to as "**nonessential functions,**" even though we might argue that they are essential to a community. Finally, government may sell bonds to finance "**private activities**"—industrial development projects, trade and convention centers, and sports arenas.

When governments borrow using bonds, they must pay back the investors who loan them the money, plus interest. (Most individual investors invest in government bonds through mutual funds.) Governments can borrow money more cheaply if they have higher **credit ratings**; the better the credit rating, the lower the interest rate. To get a credit rating on the proposed project for which the government is borrowing, state and local governments can hire three major rating firms: Standard & Poor's, Fitch, or Moody's Investors Service. These firms analyze five factors: the local economy, debt already incurred, financial condition of the government, the demographic makeup of the community, and management practices.

Constitutional Restrictions

State constitutions may place restrictions on these debts in the form of **debt ceilings**, limiting the total amount of money that a government can borrow (usually expressed as a percentage of the total assessed value of taxable property in the community); and **bond referenda provisions**, requiring that any bonded indebtedness (and the taxes imposed to pay off this indebtedness) be approved by the voters in a referendum. These restrictions usually apply only to general obligation bonds.

General Obligation versus Revenue Bonds

Bonds issued by state and local governments may be either general obligation bonds or revenue bonds. **General obligation (GO) bonds** are backed by the "full faith and credit" of the government that issues them. This pledges the full taxing powers of the government to pay both the principal and interest due on the bonds. Because these bonds are more secure, lenders are willing to accept lower interest rates on them. This saves the government (and the taxpayer) money in interest payments. **Revenue bonds** are not guaranteed by the issuing government but instead are backed by whatever revenues the project itself generates. Both the interest and principal of revenue bonds are paid from fees, and charges or rents ("revenues") generated by the project, rather than tax revenues of the government. Because these bonds are not backed by the full taxing powers of the government, lenders face greater risks and therefore require higher interest payments. Revenue bonds are not usually subject to constitutional debt ceilings or referendum requirements, although when the proposed project is extremely costly, elected officials may choose to let the voters decide (e.g., sports stadiums).

Industrial Development Bonds

Competition between municipalities for economic development has led to a vast expansion in **industrial development bonds (IDBs)**. These are revenue bonds issued by a municipality to obtain funds to purchase land and build facilities for private businesses. **Pollution control revenue bonds** are issued by municipalities to obtain funds to provide industries with air and water

Many local governments sell bonds to pay for sports stadiums, roads, libraries, prisons, parks, and other expensive capital improvement projects. The Washington-King County Stadium Authority sold bonds to finance part of the construction of Safeco Field, home of the Seattle Mariners. The rest of the financing came from the owner.

pollution control facilities. Municipalities sometimes issue **single-family mortgage revenue bonds** to assist homebuyers, builders, and developers. Municipalities may issue **hospital revenue bonds** to assist private as well as public hospitals in the community. These types of revenue bonds blur the distinction between public and private business. At one time most state and local indebtedness was in the form of general obligation bonds. But industrial development, pollution control, mortgage revenue, and hospital bonds have become so popular that these nonguaranteed revenue bonds now constitute well over half of the outstanding municipal debt in the nation.

Municipal Bond Interest Deductibility

Traditionally, the federal government did not levy individual or corporate income taxes on the interest that lenders received from state and local government bonds. All municipal bond interest income was deductible from gross income for federal tax purposes. The original rationale for this deductibility was based on the federal ideal: The national government should not interfere with the operations of state governments and their subdivisions. "The power to tax is the power to destroy,"[14] and therefore neither level of government should tax the instrumentalities of the other. Later, this rationale was replaced by more practical considerations: By not taxing municipal bond interest, the federal government was providing an incentive for investment in public infrastructure—schools, streets, hospitals, sewers, and airports. Because the federal government forgoes taxing municipal bond income, we might consider these lost federal revenues as a subsidy to state and local governments and the people who lend money to them.

The deductibility of municipal bond interest from federal income taxation makes these bonds attractive to high-income investors. This attraction allows state and local governments to pay out less interest on their tax-free bonds than corporations must pay out on comparable taxable corporate bonds. Thus, for example, if average *corporate* AAA-rated 30-year bonds are paying 7 percent interest (taxable), average *municipal* AAA-rated 30-year bonds might only pay 5 percent interest (tax free). Many investors would prefer the lower rate because it is tax free. In short, federal deductibility allows state and local governments to borrow money relatively cheaply.

Public Bonds for Private Uses

But controversy arises when private businesses ask municipal governments to issue revenue bonds on their behalf—bonds that businesses use to finance everything from the purchase of single-family homes and the development of luxury apartments, to the building of industrial plants and commercial offices. Business prefers municipal revenue bond financing over its own direct financing because municipal bond interest rates are cheaper owing to federal deductibility. In other words, the issuance of municipal "private-purpose" revenue bonds is really a device to obtain cheaper interest rates for business at the expense of lost revenues to the federal government.

Federal Tax Reform and Municipal Finance

The Federal Tax Reform Act of 1986 distinguishes between **"essential function"** bonds (bonds issued for roads, schools, parks, libraries, prisons, and government buildings), **"nonessential function"** bonds (bonds issued for water and sewer, transportation, multifamily housing, hazardous waste disposal, and health and education facilities), and **"private activities"** bonds (bonds for industrial development, pollution control, parking facilities, and sports and convention centers). Only essential function bond income is completely free of all federal income taxation. Nonessential bond income is subject to the federal alternate minimum tax (AMT), which means it may be taxable if the taxpayer has a large amount of tax-free income. And income from "private-purpose" municipal bonds no longer enjoys tax-free status. These separate treatments complicate the municipal bond market for both governments and investors.

Debt Patterns

In examining total indebtedness, we should consider both general obligation and revenue indebtedness. The total debt per person of all governments within a state ranges from $3,919 in Idaho to $16,364 in New York. (See "*Rankings of the States:* Spending and Borrowing.") Of course, some local governments avoid debt altogether, preferring **"pay-as-you-go" (PAYGO) financing** of capital projects. Indebtedness appears to be greater in cities in the Northeast, cities that undertake a wide variety of functions and services, and cities under fiscal strain.[15]

> **"PAY-AS-YOU-GO" (PAYGO) FINANCING**
> Requires newly proposed expenditures or tax cuts to be accompanied by commensurate increases in revenue or a reduction elsewhere in the budget.

WHEN A LOCAL GOVERNMENT GOES BUST

14.7

Describe what happens when a local government faces bankruptcy, and assess the financial health of U.S. cities in the wake of the Great Recession.

What happens when a city continually spends more than it receives in revenues, when its annual deficits pile up into a huge city debt, when banks and other lenders finally decide not to lend a city any more money? A number of large American cities have gone bust or come close to it, including New York City in 1975, Cleveland in 1979, Philadelphia in 1991, and Washington, DC in 1995. Only about half the states allow their cities to file for bankruptcy.[16] But since 2010, over 30 municipalities and counties have had to declare bankruptcy, including Stockton, California, Harrisburg, Pennsylvania, and Boise County, Idaho.[17]

Instead of officially declaring bankruptcy and having federal bankruptcy courts take over fiscal control, some cities in deep financial trouble have been "rescued" by state and federal governments. Rescue, however, generally requires the city to turn over control of its financial affairs to a control board. Control board members are appointed by the state or federal government. In exchange for an infusion of state or federal money, the control board imposes fiscal discipline on the city. Such a board oversaw New York City's financial recovery. But in the case of Detroit (2013), Michigan Governor Rick Snyder (R) Michigan stepped in and appointed an emergency financial manager to "fix" the Motor City's financial mess, with Mayor David Bing's (D) approval. The governor's appointee, Kevyn Orr, was a 54-year-old African American lawyer and bankruptcy turnaround expert from Washington DC and a graduate of the University of Michigan. He described the monumental task ahead of him as "the Olympics of restructuring" and proclaimed that "If we can do this, I will have participated in one of the greatest turnarounds in the history of this country."[18] At the time Orr stepped in, Detroit was facing massive budget deficits, persistent cash-flow problems, growing long-term liabilities related to employee pension and retiree health care costs, and a poor credit rating. The city had been experiencing a shrinking population for decades. As more people and businesses left the city, there were fewer jobs for those who remained behind and a smaller tax base to support the rising costs of service and infrastructure demands.[19]

Slow Recovery from the Great Recession

It has taken many states and their local governments a long while to recover from the Great Recession, which was the longest and worst economic downturn since the

Detroit's fiscal crisis prompted Michigan Governor Rick Snyder (left) to appoint an Emergency Manager, Kevyn Orr (right). The City of Detroit, which has billions of U.S. dollars in debt, ultimately filed for bankruptcy protection on July 18, 2013. Once the nation's fourth largest city, by the time of its bankruptcy filing, it had slipped to the 18th largest city.

Great Depression. In the past, the normal time for recovery was one to two years, but this time it has taken five years or more for many localities to bounce back.[20] Many still face formidable fiscal challenges in the years ahead, ranging from the sustainability of their public employee pensions and retiree health care benefits to concerns about possible population and job outmigration, aging infrastructure, a stagnant tax base, and the unpredictability of federal funding.

The Goal: Financial Resiliency

FINANCIALLY RESILIENT
Governments that have implemented strategies to balance service levels and resources, fund reserves, capital, and liabilities, and create a culture of flexibility and responsiveness to combat future crises.

The Government Finance Officers Association defines a **financially resilient** government as one that "has recovered its financial stability and gone on to implement strategies, control mechanisms, budgeting techniques, and early warning systems to make sure it can withstand future financial shocks."[21] To reach that status, state and local governments must: (1) balance service levels with available resources; (2) fund reserves, capital, and liabilities; and (3) create a culture that promotes flexibility and responsiveness—innovative and nimble organizations that can react to whatever crisis comes next.[22] Managing government finances is a difficult task, especially when economics collides with politics.

CHAPTER HIGHLIGHTS

- Today, total governmental spending—federal, state, and local—amounts to over one-third of the nation's gross domestic product. State and local governments direct most of their spending toward education, social services, public safety, and transportation.

- Property taxes are the largest source of revenue for *local* governments. The effect is that wealthy communities can raise more revenue with less burden on taxpayers.

- The general sales tax is the largest source of revenue for most state governments. Sales taxes are easier to impose because they are not as visible as income or property taxes.

- All but seven states tax individual income, and all but four states tax corporations (either a flat tax or a percentage of net profits). Other state revenue sources include selective sales taxes (alcohol, cigarettes, gasoline), lottery, and user charges (toll roads).

- Lotteries are popular but they bring in a small portion of total state revenue. States are hopeful they will generate more revenue now that online gambling and lottery ticket purchase is legal.

- The average total tax burden in the United States (10% of personal income) is lighter than in most other industrialized nations. Yet opinion polls regularly show that many Americans believe their taxes are "too high."

- Mindful of antitax sentiment, states have set constitutional limits on property and income taxes as well as state expenditures. In addition, some states prohibit certain taxes and allow tax exemptions (homestead).

- In budget crises, government officials may choose strategies such as imposing across-the-board cuts and hiring freezes, prioritizing programs based on community need, privatizing some services, reducing capital spending, and reducing labor.

- When budgets don't balance, state constitutions generally permit state and local governments to borrow funds for capital improvements by issuing bonds and backing them either by taxing power or the revenues generated by the bond project. The federal government's threat to make municipal bond interest earning taxable has made many local governments very nervous, fearing they would not be able to entice investors to purchase their bonds.

- When a city can no longer borrow its way out of debt, it may declare bankruptcy if state law permits. It could be taken over by the federal courts or be rescued by state or local governments that take over control of its finances through an appointed control board or emergency financial manager, as was the case in Detroit.

- Recovery from the Great Recession has been considerably slower than usual for many states and localities. Many are scrambling to become more sufficiently financially resilient to withstand severe economic downturns in the future.

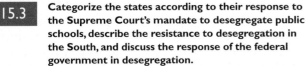

CHAPTER FIFTEEN

POLITICS AND CIVIL RIGHTS

LEARNING OBJECTIVES

15.1 Evaluate the extent to which city government policies have changed as a result of minority incorporation into the political system.

15.2 Trace the legal status of segregation from the Civil War through *Brown* v. *Board of Education*.

15.3 Categorize the states according to their response to the Supreme Court's mandate to desegregate public schools, describe the resistance to desegregation in the South, and discuss the response of the federal government in desegregation.

15.4 Demonstrate how *de facto* segregation results in racial imbalance in public schools, discuss efforts to address this imbalance through bussing, and evaluate whether and under what circumstances such efforts are worthwhile.

15.5 Explain why the Civil Rights Act and fair housing laws were necessary for ensuring the civil rights of African Americans and other minorities.

15.6 Describe how affirmative action programs are designed to increase the equality of results in the United States; outline the Supreme Court decisions related to affirmative action; explain why some are opposed to affirmative action; and discuss the efforts they have pursued to end the practice.

15.7 Describe the size of the Hispanic population in the United States; and outline the characteristics of Mexican Americans, Puerto Ricans, and Cuban Americans.

427

15.8 Trace the political mobilization and voter turnout of Hispanics, and describe their partisanship and ideology.

 15.9 Trace the history of the legal relationships between the United States and Indian nations, and describe the current status and governments of Indian nations.

15.10 Describe the extent to which the American population is disabled, and describe the protections afforded to Americans with disabilities through the Americans with Disabilities Act.

 15.11 Describe the prohibitions against age discrimination afforded to Americans.

 15.12 Describe the prohibitions against gender discrimination that are codified in federal law and Supreme Court decisions, describe the earnings gap between men and women, and evaluate whether comparable worth should be instituted to narrow this gap.

 15.13 Compare "pro-life" and "pro-choice" attitudes about abortion, trace abortion restrictions imposed by the states at various times, and discuss the Supreme Court decisions related to abortion.

 15.14 Trace the expansion of gay rights from the Stonewall riots through the Supreme Court's recent decision about the Defense of Marriage Act, and list various gay rights issue areas that are covered by state laws.

15.1

Evaluate the extent to which city government policies have changed as a result of minority incorporation into the political system.

FROM PROTEST TO POWER

African Americans and Hispanics have made significant progress in urban politics in recent years. The progress of these minorities in city government has important implications for the future of the American political system because these are the two largest minority groups in the country. Minorities were almost totally excluded from significant influence in city politics prior to the 1960s. We have already discussed increases in minority representation in city councils (Chapter 11) and state legislatures (Chapter 6), and minority political power in the nation's largest cities is a recognized fact of American politics. As former Atlanta Mayor Andrew Young said, "It's like the old preacher says: we ain't what we oughta be; we ain't what we gonna be; but thank God we ain't what we was."[1] While the earliest civil rights fights in the states primarily focused on racial discrimination, in recent years the battles have extended to gender, age, disability, and sexual preference.

Policy Consequences of Minority Representation

Do city government policies change as a result of minority incorporation into the political system? Black elected officials in cities perceive poverty and unemployment as more severe problems than do white officials in the same cities; and black officeholders are more likely to add race relations and racial balance in the distribution of city jobs and services to the policy agenda.[2] Another consequence of the election of blacks to public office, especially the mayor's office, is an increase in political participation among black citizens.[3] And it appears that the election of black mayors reduces fears among whites about the consequences of electing blacks and reduces racial polarization in voting.[4]

But many city government policies, especially taxing and spending policies, are severely constrained by economic conditions and by limits and mandates set by the state and federal governments.[5] So it is unrealistic to expect major shifts in these policies to accompany the election of African Americans or Hispanics to city office. The policies that respond to minority representation in city government are those that deal directly with minority presence in government. Broad taxing and spending policies are largely unaffected by minority influence in government. Examples of the kind of policy changes directly attributable to minority representation in government include the creation of police review boards, the appointment of more minorities to city boards and commissions, increasing use of minority contractors, and a general increase in the number of programs oriented toward minorities. Perhaps the most significant policy impact of minority representation on city councils is an increase in the number of minorities in city employment and their employment in higher-grade positions.[6] Even though minorities are still underrepresented in some communities, their gains have been impressive, especially in light of the legal barriers that existed for decades.

THE STRUGGLE AGAINST SEGREGATION

Trace the legal status of segregation from the Civil War through *Brown v. Board of Education*.

The Fourteenth Amendment of the U.S. Constitution declares:

> All persons born or naturalized in the United States, and subject to the jurisdiction thereof, are citizens of the United States and of the State wherein they reside. No State shall make or enforce any law which shall abridge the privileges or immunities of citizens of the United States; nor shall any State deprive any person of life, liberty, or property, without due process of law; nor deny to any person within its jurisdiction the equal protection of the laws.

The language of the Fourteenth Amendment and its post–Civil War historical context leave little doubt that its original purpose was to achieve the full measure of citizenship and equality for African Americans. Some "radical" Republicans were prepared in 1867 to carry out the revolution in southern society that this amendment implied. Under military occupation, southern states adopted new constitutions that awarded the vote and full civil liberties to African Americans, and southern states were compelled to ratify the Thirteenth, Fourteenth, and Fifteenth Amendments to the U.S. Constitution. African Americans were elected to southern state legislatures and to the Congress; the first African American to serve in Congress, Hiram R. Revels, took over the U.S. Senate seat from Mississippi previously held by Confederate President Jefferson Davis.

However, by 1877 Reconstruction was abandoned. The national government was not willing to carry out the long and difficult task of really reconstructing society in the 11 states of the former Confederacy.[7] In what has been described as the "Compromise of 1877," the national government agreed to end military occupation of the South, give up its efforts to rearrange southern society, and lend tacit approval to white supremacy in that region. In return, the southern states pledged their support of the Union, accepted national supremacy, and agreed to permit the Republican candidate, Rutherford B. Hayes, to assume the presidency after the disputed election of 1876.

"Separate but Equal"

The U.S. Supreme Court adhered to the terms of the compromise. The result was an inversion of the meaning of the Fourteenth Amendment so that by 1896 it had become a bulwark of **segregation**. State laws segregating the races were upheld so long as persons in each of the separated races were treated equally. The constitutional argument on behalf of segregation under the Fourteenth Amendment was that the phrase "equal protection of the laws" did not prevent state-enforced separation of the races. Schools and other public facilities that were **"separate but equal"** won constitutional approval.[8] This separate but equal doctrine remained the Supreme Court's interpretation of the Equal Protection Clause of the Fourteenth Amendment until 1954.

As a matter of fact, of course, segregated facilities, including public schools, were seldom if ever equal, even with respect to physical conditions. In practice, the doctrine of segregation was "separate and unequal." The Supreme Court began to take notice of this after World War II. While it declined to overrule the segregationist interpretation of the Fourteenth Amendment, it began to order the admission of individual blacks to white public universities, where evidence indicated that separate black institutions were inferior or nonexistent.[9]

NAACP

Leaders of the newly emerging civil rights movement in the 1940s and 1950s were not satisfied with court decisions that examined the circumstances in each case to determine if separate school facilities were really equal. The National Association for the Advancement of Colored People (**NAACP**), led by Roy Wilkins, its executive director, and Thurgood Marshall, its chief counsel, pressed for a court decision that segregation itself meant inequality within the meaning of the Fourteenth Amendment, whether or not facilities were equal in all tangible respects. In short, they wanted a complete reversal of the "separate

---

SEGREGATION

Separation of people by race; mandated by law in schools and public facilities in southern states prior to the U.S. Supreme Court decision in *Brown v. Board of Education of Topeka* in 1954, and prior to the Civil Rights Act of 1964.

"SEPARATE BUT EQUAL"

The ruling by the U.S. Supreme Court in 1896 that segregated facilities were lawful as long as the facilities were equal; a ruling reversed by the Court in *Brown v. Board of Education of Topeka* in 1954.

NAACP

The largest African American civil rights organization; sponsored historic desegregation case in 1954.

The 1954 *Brown v. Board of Education* ruling by the U.S. Supreme Court declared that segregation in public schools is unconstitutional. Here the jubilant attorneys who successfully argued the case against segregation, George E. C. Hayes, Thurgood Marshall, and James Nabrit, Jr., stand arm-in-arm on the steps of the Court. Thurgood Marshall would later become a U.S. Supreme Court Justice.

but equal" interpretation of the Fourteenth Amendment, and a holding that laws *separating* the races were unconstitutional.

The civil rights groups chose to bring suit for desegregation in Topeka, Kansas, where segregated black and white schools were equal with respect to buildings, curricula, qualifications and salaries of teachers, and other tangible factors. The legal strategy was to prevent the Court from ordering the admission of a black because *tangible* facilities were not equal and to force the Court to review the doctrine of segregation itself.

Brown v. Board of Education of Topeka

On May 17, 1954, the Court rendered its decision in *Brown* v. *Board of Education of Topeka, Kansas*:

> Segregation of white and colored children in public schools has a detrimental effect upon the colored children. The impact is greater when it has the sanction of law, for the policy of separating the races is usually interpreted as denoting the inferiority of the Negro group. A sense of inferiority affects the motivation of a child to learn. Segregation with the sanction of law, therefore, has a tendency to retard the educational and mental development of Negro children and to deprive them of some of the benefits they would receive in a racially integrated school system.[10]

The symbolic importance of the original *Brown* v. *Board of Education of Topeka* decision cannot be overestimated. While it would be many years before any significant number of black children would attend formerly segregated white schools, the decision by the nation's highest court undoubtedly stimulated black hopes and expectations. African American sociologist Kenneth Clark wrote:

> This [civil rights] movement would probably not have existed at all were it not for the 1954 Supreme Court school desegregation decision which provided a tremendous boost to the morale of Negroes by its *clear* affirmation that color is irrelevant to the rights of American citizens. Until this time the Southern Negro generally had accommodated to the separatism of the black from the white society.[11]

STATE RESISTANCE TO DESEGREGATION

The Supreme Court had spoken forcefully in the *Brown* case in 1954 in declaring segregation unconstitutional. From a constitutional viewpoint, any state-supported segregation of the races after 1954 was prohibited. Article VI of the Constitution declares that the words of that document are "the supreme law of the land . . . anything in the constitution or laws of any state to the contrary notwithstanding." From a political viewpoint, however, the battle over segregation was just beginning.

Segregation in the States

In 1954, the practice of segregation was widespread and deeply ingrained in American life. Seventeen states required the segregation of the races in public schools. These 17 were:

Alabama	Louisiana	South Carolina
Arkansas	Maryland	Tennessee
Delaware	Mississippi	Texas
Florida	Missouri	Virginia
Georgia	North Carolina	West Virginia
Kentucky	Oklahoma	

The Congress of the United States required the segregation of the races in the public schools of the District of Columbia.[12] Four additional states—Arizona, Kansas, New Mexico, and Wyoming—authorized segregation upon the option of local school boards. (See Figure 15–1.)

Thus, in deciding *Brown* v. *Board of Education of Topeka, Kansas* the U.S. Supreme Court struck down the laws of 21 states and the District of Columbia in a single opinion. Such a far-reaching decision was bound to meet with difficulties in implementation. The Supreme Court did not order immediate nationwide desegregation, but instead it turned over the responsibility for desegregation to state and local authorities under the supervision of federal district courts.

The six border states with segregated school systems—Delaware, Kentucky, Maryland, Missouri, Oklahoma, and West Virginia—together with the school districts in Kansas, Arizona, and New Mexico that had operated segregated schools, chose not to resist desegregation. The District of Columbia also desegregated its public schools the year following the Supreme Court's decision.

Resistance

Resistance to school integration was the policy of the 11 states of the Old Confederacy. Refusal of a school district to desegregate until it was faced with a federal court injunction was the most common form of delay. Other schemes included state payment of private school tuition in lieu of providing public schools, amending compulsory attendance laws to provide that no child shall be required to attend an integrated school, requiring schools faced with desegregation orders to cease operation, and the use of pupil-placement laws to avoid or minimize the extent of integration. State officials also attempted to delay desegregation on the grounds that it would endanger public safety.[13] On the whole, those states that chose to resist desegregation were quite successful in doing so during the 10-year period from 1954 to 1964. Ten years after *Brown* v. *Board of Education of Topeka,* only about 2 percent of the black schoolchildren in the 11 southern states were attending integrated schools.

FIGURE 15–1 Segregation Laws in the United States in 1954

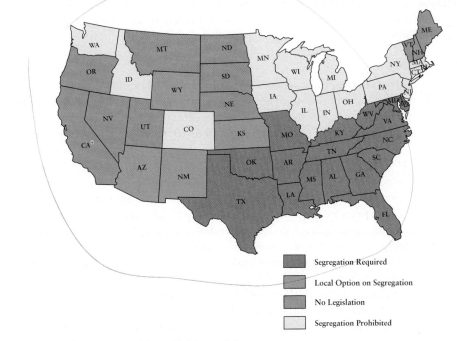

Segregation Required
Local Option on Segregation
No Legislation
Segregation Prohibited

Source: Library of Congress United States, Washington, DC.

Federal Funds

In the Civil Rights Act of 1964, Congress finally entered the civil rights field in support of court efforts to achieve desegregation. Among other things, the Civil Rights Act of 1964 provided that every federal department and agency must take action to end segregation in all programs and activities receiving federal financial assistance. It was specified that this action was to include termination of financial assistance if states and communities receiving federal funds refused to comply with federal desegregation orders. Acting under the authority of Title VI of the Act, the U.S. Office of Education (now the Department of Education) required all school districts in the 17 formerly segregated states to submit desegregation plans as a condition of federal assistance. Progress toward desegregation was speeded up.

Unitary Schools

The last vestige of legal justification for delay in implementing school desegregation collapsed in 1969 when the U.S. Supreme Court rejected a request by Mississippi school officials for a delay in implementing school desegregation plans in that state. The Supreme Court declared that every school district was obligated to end dual school systems "at once" and "now and hereafter" to operate only unitary schools.[14] The effect of the decision—15 years after the original *Brown* case—was to eliminate any further legal justification for the continuation of segregation in public schools.

15.4

Demonstrate how *de facto* **segregation results in racial imbalance in public schools, discuss efforts to address this imbalance through bussing, and evaluate whether and under what circumstances such efforts are worthwhile.**

DE FACTO SEGREGATION

Racial imbalances not directly caused by official action but rather by neighborhood residential patterns.

BUSING

In public schools, the attempt to overcome racial imbalances by assigning pupils to schools by race rather than residence and therefore requiring the busing of students.

RACIAL BALANCING IN SCHOOLS

In *Brown* v. *Board of Education of Topeka, Kansas,* the Supreme Court found that segregation had "a tendency to retard the educational and mental development of Negro children and to deprive them of some of the benefits they would receive in a racially integrated school system." The U.S. Civil Rights Commission reported that even when segregation was **"de facto,"** that is, a product of segregated housing patterns and neighborhood schools rather than direct discrimination, the adverse effects on African American students were still significant.[15] In northern urban school districts, the commission reported, predominantly black schools were less likely to have good libraries or advanced courses in the sciences and languages than predominantly white schools and more likely to have overcrowded classrooms, poorly trained teachers, and teachers who were dissatisfied with their school assignments.

Racial Balance

Ending racial isolation in the public schools frequently involved **busing** schoolchildren into and out of segregated neighborhoods. The objective was to achieve a racial "balance" in public schools, so that each had roughly the same percentages of minorities and whites as are found in the total population of the entire school district.

Federal Court Supervision

Federal district judges enjoy wide freedom in fashioning remedies for past or present discriminatory practices by governments. If a federal district court anywhere in the United States finds that any actions by governments or school officials have contributed to racial imbalances (e.g., in drawing school district attendance lines), the judge may order the adoption of a desegregation plan to overcome racial imbalances produced by official action. A large number of cities have come under federal district court orders to improve racial balances in their schools through busing.

   In the case of *Swan* v. *Charlotte–Mecklenburg Board of Education,* the Supreme Court upheld (1) the use of racial balance requirements in schools and the assignment of pupils to schools based on race, (2) "close scrutiny" by judges of schools that are predominantly of one race, (3) gerrymandering of school attendance zones as well as "clustering" or "grouping" of schools to achieve equal balance, and (4) court-ordered busing of pupils to achieve racial balance.[16] The Court was careful to note, however, that racial imbalance in schools is not itself grounds for ordering these remedies, unless it is also shown that some present or past governmental action contributed to the imbalance.

Cross-District Busing

In the absence of any governmental actions contributing to racial imbalance, states and school districts are *not* required by the Fourteenth Amendment to integrate their schools. Thus, for example, where central-city schools are predominantly black, and suburban schools are predominantly white, owing to residential patterns, cross-district busing is not constitutionally required, unless it is shown that some official action brought about these racial imbalances. The Supreme Court threw out a lower federal court order for massive busing of students between Detroit and 52 suburban school districts. Although Detroit city schools were 70 percent black, none of the Detroit-area suburban school districts segregated students within their own boundaries.[17] This important decision means the largely black central cities, surrounded by largely white suburbs, will remain de facto segregated because there are not enough white students living within the city to achieve integration.

When Is Desegregation Complete?

Many school districts in the South and elsewhere have operated under federal court supervision for many years. How long should court supervision continue, and what standards are to be used in determining when desegregation has been achieved once and for all? In recent years, the Supreme Court has undertaken to free some school districts from direct federal court supervision. Where the last vestiges of state-sanctioned discrimination have been removed "as far as practicable," the Supreme Court has allowed lower federal courts to dissolve racial balancing plans even though imbalances due to residential patterns continue to exist.[18]

When Is Racial Balancing Constitutional?

All racial classifications by governments are subject to **strict scrutiny** by the courts. This means that racial classifications must be "narrowly tailored" to achieve a "compelling government interest."[19] School districts that engage in racial balancing must show that the interest they seek to achieve is a compelling one and that the means they have chosen are the least disruptive of all the means available.

When a Seattle school district voluntarily adopted student assignment plans that relied on race to determine which schools certain children would attend, the U.S. Supreme Court held that the district had violated the Fourteenth Amendment's guarantee of equal protection of the laws.[20] (In as much as the Seattle district had no history of segregation, its racial balancing was subject to the strict scrutiny test.) The Court reasoned that although achieving "diversity" in the student body may be a compelling interest in a university context,[21] it was not proven to be a compelling interest in public elementary and secondary schools. Moreover, the Seattle district's racial balancing plan was not narrowly tailored; the district failed to consider race-neutral assignment plans that might achieve the same interest in racial diversity. The Court noted that the Seattle plan considered race exclusively and not in a broader definition of diversity. The effect of the decision is to force school districts across the country to reconsider voluntary racial balancing plans.

STRICT SCRUTINY
Supreme Court standard used to determine whether a law has violated a person's or group's rights under the due process and equal protection clause of the U.S. Constitution

Continuing Racial Separation and "White Flight"

Minority students now comprise the overwhelming majority of public school pupils in many large cities (including Detroit, Philadelphia, Boston, Atlanta, Chicago, Baltimore, Cleveland, Memphis, New Orleans, Newark (NJ), Richmond, St. Louis, and Washington, DC). In some

"WHITE FLIGHT"

The movement of white residents to suburbs in response to increasing numbers and percentages of minorities in neighborhoods and schools in the central cities.

cities, where extensive busing was employed, **"white flight"** from the public schools was so widespread that the schools ended up more racially separated than before racial balancing was imposed.[22] Racial separation in public schools has actually *increased* in many areas where neighborhoods have become more segregated. Some 43 percent of Latinos and 38 percent of African American students attend schools where fewer than 10 percent of their classmates are white. Reflecting residential patterns, segregation of Latino students is most common in California, New York, and Texas. For AfricanAmericans, it is highest in Atlanta, Chicago, Detroit, Houston, Philadelphia, and Washington, DC.[23]

15.5 THE CIVIL RIGHTS ACT OF 1964

Explain why the Civil Rights Act and fair housing laws were necessary for ensuring the civil rights of African Americans and other minorities.

The initial objective of the civil rights movement in America was to prevent discrimination and segregation as practiced by or supported by *governments*, particularly states, municipalities, and school districts. However, even while important victories for the civil rights movement were being recorded in the prevention of discrimination by governments, particularly in the *Brown* case, the movement began to broaden its objectives to include the elimination of discrimination in all segments of American life, private as well as public.

The Constitution does not govern the activities of private individuals. It is the laws of Congress and the states that govern the conduct of private individuals. When the civil rights movement turned to combating private discrimination, it had to carry its fight into the legislative branch of government. The federal courts could help restrict discrimination by state and local governments and school authorities, but only Congress, state legislatures, and city councils could restrict discrimination practiced by private owners of restaurants, hotels and motels, private employers, and other individuals who were not government officials.

The Civil Rights Act of 1964 passed both houses of Congress by better than a two-thirds favorable vote; it won the overwhelming support of both Republican and Democratic members of Congress. It was signed into law on July 4, 1964. It ranks with the Emancipation Proclamation, the Fourteenth Amendment, and *Brown* v. *Board of Education of Topeka* as one of the most important steps toward full equality for African Americans in America. (See "*People in Politics*: Martin Luther King, Jr.")

Among other things, the Civil Rights Act of 1964 provides:

The fight against racial discrimination has become an international effort.

- That it is unlawful to discriminate or segregate persons on the grounds of race, color, religion, or national origin in any place of public accommodation, including hotels, motels, restaurants, movie theaters, sports arenas, entertainment houses, and other places that offer to serve the public. This prohibition extends to all establishments whose operations affect interstate commerce or whose discriminatory practices are supported by state action. (Title II)

- That each federal department and agency shall take action to end discrimination in all programs or activities receiving federal financial assistance in any form. This action shall include termination of financial assistance. (Title VI)

- That it shall be unlawful for any employer or labor union with twenty-five or more persons after 1965 to discriminate against any individual in any fashion in employment, because of the person's race, color, religion, sex, or national origin, and that an Equal Employment Opportunity Commission shall be established to enforce this provision by investigation, conference, conciliation, persuasion, and, if need be, civil action in federal court. (Title VII)[24]

Fair Housing

Discrimination in the sale and rental of housing was the last major civil rights problem on which Congress took action. Discrimination in housing had not been mentioned in any previous legislation; even the comprehensive

Martin Luther King, Jr.

The leadership in the struggle to eliminate discrimination and segregation from private life was provided by a young African American minister, Martin Luther King, Jr. King's father was the pastor of one of the South's largest and most influential congregations, the Ebenezer Baptist Church in Atlanta, Georgia. Martin Luther King, Jr., received his doctorate from Boston University and began his ministry in Montgomery, Alabama. In 1955 the black community of Montgomery began a yearlong boycott with frequent demonstrations against the Montgomery city buses over segregated seating practices. The dramatic appeal and the eventual success of the boycott in Montgomery brought nation-wide attention to its leader and led to the creation in 1957 of the Southern Christian Leadership Conference.

Nonviolent Direct Action

Under King's leadership, the civil rights movement developed and refined political techniques for minorities in American politics, including *nonviolent direct action.* Nonviolent direct action is a form of protest that involves breaking "unjust" laws in an open, "loving," nonviolent fashion. The general notion of civil disobedience is not new; it played an important role in American history from the Boston Tea Party to the abolitionists who illegally hid runaway slaves, to the suffragettes who demonstrated for women's voting rights, to the labor organizers who formed the nation's major industrial unions, to the civil rights workers of the early 1960s who deliberately violated segregation laws. The purpose of nonviolent direct action is to call attention, or to "bear witness," to the existence of injustice. In the words of Martin Luther King, Jr., civil disobedience "seeks to dramatize the issue so that it can no longer be ignored." There should be no violence in true civil disobedience, and

only "unjust" laws are broken. Moreover, the law is broken "openly, lovingly," with a willingness to accept the penalty.[a]

Marches in Birmingham and Washington

Perhaps the most dramatic confrontation between the civil rights movement and the southern segregationists occurred in Birmingham, Alabama, in the spring of 1963. In support of a request for desegregation of downtown eating places and the formation of a biracial committee to work out the integration of public schools, Martin Luther King, Jr., led several thousand Birmingham blacks in a series of orderly street marches. The demonstrators were met with strong police action, including fire hoses, police dogs, and electric cattle prods. Newspaper pictures of blacks being attacked by police and bitten by dogs were flashed all over the world. More than 2,500 demonstrators, including Dr. King, were jailed.

The Birmingham protest set off demonstrations in many parts of the country; the theme remained one of nonviolence, and it was usually whites rather than blacks who resorted to violence in these demonstrations. The culmination of the nonviolent philosophy was a giant, yet orderly, march on Washington, held on August 28, 1963. More than 200,000 blacks and whites participated in the march, which was endorsed by various labor leaders, religious groups, and political figures. The march ended at the Lincoln Memorial where Martin Luther King, Jr., delivered his most eloquent appeal, "I Have a Dream."[b]

It was in response to this march that President John F. Kennedy sent a strong civil rights bill to Congress, which was passed after his death—the landmark Civil Rights Act of 1964. On the night of April 4, 1968, the world's leading voice of nonviolence was killed by an assassin's bullet.

[a]Martin Luther King, Jr., "Letter from Birmingham City Jail," April 16, 1963.
[b]Martin Luther King, Jr., August 28, 1963, at the Lincoln Memorial, Washington, DC.

Civil Rights Act of 1964 made no reference to housing. Prohibiting discrimination in the sale or rental of housing affected the constituencies of northern members of Congress more than any of the earlier, southern-oriented legislation. The prospects for a **fair housing** law were not very good at the beginning of 1968. When Martin Luther King, Jr., was assassinated, however, the mood of the nation and of Congress changed dramatically, and many felt that Congress should pass a fair housing law as a tribute to the slain civil rights leader. The Civil Rights Act of 1968 prohibited the following forms of discrimination:

FAIR HOUSING
Anti-discrimination in the sale and rental of housing to minorities.

- Refusal to sell or rent a dwelling to any person because of race, color, religion, or national origin.
- Discrimination against a person in the terms, conditions, or privileges of the sale or rental of a dwelling, or advertising the sale or rental of a dwelling indicating a preference or discrimination based on race, color, religion, or national origin.

The Act applied to all apartments and houses, rented or sold by either real estate developers or by private individuals who used the services of real estate agents. It exempted private individuals who sold their own homes without the services of a real estate agent, provided they did not indicate any preference or discrimination in advertising in the sale or rental of a house.

15.6

AFFIRMATIVE ACTION BATTLES

Describe how affirmative action programs are designed to increase the equality of results in the United States; outline the Supreme Court decisions related to affirmative action; explain why some are opposed to affirmative action; and discuss the efforts they have pursued to end the practice.

Although the gains of the civil rights movement were immensely important, they were primarily gains in *opportunity* rather than in *results*. The civil rights movement of the 1960s did not bring about major changes in the conditions under which most African Americans lived in America. Racial politics today center on the actual inequalities between minorities and whites in incomes, jobs, housing, health, education, and other conditions of life.

Continuing Inequalities

The issue of black-white inequality is often posed today as differences in the "life chances" of whites, blacks, and Hispanics. Figures can reveal only the bare outline of the life chances in American society. (See Table 15–1.) The median income of a black family is 63 percent of the average white family's income. Over 20 percent of all black families are below the recognized poverty line, while less than 10 percent of white families live in poverty. The unemployment rate for blacks is almost twice as high as that for whites. Blacks and Hispanics are less likely to hold prestigious white-collar jobs in professional, managerial, clerical, or sales work. They do not hold many skilled craft jobs in industry but are concentrated in operative, service, and laboring positions. The civil rights movement opened up new opportunities for black and Hispanic Americans. But equality of *opportunity* is not the same as *absolute* equality.

Policy Choices

What public policies should be pursued to achieve equality in America? Is it sufficient that government eliminate discrimination, guarantee "equality of opportunity," and apply "color-blind" standards to both minorities and whites? Or should government take "affirmative action" to overcome the results of past unequal treatment of minorities—that is, preferential or compensatory treatment to assist minority applicants for university admissions and scholarships, job hiring and promotion, and other opportunities for advancement in life?

The early emphasis of government policy, of course, was nondiscrimination. This approach began with President Harry Truman's decision to desegregate the armed forces in 1948 and was carried through to Title VI and Title VII of the Civil Rights Act of 1964 to eliminate discrimination in federally aided projects and private employment. Gradually, however, policy shifted from the traditional aim of *equality of opportunity* through nondiscrimination alone to affirmative action to establish "goals and timetables" to achieve greater *equality of results* between minorities and whites. While avoiding the term quota, the notion of affirmative action tests the success of equal opportunity by observing whether minorities achieve admissions, jobs, and promotions in proportion to their numbers in the population.

Constitutional Issues—The Bakke Case

The constitutional question posed by "**affirmative action**" programs is whether or not they discriminate against whites in violation of the Equal Protection Clause of the Fourteenth Amendment. The U.S. Supreme Court first dealt directly with this question in *Regents of the University of California v. Bakke* (1978).[25] The Court struck down a special admissions program for minorities at a state medical school on the grounds that it excluded a white applicant because of his race and violated his rights under the Equal Protection Clause. Allan

AFFIRMATIVE ACTION

Programs pursued by governments or private businesses to overcome the results of past discriminatory treatment of minorities and/or women by giving these groups special or preferential treatment in employment, promotion, admissions, and other activities.

REGENTS OF THE UNIVERSITY OF CALIFORNIA V. BAKKE

Early case challenging affirmative action; ruling that race may be *considered* a "plus" factor but banning specific quotas.

TABLE 15–1 Minority Life Chances

Median Income of Families				
Race	1980	1990	2000	2009
White	38,621	41,668	45,860	51,861
Black	22,250	24,917	30,980	32,584
Asian and Pacific Islander	N/A	51,299	58,255	65,469
Hispanic[a]	28,218	29,792	34,636	38,039

Percentage of Persons below Poverty Level				
Race	1980	1990	2000	2009
White	10.2	10.7	9.5	9.3
Black	32.5	31.9	22.5	22.7
Asian and Pacific Islander	N/A	12.2	9.9	9.4
Hispanic[a]	25.7	28.1	21.5	22.7

Unemployment Rate			
Race	1992	2000	2010
White	5.5	2.6	8.7
Black	11.0	5.4	16
Asian and Pacific Islander	N/A	2.7	7.5
Hispanic[a]	9.8	4.4	12.5

[a]Persons of Hispanic origin may be any race.
Source: U.S. Census Bureau, Statistical Abstract of the United States, 2012, Tables 622, 690, 715. Available at http://www.census.gov/compendia/statab/2012edition.html.

Bakke applied to the University of California Davis Medical School two consecutive years and was rejected; in both years black applicants with significantly lower grade point averages and medical aptitude test scores were accepted through a special admissions program that reserved sixteen minority places in a class of one hundred.[26] The University of California did not deny that its admission decisions were based on race. Instead, it argued that its racial classification was "benign," that is, designed to assist minorities, not to hinder them. The Supreme Court held that race and ethnic origin *may* be considered in reviewing applications to a state school without violating the Equal Protection Clause. However, the Court held that a *separate* admissions program for minorities with a specific quota of openings that were unavailable to white applicants violated the Equal Protection Clause. The Court ordered Bakke admitted to medical school and the elimination of the special admissions program. It recommended that California consider an admissions program developed at Harvard that considered disadvantaged racial or ethnic background as a "plus" in an overall evaluation of an application but did not set numerical quotas or exclude any persons from competing for all positions. Since the Bakke decision, there been a number of challenges to the continued use of affirmative action in university admissions. (See "*Up Close:* "Diversity" in Universities: Continued Legal Challenges to Affirmative Action in Admissions.")

Affirmative Action as a Remedy for Past Discrimination

The Supreme Court has generally approved of affirmative action programs when there was evidence of past discriminatory practices. In *United Steelworkers of America* v. *Weber* (1979), the Supreme Court approved a plan developed by a private employer and a union to reserve 50 percent of higher paying, skilled jobs for minorities.[27] In *United States* v. *Paradise* (1987), the Court upheld a rigid 50 percent black quota system for promotions

"Diversity" in Universities: Continued Legal Challenges to Affirmative Action in Admissions

Most colleges and universities in the United States—public as well as private—specify "diversity" as an institutional goal. The term refers to racial and ethnic representation in student body and faculty.

University administrators argue that students benefit when they interact with others from different cultural heritages. There are claims that racial and ethnic diversity on the campus improve students' "self-evaluation," "social-historical thinking," and "intellectual engagement." There is some evidence that students admitted under policies designed to increase diversity do well in post-college careers. But despite numerous efforts to develop scientific evidence that racial or ethnic diversity on the campus improves learning, no definitive conclusions have emerged. Educational research on this topic is clouded by political and ideological conflict. There is no conclusive evidence that racial diversity does in fact promote the expression of ideas on campus or change perspectives or viewpoints of students.

Diversity requires racial classifications and the U.S. Supreme Court has held that such classifications be subject to "strict scrutiny." The Supreme Court held in 2003 that diversity may be a "compelling government interest" because it "promotes cross-racial understanding, helps break down racial stereotypes, and enables [students] to better understand persons of different races." This opinion was written by Justice Sandra Day O'Connor in a case involving the University of Michigan Law School's affirmative action program. In a 5–4 decision, O'Connor said that the Constitution "does not prohibit the law school's narrowly tailored use of race in admissions decisions to further a compelling interest in obtaining the educational benefits that flow from a diverse student body."[a]

However, in a case involving University of Michigan's affirmative action program for *undergraduate* admissions, the Supreme Court held that the admissions policy was "not narrowly tailored to achieve the asserted interest in diversity" and therefore violated the Equal Protection Clause of the Fourteenth Amendment.[b] The Court rejected the University's affirmative action plan that made race the *decisive* factor for even minimally qualified minority applicants. Yet the Court restated its support for limited affirmative action programs that use race as a "plus" factor, the position the Court has held since the *Bakke* case in 1978.

The 2003 Michigan ruling did not end court battles over affirmative action in U.S. universities. Ten years later, the U.S. Supreme Court heard a case (*Fisher* v. *University of Texas*) challenging the use of race-conscious admission criteria. The case was filed by a white student who was denied admission to UT. The Supreme Court reaffirmed its "strict scrutiny" doctrine in 2013 in holding that the University of Texas, Austin, program that used race as part of an "index" for evaluating admissions applications was unconstitutional. The burden of proof that racial classifications meet strict scrutiny requirements rests with universities; lower federal courts cannot simply assume that universities are in compliance.

Can colleges and universities achieve diversity without using preferences? The U.S. Department of Education under President George W. Bush recommended (1) preferences based on socioeconomic status, (2) recruitment outreach efforts targeted at students of traditionally low-performing schools, and (3) admissions plans for students who finished in the top of their high school classes without regard to SAT scores.

[a]*Grutter* v. *Bollinger*, 539 U.S. 306 (2003).
[b]*Gratz* v. *Bollinger*, 523 U.S. 244 (2003).

in the Alabama Department of Safety, which had excluded blacks from the ranks of state troopers prior to 1972 and had not promoted any blacks higher than corporal prior to 1984. In a 5 to 4 decision, the majority stressed the long history of discrimination in the agency as a reason for upholding the quota system. Whatever burdens were imposed on innocent parties were outweighed by the need to correct the effects of past discrimination.[28]

Cases Questioning Affirmative Action

Yet the Supreme Court has continued to express concern about whites who are directly and adversely affected by government action solely because of their race. In *Firefighters Local Union* v. *Stotts* (1984), the Court ruled that a city could not lay off white firefighters in favor of black firefighters with less seniority.[29] In *Richmond* v. *Croson* (1989), the Supreme Court held that a minority set-aside program in Richmond, Virginia, which mandated that 30 percent of all city construction contracts must go to "blacks, Spanish-speaking, Orientals, Indians, Eskimos, or Aleuts" violated the Equal Protection Clause of the Fourteenth Amendment.[30]

Affirmative Action and "Strict Scrutiny"

It is important to note that the Supreme Court has never adopted the color-blind doctrine first espoused by Justice John Harlan in his *dissent* from *Plessy* v. *Ferguson*—that "our constitution is color-blind and neither knows nor tolerates classes among citizens." If the Equal Protection Clause requires that the laws of the United States and the states be truly color-blind, then *no* racial preferences, goals, or quotas would be tolerated. This view has occasionally been expressed in minority dissents and concurring opinions.[31]

However, the Court has held that racial classifications in law must be subject to "strict scrutiny." This means that race-based actions by government—any disparate treatment of the races by federal, state, or local public agencies—must be found necessary to remedy past proven discrimination, or to further clearly identified, compelling, and legitimate government objectives. Moreover, it must be "narrowly tailored" so as not to adversely affect the rights of individuals. In striking down a federal construction contract **"set-aside" program** for small businesses owned by racial minorities, the Court expressed skepticism about governmental racial classifications: "There is simply no way of determining what classifications are 'benign' and 'remedial' and what classifications are in fact motivated by illegitimate notions of racial inferiority or simple racial politics."[32] The membership of the Supreme Court appears to be closely split over the meaning and use of "strict scrutiny" in affirmative action cases.

"SET-ASIDE" PROGRAM Governments requiring a certain percentage of contracts to go to minority contractors.

Ending Racial Preferences by Initiative and Referenda

While leaders in business and government generally support affirmative action, many voters oppose granting preferential treatment to minorities. The initiative and referenda devices in American state politics allow voters to bypass political leadership (see Chapter 2).

California voters led the way in 1996 with a citizens' initiative (Proposition 209) that added the following phrase to that state's constitution:

> Neither the State of California nor any of its political subdivisions or agents shall use race, sex, color, ethnicity or national origin as criterion for either discriminating against, or granting preferential treatment to, any individual or group in the operation of the State's system of public employment, public education or public contracting.

The key words are "or granting preferential treatment to." Supporters of this "California Civil Rights Initiative" argued that it leaves all existing federal and state civil rights protections intact, while extending the rights of specifically protected groups to all of the state's citizens. They contended that governmental racial classifications violate the fundamental principle of equality under the law—that America cannot "make up" for past discrimination by "discrimination in the opposite direction." Even some early supporters of affirmative action argued that race-conscious programs are no longer necessary, that disadvantages in society today are more class-based than race-based, and that if preferences are to be granted at all they should be based on economic disadvantage, not race. In addition, it was argued that affirmative action may unfairly stigmatize the supposed beneficiaries, resulting in stereotyping that "stamps minorities with a badge of inferiority that may cause them to develop dependencies or to adopt an attitude that they are 'entitled' to preferences."[33]

CALIFORNIA CIVIL RIGHTS INITIATIVE An initiative that changed California's constitution to include a ban on race or gender preferences, which made some forms of affirmative action illegal.

Opponents argued that it sets back the civil rights movement, that it will end the progress of minorities in education and employment, and that it denies minorities the opportunity to seek assistance and protection from government. Supporters of racial preferences argue that discrimination still exists in American society. Race-conscious policies are a continuing necessity to remedy current discrimination as well as the effects of past discrimination. They contended that America is not now nor has ever been a "color-blind" society, and that racial preferences remain a necessary tool in achieving equality of opportunity.

Following its adoption, opponents of the California Civil Rights Initiative filed suit in federal court arguing that it violated the Equal Protection Clause of the U.S. Constitution because it denied minorities and women an opportunity to seek preferential treatment by government. But a federal Circuit Court of Appeals held, and the U.S. Supreme Court affirmed, that a "ban on race or gender preferences, as a matter of law or logic, does not violate the Equal Protection Clause [of the Constitution]." The Court reasoned that the Constitution allows some race-based preferences to correct past discrimination, but does not prevent states from banning racial preferences altogether.[34]

California voters approved of this initiative by a margin of 54 to 46 percent. But the overall margin of victory obscured serious divisions within the California electorate over racial preferences. Men voted in favor of the ban (61–39%) while women opposed it (48–52%). Whites voted for it (63–37%), while blacks voted against it (26–74%). Hispanics also opposed it (24–76%).

The success of the California Civil Rights Initiative inspired similar mass movements in other states: Washington adopted a similarly worded state constitutional amendment in 1998, and Michigan approved a statewide ban on racial preferences in public education, employment, and state contracts in 2006. In Michigan this initiative was opposed by elites in the political, business, and academic worlds, including both Democratic and Republican gubernatorial candidates. Nonetheless, 58percent of Michigan voters favored banning racial preferences. "Proposition 2" in that state gathered the most support from men (60–40%) and whites (59–39%). It gathered less support from women (47–53%) and very little support from blacks (14–86%). Following voter approval of the referendum, the president of the University of Michigan announced her intention "not to allow our University" to end its affirmative action efforts. Ultimately, the question of whether the results of the referendum were constitutional ended up in the U.S. Supreme Court in 2013 (*Schuette* v. *Michigan Coalition to Defend Affirmative Action*).

15.7 HISPANICS IN AMERICA

Describe the size of the Hispanic population in the United States; and outline the characteristics of Mexican Americans, Puerto Ricans, and Cuban Americans.

HISPANIC

A general reference to persons of Spanish-speaking ancestry and culture. Hispanics are an ethnic group, not a race. For example, there are black Hispanics.

Hispanics—persons of Spanish-speaking ancestry and culture—are now the nation's largest minority (see Table 15–2). When adult Hispanics were asked in a 2011 national poll which term they use to describe themselves, their country of origin, Latino/Hispanic, or American, the results were country of origin—51percent, Latino/Hispanic—24percent, and other—3 percent.[35] Most are of Mexican descent (62%) and reside in California, Texas, Arizona, and New Mexico. Puerto Ricans (9%) are concentrated in New York and Cuban Americans (4%) are concentrated in South Florida. Increasing immigration from other Latin American countries also contributes (24%) to the nation's Hispanic population.

Over two-thirds of Hispanics in the United States acknowledge that they represent different cultures rather than a common culture.[36] But if all Hispanics are grouped together

TABLE 15–2 Minorities in America

Race/Ethnicity	Number	Percentage of U.S. Population
White[a]	196,817,552	63.7
Hispanics	50,477,594	16.3
African Americans	38,929,319	12.6
Asians	14,674,252	4.8
All Other[b]	1,007,384	2.6
Total Population	308,745,538	100.0

Note: Data are for 2010.

[a]White alone, not of Hispanic origin.

[b]Includes American Indian, Alaska Native, Hawaiian and Pacific Islander, and persons identified as being of two or more races.

Source: U.S. Census Bureau, "Overview of Race and Hispanic Origin, 2010," March 2011, Table 1. Available at http://www.census.gov/prod/cen2010/briefs/c2010br-02.pdf.

for statistical comparisons, their median family income level is below that of whites (see Table 15–1). Hispanic poverty and unemployment rates are also higher than those of whites. The percentage of Hispanics completing high school and college is below that of both whites and blacks, suggesting that language or other cultural obstacles adversely affect education.

Mexican Americans

For many years, agricultural business encouraged immigration of Mexican farm laborers willing to endure harsh conditions for low pay. Many others came to the United States as *indocumentados*—undocumented immigrants. In the Immigration Reform Act of 1986 Congress offered amnesty to all undocumented workers who had entered the United States prior to 1982. But the Act also required employers, under threat of penalties, to hire only people who can provide documentation of their legal status in the country. The result has been a booming business in counterfeit green (employment) and Social Security cards.

Although Mexican Americans have served as governors of Arizona, Nevada, and New Mexico and have won election to the U.S. Congress, their political power does not yet match their population percentages. Mexican American voter turnout is lower than for other ethnic groups, perhaps because many are resident aliens or undocumented immigrants not eligible to vote, or perhaps because of cultural factors that discourage political participation.

Puerto Ricans

Puerto Rico is a commonwealth of the United States. Its commonwealth government resembles that of a state, with a constitution and elected governor and legislature, but the island has no voting members of the U.S. Congress and no electoral votes for president (see "The Commonwealth of Puerto Rico" in Chapter 1). As citizens, Puerto Ricans can move anywhere in the United States; many have immigrated to New York City, Philadelphia, Boston, Orlando, and Tampa. A growing, although still small, number are being elected to political offices at all levels.

Puerto Ricans have long debated whether to remain a commonwealth of the United States, apply for statehood, or seek complete independence from the United States. All of the participants in the debate agree that Puerto Ricans themselves should vote on the matter by referendum. For the island to become the nation's 51st state, the U.S. Congress would have to approve it.

Cuban Americans

Many Cuban Americans, especially those in the early waves of refugees from Castro's revolution in 1959, were skilled professionals and businesspeople, and they rapidly set about building Miami into a thriving economy. Although Cuban Americans are the third-largest Hispanic subgroup, today they are better educated and enjoy higher incomes than the others. They are well organized politically, and they have succeeded in electing Cuban Americans to state and local offices in Florida and to the U.S. Senate and House of Representatives.

HISPANIC POLITICS

Hispanic voters are a growing force in American politics. While Hispanic voter turnout has been low, population projections forecast a growing role for Hispanics in state, national, and local politics.

Political Mobilization

For many decades, American agriculture encouraged Mexican American immigration, both legal and illegal, to labor in fields as *braceros*. Most of these migrant farm workers lived and worked under difficult conditions; they were paid less than minimum wages for

15.8

Trace the political mobilization and voter turnout of Hispanics, and describe their partisanship and ideology.

backbreaking labor. Farm workers were not covered by the federal National Labor Relations Act and therefore not protected in the right to organize labor unions. But civil rights activity among Hispanics, especially among farmworkers, grew during the 1960s under the leadership of Cesar Chavez and his United Farm Workers union. Chavez organized a national boycott of grapes from California vineyards that refused to recognize the union or improve conditions. *La Raza*, as the movement was called, finally ended in a union contract with the growers and later a California law protecting the right of farm workers to organize unions and bargain collectively with their employers. More important, the movement galvanized Mexican Americans throughout the Southwest to engage in political activity.[37]

However, inasmuch as many Mexican American immigrants were noncitizens, and many were *indocumentados*, the voting strength of Mexican Americans never matched their numbers in the population. The Immigration Reform and Control Act of 1986 granted amnesty to illegal aliens living in the United States in 1982. But the same Act also imposed penalties on employers who hired illegal aliens. The effect of these threatened penalties on many employers was to make them wary of hiring Hispanics, especially as permanent employees. At the same time, industries in need of cheap labor—agriculture, health and hospitals, restaurants, clothing manufacturers—continued to encourage legal and illegal immigration to fill minimum- and even subminimum-wage-level jobs with few, if any, benefits.

In 1994 California voters approved a referendum, Proposition 187, which would have barred welfare and other benefits to persons living in the state illegally. Most Hispanics opposed the measure, believing that it was motivated by prejudice. A federal court later declared major portions of Proposition 187 unconstitutional; and earlier the U.S. Supreme Court held that a state may not bar the children of illegal immigrants from attending public schools.[38] Although Proposition 187 won, the battle over it in California helped to mobilize Hispanic voters everywhere.[39]

Voter Turnout

Hispanic voters made up 10 percent of the electorate in the 2012 presidential election, up from just 7.4 percent in 2008. In spite of the gain, the Hispanic share of the total electorate is still below the Hispanic percentage of the general population. Various explanations have been advanced for the lower participation rate of Hispanics. Language barriers may still discourage some voters, even though ballots in many states are now available in the Spanish language. Undocumented immigrants, of course, cannot vote. Lower education and income levels are also associated with lower voter turnout.

The Voting Rights Act of 1965, as later amended and as interpreted by the U.S. Supreme Court, extends voting right protections to "language minorities," including Hispanics. This ensures that Spanish-speaking minorities cannot have their vote diluted in redistricting plans (see "Legislative Apportionment and Districting" in Chapter 6). Hispanics did gain some seats in Congress and some state legislatures as a consequence of redistricting following the 2010 Census.

Partisanship

Overall, most Hispanics identify with the Democratic Party. Among Hispanic groups, only Cuban Americans tend to identify with the Republican Party. The Republican Party under President George W. Bush sought "outreach" to Hispanic voters. (President Bush and former Governor Jeb Bush of Florida both speak Spanish.) In Texas gubernatorial elections, George W. Bush won nearly half of the Mexican American vote. In the 2000 and 2004 presidential elections, Bush won over 35 percent of the Hispanic vote nationwide. But these Republican inroads disappeared in 2008 when Hispanic voters strongly supported Democratic presidential candidate Barack Obama. And in 2012, Obama received over 70 percent of the Hispanic vote in his successful bid for reelection. To the extent that

Republican officeholders oppose comprehensive immigration reform, and support stringent anti-immigration laws, like Arizona's, the prospects for future Republican capture of any significant share of Hispanic voters appears dim, in spite of the efforts of Hispanic Republican U.S. Senators Marco Rubio (Florida) and Ted Cruz (Texas).

Ideology

Polls suggest that Hispanics are generally conservative on social issues (opposing abortion, favoring government support of credits to pay parochial school tuition), but liberal on economic issues (favoring government provision of health insurance for all, favoring government spending for various services). And most Hispanics favor comprehensive immigration reform, including proposals that provide a pathway for the nation's millions of undocumented aliens to acquire citizenship.

NATIVE AMERICANS AND TRIBAL GOVERNMENT

15.9

Trace the history of the legal relationships between the United States and Indian nations, and describe the current status and governments of Indian nations.

Christopher Columbus erred in his estimate of the circumference of the globe. He believed he had arrived in the Indian Ocean when he first came to the Caribbean. He mistook the Arawaks for people of the East Indies, calling them "Indios," and this Spanish word passed into English as Indians—a word that came to refer to all Native American peoples. But at the time of the first European contacts, these peoples had no common identity; there were hundreds of separate cultures and languages thriving in the Americas.

Although estimates vary, most historians believe that in the fifteenth century, 7–12 million people lived in the land that is now the United States and Canada; 25 million more lived in Mexico; and 60–70 million lived in the Western Hemisphere, a number comparable to Europe's population at the time. But in the centuries that followed, the native population of the Americas was devastated by warfare, famine, and, most of all, by epidemic diseases brought from Europe. Overall, the native population fell by 90 percent, the greatest human disaster in world history.

The Trail of Broken Treaties

In the Northwest Ordinance of 1787, Congress, in organizing the western territories of the new nation, declared that "The utmost good faith shall always be observed toward the Indians. Their lands and property shall never be taken from them without their consent."

And later, in the Intercourse Act of 1790, Congress declared that public treaties between the U.S. government and the independent Indian "nations" would be the only legal means of obtaining Indian land. As president, George Washington forged a treaty with the Creeks: In exchange for land concessions, the United States pledged to protect the boundaries of the "Creek Nation" and allow the Creeks themselves to punish all violators of their laws within these boundaries. This semblance of legality was reflected in hundreds of treaties to follow. (And indeed, in recent years some Indian tribes have successfully sued in federal court for reparations and return of lands obtained in violation of the Intercourse Act of 1790 and subsequent treaties.) Yet, Indian lands were constantly invaded by whites. The resulting Indian resistance typically led to wars that ultimately resulted in great loss of life among warriors and their families and to further loss of tribal land. The cycle of invasion, resistance, military defeat, and further land concessions continued for a hundred years.

Indian Wars

The "Indian wars" were fought between the Plains Indian tribes and the U.S. Army between 1864 and 1890. Following the Civil War, the federal government began to assign boundaries to each tribe and created a Bureau of Indian Affairs (BIA) to "assist and protect" Indian peoples on their "reservations." But the reservations were repeatedly reduced in size until subsistence by hunting became impossible. Malnutrition and demoralization of the native peoples were aided by the mass slaughter of the buffalo; vast herds, numbering perhaps as many as 70 million, were exterminated over the years. The most storied engagement of the long war occurred at the Little Big Horn River in Montana on June 25, 1876, where Civil War hero General George Armstrong Custer led elements of the U.S. Seventh Cavalry to destruction at the hands of Sioux and Cheyenne warriors led by Chief Crazy Horse, Sitting Bull, and Gall. But Custer's Last Stand inspired renewed army campaigns against the Plains tribes; the following year Crazy Horse was forced to surrender. In 1881, destitute Sioux under Chief Sitting Bull returned from exile in Canada to surrender themselves to reservation life. Among the last tribes to hold out were the Apaches, whose famous warrior, Geronimo, finally surrendered in 1886. Sporadic fighting continued until 1890, when a small, malnourished band of Lakota Sioux were wiped out at Wounded Knee Creek.

Federal Policy Reversals

The Dawes Act of 1887 governed federal Indian policy for decades. The thrust of the policy was to break up tribal lands, allotting acreage for individual homesteads in order to assimilate Indians into the white agricultural society. Farming was to replace hunting, and tribal life and traditional customs were to be shed for English language and schooling. But this effort to destroy Indian culture never really succeeded. While Indian peoples lost over half of their 1877 reservation land, few lost their communal ties or accumulated much private property. The Dawes Act remained federal policy until 1934, when Congress finally reversed itself in the Indian Reorganization Act of 1934 and reaffirmed tribal ownership of land. Life on the reservations was often disparate. Indians suffered the worst poverty of any group in the nation, with high rates of infant mortality, alcoholism, and other diseases. The BIA, notoriously corrupt and mismanaged, encouraged dependency and regularly interfered with Indian religious affairs and tribal customs.

In 2010, Congress passed the Tribal Law and Order Act, reversing the long-standing 1885 Major Crimes Act. The old law gave federal authorities the sole responsibility for prosecuting felony crimes committed on Indian reservations, but U.S. attorneys often failed to do so because of being based in cities quite some distance away from reservations. Under the new law, Tribal police and courts are given more authority (although still limited) to investigate some serious crimes, then to prosecute and sentence the guilty individual.

Native Americans Today

Today almost 3 million people—less than 1 percent of the nation's population—identify themselves as American Indians or Alaska Natives. (The Census defines these persons as having origins in any of the original peoples of North and South America, including Central America, who maintain tribal affiliation or community attachment.[40]) The 10 states with the largest American Indian and Alaska Native populations are California, Oklahoma, Arizona, Texas, New York, New Mexico, Washington, North Carolina, Florida, and Michigan. There are 324 federally recognized American Indian reservations. Less than half of the American Indian population lives on tribal reservations and trust land, the largest of which is the Navaho and Hopi enclave in the southwestern United States. (See Figure 15–2.) Yet these peoples remain the poorest and least healthy in America, with high incidences of infant mortality, suicide, and alcoholism. Approximately half of all Indians live below the poverty line. The median income of American Indian and Alaska Native households is $35,192 compared to $50,502 for the nation as a whole.[41]

Tribal Government

There are 566 federally recognized American Indian tribes. The largest (in descending order) are Cherokee, Navajo, Choctaw, Mexican American Indian, Chippewa, Sioux, Apache, and Blackfeet.[42] The U.S. Constitution (Article I, Section 8) grants Congress the full power "to regulate Commerce . . . with the Indian Tribes." States are prevented from regulating or taxing Indian tribes or extending their courts' jurisdiction over them, unless

FIGURE 15-2 Native American Reservations and Trust Land

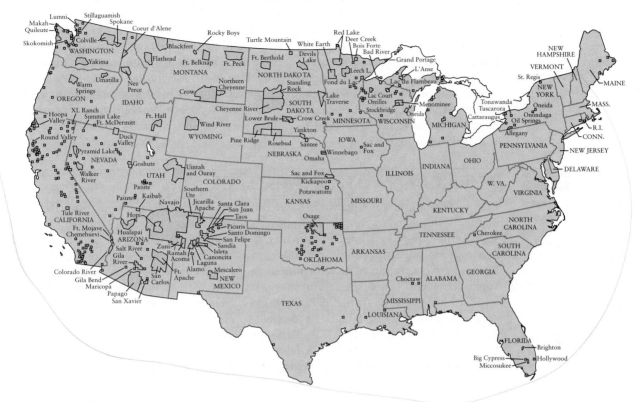

Source: U.S. Bureau of the Census.

authorized by Congress. The Supreme Court recognizes Native Americans "as members of quasi-sovereign tribal entities"[43] with powers to regulate their own internal affairs, establish their own courts, and enforce their own laws, all subject to congressional supervision. Thus, for example, many Indian tribes chose to legalize gambling, including casino gambling, on reservations in states that otherwise prohibited the activity. As American citizens, Indians have the right to vote in state as well as national elections. Indians living off of reservations have the same rights and responsibilities as anyone else. Indians enrolled as members of tribes and living on reservations are entitled to certain benefits established by law and treaty.

The Bureau of Indian Affairs (BIA) in the Department of Commerce continues to supervise reservation life. But it is the U.S. Departments of the Interior and Treasury that oversee Indian lands and collect monies from companies holding leases and extracting minerals, timber, oil and gas, and other resources from the lands. In 2012, the federal government agreed to pay tribes more than $1 billion for the mismanagement of funds and natural resources that the government holds in trust. The settlement went to 41 tribes, mostly located in the West, but another 60 similar lawsuits have yet to be settled. In most cases, tribal councils—the elected governing bodies—will decide how to spend the money.[44]

Tribes versus States

In recent years, many tribal governments have reasserted their sovereignty and rights to self-government. The result has often led to strained relations with state and local governments. Disputes with **tribes** have arisen over casino gambling on reservations; state collection of taxes on gasoline, liquor, and cigarettes sold on reservations; and the enforcement

TRIBES

Semi-sovereign Native American nations recognized by the U.S. government and exercising self-government on trust lands and reservations.

of state environmental, natural resource, and wildlife protection laws within reservations. Some states have succeeded in negotiating compacts and agreements with tribal governments.

Under federal law, the Indian Gaming Regulatory Act of 1988, tribes must enter into compacts with states before they can open gambling casinos on tribal land. States must bargain "in good faith" in negotiating these compacts. States cannot tax the income from Indian casinos, but they may negotiate reimbursement for regulation and administration. About half of the states have negotiated such compacts. But in several states, including California, Texas, and Florida, tribes have opened casinos without state approval. State governments have been reluctant to enforce prohibitions on tribes: "I don't want another war with the Seminoles."[45]

15.10 AMERICANS WITH DISABILITIES

Describe the extent to which the American population is disabled, and describe the protections afforded to Americans with disabilities through the Americans with Disabilities Act.

Fifty-seven million Americans (19% of the noninstitutionalized population) have a disability. With regard to specific disabilities, 31 million have difficulty walking or climbing stairs, 8 million have a hearing difficulty, 8 million have a vision problem, and 4 million must use a wheelchair to move around. The oldest Americans (65 or older) are much more likely to have a disability of some type than the youngest cohort (under 15)—50 percent versus 8 percent. Just 41 percent of people 21 to 64 with a disability are employed.[46]

Throughout most of our nation's history, little thought was given to making public or private buildings or facilities accessible to people with disabilities, such as impaired vision, hearing, or mobility.[47] But in 1990, Congress passed the sweeping Americans with Disabilities Act (ADA), which prohibits discrimination in private employment, government programs, public accommodations, transportation, commercial facilities, state and local government services, and telecommunications.

Americans with Disabilities Act (ADA)

The Act is vaguely worded in many of its provisions, requiring "reasonable accommodations" for people with disabilities that do not involve "undue hardship." But the ADA mandates that people with disabilities

1. cannot be denied employment or promotion if, with "reasonable accommodation," they can perform the duties of the job.

2. cannot be denied access to government programs or benefits. New buses, taxis, and trains must be accessible to people, including those in wheelchairs.

3. must enjoy "full and equal" access to hotels, restaurants, stores, schools, parks, museums, auditoriums, and the like. To achieve equal access, owners of existing facilities must alter them "to the maximum extent feasible"; builders of new facilities must ensure that they are readily accessible unless doing so is structurally impossible.

These federal mandates for accommodating people with disabilities were not accompanied by any federal funds to employers or state and local governments to implement them (see "Coercive Federalism: Preemptions and Mandates" in Chapter 3).

Mental and Learning Disabilities

The ADA protects the rights of people with learning and psychiatric disabilities, as well as physical disabilities. States vary considerably in the size of their disabled population. The U.S. Equal Employment Opportunity Commission has received almost as many complaints about workplace discrimination against people with mental disabilities as it has received from people claiming back injuries. But it is far more difficult for employers to determine how to handle a depressed or anxiety-ridden employee than an employee with a visible physical disability. How can employers distinguish uncooperative employees from those with psychiatric disorders?

The American Council on Education reports that the percentage of students in colleges and universities claiming a "learning disability" jumped from 3 to 10 percent after the enactment of ADA.[48] A decision by the U.S. Department of Education that "attention-deficit disorder" is covered by the ADA has resulted in another significant rise in students claiming disabilities. Colleges and universities are required to provide special accommodations for students with disabilities, including tutors, extra time on examinations, and oral rather than written exams.

Lawsuits

In recent years the ADA has produced a flood of lawsuits against private businesses, claiming that their facilities were not reasonably accessible to employees or customers. The law requires buildings open to the public to have designated parking for people with disabilities and no steps or curbs blocking the entrance. Bathrooms and aisles must be able to accommodate patrons in wheelchairs. Counters cannot be too high. The law allows attorneys to file lawsuits on behalf of clients with disabilities and collect damages and fees from offending businesses. Many business owners complain that frivolous lawsuits are being driven by lawyers' fees. Like businesses, state and local governments have been subjected to lawsuits challenging their compliance with a wide range of ADA-related requirements.

AGE DISCRIMINATION

15.11

Describe the prohibitions against age discrimination afforded to Americans.

The issue of age discrimination was first addressed in the Age Discrimination in Employment Act (ADEA) of 1967. The ADEA and its amendments forbid age discrimination against people who are *40 or older*. As noted by the U.S. Equal Employment Opportunity Commission, the ADEA makes it against the law to discriminate against a person because of his/her age with respect to any term, condition, or privilege of employment, including hiring, firing, promotion, layoff, compensation, fringe benefits, job assignments, and training. It is also unlawful to retaliate against an individual for opposing employment practices that discriminate based on age or for filing an age discrimination charge, testifying, or participating in any way in an investigation, proceeding, or litigation under the ADEA. The ADEA applies to employers with 20 or more employees, *including state and local governments*.

The number of complaints about age discrimination is on the upswing. Nearly 23,000 complaints were filed with EEOC in 2012 alone and projections are that the number will continue to climb as the American population ages. Baby boomers and seniors (65 and older) now make up almost 40 percent of the population. Nearly two-thirds of older workers age 45 to 74 say they have seen or experienced age discrimination in the workplace.[49] Their concerns escalated during the Great Recession when higher paid older workers were often the first to be laid off and the last to be rehired. At the height of the recession, the average length of unemployment between jobs for older workers was 60 weeks, compared with 38.5 weeks for younger workers.[50] Employers' hesitancy to rehire older workers stems from concerns about seniors' technical skills, their impact on a company's health care costs, and uncertainties about how long they will stay on the job. Advocates for older workers say these concerns are off base.

Proving age discrimination is much more difficult than proving racial or gender discrimination. In 2009, a divided (5–4) U.S. Supreme Court ruling (*Gross* v. *FBL Financial Services*) actually weakened the ADEA. The controversial ruling requires an aggrieved older worker to prove that age was *the* decisive factor for an employer's discriminatory action, rather than simply one factor. In 2013, the U.S. Supreme Court agreed to hear an age discrimination-related case (*Madigan* v. *Levin*). At issue is whether state and local government employees can bring cases of age discrimination directly to federal court under the U.S. Constitution's Fourteenth Amendment Equal Protection Clause or whether they have to go through procedures established by the ADEA. If the Court rules that age discrimination cases can be brought under the equal protection clause, it would "put age discrimination claimants on a more even playing field with employees suing for sex and race discrimination."[51]

15.12 GENDER EQUALITY

Describe the prohibitions against gender discrimination that are codified in federal law and Supreme Court decisions, describe the earnings gap between men and women, and evaluate whether comparable worth should be instituted to narrow this gap.

Traditionally, gender issues were decided largely by *states,* particularly state laws governing marriage, divorce, employment, and abortion. State laws frequently differentiated between the rights and responsibilities of men and women. Women had many special protections in state laws, but often these protections limited opportunities for advancement and encouraged dependence upon men. State laws governing employment considered women as frail creatures in need of special protections against long hours, heavy work, night work, and other conditions.

Employment

Today, Title VII of the federal Civil Rights Act of 1964 prohibits sexual (as well as racial) discrimination in hiring, pay, and promotions. The Equal Employment Opportunity Commission, which is the federal agency charged with eliminating discrimination in employment, has established guidelines barring stereotyped classifications of "men's jobs" and "women's jobs." State laws and employer practices that differentiate between men and women in hours, pay, retirement age, and other factors have been struck down.

Gender Classifications

Over the years, the Supreme Court ruled that states could no longer set different ages for men and women to become legal adults[52] or purchase alcoholic beverages;[53] women could not be barred from police or firefighting jobs by arbitrary height and weight requirements;[54] insurance and retirement plans for women must pay the same monthly benefits even though women on the average live longer;[55] and schools must pay coaches in girls' sports the same as coaches in boys' sports.[56] However, all-male and all-female schools are still permitted;[57] and Congress may draft men for military service without drafting women.[58] Gender protection under the Equal Protection Clause was also extended to men: The Supreme Court struck down a state law that allowed wives to obtain alimony from husbands but did not permit husbands to obtain alimony from wives.[59]

Education

Title IX of the Federal Education Act Amendment of 1972 dealt with sex discrimination in education. This federal law barred discrimination in admissions, housing, rules, financial aid, faculty and staff recruitment, pay, and athletics. The latter problem has proven difficult because men's football and basketball programs have traditionally brought in the money to finance all other sports and have received the largest share of school athletic budgets. (See also *"Up Close:* Sexual Harassment.")

The Earnings Gap

The federal Equal Pay Act of 1963 prevents employers from discriminating against women by paying them less than men for work performed under similar conditions that require "equal skill, effort and responsibility." When it was signed, women were earning about 59 cents for every dollar earned by a man.

Today, women earn annually about 77 percent of what men earn. Despite federal laws barring direct gender discrimination

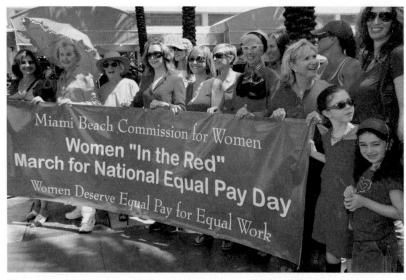

The wage gap between men and women is narrowing. But women today still earn annually 77 percent of what men earn. The existence of a "dual" labor market is a large part of the problem. Female-dominated jobs pay less than male-dominated occupations.

The Civil Rights Act of 1964 (Title VII) makes it "an unlawful employment practice to discriminate against any individual with respect to . . . conditions or privileges of employment because of an individual's race, color, religion, *sex*, or national origin." The U.S. Supreme Court has declared that "sexual harassment" is a condition of employment that is outlawed by the Civil Rights Act. But what constitutes "sexual harassment"?

The Supreme Court has wrestled with the question over the years. In 1986, the Court provided the following definition:

> Unwelcome sexual advances, requests for sexual favors, and other verbal or physical conduct of a sexual nature constitute sexual harassment when (1) submission to such conduct is made either explicitly or implicitly a term or condition of an individual's employment; (2) submission to or rejection of such conduct by an individual is used as the basis for employment decisions affecting such individual; or (3) such conduct has the purpose or effect of unreasonably interfering with an individual's work performance or creating an intimidating, hostile, or offensive working environment.[a]

There is no real difficulty in defining sexual harassment when jobs or promotions are conditioned on the granting of sexual favors. But problems arise in defining what is an "intimidating, hostile, or offensive working environment." This phrase may include dirty jokes, sexual innuendoes, the display of X-rated photos, or perhaps even unwanted proposals for dates. All of these definitions raise First Amendment questions regarding how far speech may be curtailed by law in the workplace. Moreover, some of these definitions about what is "offensive" or "unwanted" depend more on the subjective feelings of the individual employee than any objective standard of law.

[a]*Meritor Savings Bank v. Vinson,* 477 U.S. 57 (1986).
[b]*Harris v. Forklift,* 510 U.S. 17 (1993).

Justice Sandra Day O'Connor tried to clarify some of these questions in 1993. Writing for the Court majority, she held that the particular words or actions objected to must be serious enough to make a "reasonable person," not just the plaintiff, perceive the work environment to be hostile. She indicated that a single incident is unlikely to constitute harassment; rather, courts should consider "the frequency of the discriminatory conduct, . . . its severity," and whether it "unreasonably interferes with an employee's work performance."[b]

What does a "reasonable person" believe to be sexual harassment? Some polls show that neither women nor men are likely to believe that sexual harassment includes repeated requests for a date, or the telling of dirty jokes, or comments on attractiveness—even though these behaviors often inspire formal complaints. Many college and university policies go well beyond the Supreme Court definition of sexual harassment, including the following:

- Remarks about the person's clothing
- Suggestive or insulting sounds
- Leering or ogling a person's body
- Remarks that degrade a person's gender

Overly broad and vague definitions of sexual harassment can undermine academic freedom and inhibit classroom discussions of important yet sensitive topics. Both faculty and students must feel free to express their views without fear of being labeled "insensitive" or charged with making others feel "uncomfortable." Students especially must feel free to express themselves on matters of gender, whether or not their ideas are immature or crudely expressed.

---

in employment, the existence of a "dual" labor market, with male-dominated "blue-collar" jobs distinguishable from female-dominated "pink-collar" jobs, continues to be a major obstacle to economic equality between men and women. These occupational differences can be attributed to cultural stereotyping, social conditioning, and training and education that narrow the choices available to women. While significant progress has been made in recent years in reducing occupational sex segregation, many observers doubt that sexually differentiated occupations will be eliminated soon.

Comparable Worth

As a result of a growing recognition that the wage gap is more a result of occupational differentiation than direct discrimination, some feminist organizations have turned to another approach—the demand that pay levels in various occupations be determined by "**comparable worth**" rather than by the labor market. Comparable worth means more than paying men and women equally for the same work; it means paying the same wages for jobs of comparable value to the employer. It means that traditionally male and female jobs would be evaluated by governmental agencies or courts to determine their "worth" to

COMPARABLE WORTH
The argument that pay levels for traditionally male and traditionally female jobs should be equalized either by employers or by government laws and regulations.

the employer, perhaps by considering responsibilities, effort, knowledge, and skill requirements. Jobs judged to be comparable would have equal wages. Government agencies or the courts would replace the labor market in the determination of wage rates.

To date, the U.S. Equal Employment Opportunity Commission has rejected the notion of comparable worth and declined to recommend wages for traditionally male and female jobs. And so far the federal courts have refused to declare that different wages in traditionally male and female occupations are evidence of sexual discrimination in violation of federal law. However, some state governments and private employers have undertaken to review their own pay scales to determine if traditionally female occupations are underpaid.

15.13

BATTLES OVER ABORTION

Compare "pro-life" and "pro-choice" attitudes about abortion, trace abortion restrictions imposed by the states at various times, and discuss the Supreme Court decisions related to abortion.

Abortion has been one of the nation's most debated issues, with the most intense battles often occurring in state legislatures. Arguments over abortion touch on fundamental moral and religious principles. Proponents of legalized abortion, who often refer to themselves as **"pro-choice,"** argue that a woman should be permitted to control her own body and should not be forced by law to have unwanted children. They cite the heavy toll in lives lost in criminal abortions and the psychological and emotional pain of an unwanted pregnancy. Opponents of abortion, who often refer to themselves as **"pro-life,"** generally base their belief on the sanctity of life, including the life of the unborn child, which they believe deserves the protection of law—"the right to life." Many believe that the killing of an unborn child for any reason other than the preservation of the life of the mother is murder.

Many Americans have mixed opinions about abortion. A Pew Research Center poll taken in 2013 (the 40th anniversary of the U.S. Supreme Court's *Roe* v. *Wade* ruling permitting abortion) found that 63 percent do not want to see the ruling completely overturned. But at the same time, nearly half (47%) think it is morally wrong to have an abortion.[60]

PRO-CHOICE

Those who feel that a woman should be permitted to make choices about her own body, including whether to have an abortion.

PRO-LIFE

Those who support a ban on most abortions, generally based on their belief in the sanctity of life, including the life of the unborn child, which they believe deserves the protection of law.

Early State Laws

Historically, abortions for any purpose other than saving the life of the mother were criminal offenses under state law. About a dozen states acted in the late 1960s to permit abortions in cases of rape or incest, or to protect the physical health of the mother, and in some cases her mental health as well. Relatively few legal abortions were performed under these laws, however, because of the red tape involved—review of each case by several concurring physicians, approval of a hospital board. Then, in 1970, New York, Alaska, Hawaii, and Washington enacted laws that in effect permitted abortion at the request of the woman involved with the concurrence of her physician.[61]

Roe v. Wade

The U.S. Supreme Court's decision in *Roe* v. *Wade* was one of the most important and far-reaching in the Court's history.[62] The Supreme Court ruled that the constitutional guarantee of "liberty" in the Fifth and Fourteenth Amendments included a woman's decision to bear or not to bear a child. The Supreme Court ruled that the word *person* in the Constitution did not include the unborn child. Therefore, the Fifth and Fourteenth Amendments to the Constitution, guaranteeing "life, liberty and property," did not protect the "life" of the fetus. The Court also ruled that a state's power to protect the health and safety of the mother could not justify *any* restriction of abortion in the first three months of pregnancy. Between the third and sixth month of pregnancy, a state could set standards for abortion procedures in order to protect the health of women, but a state could not prohibit abortions. Only in the final three months could a state prohibit or regulate abortion to protect the unborn.

Reactions in the States

The Supreme Court's decision did not end the controversy over abortion. Congress declined to pass a constitutional amendment restricting abortion or declaring that the guarantee of life begins at conception. However, Congress banned the use of federal funds under Medicaid (medical care for the poor) for abortions (except to protect the life of a woman, and later, in cases of rape and incest). The Supreme Court upheld the constitutionality of federal and state laws *denying tax funds for abortions.*[63] While women retained the right to an abortion, the Court held that there was no constitutional obligation for governments to pay for abortions; the decision about whether to pay for abortions from tax revenues was left to Congress and the states.[64] However, efforts by the states to directly restrict abortion ran into Supreme Court opposition.[65]

Issues that touch on a person's moral and religious beliefs often generate the most intense courtroom battles. Abortion has been just such an issue for several decades, creating intense and emotionally charged debates between Americans described as "pro-life" and those who consider themselves "pro-choice." Meanwhile, public opinion surveys show that many in the public at large have mixed views on the subject.

Abortions in the States Declining; Use of Contraception Rising

Over 1 million abortions are performed each year in the United States. About 85 percent of all abortions are performed at abortion clinics; others are performed in physicians' offices or in hospitals, where the cost is significantly higher. Most of these abortions are performed in the first three months; about 10 percent are performed after the third month. Abortion rates are highest in New York and lowest in Mississippi.

Why are abortions more frequent in some states than in others? An early study of this question by political scientist Susan B. Hansen revealed that abortion rates were *not* related to unwanted pregnancies, that is, the "demand" for abortions.[66] Rather, abortion rates were related to state policies affecting the availability of abortion services, that is, to government policies affecting the "supply" of abortions. Among the reported findings were that abortion rates are higher in states that permitted abortion before *Roe* v. *Wade;* some states with low abortion rates (Utah and Idaho) have large Mormon populations; and greater state legislative support for abortion facilities and health services leads to higher abortion rates.

The abortion rate has been steadily declining since 2000. Greater use of effective contraceptives (pills, patch) by teenage girls is one reason, along with the growing use of IUDs (intrauterine devices), and easier access to the morning-after pill (over the counter).[67] Today, nearly 90 percent of women who are at risk of an unintended pregnancy use contraceptives.[68]

Abortion Restrictions

Opponents of abortion won a victory in the *Webster* v. *Reproductive Health Services* case in 1989 when the Supreme Court upheld a Missouri law sharply restricting abortions.[69] The right to abortion under *Roe* v. *Wade* was not overturned, but narrowed in application. The effect of the decision was to return the question of abortion restrictions to the states for decision.

The Court held that Missouri could deny public funds for abortions that were not necessary for the life of the woman and could deny the use of public facilities or public employees in performing or assisting in abortions. More important, the Court upheld the requirement for a test of "viability" after 20 weeks and a prohibition of an abortion of a viable fetus except to save a woman's life. The Court recognized the state's "interest in the protection of human life when viability is possible."

Reaffirming *Roe v. Wade*

Abortion has become such a polarizing issue that pro-choice and pro-life groups are generally unwilling to search out a middle ground. Yet the current Supreme Court appears to have chosen a policy of affirming a woman's right to abortion while upholding modest restrictions.

Pennsylvania is a state where pro-life forces won the support of the governor and legislature for a series of restrictions on abortion—physicians must inform women of risks and alternatives; a 24-hour waiting period is required; minors must have consent of parents or a judge; spouses must be notified. These restrictions reached the Supreme Court in the case of *Planned Parenthood of Pennsylvania* v. *Casey* in 1992.[70]

Justice Sandra Day O'Connor took the lead in forming a moderate, swing bloc on the Court; her majority opinion strongly reaffirmed the fundamental right to abortion:

> Our law affords constitutional protection to personal decisions relating to marriage, procreation, contraception, family relationships, child rearing, and education. . . . These matters, involving the most intimate and personal choices a person may make in a lifetime, choices central to personal dignity and autonomy, are central to the liberty protected by the Fourteenth Amendment. . . . A woman's liberty is not so unlimited, however, that from the outset the State cannot show its concern for the life of the unborn, and at a later point in fetal development the State's interest in life has sufficient force so that the right of the woman to terminate the pregnancy can be restricted. We conclude the line should be drawn at viability, so that before that time the woman has a right to choose to terminate her pregnancy. . . .[71]

Justice O'Connor went on to establish a standard for constitutionally evaluating state restrictions: They must not impose an "undue burden" on women seeking abortion or place "substantial obstacles" in her path. All of Pennsylvania's restrictions were upheld except spousal notification.

It is sometimes argued that abortion rates could be lowered by expanding child care, health care, family leave laws, and other economic benefits for families, thereby encouraging disadvantaged women to carry their pregnancies to term. It is true that low-income women abort at higher rates than middle- and upper-income women. But careful research suggests that these "pro-family" policies have little direct effect on abortion rates.[72]

"Partial-Birth" Abortions

But perhaps the most inflamed arguments have been inspired by efforts in the states to ban "partial-birth" abortions of viable fetuses. The procedure is relatively rare. A physician induces a breech delivery with forceps, pulls out the fetus's legs and body, and then pierces the as-yet-undelivered skull and vacuums out the brain; the delivery is then completed. In 1996 and 1997, Congress passed national bans on the procedure, only to have them vetoed by President Bill Clinton. The "partial-birth" abortion issue energized anti-abortion pro-life supporters in the states to seek bans on the procedure. By 2000, over half of the states had enacted such bans. The U.S. Supreme Court decided in 2000 (by a 5–4 decision) that a Nebraska law prohibiting "partial-birth abortion" was an unconstitutional "undue burden" on a woman's right to choose whether to have an abortion.[73] The Nebraska law failed to make an exception for the procedure when it was considered necessary to save a woman's life.

Congress passed and President George W. Bush signed into law a Partial Birth Abortion Ban Act in 2003 that carefully defines the procedure as "deliberately and intentionally vaginally [delivering] a living fetus until, in the case of a head-first presentation, the entire fetal head is outside the body . . . for the purpose of performing an overt act that the person [doctor] knows will kill the partially delivered living fetus." Moreover, the Act makes an exception for the procedure where it is determined by appropriate medical authorities to be "necessary to save the life of a mother."

Lower courts initially declined to enforce the ban, believing that it was an unconstitutional undue burden on a woman's right to choose an abortion. But in 2007, the Supreme Court upheld the Act, citing it specifically in describing the prohibited procedure and granting an exception for the preservation of a woman's life.[74] The case was decided by a 5–4 margin with President Bush's new appointees, Justices Roberts and Alito, joining the majority. The decision upholding the ban reignited efforts in the states not only to prohibit partial-birth abortions, but also to enact other limitations on abortion.

Abortion Battles in the States

Contentious debates over abortion continue in virtually all state capitals. Various legal restrictions on abortions have been passed in the states, including (1) *denial of public financing:* prohibitions on public financing of abortions; (2) *conscience laws:* laws granting permission to doctors and hospitals to refuse to perform abortions; (3) *fetal disposal:* laws requiring humane and sanitary disposal of fetal remains; (4) *informed consent:* laws requiring physicians to inform patients about the development of the fetus and the availability of assistance in pregnancy; (5) *parental notification:* laws requiring that parents of minors seeking abortion be informed (upheld by the U.S. Supreme Court); (6) *spousal verification:* laws requiring spouses to be informed (struck down by the U.S. Supreme Court);[75] (7) *hospitalization requirement:* laws requiring that late abortions be performed in hospitals; and (8) *clinic licensing:* laws setting standards of cleanliness and care in abortion clinics.

More recently, beginning in 2011, state legislatures in a number of conservative one-party-controlled states have passed a wide range of tougher restrictions on abortion. (See *Rankings of*

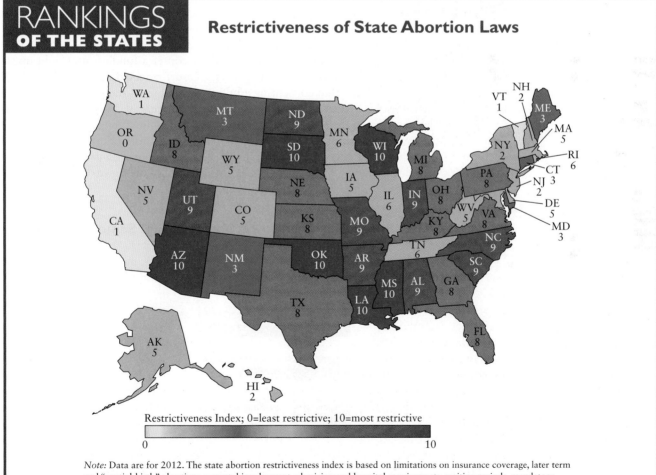

RANKINGS
OF THE STATES

Restrictiveness of State Abortion Laws

WA 1
MT 3
ND 9
MN 6
WI 10
MI 8
NY 2
VT 1
NH 2
ME 3
MA 5
RI 6
CT 3
NJ 2
DE 5
MD 3
OR 0
ID 8
WY 5
SD 10
IA 5
IL 6
IN 9
OH 8
PA 8
WV 5
VA 8
NV 5
UT 9
CO 5
NE 8
KS 8
MO 9
KY 8
NC 9
CA 1
AZ 10
NM 3
OK 10
AR 9
TN 6
SC 9
MS 10
AL 9
GA 8
TX 8
LA 10
FL 8
AK 5
HI 2

Restrictiveness Index; 0=least restrictive; 10=most restrictive

0   10

Note: Data are for 2012. The state abortion restrictiveness index is based on limitations on insurance coverage, later term and "partial-birth" abortions, parental involvement, physician and hospital requirements, waiting periods, mandatory counseling, scarcity of abortion providers, targeted regulation of abortion providers, ultrasound requirements, limits on public financing, and near-total abortion ban unenforceable per *Roe v. Wade.*

Source: Guttmacher Institute, Center for Reproductive Rights, NARAL Pro-Choice America, 2012. Available at http://www.remappingdebate.org/map-data-tool/dozens-new-state-limits-abortions-added-2012?page=0,1. Reprinted Courtesy of Remapping Debate (remappingdebate.org).

the States: Restrictiveness of State Abortion Laws for a comparison of abortion law restrictiveness.) Depending on the state, these restrictions may impose earlier bans tied to when a fetus can feel pain, require ultrasound tests before an abortion, mandate counseling sessions discussing the potential risks of breast cancer or mental health problems (including suicide), increase state oversight of abortion clinics, restrict physicians from prescribing drugs to induce abortion unless in the room with the patient, and require longer waiting periods between counseling and abortions.[76] One of the fiercest fights took place in the Texas Legislature and garnered national attention. Though Republicans controlled the state Senate, a female senator (Democrat) tried to block (unsuccessfully) a restrictive abortion bill with a 13-hour filibuster. Many of these new, more restrictive, laws are likely to be challenged in court by supporters of abortion rights.

15.14   POLITICS AND SEXUAL ORIENTATION

Trace the expansion of gay rights from the Stonewall riots through the Supreme Court's recent decision about the Defense of Marriage Act, and list various gay rights issue areas that are covered by state laws.

The political movement on behalf of gay and lesbian rights is often traced back to the 1969 Stonewall riots in New York City, where gays confronted police in an effort to halt harassment. Since that time gays have made considerable strides in winning public acceptance of their lifestyle and in changing public policy. (See Figure 15–3.) Today, nearly 60 percent of Americans acknowledge they have a family member or close friend who is gay or lesbian.[77]

Privacy Rights X

Historically, "sodomy" was defined as "an act against the laws of human nature" and criminalized in most states. As late as 1986, the U.S. Supreme Court upheld a Georgia law against sodomy, holding that "the Constitution does not confer a fundamental right upon homosexuals to engage in sodomy."[78] But the Supreme Court reversed its position in 2003 in *Lawrence* v. *Texas,* holding that consenting adults "engaged in sexual practices common to a homosexual lifestyle . . . are entitled to respect for their private lives. . . . Their right to liberty under the Due Process Clause gives them the full right to engage in their conduct without the intervention of the government."[79] The Court noted that since its earlier decision most of the states had repealed their laws against sodomy. *Lawrence* v. *Texas* is a landmark decision that is likely to affect every type of case involving sexual orientation, including employment, marriage, child custody, and adoption.

FIGURE 15–3 Generation Gap: Changing Attitudes toward Same-Sex Marriage

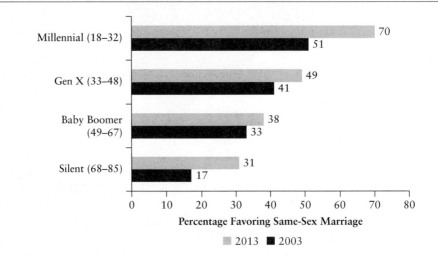

Note: Data are from a telephone interview with 1,501 adults conducted March 13–17, 2013. Margin of error ±3 percentage points.
Source: Pew Research Center, "Growing Support for Gay Marriage: Changed Minds and Changing Demographics," March 20, 2013. Available at http://www.people-press.org/2013/03/20/growing-support-for-gay-marriage-changed-minds-and-changing-demographics/.
© 2013 National Conference of State Legislatures.

However, the Court has refused to interfere with private or religious organizations that ban avowed gays or lesbians. In *Boy Scouts of America* v. *Dale* in 2000, the Court upheld a Boy Scout prohibition against gays becoming scout leaders.[80] It also upheld the decision by the organizers of New York's annual St. Patrick's Day Parade to exclude a gay marching contingent. But public protests against these policies have intensified as support for gay rights has broadened. The Boy Scouts of America organization has begun to reexamine its restrictive policies on the sexual orientation of employees, volunteers, and members. Resistance to change has largely come from religious organizations who sponsor and fund many of the Boy Scouts' activities. Similarly, opposition to including gays and lesbians in Irish Catholic St. Patrick's Day parades across the United States has historically been on religious grounds.[81]

"Don't Ask, Don't Tell"

Upon taking office in 1993, President Bill Clinton announced his intention to overturn the military's existing ban on gays serving in the military. Gay rights groups had donated heavily to the Clinton campaign, ranking them along with the Jewish community, the entertainment industry, and environmentalists as the Democratic Party's biggest contribu-

Houston, the nation's fourth largest city, elected Annise Parker as mayor, making her the nation's first openly gay mayor of a major U.S. city.

tors. But military professionals at the time strongly objected to this move, and veterans groups including the American Legion and the Veterans of Foreign Wars criticized the plan. Clinton was obliged to compromise the issue and the policy of "don't ask, don't tell" emerged. The policy was that the military would no longer inquire into the sexual orientation of service personnel or recruits as long as they do not make their orientation public. In 2010, Congress passed and President Obama signed a law repealing the policy once it has shown to be "consistent with the standards of military readiness, military effectiveness, unit cohesion, and recruiting and retention of the Armed Forces." In November 2010, the Defense Department's report affirmed the policy would have no harmful impact and steps to fully implement the repeal began.

Same-Sex Marriage

In 2003, the Massachusetts Supreme Court ruled that same-sex couples had a right to marriage under the Massachusetts state constitution. Immediately thereafter, many states passed laws or constitutional amendments defining marriage as between a man and a woman. Later, reflective of changing attitudes, a number of states began moving in the opposite direction, approving more liberal policies such as same sex marriage and civil unions. A legal challenge to California voters' rejection of same sex marriage (see Chapter 2) ended up in the U.S. Supreme Court (*Hollingsworth* v. *Perry*, 2013). In early 2013, the Court heard oral arguments on whether states have the authority to ban same-sex marriage. In 2008, the California Supreme Court had held that banning same-sex marriages was an unconstitutional denial of the Equal Protection Clause of the 14th Amendment. But that same year, California voters passed a state constitutional amendment, Proposition 8, declaring that "only marriage between a man and a woman is valid or recognized in California." California officials, including the governor, refused to defend Proposition 8 in federal courts. Lower federal courts held that Proposition 8 was unconstitutional. But when the case was presented to the U.S. Supreme Court, it held on a technicality that the parties to the case had no "standing" before the Court. But the effect of the Courts decision was to let the lower federal courts' rulings stand, thus approving same-sex marriages in California. Same-sex marriages in California resumed on July 28, 2013. The U.S. Supreme Court's ruling in that case was restricted to California and did not prevent other states from banning same-sex marriages.

Defense of Marriage Act (DOMA)

Anticipating that some states might pass laws allowing same-sex marriage, or that some state courts might rule that such marriages were constitutionally protected in their states, Congress passed a Defense of Marriage Act in 1996. This Act declared that marriage is between a man and a woman and that "no state . . . shall be required to give effect to any public act, record, judicial proceeding of any other state respecting a relationship between persons of the same sex that is treated as marriage." This provision is designed to circumvent the Full Faith and Credit Clause of Article IV of the U.S. Constitution that requires each state to recognize the "public acts, records, and judicial proceedings of every other state." (Article IV does, however, include a provision that Congress may "prescribe the manner in which such acts records and proceedings shall be proved, and the effect thereof.")

The gay rights movement was bitterly opposed to the Defense of Marriage Act from the outset. In 2013, the U.S. Supreme Court heard a case challenging DOMA's definition of marriage as between a man and a woman and its prohibition against federal recognition of legal state same-sex marriagelaws (*United States* v. *Windsor*).The case, brought by a gay couple from New York, challenged the federal government's DOMA-based denial of a federal tax exemption for property inherited by one of the couple upon the death of another. The complex case involved questions of both individual liberty and the federal-state relationship.[82] Former president Bill Clinton, who had originally signed the Defense of Marriage Act in 1996, disavowed the Act right before it went to the Supreme Court in an op-ed in the *Washington Post*. He attributed his change of heart to his daughter, Chelsea, and her gay friends.[83]

The Defense of Marriage Act (DOMA) passed by Congress had declared that marriage is between a man and a woman and that "no state shall be required to give effect to any public act, record, or judicial proceeding of any other state respecting a relationship between persons of the same sex that is treated as a marriage." The effect of DOMA was to allow states to reject marriages between same-sex partners that had been performed in other states. It also denied spousal benefits under a wide variety of federal laws, including estate tax laws. President Barack Obama said his views on same-sex marriage were "evolving," and he ordered the U.S. Justice Department not to defend DOMA in federal court.

The U.S. Supreme Court ruled in 2013 that DOMA was an unconstitutional deprivation of due process and equal protection of the law. A same-sex couple legally married in New York could not be denied spousal benefits under federal law. Historically, federal law has deferred to state law in domestic relations, and the New York legislature had approved same-sex marriage. The Court argued that DOMA required the states to treat same-sex couples unequally. "The avowed purpose and practical effect of the law is to impose a disadvantage, a separate status, and so a stigma upon all who enter into same-sex marriages made lawful by the unquestioned authority of the states." Thus, the Court ruled DOMA to be unconstitutional with respect to its application to *federal* laws and regulations. However, the court did not rule that states were forbidden to deny marriage licenses to same-sex couples. As in the *Hollingsworth* decision, the Court's decision in the *Windsor* case was not a clear-cut ruling in favor of same-sex marriages in every state.

Regardless of the two court rulings, Same-sex marriages are increasingly being recognized in the states. As of 2013, 13 states allowed same-sex marriages. In three of these states—Maine, Maryland, and Washington—voters approved same-sex marriage by referendum. Polls showed that by 2011 a majority of Americans supported same-sex marriage.

AIDS

The gay rights movement was threatened in the early 1980s by the spread of the HIV virus and the deadly disease, acquired immune deficiency syndrome, or AIDS. Gay men were identified as one of the high-risk groups in the United States. The medical consensus was that the disease is spread through sexual activity especially prevalent among male homosexuals, as well as through the sharing of contaminated needles among intravenous drug users and through blood infusions. Casual contact (touching, kissing, using common utensils) does not transmit the disease. But the gay rights movement was successful in its campaign to convince Americans that "anyone could get AIDS," and over time it won the sympathy and support of the American public. Funding for AIDS research rose dramatically. The Centers for Disease Control and Prevention (CDC) gave priority to the search for antidotes to the virus, and at the same time, instituted a public education effort aimed at changing sexual behavior. Gay organizations across the nation distributed material describing safe-sex practices. Over time deaths from AIDS declined and the feared epidemic was held in check.

State Laws

Much of the conflict over gay rights occurs at the state level—in referenda, legislative enactments, and in court—yielding a complex mosaic of laws involving sexual orientation throughout the nation. Among the issues confronting the states:

- *Adoption.* Should gay and lesbian couples be allowed to adopt children?
- *Hate crimes.* Should hate crime laws also protect gays?
- *Health.* Should health insurance companies be required to extend benefits to gay spouses?
- *Employment.* Should laws against job discrimination be extended to protect gays?
- *Housing.* Should laws against discrimination in housing be extended to protect gays?
- *Marriage.* Should gay and lesbian couples be allowed to marry?
- **Civil unions.** Should gay and lesbian couples be allowed to legally form civil unions, giving them many of the rights of married couples?

State laws differ on each of these issues, although recent changes have generally benefited gays and lesbians.[84]

CIVIL UNIONS
A legal status some states give to same-sex couples that provide rights, responsibilities, and benefits similar to those of opposite-sex civil marriages.

The Politics of Sexual Orientation

The gay movement includes a loose coalition of groups, including lesbian gay bisexual and transgender (LGBT) centers; National Gay and Lesbian Task Force; Queer Nation; AIDS Coalition to Unleash Power (ACT-UP); and Gay Lesbian Alliance Against Discrimination (GLAAD). Many of these groups have affiliates in colleges, universities, and communities across the country.

The goals of the gay movement have evolved over the years from initially seeking protection against government restrictions on private behavior; to later seeking government protection of gays and lesbians from discrimination; to still later seeking societal approval of homosexuality as a morally equivalent lifestyle.[85] Over time public opinion has become much more supportive of gay and lesbian goals. Support is especially strong among the Millennial Generation.

CHAPTER HIGHLIGHTS

- The earliest civil rights battles in the states primarily focused on racial discrimination. In recent years, the struggles have extended to gender, disability, age, and sexual preference. While the federal laws and court rulings were instrumental in legally ending discrimination, states and localities were responsible for making it happen. Some did it faster than others.
- A landmark case in civil rights occurred in 1954 when the U.S. Supreme Court declared in *Brown* v. *Board of Education of Topeka, Kansas* that segregation in America's public schools which were "separate but equal" was unconstitutional. Even so, the eleven states of the old Confederacy resisted integration for over a decade until forced by court orders.

- In 1971 the U.S. Supreme Court upheld cross-district busing to achieve racial balance in schools in cases where governments had historically contributed to racial isolation. But busing was not required when racial imbalances occurred as a result of residential patterns.

- Some cities that used extensive busing experienced such massive "white flight" from the public schools that the schools have ended up even more racially separated than before busing. And racial imbalance continues to increase in the schools in neighborhoods that have become more segregated.

- Congress entered the fight for equality by passing the Civil Rights Act of 1964, which prohibited discrimination in public accommodations (hotels and restaurants), employment, and all government programs receiving federal financial assistance. A 1965 law banned voting restrictions, and a 1968 law prohibited discrimination in housing.

- In the 1970s, policy shifted from seeking equality of *opportunity* to achieving greater equality of *results* between minorities and whites through affirmative action plans. The goal was minority representation in education and employment in proportion to a minority's numbers in the population.

- *Bakke* and other cases have led to changes in affirmative action programs to avoid discrimination against whites under the Equal Protection Clause of the Fourteenth Amendment. At least three states, led by a California citizens' initiative in 1996, have constitutional bans on the use of racial preferences. But legal challenges are still ongoing.

- The success of Cesar Chavez in organizing the United Farm Workers union in California plus opposition to a ban on children of immigrants attending public schools galvanized Mexican Americans throughout the Southwest to engage in political activity. Puerto Ricans and younger Cubans have been mobilized by anti-immigrant statements made by elected officials in certain parts of the country. (A majority of Hispanics prefer to describe themselves by their country of origin.)

- Hispanic voter turnout remains low, perhaps because of lower educational levels, language difficulties, or questions about immigration status. But Hispanics now form the nation's largest minority and are expected to exert growing political power at all levels of government, although they are not as cohesive as African Americans in their voting patterns.

- After decades of broken treaties, wars, and poverty on reservations, many Native American tribal governments have reasserted their sovereignty, notably in establishing casinos, often straining relationships with state and local governments. The tribes also successfully fought and won a complaint against the federal government for mismanagement of Indian-owned lands leased out to various companies extracting natural resources.

- The Americans with Disabilities Act of 1990 prohibits discrimination in private employment, government programs, public accommodations, and telecommunications because of a person's disability—not only physical but also learning and mental disability.

- The Age Discrimination in Employment Act of 1967 makes it against the law for companies to discriminate against a person because of age in hiring, promotions, layoffs, firings, pay, fringe benefits, job assignments or training. Age discrimination lawsuits are increasing, largely driven by the baby boomers. Proving age discrimination is harder than proving race discrimination.

- Federal law prohibits discrimination against women in employment and education, and the U.S. Supreme Court has had to clarify what constitutes sexual harassment. But so far the federal courts have refused to consider the concept of "comparable worth" in overcoming lower pay for women.

- In the landmark *Roe* v. *Wade* in 1973, the U.S. Supreme Court declared that the constitutional guarantee of "liberty" in the Fifth and Fourteenth Amendments includes a woman's decision about whether to bear a child. As contraceptives have become more easily available, the abortion rate has declined. It is still a divisive issue and conservative one-party controlled states continue to pass tougher restrictions.

- In the aftermath of a Supreme Court ruling in 2003 that intimate acts of consenting gay and lesbian adults are a liberty protected by the Fourteenth Amendment, states are considering whether gays may marry, adopt children, be protected against discrimination in housing and employment, and receive the same benefits given to married couples. Liberal states have been far quicker to embrace same sex marriage and other gay rights than conservative states.

CHAPTER SIXTEEN

THE POLITICS OF EDUCATION

LEARNING OBJECTIVES

 16.1 Describe the three main goals in education policy.

 16.2 Discuss the various educational performance measures, and assess the quality of student outcomes in the United States.

 16.3 Analyze the effectiveness of efforts to reform education through increased spending, magnet schools, and charter schools.

 16.4 Explain how school vouchers work, evaluate the arguments for and against them, and describe how voters and the courts have reacted to voucher programs.

 16.5 Explain how virtual schools work, and evaluate the arguments for and against them.

16.6 Outline the Common Core educational standards that have been adopted by most states.

16.7 Trace the expansion of federal involvement in education policy, and describe the financial contributions for education by federal, state, and local governments.

 16.8 Discuss the core features of No Child Left Behind and the Obama administration's position on the law.

 16.9 Describe Obama's Race to the Top initiative, and contrast it with George W. Bush's No Child Left Behind.

16.10 Outline the organizational structure that states have developed to provide public education, and describe the financial contributions states provide to local school districts.

 16.11 Describe the inequality in "per student" school funding across states and school districts, evaluate why such inequalities exist, and assess the impact of these inequalities on educational outcomes.

 16.12 Outline the decision-making processes used in school districts, and assess the impact of teachers unions on these processes.

 16.13 Describe the reach of higher education in the United States, the organizational structure of the higher education system, and the policies enacted by both federal and state governments to fund higher education and student loans.

 16.14 Evaluate the arguments for and against public support for private schools, discuss the constitutional limits on such support as determined by the U.S. Supreme Court, and summarize the current status of prayer in public schools.

 16.15 Outline the challenges schools face in protecting students from criminals and bullies while at school.

 16.1

Describe the three main goals in education policy.

GOALS IN EDUCATIONAL POLICY

The primary responsibility for American public education rests with the 50 state governments and their local school districts. It is one of the largest and most costly of state functions. Today, about 56 million pupils are in grade schools and high schools in America. About 50 million are in public schools and 6 million in private schools. Nearly 22 million students are enrolled in institutions of higher education: community colleges, colleges, and universities. Education is a top priority for many state and local officials who see it as a key to an area's economy. Their goal is to create an educational system that prepares students for a satisfying and productive life and helps them succeed in the increasingly competitive global economy. Two-thirds of the public agree that "a world-class education is the single most important factor in determining whether our kids can compete for the best jobs and whether America can outcompete countries around the world."[1]

Educating Citizens

In 1647, the Massachusetts colonial legislature first required towns to provide for the education of children out of public funds. The rugged individualists of earlier eras thought it outrageous that one person should be taxed to pay for the education of another person's child. They were joined in their opposition to public education by those aristocrats who were opposed to arming the common people with the power that knowledge gives. However, the logic of democracy led inevitably to public education. The earliest democrats believed that the safest repository of the ultimate powers of society was the people themselves. If the people make mistakes, the remedy was not to remove power from their hands, but to help them in forming their judgment through education. Congress passed the **Northwest Ordinance** in 1787 offering land grants for public schools in the new territories and giving succeeding generations words to be forever etched on grammar school cornerstones: "Religion, morality, and knowledge being necessary to good government and the happiness of mankind, schools and the means for education shall ever be encouraged." When American democracy adopted universal suffrage, it affected every aspect of American life, and particularly education. If the people were to be granted the right of suffrage, they must be educated to the task. This meant that public education had to be universal, free, and compulsory.

NORTHWEST ORDINANCE

The first recognition by Congress in 1787 of the importance of education to democracy; provided grants of federal land to states for public schools.

Advancing Social Goals

If there ever was a time when schools were expected only to combat ignorance and illiteracy, that time is far behind us. Today, schools are expected to do many things: resolve racial conflict and build an integrated society; improve the self-image of minority children; inspire patriotism and good citizenship; offer various forms of recreation and mass entertainment (football games, bands, choruses, drama clubs, and the like); teach children to get along well with others and appreciate multiple cultures; reduce the highway accident toll by teaching students to be good drivers; eliminate unemployment and poverty by teaching job skills; end malnutrition and hunger through school lunch and milk programs; produce scientists and other technicians to continue America's progress in science and technology; fight drug abuse and educate children about sex and sexually transmitted diseases; and act as custodians for teenagers who have no interest in education, but are not permitted to work or roam the streets unsupervised. In other words, nearly all the nation's problems are reflected in demands placed on schools. And, of course, these demands are frequently conflicting.

Strengthening the Economy

Governors, legislators, and candidates for almost every office regularly extol education as the key to economic development in their states. As governor of Arkansas, Bill Clinton was once quoted as saying, "Low education levels of the workforce are perhaps the biggest stumbling block to economic growth."[2] It is theorized that a well-educated workforce creates the "human capital" that becomes the stimulus to economic development, especially in the "information age." University-based "research parks" are promoted in the states as a magnet for high-tech industry.[3]

But regrettably there is little systematic evidence that state spending for education—for either public elementary and secondary schools or for higher education—has any *direct* impact on economic growth rates in the states.[4] (Even average state SAT scores are *un*related to economic growth rates.) Direct state investment in physical infrastructure, especially transportation, is the only public expenditure that consistently correlates with economic growth in the states.[5] However, over the long run education and economic development are related. "If you think education is expensive, you should try ignorance."

INPUTS
Measures of resources expended on education.

OUTPUTS
Measures of what, if anything, pupils are learning.

EDUCATIONAL PERFORMANCE MEASUREMENT

16.2

Too often educational reports focus on "**inputs**"—measures of resources expended on education—rather than "**outputs**"—measures of what, if anything, pupils are learning. Professional educators frequently resist performance measurement, especially comparisons between states or school districts. It is true that many performance measures, especially test scores, are controversial; many commentators argue that they do not measure the

Discuss the various educational performance measures, and assess the quality of student outcomes in the United States.

qualitative goals of education or that they are biased in one fashion or another. Certainly all interested citizens will welcome future refinements in educational performance measurement. But we cannot ignore performance simply because our measures are unrefined. We need to make reasoned use of the best available comparative measures of educational performance, including measures of teacher performance. (See "*People in Politics: Jeff Charbonneau*—"Mr. Robot," The Nation's Best Teacher.")

Educational Attainment

Educational attainment is measured by the years of school completed, rather than by student knowledge. In educational attainment, the nation has an enviable record, with 78 percent of the overall population now graduating from high school. Discrepancies between white and

Intense debates among teachers, students, and parents over how to measure student achievement are ongoing. Any sort of testing tied to graduation is seen by some as "unfair" but to others it is regarded as an essential element of holding schools accountable for educating students.

Jeff Charbonneau—"Mr. Robot," The Nation's Best Teacher

Jeff Charbonneau, 63rd National Teacher of the Year

Jeff Charbonneau teaches 9th–12th grade Chemistry, Physics, and Engineering at Zillah High School (a small rural high school) in Zillah, Washington—a city of around 3,000 residents located in Washington's Yakima Valley. Jeff's teaching philosophy:

> I greet my students in class every day by saying 'Welcome back to another day in paradise. The reality is that paradise must be built, maintained and improved each day. It removes the words 'can't,' 'too hard' and 'impossible' from our vocabulary. This concept has become my philosophy of teaching, as I foster self-confidence, academic success, collaboration and dedication within my classroom, school and greater community.

This outstanding teacher founded a statewide robotics competition. "Mr. Robot" admitted his subject matter was initially intimidating to many students: "I fight a stigma. Students hear the words 'quantum mechanics' and instantly think 'too hard' and 'no way.' It is my job to convince them that they are smart enough, that they can do anything."

Measuring Teacher Performance

The challenge facing many states is how to measure teacher performance and how to reward the best teachers. The Council of Chief State School Officers has been doing it for years through its National Teacher of the Year Program which began in 1952. So just what are the criteria the Council uses to make its selection?

> A candidate for National Teacher of the Year is a State Teacher of the Year who is an exceptionally dedicated, knowledgeable, and skilled teacher in any state-approved or accredited school: prekindergarten through grade 12, who is planning to continue in an active teaching status. The National Teacher of the Year should:

- Inspire students of all backgrounds and abilities to learn.
- Have the respect and admiration of students, parents, and colleagues.
- Play an active and useful role in the community as well as in the school.
- Be poised, articulate, and possess the energy to withstand a taxing schedule.

Sources: Elizabeth Chuck, "Innovative Science Teacher Honored as National Teacher of the Year," NBC News, April 23, 2013.

Council of Chief State School Officers, "About the National Teacher of the Year Program," and "WA Teacher Named 2013 National Teacher of the Year." Available at www.ccsso.org; accessed May 3, 2013.

Source: National Education Association. Available at http://neatoday.org/2013/04/23/2013-teacher-of-the-year-jeff-charbonneau-honored-at-white-house/

black educational attainment have diminished. (See Figure 16–1.) High school graduation rates of blacks and whites are nearing parity. Only Hispanic education levels still appear to lag. States with the highest graduation rates are Iowa, Vermont, and Wisconsin, the lowest are in Nevada and New Mexico. States with lower graduation rates have more diverse student populations—with larger proportions of low-income, disadvantaged, less English-fluent students.[6]

A college education is now fairly common. Asian Americans have the highest graduation rate (52%). The white college graduation rate has reached 30 percent and the black college graduation rate almost 20 percent. Again, the Hispanic rate seems to lag. As late as 2000, women's educational attainment rates were below those of men. But that condition has changed; today, women have higher educational attainment rates than men. Women now comprise 56 percent of all college students.

The Dropout Rate

Certainly one measure of an educational system's performance is its ability to retain and graduate its students. National studies have consistently shown that high school dropouts tend to

FIGURE 16–1 Educational Attainment by Race

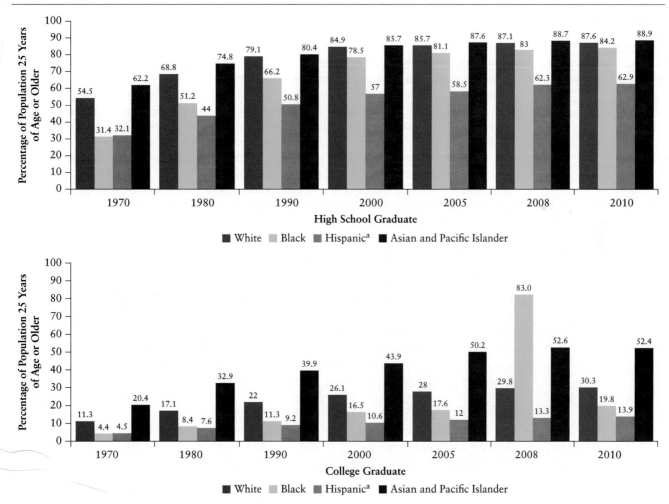

[a]Persons of Hispanic origin may be of any race.
Source: U.S. Census Bureau, Statistical Abstract of the United States, 2012, Table 229. Available at http://www.census.gov/prod/2011pubs/12statab/educ.pdf.

experience more unemployment and earn less over a lifetime than high school graduates. Yet often schools fail to convince young people that staying in school is a worthwhile endeavor.

The conflict over dropouts begins with arguments over how to measure the dropout rate. Three separate measures are regularly employed:

1. *Event Dropouts:* Persons who are recorded by the schools as having stopped attending during the 10th, 11th, and 12th grades, as a percentage of total attendance. This figure is preferred by professional educators because it is very low, at nearly 3 percent.

2. *Status Dropouts:* Persons age 18 to 24 who are not attending school and have not graduated from high school, as a percentage of all persons in that age group. The national status dropout rate is about 13 percent.

3. *High School Graduation Rate:* The number of high school graduates as a percentage of ninth graders four years earlier. The high school graduation rate is only 78 percent nationwide, indicating that about one-quarter of high school students drop out.

The good news is that high school dropout rates are declining over time, however they are measured. Even so, dropout rates differ by race and ethnicity. Dropout rates for blacks and Hispanics remain higher than those for whites and Asians. Dropout rates are higher than the national average in southern states and states with large Hispanic populations.

SAT Scores

For many years critics of modern public education cited declining scores on standardized tests, particularly the Scholastic Assessment Test (SAT), as evidence of the failure of the schools to teach basic reading and mathematics skills.[7] **SAT scores** declined dramatically during the 1960s and 1970s, ironically during a period in which per pupil educational spending was rising and the federal government initiated federal aid to education. (See Figure 16–2.) When the decline ended in 1982, it was attributed to increasing emphasis on basic skills and standardized testing. But changes in these test scores are also a function of how many students take the test. During the declining years, increasing numbers of students were taking the test—students who never aspired to college in the past and whose test scores did not match those of the earlier, smaller group of college-bound test takers.

Professional educators generally oppose efforts to assess state educational performance by comparing average SAT scores. Indeed, the College Board "strongly cautions against comparing states based on SAT scores alone" (but see "*Rankings of the States: Educational Performance*"). In some states, more than 75 percent of graduating students take the test, while in other states fewer than 20 percent do so. Average scores are higher when only a small select group takes the test.

SAT score increases in recent years have been attributed to the increased emphasis in schools on testing for basic skills. An influential 1983 report by the Commission on Excellence in Education titled "A Nation at Risk" recommended, among other things, standardized tests for promotion and graduation.[8] Many states responded to the demand for greater achievement in basic skills by requiring minimum competency testing in the schools. The U.S. Department of Education began giving tests each year to a sample of 4th-, 8th-, and 12th-grade students and publishing the results. This National Assessment of Educational Progress gave added emphasis to the testing movement. But testing finally became nationwide with the passage of the No Child Left Behind Act in 2001 (see "No Child Left Behind" later in this chapter).

Minority group leaders often charge that tests are racially biased. Average scores of African American students are frequently lower than those of white students on standardized tests. (See Figure 16–3.) Larger percentages of black students are held back from promotion and graduation by testing than are white students. However, to date, federal courts have declined to rule that testing requirements for promotion or graduation are discriminatory, as long as sufficient time and opportunity have been provided for all students to prepare for the examinations.

FIGURE 16–2 SAT Score Trends

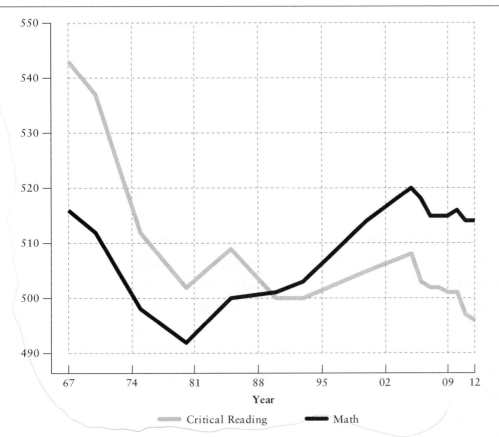

FIGURE 16–3 Average SAT Scores by Race/Ethnicity

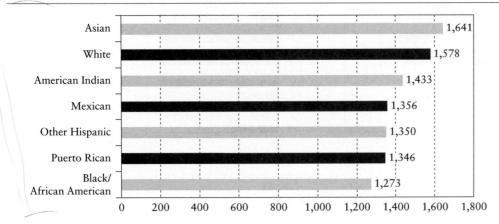

Note: Data are for 2012. Based on the 2400 Scale.

Educational Performance

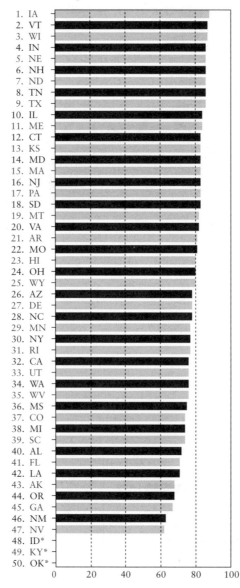

High School Graduation Rate (%)

1. IA
2. VT
3. WI
4. IN
5. NE
6. NH
7. ND
8. TN
9. TX
10. IL
11. ME
12. CT
13. KS
14. MD
15. MA
16. NJ
17. PA
18. SD
19. MT
20. VA
21. AR
22. MO
23. HI
24. OH
25. WY
26. AZ
27. DE
28. NC
29. MN
30. NY
31. RI
32. CA
33. UT
34. WA
35. WV
36. MS
37. CO
38. MI
39. SC
40. AL
41. FL
42. LA
43. AK
44. OR
45. GA
46. NM
47. NV
48. ID*
49. KY*
50. OK*

0   20   40   60   80   100

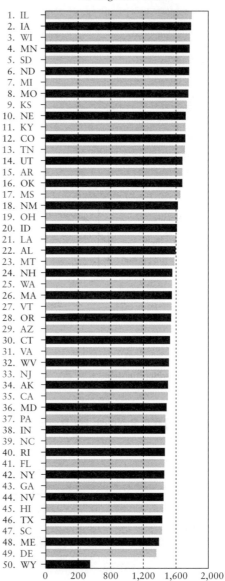

Average SAT Scores

1. IL
2. IA
3. WI
4. MN
5. SD
6. ND
7. MI
8. MO
9. KS
10. NE
11. KY
12. CO
13. TN
14. UT
15. AR
16. OK
17. MS
18. NM
19. OH
20. ID
21. LA
22. AL
23. MT
24. NH
25. WA
26. MA
27. VT
28. OR
29. AZ
30. CT
31. VA
32. WV
33. NJ
34. AK
35. CA
36. MD
37. PA
38. IN
39. NC
40. RI
41. FL
42. NY
43. GA
44. NV
45. HI
46. TX
47. SC
48. ME
49. DE
50. WY

0   200   800   1,200   1,600   2,000

Note: Data are for 2011 school year. High School Graduation Rate is a percent of students who graduated as part of a four-year cohort, adjusted for students transferring in and out of the class.

[a]Idaho, Kentucky, and Oklahoma received extensions for data submission and data are not available.

Source: U.S. Department of Education "States Report New High School Graduation Rates Using More Accurate, Common Measure," November 26, 2012. Available at http://www2.ed.gov/documents/press-releases/state-2010-11-graduation-rate-data.pdf.

Note: Data are for 2012. Scores are based on a maximum score of 2,400.
Source: 2012 College Bound Seniors: Total Group Profile Report. Copyright © 2012. The College Board. www.collegeboard.org. Reproduced with permission.

EDUCATIONAL REFORM

How can the quality of education be improved? Systematic research has made it clear that money alone does not guarantee good educational performance. The early landmark work of sociologist James Coleman, *Equality of Educational Opportunity* (popularly known as the **Coleman report**), demonstrated that per pupil expenditures, teacher salaries, classroom size, facilities, and materials were *un*related to student achievement.[9] Student success is more closely related to characteristics of the home environment than to those of the schools. However, Coleman later demonstrated that student achievement levels are higher in schools in which there is a high expectation for achievement, an orderly and disciplined learning environment, an emphasis on basic skills, frequent monitoring of student progress, and teacher–parent interaction and agreement on values and norms.[10]

COLEMAN REPORT

Work of sociologist James Coleman that demonstrated that pupil expenditures, teacher salaries, classroom size, facilities, and materials were unrelated to student achievement.

Educational Spending

There is no evidence that increased spending for public education improves student achievement. Public elementary and secondary school spending per pupil has risen dramatically over the years. Indeed, since 1980 spending per pupil has quadrupled, yet SAT scores have improved only modestly. (See Figure 16–2.) Even the public has become somewhat skeptical of the link between spending and student achievement; just 36 percent think student performance in America will improve if more money is spent on schools and education programs, 40 percent do not, and 24 percent are not sure.[11] The apparent failure of money alone, including federal aid, to significantly affect student achievement directed the focus of educational improvements to new and sometimes controversial reforms.

Magnet Schools

A common reform proposal is the "**magnet school**." High schools choose to specialize, some emphasizing math and science, others the fine arts, others business, and still others vocational training. Some schools might be "adopted" by businesses, professional organizations, or universities. Magnet schools, with reputations for quality and specialized instruction, are frequently recommended for inner-city areas in order to attract white pupils and reduce racial isolation.

MAGNET SCHOOLS

Schools emphasizing instruction in particular areas in an effort to improve quality and attract students.

Charter Schools

Yet another reform that has been advanced is the **charter school**. Community educational groups, including public school teachers and parents, receive a "charter" from their school district or state education department to establish their own school. They receive waivers from most state and school district regulations to enable them to be more innovative; in exchange for this flexibility they promise to show specific student achievement. They receive tax money from the state and school district based on their enrollment. Minnesota was the first state to permit charter schools (1991); now most states have them.[12] Nearly 2 million students across the United States are enrolled in over 5,000 charter schools.

CHARTER SCHOOLS

Schools operated with public funds by private community groups under a charter from public school districts or other granting agency.

The experience with charter schools to date is uneven. There is no clear evidence that pupils transferring to charter schools improve their performance on achievement tests, although parents of charter school pupils express greater satisfaction with their children's education.[13] Opponents—primarily public school officials and teachers' unions—argue that charter schools divert much-needed funds from public schools. A study released by the National Center for Education Statistics found that charter schools fail to boost educational achievement when demographic controls are employed in the analysis.[14] Another study by the Center for Research on Education Outcomes at Stanford University found that 17 percent of charter schools were better at educating kids than public schools,

46 percent were about the same, and 37 percent were worse, although in the *long term*, charter school students did better than their public school counterparts.[15] Many charter schools have initiated unorthodox curricula, and many have employed teachers with little or no background in education.[16] Although charter schools promise results, there are few ways to hold them accountable; theoretically, charters can be revoked, but revocation has proven difficult. It has prompted a number of states to pass legislation focused more on improving charter school accountability and quality.

The charter school movement was given strong impetus by the Obama administration's Race to the Top program (see "Race to the Top" later in the chapter). In this federal program, competitive grants are offered to the states based on a variety of reforms, among them the enactment of rigorous charter school laws. Charter school growth is part of the "scorecard" produced by the U.S. Department of Education ranking of the states for consideration for the award of federal money.[17]

EDUCATIONAL VOUCHERS

Vouchers given to parents to pay for their children's education at schools of their own choosing, redeemable by the schools in public funds from the state and school district.

16.4

THE DEBATE OVER SCHOOL VOUCHERS

Explain how school vouchers work, evaluate the arguments for and against them, and describe how voters and the courts have reacted to voucher programs.

An even more controversial reform involves **educational vouchers** that are given to parents to spend at any school they choose, public or private. State governments would redeem the vouchers submitted by schools by paying specified amounts for each student enrolled—perhaps the equivalent of the state's average per pupil educational spending (the U.S. average is over $11,000). Today, 17 states offer 33 programs that allow parents to use taxpayer money to send their children to private schools, according to the American Federation for Children—a nonprofit advocacy group favoring school vouchers and tax-credit scholarship programs.[18]

"My child, my choice" reflects the sentiment of school voucher supporters. Among the strongest proponents are parents from poor or disadvantaged homes whose children do not have the same option as children from more affluent homes of fleeing poorly performing public schools and enrolling in private schools.

The Pro-Voucher Argument

Proponents of vouchers argue that parental choice among schools would promote competition and enhance achievement. Vouchers would inspire both public and private schools to compete equally for students. State education funds would flow to those schools that successfully enrolled more students. Competition would encourage all schools to satisfy parental demands for excellence. Racial or religious or ethnic discrimination would be strictly prohibited in any private or public school receiving vouchers. It is argued that providing vouchers for children from poor or disadvantaged homes, or children who are currently attending poor public schools, is the most effective way of serving their needs. These children currently do not have the same option as children from more affluent homes of fleeing the public schools and enrolling in private academies.[19]

Opposition to Vouchers

Yet there is strong opposition to the voucher idea.[20] The most vocal opposition comes from professional school administrators, state education agencies, and teachers unions. They argue that giving parents the right to move their children from school to school disrupts educational planning and threatens the viability of schools that are perceived as inferior. It may lead to a stratification of schools into popular schools that attract the best students, and less popular schools that are left with the task of educating students whose parents are unaware of or uninterested in their children's education. Other opponents of choice plans fear that public education may be undermined by diverting public money from public to private schools.

Voters Reject Vouchers

The voucher movement was dealt a major setback in 1993 when California voters soundly defeated a citizens' initiative known as Proposition 174, Parental Choice in Education. Professional educators, teachers' unions, and liberal groups joined together to mount an expensive, highly publicized campaign to defeat the measure. Proposition 174 promised to "empower parents" by granting each schoolchild a "scholarship" (voucher) equal to about one-half of the average amount of state and local government aid per pupil in California. The money was to be paid directly to the schools in which parents chose to enroll their children. Either public or private schools could qualify as "scholarship-redeeming schools"; schools that discriminated on the basis of race, ethnicity, color, or national origin would not be eligible. Opposition groups, including the powerful California Teachers Association, argued that the proposal would create a "two-tier system of schools, one for the haves, one for the have-nots." They portrayed vouchers as "an entitlement program offering wealthy families a private-school subsidy for their children, paid for by the taxpayers,"[21] noting that there was no means test for the vouchers.

Vouchers as a Constitutional Issue

School vouchers paid to religious schools by states raised the issue of whether or not these payments violated the First Amendment's prohibition against the "establishment of religion." Earlier Supreme Court decisions had invalidated programs that provided *direct* government subsidies to religious schools. But the Court had approved of state and federal scholarships granted directly to students who then used them to enroll in religious colleges and universities.

Opponents of vouchers argue that public education will be harmed by diverting public money from public to private schools.

When Ohio initiated a "Scholarship Program" that provided tuition aid to certain students in the Cleveland City School District who could choose to use this aid to attend either public or private or religious schools of their parents' choosing, opponents challenged the program in federal court, arguing that it "advanced a religious mission" in violation of the No Establishment Clause of the First Amendment. Although parents could use the vouchers to send their children to other public schools or nonreligious private schools, over 90 percent of the students participating in the scholarship program were enrolled in religiously affiliated schools. Sixty percent of the students were from families at or below the poverty line. In 2002 the U.S. Supreme Court held (in a narrow 5–4 decision) that the program did *not* violate the Constitution. The Court reasoned that the program was neutral with respect to religion and provided assistance directly to citizens who, in turn, directed this aid to religious schools wholly as a result of their own independent private choices. The incidental advancement of a religious mission is reasonably attributed to the individual recipients, not the government, "whose role ends with the distribution of benefits."[22]

VIRTUAL SCHOOL
School where classes are taught entirely through online methods.

VIRTUAL SCHOOLS

16.5

The newest reform is the virtual school which provides online or cyber learning opportunities for K–12 students, as well as college students. A **virtual school** is "an institution that teaches courses entirely through online methods. Unlike a traditional brick-and-mortar school, the student attends a virtual classroom at any location by logging on to their computer and receiving instructions over the Internet."[23] In 31 states, students can enroll in a

Explain how virtual schools work, and evaluate the arguments for and against them.

full-time virtual school. The number of K–12 students enrolled in virtual schools is still relatively small, but millions are taking at least some classes online. Online classes have two formats: **fully online classes** (all course interaction is done through the computer) or **blended learning classes** (a mixture of in-person and online instruction).

Proponents see the move toward virtual schools as both inevitable and beneficial, especially to "the seriously ill, the shy, the bullied, the Olympians, the artists, the hackers, the connected learners, and others [who] might find online schools the best pathway to educational success."[24] Virtual schools can also greatly benefit smaller school districts as they are a more affordable way to offer more a wider range of educational opportunities such as foreign languages, AP classes, and other specialized learning.

Some opponents see virtual schools as just the latest effort by lawmakers across the country to redefine public education. "Instead of simply financing a traditional system of neighborhood schools, legislators and some governors are headed toward funneling public money directly to families, who would be free to choose the kind of schooling they believe is best for their children, be it public, charter, private, religious, online or at home."[25] Many of the same controversies that have surfaced with regard to charter schools and vouchers are evident in the battle for virtual schools, particularly at the elementary and secondary levels. Among the foremost concerns are how to assess student performance and ensure accountability. Thus far, results on student performance are mixed.[26]

16.6 THE COMMON CORE STATE STANDARDS INITIATIVE

Outline the common core educational standards that have been adopted by most states.

Governors and state education commissioners, through the National Governors Association and the Council of Chief State School Officers, worked together to create a set of common core standards in English language arts (writing, speaking and listening, language) and mathematics to be used at the K–12 level to prepare students for success in college, work, and life. These common standards (as listed on State of Washington's Office of Superintendent of Public Instruction's Website) are to provide (1) consistent learning expectations for all students, (2) clear standards that focus on understanding over memorization, (3) an emphasis on the critical topics students need to succeed after high school, and (4) faster testing results with a better, more focused online assessment system. The goal is to provide teachers, parents, and students with the same set of high standards. The expectation is that these common standards will enable collaboration between states on everything from developing textbooks and digital media to improving testing systems that more accurately gauge student performance. To date, 45 states, the District of Columbia, the Department of Defense Education Systems, and four U.S. territories have adopted these standards.[27]

The Common Core Standards have generated the same criticisms as other reforms. Critics are fearful the Standards will not improve student performance, will be difficult and too expensive to implement and monitor, will create a national curriculum based on the erroneous assumption that "one size fits all 50 states," and will involve the federal government too much. Concerns about the Standards have led several states to reject them (Alaska, Nebraska, Texas, and Virginia) or delay their implementation (Indiana, and Pennsylvania). While the federal Race to the Top program offers a fiscal incentive for states to adopt the standards, some states are fearful the federal monies will be insufficient.

16.7 THE FEDERAL ROLE IN EDUCATION

Trace the expansion of federal involvement in education policy, and describe the financial contributions for education by federal, state, and local governments.

Traditionally, education in America was a community responsibility. But today state governments have taken major responsibility for public education. The federal government has taken the lead in guaranteeing racial equality in education and separating religion from public schools, but it has never assumed any significant share of the costs of education. The federal share of educational spending is just over 10 percent. (See Table 16–1.)

TABLE 16–1   Sources of Funds for Public Education in the United States

Percentage of Public Educational Revenues by Source

	1980	1985	1990	1995	2000	2005	2007	2009
Federal	9.2	6.7	6.3	6.9	7.1	8.6	8.8	10.1
State	49.1	49.0	48.3	47.6	49.8	48.0	47.2	46.3
Local	41.7	44.3	45.4	45.4	43.1	43.4	44.0	43.6

Source: U.S. Census Bureau, Statistical Abstract of the United States, 2012, Table 262. Available at http://www.census.gov/prod/2011pubs/12statab/educ.pdf.

Early Federal Aid

The federal government's role in education, however, is a long-standing one. As mentioned earlier, the famous Northwest Ordinance of 1787 offered land grants for public schools in the new territories. Then in 1862 the Morrill Land Grant Act provided grants of federal land to each state for the establishment of colleges specializing in agricultural and mechanical arts. These became known as "**land grant colleges**." In 1867, Congress established a U.S. Office of Education, which became the Department of Education in 1979. The Smith-Hughes Act of 1917 set up the first program of federal grants-in-aid to promote vocational education and enable schools to provide training in agriculture, home economics, trades, and industries. In the National School Lunch and Milk programs, begun in 1946, federal grants and commodity donations are made for nonprofit lunches and milk served in public and private schools. In the Federal Impacted Areas Aid Program, begun in 1950, federal aid is authorized in "federally impacted" areas of the nation. These are areas where federal activities create a substantial increase in school enrollments or a reduction in taxable resources because of federally owned property. In response to the Soviet Union's success in launching *Sputnik,* the first satellite into space, in 1957, Congress became concerned that the American educational system might not be keeping abreast of advances made in other nations, particularly in science and technology. In the National Defense Education Act (NDEA) of 1958, Congress provided financial aid to states and public school districts to improve instruction in science, mathematics, and foreign languages.

LAND GRANT COLLEGES
Colleges established by federal land grants to promote study of the agricultural and mechanical arts.

ELEMENTARY AND SECONDARY EDUCATION ACT (ESEA) OF 1965
The federal Elementary and Secondary Education Act, later amended into a federal block grant (Title I) to states to improve education.

Elementary and Secondary Education Act (Title I)

The **Elementary and Secondary Education Act (ESEA) of 1965** marked the first large breakthrough in federal aid to education. Yet even ESEA was not a *general* aid-to-education program—one that would assist all public and private schools in school construction and teachers' salaries. The main thrust of ESEA is in "poverty-impacted" schools, instructional materials, and educational research and training. The Education Consolidation and Improvement Act of 1981 consolidated ESEA and related education programs into a single "Title I" block grant allowing the states greater discretion in how federal funds can be spent for compensatory education. This remains

Early childhood education first got a lot of attention under the federal Head Start program. Today state and local officials are also focusing more attention on pre-K and kindergarten as research has shown positive results from early childhood learning programs.

the largest federal aid-to-education program, accounting for over half of all federal elementary and secondary education spending.

However, it is difficult to demonstrate that federal aid programs improve the quality of education in America. Indeed, during the years in which federal aid was increasing, student achievement scores were *declining*. Raising the educational achievement levels of America's youth depends less on the amount spent than on how it is spent.

Head Start

The most popular federal educational aid program is Head Start, which began in President Lyndon B. Johnson's "War on Poverty" in the 1960s. Its purpose is to provide special preschool preparation to disadvantaged children before they enter kindergarten or first grade. Over the years it has enjoyed great popularity among parents, members of Congress, and both Republican and Democratic presidents. However, despite an avalanche of research by professional educators seeking to prove the value of the program, the results can best be described as mixed. Much of the value of Head Start preparation disappears after a few years of schooling; disadvantaged pupils who attend Head Start do not perform much better in later years than disadvantaged pupils who did not attend. Nevertheless, Head Start remains politically popular.

16.8

Discuss the core features of No Child Left Behind and the Obama administration's position on the law.

NO CHILD LEFT BEHIND (NCLB)

Upon taking office, President George W. Bush made education his first domestic priority. His approach to comprehensive educational reform is embodied in the No Child Left Behind Act of 2001. While this Act is officially only an amendment to Title I of the Elementary and Secondary Education Act of 1965, it really defines the federal role in public education.

Testing

The No Child Left Behind Act relies primarily on testing as a means to improve performance of America's elementary and secondary schools. The preferred phraseology is "accountability"—requiring states to establish standards in reading and mathematics and undertaking to annually test all students in grades three through eight. (Testing under this Act is in addition to the U.S. Department of Education's National Assessment of Educational Progress tests given each year to a sample of public and private school students in the 4th, 8th, and 12th grades; results of these NAEP tests are frequently cited as indicators of educational achievement for the nation.) One of the goals of testing is to make sure that every child can read by the end of third grade.

Test results and school progress toward proficiency goals are published, including results broken out by poverty, race, ethnicity, disability, and limited English proficiency, in order to ensure that no group is "left behind." School districts and individual schools that fail to make adequate yearly progress (AYP) toward statewide proficiency goals face "corrective action" and "restructuring measures" designed to improve their performance. Student achievement and progress are measured according to tests given to every child every year. Annual report cards on school performance aim to give parents information about their child's school and all other schools in their district.

Parental Choice

Parents whose children attend schools that fail to make AYP are given the opportunity to send their children to another public school or a public charter school within the school district. The school district is required to use its own money for transportation to the new school and to use Title I federal funds to implement school choice and supplemental educational services to the students. The objective is to ensure that no pupil is "trapped" in a failing school, and in addition to provide an incentive for low performing schools to improve. Schools that wish to avoid losing students, along with a portion of their annual budgets typically associated with these students, are required to make AYP. Schools that fail to make AYP for five years run the risk of "restructuring."

State Flexibility

The No Child Left Behind Act promises the states "flexibility in accountability." It allows the states to design and administer tests and decide what constitutes low performance and adequate yearly progress. Some states have objected to the Act as an "unfunded mandate," some have sought federal waivers from various provisions, and others have threatened court challenges.[28] But many supporters of the Act contend that it grants too much flexibility, that state tests are not sufficiently rigorous, and that national standards are needed.

Controversy

The No Child Left Behind Act (NCLB) has inspired considerable controversy in Washington, state capitols, and educational circles. The National Education Association—the powerful teachers' union—contends that NCLB is "fundamentally flawed." Professional educators object, first of all, to the emphasis on testing for basic skills, reading, and mathematics. They argue that this emphasis leads to narrow "test-taking" education rather than "comprehensive" preparation for life. Teachers are obliged to neglect other instructional topics in order to concentrate on reading and mathematics. Even some supporters of NCLB urge that history and civics as well as science be added to the tests.

The federal No Child Left Behind Act of 2001 is actually an amendment to Title I of the Elementary and Secondary Education Act of 1965. It has become highly controversial, primarily because of its heavy reliance on testing as a measure of how well teachers and the school system overall are performing and its use of test scores over time for funding decisions. Proponents argue that it is working—student test scores are rising and the gap between minority and white students' scores is narrowing. The bottom line is that the Act has become a key issue in local school board elections.

Professional educators also argue that states, school districts, and schools should all participate in developing "accountability systems" based on multiple measures of student success. States should have greater "flexibility" in implementing NCLB. Moreover, measures of progress, or lack of it, should not be used to penalize schools or teachers. Measures of AYP should be used to provide increased support and assistance to schools needing help, not to penalize them. The National Education Association strongly opposes providing transfers or vouchers to students in low-performing schools.

Opposition to testing has also arisen from minority group leaders who charge that the tests are racially biased. Average black student scores are frequently lower than average white student scores. Denying a disproportionate number of black students' advancement because of the school's failure to teach basics is viewed as a form of discrimination. Proponents of NCLB argue that testing for basic skills has improved student performance in recent years. AYP measures inspire school administrators and teachers to bring about improvement in student achievement. And proponents also contend that disparities between whites and minorities in test scores have been narrowing as teachers concentrate more on instruction in basic skills.

No Child Left Behind Waivers

Responding to teachers unions, state education officials, and other critics of NCLB, President Obama began issuing "waivers" in 2012 to states, freeing them from certain No Child Left Behind requirements. In exchange for new flexibility, states agree to support "rigorous and comprehensive state-developed plans designed to improve educational outcomes for all students, close achievement gaps, increase equity, and improve the quality of instructions." By 2013 some 34 states and the District of Columbia had received waivers. Each state's waiver plan is slightly different. But all appear to weaken the original No Child Left Behind requirements.

16.9

Describe Obama's Race to the Top initiative, and contrast it with George W. Bush's No Child Left Behind.

OBAMA'S EDUCATION AGENDA

The Obama administration laid out an ambitious agenda for education—an agenda that envisions spending additional billions of dollars of federal monies for a wide variety of programs. The bulk of this new spending is to go to poor inner-city schools.

Race to the Top

To implement his agenda, the president has allocated billions of dollars in competitive grants to states in a Race to the Top Fund. This is a national competition for federal dollars designed to encourage specific reforms, including:

- Tying teacher and principal pay to student test scores.
- Adopting international benchmark standards and assessments.
- Finding effective programs to turn around failing schools.
- Building data systems that measure student success and track students throughout their educational career.
- Loosening legal requirements for charter schools.

In practice, awards have been made to states with effective programs to turn around failing schools and to states with meaningful teacher evaluation systems linked to student achievement. States have offered various reforms as part of the competition: closing poor-performing schools and reopening them as charters or transferring pupils to higher performing schools; evaluating students on "learning gains" observed in pre- and post-course exams; basing merit pay for teachers on student gains; and eliminating seniority as a basis for teacher retention and pay increases.

The Race to the Top is not without its critics. Teacher unions—the National Education Association and the American Federation of Teachers and their state and local affiliates—have been reluctant partners in state competition for the Race to the Top. They generally oppose educational evaluation based on test results, teacher testing, merit pay for teachers based on student performance, the closing of low-performing schools, and the establishment of charter schools. But support of the unions is one of the criteria that the Obama administration uses to judge requests for funding. Another source of opposition is from state officials who fear that the program is a "federal takeover" of education in America. And the support for charter schools has irked critics who say that the federal government is promoting schools that have not shown consistent evidence of success. Finally, educators worry that much Race to the Top money could simply disappear into state budgets as legislators scramble to close deficits.

16.10

Outline the organizational structure that states have developed to provide public education, and describe the financial contributions states provide to local school districts.

ORGANIZING PUBLIC EDUCATION IN THE STATES

The 50 state governments, by means of enabling legislation, establish local school districts and endow them with the authority to operate public schools. There are about nearly 14,000 local school districts, governed by over 90,000 school board members, who are chosen usually, but not always, by popular election. State laws authorize these boards to levy and collect taxes, borrow money, engage in school construction, hire instructional personnel, and make certain determinations about local school policy.

Only Hawaii governs its schools centrally from the state capital. Other states vary considerably in the number of local school districts functioning within their boundaries. For example, Texas has 1,043 local school boards while Delaware has but 15.

State Supervision

Yet, in every state, the authority of local school districts is severely limited by state legislation. State law often determines the types and rates of taxes to be levied, the maximum debt that can be incurred, the number of days schools shall remain open, the number of years of compulsory school attendance, the minimum salaries to be paid to teachers, the types of schools to be operated by the local boards, the number of grades to be taught, the qualifications of teachers, and the general content of curricula. In addition, many states choose the textbooks, establish course outlines, recommend teaching methods, establish statewide examinations, set teacher–pupil ratios, and stipulate course content in great detail. In short, the responsibility for public education is firmly in the hands of state governments.

State responsibility for public education is no mere paper arrangement. States ensure local compliance with state educational policy through (1) bureaucratic oversight, involving state boards of education, state commissioners or superintendents of education, and state departments of education; and (2) financial control through state allocation of funds to local school districts.

State Boards of Education

Traditionally, state control over education was vested in state boards of education. In most states these boards are appointed by the governor; in some states they are composed of state officials; and in 10 states (Alabama, Colorado, Hawaii, Kansas, Michigan, Nebraska, Nevada, New Mexico, Texas, and Utah) they are directly elected by the voters. These boards generally have the formal power to decide everything from teacher certification to textbook selection. These formal powers can lead to controversial decisions about state curriculum requirements. However, in practice these boards rely heavily on the recommendations of the state commissioner of education and the state department of education.

State Commissioners of Education

All states have chief education officers, variously titled commissioner of education, state school superintendent, or superintendent of public instruction. In 14 states this official is elected (Arizona, California, Georgia, Idaho, Indiana, Montana, North Carolina, North Dakota, Oklahoma, Oregon, South Carolina, Washington, Wisconsin, and Wyoming). In other states the official is appointed by the governor or the state education board. The chief education officer may exercise the most important influence over education in the state, as public spokesperson for education, in testimony before the legislature, and as the head of the state department of education.

State Departments of Education

State educational bureaucracies have greatly expanded in size and power over the years. They disburse state funds to local schools, prepare statewide curricula, select textbooks and materials, determine teacher qualifications, establish and enforce school building codes, and supervise statewide testing. Their main tool in enforcing their control over local schools is the allocation of state education money.

School District Consolidation

One of the most dramatic reorganization and centralization movements in American government in this century was the successful drive to reduce, through consolidation, the number of local school districts in the United States. In a 30-year period (1950–1980), three out of every four school districts were eliminated through consolidation. Support for school district consolidation came from *state* school officials in every state. Opposition to consolidation was *local* in character. Loss of control was the major reason local officials opposed it. From the states' perspective, saving money was the biggest reason to consolidate. New research by the Center for Policy Research at Syracuse University has found that consolidation is most effective at cutting costs when the districts involved range from 1,000 to 3,500 pupils.[29]

State Financial Control

States ensure the implementation of state educational policies through state grants of money to local school districts. Every state provides grants in one form or another to local school districts to supplement locally derived school revenue. This places the superior taxing powers of the state in the service of public schools operated at the local level. In every state, an equalization formula in the distribution of state grants to local districts operates to help equalize educational opportunities in all parts of the state. This enables the state to guarantee a minimum "foundation" program in education throughout the state. In addition, since state grants to local school districts are administered through state departments of education, state school officials are given an effective tool for implementing state policies, namely, withholding or threatening to withhold state funds from school districts that do not conform to state standards. The growth of state responsibility for school policy was accomplished largely by the use of money—state grants to local schools.

States also have the authority to step in and take charge of local school districts that are in financial difficulty and/or poorly performing. New Jersey Governor Chris Christie (R) put the educational and fiscal management of the Camden School District under state control and limited the local school board role to an advisory one. It was the fourth New Jersey city put under state control. The Ohio Department of Education appointed a five-person academic distress commission to take control of the Cleveland School District. Similar actions have been taken in other states.

16.11

BATTLES OVER SCHOOL FINANCES

Describe the inequality in "per student" school funding across states and school districts, evaluate why such inequalities exist, and assess the impact of these inequalities on educational outcomes.

Public elementary and secondary schools enroll about 50 million students. Nationwide over $11,000 per year is spent on the public education of each child. Yet national averages can obscure as much as they reveal about the record of the states in public education. Fifty different state school systems establish policy for the nation, and this decentralization results in variations from state to state in educational policy. Only by examining public policy in all 50 states can the full dimension of American education be understood.

Variation among States

In 2012, for example, public school expenditures for each pupil ranged from $6,683 in Arizona to $18,616 in New York. (See "*Rankings of the States:* Financing Public Schools.") Why is it that some states spend more than three times as much on the education of each child as other states? Economic resources are the main determinant of a state's willingness and ability to provide educational services.

Inequalities among School Districts

A central issue in the struggle over public education is that of distributing the benefits and costs of education equitably. In every state except Hawaii, local school boards must raise money from property taxes to help finance their schools. This means that communities that do *not* have much taxable property cannot finance their schools as well as communities that are blessed with great wealth. Frequently, wealthy communities can provide better education for their children at lower tax rates than poor communities can provide at higher tax rates, simply because of disparities in the value of taxable property from one community to the next. Disparities in educational funding among school districts *within* states can be quite large.

School Inequalities as a Constitutional Issue

Do disparities among school districts within a state deny "equal protection of laws" guaranteed by the Fourteenth Amendment of the U.S. Constitution and similar guarantees found in most state constitutions? The U.S. Supreme Court ruled that disparities in financial resources between school districts in a state, and resulting inequalities in educational spending per

While research has shown that money alone is not the answer to improving schools, any proposal to cut back funding is likely to generate protests against it by persons of all ages and headlines in local newspapers.

Financing Public Schools

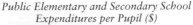

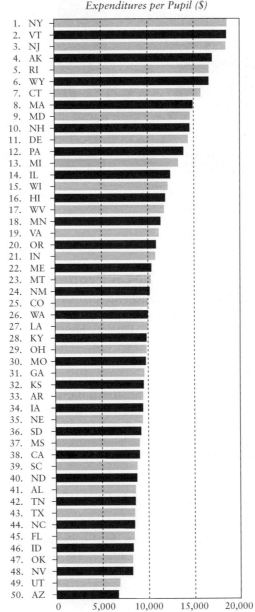

Public Elementary and Secondary School
Expenditures per Pupil ($)

1. NY	
2. VT	
3. NJ	
4. AK	
5. RI	
6. WY	
7. CT	
8. MA	
9. MD	
10. NH	
11. DE	
12. PA	
13. MI	
14. IL	
15. WI	
16. HI	
17. WV	
18. MN	
19. VA	
20. OR	
21. IN	
22. ME	
23. MT	
24. NM	
25. CO	
26. WA	
27. LA	
28. KY	
29. OH	
30. MO	
31. GA	
32. KS	
33. AR	
34. IA	
35. NE	
36. SD	
37. MS	
38. CA	
39. SC	
40. ND	
41. AL	
42. TN	
43. TX	
44. NC	
45. FL	
46. ID	
47. OK	
48. NV	
49. UT	
50. AZ	

Note: Data are for 2012.
Source: National Education Association, "Rankings and Estimates," December 2012. Available at http://www.nea.org/assets/img/content/
NEA_Rankings_And_Estimates-2013_(2).pdf.

Polls show that Americans prefer smaller classes and expect smaller class size to improve student learning. Smaller class size mandates approved by voters require building more classrooms and hiring more teachers. This is not always easy, especially when the economy is in a slump.

pupil across a state, do *not* violate the Equal Protection Clause of the Fourteenth Amendment. There is no duty under the U.S. Constitution for a state to equalize educational resources within the state.[30]

However, in recent years *state courts* have increasingly intervened in school financing to ensure equality among school districts based on their own interpretation of *state* constitutional provisions. Beginning with an early California state supreme court decision requiring that state funds be used to help equalize resources among the state's school districts,[31] many state courts have pressured their legislatures to come up with equalization plans in state school grants to overcome disparities in property tax revenues among school districts. State court equalization orders are generally based on *state* constitutional provisions guaranteeing equality.

State Funds versus Local Property Taxes

Local school district reliance on property taxation, combined with inequalities in property values among communities, creates an equity problem: Should less money be spent on children in poorer districts because of where their parents live? Heavy reliance on local property taxes to fund schools generally ensures that fiscal disparities among school districts will exist. But many school districts across the country have sued their respective state governments, claiming that heavy reliance on local property taxes to fund schools discriminates unfairly against poorer communities. A number of state Supreme Courts in recent years have agreed, and cases are currently pending in many other states. To achieve equity in school funding among communities, state courts are increasingly ordering their legislatures to substitute state general revenues for local property taxes.

16.12

GOVERNING LOCAL SCHOOLS

Outline the decision-making processes used in school districts, and assess the impact of teachers unions on these processes.

Responsibility for many basic decisions in public education lies with the nearly 14,000 separate school districts in America. In theory, these school districts are under local control. The people of the local school district are supposed to exercise that control through an elected **school board** and an elected or appointed **school superintendent** who acts as the chief executive of the community schools. There is some variation to that pattern—in some of the nation's school districts (mostly larger ones), the boards are appointed rather than elected, usually by city councils, county commissions, mayors, or even judges. In theory, school boards exercise control over the curriculum (that is, what should be taught in the schools), buildings and facilities, personnel (including both administrators and teachers), and perhaps most important of all, financing. They are "the accountable agents for the $500 billion annual public investment in elementary and secondary education through federal, state, and local tax revenue."[32] In practice, however, as we have already seen, the concept of local control over education is heavily circumscribed by both state and federal laws.

SCHOOL BOARD

The governing body of a school district; most are elected, but some are appointed.

SCHOOL SUPERINTENDENT

The chief executive officer of a school district; may be directly elected or appointed by the school board.

The School District Superintendents

School district superintendents are usually professionally trained educators, either appointed by the local school board or separately elected on a nonpartisan ballot. The superintendent is responsible for the management of the public schools—hiring and supervising teachers and principals, planning and organizing the schools, preparing budgets and overseeing expenditures, and recommending policy to the board.

School superintendents have three major responsibilities. First, the superintendent sets the agenda for school board decisions. Second, the superintendent makes policy recommendations. Most agenda items will carry a recommendation. Third, the superintendent implements board decisions. In performing these responsibilities, superintendents, even more than city managers, provide strong leadership—advocating policy changes and selling programs to the community. Moreover, many superintendents, in contrast to city managers, involve themselves in school board elections, providing encouragement to candidates whom they respect.

Professional superintendents do not expect to be overruled by their boards. Many of them have a "trust me or fire me" attitude that often makes compromise difficult. The average tenure of school superintendents in large urban school districts is just over three years. However, not all leave because of tangling with their school boards. Some simply choose to retire because of decreased funding and the stress that comes along with having to slash budgets.[33]

Attracting and keeping good teachers is a major challenge for local school systems.

School Boards

Even if we accept the notion that schools should be governed by a democratically elected board, how can we know whether board members are accurately reflecting their constituents' desires and aspirations?[34]

Like most decision makers, the nation's 90,000 school board members are unrepresentative of their constituents in socioeconomic background. Specifically, board members come disproportionately from "educational families"; many members have relatives in education, usually their spouse, but more than a quarter are current or former educators themselves. Many school board members report that they were first prompted to run for the school board by friends already on the board; this suggests a perpetuation of similar kinds of people on school boards. Seventy-five percent have at least a bachelor's degree. Seventy percent are 50 or older, which explains why just 36 percent have children in the school district they govern. Women make up 44 percent of all board members.

In large districts, 22 percent are African American and 6 percent are Latino.[35] Black membership on the nation's large central-city school district boards reflects fairly accurately the black population in central cities.[36] Black representation on school boards has been linked to a variety of school policies: increased employment of black teachers; fewer black students disciplined, suspended, or dropping out; fewer black students assigned to special education classes; and more black students in gifted programs. Hispanic and Asian board members, while more underrepresented, most likely have similar impacts.

The average tenure of board members is about five years. School board members do not ordinarily aspire to, or gain, higher political office. Two-thirds of them leave office, rather than being defeated in an election which makes it difficult to hold members accountable through the threat of electoral defeat.

Most school board elections are nonpartisan, although partisan politics is becoming more evident in school elections just as it is in municipal elections. Historically, school board races have not received a lot of media attention nor required high levels of fundraising.

Teachers' unions are very active in politics, most often in support of Democratic Party candidates. However, not all teachers support the union's goals and tactics, particularly when it comes to partisan campaigns. The U.S. Supreme Court has ruled that states may require a nonunion member's *affirmative consent* before a public sector union (the teachers union) may use fees paid by nonmembers for collective bargaining for political purposes. (Unions collect fees from all teachers, regardless of whether they are members, for representing them in collective bargaining.) (*Washington* v. *Washington Education Association* and *Davenport* v. *Washington Education Association*, 2007.)

A 2010 survey conducted by the National School Boards Association found that three-fourths of those surveyed spent less than $1,000 on their races and 87 percent spent less than $5,000.[37] But that, too, is changing as the battle over education reform has intensified. There have been several high-profile and high-spending clashes between teacher unions and more conservative education reform groups over control of local school boards in New Orleans, Denver, Memphis, and Los Angeles. (Labor unions and outside conservative groups poured $5 million into Los Angeles school board races in 2013.)

Teachers Unions

The struggle for power over the schools between interested citizens, school board members, and professional educators has now been joined by still another powerful force—the nation's teachers unions. Most of the nation's 4 million teachers are organized into either the older, larger National Education Association (NEA) or the smaller American Federation of Teachers (AFT), an affiliate of the AFL-CIO. Since its origin, the AFT has espoused the right to organize, bargain collectively, and strike, in the fashion of other labor unions. The AFT is small in numbers, but its membership is concentrated in the nation's largest cities, where it exercises considerable power. Traditionally, the NEA was considered a "professional" organization of both teachers and administrators. However, today state and district chapters of the NEA are organized as labor unions, demanding collective bargaining rights for their members and threatening to strike to achieve them. Both AFT and NEA chapters have shut down schools to force concessions by superintendents, board members, and taxpayers—not only in salaries and benefits, but also in pupil–teacher ratios, classroom conditions, school discipline, and other educational matters. As the teacher unions have grown stronger, the tug-of-war between union members and supporters of alternative schooling options (charters, virtual, voucher-supported private schools) has become more intense as student achievement levels have not improved significantly.

16.13

THE POLITICS OF HIGHER EDUCATION

Describe the reach of higher education in the United States, the organizational structure of the higher education system, and the policies enacted by both federal and state governments to fund higher education and student loans.

Higher education in America is mass education. No other nation sends so large a proportion of its young people to college. Over 20 million Americans are enrolled in colleges and universities. (See Table 16–2.) Two-thirds of all high school graduates enroll in college.

Community Colleges

In most states, community colleges are separate from state colleges and universities; the community colleges are really part of local government. They receive revenue from local

TABLE 16–2 Higher Education in America

Institutions (Number)	1970	1980	1990	2000	2005	2007	2009
Total	2,556	3,231	3,559	4,182	4,276	4,352	4,495
Four-year colleges and universities	1,665	1,957	2,141	2,450	2,582	2,675	2,774
Two-year colleges	891	1,274	1,418	1,732	1,694	1,677	1,721
Faculty (thousands)	474	686	817	990	1,290	(N/A)	1,439
Percent full-time faculty	75	66	61	(N/A)	52	(N/A)	51

Enrollment (Thousands)	1970	1980	1990	2000	2005	2007	2009
Total	8,581	12,097	13,819	15,312	17,487	18,248	20,428
Four-year colleges and universities	6,290	7,571	8,579	9,364	10,999	11,630	12,906
Two-year colleges	1,630	4,526	5,240	5,948	6,488	6,618	7,521
Public	5,800	9,457	10,845	11,753	13,022	13,491	14,811
Private	2,120	2,640	2,974	3,560	4,466	4,757	5,617
Undergraduate	7,376	10,495	11,959	13,155	14,964	15,604	17,565
Graduate	1,031	1,343	1,586	1,850	2,186	2,294	(N/A)

Source: U.S. Census Bureau, *Statistical Abstract of the United States: 2012*, Table 278. Available at http://www.census.gov/prod/2011pubs/12statab/educ.pdf.

property taxes as well as grants from the state and federal government. They are usually governed by a local board, whose members are elected or appointed from the communities served by the college.

Community colleges are designed to reflect the local area's requirements for higher education, and they usually offer both a general undergraduate curriculum that fulfills the first two years of a baccalaureate degree, and vocational and technical programs that fulfill community needs for skilled workers. Moreover, community colleges usually offer special programs and courses in adult higher education, often in association with community groups.

University Governance

The organization and governance of public higher education varies a great deal from state to state. Most states have established "**boards of trustees/regents**" with authority to govern the state universities. One of the purposes of the boards is to insulate higher education from the vicissitudes of politics. Prominent citizens who are appointed to these boards are expected to champion higher education with the public and the legislature, as well as set overall policy guidelines for colleges and universities. In the past, there were separate boards for each institution and separate consideration by the governor's office and the legislature of each institution's budgetary request. However, the resulting competition caused state after state to create unified "university system" boards to coordinate higher education. These university system boards consolidate the budget requests of each institution, determine systemwide priorities, and

BOARD OF TRUSTEES/ REGENTS
A governing body with the authority to govern a state's universities.

On many college campuses in states with sizable undocumented immigrant populations, there is strong support for the DREAM Act.

present a single budget for higher education to the governor and the legislature. The stronger and more independent the university system board, the less likely that university and college funding will be distributed in a pork-barrel fashion by legislators seeking to enhance their local constituencies.

University Presidents

The key figures in university politics are the **presidents**. They are the chief spokespersons for higher education, and they must convince the public, the regents, the governor, and the legislature of the value of state universities. The presidents' crucial role is one of maintaining support for higher education in the state; they frequently delegate administrative responsibilities for the internal operation of the university to the vice presidents, provosts, and deans.

The Faculty

Faculty members traditionally identified themselves as professionals with strong attachments to their institutions. The historic pattern of college and university government included faculty participation in policymaking—not only in determining academic requirements but also in budgeting, the hiring and firing of personnel, and building programs. However, government by faculty committee has proven cumbersome, unwieldy, and time-consuming in an era of large-scale enrollments, multimillion-dollar budgets, and increases in the size and complexity of academic administration. Increasingly, concepts of public "accountability," academic "management," cost control, centralized budgeting, and purchasing have transferred power in colleges and universities from faculty to professional academic administrators.

Yet another infringement on the powers of faculty is the increasing employment by colleges and universities of part-time or **adjunct faculty**. In 1969, 78 percent of faculty at American colleges and universities held full-time tenure-track positions. Today, adjuncts and graduate students studying for advanced degrees make up nearly three-fourths of instructional staff. The use of adjuncts is highest at community colleges.[38] Employing adjuncts and graduate students rather than full-time faculty saves money for the institution. Adjuncts are paid on a per-course-taught basis, almost always much less than full-time faculty teaching the same number of courses. And adjuncts rarely receive medical, retirement, or other benefits. Whether or not these savings result in diminished quality of teaching is a hotly debated topic on many campuses.

The Unions

The traditional organization for faculty was the American Association of University Professors (AAUP); historically, this group confined itself to publishing data on faculty salaries and officially "censoring" colleges or universities that violated long-standing notions of academic freedom or tenure. (**Tenure** ensures that faculty members who have demonstrated their competence in a college or university position for three to seven years cannot thereafter be dismissed except for "cause"—a serious infraction of established rules or dereliction of duty, provable in an open hearing.) In recent years, some faculty have become convinced that traditional patterns of *individual* bargaining over salaries, teaching load, and working conditions in colleges and universities should be replaced by *collective* bargaining in the style of unionized labor. The American Federation of Teachers of the AFL-CIO, as well as the National Education Association and the AAUP, has sought to represent faculty in collective bargaining. Many states now authorize collective bargaining with the faculty of public colleges and universities if the faculty votes for such bargaining.

State Legislatures

The costs of public higher education are borne largely by taxpayers. Rarely does tuition at state colleges and universities pay for more than one-quarter of the costs of providing an education. Each year's higher education appropriations bill provides state legislatures with the opportunity to exercise their oversight of the state university system.

In recent years, public higher education has faced increased austerity as the demands for state spending on Medicaid, social services, and prison construction have risen dramatically. In most states, higher education currently receives a *smaller* share of the state budget than in previous years. Moreover, state legislatures are increasingly interjecting themselves into college and university policymaking, often intruding on the traditional powers of independent trustees and regents, as well as presidents and faculty.

The thrust of legislative interventions is to increase teaching loads and responsibilities of faculty. State legislators are rarely impressed with the research activities of faculty, even when these activities are funded by grants and contracts from federal agencies or private foundations. (However, university administrators are more than happy to tout such achievements.) And legislators are more concerned with teaching *under*-graduates than graduate students. Legislators often receive complaints about closed or overcrowded classes encountered by the sons and daughters of their constituents, or the inability of a state university to admit qualified students. So many state legislators are demanding greater faculty "productivity," usually defined as teaching more class-room hours each week to more undergraduate students.[39] In some states, legislators are increasingly asking students to do more as well, by hiking their tuition and fees. Even with tuition increases, tuition revenue accounts for less than half of all educational funding at public colleges.[40]

In some states, governors have urged legislatures to tie some higher education funding to graduates' success in finding jobs. They have questioned the economic value of certain majors, like anthropology and philosophy. North Carolina Governor Tim McCrory (R) stated he did not want the legislature to subsidize any major that does not easily translate into a job. He even suggested that students interested in those fields go to a private university. Other governors, like Vermont Governor Peter Shumlin (D) and New Hampshire Governor Maggie Hassan (D), have questioned the overemphasis on funding four-year college degrees at the expense of technical degrees and STEM (Science, Technology, English, Math) high schools.[41]

Federal Role

Federal aid to colleges and universities comes in a variety of forms. Historically, the Morrill Act of 1862 provided the groundwork for federal assistance in higher education. In 1890 Congress initiated several federal grants to support the operations of the land-grant colleges, and this aid, although modest, continues to the present. Federal support for scientific research has also had an important impact on higher education. In 1950 Congress established the National Science Foundation (NSF) to promote scientific research and education through direct grants to university faculty and departments. (In 1965 Congress established a National Endowment for the Arts and Humanities, but these fields receive only a fraction of the amounts given to NSF.) In addition to NSF, many other federal agencies—the Department of Defense, the Department of Education, the U.S. Public Health Service, the Department of Health and Human Services, and the Department of Housing and Urban Development—grant research contracts to universities for specific projects. Thus, research has become a big item in university life.

Federal Student Aid

The federal government directly assists students with a variety of federal grant and loan programs. Federal "Pell Grants" (named for the program's original sponsor Senator

Claiborne Pell, D-RI) offer students in good standing a money grant each year, based on the amount their families could reasonably be expected to contribute to their educational expenses. Today, over 9 million students receive Pell grants, worth an average of about $3,500; grants do not need to be repaid. In addition, a Federal Family Education Loan (FFEL) program allows students to borrow money with no interest charged while the student is in college; repayment is delayed until after the student leaves school. (The Obama administration succeeded in getting Congress to federalize the program in 2010; loans are now made directly by the U.S. Department of Education rather than private banks.) And a national work-study program uses federal funds to allow colleges and universities to employ students part time while they continue to go to school.

16.14

READING, WRITING, AND RELIGION

Evaluate the arguments for and against public support for private schools, discuss the constitutional limits on such support as determined by the Supreme Court, and summarize the current status of prayer in public schools.

The First Amendment to the Constitution of the United States contains two important guarantees of religious freedom: (1) "Congress shall make no law respecting an establishment of religion, . . ." and (2) "Or prohibiting the free exercise thereof." The Due Process Clause of the Fourteenth Amendment made these guarantees of religious liberty applicable to the states and their subdivisions as well as to Congress.

"Free Exercise" and Private Religious Schools

NO ESTABLISHMENT CLAUSE

The First Amendment clause of the U.S. Constitution, interpreted by the U.S. Supreme Court to prohibit government from aiding religious education or conducting religious ceremonies in public schools.

Most of the debate over religion in the public schools centers on the **No Establishment Clause** of the First Amendment rather than the Free Exercise Clause. However, it was respect for the **Free Exercise Clause** that caused the Supreme Court in 1925 to declare unconstitutional an attempt on the part of a state to prohibit private religious schools and to force all children to attend public schools. In the words of the Supreme Court, "The fundamental theory of liberty upon which all governments in this Union repose excludes any general power of the state to standardize its children by forcing them to accept instruction from public teachers only. The child is not the mere creature of the state."[42] It is this decision that protects the entire structure of private religious schools in this nation.

The Meaning of "No Establishment"

FREE EXERCISE CLAUSE

The First Amendment clause of the U.S. Constitution, interpreted by the U.S. Supreme Court to prohibit states from closing religious schools or forcing all students to attend public schools.

A great deal of religious conflict in America has centered on the meaning of the No Establishment Clause, and the public schools have been the principal scene of this conflict. One interpretation of the clause holds that it does not prevent government from aiding religious schools or encouraging religious beliefs in the public schools, so long as it does not discriminate against any particular religion. Another interpretation of the No Establishment Clause is that it creates a "wall of separation" between church and state in America, which prevents government from directly aiding religious schools or encouraging religious beliefs in any way.

Support for Public Aid to Religious Schools

The Catholic Church in America enrolls about half of all private school students in the nation, and the Catholic Church has led the fight for an interpretation of the No Establishment Clause that would permit government to aid religious schools. As Catholic spokespeople see it, Catholic parents have a right to send their children to Catholic schools; and since they are taxpayers, they also expect that some tax monies should go to the aid of church schools. To do otherwise, they argue, would discriminate against parents who choose a religious education for their children.

Those who favor government aid to religious schools frequently refer to the language found in several cases decided by the Supreme Court, which appears to support the idea that government can *in a limited fashion* support the activities of church-related schools. In *Cochran* v. *Board of Education* (1930), the Court upheld a state law providing free textbooks for children attending both public and parochial schools on the grounds that this aid benefited the *children* rather than the Catholic Church and hence did not constitute an "establishment" of religion within the meaning of the First Amendment.[43] In *Everson* v. *Board of Education* (1947), the Supreme Court upheld the provision of school bus service to parochial schoolchildren at public expense on the grounds that the "wall of separation between church and state" does not prohibit the state from adopting a general program that helps *all* children, regardless of religion, to proceed safely to and from schools.[44] In *Mueller* v. *Allen* (1983) the Court upheld a state income tax deduction for educational expenses even though the vast majority of deductions were used for religious school expenses.[45] These cases suggest that the Supreme Court is willing to permit some forms of aid to parochial school*children* that indirectly aids religion, so long as this is not directly used for the teaching of religion.

Proponents of public aid for church schools argue that these schools render a valuable public service by instructing millions of children who would have to be instructed by the state, at additional expense, if church schools were not available. Moreover, there are many precedents for public support of religious institutions: Church property has always been exempt from taxation; church contributions are deductible from federal income taxes; chaplains are provided in the armed forces as well as in the Congress of the United States; student federal grant and loan monies can be used to finance college educations in Catholic and other religious universities.

Opposition to Public Aid to Religious Schools

Opponents of aid to church schools argue that free public schools are available to the parents of all children regardless of religious denomination. If religious parents are not content with the type of school that the state provides, they should expect to pay for the establishment and operation of special schools. The state is under no obligation to finance the religious preferences in education of religious groups, and it is unfair to compel taxpayers to support religion directly or indirectly. Furthermore, the diversion of any substantial amount of public education funds to church schools would weaken the public school system.

The Supreme Court has also voiced the opinion that the No Establishment Clause of the First Amendment should constitute a "wall of separation" between church and state. In the words of the Court:

> Neither a state nor the federal government can set up a church. Neither can pass laws which aid one religion, aid all religions, or prefer one religion over another. Neither can force nor influence a person to go to or to remain away from church against his will, or force him to profess a belief or disbelief in any religion. No person can be punished for entertaining or professing religious beliefs or disbeliefs, for church attendance or nonattendance. No tax in any amount, large or small, can be levied to support any religious activities or institutions, whatever they may be called, or whatever form they may adopt to teach or practice religion. Neither a state nor the federal government can openly or secretly, participate in the affairs of any religious organizations or groups, and vice versa.[46]

"Excessive Entanglement" and the "Lemon Test"

One of the more important U.S. Supreme Court decisions in the history of church–state relations in America came in 1971 in the case of *Lemon* v. *Kurtzman*.[47] The Supreme Court set forth a three-part *Lemon test* for determining whether a particular state law constitutes "establishment" of religion and thus violates the First Amendment. To be constitutional, a law affecting religious activity:

- Must have a secular purpose.
- As its primary effect, must neither advance nor inhibit religion.
- Must not foster "an excessive government entanglement with religion."

Using this three-part test the Supreme Court held that it was unconstitutional for a state to pay the costs of teachers' salaries or instructional materials in parochial schools. The justices argued that this practice would require excessive government controls and surveillance to ensure that funds were used only for secular instruction and thus would create an "excessive entanglement between government and religion."

However, the Supreme Court has upheld the use of tax funds to provide students attending church-related schools with nonreligious textbooks, lunches, transportation, sign language interpreting, and special education teachers. And the Court has upheld a state's granting of tax credits to parents whose children attend private schools, including religious schools.[48] The Court has also upheld government grants of money to church-related colleges and universities for secular purposes.[49] The Court has ruled that if school buildings are open to use for secular organizations, they must also be open to use by religious organizations.[50] And the Court has held that a state institution (the University of Virginia) not only can but must grant student activity fees to religious organizations on the same basis as it grants these fees to secular organizations.[51] But the Court held that a Louisiana law requiring the teaching of creationism along with evolution in the public schools was an unconstitutional establishment of a religious belief.[52]

Prayer in the Schools

Religious conflict in public schools also centers on the question of prayer and Bible-reading ceremonies conducted by public schools. The practice of opening the school day with prayer and Bible-reading ceremonies was once widespread in American public schools. Usually the prayer was a Protestant rendition of the Lord's Prayer, and Bible reading was from the King James version. To avoid the denominational aspects of these ceremonies, the New York State Board of Regents substituted a nondenominational prayer, which it required to be said aloud in each class in the presence of a teacher at the beginning of each school day:

> Almighty God, we acknowledge our dependence upon Thee, and we beg Thy blessings upon us, our parents, our teachers, and our country.

New York argued that this prayer ceremony did not violate the No Establishment Clause because the prayer was denominationally neutral and because student participation in the prayer was voluntary. However, in *Engle* v. *Vitale* (1962), the Supreme Court stated that "the constitutional prohibition against laws respecting an establishment of a religion must at least mean in this country it is no part of the business of government to compose official prayers for any group of the American people to recite as part of a religious program carried on by government."[53] The Court pointed out that making prayer voluntary did not free it from the prohibitions of the No Establishment Clause; that clause prevented the *establishment* of a religious ceremony by a government agency, regardless of whether the ceremony was voluntary or not:

> Neither the fact that the prayer may be denominationally neutral, nor the fact that its observance on the part of the students is voluntary can serve to free it from the limitations of the establishment clause, as it might from the free exercise clause, of the First Amendment, both of which are operative against the states by virtue of the 14th Amendment.... The establishment clause, unlike the free exercise clause, does not depend on any showing of direct governmental compulsion and is violated by the enactment of laws which establish an official religion whether those laws operate directly to coerce nonobserving individuals or not.[54]

One year later, in the case of *Abbington Township* v. *Schempp*, the Court considered the constitutionality of Bible-reading ceremonies in the public schools.[55] Here again, even though the children were not required to participate, the Court found that Bible reading as an opening exercise in the schools was a religious ceremony. The Court went to some trouble in its opinion to point out that they were not "throwing the Bible out of the school," for they specifically stated that the study of the Bible or of religion, when presented objectively as part of a secular program of education, did not violate the First Amendment, but religious *ceremonies* involving Bible reading or prayer, established by a state or school, did so.

State efforts to encourage "voluntary prayer" in public schools have also been struck down by the Supreme Court as unconstitutional. When the state of Alabama authorized a period of silence for "meditation or voluntary prayer" in public schools, the Court ruled that this was an "establishment of religion." The Court said the law had no secular purpose, that it conveyed "a message of state endorsement and promotion of prayer," and that its real intent was to encourage prayer in public schools.[56] (In a stinging dissenting opinion, then chief justice Warren Burger noted that the Supreme Court itself opened its session with a prayer, that both houses of Congress opened every session with prayers led by official chaplains paid by the government: "To suggest that a moment of silence statute that includes the word *prayer* unconstitutionally endorses religion, manifests not neutrality but hostility toward religion.") In 2000, the Supreme Court ruled that student delivery of an invocation at public high school football games over the school's public address system was an unconstitutional state-sponsored endorsement of religion.[57]

NEW CHALLENGE: CREATING SAFE LEARNING ENVIRONMENTS

16.15

Outline the challenges schools face in protecting students from criminals and bullies while at school.

Everyone agrees that "our nation's schools should be safe havens for teaching and learning, free of crime and violence. Any instance of crime or violence at school not only affects the individuals involved, but also may disrupt the educational process and affect bystanders, the school itself, and the surrounding community."[58] Mass shootings at Columbine High School (1999), Virginia Tech University (2007), and Sandy Hook Elementary School (2012), along with more incidences of bullying (see Table 16–3), sexual assaults, and other crimes, have frightened, angered, and mobilized many citizens. Making schools safe learning environments has become a very difficult—but vital—task for state lawmakers, local school officials, and college and university administrators. Security has become a 24/7 operation.

Demands for heightened security systems have escalated, and at the same time many schools are experiencing budget shortfalls. Yet, as the Skokie, Illinois School Superintendent explained, "I don't know that there's too big a price tag to put on kids being as safe as they can be… So often we hear we can't afford it, but what we can't afford is another terrible incident."[59] In the immediate aftermath of crises like the Sandy Hook shootings, many school systems react with short-term solutions, like hiring more security personnel, limiting access to school facilities and events, requiring visitor background checks and tracking systems, installing panic buttons and video cameras, even arming a limited number of school officials (although that is certainly more controversial). Other districts choose to contract with professional school security experts to conduct in-depth school security assessments for each school in their district. One well-known consulting firm's Website details what such an assessment entails: "Practical and cost-effective recommendations for security and crisis preparedness planning, violence prevention, physical security (access control, communications, perimeter security, after hours safety, physical design), school safety training, security staff and police operations, linking security with prevention and intervention, school-community collaboration, and support service roles in school safety."[60]

What officials often cannot agree on are the most effective ways to combat security shortcoming and create safe learning environments. Besides philosophical and intense

	Percentage of Reporting Being Bullied at School[a]	Percentage of Reporting Being Cyberbullied Anywhere[b]	Percentage of Reporting Being either Bullied at School or Cyberbullied
Total	28.0	6.0	29.0
Sex			
Male	26.6	4.9	27.8
Female	29.5	7.2	30.2
Race/Ethnicity			
White	29.3	6.8	30.3
Black	29.1	5.5	30.3
Hispanic	25.5	5.0	26.5
Asian	17.3	2.9*	17.8
Other[c]	26.7	4.2*	26.7
Urbanicity[d]			
Urban	27.4	5.7	28.8
Suburban	27.5	6.3	28.6
Rural	30.7	5.7	30.8
Sector			
Public	28.8	6.2	29.8
Private	18.9	4.0	20.1

Note: Data are for 2009. Survey of students ages 12-18. Most recent data available at time of publication.

*The coefficient variation (CV) for this estimate is 30% or greater, interpret data with caution.

[a]"At school" includes inside the school building, on school property, on a school bus, or going to and from school.

[b]"Cyberbullying" includes students who responded that another student posted hurtful information on the Internet, students who were harassed via instant messaging, text messaging, emails, or while gaming, and students who responded that they were excluded online.

[c]Other includes Native American, Alaska Native, Pacific Islander, and two or more races.

[d]Urbanicity refers to the Standard Metropolitan Statistical Area (MSA) status of the respondent's household as defined in 2009 by the U.S. Census Bureau.

Source: U.S. Department of Education National Center for Education Statistics and the U.S. Department of Justice Bureau of Justice Statistics, "Indicators of School Crime and Safety: 2011," February 2012, Tables 11.1 and 11.3. Available at http://nces.ed.gov/programs/crimeindicators/crimeindicators2011/index.asp.

political differences on contentious issues like whether to arm teachers (and students on some university campuses), researchers have often come to different conclusions about the effectiveness of other issues. To date, evidence on the impacts of armed security guards, zero-tolerance policies for certain types of infractions, self-defense and/or gun-use training for school personnel and students, and efforts to monitor off-campus incidents (cyberbullying) potentially affecting in-school learning is mixed.[61] What works well in one school system may not work well in another; there is no "one size fits all" approach to school security. What has yet to be studied is the degree to which mental health–based interventions might make schools safer and a better place to learn. (See Chapter 17 "*Up Close: Mental Health and Mass Murders.*") State and local lawmakers are already being pressured to spend more on mental health programs.

Education is one of the most important functions of state and local governments. It is also one of the most difficult to deliver in an effective, efficient, and equitable manner. Differences in opinions as to what works best vary considerably within and across states and school districts.

- Education is a high priority for many state and local officials who see it as the key to a strong economy.

- Universal suffrage requires universal, free, and compulsory education. In addition to advancing literacy, education today is expected to fulfill social goals such as alleviating hunger, combating drug abuse, and seeing student mental health needs.

- State and local officials extol a well-educated workforce as essential to economic development.

- The education system is usually evaluated by educational attainment (high school or college diploma), the dropout rate, and SAT scores.

- The high school dropout rate varies according to how it's calculated: (1) event (no attendance during grades 10 to 12), 3 percent; (2) status (nonattendance or nongraduation of 18- to 24-year-olds), 13 percent; and (3) graduation rate (graduates as a percentage of ninth graders four years earlier), 25 percent.

- Efforts to improve education have included increased spending, school-based management, magnet schools, charter schools, and virtual schools. These reforms have had mixed results.

- School voucher proponents argue that parental choice would enhance achievement; opponents argue that vouchers would create a two-tier system of schools—one for the haves and one for the have-nots.

- Forty-five states are participating in the Common Core State Standards Initiative. Proponents argue that common standards will better prepare students to succeed in today's global economy whether they are educated in New York, Kansas, or any other state. Opponents are skeptical it will improve student performance, convinced it will cost too much to implement and track, and worried it will erode local control.

- The federal government assists with education for low-income students through its preschool Head Start program and Title I funding to elementary and secondary schools.

- The federal No Child Left Behind Act of 2001 relies primarily on testing to improve education and asserts that every child should be able to read by the end of third grade. Proponents say the law has improved students' basic skills, and opponents argue that test results should be used to help low-performing schools, not penalize them. The overly ambitious program ended up granting many states waivers from certain requirements.

- The Obama administration's education policy includes testing, a focus on inner-city schools, greater support to charter schools, and linking teacher pay to student test scores.

- The Race to the Top program allows states to compete for funds to turn around failing schools.

- States have the major responsibility for public education. States ensure local compliance with state educational policy through bureaucratic oversight and allocation of funding to local school districts. States may take over failing school districts.

- Annual per-pupil expenditures for public education range from $6,683 in one state to more than $18,000 in another, depending on a state's economic resources.

- Within a state, district revenues vary widely because communities with high-value taxable property can finance their schools better than communities with low-value property. State courts are increasingly ordering their legislatures to substitute state general revenues for local property taxes in funding education.

- At the local district level, policymaking is led by the superintendent and the local school board with input from interested citizens and teacher unions.

- As the battle over education reform has intensified, school board races have become more highly visible, contentious, and expensive.

- Two-thirds of America's high school graduates enroll in college. Three-quarters of higher education enrollment is in public colleges and universities.

■ Taxpayers foot most of the bill for a college education; tuition pays for only about a quarter of it. Federal assistance includes grants for research and student aid.

■ The Supreme Court has upheld the provision of nonreligious textbooks, lunches, transportation, and other services to church-related schools because funding does not benefit religion directly. But the Court has disallowed prayer (including voluntary prayer and silence) and Bible-reading ceremonies as a violation of the First Amendment's No Establishment Clause.

■ Creating safe learning environments has become a huge challenge for public schools, colleges, and universities. Mass shootings on campuses have created intense debates over how best to protect students, including whether to arm faculty, staff, and students.

CHAPTER SEVENTEEN

THE POLITICS OF POVERTY, WELFARE, AND HEALTH

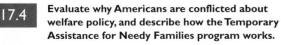

LEARNING OBJECTIVES

 17.1 Describe the extent to which Americans live in poverty, and compare poverty rates among the states.

 17.2 Establish the link between poverty rates and demographic characteristics, including family structure, race, ethnicity, and age; and describe how poverty rates have been impacted by the Great Recession.

17.3 Outline the various government programs that provide assistance to families to help combat or avoid poverty.

 17.4 Evaluate why Americans are conflicted about welfare policy, and describe how the Temporary Assistance for Needy Families program works.

17.5 Outline the various policies enacted by the federal, state, and local governments to provide health care to certain Americans.

 17.6 Describe the efforts by state government to expand health insurance to more Americans and to reign in health care costs.

 17.7 Outline the policies established by the Patient Protection and Affordable Care Act, and explain why so many Americans dislike the law.

17.8 Explain the responsibilities given to states for implementing the Affordable Care Act, and discuss the efforts by some states to weaken or repeal the law.

 17.9 Describe the role of the federal and state governments in protecting citizens suffering from mental health issues, and evaluate whether or not these measures have been effective.

491

POVERTY IN AMERICA

Political conflict over poverty in America begins with disagreement over its nature and extent, and then it proceeds to disputes over its causes and remedies. While many antipoverty programs are largely regarded as federal programs, many allow states to set their own eligibility criteria and benefit levels and are a blend of federal and state government funds.

OFFICIAL POVERTY RATE

The percentage of the population whose annual cash income falls below that which is required, according to the federal government, to maintain a decent standard of living.

How Many Poor?

How much poverty really exists in America? According to the U.S. Census Bureau, there are over 46 million poor people in the United States. The **official poverty rate** (the number of people living in poverty as a percentage of the total population) has ranged between 11 and 15 percent in recent years. (See Figure 17–1.) This official definition of poverty includes all those Americans whose annual cash income falls below that which is required to maintain a decent standard of living. The dollar amounts of the poverty level change each year to take into account the effect of inflation. In 2013, it was $11,945 per year for a single person, and $23,283 for a family of four. Poverty can be **episodic** (hard times for brief spells) or more permanent (**chronic poverty**). Temporary poverty is more common than chronic poverty (around 5% of the population).

EPISODIC POVERTY

Poverty conditions that are temporary; hard times occurring for a brief time.

CHRONIC POVERTY

Permanent, persistent poverty conditions.

Variations among the States

The official poverty rate varies considerably among the states. (See "*Rankings of the States: Poverty Rates.*") Poverty in some states (notably Mississippi, New Mexico, and Louisiana) is over 20 percent. Inasmuch as minority populations tend to experience poverty in greater proportions than others, it is not surprising that southern states with larger African American populations and southwestern states with larger Hispanic populations have higher poverty rates.

FEMINIZATION OF POVERTY

The concept that poverty is most common among female-headed families.

WHO ARE THE POOR?

Poverty occurs in many kinds of families and in all races and ethnic groups. However, some groups experience poverty in greater proportions than the national average.

Family Structure

Poverty is most common among female-headed families. The incidence of poverty among these families is over 30 percent, compared to about 6 percent for married couples. (See Table 17–1.) These women and their children comprise over two-thirds of all of the persons living in poverty in the United States. These figures describe the "**feminization of poverty**"

FIGURE 17–1 Poverty in America

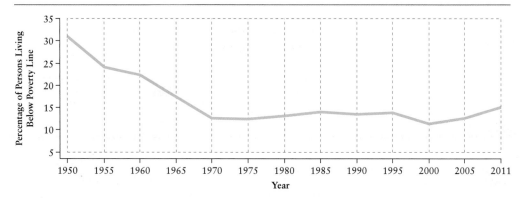

Source: U.S. Census Bureau, "Income, Poverty, and Health Insurance Coverage in the United States: 2011," September 2012: p. 16. Available at http://www.census.gov/newsroom/releases/pdf/20120912_ip_%20slides_wplotpoints.pdf.

Poverty Rates

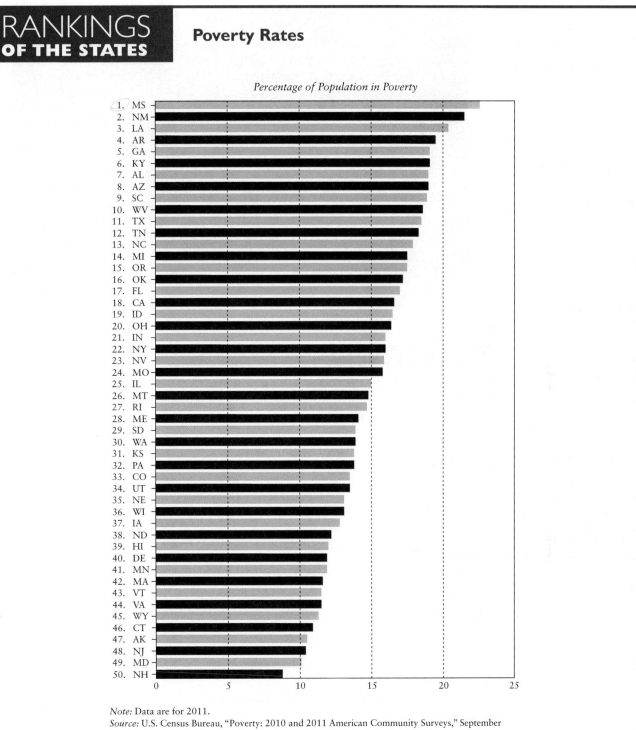

Percentage of Population in Poverty

1. MS	
2. NM	
3. LA	
4. AR	
5. GA	
6. KY	
7. AL	
8. AZ	
9. SC	
10. WV	
11. TX	
12. TN	
13. NC	
14. MI	
15. OR	
16. OK	
17. FL	
18. CA	
19. ID	
20. OH	
21. IN	
22. NY	
23. NV	
24. MO	
25. IL	
26. MT	
27. RI	
28. ME	
29. SD	
30. WA	
31. KS	
32. PA	
33. CO	
34. UT	
35. NE	
36. WI	
37. IA	
38. ND	
39. HI	
40. DE	
41. MN	
42. MA	
43. VT	
44. VA	
45. WY	
46. CT	
47. AK	
48. NJ	
49. MD	
50. NH	

Note: Data are for 2011.
Source: U.S. Census Bureau, "Poverty: 2010 and 2011 American Community Surveys," September 2012, Table 1. Available at http://www.census.gov/prod/2012pubs/acsbr11-01.pdf.

Families headed by single moms are more likely to be poor than two-parent households.

TABLE 17–1 Poverty in America	
Poverty definition[a]	$23,021
Number of poor	46.2 million
Poverty rate	15
Race (% poor)	
White	9.8
Black	27.6
Asian	12.3
Hispanic	25.3
Age (% poor)	
Under 18	21.9
Over 65	8.7
Family (% poor)	
Married couple	6.2
Single parent, mother only	31.2
Single parent, father only	16.1

Note: Data are for 2011.
[a]Poverty threshold for four-person family unit.
Source: U.S. Census Bureau, "Income, Poverty, and Health Insurance Coverage in the United States: 2011," September 2012: p. 14. Available at http://www.census.gov/prod/2012pubs/p60-243.pdf.

in America. Clearly, poverty is closely related to the family structure. Many believe the disintegration of the traditional husband–wife family is the single most influential factor contributing to poverty. Hunger and homeless rates among single mother–headed families with small children have steadily climbed over the past decade. In some large metropolitan areas, homeless families on average spend more than a year in a shelter.

Race/Ethnicity

African Americans, Hispanics, and Native Americans experience poverty in much greater proportions than whites. Chronic poverty is also more pervasive among minorities. Over the years the poverty rate among blacks and Hispanics in the United States has been over twice the poverty rate among whites.

Age

The aged in America experience *less* poverty than the nonaged. The aged are not poor, despite the popularity of the phrase "the poor and the aged." The poverty rate for persons over 65 years of age is *below* the national average. Moreover, the aged are much wealthier than middle age and younger Americans. They are more likely than younger people to own homes with paid mortgages. Medicare pays a large portion of their medical expenses. With fewer expenses, the aged, even with relatively smaller cash incomes, experience poverty in a different fashion than young mothers with children. Continuing increases in Social Security benefits over the years are largely responsible for this singular "victory" in the war against poverty.

Wealth

Wealth is the net worth of all one's possessions—home value minus mortgage, auto value minus loan, business value minus debts, money in bank accounts, savings, stocks and bonds, and real estate. All calculations of poverty consider income, not wealth. It is theoretically possible for persons to have considerable wealth (e.g., to own a mortgage-free home and a loan-free automobile and have money in savings and investments), yet fall within the official definition of poverty because current cash income is low. Indeed, many of the *aged* who are counted as poor because their incomes are low have substantial accumulations of wealth. But even seniors' net worth dropped 13 percent during the Great Recession when the value of stocks, bonds, and housing fell.[1]

The Great Recession took its toll on everyone. The median net worth of all Americans fell to a 43-year low ($57,000). Especially hard hit was the shrinking middle class, which gave rise to a widening wealth gap. Sixty percent of the job losses during that time occurred in middle-income jobs. Middle-income households (defined as those where incomes are 67 to 200% of the national median) were 54 percent of all households in 1980 but only 48 percent in 2010. At the same time, upper-income households grew from 15 percent in 1980 to 20 percent in 2010.[2] Americans' sensitivity to the wealth gap is reflected in polls showing that two-thirds believe the gap has grown over the past decade and that it is a bad thing for the country. At the same time, "overwhelming majorities of self-described middle- and lower-class Americans say they admire people who get rich by working hard (92 percent and 84 percent, respectively)."[3]

Americans are somewhat conflicted when it comes to their views on the government's role in helping the poor. Nearly two-thirds of American adults think there are too many Americans dependent on the government for financial aid, including a majority of those earning less than $30,000 a year. Even among these low-income adults, there is some skepticism about whether antipoverty programs really work; over 40 percent believe they only make the problem worse.[4] But Americans are favorably disposed toward government-subsidized jobs. A majority of Americans favor redirecting some government funds supporting social welfare programs to guaranteeing a minimum wage government job doing projects for someone who cannot find a job and wants to work.[5]

WEALTH
The net worth of all one's possessions.

AN OVERVIEW OF WELFARE POLICY

Public welfare has been a recognized responsibility of government in the United States since colonial days. As far back as the Poor Relief Act of 1601, the English Parliament provided workhouses for both the "able-bodied poor" (the unemployed) and poorhouses for widows and orphans, the aged, and the handicapped. Today, about half of all families in America receive some type of government payments. (See Table 17–2.) However, the

17.3

Outline the various government programs that provide assistance to families to help combat or avoid poverty.

TABLE 17-2 Social Welfare for Everyone

U.S. Population Receiving Government Payments

Social Insurance Programs (No Means Test for Entitlement to Benefits)	Beneficiaries (Millions)
Social Security	54.0
Medicare	47.5
Federal Government Retirement	2.8
State and Local Government Retirement	7.7
Veterans' Benefits	2.7
Unemployment Compensation	13.0

Public Assistance Programs (Means-Tested Entitlement)	Beneficiaries (Millions)
Cash Aid	
Temporary Assistance for Needy Families (formerly AFDC)	4.2
SSI	7.7
Medical Care	
Medicaid	61.8
SCHIP (State Children's Health Insurance Program)	7.7
Food Benefits	
Food stamps	40.3
School lunches	32
School breakfasts	12
Women, infants, children	9.2
Education Aid	
Federal loans	24.2
Pell Grants	9.4
Head Start	0.9

Source: U.S. Census Bureau, *Statistical Abstract of the United States,* 2012, Tables 145, 151, 291, 564, 565, 570, 574. Available at http://www.census.gov/compendia/statab/2012edition.html.

percentage of people receiving aid varies considerably among the states. (See "*Rankings of the States:* TANF (Temporary Assistance for Needy Families) and Medicaid Recipients.") The number of households receiving government benefits has continued to rise. Total federal and state welfare spending rose from $431 billion in 2000 to $927 billion in 2011 and amounted to $20,610 for every poor person in the United States.[6]

Social Security

The key feature of the Social Security Act is the Old-Age, Survivors, and Disability Insurance (OASDI) program; this is a compulsory social insurance program that gives individuals a legal right to benefits in the event of certain occurrences that cause a reduction in their income: old age, death of the head of the household, or permanent disability.[7] Both employees and employers must pay equal amounts toward employees' OASDI insurance. Upon retirement, an insured worker is entitled to monthly benefit payments based on age at retirement and the amount earned during his or her working years. OASDI also ensures benefit payments to survivors of an insured worker, including the spouse if there are dependent children. However, if the spouse has no dependent children, benefits will not begin until he or she reaches retirement age. Finally, OASDI ensures benefit payments to people who suffer permanent and total disabilities that prevent them from working more than one year. Almost one-third of Americans receive Social Security—a percent that is

TANF (Temporary Assistance for Needy Families) and Medicaid Recipients

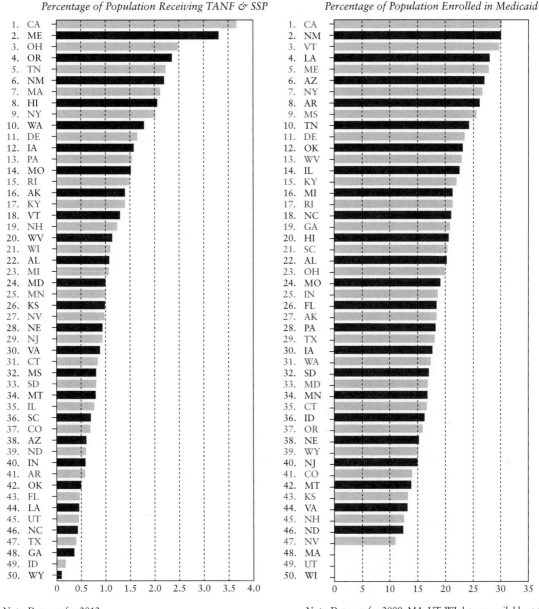

Percentage of Population Receiving TANF & SSP

1.	CA
2.	ME
3.	OH
4.	OR
5.	TN
6.	NM
7.	MA
8.	HI
9.	NY
10.	WA
11.	DE
12.	IA
13.	PA
14.	MO
15.	RI
16.	AK
17.	KY
18.	VT
19.	NH
20.	WV
21.	WI
22.	AL
23.	MI
24.	MD
25.	MN
26.	KS
27.	NV
28.	NE
29.	NJ
30.	VA
31.	CT
32.	MS
33.	SD
34.	MT
35.	IL
36.	SC
37.	CO
38.	AZ
39.	ND
40.	IN
41.	AR
42.	OK
43.	FL
44.	LA
45.	UT
46.	NC
47.	TX
48.	GA
49.	ID
50.	WY

Percentage of Population Enrolled in Medicaid

1.	CA
2.	NM
3.	VT
4.	LA
5.	ME
6.	AZ
7.	NY
8.	AR
9.	MS
10.	TN
11.	DE
12.	OK
13.	WV
14.	IL
15.	KY
16.	MI
17.	RI
18.	NC
19.	GA
20.	HI
21.	SC
22.	AL
23.	OH
24.	MO
25.	IN
26.	FL
27.	AK
28.	PA
29.	TX
30.	IA
31.	WA
32.	SD
33.	MD
34.	MN
35.	CT
36.	ID
37.	OR
38.	NE
39.	WY
40.	NJ
41.	CO
42.	MT
43.	KS
44.	VA
45.	NH
46.	ND
47.	NV
48.	MA
49.	UT
50.	WI

Note: Data are for 2012.
Source: Office of Family Assistance, Administration of Children and Families, "Caseload Data 2012." Available at http://www.acf.hhs.gov/programs/ofa/resource/caseload-data-2012.

Note: Data are for 2009. MA, UT, WI data unavailable at the time of publication.
Source: Medicaid.gov. Available at http://www.medicaid.gov/Medicaid-CHIP-Program-Information/By-State/By-State.html.

sure to rise with the baby-boomer generation now beginning to hit retirement age. The future solvency of **Social Security** has become a big issue, one that is creating generational conflicts between the young and the old.

OASDI is a completely federal program, administered by the Social Security Administration in the Department of Health and Human Services. However, OASDI has an important indirect effect on state and local welfare programs by removing people in whole or in part from welfare roles. Social Security has doubtlessly reduced the welfare problems that state and local governments would otherwise face.

Unemployment Compensation

Another feature of the Social Security Act was that it induced states to enact unemployment compensation programs through the imposition of the **payroll tax** on all employers. A federal unemployment tax was levied on the payroll of employers of four or more workers, but employers paying into state insurance programs that meet federal standards could use these state payments to offset their federal unemployment tax. In other words, the federal government threatened to undertake an unemployment compensation program and tax if the states did not do so themselves. This federal program succeeded in inducing all 50 states to establish unemployment compensation programs.

The states have some flexibility in shaping their own unemployment programs. Unemployed workers must show that they are willing and able to work in order to receive unemployment compensation benefits. This usually means that they must register for work at state unemployment offices; they must not refuse an offer of "suitable work" without good cause. Disqualification may also result from voluntarily quitting work without good cause or being discharged for misconduct. States cannot deny workers' benefits for refusing to work as strike breakers or refusing to work for rates lower than prevailing rates.

Benefits are calculated by each state based on prevailing wage rates. Nationwide benefit payments average about $300 per week. Traditionally, benefits can be extended for a maximum of 39 weeks, but during economic downturns, Congress regularly extends the benefit period. In 2010, benefits were extended to almost two years. But in 2012, Congress reduced the maximum duration of state and federal benefits from 99 to 73 weeks.

Supplemental Security Income

The federal government also directly aids certain categories of welfare recipients—people who are aged, blind, or disabled—under a program called **Supplemental Security Income (SSI)**. A loose definition of "disabled"—including alcoholism and drug abuse among adults and attention deficiency among children—has led to rapid growth in the number of SSI recipients.

Family Assistance

Family Assistance, officially Temporary Assistance for Needy Families, (formerly AFDC, or Aid to Families with Dependent Children), is a grant program to enable the *states* to assist needy families. States now operate the program and define "need"; they set their own benefit levels and establish (within federal guidelines) income and resource limits. Prior to welfare reform in 1996, AFDC was a *federal* entitlement program.

Food Stamps (SNAP)

The federal food stamp program, officially the Supplemental Nutrition Assistance Program (SNAP), now distributes billions in federal monies to improve food and nutrition among the poor. Eligible persons may receive a SNAP card, generally from state or county welfare departments, which may be used to purchase food at supermarkets. This program has mushroomed rapidly since its origins; eligibility for food stamp cards now extends to many people who are not poor enough to qualify for public assistance. Today, almost one out of every six Americans is receiving food stamps.

Earned Income Tax Credit

The **Earned Income Tax Credit** (EITC) is designed to assist the working poor. It not only refunds their payroll taxes, but also provides larger refunds than they actually paid in taxes during the previous year. Thus, the EITC is in effect a "negative" income tax. The program applies only to those poor who actually work and who apply for the credit when filing their income tax.

Other Social Programs

Public assistance recipients are generally eligible for participation in a variety of other social programs. These include school lunch and milk; housing assistance; job training; various educational and child-care programs and services; special food programs for women, infants, and children (WIC); home heating and weatherization assistance; free legal services; and more.

EARNED INCOME TAX CREDIT

A refundable federal income tax credit for low-income working individuals and families: when the EITC amount exceeds taxes owed, a refund is made to those claiming credit on their income tax return.

WELFARE REFORM

Political conflict over welfare policy arises in part from a clash of values over individual responsibility and social compassion. As Harvard sociologist David Ellwood explains:

> Welfare brings some of our most precious values—involving autonomy, responsibility, work, family, community and compassion—into conflict. We want to help those who are not making it but in so doing, we seem to cheapen the efforts of those who are struggling hard just to get by. We want to offer financial support to those with low incomes, but if we do we reduce the pressure on them and their incentive to work. We want to help people who are not able to help themselves but then we worry that people will not bother to help themselves. We recognize the insecurity of single-parent families but, in helping them, we appear to be promoting or supporting their formation.[8]

A political consensus developed over the years that welfare policy in America was in need of reform. A variety of problems were commonly cited: the work disincentives created by the pyramiding of multiple forms of public assistance, the long-term social dependency that welfare programs seemed to encourage, and the adverse effects welfare assistance appeared to have on families.

17.4

Evaluate why Americans are conflicted about welfare policy, and describe how Temporary Assistance for Needy Families works.

WELFARE REFORM

Officially, the Temporary Assistance for Needy Families (TANF) program enacted in 1996, which included the "devolution" of responsibility for cash assistance programs to the states.

Welfare Reform

After a great deal of controversy and two presidential vetoes, welfare reform finally became law in 1996. It was passed by a Republican Congress and signed by Democratic President Bill Clinton, but it was bitterly opposed by groups representing social workers, minorities, and the poor.

Welfare reform—officially **Temporary Assistance for Needy Families (TANF)**—ended the 60-year-old federal cash entitlement program for low-income families with children—Aid to Families with Dependent Children (AFDC). TANF reflects the philosophy of "devolution" of responsibility to the states. TANF is essentially a federal block grant program that allocates lump sums to the states for cash welfare payments. Benefits and

Welfare reform was a bipartisan effort. A Republican Congress passed the legislation and Democrat President Bill Clinton signed it into law in 1996.

Welfare Reform Success Tied to Work

Supporters of welfare reform have declared it a success. Their claim is based primarily on the exodus of over 8 million people from the nation's welfare rolls (see the figure below).

The number of welfare recipients in the nation has dropped to just over 4 million, although it rose slightly during the Great Recession. Today, around 7 percent of Americans receive cash welfare.

Virtually all states have now developed work programs for welfare recipients. Applicants for welfare benefits are now generally required to enter job-search programs, to undertake job training, and to accept jobs or community service positions.

Yet, although nearly everyone agrees that getting people off welfare rolls and onto payrolls is the main goal of reform, there are major obstacles to the achievement of this goal. First of all, many long-term welfare recipients have obstacles—physical disabilities, chronic illnesses, learning disabilities, alcohol or drug abuse problems—that prevent them from holding a full-time job. Many long-term recipients have no work experience at all, and two-thirds of them did not graduate from high school. Almost half have three or more children, making day-care arrangements a major obstacle. It is unlikely that any counseling, education, job training, or job placement programs could ever succeed in getting these people into productive employment.

Early studies of people who left the welfare rolls following welfare reform suggest that over half and perhaps as many as three-quarters have found work, although most at minimum or near-minimum wages.[a] As projected, the early dramatic reductions in welfare case loads (see figure) began to level off after 2000. There are probably 4–5 million people who have so many physical, psychological, and social problems that it is simply impossible for them to work.

[a]*Governing* (April 1999): 21–26.

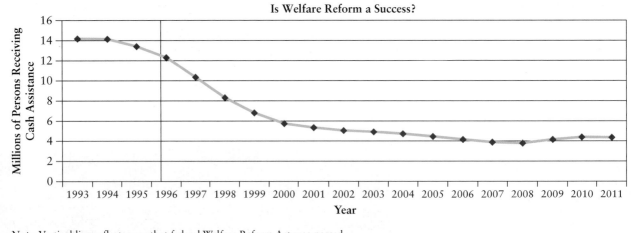

Is Welfare Reform a Success?

Note: Vertical line reflects year that federal Welfare Reform Act was passed.
Sources: U.S. Census Bureau, *Statistical Abstract of the United States*, 2012, Table 565. Available at http://www.census.gov/prod/2011pubs/12statab/socins.pdf. 2010 and 2011 data from U.S. Department of Health and Human Services, Office of Family Assistance, "TANF: Total Number of Adult Recipients," Fiscal and Calendar Year 2010 and 2011. Available at http://www.acf.hhs.gov/programs/ofa/resource/2010-adult-tan; http://www.acf.hhs.gov/programs/ofa/resource/2011-adult-tan.

TEMPORARY ASSISTANCE FOR NEEDY FAMILIES (TANF)

Federal aid for state programs of cash assistance to poor families; replaced the AFDC federal entitlement program.

eligibility requirements for cash assistance are now largely decided by the states. However, conservatives in Congress imposed some tough-minded "strings" to this federal aid, including a two-year limit on continuing cash benefits and a five-year lifetime limit; a "family cap" that denies additional cash benefits to women already on welfare who bear more children; and the denial of cash welfare to unwed parents under 18 years of age unless they live with an adult and attend school. Liberals in Congress obtained some modifications to the welfare reform act: exemptions from time limits and work requirements for some portion of welfare recipients, and community service alternatives to work requirements. (See *Did You Know?: Welfare Reform Success Tied to Work*.)

HEALTH CARE

Health care costs governments at all levels—federal, state, and local—billions of dollars. Overall, almost 18 percent of the U.S. gross domestic product (GDP) is spent on health.

Good health correlates best with factors over which doctors and hospitals have no direct control: heredity, lifestyle (smoking, eating, drinking, exercise, stress), and the physical environment. Historically, most of the reductions in death rates have resulted from public health and sanitation improvements, including immunization against smallpox, clean public water supplies, sanitary sewage disposal, and increased standards of living. Many of the leading causes of death today, including heart disease, stroke, cirrhosis of the liver, AIDS, accidents, and suicides, are closely linked to personal habits and lifestyles. Over 65 percent of the nation's population is overweight or obese.[9] Thus, for many, the greatest contribution to better health is likely to be found in altered personal habits and lifestyles, rather than in more medical care.

Community Public Health and Hospitals

Public health and sanitation are among the oldest functions of local government. Keeping clean is still one of the major tasks of cities today, a task that includes street cleaning, sewage disposal, garbage collection, and the provision of a clean water supply. Often these services are taken for granted in the United States, but in many underdeveloped countries of the world, health and sanitation are still major concerns.

Local public health departments are directly concerned with the *prevention* of disease. They engage in vaccination and immunization, as well as regulatory activity and the safeguarding of water supplies.

In addition to the preventive activities of public health departments, state and local governments also provide extensive, tax-supported hospital care. State and local governments provide both general and specialized hospitals, health centers, and nursing homes and often subsidize private hospitals and medical facilities as well. New York City operates the nation's largest city hospital system, but almost every community subsidizes hospital facilities in some way. City and county hospitals and heavily subsidized private hospitals are expected to provide free emergency care to indigent patients. Thus, when revenue shortfalls hit local governments, the impact can be quite negative for governments, hospitals, doctors who may not get reimbursed, and the poor.

Medicare

The federal government added Medicare to the Social Security program in 1965. **Medicare** provides for prepaid hospital insurance for the *aged* and low-cost voluntary medical insurance for the aged under federal administration. Medicare includes (1) a compulsory basic health insurance plan covering hospital costs for the aged, which is financed through payroll taxes collected under the Social Security system; and (2) a voluntary but supplemental medical program that will pay doctors' bills and additional medical expenses, financed in part by contributions from the aged and in part by the general tax revenues. Only persons 65 and over are covered by Medicare. Reflective of the aging of Americans, nearly 30 percent of all households are eligible for Medicare—again, a figure destined to rise as the large baby-boomer generation reaches 65.

MEDICARE
Federal health insurance for the aged.

Medicaid

The federal government also provides funds under **Medicaid** to enable states to guarantee medical services to the *poor.* Each state operates its own Medicaid program. Unlike Medicare, Medicaid is a welfare program designed for needy persons; no prior contributions are required, and recipients of Medicaid services are generally welfare recipients. States can extend coverage to other medically needy persons if they choose to do so. Medicaid pays virtually all health care costs, including nursing home care.

MEDICAID
Federal aid to the states to provide health insurance for the poor.

Medicaid is a federally funded program that requires states to provide medical services to the poor—regardless of their age.

Medicaid in the States

Medicaid is the costliest of all public assistance programs. States must pay about 45 percent of Medicaid's costs, with the federal government paying the remainder. Medicaid is the most rapidly growing item in the budget of most states.

Medicaid is increasingly becoming the last resort for people who have no medical insurance and for those whose insurance does not cover long-term illness or nursing home care. People confronted with serious or "catastrophic" illnesses that exhaust their private insurance or Medicare coverage are often forced to impoverish themselves in order to qualify for Medicaid. (Medicare pays for only 60 days of hospital care and 100 days of nursing home care.) Moreover, as the number and proportion of the very old in society rise (those 80 years and over comprise the nation's fastest-growing age group), the need for long-term nursing home care grows. Medicaid is the only program that covers nursing home care, but middle-class people must first "spend down" their savings or transfer their wealth to others in order to qualify for Medicaid. Nursing home care is now the single largest item in Medicaid spending.

Medicaid Expansion

The Patient Protection and Affordable Care Act of 2010 ("ObamaCare") provides for nationwide expansion of Medicaid eligibility. People with family incomes up to 133 percent of the federal poverty level ($30,675 in 2012 for a family of four) will qualify for Medicaid. This expansion will be particularly beneficial for childless adults under age 65, who in many states did not previously qualify for Medicaid. (Children were covered by SCHIP and persons 65 and over by Medicare.) The federal government will pay for the first three years of the expansion, but afterward the states will be obliged to pick up a share of the costs.

In the original version of the Act, the states would lose all of their federal Medicaid funds if they did not adopt the expansion. But the U.S. Supreme Court ruled in 2012 that threatening to cut off all Medicaid assistance to nonparticipating states was a penalty, and that the federal government had no power to penalize states for not participating in a federal program.[10] The effect of the decision was to make state participation optional. But states that chose not to participate would still lose considerable federal funding and significant portions of their populations would be without health care insurance. Most states are expected to participate. But all are frantically seeking ways to contain the rising costs of Medicaid, which continue to overwhelm state budgets. Among the most common cost containment approaches being used are limiting eligibility, shifting eligibles to managed care organizations, altering provider reimbursements, and aggressively tackling the fraud and abuse issue.[11]

SCHIP

STATE CHILDREN'S HEALTH INSURANCE PROGRAM (SCHIP)
Federal grants to states to extend health insurance to children who would not otherwise qualify for Medicaid.

Under the **State Children's Health Insurance Program (SCHIP)** the federal government provides grants to states to extend health insurance to children who would not otherwise qualify for Medicaid. The program is generally targeted toward families with incomes below 200 percent of the poverty level. However, each state may set its own eligibility limits and each state has flexibility in the administration of the program.[12] States may expand their Medicaid programs to include children or develop separate child health programs.

STIMULUS TO HEALTH CARE REFORM

Traditionally, health care reform centered on two central problems: controlling costs and expanding access. These problems were related: Expanding access to Americans who were currently uninsured and closing gaps in coverage required increases in costs, even while the central thrust of reform was to bring down overall health care costs.

Approximately 86 percent of the population of the United States was covered by either private health insurance, mostly through their employers, or government health insurance, including Medicare and Medicaid. However, about 14 percent of the population had *no* medical insurance. (Among age categories, young people 18 to 24 were the least likely to have insurance.) Most of the uninsured were working Americans and their families—people who were neither poor enough to qualify for Medicaid nor old enough to qualify for Medicare. These people might postpone or go without needed medical care or be denied medical care except in emergencies. Confronted with serious illnesses, they might be obliged to impoverish themselves in order to become eligible for Medicaid. Their unpaid medical bills had to be absorbed by hospitals and state and local government support of them, or be shifted to paying patients and their insurance companies.

State Reforms

For many years, the states, rather than the federal government, took the lead in heath care reform. Inasmuch as states cannot run deficits in the fashion of the federal government, considerable effort was made in the states to contain Medicaid costs. Prior to 1997 states were required to obtain "waivers" from the U.S. Department of Health and Human Services in order to experiment with Medicaid cost containment. But in that year Congress eliminated the waiver requirement and states began to place their Medicaid recipients in managed care plans. Nationwide, about 60 percent of all Medicaid patients were in managed care plans.

Managed Care

State managed care programs vary widely, but most resemble private health insurance organizations, known as **Health Maintenance Organizations (HMOs)**. The states pay

HEALTH MAINTENANCE ORGANIZATIONS (HMOs)
Private health care organizations that provide medical services for fixed fees.

health insurance organizations a fixed amount for each person enrolled. These organizations have financial incentives to limit costs, by monitoring patient care, often requiring primary care physicians to first obtain permission before referring patients to specialists or before performing specific procedures. The object is to minimize unnecessary care and costs, but, of course, physicians, hospitals, and patients themselves are often frustrated with delays and adverse decisions by outside personnel who have no direct contact with patients. Moreover, overall Medicaid spending continues to rise dramatically.

Massachusetts Mandated Health Insurance

Massachusetts led the way with mandated health insurance. The aged are covered by Medicare, the poor by Medicaid,

Mentally incapacitated people living out of shopping carts are often taken off the streets and put in jail because there is no housing for them.

employers with more than ten workers are required to provide health insurance, and those who cannot afford private insurance qualify for a state health insurance program. Massachusetts was the first state in the nation to experiment with this approach to health care reform. In 2006, Republican Governor Mitt Romney and the Democratic-controlled state legislature, together with an unlikely alliance of business leaders and consumer advocates, agreed on this "bold, positive, and necessary" program. Beginning in 2008, Massachusetts residents were required to provide health insurance information on their state income tax forms or face a financial penalty. Since its passage, support for the state's universal health care system has remained strong.

OBAMACARE: HEALTH CARE TRANSFORMATION

17.7

Outline the policies established by the Patient Protection and Affordable Care Act, and explain why so many Americans dislike the law.

President Barack Obama and a Democratic-controlled Congress acted to transform health care in America with the comprehensive Patient Protection and Affordable Care Act of 2010. National health care had been attempted unsuccessfully by past presidents, including Franklin D. Roosevelt, Harry Truman, and Bill Clinton. According to President Obama, "Moving to provide all Americans with health insurance is not only a moral imperative, but it is also essential to a more effective and efficient health care system."[13]

America's health care system will continue to rely primarily on private health insurance companies. However, private insurers will no longer be permitted to deny insurance for preexisting conditions, or to drop coverage when patients get sick, or to place lifetime limits on coverage. Dependent children under age 26 can be covered under their parents' insurance plan. These particular reforms faced no serious opposition in Congress.

Provisions

Many other provisions in the 2,500-page bill stirred intense controversy. Republicans in both the U.S. House and Senate were unanimous in their opposition to the overall bill. Among its many provisions:

- *Individual Mandate.* Every American is required to purchase health insurance or face a tax penalty up to 2.5 percent of their household income. The Internal Revenue Service is charged with enforcing this individual mandate.
- *Employer Mandate.* Employers with 50 or more workers are obliged to provide health insurance to their employees. Companies that fail to do so will face substantial fines. Small businesses are offered tax credits for offering their employees health insurance.
- *Medicaid Expansion.* State Medicaid eligibility is expanded to include all individuals with incomes up to 133 percent of the federal poverty level. The federal government will initially fund this new state mandate, but eventually the states must fund increasing shares of it themselves.
- *Health Insurance Exchanges.* The federal government assists states in creating "exchanges" or marketplaces where individuals can purchase health insurance from private companies. Health plans offered through the exchanges must meet federal requirements, including coverage for preventative care. Federal subsidies are available for individuals who earn between 133 and 400 percent of the federal poverty level. High-risk pools are created to cover individuals with preexisting conditions.
- *Taxes.* A surtax of 3.8 percent is imposed on personal investment income of individuals with adjusted gross income of $200,000 or more and couples with adjusted gross income of $250,000 or more. An excise tax is placed on high-cost ("Cadillac") private health care plans, as well as on medical devices. New fees are imposed on health insurance companies and on brand-name drug manufacturers.
- *No "Public Option."* Congress rejected President Obama's proposed "public option"—a government-run nonprofit health insurance agency that would compete with private insurers.

The president had argued that a public option was necessary "to keep them honest" by offering reasonable coverage at affordable prices. But critics warned that the public option threatened a "government takeover" of the nation's health care system. Over time, private insurance companies would lose out to the public program, eventually creating a single national health insurance system or "socialized medicine." Liberals in Congress were disappointed when the public option was dropped from the bill.

■ *Costs.* The Congressional Budget Office estimated the cost of health care reform at nearly $1 trillion. President Obama argued that the cost of health care reform could be recovered in savings from the existing health care system—"a system that is currently full of waste and abuse." The president claimed that eliminating waste and inefficiency in Medicare and Medicaid could pay for most of his plan. But critics doubted that such savings exist. Indeed, the proposal to cut waste and abuse in Medicare inspired critics to claim that health care reform is coming at the expense of the elderly.

Some opponents of the federal health care plan (ObamaCare) believe it will lead to long waits at hospitals and clinics across the states.

Coverage

Health care reform will expand health insurance coverage to virtually all Americans. About 35 million people will be brought into the nation's health insurance system. But critics fear that this influx of patients will overload doctors and hospitals, leading to long waits and perhaps "rationing" of care. Government-imposed limits on physicians' fees may cause many doctors to turn away Medicare, Medicaid, and government-subsidized patients.

Tort Reform Missing

Health care reform largely fails to contain the nation's burgeoning health care costs. Congress failed to include any provision for the reform of medical malpractice litigation. Lawsuits against physicians, hospitals, and insurers are a major cause of increased health care costs. Physicians must pay exorbitant fees for malpractice insurance. More importantly, physicians are inspired by fear of lawsuits to order numerous tests and procedures not necessary for good medical practice. Tort reform would pay for the actual lifetime costs of medical errors but place a cap on "pain and suffering" damages.

THE STATES AND "OBAMACARE"

The states play an important role in the Patient Protection and Affordable Care Act. They are encouraged to participate in Medicaid expansion by the offer of full federal funding for the first three years. And they are authorized to establish health insurance exchanges to assist in providing coverage to middle-income families not covered by Medicaid or Medicare.

17.8

Explain the responsibilities given to states for implementing the Affordable Care Act, and discuss the efforts by some states to weaken or repeal the law.

State Compliance with Medicaid Expansion

The U.S. Supreme Court held that state participation in Medicaid expansion was optional. The availability of full federal funding for three years is a strong incentive for states to

Freedom to choose one's own doctor has always been a concern of citizens against the nationalization of health care.

participate. But general opposition to "ObamaCare" has inspired a few (Republican) governors and legislatures to declare that their states will not participate. Governor Rick Perry of Texas labeled the Medicaid program as "broken" and argued that its expansion would place further heavy burdens on the state government's budget.

State Participation in Exchanges

States are authorized to set up their own healthcare exchanges to provide insurance for families with incomes up to 400 percent of the federal poverty level. Several states have chosen not to create these exchanges on their own. But the Act provides for the federal Department of Health and Human Services to step in and create exchanges in any states that refuse to do so.

States Lose Their Challenge to the Individual Mandate

At the heart of ObamaCare is a requirement that every American purchase health insurance or face a fine of up to 2.5 percent of their income at income tax time. The health-insurance industry itself strongly supported this provision; it generates customers including younger and healthier people. It also enables insurers to accept the risks of covering people with costly preexisting conditions.

However, attorneys general in 26 states, together with the Federation of Independent Business, brought suit in federal court challenging the constitutionality of the Patient Protection and Affordable Care Act. They argued that it was an unconstitutional expansion of the meaning of the Interstate Commerce Clause, and that it infringed on the "reserved powers" of the states under the Tenth Amendment. (See "The States Lose Their Fight against ObamaCare" in Chapter 3.) But the states lost their case. Chief Justice John Roberts held in 2012 in a 5–4 decision that the Act's "penalty" for noncompliance was actually a "tax" and constitutional under the Congress's power to "lay and collect taxes" (Art. I, Sect.8).[14] The Supreme Court's decision paved the way for the implementation of ObamaCare.

17.9   RENEWED FOCUS ON MENTAL HEALTH

Describe the role of the federal and state governments in protecting citizens suffering from mental health issues, and evaluate whether or not these measures have been effective.

Mental illness is much more extensive than most Americans realize. According to the National Alliance on Mental Illness, in any given year, one in four adults will experience some type of mental health problem. (These disorders range from depression and anxiety to attention-deficit hyperactivity disorder, anorexia, schizophrenia, post-traumatic stress disorder, and drug abuse.) The American Academy of Pediatrics estimates that one in five children has a "diagnosable mental illness."[15] Three-fourths of mental illnesses emerge by age 24.[16] Overall, just 38 percent of adults and fewer than one in five youths receive treatment.

The mass killings at Sandy Hook Elementary School drew national attention to the growing mental health problem. In fact, a plurality of citizens surveyed after the killings said that better treatment of mental illness would be more effective in reducing mass murders than stricter gun control. (See Figure 17–2.) While only a very small proportion of

FIGURE 17–2 Best Way to Reduce Mass Murders

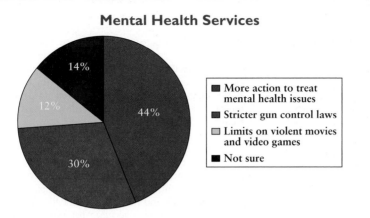

Mental Health Services

- More action to treat mental health issues — 44%
- Stricter gun control laws — 30%
- Limits on violent movies and video games — 12%
- Not sure — 14%

Note: Respondents were asked "What will do the most to reduce the number of mass murders like the school shootings in Connecticut?"
Source: Rasmussen Reports, "52% Think It's Possible to Watch Mentally Ill Closer without Violating Their Rights," January 10–11, 2013. Available at http://www.rasmussenreports.com/public_content/politics/general_politics/january_2013/52_think_it_s_possible_to_watch_mentally_ill_closer_without_violating_their_rights.

mentally ill Americans are mass killers, the severity and heinous nature of the crime made mental health the focal point of discussions in Congress and in many state legislatures. (*See Up Close:* Mental Health and Mass Murders.)

The federal government's stepped up involvement in mental illness policy began in 2008 with passage of the Mental Health Parity Act requiring large insurance plans to treat mental health benefits on par with physical health benefits. But implementation regulations were slow to come. Later, President Obama's Affordable Health Care Act mandated that both Medicaid and private health insurance plans must include mental health benefits by 2014.

Well before passage of the either the federal Parity or the Affordable Health Care Acts, most states had been offering limited mental health-related programs. But the realities of the Great Recession prompted many to cut back on funding. From 2009 to 2012, the states' spending on mental health fell by over $4 billion.[17] In some states, that meant reduced funding for state charity hospitals, state psychiatric hospitals, mental health counselors in schools, crisis centers, and community and mental health centers.[18] At the time of the Sandy Hook shootings, the nation's mental health system was described by many as "underfunded, overburdened, and ineffective" and "painfully, tragically broken."

Mental health advocates quickly mobilized and began pressuring their state officials to "do something fast." Several states whose finances have improved have begun restoring some funding for mental health, adding beds at psychiatric hospitals, improving treatment for inmates with behavioral disorders, giving "mental-health first aid" training to teachers and first responders, creating statewide mental-health crisis hotlines, walk-in centers, and housing vouchers for the severely mentally ill, and putting more mental-health professionals in middle schools.[19] But as in other policy areas, like education, the environment, and social services, not everyone agrees on which changes are the most urgent and which will be the most effective.

Mental Health and Mass Murders

Mass killings, such as the Sandy Hook Elementary School shooting in Newton, Massachusetts, in 2012, have focused public attention on mental health policy as well as gun control. The Congressional Research Service has identified 78 public mass shootings since 1983—shootings in public places involving four or more deaths and a gunman who indiscriminately selects victims.[a] Among the most publicized:

- Sandy Hook Elementary School, Newton, MA, 2012
    Adam Lanza, 20, shot his mother and then killed 20 children and 6 adults before committing suicide.
- Sikh Temple, Oak Ridge, WI, 2012.
    Army veteran Michael Page, 40, killed 12 people before committing suicide.
- Aurora Theater, Aurora, CO, 2012.
    James Holmes, 20, opened fire in a theater killing 70 people.
- Tucson shooting, Tucson AZ, 2011.
    Jerod Loughner, 22, fired on an open constituent meeting with Congresswoman Gabrielle Giffords, killing 6 and wounding 12 others.
- Fort Hood, TX, 2009.
    U.S. Army psychiatrist Nidal Hasan, 39, opened fire in an Army mess hall killing or injuring 43 before being arrested.
- Virginia Tech University, Blacksburg, VA, 2007
    Student Seuing Ho Cho, 23, opened fire on campus killing or injuring 56 before committing suicide.
- Columbine High School, Little, CO, 1999
    Eric Harris, 18 and Dylan Klebold, 17, shot and killed 14 students (including themselves) and one teacher and wounded 23 others.

A majority of the killers in all of the mass killings since 1983 have been mentally ill, and many have shown signs of it before setting out to kill. Pima County College in Arizona had previously suspended Jerod Loughner and advised his parents to remove guns from his home. Loughner went back to the gun store, submitted to a background check, and purchased a semiautomatic Glock pistol. Similar warnings had been raised regarding other mass killers before they committed their murderous acts.

The common thread among these mass killings is not the guns used or how they were obtained, but rather it is the killers' history of mental illness. The history of public mental health care in America is a long and troublesome one. Prior to the 1950s large numbers of people were incarcerated in mental health institutions run by states. Stories of inhuman conditions inspired many states to provide better care, but the institutional philosophy of mental health treatment continued.

But by the late 1950s the development and improvement of psychotherapeutic drugs allowed hospital staff to reduce restrictions on patients, as well as to limit the need for hospitalization. The widespread outpatient use of psychotherapeutic drugs provided the groundwork for the Community Mental Health Act of 1963. The Act promised improved community services for people with mental illness, a reduction in state hospital care, and *deinstitutionalization* of patients who were believed to be of no danger to themselves or others. The Act established Community Mental Health Centers (CMHAs) to make mental health services more widely available.

Yet another contributing factor to nationwide deinstitutionalization was in 1975 U.S. Supreme Court case of *O'Connor* v. *Donaldson*,[b] that placed severe restrictions on involuntary commitment of the mentally ill to institutions. It effectively prevented involuntary confinement of persons who were not a danger to themselves or others. It established stringent due process procedures regarding involuntary confinement. Such confinement can only be for short periods followed by additional court procedures. States differ in periods of involuntary confinement from 72 hours to 30 days or more. Testimony is taken from duly authorized licensed professionals. Judges make the final decisions.

In theory, deinstitutionalization, outpatient drug treatment, and community mental health centers, can reduce mental health tragedies. But too many mentally ill persons have been left "to die with their rights on."[c] The vast majority of homeless people in the United States suffer from mental illness or drug dependency.[d] They do not seek out mental health assistance. Even many of those who have done so have quit taking their medicines. They languish in back bedrooms, jail cells, and homeless shelters, as well as the streets. They are far too paranoid to seek help. One-half of the people with psychotic illnesses do not acknowledge that there's anything wrong with them.[e] They do not know they need care in the first place. They are not all mass killers, of course, but mental illness remains a key factor in violent crime.

Sources: Rasmussen Reports, *"52% Think It's Possible to Watch Mentally Ill Closer without Violating Their Rights,"* January 10–11, 2013. Available at http://www.rasmussenreports.com/public_content/politics/general_politics/january_2013/52_think_it_s_possible_to_watch_mentally_ill_closer_without_violating_their_rights.

[a]Congressional Research Service, *Public Mass Shootings in the United States,* March 18, 2013. Accessed at www.fas.org/sgp/crs/

[b]O'Conner v. Donaldson 422 U.S. 563 (1975).

[c]See Charlotte Low, "A Rude Awakening from Civil Liberties," *Insight,* March 21, 1988, pp. 7–8; also cited in Dianna DiNitto, *Social Welfare,* 6th ed. (New York: Pearson Education, 2007), p. 405.

[d]U.S. Conference of Mayors, *Report of the Taskforce on Hunger and Homelessness,* December, 2002.

[e]Sally Satel and Mary Zdanowicz, "Commission's Omission: The President's Mental Health Commission in Denial," *National Review,* July 19, 2003, pp. 17–19.

CHAPTER HIGHLIGHTS

- The official U.S. poverty rate has ranged between 11 and 15 percent in recent years. African Americans and Hispanics experience poverty in much greater proportions than whites.

- Many believe the single most influential factor contributing to poverty is the disintegration of the traditional husband–wife family. Single mother–headed households have higher poverty levels.

- People older than 65 have a low poverty rate largely because of continuing increases in Social Security and Medicare benefits over the years.

- The middle class has been shrinking as the wealth gap has widened. Middle-income Americans were hurt hardest by the Great Recession.

- Individuals and families may receive government aid through such programs as Social Security, unemployment compensation, Supplemental Security Income, food stamps, and Temporary Assistance for Needy Families. Other programs provide tax credits, housing, food, job training, and other assistance. Many believe Americans are too dependent upon government programs that aren't particularly effective at eliminating poverty.

- Generational conflicts over federal entitlement programs aimed at older Americans (like Social Security) are intensifying.

- Concerns about possible negative effects of government aid (work disincentives, social dependency) led to the passage of welfare reform in 1996. The number of welfare recipients drastically decreased after its passage but rose again in the midst of the Great Recession.

- Local government responsibility for health care consists largely of preventing disease through public sanitation and operating public clinics and hospitals.

- The federal Medicare program provides health care for the elderly, and the federal-state Medicaid program provides health care for the poor. Medicaid also covers nursing home care (middle-class families can qualify by spending down assets) and health care for children of eligible working-class families. Medicaid is the fastest growing portion of many states' budgets. Federal funding is available to states that promise to expand their Medicaid programs, but after three years, states will have to share the costs.

- Health care reform traditionally has centered on expanding access and containing costs. States have turned to managed care plans for Medicaid recipients. It was Massachusetts in 2006 that was first to mandate health insurance coverage for everyone—a predecessor to ObamaCare.

- The Patient Protection and Affordable Care Act of 2010 ("ObamaCare")—the federal health care reform bill passed in 2010—expanded access to virtually all Americans but stirred controversy with the requirement that everyone purchase health insurance. A number of states challenged the constitutionality of the provision, seeing it as violating the Interstate Commerce Clause in the U.S. Constitution. The U.S. Supreme Court rejected their claim.

- Mental illness in the United States is more pervasive than many citizens realize. Funding for mental health programs had been steadily cut back during the Great Recession, but mass killings by persons judged to be suffering from mental illness renewed demands on both the federal and state governments to restore funding. Under ObamaCare both Medicaid and private insurance plans must offer mental health benefits by 2014. Several states have expanded mental health prevention and intervention programs.

NOTES

CHAPTER I

1. U.S. Census Bureau, *The 2010 Statistical Abstract.* Available at http://www.census.gov/compendia/statab/2010edition.html; U.S. Census Bureau, *Population Distribution and Change 2000 to 2010.* Available at http://www.census.gov/prod/cen2010/briefs/c2010br-01.pdf.

2. U.S. Census Bureau, *American Community Survey 2010.* Available at http://factfinder2.census.gov/faces/nav/jsf/pages/searchresults.xhtml?refresh=t.

3. Kim Geron, *Latino Political Power* (Boulder, CO: Lynne Rienner, 2005).

4. Wendy K. Tam Cho and Suneet P. Lad, "Subcontinential Divide: Asian Indians and Asian American Politics," *American Politics Quarterly* 32 (May 2004): 239–263.

5. "Native American Nations," available at www.tribal-institute.org/lists/nations.htm, May 10, 2005; U.S. Census Bureau, "The American Indian and Alaska Native Population: 2000," *Census 2000 Brief,* February 2002.

6. Michael Hoffer, Nancy Rytina, and Bryan C. Baker. "Estimates of the Unauthorized Immigrant Population Residing in the United States," *U.S. Department of Homeland Security,* January 2011. Available at http://www.dhs.gov/xlibrary/assets/statistics/publications/ois_ill_pe_2011.pdf.

7. *Plyer v. Doe,* 457 U.S. 202 (1982).

8. For a debate over how to measure a state's ideology and whether it changes, see a series of articles in *State Politics and Policy Quarterly* 7(2) (Summer 2007): 111–166. Also see Thomas M. Carsey and Jeffrey J. Harden, "New Measures of Partisanship, Ideology, and Policy Mood in the American States," *State Politics and Policy Quarterly* 10(2) (Summer 2010): 136–156.

9. Virginia Gray, "The Socioeconomic and Political Context of States," in Virginia Gray and Russell L. Hanson, eds., *Politics in the American States: A Comparative Analysis,* 8th ed. (Washington, DC: CQ Press, 2004), pp. 1–30.

10. Frank Newport, "Alabama, North Dakota, Wyoming Most Conservative States," *The Gallup Organization.* Available at http://www.gallup.com/poll/160196/alabama-north-dakota-wyoming-conservative-states.aspx#2.

11. Ibid.

12. Gerald C. Wright, Robert S. Erikson, and John P. McIver, "Public Opinion and Policy Liberalism in the American States," *American Journal of Political Science* 31 (November 1987): 980–1001. See also William D. Berry et al., "Measuring Citizen and Government Ideology in the American States," *American Journal of Political Science* 42 (January 1998): 327–348; William D. Berry et al., "Measuring Citizen and Government Ideology in the U.S. States: A Re-appraisal," *State Politics and Policy Quarterly* 10(2) (Summer 2010): 117–135.

13. Joel Lieske, "The Changing Regional Subcultures of the American States and the Utility of a New Cultural Measure," *Political Research Quarterly* 63 (2010): 538–552. See also Daniel Elazar, *American Federalism: A View from the States,* 3rd ed. (New York: Harper and Row, 1984).

14. Robert P. Jones, Daniel Dox, Juhem Navarro-Rivera, E. J. Dionne, and William A. Galston, *Citizenship, Values, & Culture Concerns: What Americans Want from Immigration Reform* (Washington, DC: Public Religion Research Institute and The Brookings Institution, 2013), p. 36.

15. See Kenneth D. Wald, *Religion and Politics in the United States,* 4th ed. (New York: Rowman and Littlefield, 2003).

16. John C. Green, "The American Religious Landscape and Political Attitudes: A Baseline for 2004," *The University of Akron.* Available at https://www.uakron.edu/pages/bliss/docs/Religious_Landscape_2004.pdf. The Pew Forum on Religion and Public Life, *A Faith-Based Partisan Divide* (Washington, DC: Pew Research Center, 2005).

17. "How Religious Is Your State?," *The Pew Research Forum on Religion and Public Life.* Available at http://pewforum.org/How-Religious-Is-Your-State-.aspx.

18. Alexander Hamilton, *The Federalist,* Number 43. Available at http://avalon.law.yale.edu/18th_century/fed43.asp.

19. For further reading on U.S. territories, see Pedro A. Malavet, *America's Colony: The Political and Cultural Conflict Between the United States and Puerto Rico* (New York: New York University Press, 2004); Arnold H. Leibowitz, *Defining Status: A Comprehensive Analysis of United States Territorial Possessions* (New York: Springer Publishing Company, 1989).

CHAPTER 2

1. Bil's Blog, November 1, 2004.

2. See Bruce E. Cain and Roger G. Noll, eds., *Constitutional Reform in California* (Berkeley, CA: Institute of Governmental Studies, 1995).

3. For a history of the initiative, see Joseph F. Zimmerman, *The Initiative: Citizen Law-Making* (Westport, CT: Praeger, 1999).

4. See Richard Hofstadter, *The Age of Reform* (New York: Knopf, 1955).

5. For a balanced summary and evaluation of direct democracy, see Thomas E. Cronin, *Direct Democracy: The Politics of Initiative, Referendum and Recall* (Cambridge, MA: Harvard University Press, 1989).

6. Ibid., p. 227.

7. Joshua J. Dyck, "Initiated Distrust: Direct Democracy and Trust in Government," *American Politics Research* 37(4) (July 2009): 539–568.

8. Chief Justice Ronald M. George, "The Perils of Direct Democracy: The California Experience," remarks at the induction ceremony for the American Academy of Arts and Sciences, Cambridge, MA, October 10, 2009.

9. Rasmussen Research poll, March 3, 1998. See also John R. Hibbing and Elizabeth Thiess-Morse, "Policy Preferences and American Politics," *American Political Science Review* 95 (March 2001): 145–153.

10. Alan Rosenthal, *The Decline of Representative Democracy* (Washington, DC: Congressional Quarterly Press, 1998), p. 337.

11. Daniel A. Smith, "Initiatives and Referendums: The Effects of Direct Democracy on Candidate Elections," paper presented at the Graduate Program in Political Campaigning, University of Florida, Gainesville, February 24–25, 2005.

12. Susan B. Hansen, *The Politics of Taxation* (New York: Praeger, 1983).

13. Jerry Seper, "Arizona Initiative Inspires Others," *Washington Times,* November 10, 2004.

14. William Fulton, "Eminent Domain Outrage in Connecticut," *Governing,* January 2010.

15. The U.S. Supreme Court has held that a state may not prohibit financial payments for the circulation of petitions. *Meger* v. *Grant,* 486 U.S. 414 (1988).

16. Frederick J. Boehmke, "Sources of Variation in the Frequency of Statewide Initiatives: The Role of Interest Group Populations," *Political Research Quarterly* 58(4) (December 2005): 565–576; Shaun Bowler and Robert Hanneman, "Just How Pluralist Is Direct Democracy? The Structure of Interest Group Participation in Ballot Proposition Elections," *Political Research Quarterly* 59(4) (December 2006): 557–568.

17. Council of State Governments, *Book of the States, 1994–95* (Lexington, KY: Council of State Governments, 1995), p. 286.

18. Kellyanne Conway, president and CEO of the Polling Company, quoted in Elizabeth Fulk, "State Ballot Initiatives May Play Large Role in '04 Elections; Candidates Ignore Them 'at Their Own Peril,' Pollster Says," *The Hill,* September 23, 2004. Available at http://thehill.com/homenews/news/10979-state-ballot-initiatives-may-play-large-role-in-04-elections.

19. Stephen Nicholson, *Voting the Agenda: Candidates, Elections, and Ballot Propositions* (Princeton, NJ: Princeton University Press, 2005).

20. Political consultant David Hill quoted in Elizabeth Fulk, "State Ballot Initiatives May Play Large Role in '04 Elections; Candidates Ignore Them 'at Their Own Peril,' Pollster Says," *The Hill,* September 23, 2004. Available at www.thehill.com/news/092304/ballot.aspx.

21. Caroline Tolbert, Ramona McNeal, and Daniel A. Smith, "Enhancing Civic Engagement: The Effect of Direct Democracy on Political Participation and Knowledge," *State Politics and Policy Quarterly* 3 (2003): 23–41; Todd Donovan and Daniel A. Smith, "Turning On and Turning Out: Assessing the Indirect Effects of Ballot Measures on Voter Participation," paper presented at the Conference on State Politics and Policy, Kent State University, Kent, OH, April 30–May 2, 2004; Robert J. Lacey, "The Electoral Allure of Direct Democracy: The Effect of Initiative Salience on Voting, 1990–96," *State Politics and Policy Quarterly* 5(2) (Summer 2005): 168–181.

22. Elizabeth A. Gerber, "Legislative Response to the Threat of Popular Initiatives," *American Journal of Political Science* 40 (February 1996): 99–128. However, for evidence that public policy and public opinion are no closer in initiative states than noninitiative states (i.e., for evidence that initiative states are no more "responsive" than noninitiative states), see Edward L. Lascher, Jr. et al., "Gun Behind the Door? Ballot Initiatives, State Politics and Public Opinion," *Journal of Politics* 58 (August 1996): 760–775.

23. Scott W. Rasmussen, *Rasmussen Research,* March 3, 1998.

24. *Bates* v. *Jones,* U.S. Ninth Circuit Court of Appeals, December 1997.

25. *Bates* v. *Jones,* U.S. Supreme Court, March 23, 1998.

26. Quotation from *U.S. Term Limits* v. *Thornton* (1995).

27. Lydia Saad, "Americans Call for Term Limits, End to Electoral College," Gallup Organization, January 18, 2013. Available at http://www.gallup.com/poll/159881/americans-call-term-limits-end-electoral-college.aspx?version=print.

28. National Conference of State Legislatures, "NCSL's Online Term Limits Poll," November 2000.

29. Marjorie Sarbaugh-Thompson, "Measuring 'Term Limitedness' in U.S. Multi-State Research," *State Politics and Policy Quarterly* 10(2) (Summer 2010): 199–217.

CHAPTER 3

1. Other definitions of federalism in American political science include: "Federalism refers to a political system in which there are local (territorial, regional, provincial, state, or municipal) units of government as well as a national government, that can make final decisions with respect to at least some governmental authorities and whose existence is especially protected." James Q. Wilson, *American Government,* 4th ed. (Lexington, MA: D.C. Heath, 1989), p. 47; "Federalism is the mode of political organization that unites smaller polities within an overarching political system by distributing power among general and constituent units in a manner designed to protect the existence and authority of both national and subnational systems enabling all to share in the overall system's decision-making and executing processes." Daniel J. Elazar, *American Federalism: A View from the States* (New York: Thomas Y. Crowell, 1966), p. 2.

2. James Madison, Alexander Hamilton, and John Jay, *The Federalist,* Number 51 (New York: Modern Library, 1958).

3. David Osborne, *Laboratories of Democracy* (Cambridge, MA: Harvard Business School, 1988).

4. The arguments for "competitive federalism" are developed at length in Thomas R. Dye, *American Federalism: Competition Among Governments* (Lexington, MA: Lexington Books, 1990). The book argues that competitive decentralized government has many advantages over centralized "monopoly" governments: greater overall responsiveness to citizen preferences; incentives for government to become efficient and provide quality services at the lowest costs; restraints on the overall burdens of taxation and nonproportional taxes; encouragement of economic growth; and innovation in policies designed to improve the well-being of citizens.

5. For conflicting arguments, see Paul E. Peterson and Mark C. Rom, *Welfare Magnets* (Washington, DC: Brookings Institution, 1990); Scott W. Allard and Sheldon Danzinger, "Welfare Magnets: Myth or Reality?" *Journal of Politics* 62 (May 2000): 350–368; Robert R. Preuhs, "State Policy Components of Interstate Migration in the States," *Political Research Quarterly* 52 (September 1999): 527–549; Robert C. Lieberman and Greg M. Shaw, "Looking Inward, Looking Outward: The Politics of State Welfare Innovation under Devolution," *Political Research Quarterly* 52 (June 2000): 215–240.

6. *Texas* v. *White*, 7 Wallace 700 (1869).

7. See Val Burris, "Who Opposed the ERA? An Analysis of the Social Basis for Antifeminism," *Social Science Quarterly* 64 (June 1983): 305–317.

8. See Ruth Ann Strickland, "The Twenty-Seventh Amendment and Constitutional Change by Stealth," *PS: Political Science and Politics* 26 (December 1993): 716–722.

9. *Massachusetts* v. *Mellon*, 262 U.S. 447 (1923).

10. See Daniel J. Elazar, *The American Partnership: Inter-Governmental Cooperation in Nineteenth-Century United States* (Chicago: University of Chicago Press, 1962).

11. Laurence J. O'Toole Jr. and Robert K. Christensen, eds. *American Intergovernmental Relations*, 5th ed. (Washington, DC: CQ Press, 2013).

12. Veronique de Rugy, "The Fiscal Interplay Between Federal, State, and Local Governments," Mercatus Center, George Mason University, July 30, 2012.

13. Robert M. Stein, "The Allocation of Federal Aid Monies: The Synthesis of Demand-Side and Supply-Side Explanations," *American Political Science Review* 75 (June 1981): 334–343.

14. John Kincaid, "Trends in Federalism: Continuity, Change and Polarization," in The Council of State Governments, eds., *The Book of the States,* 2004 edition, Vol. 36 (Lexington, KY: The Council of State Governments, 2004), pp. 21–27.

15. J. Edwin Benton, "George W. Bush's Federal Aid Legacy," *Publius: The Journal of Federalism* 37(3) (Summer 2007): 371–389.

16. Morton Grodzins, *The American System* (Chicago: Rand McNally, 1966), pp. 8–9.

17. Ibid., p. 265.

18. Charles Press, *State and Community Governments in the Federal System* (New York: John Wiley, 1979), p. 78.

19. *Garcia* v. *San Antonio Metropolitan Transit Authority,* 469 U.S. 528 (1985).

20. *Gregory* v. *Ashcraft,* 11 S. Ct. 2395 (1991).

21. *Tarbels Case,* 13 Wall. 397 (1872). Also cited and discussed in Deil S. Wright, *Understanding Intergovernmental Relations* (Boston: Duxbury Press, 1978), p. 22.

22. Paul Posner, "The Politics of Coercive Federalism in the Bush Era," *Publius: The Journal of Federalism* 37(3) (Summer 2007): 390–412; Tim Conlan and John Dinan, "Federalism, the Bush Administration, and the Transformation of American Conservatism," *Publius: The Journal of Federalism* 37(3) (Summer 2007): 279–303.

23. *Pollock* v. *Farmers Loan and Trust Company,* 157 U.S. 429 (1895).

24. *South Carolina* v. *Barker,* 485 U.S. 505 (1988).

25. Joseph F. Zimmerman, "The Nature and Political Significance of Preemption," *PS: Political Science and Politics* 38 (July 2005): 358–362, and "Congressional Preemption: Removal of State Regulatory Powers," pp. 375–378; in the same volume, see also Paul L. Posner, "The Politics of Preemption: Propects for the States," *PS: Political Science and Politics* 38 (July 2005): 371–374.

26. John Kincaid, "Trends in Federalism: Continuity, Change and Polarization," in The Council of State Governments, eds., *The Book of the States,* 2004 edition, Vol. 36 (Lexington, KY: The Council of State Governments, 2004), pp. 21–27.

27. Shama Gamkhar and J. L. Mitchell Pickerill, "The State of American Federalism 2011–2012: A Fend for Yourself and Activist Form of Bottom-Up Federalism," *Publius: The Journal of Federalism* 42(3) (Summer 2012): 357–386; Alice M. Rivlin, "Rethinking Federalism for More Effective Government," *Publius: The Journal of Federalism* 42(3) (Summer 2012): 387–400.

28. Lori Riverstone-Newell, "Bottom-Up Activism: A Local Political Strategy for Higher Policy Change," *Publius: The Journal of Federalism* 42(3) (Summer 2012): 401–422.

29. Sean Nicholson-Crotty, "Leaving Money on the Table: Learning from Recent Refusals of Federal Grants in the American States," *Publius: The Journal of Federalism* 42(3) (Summer 2012): 449–466.

30. Alexandria Jaffe, "White House Responds to Secession Petitions, Calls for Unity Instead," *The Hill,* January 12, 2013.

31. Jake Grovum, "Social Issues Challenge State-Federal Relationship," *Pew Center on the States,* January 24, 2013. Available at http://www.pewstates.org/projects/stateline/headlines/social-issues-challenge-state-federal-relationship-85899445047.

32. Peter A. Harkness, "Federalism from the Bottom Up," *Governing,* March 2013, pp. 16–17.

33. See Timothy Conlan, *From New Federalism to Devolution* (Washington, DC: Brookings Institution, 1998).

34. *United States v. Lopez,* 63 L.W. 4343 (1995).

35. *Puintz v. U.S.,* 521 U.S. 890 (1997).

36. *Seminole Tribe v. Florida,* 517 U.S. 44 (1996).

37. *Aldin v. Maine,* June 23, 1999.

38. *Nevada Department of Human Resources v. Hibbs,* 123 S. Ct. 1972 (2003).

39. *U.S. v. Morrison,* May 15, 2000.

40. Crady deGolian, "Top 5 Issues for 2013: Interstate Compacts," *The Council of State Governments Knowledge Center,* January 7, 2013. Available at http://knowledgecenter.csg.org.

CHAPTER 4

1. Richard Niemi and Michael Hanmer, "Voter Turnout Among College Students: New Data and a Rethinking of Traditional Theories," *Social Science Quarterly* 91(2) (June 2010): 301–323; Jesse Richman and Andrew Pate, "Can the College Vote Turn Out? Evidence from the U.S. States, 2000–08," *State Politics and Policy Quarterly* 10(1) (Spring 2010): 51–68.

2. Lee Sigelman et al., "Voting and Nonvoting: A MultiElection Perspective," *American Journal of Political Science* 29 (November 1985): 749–765.

3. Susan A. MacManus, *Targeting Senior Voters: Campaign Outreach to Elders and Others with Special Needs* (Lanham, MD: Rowman and Littlefield, 2000).

4. Sara E. Helms, "Youth Volunteering in the States: 2002 and 2003," *Fact Sheet, Center for Information and Research on Civic Learning and Engagement,* August 2004.

5. William H. Riker and Peter C. Ordeshook, "A Theory of the Calculus of Voting," *American Political Science Review* 62 (March 1968): 25–42.

6. J. A. Ferejohn and Morris Fiorina, "The Paradox of Voting," *American Political Science Review* 18 (March 1974): 525–536.

7. For an excellent review of this literature, see Jan E. Leighley and Arnold Vedlitz, "Race, Ethnicity, and Political Participation: Competing Models and Contrasting Explanations," *Journal of Politics* 61 (November 1999): 1092–1114.

8. James G. Gimpel and Jason E. Schuknecht, "Interstate Migration and Electoral Politics," *Journal of Politics* 63 (February 2001): 207–231.

9. Robert D. Brown, Robert A. Jackson, and Gerald C. Wright, "Registration, Turnout, and State Party Systems," *Political Research Quarterly* 52 (September 1999): 463–479.

10. Douglas L. Kruse, Kay Schriner, Lisa Schur, and Todd Shields, *Empowerment Through Civic Participation: A Study of the Political Behavior of People with Disabilities,* Final Report to the Disability Research Consortium, Bureau of Economic Research, Rutgers University and New Jersey Developmental Disabilities Council, April 1999; Susan A. MacManus, *Targeting Senior Voters: Campaign Outreach to Elders and Others with Special Needs* (Lanham, MD: Rowman and Littlefield, 2000); United States General Accounting Office, *Voters with Disabilities: Access to Polling Places and Alternative Voting Methods* (Washington, DC: GAO, October 2001).

11. George Pillsbury and Julian Johannesen, "America Goes to the Polls 2012," *NonprofitVOTE,* March 2013. Available at www.nonprofitvote.org/.../america-goes-to-the-polls-2012.html.

12. Warren J. Mitofsky, "Fool Me Twice: An Election Nightmare," *Public Perspective* 12 (May/June 2001): 35–38.

13. National Conference of State Legislatures, "Same-Day Registration," February 21, 2013. Available at www.ncsl.org.

14. George Pillsbury and Julian Johannesen, "America Goes to the Polls 2012," *NonprofitVOTE,* March 2013. Available at www.nonprofitvote.org/.../america-goes-to-the-polls-2012.html.

15. Susan A. MacManus, "Election Reform in Florida," *New England Journal of Political Science* 6(2) (Fall 2012): 237–292.

16. See Staci L. Rhine, "Registration Reform and Turnout Change in the American States," *American Politics Quarterly* 23 (October 1995): 409–426; Stephen Knack, "Does Motor-Voter Work? Evidence from State Level Data," *Journal of Politics* 57 (August 1995): 796–811.

17. Benjamin Highton and Raymond E. Wolfiner, "Estimating the Effects of the National Voter Registration Act of 1993," *Political Behavior* 20(2) (1998): 79–104.

18. Robert D. Brown, Robert A. Jackson, and Gerald C. Wright, "Registration, Turnout, and State Party Systems," *Political Research Quarterly* 52 (September 1999): 477.

19. Raymond E. Wolfinger, Benjamin Highton, and Megan Mullin, "How Postregistration Laws Affect the Turnout of Citizens Registered to Vote," *State Politics and Policy Quarterly* 5(1) (Spring 2005): 1–23.

20. George Pillsbury and Julian Johannesen, "America Goes to the Polls 2012," *NonprofitVOTE,* March 2013. Available at www.nonprofitvote.org/.../america-goes-to-the-polls-2012.html.

21. Sean Richey, "Voting by Mail: Turnout and Institutional Reform in Oregon," *Social Science Quarterly* 89(4) (2008): 902–915.

22. For excellent analyses of the states' implementation of HAVA, see Sarah F. Liebschutz and Daniel J. Palazzolo, "HAVA and the States," editors of a special issue of *Publius: The Journal of Federalism* 35(4) (Fall 2005); Daniel J. Palazzolo and Vincent G. Moscardelli, "Policy Crisis and Political Leadership: Election Law Reform in the States After the 2000 Presidential Election," *State Politics and Policy Quarterly* 6(3) (Fall 2006): 300–321.

23. Barry C. Burden, David T. Canon, Kenneth R. Mayer, and Donald P. Moynihan, "The Effects of Early Voting, Election Day Registration, and Same Day Registration in the 2008 Elections," report to the Pew Charitable Trusts, 2009.

24. The Verified Voting Foundation monitors the security, accuracy, and transparency of voting systems. Its Web site is verifiedvotingfoundation.org.

25. See John Fund, *Stealing Elections: How Voter Fraud Threatens Our Democracy* (San Francisco: Encounter Books, 2004); Tom Curry, "Do Absentee Ballots Facilitate Fraud?" October 16, 2008. Available at www.msnbc.msn.com/id/27166150.

26. Susan A. MacManus, "Election Reform in Florida," *New England Journal of Political Science* 6(2) (Fall 2012): 237–292.

27. George Pillsbury and Julian Johannesen, "America Goes to the Polls 2012," *NonprofitVOTE*, March 2013. Available at www.nonprofitvote.org/.../america-goes-to-the-polls-2012.html.

28. National Conference of State Legislatures, *Voter Identification Requirements*. Constant updates available at http://www.ncsl.org/legislatures-elections/elections/voter-id.aspx.

29. Emily Schultheis, "Study Finds Voter ID Laws Hurt Young, Minorities," *Politico*, March 12, 2013. The author cites a study by Cathy J. Cohen and Jon C. Rogowski. Also see Liz Kennedy, "Protecting the Freedom to Vote," *National Civic Review* 101(3) (Fall 2012): 31–37.

30. Pew Center on the States, "Infographic: The Wait to Vote," December 10, 2012. Available at http://www.pewstates.org/research/data-visualizations/the-wait-to-vote-85899435488.

31. Wendy Underhill, "Short Answers to Long Lines," *National Conference of State Legislatures*, February 2013; Robert M. Stein and Greg Vonnahme, "When, Where, and How We Vote: Does it Matter?" *Social Science Quarterly* 93(3) (September 2012): 692–712.

32. The rest vote on hand-counted paper ballots (4 percent) or punch cards (0.02 percent). "Voting Machines: Voting Systems & Use: 1980–2012," ProCon.org. Available at http://votingmachines.procon.org/view.resource.php?resourceID=000274. For the history of voting machines in the U.S., see National Conference of State Legislatures, "Voting Technology: Current and Future Choices," June 2012.

33. Laurence Arnold, "Carter-Baker Commission Weighs U.S. Voting Changes (Update 1)," Bloomberg.com, April 18, 2005.

34. Jill E. Fuller, "Equality in Cyberdemocracy? Gauging Gender Gaps in On-Line Civic Participation," *Social Science Quarterly* 85 (December 2004): 938–957.

35. "Datapoints: Military and Overseas Voters in 2012," *The Pew Charitable Trusts State and Consumer Initiatives*, January 31, 2013.

36. Breanna Edwards, "Report: Voting Cyberattack in Florida," *Politico*, March 18, 2013.

37. National Conference of State Legislatures, "Internet Voting: Not Ready for Prime Time," *The Canvass*, February 2013. Available at http://www.ncsl.org/documents/legismgt/elect/Canvass_Feb_2013_No_37.pdf.

38. Yvette Alex-Assensoh and A. B. Assensoh, "Inner-City Contexts, Church Attendance, and African-American Political Participation," *Journal of Politics* 63 (August 2001): 886–901; Peter W. Wielhouwer, "Releasing the Fetters: Parties and the Mobilization of the African-American Electorate," *Journal of Politics* 62 (February 2000): 206–222; Avaluara L. Gaither and Eric C. Newburger, *The Emerging American Voter: An Examination of the Increase in the Black Vote in November 1998*, Population Division Working Paper No. 44 (Washington, DC: U.S. Census Bureau, June 2000); Priscilla Southwell and Kevin Pirch, "Defying the National Trend: Rising Voter Turnout Among Blacks," paper presented at the annual meeting of the American Political Science Association, 2001.

39. John R. Arvizu and F. Chris Garcia, "Latino Voting Participation: Explaining and Differentiating Latino Voting Turnout," *Hispanic Journal of Behavioral Sciences* 18 (May 1996): 104–128; Robert A. Jackson, "Latino Electoral Participation," paper presented at the annual meeting of the Southern Political Science Association, 2001; David L. Leal, Matt A. Barreto, Jongho Lee, and Rodolfo O. de la Garza, "The Latino Vote in the 2004 Election," *PS: Political Science and Politics* 38(1) (January 2005): 41–50.

40. Atiya Kai Stokes-Brown, "Racial Identity and Latino Vote Choice," *American Politics Research* 34(5) (September 2006): 627–652.

41. Wendy K. Tam Cho, "Naturalization, Socialization, Participation: Immigrants and (Non-) Voting," *Journal of Politics* 61 (November 1999): 1140–1155; Louis DeSipio, "Making Citizens or Good Citizens? Naturalization as a Predictor of Organizational and Electoral Behavior Among Latino Immigrants," *Hispanic Journal of Behavioral Sciences* 18 (May 1996): 194–213.

42. Matt Barreto, Ricardo Ramirez, and Nathan D. Woods, "Are Naturalized Voters Driving the California Latino Electorate? Measuring the Effect of IRCA Citizenship on Latino Voting," *Social Science Quarterly* 86(4) (December 2005): 792–811; Matt Barreto, "Latino Immigrants at the Polls: Foreign Born Voter Turnout in the 2002 Election," *Political Research Quarterly* 58(1) (March 2005): 79–86.

43. *Voting and Registration in the Election of November 2008* (Washington, DC: U.S. Census Bureau).

44. N. Kim Nguyen and James C. Garand, "Partisan Strength and Nonpartisanship Among Asian Americans," *American Politics Research* 37(3): 375–408; Paul M. Ong and Don T. Nakanishi, "Becoming Citizens, Becoming Voters: The Naturalization and Political Participation of Asian Pacific Immigrants," in Bill Ong Hing and Ronald Lee, eds., *Reframing the Immigration Debate* (Los Angeles, CA: LEAP Public Policy Institute and UCLA Asian American Studies Center, 1996), pp. 275–305.

45. Pew Research Center, "The Rise of Asian Americans," *Pew Research Social & Demographic Trends,* June 19, 2012. Available at http://www.pewsocialtrends.org/2012/06/19/the-rise-of-asian-americans/.

46. *Smith* v. *Allright,* 321 U.S. 649 (1944).

47. *Harper* v. *Virginia State Board of Elections,* 383 U.S. 663 (1966).

48. *South Carolina* v. *Katzenbach,* U.S. 301 (1966).

49. United States Department of Justice, Civil Rights Division, Voting Section. "Introduction to Federal Voting Rights Laws," Available at www.usdoj.gov/crt/voting/intro/intro_c.htm, January 18, 2002; Pei-te Lien, Dianne M. Pinderhuges, Carol Hardy-Fanta, and Christine M. Sierra, "The Voting Rights Act and the Election of Nonwhite Officials," *PS: Political Science and Politics* 40 (July 2007): 489–494.

50. Congress had earlier passed the Voting Rights Act of 1970, which (1) extended the vote to 18-year-olds regardless of state law; (2) abolished residency requirements in excess of 30 days; and (3) prohibited literacy tests. However, there was some constitutional debate about the power of Congress to change state laws on voting age. While Congress can end *racial* discrimination, extending the vote to eighteen-year-olds was a different matter. All previous extensions of the vote had come by constitutional amendment. Hence, Congress quickly passed the Twenty-sixth Amendment.

51. George Pillsbury and Julian Johannesen, "America Goes to the Polls 2012," *NonprofitVOTE,* March 2013. Available at www.nonprofitvote.org/.../america-goes-to-the-polls-2012.html.

52. *Mobile* v. *Bolden,* 446 U.S. 50 (1980).

53. See Susan A. MacManus, "Racial Representation Issues," *Political Science and Politics* 18 (Fall 1985): 759–769.

54. *Thornburg* v. *Gingles,* 478 U.S. 30 (1986).

55. Kevin A. Hill, "Does the Creation of Majority Black Districts Aid Republicans?" *Journal of Politics* 57 (May 1995): 384–401.

56. *Shaw* v. *Reno* (1993).

57. *Miller* v. *Johnson* (1995).

58. Bernard Grofman and Lisa Handley, "The Impact of the Voting Rights Act on Black Representation in Southern State Legislatures," *Legislative Studies Quarterly* 16 (February 1991): 111–128; Benjamin Radcliff and Martin Saiz, "Race, Turnout, and Public Policy in the States," *Political Research Quarterly* 48 (December 1995): 775–794; Baodong Liu, "Whites as a Minority and the New Racial Coalition in New Orleans and Memphis,"*PS: Political Science and Politics* 39(1) (January 2006): 69–76; Robert M. Stein, Stacey G. Ulbig, and Stephanie Shirley Post, "Voting for Minority Candidates in Multiracial /Multiethnic Communities," *Urban Affairs Review* 41(2) (November 2005): 157–181.

59. Phil Tajitsu Nash, "Reaching Out to Asian Americans and Latinos," *Campaigns & Elections,* February 2003, pp. 40–42; Atiya Kai Stokes, "Latino Group Consciousness and Political Participation," *American Politics Research* 31 (July 2003): 361–378.

60. Center for American Women and Politics, "Statewide Elective Executive Women 2013," March 2013. Available at http://www.cawp.rutgers.edu/fast_facts/levels_of_office/documents/stwide.pdf.

61. Center for American Women and Politics, "Women in Elective Office 2013," March 2013. Available at http://www.cawp.rutgers.edu/fast_facts/levels_of_office/documents/elective.pdf.

62. Kira Sanbonmatsu, "Gender Pools and Puzzles: Charting a 'Women's Path' to the Legislature," *Politics and Gender* 2(3) (September 2006): 387–399.

63. Kira Sanbonmatsu, "Do Parties Know that 'Women Win'? Party Leader Beliefs About Women's Electoral Chances," *Politics and Gender* 2(4) (December 2006): 431–450.

64. Sue Thomas, "The Impact of Women on State Legislative Policies," *Journal of Politics* 53 (November 1991): 958–976. See also Michelle A. Saint-Germain, "Does Their Difference Make a Difference?" *Social Science Quarterly* 70 (December 1989): 956–968; Sue Tolleson-Rinehart and Jyl J. Josephson, eds., *Gender and American Politics,* 2nd ed. (Armonk, NY: M.E. Sharpe, 2005).

65. Lyn Kathlene, "Alternative Views of Crime: Legislative Policymaking in Gendered Terms," *Journal of Politics* 57 (August 1995): 696–723.

66. Pew Research Center for the People & the Press, "The Generation Gap and the 2012 Election," November 3, 2011. Available at http://www.people-press.org/2011/11/03/the-generation-gap-and-the-2012-election-3/.

67. George Pillsbury and Julian Johannesen, "America Goes to the Polls 2012," *NonprofitVOTE,* March 2013. Available at www.nonprofitvote.org/.../america-goes-to-the-polls-2012.html.

68. Pew Research Center for the People & the Press, "Young Voters Supported Obama Less, But May Have Mattered More," November 26, 2012. Available at http://www.people-press.org/2012/11/26/young-voters-supported-obama-less-but-may-have-mattered-more/.

69. Susan A. MacManus, *Young vs. Old: Generational Conflict in the 21st Century* (Boulder, CO: Westview Press, 1996), p. 23.

70. Andrea Louise Campbell, "The Non-distinctiveness of Senior Voters in the 2004 Election," *Public Policy and Aging Report* 15 (Winter 2005): 1, 3–6; Lawrence R. Jacobs and Melanie Burns, "Don't Lump Seniors," *Public Policy and Aging Report* 15 (Winter 2005): 7–9; Susan A. MacManus, "Florida's Senior Voters in Election 2004: Results, Top Issues, Reforms, and New Concerns," *Public Policy and Aging Report* 15 (Winter 2005): 10–13.

71. See Benjamin Radcliff and Martin Saiz, "Labor Organization and Public Policy in the American States," *Journal of Politics* 60 (February 1998): 113–125.

72. Quotations reported in *Tallahassee Democrat,* January 12, 1992.

73. Christopher A. Cooper, Anthony J. Nownes, and Martin Johnson, "Interest Groups and Journalists in the States," *State Politics and Policy Quarterly* 7(1) (Spring 2007): 39–53.

74. Anthony J. Nownes and Patricia Freeman, "Interest Group Activity in the States," *Journal of Politics* 60 (February 1998): 86–112.

75. See, for example, William P. Browne, "Variations in the Behavior and Style of State Lobbyists and Interest Groups," *Journal of Politics* 47 (May 1985): 450–468.

76. Quotations from legislators in Lester Milbrath, *The Washington Lobbyists* (Chicago: Rand McNally, 1963), pp. 241–243.

77. Alan J. Cigler and Burdett A. Lomis, *Interest Group Politics,* 4th ed. (Washington, DC: Congressional Quarterly Press, 1995), p. 395.

78. Anthony J. Nownes and Patricia Freeman, "Interest Group Activity in the States," *Journal of Politics* 60 (February 1998): 86–112.

79. Stacy B. Gordon, "All Votes Are Not Created Equal: Campaign Contributions and Critical Votes," *Journal of Politics* 63 (February 2001): 249.

80. Benjamin Radcliff and Martin Saiz, "Labor Organizations and Public Policy in the American States," *Journal of Politics* 60 (February 1998): 113–125.

81. Robert E. Hogan, "State Campaign Finance Laws and Interest Group Electioneering Activities," *Journal of Politics* 67(3) (August 2005): 887–906.

82. Clive S. Thomas and Robert J. Hrebenar, "Interest Groups in the States," in Virginia Gray et al., eds., *Politics in the American States,* 5th ed. (New York: HarperCollins, 1990), p. 141.

83. Sarah McCally Morehouse, *State Politics, Parties and Policy* (New York: Holt, Rinehart and Winston, 1981), p. 118.

84. See Charles W. Wiggins, Keith E. Harmun, and Charles G. Bell, "Interest-Group and Party Influence Agents in the Legislative Process: A Comparative State Analysis," *Journal of Politics* 54 (February 1992): 82–100.

85. See Special Issue on the Impact of State Legislative Term Limits, *State Politics and Policy Quarterly* 6(4) (Winter 2006); Thad Kousser, "The Limited Impact of Term Limits: Contingent Effects on the Complexity and Breadth of Laws," *State Politics and Policy Quarterly* 6(4) (Winter 2006): 410–429.

86. William Safire, "Netroots," *New York Times,* November 19, 2006. Available at nytimes.com/2006/11/19/magazine/19wwln_safire.html.

87. For an inspiring essay on "nonviolent direct action" and civil disobedience in a modern context, read Martin Luther King, Jr., "Letter from Birmingham City Jail," April 16, 1963.

88. For a more detailed examination of the purposes, functions, and rationale of civil disobedience, see Paul F. Power, "Civil Disobedience as Functional Opposition," *Journal of Politics* 34 (February 1972): 37–55; "On Civil Disobedience in Recent American Thought," *American Political Science Review* 64 (March 1970): 35–47.

89. Michael Lipsky, *Protest in City Politics* (Chicago: Rand McNally, 1970); Peter K. Eisinger, "The Conditions of Protest Behavior in American Cities," *American Political Science Review* 67 (March 1973): 11–29; Paul D. Schumaker, "Policy Responsiveness to Protest Group Demands," *Journal of Politics* 37 (May 1975): 488–521.

90. Michael Lipsky, "Protest as a Political Resource," *American Political Science Review* 62 (December 1968): 1144–1158.

CHAPTER 5

1. E. E. Schattschneider, *Party Government* (New York: Rinehart, 1942), p. 1.

2. John C. Green and Paul S. Herrnson, eds., *Responsible Partisanship? The Evolution of American Political Parties Since 1950* (Lawrence: University Press of Kansas, 2003); John C. Green and Rick Farmer, eds., *The State of the Parties: The Changing Role of Contemporary American Parties,* 4th ed. (Lanham, MD: Rowman & Littlefield, 2003); Gerald M. Pomper, "Parliamentary Government in the United States: A New Regime for a New Century?" in *The State of the Parties: The Changing Role of Contemporary American Parties,* 4th ed. (Lanham, MD: Rowman & Littlefield, 2003), pp. 267–286.

3. See John F. Bibby, "State and Local Parties in a Candidate-Centered Age," in Robert E. Weber and Paul Brace, eds., *American State and Local Politics* (New York: Chatham House, 1999), pp. 194–211.

4. John F. Bibby and Thomas M. Holbrook, "Parties and Elections," in Virginia Gray and Russell L. Hanson, eds., *Politics in the American States: A Comparative Analysis,* 8th ed. (Washington, DC: CQ Press, 2004), p. 62.

5. *California Democratic Party et al. v. Jones,* 120 S.Ct. 2402 (2000).

6. See Charles S. Bullock and Loch K. Johnson, "Sex and the Second Primary," *Social Science Quarterly* 66 (December 1985): 933–942.

7. Charles S. Bullock and A. Brock Smith, "Black Success in Local Runoff Elections," *Journal of Politics* 52 (November 1990): 1205–1220.

8. Charles S. Bullock, III and Loch Johnson, *Runoff Elections in the United States* (Chapel Hill: University of North Carolina Press, 1992); Joseph Stewart, James F. Sheffield, and Margaret E. Ellis, "The Mechanisms of Runoff Primary Disadvantage," *Social Science Quarterly* 76 (December 1995): 807–822.

9. Robert J. Huckshorn, *Party Leadership in the States* (Amherst: University of Massachusetts Press, 1976), p. 1.

10. Joel Paddock, "Explaining State Variation in Interparty Ideological Differences," *Political Research Quarterly* 51 (September 1981): 765–780.

11. See Harold Clarke, Frank B. Feigert, and Marianne C. Stewart, "Different Contents, Similar Packages:

The Domestic Political Beliefs of Southern Local Party Activists," *Political Research Quarterly* 48 (March 1995): 151–167.

12. John F. Bibby, "State and Local Parties in a Candidate-Centered Age," in Ronald E. Weber and Paul Brace, *American State and Local Politics* (New York: Chatham House, 1999), p. 209.

13. Robert J. Huckshorn, *Party Leadership in the States* (Amherst: University of Massachusetts Press, 1976), p. 46.

14. James L. Gibson et al., "Whither the Local Parties?" *American Journal of Political Science* 29 (February 1985): 139–160.

15. Lydia Saad, "Heavily Democratic States Are Concentrated in the East," *State of the States, Gallup,* August 3, 2012. Available at http://www.gallup.com/poll/156437/heavily-democratic-states-concentrated-east.aspx.

16. Alan Greenblatt, "A State Apart And, Politically, A World Away," *National Public Radio,* April 1, 2013. Available at http://www.npr.org/blogs/itsallpolitics/2013/03/29/175698193/a-state-apart-and-politically-a-world-away.

17. See Kerin M. Leyden and Stephen A. Borrelli, "The Effect of State Economic Conditions on Gubernatorial Elections: Does Unified Government Make a Difference?" *Political Research Quarterly* 48 (June 1995): 275–290.

18. Cynthia J. Bowling and Margaret R. Ferguson, "Divided Government, Interest Representation, and Policy Differences," *Journal of Politics* 63 (February 2001): 182–206.

19. Charlie Cook, "Driving into the Ditch," *National Journal,* June 26, 2010.

20. See also Robert D. Brown, "Party Cleavages and Welfare Effort in the American States," *American Political Science Review* 89 (March 1995): 23–33.

21. Costas Panagopoulos, "Political Consultants, Campaign Professionalization, and Media Attention," *PS: Political Science and Politics* 39(4) (October 2006): 867–870.

22. Judith S. Trent and Robert V. Friedenberg, *Political Campaign Communication,* 5th ed. (Boulder, CO: Rowman & Littlefield, 2004).

23. Bill Adair, "Steal the Playbook, Democrats," *St. Petersburg Times,* December 5, 2004.

24. Barbara Allen, Daniel P. Stevens, Gregory Marfleet, John Sullivan, and Dean Alger, "Local News and Perceptions of the Rhetoric of Political Advertising," *American Politics Research* 35(4) (July 2007): 506–540.

25. Pew Research Center, *Trends 2005,* Chapter 5 ("More Voices, Less Credibility"), 2005. Available at http://www.pewresearch.org/2005/01/20/trends-2005/.

26. Kim L. Fridkin and Patrick J. Kenney, "Do Negative Messages Work? The Impact of Negativity on Citizens' Evaluations of Candidates,"*American Politics Research* 32 (September 2004): 570–605. See also Ted Brader, "Striking a Responsive Chord: How Political Ads Motivate and Persuade Voters by Appealing to Emotions," *American Journal of Political Science* 49 (April 2005): 388–405.

27. Erika Franklin Fowler and Travis N. Ridout, "Negative, Angry, and Ubiquitous: Political Advertising in 2012," *The Forum* 10(4) (February 2013): 51–61.

28. Darrell M. West, "M-Campaigning: Mobile Technology and Public Outreach," *Issues in Technology Innovation* (Washington, DC: The Brookings Institution, February 2012).

29. Ibid.

30. Ron Faucheux, "Ask, and You Shall Receive: Seven Fundamentals of Candidate Fund Raising," *Campaigns and Elections* 26 (April 2005): 25.

31. See Sarah M. Morehouse, "Money versus Party Effect: Nominating for Governor," *American Journal of Political Science* 34 (August 1990): 706–724.

32. W. P. Welch, "The Effectiveness of Expenditures in State Legislative Races," *American Politics Quarterly* 4 (July 1976): 333–356.

33. Frank J. Sorauf, *Money in American Elections* (Boston: Scott, Foresman, 1988).

34. W. P. Welch, "The Effectiveness of Expenditures in State Legislative Races," *American Politics Quarterly* 4 (July 1976): 333–356.

35. Peter Quist, "The Role of Money & Incumbency in 2007–2008 State Elections," National Institute on Money in State Politics, May 6, 2010. Available at www.followthemoney.org/press/PrintReportView.phtml?r=423.

36. Michael J. Malbin, *Money and Politics in the United States* (Washington, DC: American Enterprise Institute, 1984).

37. Ruth S. Jones and Anne H. Hopkins, "State Campaign Fund Raising," *Journal of Politics* 47 (May 1985): 427–449.

38. Anne Bauer, "The Efficacy of Self-Funding a Political Campaign," National Institute on Money in State Politics, June 22, 2010. Available at www.followthemoney.org/press/PrintReportView.phtml?r=429.

39. Thad Beyle, "Governors, Elections, Campaign Costs, and Winning Governors," in The Council of State Governments, eds., *The Book of the States 2012* (Lexington, KY: Council of State Governments, 2012), pp. 203–213.

40. Peter Quist, "Monetary Competitiveness in 2009–2010 State Legislative Races," National Institute on Money in State Politics, July 3, 2012. Available at http://www.followthemoney.org/press/ReportView.phtml?r=490&ext=10.

41. Matthew Stone, "2012 Legislative Races Most Expensive in History; Targeted Spending Led to Democrats Retaking Control of Legislature," *Bangor Daily News,* November 9, 2012. Available at http://bangordailynews.com/2012/10/24/politics/bangor-senate-race-marked-by-largest-amount-of-outside-money/?ref=inline;

National Institute on Money in State Politics, Follow the Money.org, "Candidates-Maine 2012." Available at http://www.followthemoney.org/database/StateGlance/state_candidates.phtml?f=S&y=2012&s=ME; National Conference of State Legislators, "2012 NCSL Legislator Compensation Data." Available at http://www.ncsl.org/legislatures-elections/legisdata/2012-ncsl-legislator-compensation-data.aspx.

42. National Institute on Money in State Politics, Follow the Money.org, "Idaho 2012." Available at http://www.followthemoney.org/database/state_overview.phtml?s=ID&y=2012.

43. Anne Bauer, "Third-Party Candidates Face Long Odds," National Institute on Money in State Politics, May 18, 2010. Study of third-party candidates from 2000 to 2009.

44. Michael McDonald, "Multi-Partyism in American Politics?" May 13, 2010. Available at www.pollster.com/blogs/michael-mcdonald/2010/05/09-week/; Pew Center for the People & the Press, "Distrust, Discontent, Anger, and Partisan Rancor," April 18, 2010. Available at http://people-press.org/report/606/trust-in-government.

45. Eric Kelderman, "Report Ranks Campaign Disclosure Laws," October 17, 2007. Available at www.stateline.org.

46. National Conference of State Legislatures, "State Limits on Contributions to Candidates 2011–2012," Updated June 1, 2012. Available at http://www.ncsl.org/Portals/1/documents/legismgt/Limits_to_Candidates_2011-2012v2.pdf.

47. National Conference of State Legislatures, "Public Financing of Campaigns: An Overview," Updated January 23, 2013. Available at http://www.ncsl.org/legislatures-elections/elections/public-financing-of-campaigns-overview.aspx.

48. Ibid.

49. United States General Accounting Office, "Experiences of Two States [Maine, Arizona] That Offered Full Public Funding for Political Candidates," *GAO-10-390*, May 2010; Peter Quist, "Monetary Competitiveness in 2009–2010 State Legislative Races," National Institute on Money in State Politics, July 3, 2012. Available at http://www.followthemoney.org/press/ReportView.phtml?r=490&ext=10.

50. *Buckley* v. *Valeo* 424 U.S. 1 (1976).

51. *McConnell* v. *Federal Elections Commission* 540 U.S. 93 (2003).

52. *Federal Elections Commission* v. *Wisconsin Right to Life*, June 25, 2007.

53. Kristin Sullivan and Terrance Adams, "Summary of Citizens United v. Federal Election Commission," *OLD Research Report*, March 2, 2010. Available at www.cga.ct.gov/2010/rpt/2010-R-0124.htm; also see L. Paige Whitaker et al., "Legislative Options After Citizens United v. FEC: Constitutional and Legal Issues, Congressional Research Service, March 8, 2010, R41096; Dan Eggen, "Poll: Large Majority Opposes Supreme Court's Decision on Campaign Financing," *Washington Post*, February 17, 2010.

54. Deborah Tedford, "Supreme Court Rips Up Campaign Finance Laws," *National Public Radio*, January 21, 2010. Available at www.npr.org/templates/story/story.php?storyId=122805666.

55. Under BCRA, televised communication funded by anyone other than a candidate for office must include a clear, readable disclaimer displayed on the screen for at least four seconds. The disclaimer must identify the person or organization responsible for the advertisement, that person or organization's address or Web site, and a statement that the advertisement "is not authorized by any candidate or candidate's committee." Kristin Sullivan and Terrance Adams, "Summary of Citizens United v. Federal Election Commission," *OLD Research Report*, March 2, 2010, p. 2. Available at www.cga.ct.gov/2010/rpt/2010-R-0124.htm.

56. Denise Roth Barber, "Citizens United v. Federal Election Commission: The Impacts—and Lack Thereof—on State Campaign Finance Law," National Institute on Money in State Politics, March 2, 2010. Available at www.followthemoney.org/press/PrintReportView.phtml?r=414.

57. For a detailed list of these states, see National Conference of State Legislatures, "Life After Citizen United," June 15, 2010. Available at www.ncsl.org/default.aspx?tabid=19607.

58. *Randall* v. *Sorrell*, June 26, 2006.

59. Jennifer Drage, "Do Campaign Finance Laws Make a Difference?" *State Legislatures* 26 (September 2000): 25.

60. Neil Reiff, "State and Local Party Committees: An Endangered Species?" *Campaigns & Elections* 3 (July/August 2012): 12–14.

61. Joseph E. Sandler and Neil P. Reiff, "New Campaign Finance Rules and the 2004 Elections," *Campaigns & Elections*, February 2005, pp. 35–36.

CHAPTER 6

1. The Council of State Governments, *The Book of the States*, 2012 edition, Vol. 44 (Lexington, KY: The Council of State Governments, 2012), Table 3.19.

2. National Conference of State Legislatures, "Legislator Demographics," available at http://www.ncsl.org/legislatures-elections/legisdata/legislator-demographics.aspx, April 16, 2013.

3. *Tampa Tribune*, July 27, 1987.

4. National Conference of State Legislatures, "Legislator Demographics," accessed at http://www.ncsl.org/legislatures-elections/legisdata/legislator-demographics.aspx, April 16, 2013.

5. See Paul J. Hain and James E. Pierson, "Lawyers and Politics Revisited: Structural Advantages of Lawyer-Politicians," *American Journal of Political Science* 19 (February 1975): 41–51.

6. National Conference of State Legislatures, "Full and Part-time Legislatures," June 2009, available at http://www.ncsl.org/legislatures-elections/legislatures/full-and-part-time-legislatures.aspx#average, April 16, 2013.

7. Wayne L. Francis, "Costs and Benefits of Legislative Service in the American States," *American Journal of Political Science* 29 (August 1985): 626–642.

8. Karl T. Kurtz, Gary Moncrief, Richard G. Niemi, and Lynda W. Powell, "Full-Time, Part-Time, and Real Time: Explaining State Legislators' Perceptions of Time on the Job," *State Politics and Policy Quarterly* 6(3) (Fall 2006): 322–338.

9. Karl Kurtz and Brenda Erickson, "Legislaturs: All Over the Map," *State Legislaturs* 39(1) (January 2013): 5.

10. Minority statistics (as of 2009) are from the National Conference of State Legislatures, "Numbers of African American Legislators 2009." Available at http://www.ncsl.org/default.aspx?tabid=l14781; National Conference of State Legislatures, "Latino Legislators 2009." Available at http://www.ncsl.org/default.aspx?tabid=14776; statistics on women (as of March 2010) are from the Center for American Women and Politics, "Women in State Legislative Office 2010." Available at http://www.cawp.rutgers.edu/fast_facts/levels_of_office/documents/stleg.pdf.

11. Byron D'Andra Orey, L. Marvin Overby, and Christopher W. Larimer, "African-American Committee Chairs in U.S. State Legislatures," *Social Science Quarterly* 88(3) (September 2007): 619–639; Robert R. Preuhs, "The Conditional Effects of Minority Descriptive Representation: Black Legislators and Policy Influence in the American States," *Journal of Politics* 68(3) (August 2006): 585–599.

12. Mary Herring, "Legislative Responsiveness to Black Constituents in Three Southern States," *Journal of Politics* 52 (August 1990): 740–758; for a report on the differing experiences of black legislators, see David Hedge, James Button, and Mary Spear, "Accounting for the Quality of Black Legislative Life," *American Journal of Political Science* 40 (February 1996): 82–98. See also Kerry L. Haynie, *African American Legislators in the American States* (New York: Columbia University Press, 2001).

13. Center for American Women and Politics, "Women of Color in Elective Office 2013," April 2013. Available at http://www.cawp.rutgers.edu/fast_facts/levels_of_office/documents/color.pdf.

14. See Emmy F. Werner, "Women in State Legislatures," *Western Political Quarterly* 21 (March 1968): 40–50; Paula J. Dubeck, "Women and Access to Political Office," *Sociological Quarterly* 17 (March 1976): 42–52; Susan Welch, "The Recruitment of Women to Public Office," *Western Political Quarterly* 19 (June 1978): 372–380.

15. Wilma Rule, "Why More Women Are State Legislators," *Western Political Quarterly* 43 (June 1990): 437–448.

16. Sue Vandenbosch, "A Negative Relationship Between Religion and the Percentage of Women State Legislators in the United States," *Journal of Legislative Studies* 2 (Winter 1996): 322–338.

17. Susan A. MacManus, Charles S. Bullock, III, Karen Padgett, and Brittany Penberthy, "Women Winning at the Local Level: Are County and School Board Positions Becoming More Desirable and Plugging the Pipeline to Higher Office?" in Lois Duke Whitaker, ed., *Women in Politics,* 4th ed. (Upper Saddle River, NJ: Prentice-Hall, 2005). See also H. W. Jerome Maddox, "Opportunity Costs and Outside Careers in U.S. State Legislatures," *Legislative Studies Quarterly* 29 (November 2004): 517–544.

18. Susan Welch, et al., "The Effect of Gender on Electoral Outcomes in State Legislative Races," *Western Political Quarterly* 38 (September 1985): 464–475.

19. Susan Welch and Lee Sigelman, "Changes in Public Attitudes Toward Women in Politics," *Social Science Quarterly* 63 (June 1982): 321–322.

20. Carole J. Uhlaner, "Potentiality and Representation: The Link Between Descriptive Representation and Participation in the United States," *Politics & Gender* 8(4) (December 2012): 535–541.

21. David Niven, "Throwing Your Hat Out of the Ring: Negative Recruitment and the Gender Imbalance in State Legislative Candidacy," *Politics and Gender* 2(4) (December 2006): 473–491.

22. Virginia Sapiro, "Private Costs of Public Commitments: Family Roles Versus Political Ambition," *American Journal of Political Science* 26 (May 1982): 265–279.

23. Carol Nechemias, "Geographic Mobility and Women's Access to State Legislatures," *Western Political Quarterly* 38 (March 1985): 119–131.

24. Kevin Arceneaux, "The Gender Gap in State Legislature Representation," *Political Research Quarterly* 54 (March 2000): 143–160.

25. Lesley Dahlkemper, "Growing Accustomed to Her Face," *State Legislatures* (July/August 1996): 37–45.

26. R. Darcy, "Women in the State Legislative Power Structure," *Social Science Quarterly* 77 (December 1996): 888–898.

27. Sue Thomas, *How Women Legislate* (New York: Oxford University Press, 1994).

28. Lyn Kathlene, "Power and Influence in State Legislative Policymaking: The Interaction of Gender and Position in Committee Hearing Debates," *American Political Science Review* 88 (September 1994): 560–576.

29. Michelle Swers, "Understanding the Policy Impact of Electing Women," *PS: Political Science and Politics* 34 (June 2001): 217–220. See also Beth Reingold, *Representing Women: Sex, Gender, and Legislative Behavior in Arizona and California* (Chapel Hill: University of North Carolina Press, 2000); Kathleen A. Bratton and Kerry L. Haynie, "Agenda Setting and Legistative Success in State Legislatures," *Journal of Politics* 61 (August 1999): 658–679.

30. Beth Reingold, *Representing Women: Sex, Gender, and Legislative Behavior in Arizona and California* (Chapel Hill: University of North Carolina Press, 2000).

31. Peter Quist, "Monetary Competitiveness in 2009–2010 State Legislative Races," National Institute on Money in State Politics, July 3, 2012. Available at http://www.followthemoney.org/press/ReportView.phtml?r=490&ext=1.

32. Zach Patton, "Chasing the Shadow," *Governing* 19(9) (June 2006): 43–45; Peter Quist, "The Role of Money & Incumbency in 2007–2008 State Elections," National Institute on Money in State Politics, May 6, 2010. Available at www.followthemoney.org/press/PrintReportView.phtml?r=423.

33. Alan E. Wiseman, "Partisan Strategy and Support in State Legislative Elections: The Case of Illinois," *American Politics Research* 33(3) (May 2005): 376–403.

34. Robert E. Hogan, "Sources of Competition in State Legislative Primary Elections," *Legislative Studies Quarterly* 28 (February 2003): 103–126.

35. Ronald E. Weber, "The Quality of State Legislative Representation," *Journal of Politics* 61 (August 1999): 609–627.

36. David Ray and John Havick, "A Longitudinal Analysis of Party Competition in State Legislative Elections," *American Journal of Political Science* 25 (February 1981): 119–128.

37. Ronald Weber, Harvey Tucker, and Paul Brace, "Vanishing Marginals in State Legislative Elections," *Legislative Studies Quarterly* 16 (February 1991): 29–47.

38. John J. McGlennon and Ian Mahoney, "State Legislative Competition in 2012: Redistricting and Party Polarization Drive Decrease in Competition," Thomas Jefferson Program in Public Policy at the College of William 7 Mary, October 17, 2012.

39. Alan Abramowitz, "Don't Blame Redistricting for Uncompetitive Elections," *Sabato's Crystal Ball* 111(10), available at http://www.centerforpolitics.org/crystalball, May 26, 2005.

40. Malcolm E. Jewell, "State Legislative Elections," *American Politics Quarterly* 22 (October 1994): 483–509.

41. Emily Van Dunk, "Challenger Quality in State Legislative Elections," *Political Research Quarterly* 50 (December 1997): 793–807.

42. Peter Quist, "The Role of Money & Incumbency in 2007–2008 State Elections," National Institute on Money in State Politics, May 6, 2010. Available at www.followthemoney.org/press/PrintReportView.phtml?r=423.

43. Quotations of legislators from William J. Keefe and Morris S. Ogul, *The American Legislative Process: Congress and the States*, 8th ed. (Englewood Cliffs, NJ: Prentice Hall, 1993).

44. William B. Berry, Michael B. Berkman, and Stewart Schneiderman, "Legislative Professionalism and Incumbent Reelection," *American Political Science Review* 94 (December 2000): 859–874.

45. Jennifer A. Steen, "The Impact of State Legislative Term Limits on the Supply of Congressional Candidates," *State Politics and Policy Quarterly* 6(4) (Winter 2006): 430–447.

46. Michael Berkman and James Eisenstein, "State Legislators as Congressional Candidates," *Political Research Quarterly* 52 (September 1999): 481–498.

47. For a comprehensive look at the ins and outs of redistricting, see the series of articles published in *PS: Political Science and Politics* 39(1) (January 2006).

48. H. W. Jerome Maddox, "Opportunity Costs and Outside Careers in U.S. State Legislatures," *Legislative Studies Quarterly* 29 (November 2004): 517–544. He concludes that the prevalence of outside careers declines as legislative salary increases, regardless of party, education, or sex.

49. Richard A. Clucas, "Legislative Professionalism and the Power of State House Leaders," *State Politics and Policy Quarterly* 7(1) (Spring 2007): 1–19.

50. Alan Rosenthal, *Governors and Legislatures* (Washington, DC: CQ Press, 1990), p. 63.

51. *Baker v. Carr*, 369 U.S. 186 (1962).

52. *Reynold v. Sims*, 84 S. Ct. 1362 (1964).

53. *Wesberry v. Sanders*, 84 S. Ct. 526 (1964).

54. *Gray v. Sanders*, 83 S. Ct. 801 (1963), p. 809.

55. *Karchev v. Daggett*, 462 U.S. 725 (1983).

56. *Brown v. Thompson*, 462 U.S. 835 (1983).

57. For an excellent discussion of the issues and rulings, see National Conference of State Legislatures, "Shifting Sands of Redistricting Law," 2005, available at http://www.ncsl.org/research/redistricting/washington-dc-redistricting-seminar-presentions.aspx, May 30, 2005.

58. Kevin B. Smith, Alan Greenblatt, and John Buntin, *Governing States and Localities* (Washington, DC: CQ Press, 2005), p. 193.

59. *Davis v. Bandemer*, 106 S. Ct. 2797 (1986).

60. Charles Backstrom, Samuel Krislov, and Leonard Robins, "Desperately Seeking Standards: The Court's Frustrating Attempts to Limit Political Gerrymandering," *PS: Political Science and Politics* 39(3) (July 2006): 409–416.

61. *Vieth v. Jubelirer*, 241 F. Supp. 2d 478 (2004).

62. See Harry Basehart, "The Seats/Vote Relationship and the Identification of Partisan Gerrymandering in State Legislature," *American Politics Quarterly* 15 (October 1987): 484–498. See also Gerard S. Gryski, Bruce Reed, and Euel Elliot, "The Seats–Vote Relationship in State Legislative Elections," *American Politics Quarterly* 18 (April 1990): 141–157, for an estimate of bias for each state prior to 1990 redistricting.

63. *Davis v. Bandemer*, 106 S. Ct. 2797 (1986).

64. *Fortson v. Dorsey*, 179 U.S. 433 (1965).

65. *Thornburg v. Gingles*, 478 U.S. 30 (1986).

66. *Hunt v. Cromartie*, 532 U.S. 234 (2001).

67. For an excellent review of redistricting court cases, see *National Redistricting Law 2010* (Washington, DC: National Conference of State Legislatures, 2010);

Charles S. Bullock III, *Redistricting: The Most Political Activity in America* (Boulder, CO: Rowman & Littlefield, 2010).

68. Thomas F. Schaller, "Multi-Member Districts: Just a Thing of the Past?" *Sabato's Crystal Ball,* March 21, 2013. Available at http://www.centerforpolitics.org /crystalball/articles/multi-member-legislative-districts-just-a-thing-of-the-past/.

69. Justin H. Kirkland, "Multimember Districts' Effect on Collaboration Between U.S. State Legislators," *Legislative Studies Quarterly* 37(3) (August 2012): 329–353.

70. *Connor v. Johnson,* 407 U.S. 640 (1971).

71. *White v. Regester,* 412 U.S. 755 (1973).

72. National Conference of State Legislatures, "2010 Constituents Per State Legislative District." Available at http://www.ncsl.org/legislatures-elections/legislatures /2010-constituents-per-state-legislative-district.aspx.

73. National Conference of State Legislatures, "Shifting Sands of Redistricting Law," 2005, available at http:// www.ncsl.org/research/redistricting/washington-dc-redistricting-seminar-presentions.aspx, May 30, 2005.

74. Anjeanette Damon and Andrew Doughman, "Banishment Ends Brooks Saga: 'We Did Not Feel Safe,' " *Las Vegas Sun,* March 29, 2013.

75. Harvey J. Tucker, "Legislative Logjams: A Comparative State Analysis," *Western Political Quarterly* 38 (September 1985): 432–446.

76. The "institutionalization" theme was first developed to understand changes in the U.S. House of Representatives by Nelson Polsby, "The Institutionalization of the U.S. House of Representatives," *American Political Science Review* 62 (March 1968): 144–168.

77. Peverill Squire, "Measuring State Legislative Professionalism: The Squire Index Revisited," *State Politics and Policy Quarterly* 7(2) (Summer 2007): 211–227.

78. Neal D. Woods and Michale Baranowski, "Legislative Professionalism and Influence on State Agencies," *Legislative Studies Quarterly* 31(4) (November 2006): 585–610; Neil Malhotra, "Government Growth and Professionalism in U.S. State Legislatures," *Legislative Studies Quarterly* 31(4) (November 2006): 563–584.

79. William D. Berry, Michael B. Berkman, and Stuart Schneiderman, "Legislative Professionalism and Incumbent Reflection," *American Political Science Review* 94 (December 2000): 859–865.

80. Alan Rosenthal, *Governors and Legislatures: Contending Powers* (Washington, DC: CQ Press, 1990), p. 63.

81. For a good overview of a job description for a legislative staffer, see "Career Prospects in Virginia: Legislative Staffers," April 7, 2005, available at http://www.career-prospects.org/briefs/Print /K-O/LegislativeStaff.shtml, May 28, 2005.

82. Karl Kurtz and Tim Rice, "Facing the Future" [Legislative Staffers], *State Legislatures* 38(7) (July/August 2013): 38–40.

83. Kim U. Hoffman, "Legislative Fiscal Analysts: Influence in State Budget Development," *State and Local Government Review* 38(1) (2006): 41–51.

84. Tim Storey, "Democrats Bounce Back," *State Legislatures* 38(10) (December 2012): 14–17.

85. James Coleman Battista, "Committee Theories and Committee Votes: Internal Committee Behavior in the California Legislature," *State Politics and Policy Quarterly* 6(2) (Summer 2006): 117–150.

86. James Coleman Battista, "State Legislative Committees and Economic Connections: Expertise and Industry Service," *State Politics & Policy Quarterly* 12(3) (September 2012): 284–302.

87. L. Marvin Overby and Thomas A. Kazee, "Outlying Committees in the Statehouse," *Journal of Politics* 62 (August 2000): 701–728; L. Marvin Overby, Thomas A. Kazee, and David W. Prince, "Committee Outliers in State Legislatures," *Legislative Studies Quarterly* 29 (February 2004): 81–108.

88. Keith E. Hamm, Ronald D. Hedlund, and Nancy Martorano, "Measuring State Legislative Committee Power: Change and Chamber Differences in the 20th Century," *State Politics and Policy Quarterly* 6(1) (Spring 2006): 88–111.

89. Thomas H. Little, "A Systematic Analysis of Members' Environments and Their Expectations of Elected Leaders," *Political Research Quarterly* 47 (September 1994): 733–747.

90. Mark Wolf, "Top 10 of 2013," *State Legislatures* 39(1) (January 2013): 18–21.

91. Christopher A. Cooper and Lilliard E. Richardson, Jr., "Institutions and Representational Roles in American State Legislatures," *State Politics and Policy Quarterly* 6(2) (Summer 2006): 174–194.

92. Hanna Pitkin, *The Concept of Representation* (Berkeley: University of California Press, 1967), p. 154.

93. Ronald D. Hedlund and H. Paul Friesma, "Representatives' Perceptions of Constituency Opinion," *Journal of Politics* 34 (August 1971): 730–752.

94. Robert S. Erikson, Norman R. Luttbeg, and William V. Holloway, "Knowing One's District: How Legislators Predict Referendum Voting," *American Journal of Political Science* 19 (May 1975): 231–241.

95. John M. Carey, Richard G. Niemi, Lynda W. Powell, and Gary F. Moncrief, "The Effects of Term Limits on State Legislatures: A New Survey of the 50 States," *Legislative Studies Quarterly* 31(1) (February 2006): 105–134.

96. D. E. Appollonio and Raymond J. La Raja, "Term Limits, Campaign Contributions, and the Distribution of Power in State Legislatures," *Legislative Studies Quarterly* 31(2) (May 2006): 259–282.

97. Marjorie Sarbaugh-Thompson, Lyke Thompson, Charles D. Elder, Meg Comins, Richard C. Elling, and John Strate, "Democracy Among Strangers: Term Limits' Effects on Relationships Between State Legislators in

Michigan," *State Politics and Policy Quarterly* 6(4) (Winter 2006): 384–409.

98. Thad Kousser, "The Limited Impact of Term Limits: Contingent Effects on the Complexity and Breadth of Laws," *State Politics and Policy Quarterly* 6(4) (Winter 2006): 410–429.

99. Daniel C. Lewis, "Legislative Term Limits and Fiscal Policy Performance," *Legislative Studies Quarterly* 37(3) (August 2012): 305–328.

100. Rebekah Herrick and Sue Thomas, "Do Term Limits Make a Difference?" *American Politics Research* 33(3) (September 2005): 726–747.

101. William M. Salka, "Term Limits and Electoral Competition: An Analysis of California Legislative Races," *State and Local Government Review* 37(2) (2005): 116–127.

102. Jeffrey Lazarus, "Term Limits' Multiple Effects on State Legislators' Career Decisions," *State Politics and Policy Quarterly* 6(4) (Winter 2006): 357–383.

103. National Conference of State Legislatures, "The Term Limited States," January 2013. Available at http://www.ncsl.org/legislatures-elections/legisdata/chart-of-term-limits-states.aspx.

104. Lilliard E. Richardson, Jr., David Valentine, and Shannon Daily Stokes, "Assessing the Impact of Term Limits in Missouri," *State and Local Government Review* 17(1) (2005): 177–192. Scot Schraufnagel and Karen Halperin, "Term Limits, Electoral Competition, and Representational Diversity: The Case of Florida," *State Politics and Policy Quarterly* 6(4) (Winter 2006): 448–462.

105. National Conference of State Legislatures, "Ethics Issues Overview," 2005, accessed at ncsl.org.

106. National Conference of State Legislatures, "Ethics: State Ethics Commissions," October 2011, available at http://www.ncsl.org/legislatures-elections/ethicshome/state-ethics-commissions.aspx, April 16, 2013.

107. Natalie Wood, "From the Campaign to the Capitol," *State Legislatures* 38(1) (December 2012): 29–31.

108. Alan Greenblatt, "Whither the Purple States?" *Governing* 26(4) (January 2013): 9.

109. Karl Kurtz, "The Most Frustrating Job in the World, The Thicket of State Legislatures," *National Conference of State Legislatures,* February 27, 2013. Available at http://ncsl.typepad.com/.

110. Christopher A. Cooper, "Media Tactics in the State Legislature," *State Politics and Policy Quarterly* 2 (Winter 2002): 353–371.

111. Nicole Casal Moore, "Adversaries Always," *State Legislatures* 31 (May 2005): 21.

112. Ibid.

113. Steven Walters, "Ready, Set, PAN," *State Legislatures* 39(1) (January 2013): 32–34.

114. The Irrigation Association, "State Lobbying: Vital for Our Industry and Your Livelihood," *The Irrigation Association Statesman* (September/October 2002): 1–2.

115. Ibid.

116. Christopher A. Mooney, "Peddling Information in the State Legislature: Closeness Counts," *Western Political Quarterly* 44 (June 1991): 433–444.

117. Harmon Zeigler and Michael A. Baer, *Lobbying: Interaction and Influence in American State Legislatures* (Belmont, CA: Wadsworth, 1969), p. 107.

118. Ibid.

119. Mary Ellen Klas, "Special-Interest Ties Persist," *Miami Herald,* May 22, 2005.

120. Jennifer C. Lucas and Mark S. Hyde, "Men and Women Lobbyists in the American States," *Social Science Quarterly* 93(2) (June 2012): 394–414.

121. Robert Morlino and Leah Rush, "Hired Guns: Lobbyists Spend Loads of Money to Influence Legislators—And in Many States, with Too Little Scrutiny," Public Integrity, May 15, 2003.

122. Cynthia Opheim, "Explaining the Differences in State Lobbying Regulation," *Western Political Quarterly* 44 (June 1991): 405–421.

123. Joshua Ozymy, "Keepin' on the Sunny Side: Scandals, Organized Interests, and the Passage of Legislative Lobbying Laws in the American States," *American Politics Research* 41(1) (January 2013): 3–23.

124. Kevin Bogardus, "Statehouse Revolvers," Public Integrity.com, October 12, 2006.

125. William Keefe, "Reform and the American Legislature," in Donald Herzberg and Alan Rosenthal, eds., *Strengthening the States: Essays on Legislative Reform* (New York: Doubleday & Co., 1971), p. 190.

126. Alan Rosenthal, *The Decline of Representative Democracy: Process, Participation, and Power in State Legislatures* (Washington, DC: CQ Press), p. 1997.

CHAPTER 7

1. Margaret Ferguson, "Governors and the Executive Branch," in Virginia Gray, Russell L. Hanson, and Thad Kousser, eds., *Politics in the American States,* 10th ed. (Washington, DC: CQ Press, 2013), p. 208.

2. Charles Howe, "Animal House," *Wall Street Journal,* April 14, 2005.

3. Greg D. Adams and Peverill Squire, "A Note on the Dynamics and Idiosyncrasies of Gubernatorial Popularity," *State Politics and Policy Quarterly* 1 (Winter 2001): 380; see also Robert E. Crew, Jr., David Branham, Gregory R. Weiher, and Ethan Bernick, "Political Events in a Model of Gubernatorial Approval," *State Politics and Policy Quarterly* 2 (Fall 2002): 283–297; Jay Barth and Margaret R. Ferguson, "American Governors and Their Constituents: The Relationship Between Gubernatorial Personality and Public Approval," *State Politics and Policy Quarterly* 2 (Fall 2002): 268–282.

4. Sarah McCally Morehouse, *The Governor and Party Leader* (Ann Arbor: University of Michigan Press, 1998).

5. Steve L. B. Lem and Conor M. Dowling, "Picking Their Spots: Minor Party Candidates in Gubernatorial Elections," *Political Research Quarterly* 59 (September 2000): 471–480.

6. Mark Bruse, "Michigan's First Governor Is the Youngest State Governor in American History," *Michigan Public Radio,* October 27, 2011. Available at http://www.michiganradio.org/post/michigans-first-governor-youngest-state-governor-american-history.

7. Center for American Women and Politics, Eagleton Institute of Politics, Rutgers University, "History of Women Governors," available at http://www.cawp.rutgers.edu/fast_facts/levels_of_office/documents/govhistory.pdf, April 6, 2013.

8. John A. Hamman, "Career Experience and Performing Effectively as Governor," *American Review of Public Administration* 34 (June 2004): 151–163.

9. Emily Schultheis, "Govenorships: Where Are the Women?" *Politico,* February 24, 2013. Available at http://www.politico.com/story/2013/02/governorships-a-mostly-male-domain-87982.html.

10. Thad Beyle, "The Governors," in Virginia Gray and Russell L. Hanson, eds., *Politics in the American States: A Comparative Analysis,* 8th ed. (Washington, DC: CQ Press, 2004), pp. 194–231.

11. See Robert M. Stein, "Economic Voting for Governor and U.S. Senator," *Journal of Politics* 52 (February 1990): 29–53.

12. Susan B. Hansen, "Life Is Not Fair: Governors' Job Performance Ratings and State Economies," *Political Research Quarterly* 52 (March 1999): 167–188.

13. Daniel Coffey, "Measuring Gubernatorial Ideology: A Content Analysis of State of the State Speeches," *State Politics and Policy Quarterly* 5 (Spring 2005): 97.

14. Dennis M. Simon, "Presidents, Governors and Electoral Accountability," *Journal of Politics* 51 (May 1989): 286–304; Thomas M. Holbrook-Provow, "National Factors in Gubernatorial Elections," *American Politics Quarterly* 15 (October 1987): 471–483.

15. James D. King, "Incumbent Popularity and Vote Choice in Gubernatorial Elections," *Journal of Politics* 63 (May 2001): 585–597.

16. James D. King and Jeffrey E. Cohen, "What Determines a Governor's Popularity?" *State Politics and Policy Quarterly* 5 (Fall 2005): 225–247.

17. Thomas M. Casey, *Campaign Dynamics: The Race for Governor* (Ann Arbor: University of Michigan Press, 2000).

18. Andrew D. McNitt and Jim Seroka, "Intraparty Challenges of Incumbent Governors and Senators," *American Politics Quarterly* 9 (July 1981): 321–340.

19. Thad Beyle, "Gubernatorial Elections, Campaign Costs and Winning Governors," in The Council of State Governments, eds., *The Book of the States,* 2012 edition, Vol. 44 (Lexington, KY: The Council of State Governments, 2012), pp. 203–213.

20. Susan L. Kane and Richard F. Winters, "Taxes and Voting: Electoral Retribution in the American States," *Journal of Politics* 55 (February 1993): 22–40.

21. Louis Jacobson, "What It Takes for a Governor to Lose Reelection," *Governing,* January 5, 2012. Available at http://www.governing.com/blogs/politics/what-it-takes-for-a-governor-to-lose-reelection.html.

22. Robert A. Jackson, "Gubernatorial and Senatorial Campaign Mobilization of Voters," *Political Research Quarterly* 55 (December 2002): 825–844.

23. Kedron Bardwell, "Campaign Finance Laws and the Competition for Spending in Gubernatorial Elections," *Social Science Quarterly* 84 (December 2003): 810–825.

24. State of Alaska, Division of Elections, "Election Results," available at http://www.elections.alaska.gov/ei_return.php, March 2013; California Secretary of State, "Statewide Elections," available at http://www.sos.ca.gov/elections/statewide-elections/2010-primary/, March 2013; Connecticut Secretary of State, "Election Results," available at http://www.sots.ct.gov/sots/cwp/view.asp?a=3172&q=525432, March 2013; Florida Department of State, Division of Elections, "Election Results," available at http://doe.dos.state.fl.us/elections/resultsarchive/index.asp, March 2013; Idaho Secretary of State, "Idaho Election Results," available at http://www.sos.idaho.gov/elect/results.htm, March 2013; Kentucky State Board of Elections, "Kentucky Election Results 2010–2019," available at http://elect.ky.gov/results/2010-2019/Pages/2011primaryandgeneralelectionresults.aspx, March 2013; Louisiana Secretary of State, "Election Results," available at http://www.sos.la.gov/ElectionsAndVoting/GetElectionInformation/FindResultsAndStatistics/Pages/default.aspx, March 2013; Secretary of State, Mississippi, "Election Results," available at http://www.sos.ms.gov/elections_results_2011.aspx, March 2013; Nebraska Secretary of State, "Previous Elections," available at http://www.sos.ne.gov/elec/prev_elec/index.html, March 2013; Pennsylvania Department of State, "Elections," available at http://www.electionreturns.state.pa.us/, March 2013; Texas Secretary of State, "Election Results," available at http://www.sos.state.tx.us/elections/historical/index.shtml, March 2013.

25. Kendra A. Hovey and Harold A. Hovey, *CQ's State Fact Finder, 2003* (Washington, DC: CQ Press, 2003).

26. Alan Rosenthal, *Governors and Legislatures: Contending Powers* (Washington, DC: Congressional Quarterly Press, 1990), p. 170.

27. F. Ted Hebert, Jeffrey L. Brudney, and Deil S. Wright, "Gubernatorial Influence and State Bureaucracy," *American Politics Quarterly* 11 (April 1983): 243–244.

28. Charles Barrilleaux and Michael Berkman, "Do Governors Matter? Budgeting Rules and the Politics of State Policymaking," *Political Research Quarterly* 56 (December 2003): 409–417.

29. Thad Kousser and Justin H. Phillips, *The Power of American Governors: Winning on Budgets and Losing on Policy* (Cambridge: Cambridge University Press, 2012).

30. Daniel Coffey, "Measuring Gubernatorial Ideology: A Content Analysis of State of the State Speeches," *State Politics and Policy Quarterly* 5(1) (Spring 2005): 88–103.

31. Katherine Willoughby, "The State of State Addresses: The New Normal Fosters Gobernatorial Funnel Vision," in The Council of State Governments, eds., *The Book of the States,* 2012 edition, Vol. 44 (Lexington, KY:The Council of State Governments, 2012), pp. 193–202.

32. Charles Wiggins, "Executive Vetoes and Legislative Overrides in the American States," *Journal of Politics* 42 (November 1980): 1110–1117.

33. Thad Beyle and Robert Dalton, *Being Governor: The View from the Office* (Durham, NC: Duke University Press, 1983), p. 135.

34. Ibid., pp. 47, 294, 296–298.

35. Gregory Korte, "One-Party Dominance Grows in States," *USA Today,* December 14, 2012. Available at http://www.usatoday.com/story/news/politics/2012/12/13/states-supermajority-legislatures/1758567/.

36. See Kevin M. Leyden and Stephen A. Borrelli, "The Effect of State Economic Conditions on Gubernatorial Elections: Does Unified Government Make a Difference?" *Political Research Quarterly* 48 (June 1995): 275–290.

37. See Sarah McCally Morehouse, *The Governor and Party Leader* (Ann Arbor: University of Michigan Press, 1998); Laura A. Van Assendelft, *Governors, Agenda Setting and Divided Government* (Lanham, MD: University Press of America, 1997).

38. Amy Zacks, "Recalling Governors: An Overview," Center on the American Governor, Eagleton Institute of Politics, Rutgers University, June 6, 2012; Available at http://governors.rutgers.edu/usgov/governors_recallelections.php.

39. Thad Beyle, "The Governors," in Virginia Gray and Russell L. Hanson, eds., *Politics in the American States: A Comparative Analysis,* 8th ed. (Washington, DC: CQ Press, 2004), pp. 194–231.

40. Pew Research Center's Project for Excellence in Journalism, "The State of the News Media 2013." Available at http://stateofthemedia.org/2013/overview-5/.

41. The study, *The American Journalist in the 21st Century,* was conducted by David Weaver, Randal Beam, Bonnie Brownlee, G. Cleveland Wilhoit, and Paul Voakes in collaboration with the Indiana University School of Journalism. *Source:* "Landmark Research into the Backgrounds of American Journalists Continues," *Indiana University Media Relations,* April 10, 2003. For an extensive compilation of media political leaning studies by the Media Research Center, see "Media Bias Basics," available at http://archive.mrc.org/biasbasics/biasbasics1.asp, November 8, 2013.

42. S. Robert Lichter, *The Media Elite: America's New Powerbrokers* (New York: Adler Publishing Company, 1986).

43. William T. Gormley, "Coverage of State Government in the Mass Media," *State Government* 52 (December 1979): 46–51.

44. Julia Hurst, "The Office of Lieutenant Govenor: A Bedrock Principle," in The Council of State Governments, eds., *The Book of the States,* 2012 edition, Vol. 44 (Lexington, KY: The Council of State Governments, 2012), pp. 243–245.

45. Arizona, Oregon and Wyoming designate the secretary of state as first in line in Maine, New Hampshire, Tennessee, and West Virginia, it is the senate president.

46. Richard L. Fox and Zoe Me. Oxley, "Does Running with a Woman Help? Evidence from U.S. Gubernatorial Elections," *Policies and Gender* 1(4) (December 2005): 525–546.

47. Dylan Scott, "Maryland Lt. Gov. Redefines the Job to Work For Him," *Governing,* January 30, 2013. Available at http://www.governing.com/gov-maryland-lt-gov-brown-makes-the-job-work-for-him.html.

48. Ibid.

49. National Association of Attorneys General, "Pillars of Hope: Attorneys General Unite Against Human Trafficking," in The Council of State Governments, eds., *The Book of the States,* 2012 edition, Vol. 44 (Lexington, KY: The Council of State Governments, 2012), pp. 261–264.

50. R. Kinney Poynter, "Transparency: It's Here to Stay," in The Council of State Governments, eds., *The Book of the States,* 2012 edition, Vol. 44 (Lexington, KY: The Council of State Governments, 2012), pp. 277–279.

51. Kay Stimson, "Secretaries of State Open for Business: New Initiatives to Reduce Red Tape, Create State Business Culture for Success," in The Council of State Governments, eds., *The Book of the States,* 2012 edition, Vol. 44 (Lexington, KY: The Council of State Governments, 2012), pp. 251–253.

CHAPTER 8

1. Elizabeth McNichol, "Some Basic Facts on State and Local Government Workers," *Center on Budget and Policy Priorities,* June 15, 2012. Available at http://www.cbpp.org/cms/?fa=view&id=3410.

2. David Osbourne and Ted Gaebler, *Reinventing Government* (New York: Addison-Wesley, 1992), p. 24.

3. *Elrod* v. *Burns,* 96 S. Ct. 2673 (1976); *Branti* v. *Finkel,* 445 U.S. 507 (1980).

4. David Cooper, Mary Gable, and Algernon Austin, "The Public-Sector Jobs Crisis," *Economic Policy Institute,* May 2, 2012. Available at http://www.epi.org/publication/bp339-public-sector-jobs-crisis/.

5. "Appointed Policy Makers in State Government: Glass Ceiling in Gubernatorial Appointments, 1997–2007," a report of the Center for Women in Government & Civil Society, State University of New York at Albany, Summer 2008. Available at http://www.albany.edu/womeningov/glass_ceiling_compressed.pdf.

6. Zogby International, "Nationwide Attitudes Toward Unions," for the Public Service Research Foundation, February 26, 2004.

7. Randall S. Davis, "Unionization and Work Attitudes: How Union Commitment Influences Public Sector Job Satisfaction," *Public Administration Review* 73(1) (January/February 2013): 74–84.

8. "Facts and Figures," *PublicSector, Inc.,* available at http://www.publicsectorinc.org/facts/, April 6, 2013.

9. John Barro, "How Congress Can Help State Pension Reform," *National Affairs* 12 (Summer 2012). Available at http://www.nationalaffairs.com/publications/detail/how-congress-can-help-state-pension-reform.

10. *The Municipal Year Book, 1987* (Washington, DC: ICMA, 1988), pp. 44–53.

11. Former Michigan Governor John Engler (R), quoted by Keon S. Chi, Kelley A. Arnold, and Heather M. Perkins, "Privatization in State Government: Trends and Issues," in The Council of State Governments, eds., *The Book of the States, 2004* (Lexington, KY: Council of State Governments, 2004), pp. 465–482.

12. Keon S. Chi, Kelley A. Arnold, and Heather M. Perkins, "Privatization in State Government: Trends and Issues," in The Council of State Governments, eds., *The Book of the States, 2004* (Lexington, KY: Council of State Governments, 2004), p. 465.

13. Kevin Fox Gotham, "Disaster, Inc.: Privatization and Post-Katrina Rebuilding in New Orleans," *Perspectives on Politics* 10(3) (September 2012): 633–646.

14. David Osbourne and Ted Gaebler, *Reinventing Government* (New York: Addison-Wesley, 1992), p. 24.

15. Kevin B. Smith, Alan Greenblatt, and John Buntin, *Governing States and Localities* (Washington, DC: CQ Press, 2005), p. 326.

16. Katherine Barrett and Richard Greene, "Why Haven't States and Localities Capitalized on Great Management Ideas?" *Governing,* March 2012. Available at http://www.governing.com/columns/smart-mgmt/col-great-management-ideas.html.

17. Christina McFarland, "State of America's Cities Survey on Jobs and the Economy," National League of Cities Center for Research and Innovation, May 2010.

18. National Conference of State Legislatures, "Ethics Report on State Legislature Counteracts Public Perceptions," NCSL News, 2002.

19. The Pew Center on the States and *Governing* Magazine, "Grading the States 2008: A Report Card on Government Performance." Available at www.pewcenteronthestates.org/gpp_report_card.asp.

20. Center for Digital Government, "Digital States Survey—2012 Results," October 2, 2012. Available at http://www.centerdigitalgov.com/survey/61/2012.

21. Mike Maciag, "New Transparency Grades Issued for States," *Government Technology,* March 26, 2013. Available at http://www.govtech.com/e-government/New-Transparency-Grades-Issued-for-States.html.

22. The federal government's fiscal year is October 1 to September 30.

23. David Osborne and Peter Hutchinson, "About the Book: The Price of Government: Getting the Results We Need in an Age of Permanent Fiscal Crisis," *Governing.*

24. James E. Alt and Robert C. Lowry, "Divided Government, Fiscal Institution, and Budget Deficits," *American Political Science Review* 88 (December 1994): 811–828.

CHAPTER 9

1. Melinda Gann Hall, "State Courts: Politics and the Judicial Process," in Virginia Gray, Russell L. Hanson, and Thad Kousser, eds., *Politics in the American States*, 10th ed. (Washington, DC: CQ Press, 2013), pp. 251–278.

2. A Harris Interactive Survey, "Arbitration: Simpler, Cheaper, and Faster Than Litigation," conducted for the U.S. Chamber Institute for Legal Reform, April 2005.

3. Ibid.

4. *Gitlow* v. *New York*, 268 U.S. 652 (1925).

5. See Donald R. Souger and Ashlyn Kuersten, "The Success of Amici in State Supreme Courts," *Political Research Quarterly* 48 (March 1995): 31–42.

6. John C. Kilwein and Richard A. Brisbin, Jr., "Policy Convergence in a Federal Judicial System," *American Journal of Political Science* 41 (January 1997): 122–148.

7. Valerie Hoekstra, "Competing Constraints: State Court Responses to Supreme Court Decisions and Legislation on Wages and Hours," *Political Research Quarterly* 58(2) (June 2005): 317–328.

8. National Center for State Courts, *Examining the Work of State Courts, 2003* (Williamsburg, VA: National Center for State Courts, 2003).

9. Henry R. Glick, "Courts: Politics and the Judicial Process," in Virginia Gray and Russell L. Hanson, eds., *Politics in the American States: A Comparative Analysis,* 8th ed. (Washington, DC: CQ Press, 2004), pp. 237–238.

10. National Center for State Courts, "Court Statistics Project State Caseload Statistics 2010." Available at http://www.courtstatistics.org/Other-Pages/StateCourtCaseloadStatistics.aspx.

11. National Center for State Courts, "Grand Juries: Frequently Asked Questions," 2013, available at http://www.ncsc.org/Topics/Jury/Grand-Juries/Resource-Guide.aspx, November 8, 2013.

12. *Miller-El* v. *Dretke,* _____ U.S. _____ (June 13, 2005); *Johnson* v. *California,* 545 U.S. _____ (2005) (June 13, 2005).

13. *Batson* v. *Kentucky,* 476 U.S. 79 (1986).

14. Charles Lane, "Justices Overturn Verdict, Cite Race," *Washington Post,* June 14, 2005, p. A01. Available at http://www.washingtonpost.com/wp-dyn/content/article/2005/06/13/AR2005061300531_pf.html.

15. James P. Wenzel, Shaun Bowler, and David J. Lanoue, "The Sources of Public Confidence in State Courts," *American Politics Research* 31 (March 2003): 191–211; Stefanie A. Lindquist, George W. Dougherty, and Mark

D. Bradbury, "Evaluating Performance in State Judicial Institutions: Trust and Confidence in the Georgia Judiciary," *State and Local Government Review* 38(3) (2006): 176–190.

16. Nicole L. Waters and Paula Hannaford-Agor, "Jurors 24/7: The Impact of New Media on Jurors, Public Perceptions of the Jury System, and the American Criminal Justice System," *National Center for State Courts*, 2012. Available at http://www.ncsc-jurystudies.org/What-We-Do/Jurors-and-New-Media.aspx.

17. *Gideon* v. *Wainwright*, 372 U.S. 335 (1963).

18. *Argersinger* v. *Hamlin*, 407 U.S. 25 (1972).

19. "Public-Defense Alternatives," *Seattle Times*, April 6, 2004, available at http://seattletimes.nwsource.com/news/local/unequaldefense/stories/three/alternatives.html, June 22, 2005.

20. Henry R. Glick, "Courts: Politics and the Judicial Process," in Virginia Gray and Russell L. Hanson, eds., *Politics in the American States: A Comparative Analysis*, 8th ed. (Washington, DC: CQ Press, 2004), p. 238.

21. See Gregory A. Caldereira, "On the Reputations of State Supreme Courts," *Political Behavior* 5 (1983): 89.

22. James L. Gibson, "Do Judicial Elections Really Stink?" *Campaigns & Elections* 314 (November/December 2012): 26–29.

23. Philip L. Dubois, "Voter Turnout in State Judicial Elections," *Journal of Politics* 41 (1979): 865–887.

24. Philip L. Dubois, "The Significance of Voting Cues in State Supreme Court Elections," *Law and Society Review* 13 (Spring 1979): 759–779.

25. Charles A. Johnson, Roger C. Schaefer, and R. Neal McKnight, "The Salience of Judicial Candidates and Elections," *Social Science Quarterly* 59 (September 1978): 371–378.

26. *Republican Party of Minnesota* v. *White*, 536 U.S. 765 (2002).

27. Brennan Center For Justice, "Caperton v. Massey," June 8, 2009. Available at www.brennancenter.org/content/resource/caperton_v_massey.

28. William Jenkins, "Retention Elections: Who Wins When No One Loses," *Judicature* 61 (August 1977): 79–86.

29. Ciara Torres-Spelliscy, Monique Chase, and Emma Greenma, "Improving Judicial Diversity," *The Brennan Center*, 2008. Available at http://brennan.3cdn.net/96d16b62f331bb13ac_kfm6bplue.pdf.

30. National Association of Women Judges, "2012 Representation of United States State Court Women Judges." Available at www.nawj.org/us_state_court_statistics_2012.asp.

31. Center for Justice, Law and Society at George Mason University, "Improving Diversity on the State Courts: A Report from the Bench," 2009.

32. Karen K. Peters, "An Inclusive Judiciary Is a Work in Progress," *New York Law Journal*, January 22, 2013.

Available at http://www.newyorklawjournal.com/PubArticleNY.jsp?id=1202585012528&An_Inclusive_Judiciary_Is_a_Work_in_Progress.

33. "Methods of Removing State Judges," *American Judicature Society*, available at https://www.ajs.org/judicial-ethics/impeachment/, November 8, 2013.

34. Ibid.

35. Bill Raftery, "2011 Year in Review: Record Number of Impeachment Attempts Against Judges for Their Decisions," *Gavel-to-Gavel*, December 27, 2011. Available at http://gaveltogavel.us/site/2011/12/27/2011-year-in-review-record-number-of-impeachment-attempts-against-judges-for-their-decisions/.

36. Melinda Gann Hall, "State Courts: Politics and the Judicial Process," in Virginia Gray, Russell L. Hanson, and Thad Kousser, eds., *Politics in the American States*, 10th ed. (Washington, DC: CQ Press, 2013), pp. 251–278.

37. Ibid.

38. Chris W. Bonneau, "Electoral Verdicts: Incumbent Defeats in State Supreme Court Elections," *American Politics Research* 33(6) (November 2005): 818–841; Melinda Gann Hall and Chris W. Bonneau, "Does Quality Matter? Challengers in State Supreme Court Elections," *American Journal of Political Science* 50(1) (January 2006): 20–33; Chris W. Bonneau. "Campaign Fundraising in State Supreme Court Elections," *Social Science Quarterly* 88(1) (March 2007): 68–85; Mathew Manweller, "The 'Angriest Crocodile': Information Costs, Direct Democracy Activists, and the Politicization of State Judicial Elections," *State and Local Government Review* 37(2) (2005): 86–102; Chris W. Bonneau, "What Price Justice?" Understanding Campaign Spending in State Supreme Court Elections," *State Politics and Policy Quarterly* 5(2) (Summer 2005): 107–125.

39. Austin Sarat, "Judging Trial Courts," *Journal of Politics* 39 (May 1977): 368–398.

40. Stuart Nagel, "Political Party Affiliation and Judges' Decisions," *American Political Science Association* 55 (1961): 843–851; Sidney Ulmer, "The Political Party Variable on the Michigan Supreme Court," *Journal of Public Law* 11 (1962): 352–362.

41. Paul Brace and Melinda Gann Hall, "Studying Courts Comparatively," *Political Research Quarterly* 48 (March 1995): 5–29.

42. Henry R. Glick, "Courts: Politics and the Judicial Process," in Virginia Gray and Russell L. Hanson, eds., *Politics in the American States: A Comparative Analysis*, 8th ed. (Washington, DC: CQ Press, 2004), p. 236.

43. Jerome Frank, *Law and the Modern Mind* (New York: Coward-McCann, 1930); Benjamin N. Cardozo, *The Nature of the Judicial Process* (New Haven, CT: Yale University Press, 1921); Roscoe Pound, *Justice According to Law* (New Haven, CT: Yale University Press, 1951).

44. See John Patrick Hagan, "Patterns of Activism on State Supreme Courts," *Publius* 18 (Winter 1988): 97–115.

45. John M. Scheb, Terry Bowen, and Gary Anderson, "Ideology, Role Orientations and Behavior in State Courts of Last Resort," *American Politics Quarterly* 19 (July 1991): 324–335.

46. Paul Brace, Laura Langer, and Melinda Gann Hall, "Measuring the Preferences of State Supreme Court Judges," *Journal of Politics* 62 (May 2000): 287–413.

47. Donald R. Songer and Susan J. Tabrizi, "The Religious Right in Court: The Decision Making of Christian Evangelicals in State Supreme Courts," *Journal of Politics* 61 (May 1999): 507–526.

48. Karmen Hanson, "A Pill Problem," *State Legislatures* 36 (March 2010): 22–25.

49. John Wooldredge, "State Corrections Policy," in Virginia Gray, Russell L. Hanson, and Thad Kousser, *Politics in the American States*, 10th ed. (Washington, DC: CQ Press, 2013), pp. 279–308.

50. Husna Haq, "US Crime Rate is Down: Six Key Reasons," *Christian Science Monitor*, May 24, 2010. Available at http://www.csmonitor.com/USA/2010/0524/US-crime-rate-is-down-six-key-reasons; Chris Uggen and Suzy McElrath, "Six Social Sourcies of the U.S. Crime Drop," *The Society Pages*, February 4, 2013. Available at http://thesocietypages.org/papers/crime-drop/.

51. Lauren Galek, "America's 10 Deadliest Cities 2012," *PolicyMic*, December, 2012. Available at http://www.policymic.com/articles/22686/america-s-10-deadliest-cities-2012.

52. National School Safety and Security Services, "School Related Deaths, School Shootings, and School Violence Incidents." Available at http://www.schoolsecurity.org/trends/school_violence.html.

53. Ethan Bronner, "Sentencing Ruling Reflects Rethinking on Juvenile Justice," *New York Times*, June 26, 2012.

54. U.S. Department of Justice, and Federal Bureau of Investigation, "Hate Crime Statistics 2010." Available at http://www.fbi.gov/about-us/cjis/ucr/hate-crime/2010/resources/hate-crime-2010-about-hate-crime.

55. Nathan Sandholtz, Lynn Langton, and Michale Planty, "Hate Crime Victimization, 2003–2011," *Bureau of Justice Statistics*, March 21, 2013. Available at http://bjs.gov/index.cfm?ty=pbdetail&iid=4614.

56. U.S. Bureau of Justice Statistics, *Criminal Victimization in the United States*, Annual Report (Washington, DC: U.S. Department of Justice).

57. Willaim E. Raftery, "The Quandary of Courthosue Security and public Access," *Daily Business Review*, February 25, 2013. Available at http://www.dailybusinessreview.com/PubArticleDBR.jsp?id=1202589249558&The_quandary_of_courthouse_security_and_public_access&slreturn=20130309105247.

58. Elaine B. Sharp, "Policing Urban America: A New Look at the Politics of Agency Size," *Social Science Quarterly* 87(2) (June 2006): 291–307.

59. John MacDonald and Robert J. Stokes, "Race, Social Capital, and Trust in the Police," *Urban Affairs Review* 41(1) (January 2006): 358–375.

60. National Sheriff's Association, "FAQ," available at http://www.sheriffs.org/content/faq, April 9, 2013.

61. Bureau of Labor Statistics, U.S. Department of Labor, *Occupational Outlook Handbook, 2004–05 Edition*, "Police and Detectives," available at http://www.bjs.gov/content/pub/pdf/cv08.pdf, June 21, 2005.

62. For a summary, see John J. Dilulio, Jr., "Arresting Ideas: Tougher Law Enforcement Is Driving Down Crime," *Policy Review* 74 (Fall 1995): 12–16.

63. Rasmussen Reports, "23% Think Surveillance Cameras Have Violated Their Privacy," April 26, 2013. Available at http://www.rasmussenreports.com/public_content/politics/general_politics/april_2013/23_think_surveillance_cameras_have_violated_their_privacy.

64. Jason Koebler, "Law Enforcement Blindsided by Public 'Panic' Over Drone Policy," *US News*, March 21, 2013. Available at http://www.usnews.com/news/articles/2013/03/21/law-enforcement-blindsided-by-public-panic-over-drone-privacy.

65. Rasmussen Reports, "67% Favor Limits on Drone Use," March 7, 2013. Available at http://www.rasmussen-reports.com/public_content/politics/general_politics/march_2013/67_favor_limits_on_drone_use.

66. Clearance rates are for 2011.

67. Steven W. Perry, "Prosecutors in State Courts, 2005," Bureau of Justice Statistics Bulletin, NCJ-213799, July 2006. Available at http://bjs.ojp.usdoj.gov/content/pub/pdf/psc05.pdf.

68. The following discussion relies on evidence presented by Robert A. Carp, "The Behavior of Grand Juries: Acquiescence or Justice," *Social Science Quarterly* 55 (March 1975): 853–870.

69. Bureau of Justice Statistics, "Correctional Populations in the United States, 2011." Available at http://bjs.gov/index.cfm?ty=pbdetail&iid=4537.

70. Christian Henrichson and Ruth Delaney, "The Price of Prisons: What Incarceration Costs Taxpayers," *VERA Institute of Justice, Center on Sentencing and Corrections*, July 20, 2012. Available at http://www.vera.org/sites/default/files/resources/downloads/Price_of_Prisons_updated_version_072512.pdf.

71. E. Ann Carson and William J. Sabol, "Prisoners in 2011," *Bureau of Justice Statistics*, December 2012. Available at http://bjs.gov/content/pub/pdf/p11.pdf.

72. Jeff Yates and Richard Fording, "Politics and State Punitiveness in Black and White," *Journal of Politics* 67(4) (November 2005): 1099–1121; S. Fernando Rodriguez, Theodore R. Curry, and Gang Lee, "Gender Differences in Criminal Sentencing: Do Effects Vary Across Violent, Property, and Drug Offenses?" *Social Science Quarterly* 87(2) (June 2006): 318–339.

73. John Wooldredge, "State Corrections Policy," in Virginia Gray, Russell L. Hanson, and Thad Kousser, eds., *Politics in the American States*, 10th ed. (Washington, DC: CQ Press, 2013), pp. 279–308.

74. CBS News, "The Cost of a Nation of Incarceration," April 22, 2012. Available at http://www.cbsnews.com/8301-3445_162-57418495/the-cost-of-a-nation-of-incarceration/.

75. Bureau of Justice Statistics, *Survey of State Prison Inmates, 1991.* Available at http://www.bjs.gov/index.cfm?ty=pbdetail&iid=1073.

76. John J. Dilulio, Jr., "Punishing Smarter," *Brookings Review* 7 (Summer 1989): 8.

77. Richard B. Abell, "Beyond Willie Horton: The Battle of the Prison Bulge," *Policy Review* 47 (Winter 1989): 32–35.

78. "Aged Inmates' Care Stresses State Prison Budget," *Arizona Republic,* May 9, 2005, available at http://www.tucsoncitizen.com/index.php?page=local&story_id=050805a6_prisonaging, June 22, 2005.

79. Christian Henrichson and Ruth Delaney, "The Price of Prisons: What Incarceration Costs Taxpayers," *VERA Institute of Justice, Center on Sentencing and Corrections,* July 20, 2012. Available at http://www.vera.org/sites/default/files/resources/downloads/Price_of_Prisons_updated_version_072512.pdf.

80. CBS News, "The Cost of a Nation of Incarceration," April 22, 2012. Available at http://www.cbsnews.com/8301-3445_162-57418495/the-cost-of-a-nation-of-incarceration/.

81. Annie Lowry, "True Crime Costs," *Slate,* October 21, 2010. Available at http://www.slate.com/articles/arts/everyday_economics/2010/10/true_crime_costs.single.html.

82. Angela Munoz, "U.S. Prison Population Hits All-Time High," PBS *Online NewsHour EXTRA,* available at http://www.pbs.org/newshour/extra/teachers/lessonplans/math/incarceration_story_9-05.html, June 22, 2005.

83. Natasha Lennard, "Taibbi: 'Three Strikes' Laws Are Cruel and Unusual," *Salon,* March 27, 2013. Available at http://www.salon.com/2013/03/27/taibbi_three_strikes_laws_are_cruel_and_unusual/.

84. Laura M. Maruschak and Erika Parks, "Probation and Parole in the United States, 2011," *Bureau of Justice Statistics,* November 2012. Available at http://bjs.gov/content/pub/pdf/ppus11.pdf.

85. *New York Times,* "Editorial: Keeping Parolees Out of Prison," citing a Bureau of Justice Statistics report, December 28, 2012. Available at http://www.nytimes.com/2012/12/29/opinion/keeping-parolees-out-of-prison.html?_r=0.

86. Pew Center on the States, *State of Recidivism: The Revolving Door of America's Prisons* (Washington, DC: The Pew Charitable Trusts, April 2011). Available at http://www.pewtrusts.org/uploadedFiles/wwwpewtrustsorg/Reports/sentencing_and_corrections/State_Recidivism_Revolving_Door_America_Prisons%20.pdf.

87. Death Penalty Information Center, "DPIC Summary: Innocence Protection Act of 2004," available at http://www.deathpenaltyinfo.org/article.php?scid=40&did=1234, June 22, 2005.

88. *Furman* v. *Georgia,* 408 U.S. 238 (1972).

89. *Gregg* v. *Georgia,* 428 U.S. 153 (1976).

90. *Atkins* v. *Virginia,* 536 U.S. 304 (2002).

91. *Roper* v. *Simmons,* 112 S. W. 3d 397, affirmed (2005).

92. Arline Kaplan, "When Is It 'Cruel and Unusual Punishment'? Supreme Court Bans Juvenile Death Penalty," *Psychiatric Times* 22 (May 2005), available at http://www.psychiatrictimes.com/showArticle.jhtml?articleId=164303063, June 22, 2005.

93. Kavan Peterson, "Death Penalty: Lethal Injection on Trial," stateline.org, January 17, 2007. Available at www.stateline.org/live/printable/story?contentId=171776.

94. *House* v. *Bell,* 597 U.S. (2006).

95. S. Kavan Peterson, "Death Penalty—34 States Permit Executions," Stateline.org, April 19, 2005, available at http://www.stateline.org/live/ViewPage.action?siteNodeId=136&languageId=1&contentId=25995, June 22, 2005.

CHAPTER 10

1. See David Jacobson, *Place and Belonging in America* (Baltimore: Johns Hopkins University Press, 2001); Tom Christensen and Per Laegreid, "Trust in Government: The Relative Importance of Service Satisfaction, Political Factors, and Demography," *Public Performance and Management Review* 28 (June 2005): 487–511.

2. Arizona State University, *The Phoenix Area Social Survey: Community and Environment in a Desert Metropolis* (Tempe, AZ: Center for Business Research, Center for Environmental Studies, Department of Social and Behavioral Sciences, Department of Sociology, Survey Research Laboratory, School of Planning and Landscape Architecture, March 2003), p. 3.

3. For empirical support for these speculations, see Gordon S. Black, "Conflict in the Community: A Theory of the Effect of Community Size," *American Political Science Review* 68 (September 1974): 1245–1261. See also Timothy A. Almy, "Residential Locations and Electoral Cohesion," *American Political Science Review* 67 (September 1973): 914–923, who argues that conflict is greater in communities where different social groups are residentially segregated.

4. The widely cited classic essay is Charles M. Tiebout, "The Pure Theory of Local Expenditure," *Journal of Political Economy* 64 (October 1956): 416–424.

5. David Swindell and Janet Kelly, "Performance Measurement Versus City Service Satisfaction: Intra-City Variations in Quality," *Social Science Quarterly* 86(3) (September 2005): 704–723.

6. John M. Orbell and Toru Uno, "A Theory of Neighborhood Problem Solving: Political Action versus Residential Mobility," *American Political Science Review* 66 (June 1972): 471–489; William E. Lyons and David

Lowery, "Citizen Response to Dissatisfaction in Urban Communities," *Journal of Politics* 51 (November 1989): 841–868.

7. Michigan Township Association, "Origins of Township Government," available at http://www.michigantownships.org/origin.asp, January 2002.

8. Pew Partnership, "Voices of Rural America: National Survey Results." Available at http://www.civicchange.org/pdf/voices_of_rural_america.pdf.

9. J. Edwin Benton, *Counties as Service Delivery Agents: Changing Expectations and Roles* (New York: Praeger, 2002); J. Edwin Benton et al., "Service Challenges and Governance Issues Confronting American Counties in the 21st Century: An Overview," *State and Local Government Review* 40(1) (2008): 54–68.

10. National Association of County Officials, "The History of County Government, Part I." Available at http://www.naco.org/Counties/learn/Pages/HistoryofCountyGovernmentPartI.aspx.

11. John F. Dillon, *Commentaries on the Laws of Municipal Corporations,* 5th ed. (Boston: Little, Brown, 1911), p. 448.

12. William DeSoto, Hassan Tajalli, and Cynthia Opheim, "Power, Professionalism, and Independence: Changes in the Office of the Mayor," *State and Local Government Review* 38(3) (2006): 156–164.

13. Evelina R. Moulder, "Municipal Form of Government: Trends in Structure, Responsibility, and Composition," in International City/County Management Association, eds., *The 2008 Municipal Year Book* (Washington, DC: International City/County Management Association), pp. 27–33.

14. Susan A. MacManus, "The Resurgent City Councils," in Ronald E. Weber and Paul Brace, eds., *American State and Local Politics: Directions for the 21st Century* (New York: Chatham House, 1999).

15. See Joseph F. Zimmerman, "The New England Town Meeting: Pure Democracy in Action?" *Municipal Yearbook, 1984* (Washington, DC: International City Managers' Association, 1984), pp. 102–106.

16. H. George Frederickson, Gary Alan Johnson, and Curtis Wood, "The Changing Structure of American Cities: A Study of the Diffusion of Innovation," *Public Administration Review* 64 (May/June 2004): 320 Also see Kimberly L. Nelson and James H. Svara, "Adaptation of Models Versus Variation in Form: Classifying Structures of City Government," *Urban Affairs Review* 45(4) (2010): 544–562.

17. Susan Welch and Timothy Bledsoe, "The Partisan Consequences of Nonpartisan Elections," *American Journal of Political Science* 30 (February 1986): 128–139.

18. John J. Kirlen, "Electoral Conflict and Democracy in Cities," *Journal of Politics* 37 (February 1975): 262–269.

19. Evelina R. Moulder, "Municipal Form of Government: Trends in Structure, Responsibility, and Composition," in International City/County Management Association, eds., *The 2008 Municipal Year Book* (Washington, DC: International City/County Management Association), pp. 27–33.

20. This section Is from Susan A. MacManus, "The Resurgent City Councils," in Ronald E. Weber and Paul Brace, eds., *American State and Local Politics: Directions for the 21st Century* (New York: Chatham House, 1999)

21. Richard Engstrom and Michael McDonald, "The Election of Blacks to City Councils," *American Political Science Review* 75 (June 1981): 344–355; Susan Welch, "The Impact of At-Large Elections on the Representation of Blacks and Hispanics," *Journal of Politics* 52 (November 1990): 1050–1057.

22. Susan A. MacManus and Charles S. Bullock, III. "Women and Racial/Ethnic Minorities in Mayoral and Council Positions," in *Municipal Year Book, 1993* (Washington, DC: International City/County Management Association, 1993), pp. 57–69.

23. *Mobile v. Bolden,* 446 U.S. 55 (1980).

24. For a discussion of federal court applications of these tests, see Susan A. MacManus and Charles S. Bullock, "Racial Representation Issues," *PS: Political Science and Politics* 18 (Fall 1985): 759–769.

25. *Thornburgh v. Gingles,* 106 S. Ct. 2752 (1986).

26. Edward Still and Robert Richie, *Alternative Electoral Systems as Voting Rights Remedies* (Washington, DC: Center for Voting and Democracy, 1995.)

27. Douglas J. Amy, *Behind the Ballot Box: A Citizen's Guide to Voting Systems* (Westport, CT: Praeger, 2000). See Chapter 5, "Semiproportional Voting Systems."

28. Shaun Bowler, David Brockington, and Todd Donovan, "Election Systems and Voter Turnout: Experiments in the United States," *Journal of Politics* 63 (August 2001): 902–915.

29. Albert K. Karnig, "Black Representation on City Councils," *Urban Affairs Quarterly* 12 (December 1976): 223–243; Thomas R. Dye and Theodore P. Robinson, "Reformism and Black Representation on City Councils," *Social Science Quarterly* 59 (June 1978): 133–141.

30. Susan Welch, "The Impact of At-Large Districts on the Representation of Blacks and Hispanics," *Journal of Politics* 52 (November 1990): 1050–1076. See also Charles S. Bullock and Susan A. MacManus, "Municipal Electoral Structure and the Election of Councilwomen," *Journal of Politics* 53 (February 1991): 75–89.

31. Ibid, p. 1072.

32. Albert Nylander, "National Superintendent Survey 2008" and "National Teacher Survey 2009," Superintendent Survey. Available at http://www.oldham.k12.ky.us/files/reports/National_Surveys/NationalSuperintendentSurvey2008FinalResults.pdf. Teacher Survey. Available at http://www.oldham.kyschools.us/files/reports/National_Surveys/NationalTeacherSurveyonSchoolBoards2009FinalResults.pdf.

33. Frederick M. Hess and Olivia Meeks, *School Boards Circa 2010: Governance in the Accountability Era* (Alexandria, VA: The National School Boards Association, The Thomas B. Fordham Institute, and the Iowa School Boards Foundation, 2010)

34. Education Commission of the States, "Local Superintendents," available at http://mb2.ecs.org/reports/Report.aspx?id=171, March 15, 2010.

35. Elizabeth McDonald, "Superindent Pay at Top of the Class," *FOXBusiness*, March 20, 2013. Available at http://www.foxbusiness.com/government/2013/03/19/superintendent-pay-at-top-class/.

36. Albert Nylander, "National Superintendent Survey 2008" and "National Teacher Survey 2009," Superintendent Survey. Available at http://www.oldham.k12.ky.us/files/reports/National_Surveys/NationalSuperintendentSurvey2008FinalResults.pdf. Teacher Survey. Available at http://www.oldham.kyschools.us/files/reports/National_Surveys/NationalTeacherSurveyonSchoolBoards2009FinalResults.pdf.

37. C. Cryss Brunner and Yon-Lyun Kim, "Are Women Prepared to be School Superintendents? An Essay on the Myths and Misunderstandings," *Journal of Research on Leadership Education* 5(8) (2010): 276–309.

CHAPTER 11

1. The town was Inglis, Florida. The proclamation read: "Be it known from this day forward that Satan, ruler of darkness, giver of evil, destroyer of what is good and just, is not now, nor ever again will be, a part of this town of Inglis..." Todd Lewan, Associated Press, "A Town Asks Itself: Did Banning Satan Make a Difference?," available at www.jacksonville.com/tu-online/apnews/stories/031304/D819HN580.shtml, March 13, 2004.

2. Arguments over value of direct citizen participation are as old as democracy itself. See "Direct versus Representative Democracy" in Chapter 2. And see Samuel P. Huntington, *American Politics: The Promise of Disharmony* (Cambridge, MA: Harvard University Press, 1981); Jeffrey M. Berry, Kent E. Portney, and Ken Thompson, *The Rebirth of Urban Democracy* (Washington, DC: Brookings Institution, 1993).

3. Carole Hamner, "New Survey Dispels Myths on Citizen Engagement," in Pew Partnership for Civic Change, Campaign Study Group, eds., *Ready, Willing, and Able: Citizens Working for Change* (Charlottesville, VA: Pew Partnership for Civic Change, 2001).

4. These uniquenesses of local elections are discussed in detail in Karen M. Kauffmann, *The Urban Voter: Group Conflict and Mayoral Voting Behavior in American Cities* (Ann Arbor: University of Michigan Press, 2004).

5. Zoltan L. Hajnal and Paul G. Lewis, "Municipal Institutions and Voter Turnout in Local Elections," *Urban Affairs Review* 38 (May 2003): 645–668.

6. Karen M. Kauffmann, *The Urban Voter: Group Conflict and Mayoral Voting Behavior in American Cities* (Ann Arbor: University of Michigan Press, 2004); Elaine Sharp, "Political Participation in Cities," in John P. Pelissero, ed., *Cities, Politics, and Policy: A Comparative Analysis* (Washington, DC: CQ Press, 2003), pp. 68–96.

7. Zoltan L. Hajnal and Paul G. Lewis, "Municipal Institutions and Voter Turnout in Local Elections," *Urban Affairs Review* 38 (May 2003): 645–668.

8. ICMA Municipal Form of Government Survey 2011 Summary. Available at http://icma.org/en/results/home/surveying/survey_research/survey_results.

9. Jennifer Hamilton, "Stripper Mayor Faces Stripping: Exposure Charges Pose Challenge to Stripper-Turned-Mayor," abcNEWS.com, December 4, 2001.

10. Early arguments over public-regardingness are found in James Q. Wilson and Edward C. Banfield, "Public Regardingness as a Value Premise in Voting Behavior," *American Political Science Review* 58 (December 1964): 876–887; Roger Durand, "Ethnicity, Public-Regardingness and Referenda Voting," *Midwest Journal of Political Science* 16 (May 1972): 259–268. More recent evidence that wealth and income lead citizens to be more supportive of public services is found in Evel Elliot, James Regens, and Barry Sheldon, "Exploring Variation in Public Support for Environmental Protection," *Social Science Quarterly* 76 (March 1995): 41–52.

11. Herbert C. Alexander, *Reform and Reality: The Financing of State and Local Campaigns* (New York: Twentieth Century Fund Press, 1991).

12. Timothy B. Krebs and David B. Holian, "Media and Momentum: Strategic Contributing in a Big-City Mayoral Election," *Urban Affairs Review* 40 (May 2005): 614–633.

13. Arnold Fleischmann and Lana Stein, "Campaign Contributions in Local Elections," *Political Research Quarterly* 51 (September 1998): 673–690.

14. John Metcalfe, "The Skyrocketing Costs of Running for Mayor of a Major U.S. City," *The Atlantic Cities*, November 6, 2012. Available at http://www.theatlantic-cities.com/politics/2012/11/skyrocketing-costs-running-mayor-major-us-city/3814/.

15. Timothy B. Krebs, "Urban Interests and Campaign Contributions: Evidence from Los Angeles," *Journal of Urban Affairs* 27(2) (2005): 165–176.

16. Frank Newport, "Democrats Racially Diverse; Republicans Mostly White," *Gallup, Inc.*, February 8, 2013. Available at http://www.gallup.com/poll/160373/democrats-racially-diverse-republicans-mostly-white.aspx.

17. See Raphael Sonenshein, "Bi-Racial Coalition Politics in Los Angeles," *PS: Political Science and Politics* 19 (September 1986): 582–590; "The Dynamics of Bi-Racial Coalitions," *Western Political Quarterly* 42 (June 1989): 333–353; Rufus Browning, Dale Rogers Marshall, and David Tabb, *Protest Is Not Enough* (Berkeley: University of California Press, 1984). The data reported in this paragraph are from a report titled "What Ethnic Americans Really Think: The Zogby Culture Polls." The survey was conducted by Zogby International and sponsored by the National Italian American Foundation and the Center for Study of Culture and Values at Catholic University of America. The results were reported in "Race and Politics," *American Demographics* 23 (August 2001): 11–13 See also Rufus P. Browning, Dale Rogers Marshall, and

David H. Tabb, eds., *Racial Politics in American Cities,* 2nd ed. (New York: Longman, 1997); Paula D. McClain and Joseph Stewart, Jr., *"Can We All Get Along?" Racial and Ethnic Minorities in American Politics* (Boulder, CO; Westview Press, 1998); Rufus P. Browning, Dale Rogers Marshall, and David H. Tabb, "Taken In or Just Taken? Political Incorporation of African Americans in Cities," in Richard E. Keiser and Katherine Underwood, eds., *Minority Politics at the Millennium* (New York: Garland Publishing, 2000), pp. 131–156.

18. See Paula D. McClain and Joseph Stewart, Jr., *"Can We All Get Along?" Racial and Ethnic Minorities in American Politics,* 3rd ed. (Boulder, CO: Westview Press, 2002); Rodney E. Hero, "Crossroads of Equality: Race/Ethnicity and Cities in American Democracy," *Urban Affairs Review* 40(6) (July 2005): 695–705.

19. Rodney E. Hero and Robert R. Preush, *Black-Latino Relations in U.S. National Politics: Beyond Conflict or Cooperation* (New York: Cambridge University Press, 2013).

20. Bloomberg initially ran as a Republican and won. In his second race for mayor, he ran as an independent. And in his third campaign, he ran as the nominee for both the Republican and independence parties.

21. William L. Riordan, *Plunkitt of Tammany Hall* (New York: McClure, Phillips, 1905), p. 46.

22. Ibid., p. 52.

23. Edward C. Banfield and James Q. Wilson, *City Politics* (Cambridge, MA: Harvard-MIT Press, 1963), Chapter 9.

24. See Elmer E. Cornwell, Jr., "Bosses, Machines, and Ethnic Groups," *Annals of the American Academy of Political and Social Science* 353 (May 1964): 27–39.

25. Lincoln Steffens, *Autobiography* (New York: Harcourt, Brace & World, 1931), p. 168.

26. See Richard J. Hofstadter, *The Age of Reform* (New York: Knopf, 1955); Lorin Peterson, *The Day of the Mugwump* (New York: Random House, 1961).

27. Lincoln Steffens, *The Shame of the Cities* (New York: Sagamore Press, 1957), p. 10.

28. Jim Svara, "Possible Approaches to the Model Charter Revision," *The National Civic League,* 2001; "Do We Still Need Model Charters? The Meaning and Relevance of Reform in the Twenty-First Century," *National Civic Review* 90 (Spring 2001): 19–33.

29. Roland Zullo, "Public–Private Contracting and Political Reciprocity," *Political Research Quarterly* 59(2) (June 2006): 273–281.

30. Thomas J. Gradel et al., *Corruption in Cook County: Anti-Corruption Report #3* (Chicago: University of Illinois at Chicago, Department of Political Science, and the Better Government Association, February 18, 2010).

31. Sean Richey, "The Impact of Corruption on Social Trust," *American Politics Research* 38(4) (2010): 676–690; Michael A. Genovese and Victoria A. Farrar-Myers, eds., *Corruption and American Politics* (New York: Cambria Press, 2010).

32. California Institute for Local Government, "Understanding the Basics of Public Service Ethics: Fair Process Laws and Merit-Based Decision-Making," available at www.ca-ilg.org/fairprocess, July 17, 2010.

33. Robert Wechsler, "Local Government Ethics Reform," *National Civic Review* 101(3) (Fall 2012): 26–30.

34. Liz Azyan, "Government-to-Citizen Communications: Utilising Multiple Digital Channels Effectively." Available at www.lgeoresearch.com.

35. David Campt and Matthew Freeman, "Using Keypad Polling to Make Meetings More Productive, Educational, and Participatory," *National Civic Review* 99(1) (Spring 2010): 3–11.

36. Steve Towns, "Web Bragging Rights," *Governing* 26(1) (October 2012): 72.

37. Dylan Scott, "The Trouble with Twitter," *Governing* 25(10) (July 2012): 42–46.

38. Karen Thoreson and Tracy Miller, "Tapping Technology to Connect with the Public," *Public Management* 95(11) (December 2012): 24–25.

39. Ibid, p. 24.

40. Eleonora Redaelli, "Cultural Planning in the United States: Toward Authentic Participation Using GIS," *Urban Affairs Review* 48(5) (2012): 642–669.

41. Evelina Moulder, "311 Survey: Customer Service Systems Spread to Smaller Cities and Counties," *Government Technology,* May 13, 2008. Available at www.govtech.com/gt/312912.

42. International City/County Management Association, *Citizen Surveys: How To Do Them, How To Use Them, and What They Mean,* 2nd ed. (Washington, DC: ICMA, 2000); Christine H. Roch and Theodore H. Poister, "Citizens, Accountability, and Service Satisfaction: The Influence of Expectations," *Urban Affairs Review* 41(3) (January 2006): 292–308.

43. Ricardo S. Morse, "Citizens Academies: Governments Building Capacity for Citizen Engagement," *Public Performance & Management Review* 36(1) (September 2012): 79–101.

44. Louis Ayala, "Trained for Democracy: The Differing Effects of Voluntary and Involuntary Organizations on Political Participation," *Political Research Quarterly* 53 (March 2000): 99–115; Gary M. Segura, Harry Pachon, and Nathan P. Woods, "Hispanics, Social Capital, and Civic Engagement," *National Civic Review* 90 (Spring 2001): 85–96; Tom Lando, "Public Participation in Local Government: Points of View," *National Civic Review* 88 (Summer 1999): 109–122; J. Eric Oliver, "City Size and Civic Involvement in Metropolitan America," *American Political Science Review* 94 (June 2000): 361–373.

45. For an extensive list of ways to facilitate public participation, see James L. Creighton, *The Public Participation Handbook: Making Better Decisions Through Citizen Involvement* (New York: Jossey-Bass, 2005) See also Suzanne W. Morse, *Smart Communities: How Citizens*

and Local Leaders Can Use Strategic Thinking to Build a Brighter Future (New York: Jossey-Bass, 2004).

46. Scott Hock, Sarah Anderson, and Matthew Potoski, "Invitation Phone Calls Increase Attendance at Civic Meetings: Evidence from a Field Experiment," *Public Administration Review* 73(2) (March/April 2013): 221–228.

47. Soonhee Kim and Jooho Lee, "E-Participation, Transparency, and Trust in Local Government," *Public Administration Review* 72(6) (November/December 2012): 819–828.

48. Robert G. Moore, "Religion, Race, and Gender Differences in Political Ambition," *Politics and Gender* 1(4) (December 2005): 577–596.

49. Much of the material in this section is from Susan A. MacManus, "The Resurgent City Councils," in Ronald E. Weber and Paul Brace, eds., *American State and Local Politics: Directions for the 21st Century* (New York: Chatham House, 1999), pp. 185–193.

50. Timothy Bledsoe, *Careers in City Politics: The Case for Urban Democracy* (Pittsburgh, PA: University of Pittsburgh Press, 1993); Timothy B. Krebs also notes that people are more likely to run if there is an open seat or a vulnerable incumbent in "The Political and Demographic Predictors of Candidate Emergence in City Council Elections," *Urban Affairs Review* 35 (November 1999): 279–300.

51. Susan A. MacManus, "The Resurgent City Councils," in Ronald E. Weber and Paul Brace, eds., *American State and Local Politics: Directions for the 21st Century* (New York: Chatham House, 1999), pp. 185–193.

52. James Svara, *Survey of America's City Councils* (Washington, DC: National League of Cities, 1991).

53. Rob Gurwitt, "Are City Councils a Relic of the Past?" *Governing* 16 (April 2003): 20–24.

54. Timothy B. Krebs, "The Determinants of Candidate's Vote Share and the Advantage of Incumbency in City Council Elections," *American Journal of Political Science* 42 (July 1998): 921–935.

55. See Joel Lieske, "The Political Dynamics of Urban Voting Behavior," *American Journal of Political Science* 33 (February 1989): 150–174.

56. James Svara, *Official Leadership in the City: Patterns of Conflict and Cooperation* (New York: Oxford University Press, 1990), p. 122.

57. Studies show citizens tend to contact municipal bureaucrats instead of elected officials when they are less familiar with or interested in local government. John Clayton Thomas and Julia E. Melkers, "Citizen Contacting of Municipal Officials: Choosing Between Appointed Administrators and Elected Officials," *Journal of Public Administration Research and Theory* 11(1) (2000): 51–71.

58. Leonard D. White, *The City Manager* (Chicago: University of Chicago Press, 1927).

59. See Harold A. Stone, Don K. Price, and Kathryn H. Stone, *City Manager Government in the United States* (Chicago: Public Administration Service, 1940).

60. See Timothy A. Almy, "Local-Cosmopolitanism and U.S. City Managers," *Urban Affairs Quarterly* 10 (March 1975): 243–277.

61. Alan L. Saltzstein, "City Managers and City Councils: Perceptions of the Division of Authority," *Western Political Quarterly* 27 (June 1974): 275–287.

62. David N. Ammons and Matthew J. Bosse, "Tenure of City Managers: Examining the Dual Meanings of 'Average' Tenure," *State and Local Government Review* 37(1) (2005): 61–71.

63. Barbara McCabe et al., "Turnover Among City Managers: The Role of Political and Economic Change," *Public Administration Review* 68(2): 380–386; William J. Pammer, Jr., Herbert A. Marlowe, Jr., Joseph G. Jarret, and Jack L. Dustin, "Managing Conflict and Building Conflict in Council-Manager Cities: Insights on Establishing a Resolution Framework," *State and Local Government Review* 31 (Fall 1999): 202–213; James B. Kaatz, P. Edward French, and Hazel Prentiss-Cooper, "City Council Conflict as a Cause of Psychological Burnout and Voluntary Turnover Among City Managers," *State and Local Government Review* 31 (Fall 1999): 162–172.

64. Doyle W. Buckwalter and Robert J. Parsons, "Local City Managers' Career Paths: Which Way to the Top?" in International City/County Management Association, eds., *The 2000 Municipal Year Book* (Washington, DC: ICMA, 2000), pp. 20–21.

65. Jeffrey L. Pressman, "Preconditions of Mayoral Leadership," *American Political Science Review* 66 (June 1972): 511–524.

66. See Melvin G. Holli, "American Mayors: The Best and the Worst Since 1960," *Social Science Quarterly* 78 (March 1997): 149–157. The five best: Richard J. Daley (Chicago, 1955–76); Henry Cisneros (San Antonio, 1981–89); Tom Bradley (Los Angeles, 1973–93); Dianne Feinstein (San Francisco, 1978–87); and Andrew Young (Atlanta, 1982–90).

67. Haya El Nasser, "Few Big Names Run Big Cities Now," *USA Today,* March 24, 2004, p. 3A.

68. Neil Kraus and Todd Swanstrom, "The Continuing Significance of Race: Black and Hispanic Mayors, 1967–1999," paper presented at the annual meeting of the American Political Science Association, August 30–September 2, 2001; Nicholas O. Alozie, "The Promise of Urban Democracy: Big-City Black Mayoral Service in the Early 1990s," *Urban Affairs Review* 35 (January 2000): 422–434.

69. David A. Bositis, *Black Elected Officials: A Statistical Summary 2001* (Washington, DC: The Joint Center for Political and Economic Studies, 2003).

70. Melissa J. Marshall and Anirudh V. S. Ruhil, "The Pomp of Power: Black Mayoralties in Urban America," *Social Science Quarterly* 87 (December 2006): 828–850.

71. David Haywood Metz and Katherine Tate, "The Color of Urban Campaigns," in Paul E. Peterson, ed., *Classifying by Race* (Washington, DC: The Brookings Institution, 1995), pp. 262–277.

72. Robert M. Stein, Stacey G. Ulbig, and Stephanie Shirley Post, "Voting for Minority Candidates in Multiracial/Multiethnic Communities," *Urban Affairs Review* 41(2) (November 2005): 157–181.

73. Baodong Liu, "Whites as a Minority and the New Racial Coalition in New Orleans and Memphis," *PS: Political Science and Politics* 39(1) (January 2006): 69–76.

74. Susan Welch, "The Impact of At-Large Elections on the Representation of Blacks and Hispanics," *Journal of Politics* 52 (November 1990): 1050–1076.

75. See Rufus P. Browning, Dale Rodgers Marshall, and David H. Tabb, *Protest Is Not Enough* (Berkeley: University of California Press, 1984); Rodney E. Hero, "Hispanics in Urban Government," *Western Political Quarterly* 43 (June 1990): 403–414; Jerry L. Polinard, Robert D. Wrinkle, and Thomas Longovia, "The Impact of District Elections on the Mexican American Community," *Social Science Quarterly* 72 (September 1991): 609–614.

76. Charles S. Bullock, III, "The Opening Up of State and Local Election Processes," in Ronald E. Weber and Paul Brace, eds., *American State and Local Politics: Directions for the 21st Century* (New York: Chatham House, 1999), pp. 220–221.

77. Kim Geron and James S. Lai, "Transforming Ethnic Politics: A Comparative Analysis of Electoral Support for and Policy Priorities of Asian American and Latino Elected Officials," paper presented at the annual meeting of the American Political Science Association, August 30–September 2, 2001.

78. Ibid., p. 7.

79. Ibid.

80. Thomas R. Dye and James Renick, "Political Power and City Jobs," *Social Science Quarterly* 62 (September 1981): 475–486. See also Matthew Hutchins and Lee Sigelman, "Black Employment in State and Local Government," *Social Science Quarterly* 62 (March 1981): 79–87.

81. For an argument that black and Hispanic mayors do not increase minority city employment, but that black and Hispanic council members do so, see Brinck Kerr and Kenneth Mladenka, "Does Politics Matter?" *American Journal of Political Science* 38 (November 1994): 918–943.

82. Grace Hall Saltzstein, "Black Mayors and Police Policies," *Journal of Politics* 51 (August 1989): 525–544.

83. Daniel J. Hopkins and Katherine T. McCabe, "After It's Too Late: Estimating the Policy Impacts of Black Mayoralties in U.S. Cities," *American Politics Review* 40(4) (July 2012): 665–700.

84. Susan E. Howell and Huey L. Perry, "Black Mayors/White Mayors: Explaining Their Approval," *Public Opinion Quarterly* 68 (Spring 2004): 57–80.

85. Rufus P. Browning, Dale Rodgers Marshall, and David H. Tabb, *Protest Is Not Enough* (Berkeley: University of California Press, 1984), p. 41.

86. Center for American Women and Politics, "Women Mayors in U.S. Cities 2012: CAWP Fact Sheet," *CAWP*, 2013. Available at http://www.cawp.rutgers.edu/fast_facts/levels_of_office/Local-WomenMayors.php.

87. Center for the American Woman in Politics, Eagleton Institute of Politics, Rutgers University, 1998.

88. Richard L. Clark, Charles J. Beacham, Jr., *Local Perspectives: A Report from the National Survey of County Elected Officials, 2008* (Athens, GA: National Center for the Study of Counties, University of Georgia, July 2008).

89. Ruth B. Mandel, *In the Running: The New Woman Candidate* (New Haven, CT: Ticknor and Fields, 1981), pp. 63–97.

90. Robert Darcy, Susan Welch, and Janet Clark, *Women, Elections, and Representation,* 2nd ed. (New York: Longman, 1994).

91. Linda L. M. Bennett and Stephen E. Bennett, "Changing Views About Gender Equality in Politics: Gradual Change and Lingering Doubts," in Lois Lovelace Duke, ed., *Women and Politics: Have the Outsiders Become Insiders?* 2nd ed. (Englewood Cliffs, NJ: Prentice-Hall, 1996), p. 38.

92. Bositis, *Black Elected Officials: A Statistical Summary 2001;* Christine Marie Sierra, et al., "Elected Officials of Color in the U.S.: A Portrait of Today's Leaders," *The Gender and Multi-Cultural Leadership Project,* November 7, 2007. Available at gmcl.org.

93. Melissa Deckman, "Gender Differences in the Decision to Run for School Board," *American Politics Research* 35(4) (July 2007): 541–563.

94. See James Svara, "Council Profile: More Diversity, Demands, and Frustration," *Nation's Cities Weekly* 14 (November 18, 1991): 4; Susan Adams Beck, "Rethinking Municipal Governance: Gender Distinctions on Local Councils," in Debra L. Dodson, ed., *Gender and Policymaking: Studies of Women in Office* (New Brunswick, NJ: Center for the American Women and Politics, 1991), p. 103.

95. Christopher A. Cooper, Anthony J. Nownes, and Steven Roberts, "Perceptions of Power: Interest Groups in Local Politics," *State and Local Government Review* 37(3) (2005): 206–216.

96. Paul A. Djupe and Christopher P. Gilbert, "The Resourceful Believer: Generating Civic Skills in Church," *Journal of Politics* 68(1) (February 2006): 116–127.

97. Elaine B. Sharp, "Culture, Institutions, and Urban Officials' Responses to Morality Issues," *Political Research Quarterly* 55 (December 2002): 861–884.

98. Pew Partnership for Civic Change, *Ready, Willing, and Able: Citizens Working for Change* (Charlottesville, VA: Pew Partnership for Civic Change, 2001).

CHAPTER 12

1. See John Bollens and Henry Schmandt, *The Metropolis* (New York: Harper & Row, 1985).

2. U.S. Conference of Mayors, *U.S. Metro Economies: Outlook—Gross Metropolitan Product, and Critical Role*

of Transportation Infrastructure (Washington, DC, July 2012). Available at http://usmayors.org/metroeconomies/0712/FullReport.pdf.

3. William H. Frey, "Micro Melting Pots," *American Demographics* 23 (June 2001): 21–23.

4. Jennifer S. Vey, "Restoring Prosperity: The State Role in Revitalizing America's Older Industrial Cities," *The Brookings Institution,* May 2007. Available at http://www.brookings.edu/research/reports/2007/05/metropolitanpolicy-vey.

5. William H. Lucy and David L. Phillips, *Suburbs and the Census: Patterns of Growth and Decline* (Washington, DC: The Brookings Institution Center on Urban and Metropolitan Policy, December 2001), Survey Series, p. 1.

6. Lewis Mumford, *The City in History* (New York: Harcourt, Brace, & World, 1961), p. 34.

7. Elizabeth Kneebone, *Job Sprawl Revisited: The Changing Geography of Metropolitan Employment* (Washington, DC: The Brookings Institution, April 2009).

8. Robert E. Land and Jennifer LeFurgy, *Boomburbs: The Rise of America's Accidental Cities* (Washington, DC: Brookings Institution Press, 2007).

9. Robert E. Lang and Patrick A. Simmons, " 'Boomburbs': The Emergence of Large, Fast Growing Suburban Cities in the United States," Fannie Mae Foundation Census Note 06 (June 2001).

10. Robert Puentes and David Warren, *One-Fifth of America: A Comprehensive Guide to America's First Suburbs* (Washington, DC: The Brookings Institution, February 2006), p. 1.

11. Metropolitan Policy Program, *State of Metropolitan America: On the Front Lines of Demographic Transformation* (Washington, DC: The Brookings Institution, 2010). Available at http://www.brookings.edu/~/media/Files/Programs/Metro/state_of_metro_america/metro_america_report.pdf.

12. Richard Child Hill, "Separate and Unequal: Government Inequality in the Metropolis," *American Political Science Review* 68 (December 1974): 1557–1568.

13. Kenneth Jackson, *Crabgrass Frontier: The Suburbanization of the United States* (New York: Oxford University Press, 1985).

14. Margaret Weir, Harold Wolman, and Todd Swanstrom, "The Calculus of Coalitions: Cities, Suburbs, and the Metropolitan Agenda.*Urban Affairs Review* 40(6) (July 2005): 730–760.

15. Jason C. Booza, Jackie Cutsinger, and George Galster, *Where Did They Go? The Decline of Middle-Income Neighborhoods in Metropolitan America* (Washington, DC: The Brookings Institution, June 2006).

16. Edward L. Glaeser and Jacob L. Vigdor, *Racial Segregation in the 2000 Census: Promising News* (Washington, DC: The Brookings Institution, April 2001).

18. Metropolitan Policy Program, *State of Metropolitan America: On the Front Lines of Demographic*

Transformation (Washington, DC: The Brookings Institution, 2010). Available at http://www.brookings.edu/~/media/Files/Programs/Metro/state_of_metro_america/metro_america_report.pdf.

19. William H. Frey, *Melting Pot Suburbs: A Census 2000 Study of Suburban Diversity* (Washington, DC: The Brookings Institution Center on Urban and Metropolitan Policy, Census 2000 Series, June 2001).

20. Peter Dreier, "How the Media Compound Urban Problems," *Journal of Urban Affairs* 27(2) (2005): 193–194.

21. Richard Florida, "The Fading Differentiation Between City and Suburb," *Urban Land,* January 2013. Available at http://urbanland.uli.org/Articles/2013/Jan/FloridaSuburbs.

22. Bruce Katz and Scott Bernstein, "The New Metropolitan Agenda," *Brookings Review* 16 (Fall 1998): 5.

23. Christine Todd Whitman, "The Metropolitan Challenge," *Brookings Review* 16 (Fall 1998): 3.

24. See Anthony Downs, "How America's Cities Are Growing," *Brookings Review* 16 (Fall 1998): 8.

25. Wendell Cox, "US Suburbs Approaching Jobs-Housing Balance," Newgeography.com, April 12, 2013.

26. Robert Johnson, "Why 'New Urbanism' Isn't for Everyone," *New York Times,* February 20, 2005.

27. Richard Florida, "The Fading Differentiation Between City and Suburb," *Urban Land,* January 2013. Available at http://urbanland.uli.org/Articles/2013/Jan/Florida-Suburbs.

28. For other criticisms, see John Carlisle, *The Campaign Against Urban Sprawl: Declaring War on the American Dream* (Washington, DC: National Center for Public Policy Research, report #239, April 1999).

29. Roger B. Parks and Ronald J. Oakerson, "Regionalism, Localism, and Metropolitan Governance: Suggestions from the Research Program on Local Public Economies," *State and Local Government Review* 32 (Fall 2000): 169–179. See also Donald F. Norris, "Whither Metropolitan Governance?" *Urban Affairs Review* 36 (March 2001): 532–550; David Lowery, "A Transaction Costs Model of Metropolitan Governance: Allocation Versus Redistribution in Urban America," *Journal of Public Administration Research and Theory* 10 (January 2000): 49–78.

30. John Harrigan, *Political Change in the Metropolis* (Boston: Little, Brown, 1985).

31. However, see Arthur C. Nelson and Kathryn A. Foster, "Metropolitan Governance Structure and Income Growth," *Journal of Urban Affairs* 21(3) (1999): 309–324.

32. Chuck Abernathy, "Practical Strategies for Consolidation," *Public Management* 94(9) (October 2012): 20–24.

33. Arthur C. Nelson and Robert E. Lang, *Megapolitan America: A New Vision for Understanding America's Metropolitan Geography* (Washington, DC: Planners Press, 2011); Michael Abels, "Managing Through

Collaborative Networks: A Twenty-First Century Mandate for Local Government," *State and Local Government Review* 44(1S) (2013): 29S–43S.

34. For an excellent analysis of the political values of scholars who study urban problems, see Brett W. Hawkins and Stephen L. Percy, "On Anti-Suburban Orthodoxy," *Social Science Quarterly* 72 (September 1991): 478–490.

35. For a good discussion of this view, see Stan Humphries, "Who's Afraid of the Big, Bad Firm: The Impact of Economic Scale on Political Participation," *American Journal of Political Science* 45 (July 2001): 678–699; for a somewhat different view, see Avery M. Guest, "The Mediate Community: The Nature of Local and Extralocal Ties Within the Metropolis," *Urban Affairs Review* 35 (May 2000): 603–627.

36. Charles Tiebout, "A Pure Theory of Local Expenditures," *Journal of Political Economy* 64 (October 1956): 416–424.

37. John C. Bollens and Henry J Schmandt, *The Metropolis: Its People, Politics and Economic Life* (New York: Harper & Row, 1982).

38. See Barrett A. Lee, "The Urban Unease Revisited: Perceptions of Local Satisfaction Among Metropolitan Residents," *Social Science Quarterly* 62 (December 1987): 611–629; Craig St. John and Frieda Clark, "Race and Social Class Differences in the Characteristics Desired in Residential Neighborhoods," *Social Science Quarterly* 65 (September 1984): 803–813.

39. Jered B. Carr and Richard C. Feoick, "State Annexation 'Constraints' and the Frequency of Municipal Annexation," *Political Research Quarterly* 54 (June 2001): 459–470.

40. Mary Edwards, "Annexation: A 'Winner-Take-All' Process?" *State and Local Government Review* 31 (Fall 1999): 221–231.

41. See Arnold Fleischmann, "The Politics of Annexation," *Social Science Quarterly* 67 (March 1986): 128–141; Gary J. Miller, *Cities by Contract: The Politics of Municipal Incorporation* (Cambridge, MA: MIT Press, 1981).

42. John A. Powell, "Addressing Regional Dilemmas for Minority Communities," Chapter 8 in Bruce Katz, ed., *Reflections on Regionalism* (Washington, DC: The Brookings Institution, 2000).

43. See Brett W. Hawkins and Rebecca M. Hendrick, "Do County Governments Reinforce City–Suburban Inequalities?" *Social Science Quarterly* 25 (December 1994): 755–771.

44. Mark Funkhouser, "Cities, Counties and the Urge to Merge," *Governing* 26(1) (October 2012): 74.

45. Jacqueline J. Byers, National Association of Counties, "City County Consolidation Proposals County," 2010 Also see Rae W. Archibald and Sally Sleeper, *Government Consolidation and Economic Development in Allegheny County and the City of Pittsburgh* (Santa Monica, CA: The RAND Corporation, 2008). Available at www.rand.org.

46. Neal R. Pierce, "Louisville Votes Merger—First Since Indy in 1969," *County News Online,* National Association of Counties, December 18, 2000, p. 32 Also see J. Edwin Benton and Darwin Gamble, "City-County Consolidation and Economies of Scale: Evidence from a Time Series Analysis in Jacksonville, Florida," *Social Science Quarterly* 65 (March 1985): 190–198.

47. See Mark S. Rosentraub, "City–County Consolidation and the Rebuilding of Image: The Fiscal Lessons from Indianapolis's UniGov Program," *State and Local Government Review* 32 (Fall 2000): 180–191; Timothy D. Mead, "Governing Charlotte-Mecklenburg," *State and Local Government Review* 32 (Fall 2000): 192–197; Arnold Fleischmann, "Regionalism and City–County Consolidation in Small Metro Areas," *State and Local Government Review* 32 (Fall 2000): 213–226; Jered B. Carr, Sang-Seok Bae, and Wenjue Lu, "City-County Government and Promises of Economic Development: A Tale of Two Cities," *State and Local Government Review* 38(3) (2006): 131–141.

48. Jered B. Carr, "Local Government Autonomy and State Reliance on Special District Governments: A Reassessment," *Political Research Quarterly* 59 (September 2006): 481–492.

49. For an excellent overview of the role of state rules regarding special districts, see Barbara Coyle McCabe, "Special-District Formation Among the States," *State and Local Government Review* 32 (Spring 2000): 121–131.

50. David K. Hamilton, "Organizing Government Structure and Governance Functions in Metropolitan Areas in Response to Growth and Change: A Critical Overview," *Journal of Urban Affairs* 22(1) (2000): 65–84.

51. Scott L. Minkoff, "From Competition to Cooperation: A Dyadic Approach to Interlocal Developmental Agreements," *American Politics Research* 41(2) (March 2013): 261–297.

52. James H. Seroka, "City–County Consolidation: Gaining Perspective on the Limits of Our Understanding," *State and Local Government Review* 37(1) (2005): 75. The essay reviewed two edited volumes on city–county consolidation: Suzanne M. Leland and Kurt Thurmaier, eds., *Case Studies of City–County Consolidation: Reshaping the Local Government Landscape* (Armonk, NY: M.E. Sharpe, 2004); Jered Carr and Richard Feiock, eds., *City–County Consolidation and Its Alternatives: Reshaping the Local Government Landscape* (Armonk, NY: M.E. Sharpe, 2004).

53. Laura A. Reese, "Same Governance, Different Day: Does Metropolitan Reorganization Make a Difference?" *Review of Policy Research* 21(4) (2004): 608 Also see David N. Ammons, Karl W. Smith, and Carl W. Stenberg," The Future of Local Government: will Current Stresses Bring Major, Permanent Changes?" *State and Local Government Review* 44(1S) (2013): 64S–75S.

54. William R. Potapchuk, "Building an Infrastructure of Community Collaboration," *National Civic Review* 88 (Fall 1999): 165.

55. Donald F. Norris, "Whither Metropolitan Governance?" *Urban Affairs Review* 36 (March 2001): 532–550.

56. For an excellent overview of the rise of regionalism, see entire issue of *State and Local Government Review* 32 (Fall 2000), which is a symposium on new regionalism and its policy agenda edited by H.V. Savitch and Ronald K. Vogel.

CHAPTER 13

1. Gaetano Mosca, *The Ruling Class* (New York: McGraw-Hill, 1939), p. 50.

2. Ibid., p. 51.

3. Robert Michels, *Political Parties* (Glencoe, IL: The Free Press, 1949).

4. Robert S. Lynd and Helen M. Lynd, *Middletown* (New York: Harcourt Brace & World, 1929); *Middletown in Transition* (New York: Harcourt Brace & World, 1937). Other classic community studies include W. Lloyd Warner et al., *Democracy in Jonesville* (New York: Harper & Row, 1949); August B. Hollingshead, *Elmtown's Youth* (New York: John Wiley, 1949).

5. The "X family," never identified in the Lynds' books, was actually the Ball family, glass manufacturers. As late as 1975 the Ball family exercised a controlling influence over the Ball Corporation, Ball Brothers Foundation, Ball Memorial Hospital, Muncie Aviation Corp., and Muncie Airport, Inc.; and E. F. Ball served as a director of American National Bank and Trust of Muncie, Borg-Warner Corp., Indiana Bell Telephone Co., Merchants National Bank of Muncie, and Wabash College. Ball State University in Muncie is named for the family.

6. Floyd Hunter, *Community Power Structure* (Chapel Hill: University of North Carolina Press, 1953).

7. Aaron Wildavsky, *Leadership in a Small Town* (Totowa, NJ: Bedminster Press, 1964), p. 8.

8. See Harvey Molotch, "The City as Growth Machine," *American Journal of Sociology* 82 (September 1976): 309–330; "Capital and Neighborhood in the United States," *Urban Affairs Quarterly* 14 (March 1979): 289–312.

9. Paul E. Peterson, *City Limits* (Chicago: University of Chicago Press, 1981), p. 20.

10. Ibid., p. 23.

11. Ibid., p. 29.

12. For a parallel argument, see Heywood T. Sanders and Clarence N. Stone, "Developmental Politics Reconsidered," *Urban Affairs Quarterly* 22 (June 1987): 521–539; Mark Schneider, "Undermining the Growth Machine," *Journal of Politics* 54 (February 1992): 214–230.

13. Pietro S. Nivola, *Laws of the Landscape: How Policies Shape Cities in Europe and America* (Washington, DC: Brookings Institution Press, 1999).

14. See Kent E. Portney, "Allaying the NIMBY Syndrome," *Hazardous Waste* 1 (1984): 411–421; "Coping in the Age of NIMBY," *New York Times,* June 19, 1988.

15. See publications on smart growth at the EcoOutlet, available at http://www.ecoiq.com/books/index-old.html, November 8, 2013.

16. Robert W. Wassmer and Edward L. Lascher, Jr., "Who Supports Local Growth and Regional Planning to Deal with Its Consequences?" *Urban Affairs Review* 41(5) (May 2006): 621–645.

17. See Todd Donovan and Max Neiman, "Local Growth Control Policy and Changes in Community Characteristics," *Social Science Quarterly* 76 (December 1995): 780–793.

18. For discussions of why suburban communities adopt growth controls, see Mark Baldasarre, *Trouble in Paradise* (New York: Columbia University Press, 1986); John R. Logan and Min Zhou, "The Adoption of Growth Controls in Suburban Communities," *Social Science Quarterly* 71 (March 1990): 118–129.

19. Andrew Haughwout, Richard Peach, and Joseph Tracy, "The Homeownership Gap," *Current Issues in Economics and Finance* 16(5) (2010): 1–11. Available at http://www.newyorkfed.org/research/current_issues/ci16-5.pdf.

20. See Anthony J. Catanese and James C. Snyder, *Urban Planning,* 2nd ed. (New York: McGraw Hill, 1988).

21. American Institute of Planners, *AIP Planning Policies* (Washington, DC: Author, 1977).

22. Rayman Mohamed, "The Economics of Conservation Subdivisions: Price Premiums, Improvement Costs, and Absorption Rates," *Urban Affairs Review* 41(3) (January 2006): 376–399.

23. See Arnold Fleischmann and Carol A. Pierannunzi, "Citizens, Development Interests, and Local Land-Use Regulation," *Journal of Politics* 52 (August 1990): 838–853.

24. Anthony Downs, "The Future of U.S. Ground Transportation from 2000 to 2020," testimony to the Subcommittee on Highways and Transit of the Committee on Transportation and Infrastructure, U.S. House of Representatives, March 21, 2001.

25. See Alan Ehrenhalt, "The Trouble with Zoning," *Governing* 11 (February 1998): 28–34.

26. For a good overview of the legal basis for these fees, see Bruce W. Bringardner, "Exactions, Impact Fees, and Dedications: National and Texas Law After *Dolan* and *Del Monte Dunes,*" *The Urban Lawyer* 32 (Summer 2000): 561–585.

27. Susan Fainstein, "New Directions in Planning Theory," *Urban Affairs Review* 35 (March 2000): 451–478.

28. Craig Malin, "Perspectives on Urban Sustainability: Efficiency, Diversity, Connectivity, and Restoration Define Core Commitments," *Public Management* 92(7) (2010): 20–23.

29. John Fitzgerald, *Emerald Cities: Urban Sustainability and Economic Development* (New York: Oxford University Press, 2010).

30. Ibid.

31. XiaoHu Wang, Christoper V. Hawkins, and Nick Lebredo, "Capacity to Sustain Sustainability: A Study of U.S. Cities," *Public Administration Review* 72(6) (November/December 2012): 841–853.

32. "Goal: Make Homes More Resistant to Natural Disasters," HousingPolicy.org. Available at www.housingpolicy.org/toolbox/straegy/policies/rehab_practices.html.

33. *Village of Euclid, Ohio* v. *Amber Realty Company,* 272 U.S. 365 (1926).

34. *Berman* v. *Parker,* 348 U.S. 26 (1954).

35. *Lucas* v. *South Carolina Coastal Council,* 112 Sup.Ct. 2886 (1992).

36. *Dolan* v. *City of Tigard* (1994).

37. *Kelo* v. *City of New London,* June 23, 2005.

38. Jon C. Teaford, "Urban Renewal and Its Aftermath," *Housing Policy Debate* 11(2) (2000): 443–465.

39. U.S. Department of Housing and Urban Development, "Community Development Block Grant (CDBG) Entitlement Communities Program,"www.hud.gov, February 4, 2002.

40. Ibid.

41. Spencer M. Cowan, William Roh, and Esmail Baku, "Factors Influencing the Performance of Community Development Corporations,"*Journal of Urban Affairs* 21(3) (1999): 325.

42. Marion G. Boarnet, "Enterprise Zones and Job Creation: Linking Evaluation and Practice," *Economic Development Quarterly* 15 (August 2001): 242–254; Laura Langer, "The Consequences of State Economic Development Strategies on Income Distribution in the American States, 1976–1994," *American Politics Research* 29 (July 2001): 392–415.

43. Robert C. Turner and Mark K. Cassell, "When Do States Pursue Targeted Economic Development Policies? The Adoption and Expansion of State Enterprise Zone Programs," *Social Science Quarterly* 88(1) (March 2007): 86–103.

44. Michael Greenberg, Karen Lowrie, Laura Solitare, and Latoya Duncan, "Brownfields, Toads, and the Struggle for Neighborhood Redevelopment: A Case Study of the State of New Jersey," *Urban Affairs Review* 35 (May 2000): 717–718. For other studies of the vacant land problem, see John Accordino and Gary T. Johnson, "Addressing the Vacant and Abandoned Property Problem," *Journal of Urban Affairs* 22(3) (2000): 301–315; Ann O'M. Bowman and Michael A. Pagano, "Transforming America's Cities: Policies and Conditions of Vacant Land," *Urban Affairs Review* 35 (March 2000): 559–581.

45. Michael Greenberg, Karen Lowrie, Laura Solitare, and Latoya Duncan, "Brownfields, Toads, and the Struggle for Neighborhood Redevelopment: A Case Study of the State of New Jersey," *Urban Affairs Review* 35 (May 2000): 717–718.

46. Manuel Pastor, Jr., Jim Sadd, and John Hipp, "Which Came First? Toxic Facilities, Minority Move-In, and Environmental Justice,"*Journal of Urban Affairs* 23(1) (2001): 1–12.

47. Ed Regan, "The Aging Interstate Highway System: Our Biggest Funding Challenge," *CDM Smith,* cdmsmith.com, April 12, 2013.

48. American Road & Transportation Builders Association, "Moving Ahead for Progress in the 21st Century Act: A Comprehensive Analysis," July 2012.

49. Jerome S. Legge, "Policy Alternatives and Traffic Safety," *Western Political Quarterly* 43 (September 1990): 597–612.

50. For a summary of previous research on the effects of state traffic safety, as well as well-crafted original research, see David J. Houston, Lilliard E. Richardson, and Grant W. Neeley, "Legislating Traffic Safety," *Social Science Quarterly* 76 (June 1995): 328–345.

51. Governors Highway Safety Administration, "Speed and Red Light Camera Laws," July 2010.

52. Sandy Graham, "Driving to Distraction," *Traffic Safety* 1 (November/December): 18–21.

53. Consumer Reports, "The Distraction Factor," available at www.consumerreports.org, January 23, 2002.

54. See Thomas R. Dye, "Taxing, Spending, and Economic Growth in the States," *Journal of Politics* 42 (November 1980): 1085–1087.

55. American Society of Civil Engineers, *2013 Report Card for America's Infrastructure.* Available at http://www.infrastructurereportcard.org/a/#p/home.

56. Don Chen and Nancy Jakowitsch, "Transportation Reform and Smart Growth: A Nation at the Tipping Point," Funders' Network for Smart Growth and Livable Communities, Surface Transportation Policy Project, Paper No. 6 (August 2001), p. 4.

57. Barbara McCann and Bianca DeLille, *Mean Streets 2000: Pedestrian Safety, Health and Federal Transportation Spending* (Washington, DC: Surface Transportation Policy Report, 2000).

58. John Fetto, "The Grid: Congestion Ahead," *American Demographics* 22 (June 2000): 49–50.

59. Ryan Holeywell, "Get on the Bus," *Governing* 25(11) (August 2012): 46-51.

60. U.S. Department of Transportation, Federal Railroad Administration, "Vision for High-Speed Rail in America," The High-Speed Rail Strategic Plan, The American Recovery and Reinvestment Act, April 2009.

61. American Road & Transportation Builders Association, *Moving Ahead for Progress in the 21st Century Act: A Comprehensive Analysis* (ARIBA, July 2012).

62. US Bureau of the Census, *Statistical Abstract of the United States, 2010 (*Washington, DC: Census Bureau*),* Table 366.

63. Resource Conservation and Recovery Act of 1976.

64. Environmental Protection Agency, "National Air Quality and Emission Trends 2006." Available at www.epa.gov.

65. Matthew Whittaker, Gary M. Segura, and Shaun Bowler, "Racial Group Attitudes Toward Environmental Protection," *Political Research Quarterly* 58 (September 2005): 435–447.

66. Olga Belogolova, "Keystone XL Pipeline: Just the Facts," *National Journal*, December 9, 2011. Available at http://www.nationaljournal.com/congress/keystone-xl-pipeline-just-the-facts-20111208?print=true.

CHAPTER 14

1. Council of State Governments, *Book of the States, 2009* (Lexington, KY: Council on State Governments, 2009), p. 41.

2. Jonathan Griffin, "Ready to Roll," *State Legislatures* 38(10) (December 2012): 22–25.

3. Robert McIntyre, *A Far Cry from Fair* (Washington, DC: Citizens for Tax Justice, 1991).

4. See David R. Morgan, "Tax Equity in the American States," *Social Science Quarterly* 75 (September 1994): 510–523.

5. Neil Berch, "Explaining Changes in Tax Incidence in the States," *Political Research Quarterly* 48 (September 1995): 629–642.

6. Shawn Bowler and Todd Donovan, "Popular Responsiveness to Taxation," *Political Research Quarterly* 48 (March 1995): 61–78.

7. James Cox and David Lowery, "The Impact of the Tax Revolt Era State Fiscal Caps," *Social Science Quarterly* 71 (September 1990): 492–509.

8. Phillip G. Joyce and Daniel R. Mullins, "The Changing Fiscal Structure of State and Local Public Sector: The Impact of Tax and Expenditure Limits," *Public Administration Review* 51 (May/June 1991): 240–253.

9. David T. Stanley, "Cities in Trouble," in Charles H. Levine, ed., *Managing Fiscal Stress* (Chatham, NJ: Chatham, 1980), pp. 95–122.

10. Susan K. Orahn, "On States' Ongoing Fiscal Stress," *Pew Center on the States,* March, 2009. Available at www.pewcenteronthestates.org/report_detail.aspx?id=45824.

11. See Christiana McFarland, "State of America's Cities Survey on Jobs and the Economy," *National League of Cities Research Brief on America's Cities,* May 2010; Richard L. Clark, "It's Still the Economy: County Officials' Views on the Economy in 2010," *National Center for the Study of Counties,* July 2010. Available at http://www.cviog.uga.edu/ncsc/.

12. See Stephen C. Brooks, "Urban Fiscal Stress: A Decade of Difference," Midwest Political Science Association Meeting, Chicago, 1993; Cal Clark and B. Oliver Walter, "Urban Political Cultures, Financial Stress, and City Fiscal Austerity Strategies," *Western Political Quarterly* 44 (September 1991): 676–697; Terry N. Clark and Lorna Crowley Ferguson, *City Money* (New York: Columbia University Press, 1983).

13. Gregory B. Lewis, "Municipal Expenditures Through Thick and Thin," *Publius,* special issue (May 1984): 380–390.

14. *McCulloch* v. *Maryland,* 4 Wheaton 316 (1819).

15. See Elaine B. Sharp, "The Politics and Economics of the New City Debt," *American Political Science Review* 80 (December 1986): 1241–1258.

16. Liz Farmer, "The 'B' Word: Is Municipal Bankruptcy's Stigma Fading?" *Governing* 26(6) (March 2013).

17. Eric Schulzke, "The Great Gamble," *Governing* 26(4) (January 2013): 48–51; "Municipal Bankruptcy: Viable Tool or Bad Idea?" same issue, p. S4.

18. Matt Helms and Joe Guillen, "Detroit Emergency Financial Manager Confident He Can Make Big Fixes," *Detroit Free Press,* March 14, 2013.

19. Reuters, "Credit Rating Agency S&P Lauds Detroit Takeover," March 15, 2013. Available at http://www.reuters.com/article/2013/03/15/usa-detroit-rating-idUSL1N0C77SD20130315.

20. Todd Haggerty, "It's a 'Weakovery' This Time Around," *Governing* 39(2) (February 2012): 5.

21. Kevin Knutson, "Getting Past the Quick Fix: On the Road to Financial Resiliency," *Government Finance Review* 28(5) (October 2012): 32–36.

22. Ibid.

CHAPTER 15

1. Quotation in Rufus P. Browning, Dale Rogers Marshall, and David H. Tabb, *Protest Is Not Enough: The Struggle of Blacks and Hispanics for Equality in Urban Politics* (Berkeley: University of California Press, 1984), p. 17.

2. Carmine Scavo, "Racial Integration of Local Government Leadership in Small Southern Cities," *Social Science Quarterly* 71 (June 1990): 362–372.

3. Lawrence Bobo and Franklin D. Gilliam, Jr., "Race, Sociopolitical Participation, and Black Empowerment," *American Political Science Review* 84 (June 1990): 377–386.

4. Zoltan L. Hajnal, "White Residents, Black Incumbents, and a Declining Racial Divide," *American Political Science Review* 95 (September 2001): 603–615.

5. See Paul Peterson, *City Limits* (Chicago: University of Chicago Press, 1981).

6. See Kenneth R. Mladenka, "Blacks and Hispanics in Urban Politics," *American Political Science Review* 83 (March 1989): 165–191; Thomas R. Dye and James Renick, "Political Power and City Jobs: Determinants of Minority Employment," *Social Science Quarterly* 62 (September 1981): 475–486.

7. C. Vann Woodward, *Reunion and Reaction: The End of Reconstruction* (Boston: Little, Brown, 1951).

8. *Plessy* v. *Ferguson,* 163 U.S. 537 (1896).

9. *Sweatt* v. *Painter,* 339 U.S. 629 (1950); *McLaurin* v. *Oklahoma State Regents,* 339 U.S. 637 (1950).

10. *Brown* v. *Board of Education of Topeka, Kansas,* 347 U.S. 483 (1954).

11. Kenneth B. Clark, *Dark Ghetto* (New York: Harper & Row, 1965), pp. 77–78.

12. The Supreme Court also ruled that Congress was bound to respect the equal protection doctrine imposed upon the states by the Fourteenth Amendment as part of the Due Process Clause of the Fifth Amendment. *Bolling* v. *Sharpe,* 347 U.S. 497 (1954).

13. The Supreme Court declared that the threat of violence was not sufficient reason to deny constitutional rights to black children and again dismissed the ancient interposition arguments. *Cooper* v. *Aaron,* 358 U.S. 1 (1958).

14. *Alexander* v. *Holmes County Board of Education,* 396 U.S. 19 (1969).

15. United States Commission on Civil Rights, *Racial Isolation in the Public Schools,* 2 vols. (Washington, DC: Government Printing Office, 1967) See also James S. Coleman, *Equality of Educational Opportunity* (Washington, DC: Government Printing Office, 1966).

16. *Swan* v. *Charlotte-Mecklenburg County Board of Education,* 402 U.S. 1 (1971).

17. *Milliken* v. *Bradley,* 418 U.S. 717 (1974).

18. *Oklahoma City Board of Education* v. *Dowell,* 498 U.S. 237 (1991).

19. *Adarand Construction Inc.* v. *Pena,* 515 U.S. 200 (1995).

20. *Parents Involved in Community Schools* v. *Seattle School District No. 1,* June 28, 2007.

21. *Grudder* v. *Bollinger,* 539 U.S. 306 (2003).

22. Michael W. Giles et al., "The Impact of Busing on White Flight," *Social Science Quarterly* 55 (September 1974): 493–501 See also George M. Metcalf, *From Little Rock to Boston: The History of School Desegregation* (Westport, CT: Greenwood Press, 1985).

23. "Racial, Class Segregatation Dominant in US Public Schools," *Press TV,* September 20, 2012; Reporting on study by the Civil Rights Project at the University of California, Los Angeles. Available at http://www.presstv.ir/detail/2012/09/20/262707/racial-segregation-rampant-in-us-schools/.

24. Opponents of the Civil Rights Act of 1964 argued that Congress unconstitutionally exceeded its delegated powers when it prohibited discrimination and segregation practiced by *privately owned* public accommodations and *private* employers. Nowhere among the delegated powers of Congress in Article I of the Constitution, or even in the Fourteenth or Fifteenth Amendments, is Congress specifically given the power to prohibit discrimination practiced by *private* individuals. In reply, supporters of the Act argued that Congress has the power to regulate interstate commerce. Instead of relying upon the Fourteenth Amendment, which prohibits only *state-supported* discrimination, Congress was relying on its powers over interstate commerce. In unanimous opinions in *Heart of Atlanta Motel* v. *United States* and *Katzenbach* v. *McClung* in December 1964, the Supreme Court upheld the constitutionality of the Civil Rights Act. The Court held that Congress could, by virtue of its power over interstate commerce, prohibit discrimination in any establishment that serves or offers to serve interstate travelers or that sells food or goods previously moved in interstate commerce. This power over commerce included not only major establishments, like the Heart of Atlanta Motel, but also the family-owned Ollie's Barbecue serving a local clientele. *Heart of Atlanta Motel* v. *United States,* 379 U.S. 241 (1964); *Katzenbach* v. *McClung,* 379 U.S. 294 (1964).

25. *Regents of the University of California* v. *Bakke,* 438 U.S. 265 (1978).

26. Bakke's overall grade point average was 3.46, while the average for special admission students was 2.62. Bakke's MCAT scores were verbal–96, quantitative–94, science–97, general information–72; while the average MCAT scores for special admissions students were verbal–34, quantitative–30, science–37, general information–18.

27. *United Steelworkers* v. *Weber,* 443 U.S. 193 (1979).

28. *United States* v. *Paradise,* 480 U.S. 149 (1987).

29. *Firefighters Local Union* v. *Totts,* 465 U.S. 561 (1981).

30. *Richmond* v. *Crosen,* 109 S. Ct. 706 (1989).

31. See Justice Antonin Scalia's dissent in *Johnson* v. *Transportation Agency of Santa Clara County,* 480 U.S. 616 (1987).

32. *Aderand Construction* v. *Pena* (1995).

33. American Civil Rights Initiative. Available at www.acri.org.

34. *Coalition for Economic Equity* v. *Pete Wilson,* Ninth Circuit Court of Appeals, April 1997.

35. Paul Taylor, Mark Hugo Lopez, Jessica Hamar Martinez, and Gabriel Velasco, *When Labels Don't Fit: Hispanics and Their Views of Identity* (Washington, DC: Pew Hispanic Center, April 4, 2012).

36. Ibid.

37. Peter Mathiessen, *Sal Si Puedes: Ceasar Chavez and the New American Revolution* (New York: Random House, 1969).

38. *Plyer* v. *Doe,* 457 U.S. 202 (1982).

39. Caroline J. Tolbert and Rodney E. Hero, "Race/Ethnicity and Direct Democracy," *Journal of Politics* 58 (August 1996): 806–808.

40. Tina Norris, Paula L. Vines, and Elizabeth M. Hoeffel, *The American Indian and Alaska Native Population 2010* (Washington, DC: U.S. Census Bureau).

41. Newsroom Profile American Facts for Features, *American Indian and Alaska Native Heritage Month: November 2012* (Washington, DC: U.S. Census Bureau.)

42. Ibid.

43. *Morton* v. *Mancari*, 417 U.S. 535 (1974).

44. Timothy Williams, "U.S. Will Pay a Settlement of $1 Billion to 41 Tribes," *New York Times*, April 13, 2012.

45. *Governing*, November 1998, p. 51.

46. Newsroom Profile American Facts for Features, "Anniversary of Americans with Disabilities Act: July 26," (Washington, DC: U.S. Census Bureau, July 25, 2012).

47. See Joseph P. Shapiro, *No Pity: People with Disabilities Forging a New Civil Rights Movement* (New York: Times Books/Random House, 1993).

48. *Chronicle of Higher Education*, December 8, 2000.

49. AARP, *Staying Ahead of the Curve 2013: AARP Multicultural Work and career Study, Perceptions of Age Discrimination in the Workplace—Ages 45–74* (Washington, DC: AARP, 2013).

50. Sondra L. Shapiro, "Legislation Fights Workplace Age Bias," fiftyplusadvocate.com, August 1, 2012. Available at http://fiftyplusadvocate.com/archives/6761.

51. Carlyn Kolker, "U.S. Supreme Court to Consider Age Discrimination Case," *Thomson Reuters News & Insight*, March 19, 2013.

52. *Stanton* v. *Stanton*, 421 U.S. 7 (1975).

53. *Craig* v. *Boren*, 429 U.S. 191 (1976).

54. *Dothland* v. *Raulinson*, 433 U.S. 321 (1977).

55. *Arizona* v. *Norvis*, 103 S. Ct. 3492 (1983).

56. *E.E.O.C.* v. *Madison Community School District*, 55 U.S.L.W. 2644 (1987).

57. *Vorcheheimer* v. *Philadelphia School District*, 430 U.S. 703 (1977).

58. *Rostker* v. *Goldberg*, 453 U.S. 57 (1981).

59. *Orr* v. *Orr*, 440 U.S. 268 (1979).

60. Kevin Cirilli, "Abortion Poll: Keep Roe v. Wade," *Politico,* January 2013.

61. See Christopher Z. Mooney and Mei-Hsien Lee, "Legislating Morality in the American States: Pre-Roe Abortion Reform," *American Journal of Political Science* 39 (August 1995): 599–627.

62. *Roe* v. *Wade*, 410 U.S. 113 (1973).

63. *Harris* v. *McRae*, 448 U.S. 297 (1980).

64. For a review of state funding of abortions, see Kenneth J. Meier and Deborah R. McFarlane, "The Politics of Funding Abortion," *American Politics Quarterly* 21 (January 1993): 81–101.

65. *Planned Parenthood of Missouri* v. *Danforth*, 428 U.S. 52 (1976); *Bellotti* v. *Baird*, 443 U.S. 622 (1979); *Akron* v. *Akron Center for Reproductive Health*, 103 S. Ct. 2481 (1983).

66. Susan B. Hansen, "State Implementation of Supreme Court Decisions: Abortion Rates Since *Roe* v. *Wade*," *Journal of Politics* 42 (1980): 372–395.

67. Associated Press, "U.S. Abortion Rates Down 5 Percent During Great Recession, Biggest One-Year Decrease in a Decade,"*CBS news,* November 21, 2013. Available at http://www.cbsnews.com/8301-201_162-57553119/u.s-abortion-rates-down-5-percent-during-great-recession-biggest-one-year-decrease-in-a-decade/.

68. Guttmacher Institute, "Fact Sheet: Contraceptive Use in the United States," July 2012. Available at http://www.guttmacher.org/pubs/fb_contr_use.html.

69. *Webster* v. *Reproductive Health Services* 492 U.S. 490 (1989).

70. *Planned Parenthood* v. *Casey,* 112 S. Ct. 2791 (1992).

71. Ibid.

72. See Laura S. Hussey, "Welfare Generosity, Abortion Access, and Abortion Rates," *Social Science Quarterly* 91 (March 2010): 276–283.

73. *Stenberg* v. *Carhart,* 530 U.S. 914 (2000).

74. *Gonzales* v. *Carhart*, April 18, 2007.

75. *Planned Parenthood of Pennsylvania* v. *Casey, Planned Parenthood of Missouri* v. *Danforth*, 428 U.S. 52 (1976).

76. Richard Wolf, "Rules, Laws Put Limits on Abortion Rights," *USA Today,* January 17, 2013; Louise Jacobson, "Are the States Deepening the Nation's Red-Blue Divide?"*Governing*, April 25, 2013. Available at http://www.governing.com/blogs/politics/gov-states-deepening-nations-red-blue-divide.html.

77. CNN/ORC International Poll, March 25, 2013.

78. *Bowers* v. *Hardwick*, 478 U.S. 186 (1986).

79. *Lawrence* v. *Texas*, 539 U.S. 558 (2003).

80. *Boy Scouts of America* v. *Dale*, 530 U.S. 640 (2000).

81. Erik Eckholm, "Boy Scouts to Continue Excluding Gay People," *New York Times,* July 17, 2012; Jessee Folk, "Gay, Lesbian Group Excluded from St. Patrick's Day Parade," *WCPO Digital*, March 15, 2013.

82. Dylan Scott, "Supreme Court Takes Up Gay Marriage: What States and Cities Need to Know," *Governing*, March 25, 2013.

83. Stoyan Zaimov, "Bill Clinton Receives GLAAD Award; Credits Daughter for Gay Marriage Stance," *Christian Post*, April 22, 2013. Available at www.freerepublic.com/focus/f-news/3010973/posts.

84. See Jeffrey R. Lax and Justin H. Phillips, "Gay Rights in the States: Public Opinion and Policy Responsiveness," *American Political Science Review* 103 (August 2009): 367–386.

85. See Margaret Ellis, "Gay Rights: Lifestyle or Immorality," in Raymond Tatalovich and Byron Daynes, eds., *Moral Controversies in American Politics*, 3rd ed. (Armonk, NY: M.E. Sharpe, 2005).

CHAPTER 16

1. "Education: Just 20% Think U.S. Public Schools Provide World-Class Education," *Rasmussen Reports,* March 26, 2013.

2. David Osborne, *Laboratories of Democracy* (Boston: Harvard Business School Press, 1988), p. 92.

3. Paul Brace, *State Government and Economic Performance* (Baltimore: Johns Hopkins University Press, 1993).

4. Kevin B. Smith and J. Scott Rademacker, "Expense Lessons: Education and the Political Economy of the American State," *Political Research Quarterly* 52 (December 1999): 709–727.

5. Thomas R. Dye, "Taxing, Spending, and Economic Growth in the American States," *Journal of Politics* 42 (November 1980): 1085–1107.

6. Stephanie Simon, "High School Graduation Rate Up Sharply, But Red Flags Abound," *Reuters,* February 25, 2013; Chris Farrell, "America's Schools: Graduation Rats Are Better Than You Think," *Bloomberg Businessweek,* April 2, 2013.

7. Administered nationally by the College Board, New York. The SAT was formerly named the Scholastic Aptitude Test.

8. National Commission on Excellence in Education, *A Nation at Risk* (Washington, DC: Government Printing Office, 1983).

9. James S. Coleman et al., *Equality of Educational Opportunity* (Washington, DC: Government Printing Office, 1966).

10. James S. Coleman et al., *High School Achievement* (New York: Basic Books, 1982).

11. "Voters Have Mixed Feelings About More Money for Schools," *Rasmussen Reports,* January 11, 2013.

12. National Conference of State Legislatures, "Charter Choice: September 2011." Available at www.ncsl.org/default.aspx?TabId=23446.

13. Eric Hirsch, "A New Chapter for Charters," *State Legislatures* 24 (June 1998): 20–24.

14. Linda A. Renzulli and Vincent J. Roscigno, "Charter Schools and the Public Good," *Caliber* 6 (Winter 2007): 31–36. These authors also argue that charter schools increase racial segregation.

15. Center for Research on Education Outcomes, "Charter School Growth and Replication," January 30, 2013. Available at http://credo.stanford.edu/research-reports.html.

16. Charles Mahtesian, "Charter Schools Learn a Few Lessons," *Governing* 8 (January 1998): 23–27.

17. Center for Education Reform, *Race to the Top for Charter Schools 2009* (Washington, DC: Center for Education Reform, 2010). Available at www.cer.org.

18. Fernanda Santos and Motoko Rich, "With Vouchers, States Shift Aid for Schools to Families," *New York Times,* March 27, 2013. Available at http://www.nytimes.com/2013/03/28/education/ states-shifting-aid-for-schools-to-the-families.html?pagewanted=all&_r=0.

19. Pro-voucher arguments can be found in John E. Chubb and Terry M. Moe, *Politics, Markets, and America's Schools* (Washington, DC: Brookings Institution, 1990); Paul E. Peterson and Bryan C. Hassel, eds., *Learning from School Choice* (Washington, DC: Brookings Institution, 1998).

20. Antivoucher arguments are provided in Kevin Smith and Kenneth Meier, *The Case Against School Choice* (Armonk, NY: M. E. Sharpe, 1995). But see also Robert Maranto, Scott Madison, and Scott Stevens, "Does Private School Competition Harm Public Schools?" *Political Research Quarterly* 53 (March 2000): 177–192.

21. Terry M. Moe, *School Vouchers and the American Public* (Washington, DC: Brookings Institution, 2002).

22. *Zelman* v. *Simmons-Harris,* 234 F. 3d, 945 (2002).

23. Wendl Foundation, "'What is a Virtual School?' Frequently Asked Questions on Virtual Schools." Available at http://www.wendlfoundation.org/Education/VirtualOnlineSchoolsFAQ.aspx, April 27, 2013.

24. Justin Reich, "The Solution to Virtual Schools Is to Open Them (Part II)," *EdTech Researcher, Education Week,* September 7, 2012. Available at http://blogs.edweek.org/edweek/edtechresearcher/2012/09/the_solution_to_virtual_schools_is_to_open_them_part_ii.html.

25. Fernanda Santos and Motoko Rich, "With Vouchers, States Shift Aid for Schools to Families," *New York Times,* March 27, 2013. Available at http://www.nytimes.com/2013/03/28/education/states-shifting-aid-for-schools-to-the-families.html?pagewanted=all&_r=0.

26. Patte Barth, Jim Hull, and Rebecca St. Andrie, "Searching for the Reality of Virtual Schools," National School Boards Association, Center for Public Education, May 2012.

27. Common Core State Standards Initiative, "Frequently Asked Questions Overview," available at http://www.corestandards.org/resources/frequently-asked-questions, April 27, 2013.

28. Bryan Shelley, "Rebels and Their Causes: State Resistance to No Child Left Behind," *Publius* 38 (May 2008): 444–468 See also National Education Association; Issues in Education, "ESEA: It's Time for a Change." Available at www.nea.org.

29. National Conference of State Legislatures, "School and District Consolidation," March 14, 2011. Available at http://www.ncsl.org/research/education/school-and-district-consolidation.aspx.

30. *Rodriguez* v. *San Antonio Independent School District,* 411 U.S. 1 (1973).

31. *Serrano* v. *Priest,* 5 Cal. 594 (1971).

32. Grover J. "Russ" Whitehurst, Matthew M. Chingos, and Michael R. Gallaher, *Do School Districts Matter?* (Washington, DC: Brown Center on Education Policy at Brookings, March 2013.)

33. American Association of School Administrators 2010 survey cited in Jack Weinstein, "Frequent Superintendent Turnover Not Uncommon," *Explore Steamboat*, April 16, 2011. Available at http://www.exploresteamboat.com/news/2011/apr/16/frequent-superintendent-turnover-not-uncommon/.

34. For an extended discussion of this issue, see Michael B. Berkman and Eric Plutzer, *Ten Thousand Democracies: Politics and Public Opinion in America's School Districts* (Washington, DC: Georgetown University Press, 2005).

35. Frederick M. Hess and Olivia Meeks, *Governance in the Accountability Era: School Boards Circa 2010* (Washington, DC: The National School Boards Association, The Thomas B. Fordham Institute and the Iowa Schol Boards Foundation, 2010).

36. Kenneth J. Meier and Robert E. England, "Black Representation and Educational Policy," *American Political Science Review* 78 (June 1984): 393–403. See also Rene R. Rocha and Daniel P. Hawes, "Racial Diversity, Representative Bureaucracy, and Equity in Multiracial School Districts," *Social Science Quarterly* 90 (June 2009): 306–344.

37. Frederick M. Hess and Olivia Meeks, *Governance in the Accountability Era: School Boards Circa 2010* (Washington, DC: The National School Boards Association, The Thomas B. Fordham Institute and the Iowa Schol Boards Foundation, 2010).

38. Staff Writers, "Labor of Love or Cheap Labor? The Plight of Adjunct Professors," *Online Colleges*, April 24, 2013. Available at http://www.onlinecolleges.net/2013/04/24/labor-of-love-or-cheap-labor-the-plight-of-adjunct-professors/.

39. See Charles Mahtesian, "Higher Ed: The No-Longer-Sacred Cow," *Governing* (July 1995): 20–26.

40. Ruth Simon, "Public-University Costs Soar," *Wall Street Journal*, March 6, 2013.

41. Liz Farmer, "Governors: A Four-Year Degree Doesn't Always Mean Job Growth," *Governing*, February 25, 2013; Margaret Newkirk, "Anthropology Mocked as U.S. Governors Push for Employable Grads," *Bloomberg news*, March 11, 2013.

42. *Pierce* v. *The Society of Sisters*, 268 U.S. 510 (1925).

43. *Cochran* v. *Board of Education*, 281 U.S. 370 (1930).

44. *Everson* v. *Board of Education*, 330 U.S. 1 (1947).

45. *Mueller* v. *Allen*, 463 U.S. 388 (1983).

46. Hugo Black, majority opinion in *Everson* v. *Board of Education*, 330 U.S. 1 (1947).

47. *Lemon* v. *Kurtzman*, 403 U.S. 602 (1972).

48. *Mueller* v. *Adams*, 463 U.S. 602 (1983).

49. *Tilden* v. *Richardson*, 403 U.S. 602 (1971).

50. *Lambs Chapel* v. *Center Moriches Union School District*, 528 U.S. 324 (1993).

51. *Rosenberger* v. *University of Virginia*, 515 U.S. 819 (1995).

52. *Edwards* v. *Aguillard*, 482 U.S. 578, (1987).

53. *Engle* v. *Vitale*, 370 U.S. 421 (1962).

54. Ibid.

55. *Abington Township* v. *Schempp*, 374 U.S. 203 (1963).

56. *Wallace* v. *Jaffree*, 105 S. Ct. 2479 (1986).

57. *Santa Fe Independent School District* v. *Doe*, 530 U.S. 290 (2000).

58. S. Henry, "What Is School Violence? An Integrated Definition," *Annals of the American Academy of Political and Social Science* 567 (2000): 16–29.

59. A. Perez and M. Jaffe, "School Safety: Inside One School's Extraordinary Security Measures," *ABC News*, December 19, 2012. Availabe at http://abcnews.go.com/blogs/headlines/2012/12/school-security-one-schools-extraordinary-safety-measures/.

60. National School Safety and Security Services. Available at http://www.schoolsecurity.org/school-safety-experts/company.html.

61. Hanover Research, "Best Practices in School Security," January 2013. Available at http://www.governor.virginia.gov/SchoolAndCampusSafetyTaskforce/docs/BestPracticesinSchoolSecurity.pdf.

CHAPTER 17

1. "Seniors' Household Median Net Worth Drops 13 Percent [Between 2005 and 2010]," *Financial Advisor*, April 24, 2013.

2. D'Vera Cohn, *The Middle Class Shrinks and Income Segregation Rises* (Washington, DC: Pew Research Center Social & Demographic Trends, August 2, 2012); Amy Sullivan, "The American Dream, Downsized," *National Journal*, April 26, 2013.

3. Kim Parker, *Yes, the Rich Are Different* (Washington, DC: Pew Research Center Social & Demographic Trends, August 27, 2012).

4. "64% Think Too Many Are Dependent on Government Aid," *Rasmussen Reports*, March 28, 2013.

5. "Americans Favor Work over Welfare as Response to Poverty," *Rasmussen Reports*, March 29, 2013.

6. Doug Bandow, "America on Welfare," *The American Spectator*, April 25, 2012. Available at http://spectator.org/archives/2013/04/25/america-on-welfare/print.

7. The original act did not include disability insurance; this was added by amendment in 1950. Health insurance for the aged, "Medicare," was added by amendment in 1965.

8. David Ellwood, *Poor Support: Poverty in the American Family* (New York: Basic Books, 1988), p. 6.

9. U.S. Census Bureau, *Statistical Abstract of the United States*, 2010, Table 206. Available at http://www.census.gov/compendia/statab/2010/tables/10s0206.pdf.

10. *Federation of Independent Business versus Sibelius*, June 28, 2012.

11. Melissa Hansen, "The Heat is On [Medicaid]," *State Legislatures* 38(10) (December 2012): 20–21; "Confronting Costs," *State Legislatures* 38(6) (June 2012): 30–32.

12. Robert J. McGrath, "Implementation Theory Revisited . . . Again: Lessons from the State Children's Health Insurance Program," *Politics and Policy* 37 (April 2009): 309–336.

13. Office of Management and Budget, *Budget of the United States Government 2010,* p. 28. Available at www.whitehouse.gov/omb.

14. *Federation of Independent Business versus Sibelius,* June 28, 2012.

15. Liz Szabo, "Newtown Shooting Prompts Calls for Mental Health Reform," *USA Today,* January 7, 2013. Available at http://www.usatoday.com/story/news/nation/2013/01/07/newtown-shooting-mental-health-reform/1781145/.

16. David Morgan, "U.S. Mental Health Experts Urge Focus on Early Treatment," *Reuters,* January 24, 2013. Available at http://www.reuters.com/article/2013/01/24/us-usa-healthcare-mental-idUSBRE90N0PB20130124.

17. Ellen Rolfes, "Medicaid Expansion to Boost Access to Mental Health Services," *The News Hour, PBS,* February 22, 2013. Available at http://www.pbs.org/newshour/rundown/2013/02/medicaid-expansion-will-expand-access-to-mental-illness-treatment.html.

18. Ibid.

19. Brady Dennis and Lena H. Sun, "After Newtown, Support for Mental-Health Spending Grows," *Washington Post,* February 23, 2013.

PHOTO CREDITS

COVER: Erich Schlegel/Getty Images

CHAPTER 1: 1, Jim West / Alamy; **2,** Marco Garcia/AP Images; **9,** Amber Miller/ZUMA Press/Newscom; **15,** AP Photo/J. Scott Applewhite; **20,** Alamy; **23,** Alex Wong/Getty Images; **24,** Monika Graff / The Image Works

CHAPTER 2: 27, Michael Springer/ Getty Images; **46,** AP Photo/ Marc Levy; **47,** Julie Jacobson/ AP Images; **48,** Marjorie Kamys Cotera/Bob Daemmrich Photography / Alamy; **49,** Ramin Talaie/ Corbis; **51,** AP Photo/Leslie E. Kossoff

CHAPTER 3: 55, searagen/Fotolia; **63,** Sascha Burkard/Fotolia; **66,** Arthur Grace/ZUMAPRESS/ Newscom; **70,** Reuters/Corbis; **82,** Charles Dharapak/AP Images; **83,** AP Photo/The Record of Bergen County, Chris Pedota)

CHAPTER 4: 087, FRED PROUSER/ Reuters/Corbis; **100,** ASSOCIATED PRESS/AP Images; **104,** (bl) William J. Smith/AP Images; **104,** (br) Judy Ondrey/AP Images; **105,** Dan Sullivan/Alamy **108,** Richard Ellis/ ZUMA Press/Newscom; **112,** (bl) Jim West / The Image Works **112,** (br) Mike Kahn / GreenStockMedia / The Image Works; **120,** rubberball / Getty Images

CHAPTER 5: 125, Casanova KRT/ Newscom; **128,** Patrick Herrera/ E+/Getty Images; **130,** T.J. Kirkpatrick/Getty Images; **133,** Ted Soqui/Corbis; **137,** RICK WILKING/Reuters/Corbis; **138,** ZUMA Press, Inc. / Alamy; **138,** Susan MacManus; **147,** (bl) JIM YOUNG/Reuters/Corbis; **147,** (br) Kevin Sanders/AP images; **148,** pablo Martinez Monsivais/AP images; **149,** Kevin Dietsch/UPI/ Newscom

CHAPTER 6: 159, Bob Daemmrich / Alamy; **163,** ZUMA Press, Inc. / Alamy; **167,** AP Photo/Steven Senne; **175,** Library of Congress, Prints & Photographs Division;

178, The Florida Senate Archives; **189,** JIM LO SCALZO/epa/Corbis

CHAPTER 7: 195, CARLOS JAVIER ORTIZ/epa/Corbis; **199,** The News Star, Brandi Jade Thomas/AP Images; **201,** (tr) ALEX C. HICKS JR/AP Images; **201,** (bl) Marla Brose/ZUMA Press, Inc/Alamy; **212,** Brian Baer/Sacramento Bee/ Newscom; **216,** Kiichiro Sato/ AP Images; **217,** (tl) Mary Ann Chastain/AP Images **217,** (br) Mary Altaffer/AP Images; **218,** MIKE RANSDELL/MCT/Newscom

CHAPTER 8: 223, DANIEL AGUILAR/Reuters/Corbis; **232,** Jason Todd/Getty Images; **233,** Chip Somodevilla/Getty Images; **236,** Aidaricci/Fotolia; **245,** AP Photo/Sang Tan

CHAPTER 9: 249, ZUMA Press, Inc. / Alamy; **256,** The Star-Ledger / John O'Boyle / The Image Works; **263,** Editorial Image, LLC / PhotoEdit; **268,** Buddy Mays / Alamy; **275,** DAVID SWANSON KRT/Newscom; **280,** Adam Tanner / The Image Works; **284,** AP Photo/Evan Vucci

CHAPTER 10: 289, Owen Franken/ corbis; **292,** Casey Christie/ZUMA Press/Corbis; **293,** Uriel Sinai/Getty Images; **294,** Syracuse Newspapers / D Blume / The Image Works; **315,** Dan Honda/ZUMA Press/Newscom

CHAPTER 11: 317, Jeff Greenberg / Alamy; **318,** © Syracuse Newspa- pers / L. Long / The Image Works; **330,** Ann E Parry / Alamy; **336,** Paul Kitagaki Jr./MCT/Newscom; **338,** Mark Duncan/AP Images; **342,** MATTHEW CAVANAUGH/ EPA/Newscom; **343,** TANNEN MAURY/EPA/Newscom; **345,** ZUMA Press, Inc. / Alamy; **349,** John Nordell / The Image Works

CHAPTER 12: 353, Gerald McDonald / Alamy; **356,** Margot Granitsas / The Image Works; **360,** (bl) David Grossman / Alamy; **360,** (br) Bill Bachmann / The Image Works; **366,** Erik Lesser/ZUMApress/Newscom; **372,** Cowlitz-Wahkiakum Council

of Governments; **373,** Ryan Miner / Splash News/Newscom

CHAPTER 13: 377, Visions of America, LLC / Alamy; **381,** Sean Cayton/The Image Works; **390,** JOHN BERRY/ The Post-Standard /Landov; **394,** JEFF KOWALSKY/EPA/Newscom; **407,** Les Stone/Corbis

CHAPTER 14: 409, John Bazemore/ AP Images; **412,** Editorial Image, LLC / PhotoEdit; **413,** LAURIE MATANICH/AP Images; **415,** Corey Lowenstein/MCT/Newscom; **418,** Michael Williams/ZUMA- PRESS/Newscom; **423,** Stevan Morgain/AP Images; **425,** RENA LAVERTY/EPA/Newscom

CHAPTER 15: 427, robin Nelson/ ZUMA/Alamy; **430,** Bettmann/ Corbis; **434,** Ed Kashi/Corbis; **435,** Library of Congress, Prints & Photographs Division, NYWT&S Collection, [LC-USZ62-122985]; **448,** Jeff Greenberg / Alamy; **451,** epa european pressphoto agency b.v. / Alamy; **455,** David J. Phillip/AP Images

CHAPTER 16: 459, Cliff Parnell/ Getty Images; **461,** Jim West / Alamy; **462,** MICHAEL REYNOLDS/EPA/Newscom; **468,** KENNELL KRISTA/SIPA/AP Images; **469,** Darron Cummings/AP Images; **471,** Najlah Feanny/Corbis; **473,** Elizabeth Crews / The Image Works; **476,** Chuck Nacke / Alamy; **478,** Jim West/Alamy; **479,** Bob Daemmrich / The Image Works; **480,** E. Jason Wambsgans/MCT/ Newscom; **481,** J. Emilio Flores/LA Opinion/Newscom; **503,** Rich Legg/ E+/Getty Images; **506,** MICHAEL REYNOLDS/EPA/Newscom

CHAPTER 17: 491, Ed Kashi/VII/ Corbis; **494,** CalPix/Alamy; **499,** J. Scott Applewhite/AP Images; **502,** Marjorie Kamys Cotera/Bob Daemmrich Photography / Alamy; **503,** Rich Legg/E+/Getty Images; **505,** Norma Jean Gargasz/Alamy; **506,** MICHAEL REYNOLDS/EPA/ Newscom

INDEX

Note: Locators followed by "*f*" and "*t*" referred as table and figure in the text